SHADOW
WARRIOR

ALSO BY RANDALL B. WOODS

LBJ: Architect of American Ambition

Quest for Identity: America Since 1945

*J. William Fulbright, Vietnam, and the
Search for a Cold War Foreign Policy*

Fulbright: A Biography

A Changing of the Guard: Anglo-American Relations, 1941–1946

SHADOW WARRIOR

William Egan Colby
and the CIA

Randall B. Woods

BASIC BOOKS
A MEMBER OF THE PERSEUS BOOKS GROUP
New York

Books published by Basic Books are available at special discounts for bulk
purchases in the United States by corporations, institutions, and other
organizations. For more information, please contact the Special Markets
Department at the Perseus Books Group, 2300 Chestnut Street, Suite
200, Philadelphia, PA 19103, or call (800) 810-4145, ext. 5000, or e-mail
special.markets@perseusbooks.com.

Designed by Timm Bryson

Library of Congress Cataloging-in-Publication Data
Woods, Randall Bennett, 1944–
  William Egan Colby and the CIA / Randall B. Woods.
   p. cm.
  Includes bibliographical references and index.
  ISBN 978-0-465-02194-9 (hbk. : alk. paper) — ISBN 978-0-465-
03788-9 (e-book) 1. Colby, William Egan, 1920–1996. 2. United States.
Central Intelligence Agency—Biography. 3. Intelligence officers—
United States—Biography. 4. Vietnam War, 1961–1975—Secret
service—United States. 5. World War, 1939–1945—Secret service—
United States. I. Title.
  UB271.U52C657 2013
  327.12730092—dc23
  [B]
                                   2012040332
10 9 8 7 6 5 4 3 2 1

For my daughter, Nicole Woods Olmstead

CONTENTS

THE DISAPPEARANCE

Saturday, April 27, 1996, dawned clear and warm; it was going to be a beautiful spring day on the Chesapeake Bay. Although his second wife, Sally, was away visiting her mother in Houston, Bill Colby was a happy man. William Egan Colby, former CIA director, Saigon station chief, and head of America's counterinsurgency and pacification operation in Vietnam, as well as a veteran of World War II's Office of Strategic Services (OSS), spent the day working on his 37-foot sloop, *Eagle Wing II*. The Colbys owned a vacation cottage on Neale Sound in Southern Maryland, about 60 miles south of Washington, DC, and the *Eagle Wing* was moored at the marina on Cobb Island, directly across the sound from the cottage. The seventy-six-year-old retired spy and covert operative had worked hard repairing the torn mainsail on his beloved vessel, scraping the hull, and scouring the hardware in preparation for the year's maiden voyage.

Sometime between 5:30 and 6:00 P.M., Colby knocked off and climbed into his red Fiat for the drive home. On the way, he stopped at Captain John's, a popular seafood restaurant and market, and bought a dozen clams and some corn on the cob for his dinner. He arrived at the cottage around 7:00. The house was modest, a turn-of-the-century oysterman's lodging with two bedrooms, a kitchen, and a glassed-in front porch. But the view of the sound—the white frame structure was situated on a spit of land, surrounded by water on three sides—was spectacular.

Weary but content, Colby unloaded his groceries and called Sally. The two had married in 1984. Colby, theretofore a devoted Catholic, had left Barbara Colby, his equally Catholic wife of thirty-nine years and mother of their five children, for Sally—intelligent, attractive, a former US ambassador to Grenada. The two were besotted with each other. Other than for weddings or funerals, Colby never darkened the door of a Catholic church again. The two chatted warmly but briefly over the phone. Bill told Sally that he was happy but tired; he was going to feast on clams and corn—his favorites—and then turn in.

Around 7:15, Joseph "Carroll" Wise, the cottage's off-season caretaker, turned into the driveway. He had his sister in tow and wanted her to meet his famous client. They found Colby watering his willow trees down near the water. The trio chatted briefly, and then Wise and his sister drove away. It was the last time they would see Bill Colby alive.

On Sunday afternoon, Colby's next-door neighbor, Alice Stokes, noticed that the Fiat was still parked in the driveway. She checked the jetty they shared; the aluminum ladder Colby used to climb down into his canoe was in the water. A frayed rope hung from the iron rung he used to moor his canoe, but there was no sign of the craft. Meanwhile, Kevin Akers, a twenty-nine-year-old unemployed carpenter and handyman, had taken his wife and two kids out on the sound in his small motorboat. At the point where Neale Sound turned into the Wicomico River, Akers spotted a beached green canoe. There was nothing unusual about that. Akers, who had spent all his life around the Chesapeake, had in the past picked up small craft that had broken loose from their moorings and towed them to the marina. Akers later recalled that this canoe was nearly filled with sand; it had taken him and his wife the better part of an hour to empty it. He had been out on the water the day before and had not spotted the canoe. There was no way, he mused, that two cycles of the tide could put that much sand in a canoe.

Around 7:00 Sunday evening, Alice Stokes called 911 to report a missing person. The local police arrived at half past eight. Both doors to the cottage were unlocked. Colby's computer and radio were on. Unwashed dishes and the remnants of a half-eaten meal lay in the sink. A partially filled glass of white wine sat on the counter; the bottle, with very little missing, was on the table in the sunroom. Also on the table were Colby's wallet, containing $296, and his keys. The canoe and its paddle and life jacket were missing from the nearby shed. Policewoman Sharon Walsh alerted the Coast Guard, and the search was on.

Over the next few days, a dozen navy divers, two helicopters, and more than a hundred volunteers scoured the area. They found nothing. On the morning of May 6, nine days after Colby was last seen, his body was spotted on the shoreline of Neale Sound, approximately 40 meters from where Kevin Akers had discovered the green canoe. The police announced that there were no signs of foul play. Most likely the old man had suffered a heart attack and fallen into the water. The state medical examiner's office issued a preliminary verdict of accidental death.

When Akers learned who had owned the green canoe, alarm bells began going off in his head. There was the unexplained overabundance of sand in the canoe. More significant, the boat and the body were separated by a spit of land. Given the prevailing currents, there was no way the canoe could have wound up on one side of the spit and Colby on the other. The former spook had been murdered, he concluded. Akers gathered his family and went into hiding.

The Neale Sound handyman was not the only doubter. Zalin Grant was in Paris when he heard the news of Colby's death. The former director of central intelligence (DCI) had gone paddling in his canoe at night, fallen out, and drowned? Not a chance. Grant, a Vietnam veteran, war correspondent, and author, had known Colby in Vietnam. Colby had subsequently helped the journalist write his book on counterinsurgency and the CIA. Grant admired him, agreeing with US counterinsurgency expert Edward Lansdale's observation that Colby was the most effective American—soldier or civilian—to serve in the Vietnam War. The man was fit, seasoned, and prudent, not some doddering septuagenarian. And he had enemies, some of them quite dangerous. Finally, Colby's death reminded Grant of the demise of another CIA official some twenty years earlier under eerily similar circumstances. On the moonlit night of September 23, 1978, John Arthur Paisley had vanished in the waters of the Chesapeake Bay. Paisley was last seen alive that morning, crossing a narrow section of the bay aboard his sloop *Brillig*. A week later, on October 1, a bloated and badly decomposed body was found floating in the water, a 9-millimeter gunshot wound in the back of the head and weighted diver's belts around the waist. The CIA suggested that Paisley had committed suicide, but the Maryland state coroner's office ruled that he had died of indeterminate causes.[1]

Upon his return to the States, Zalin Grant began investigating Colby's death. Throughout the summer of 1996, Grant interviewed family members, neighbors, police and sheriff's officers, the medical examiner—he even managed to locate Kevin Akers. What he got were unanswered questions.

Why would Colby, after a hard day's work, go canoeing in total darkness? Carroll Wise and his sister had left him between 7:15 and 7:30, still watering his willows. It still remained for Colby to go in the house, steam the clams, boil the corn, open the wine, and consume part of the meal. By the time he finished, it would have been at least 8:30—pitch black. Colby had said nothing to Sally about a water outing. Then there were Akers's questions about the location of the sand-filled canoe in relation to the body.

Grant was the first and only journalist to view the autopsy pictures. He had seen plenty of dead bodies in Vietnam, some of which had been dumped in the Mekong River or other waterways. Without exception, they had sunk to the bottom, begun to decompose, filled with gas, and surfaced, bloated and grossly disfigured. In the autopsy pictures, Colby's body appeared almost normal, with no bloating whatsoever. The medical examiner—who had ruled that the former DCI had had a cardiovascular incident, fallen into the water, and died either of hypothermia or drowning—admitted that the body was amazingly well preserved. Based on an analysis of the contents of the corpse's stomach, the medical examiner ruled that Colby had died between one and two hours after eating. That would have had him paddling around Neale Sound between 9:00 and 10:00 P.M. No, concluded the journalist, William Egan Colby had been killed.

Grant imagined that sometime in the early evening of Saturday the 27th, two or three men had parked near Colby's cottage, taken him by surprise, and abducted him. He would have gone quietly. Colby was the ultimate stoic, a fatalist who during his OSS days had come to view unreasoning fear as pointless and, from a practical perspective, dangerous. Some years earlier, Grant had visited Colby at his Georgetown row house. He had noticed that there were no locks on the doors, no deadbolts, nothing. When Grant had commented on the lack of security, his host had said that if anyone wanted to get him, they could do it; he wasn't going to live in a constant state of fear. In Vietnam, he had been the only high-ranking official to move about at night without an armed escort.

Grant surmised that another two or three men must have come by boat, tied on to Colby's canoe, pulled it loose from its mooring, and towed it away. Subsequently, the killers had suffocated Colby and then put him on ice. The water-borne assassins meanwhile took the canoe to the spit of land where the sound turned into the Wicomico River, placed it on the shoreline, and filled it with sand to keep it from drifting away. Sometime on the evening of May 5, Colby's killers had placed his body on the spit of land, but on the wrong side! They had selected the site because it was easily accessible both by water and by land via a branch off Rocky Point Road, which terminated just 40 meters from the water.[2]

Others had suspicions as well. Sally conducted her own informal investigation. The Agency assured her that the death was accidental but refused to share details of its investigation. As usual, the CIA had had exclusive control of the death scene until its agents were satisfied. The coroner's report, a copy of which the family obtained fifteen years later, seemed to go out of its way to reach conclusions. There was no evidence cited of a cardiovascular incident. Susan Colby, Bill's daughter-in-law, later heard rumors that a group of Vietnam veterans who haunted a bar near the marina had targeted Colby for what they believed to be their betrayal during the war. Colby's second son, Carl, would hint that he believed his father had committed suicide.

One thing was certain: Colby had lived a controversial and at times dangerous life. The former director of central intelligence was a deceptively mild-mannered, innocuous-looking man. Five feet nine inches tall, 170 pounds, with slicked-back hair and tortoise-shell glasses, he boasted finely chiseled features but described himself as someone who could not easily attract the attention of a waiter in a restaurant. The façade concealed a different persona. Colby was courageous, a natural leader of men, a veteran of conventional and unconventional combat, a patriot committed to the defense of his country, a man drawn to the sound of battle.

All wars produce casualties—killers and the killed. The conventional battlefield has its rules, but Bill Colby was an instrument of the CIA and as such participated in conflicts without rules or boundaries. During the 1960s, as Vietnam station chief and then head of the CIA's Far East Division, he had supervised the "secret war" in Laos—the United States had organized and armed a guerrilla force under the charismatic Vang Pao, unleashed it on the Ho Chi Minh Trail, and then abandoned it when the North Vietnamese Army moved into Laos in force. In 1965, Colby's Far East Division had supplied the new government in Indonesia with the names of thousands of suspected communists, who were then systematically "liquidated." Between 1968 and 1972, Colby had presided over the infamous Phoenix program in Vietnam, which had led to the deaths of at least twenty thousand Vietcong cadres. Colby had been CIA director when in 1975 the United States abandoned Vietnam. The CIA was able to extract thousands of South Vietnamese who had worked and fought for the Americans but left many thousands more behind, a number of them wives, sweethearts, or intimate friends of CIA personnel who had worked in-country.

Between 1974 and 1975, it was Colby as DCI who had made the decision to turn over the Agency's "family jewels" to Congress. The jewels were long-kept secrets regarding CIA participation in domestic spying, assassination plots against foreign leaders, experiments with mind-altering drugs, and US participation in the coup that overthrew Salvador Allende in Chile. The revelations split the intelligence community, with half regarding Colby as a traitor, and half seeing him as a savior. Among the former were James Jesus Angleton, the famed mole-hunter and head of the Agency's counterintelligence division. Angleton, brilliant, paranoid, and a political reactionary, had long viewed Colby as at best a communist dupe and at worst a Soviet mole. On the eve of the family jewels crisis, Colby had fired Angleton and the entire top brass of the counterintelligence division. Another victim of the family jewels crisis was former DCI Richard Helms, who pleaded no contest to charges that he had misled Congress concerning the CIA's role in the Allende affair. Crucial evidence implicating Helms had been turned over to the Justice Department by Colby himself. Then there was Henry Kissinger, also implicated in the Chilean affair. Kissinger seemed satisfied with having Colby fired in November 1975, but Angleton and Helms embarked on a vendetta that extended through the 1980s.

As director of central intelligence, Bill Colby had sought to change the very nature of intelligence gathering. Since the emergence of the nation-state system and the creation of the first security services, intelligence had been characterized by compartmentalization and absolute "need-to-know." A nation's spies operated outside constitutional and legal boundaries; secrecy was paramount, information restricted to the absolutely smallest number of individuals possible. Colby was remembered by his friends— and his enemies—for cooperating with Congress when it demanded that the Agency own up to its past and accept a future characterized by oversight and disclosure. Some said that Colby acted under duress; others, that he was an authentic advocate of more openness and accountability.

What got less public attention—but was far more worrisome to Angleton, Helms, and other traditionalists—was the array of internal reforms

Colby brought to the CIA. He attacked the concept of compartmental-ization, insisting on the broadest possible sharing of information among those who had expertise or a different perspective to offer. He was con-cerned with protection of sources and methods, but there were limits. Se-crets could be dangerous things. As he once remarked to Soviet leader Leonid Brezhnev, "the more we know about each other, the safer we are." From the point of view of those who made their lives in the world of espi-onage and counterespionage, Bill Colby was the ultimate subversive.[3]

But at heart, Colby was not a true spy. He came from that branch of the CIA that specialized in covert operations, political action, and nation-building. Like his father, he was a romantic of the Rudyard Kipling, Robert Baden-Powell, Theodore Roosevelt stripe. He could destroy the country's enemies, but he was much more interested in converting them, proving them wrong. As the Cold War developed in the 1950s and 1960s into a competition between two rival political and economic systems and moved from Europe to the developing world, Colby, the liberal activist, found himself in his element. He would train stay-behind networks in Scandi-navia (to offer resistance in case the Soviets overran the area), wage political warfare in Italy, and then spend nearly a dozen years trying to build a viable noncommunist society in South Vietnam. Colby was a champion of covert action, secret armies, pacification, and counterterrorism. These alternatives, he argued, were far preferable to conventional combat by main-force units, which killed tens of thousands and usually destroyed the country in which the battles were fought. Again, as far as the traditional military was con-cerned, Colby was a heretic, but for advocates of unconventional warfare, he was a prophet.

THE COLBYS AND
THE EGANS

B ill Colby's father, Elbridge, was the quintessential Yankee, descended from eight generations of Massachusetts Puritans-cum-Congrega- tionalists. A number of Colbys had been seafarers, ships' captains, and mates who were gone for years at a time as they traversed the world's oceans. Bill's grandfather, Charles Edward Colby, was the clan's first intellectual of note. Born in Massachusetts but educated in New York City's public schools, Charles had distinguished himself as an inventor and math whiz by age fourteen. He matriculated at Columbia College and subsequently rose to become professor of organic chemistry. He married Emily Lynn Carring- ton in 1882. Elbridge was born nine years later. Charles suffered from poor health throughout his adult life and died prematurely of Bright's disease.[1] Elbridge was nine years old.

The New York that Elbridge Colby grew up in was one of the most vi- brant communities in the world. It was a city of extreme wealth, high cul- ture, an emerging middle class, and a degraded underclass composed of dirty, diseased, illiterate immigrants who toiled from dawn to dusk for a pittance. While the rich reveled in the "high life," congregating at the Wal- dorf-Astoria and the opulent apartments of Fifth Avenue, and the doctors, lawyers, managers, and ministers sought refuge on Long Island or in the boroughs bordering Manhattan, the poor resided in crowded, filthy tene- ments in Five Points or the Lower East side—"Hell's Kitchen." The city produced America's first Progressive-era president, Theodore Roosevelt. Buoyed by his exploits with the Rough Riders in the Spanish American War (or at least reports of those exploits), by his embrace of the new reform movement known as Progressivism, and by his advocacy of overseas empire, Roosevelt had shot up through the ranks of the Republican Party. Even while he was president, TR continued to be an avid outdoorsman, hunting, hiking, and horseback riding whenever he could. He was the first conservationist to occupy the White House. From what he would call his "bully pulpit," TR advocated "preparedness" to his fellow Americans—which meant, for men, the willingness to forbear ease and risk their lives for their country; for women, the willingness to bear children and sacrifice for family; and for the nation, a strong military and active, independent foreign policy, coupled with laws to restrain big business and provide a degree of protection to the laboring masses. Though not of his socioeconomic class, the Colbys were enthusiastic supporters of the Rough Rider.

After his father's death, Elbridge's mother took a position in the registrar's office of New York's Hunter College. As his family clung desperately to the lower rungs of the middle class, Elbridge worked his way first through high school and then Columbia College. He received a bachelor's degree in English literature, graduating magna cum laude in 1912—the same year he became a Phi Beta Kappa—and earned a master's degree in 1913. Elbridge converted to Catholicism while in college. At Columbia, he was deeply influenced by the distinguished European historian Carlton J. H. Hayes. In 1904, Hayes, drawn by the teachings and example of John Henry Cardinal Newman, had himself converted. Elbridge's family did not approve of his conversion. Protestants to the core, his two older sisters would not speak to him for more than twenty years.[2]

In addition to Roosevelt, Hayes, and Newman, Elbridge was drawn to two other prominent figures of the post-Victorian era—the Englishmen Rudyard Kipling and Robert Baden-Powell. Kipling, one of the most popular writers of his time, was the ultimate apologist for British imperialism. Born in India, he and his parents considered themselves "Anglo-Indians." In his *Jungle Book* tales, *Kim*, and the epic poem "Gunga Din," Kipling reveled in the melding of native cultures and British civilization. His only son died in World War I. Robert Baden-Powell, first Baron Baden-Powell, was famed as the founder of modern scouting. "Lord B-P," as he became known in the press, served in the British Army from 1876 to 1910. During the early 1880s in the Natal Province of South Africa, where his regiment had been posted, Baden-Powell honed his military scouting skills amid the Zulu. In 1896, during the Second Matabele War, the Englishman met and befriended the American scout Frederick Burnham, who introduced Baden-Powell to "woodcraft," that is, the scout craft of the American Old West. Learned primarily from Native Americans, this method of scouting included among other things tracking, stealth, and survival techniques. On his return from Africa in 1903, Lord B-P found that his military training manual, *Aids to Scouting*, had become a best seller. *Scouting for Boys* was published in 1908 and sold 150 million copies during the years that followed.[3] TR, Baden-Powell, and Kipling were role models for the fatherless boy.

From 1912 to 1914, Elbridge was a Proudfit Fellow in Letters at Columbia. In 1914 he was accepted into the Ph.D. program in English at the University of Minnesota. While employed as an instructor there, he met and fell in love with Mary Margaret Egan, the daughter of one of nearby St. Paul's most prominent Catholic families. They were an unlikely couple. Elbridge, though still a young man, was evidencing that austerity, rigid self-discipline, and severity that would characterize the rest of his life. "Converts are painful people," Elbridge's granddaughter would later observe. Margaret was pretty, outgoing, liberal, and liberated. Her father, William H. Egan, born in St. Paul in 1859, was the son of Irish immigrants. Like Elbridge's Puritan ancestors, he had grown up on the frontier; the upper Midwest was the scene of the last sustained fighting between Indians and whites. As a young man, however, William Egan had learned Sioux—even producing a Sioux-English dictionary—and he had made a fortune trading with the natives rather than killing them. The family archives boasts a photo of little Margaret sitting in the lap of the famous Sitting Bull, who was clad in native garb and top hat. The Egans lived in a small mansion on Summit Avenue just down the street from railroad executive Jay Gould. By the 1890s, William had accumulated enough capital to take the family on an around-the-world tour. John, Margaret's elder brother, attended Harvard.[4]

Margaret was an English major at the University of Minnesota when she met Elbridge. It was still rare for women to go to college, and she was one of the few female students on campus. Margaret and Elbridge had very different personalities—Margaret was affectionate and carefree, and Elbridge stern and intense—but they shared common values. First, there was their Catholicism, which at that time began to emphasize the Social Gospel that later developed into the Catholic Worker Movement led by

Dorothy Day. Elbridge had inherited the educated New Englander's enlightened attitudes toward race, and the Egans were Democrats in a region where Progressivism was at its strongest. The Colby's exhibited enlightened racial attitudes early on. Elbridge's great-uncle, Lieutenant Colonel Ebenezer T. Colby of the 4th Massachusetts, writing to his brother in April 1863, had said, "Several hundreds of the able bodied men have joined the Negro Regiment forming here. Their condition arouses my sympathies. I am becoming more and more interested in this oppressed race every day. I hope the Government will adopt a liberal policy respecting them." Both Margaret and Elbridge also had a strong sense of service and a determination to make a difference.[5]

In 1915, Elbridge interrupted his studies—and his courtship—to volunteer for service with the Serbian Executive Committee of Mercy, a creation of the American Red Cross. Following the outbreak of World War I, the committee had devoted itself to aiding the wounded and displaced of the various Allied countries, especially Belgium and Serbia. Elbridge spent several months in the Balkans driving ambulances, delivering supplies, and helping to set up refugee camps. He was a Progressive abroad—a miniature Herbert Hoover—sharing American largesse and striving to make a better world. For his efforts he was awarded the Serbian Red Cross's Gold Medal and, after the Versailles Peace Conference, the Order of Mercy by Yugoslavia, Serbia's successor state.[6]

In 1916, Elbridge returned to his teaching post in Minnesota; he married Margaret the following year.[7] When America entered World War I in 1917, Elbridge enlisted, hoping to be sent to France, where he could establish a combat record. Instead, to his deep chagrin, he was posted to Panama to serve in the detachment guarding the canal. The one bright spot was that Margaret was able to accompany him. At war's end in 1919, he resigned from the army, and, with a pregnant Margaret in tow, returned to Minnesota to resume his studies and teaching duties.

William Egan Colby was born in St. Paul on January 4, 1920. A year later, Elbridge earned his doctorate and then abruptly decided to reenlist in the military. In his memoirs, Bill recalled that his father "became anxious about his ability, as a struggling writer and underpaid teacher, to support his family of my mother and myself." Indeed, so strapped was the young couple that they found it necessary to live with the Egans after returning from

Panama. "I went into the Army to keep the family decent," Elbridge would later tell one of his grandsons.[8]

It was clear that eventually Margaret would become a modest heiress, but her Yankee husband had no intention of living off his wife. There was more than machismo involved; from an early age, Elbridge had had to assume familial duties; he was raised to be responsible, to take responsibility for those dependent on him, and then, of course, to breed responsibility. The army recognized Elbridge's previous service and advanced degree and granted him a commission. Thus, at the age of twenty-nine, Second Lieutenant Elbridge Colby embarked on a military career that would span four decades; ultimately, however, he would be noted more for his intellectual and pedagogical attainments than for his battlefield achievements.

The interwar army was small and dominated by southern whites—and as such its culture was a bit alien to Yankees like Elbridge and Margaret. The Colbys bounced around from post to post, landing, in 1925, at Fort Benning, Georgia, where Elbridge became involved in a racial incident that would change the course of his career. That year the army, rather unwisely, had assigned the all-black 24th Infantry Division to Benning, which was situated in the heart of the ex-Confederacy. The 24th had been established in 1869 and at that time had included African American veterans of the Union Army as well as freed slaves. The regiment was one of the "Buffalo Soldier" outfits that had served in the Indian Wars on the western frontier, in the Spanish American War, and in General John J. Pershing's punitive expedition against Pancho Villa in 1916. In 1917, 150 members of the unit had become involved in a vicious race riot in Houston.

While Elbridge was at Benning, a black soldier from the 24th was shot dead in nearby Americus, Georgia, when he refused to give up the sidewalk to a white. Subsequently, an all-white jury acquitted the shooter. Elbridge, then serving as Benning's publicity officer, wrote an outraged letter of protest for the post's newspaper, calling upon all soldiers, black and white, to declare support for their wronged comrade. His eloquent appeal was reprinted in *The Nation* magazine, creating a national uproar. With the Georgia congressional delegation calling for Elbridge's head, the black press and the biracial NAACP came to the young officer's aid, but the army also felt that it had to act. As punishment, Elbridge was to be assigned for a period to the 24th.[9] Although the idealistic young officer hardly viewed his assignment as punishment, the Benning incident would mar his career, and many in his family, including Bill, would later believe that it had kept Elbridge from attaining the rank of general.

In 1929, Elbridge, now a captain, was assigned to the 15th Infantry Regiment in Tientsin (Tianjin), China. Bill, who was nine years old when his father received the assignment, would spend the next three years in the Orient; it would be one of the formative influences of his life.

The 15th Regiment had initially served in China as part of the relief expedition that had ended the siege of foreigners in Peking during the Boxer Uprising (1899–1900). Although the regiment was withdrawn after the Great Powers crushed the rebellion, it was ordered back to China following the collapse of the Manchu Dynasty in 1912. Headquartered in Tientsin, it took its position astride the Peking-Mukden railway in January 1912; it labored to protect American interests during the tumultuous years of the 1920s, particularly when the Chinese Nationalists ousted the ruling dynasty and then split into communist and noncommunist factions. A prolonged civil war between the two groups ended with Chiang Kai-shek and the Nationalists driving Mao Tse-tung and the communists into the far northwestern reaches of the country.[10] Despite this unrest, China was an attractive post for many Americans: alcohol was legal and plentiful, and the Great Depression lay half a world away. Elbridge was particularly excited about the assignment. China had occupied a special place in the hearts and minds of American Progressives. Bankers and businessmen dreamed of a "great China market," while missionaries and engineers like Herbert Hoover labored to bring a better life to the inhabitants of the land that Pearl S. Buck would so movingly profile in her novel *The Good Earth*. Progressives had launched the "Open Door Policy," which sought to preserve both Chinese markets and sovereignty, and many had embraced Chiang as the avatar of modernity. Tientsin promised to satisfy Elbridge's yearning for adventure and provide an outlet for his missionary impulses.

Elbridge, Margaret, and Bill began their journey to Tientsin on the East Coast in the fall, boarding a US Army Transport (USAT) in Brooklyn. The voyage proceeded down the eastern seaboard, where it encountered one of the gales that regularly visit the mid-Atlantic states with winter's approach. Farther south, the travelers encountered warmer weather and the stunning blue waters of the Caribbean. After a brief stop to allow passengers to see the Canal Zone and the sights of Panama City, which were new to Bill, the ship continued on to San Francisco. There Elbridge and his family boarded the "doughboy special," the USAT *Thomas*, a veteran of many transpacific runs. Following weeks at sea, the ship anchored at Chinwangtao, a major Chinese port on the Gulf of Chihli that served much of northern China, including Peking and Tientsin. Disembarking, the new arrivals boarded railcars for a six-hour trip along the Peking-Mukden railway to Tientsin, 167 miles to the southwest. At last, the replacements for the 15th arrived at Tientsin's East Station, there to find the regiment's service company waiting with teams of horses and baggage wagons. The new arrivals were soon marching along Victoria and Meadows Roads bound for the American compound situated in the old German concession.[11]

Tientsin, a city of four thousand foreigners and a million Chinese, was situated on a vast alluvial plain extending beyond Peking to the Gulf of Chihli on the Yellow Sea. It lay at the head of the Hai Ho, the "Sea River," a short waterway formed by the confluence of the Grand Canal entering Tientsin from the west and the Pei Ho River flowing from the northwest. The Sea River meandered 40 miles to the southeast, where its mouth was guarded by the Taku forts. The Sea River was an important commercial waterway navigated by small steamers, seagoing junks, and gunboats of the international concessionary powers, those nations that during the past century had forced various Chinese rulers to grant them territory and economic monopolies.[12]

As far as the eye could see, the surrounding countryside was absolutely flat, dotted with small villages, brick kilns, and the mounds of countless graves. The climate in northern China was harsh. Summers were stifling and winters bitterly cold. Situated on the banks of the Sea River, Tientsin was sometimes flooded, especially in typhoon season. In the spring, northeastern China choked under a veil of dust blowing in from the Gobi Desert located 65 miles to the northwest. Because it was the gateway to Peking, the imperial seat, Tientsin was known as the Ford of Heaven.

The United States had obtained a concession in Tientsin in 1860 when it had become a treaty port. The Americans had formally ended their residency in 1896, and although US troops had joined in putting down the Boxer Rebellion in 1901, there was no official presence until the United

States took over the German concession in the aftermath of World War I. By 1924, Tientsin was garrisoned by British, French, Italian, Japanese, and American troops.

Foreigners were struck by the squalor and despair of the native sections of the city. The population—as initially perceived by the soldiers, at least—consisted of masses of dirty, crippled, stinking, terrible-looking beings. The half-clothed "coolies" sweated in the summertime and shivered in the winter. There were the ever-present rickshaw drivers, while other members of the lumpen proletariat, "like beasts of burden," loaded and unloaded coal and other cargo from ships and barges. The natives' day-to-day existence seemed perpetually precarious. During times of famine, peasant families could be found around the rail station trying to sell their children.

By contrast, the foreign business sections of the city featured wide, paved streets flanked with stores whose windows displayed as varied an assortment of articles as any thriving Western city. One American, finding himself on Victoria Road in the British sector, observed that he might as well be on Bond Street in London or Fifth Avenue in New York. "The glamour of the place is beyond my power of exposition," he wrote in a letter home. "[It is] the most cosmopolitan place I . . . have ever seen. In one block one may see an English, a French, an Italian soldier, a dozen Jap soldiers, a Jew drummer, an American expatriate [sic], a Russian . . . and a Capuchin monk."[13]

Money went a long way in Tientsin. American soldiers were paid in gold, and the exchange rate was excellent. A bachelor officer could rent a room above the officer's club, but officers with families—such as Elbridge—had to find quarters outside the US compound, though still within the International Concession. The Colbys occupied an abode that would have been considered a mansion back in the States. Like other American families, they employed a domestic staff, including a "number one boy," a cook, two maids, a gardener, and an amah (nanny) to look after Bill. Almost all manual labor in the concession was performed by Chinese. Even when in the field, the 15th Regiment had coolies to set up camp and do the cooking and washing. Low rent and cheap labor, unfortunately, rode on the backs of squalor and disease. Foreigners had to take extraordinary measures to protect their health. Virulent diseases such as smallpox and cholera were constant threats. Drinking tap water "was an open invitation to the agonies of amoebic dysentery," according to the 15th's official historian.[14]

Despite his youth, Bill had the run of the city, first in the company of his nanny and later on his own. Victoria Park in the British concession was surrounded by iron railings. No Chinese were allowed into the park—except for amahs in charge of foreign children, hobbling along on their bound feet. Looming over the park was a dark gray building, half castle and half cathedral—Gordon Hall, named after General Charles George "Chinese" Gordon, who had surveyed and fixed the boundaries of the British Concession after the conclusion of the Second Opium War in 1860.[15]

The market was located on Taku Road, a dirt thoroughfare that bisected the British sector and extended into the native districts at both ends. Hundreds of Chinese mingled there. Stallkeepers hawked their wares, and the air reeked of fresh earth, cabbage stalks, aniseed, garlic, and soya. A huge granary housed the rice that came up the Grand Canal from southern China, forming one side of the marketplace. Against this building's wall, acrobats, storytellers, magicians, and conjurors performed. Next to the conjurors sat a row of men making six-inch-high figures out of different colors of clay mixed with water. The figures were called *ni ren*, which meant "mud men." You could ask for anything you wished—opera singer, dancer, mandarin, or warrior. The sculptors were especially good at soldiers.[16]

Periodically, a junk loaded with supplies—frequently arms—was hijacked on the Sea River or the Grand Canal, supposedly by pirates. The British editor of the *Peking and Tientsin Times*, however, correctly identified the brigands as members of the infamous White Lotus Society, the influential antiforeign movement whose agitation had spawned the Boxer Rebellion. One day, the sound of gunfire coming from the river brought Bill's mother, Margaret, up short. Bill was nowhere to be seen. She and Elbridge began scouring the city. They eventually found their son with some other European boys at the riverfront, where the local protection force was fighting off "pirates"—in reality White Lotuses attempting to hijack a junk full of arms.[17]

Like the other children of American and English families, Bill attended the Gordon Road School. The Empire Cinema was a favorite haunt of concession boys; on Saturday afternoons the performance always began with the same ritual. Herr Schneider, who looked just like Charlie Chaplin, would walk down the five steps into the orchestra pit, take his violin out of its case, and rest it on a small pad on his shoulder. The theater's pianist would sound the key note while Herr Schneider tuned his strings. After bowing to the cellist and second violinist, who together made up the rest of the orchestra, the maestro would turn to glance up at the cinema manager, who stood beside the film projector at the back of the gallery. It was his signal for the picture to begin, and the youngsters settled down in their seats to watch yet another installment of a serial like *Tarzan of the Apes.* Herr Schneider provided passionate background music for all of the shows until the advent of talkies.[18]

The officers and men of the regiment were encouraged to mingle with the Chinese and learn local customs. Chinese-language training was mandatory for officers, and Elbridge hired a language instructor for Margaret and Bill. The latter's CIA personnel file would later list his Chinese language skill as "fair." One family photo features father and son dressed in native Chinese garb. In the sweltering summers, the Colbys vacationed at the seaside resorts of Qinhuangdao and Weihai. In the fall there was horseback riding on the plains surrounding Tientsin. Bill would later observe that "my boyhood experiences of China . . . had prepared me for the exoticism of Asia."[19] In truth, foreign travel was a rarity for pre–World War II Americans. Bill's experiences in China would do more than prepare him for the mysteries of the Orient; it would create a lifelong craving for immersion in other cultures. Though he was just a preteen during his Tientsin experiences, young Bill was sensitized to the political, economic, and military forces that were shaping international politics.

Nationalist aspirations, conflicting ideologies, and imperial designs swirled all about the Colbys. During their posting, Elbridge, Margaret, and Bill visited Japan, traveling by steamer up through the inland sea to Hiroshima and then boarding a train to Yokohama. There they saw the giant steel mills that would fuel the burgeoning Japanese military-industrial complex. Japanese encroachment on Manchuria had begun just when the Colbys arrived in China. During the family's three years in Tientsin, the Japanese garrison in the city grew from six hundred to six thousand. "As a kid," Bill's son John recounted, "he saw the new Japanese soldier firsthand—tough, dedicated, fanatical even."[20] America would eventually have to deal with this threat, Elbridge told his son. The Republic must play its proper role in world affairs, he insisted, protecting its legitimate strategic and economic interests. Woodrow Wilson had been right: totalitarian aggression was a threat to all people, and the United States had a duty to facilitate the spread of democracy and to support the principle of national self-determination. The fate of the nation and the fate of the world were inextricably intertwined.

In 1932, Elbridge's tour of duty came to an end. Shortly after the family's return from China, he was assigned to the Reserve Officer's Training Corps (ROTC) at the University of Vermont as an instructor in military science. Burlington, the state capital and site of the university, was a charming, rustic town of some forty thousand. The community and its college were situated on the wooded eastern shore of Lake Champlain. Small and remote at the close of the Revolutionary War, Burlington had quickly attained a degree of prosperity as its economy shifted from fur trading to textile manufacturing and lumber milling. Burlington's most famous citizen had been Ethan Allen, whose Green Mountain Boys played a key role in the capture of Fort Ticonderoga during the war for American independence.[21]

Bill was as happy in Burlington as he would be anywhere in his youth, or at least as happy as an army child could be. He would later recall that the family's constant travels provided him with a unique education, but also with a sense of rootlessness. Still, his years in Burlington were ones of stability and contentment. Like most of his peers, Bill was an avid outdoorsman. In the winters he captained the high-school ski team; in the summers, he spent much of his time on or around Lake Champlain.

Shortly after the family's arrival in Vermont, Elbridge moved into a cottage he had inherited from his father at Thompson's Point on the lake. Hunting, fishing, canoeing, and camping lay just beyond the Colby's back door. When he was thirteen, Bill and a friend, Bill Cook, embarked on a ten-day canoe trip on the lake, camping on shore at night.[22] During the summer before his junior year, he and another chum embarked on a two-week biking tour around New England, visiting forts and historical landmarks by day and sleeping in fields and meadows by night. Physically, Bill Colby was unimpressive: full grown, he stood no more than five feet nine inches, and, until late in life, he never weighed more than about 150 pounds. In high school, his frame was almost waifish, accentuated by a large head on a thin neck. His fine-boned face promised a certain handsomeness in maturity, and young Colby was neat, even natty, with dark, meticulously combed hair and wire-rimmed glasses. There was an excellent mind, well-disciplined and inquisitive without being pedantic. He made excellent grades, rarely recording a C at a time when A's and B's were given to only the best students.

Bill remained an only child, which was somewhat unusual in a Catholic family. There were rumors of miscarriages. The young man spent a great deal of time with his parents. His mother—warm, gracious, mannerly without pretension—adored Bill. Her love was unconditional but not permissive. Like many strong women of her era, Margaret identified with her son and envisioned great things for him. Elbridge did not trust to love; like John and Abigail Adams, he believed in discipline and detailed guidance for his progeny. Elbridge spent his days away from his teaching duties at the university writing and exercising. John Colby later remembered his grandfather as "ramrod straight, a principled guy" who could not make small talk and who was devoid of humor. Elbridge proved a diligent and diverse, if not accomplished, scholar. Among his many published works were *The Echo Device in Literature*, *Early American Comedy*, *Problems in Trench Warfare*, *Theodore Winthrop*, and *The First Army in Europe*.[23]

Elbridge was an avid genealogist, compiling more than enough documentation to win membership in the Sons of the American Revolution. He frequently took Bill to nearby Fort Ticonderoga, which the Colbys' ancestors had helped capture from the British, and to Fort William Henry, which Colonel Jonathan Bagley, another ancestor, had helped to build. "Bill loved to go to Fort Ticonderoga . . . loved the Green Mountain Boys and the idea of these irregulars taking on this massive fort," son John recalled. "He grew up with that spirit and those stories from his father, yet he was not a martial kind of guy." As the family remembered it, Margaret and her sister Frances, who moved in permanently following her husband's death, were not much into substantive matters. While Elbridge might want to discuss the Greek origins of geometry, they preferred to talk about the latest fashions or the movies. That left young Bill as Elbridge's principal interlocutor. The father liked to argue, but he was tolerant of dissent. The son did not have the option of nonparticipation; so Bill learned how to take a point and defend it, to think clearly, and to express himself concisely. He also acquired a certain imperviousness to pressure. "My dad's father was very directed, I would not say harsh, but stern and focused," another of Elbridge's grandsons, Carl, recalled. "His mother gave Bill all the love he ever needed and he just took off from there."[24]

As an adult, Bill Colby would spend much of his time either as a participant in or an advocate for unconventional warfare. It was an appreciation bequeathed him by his father. Elbridge was fascinated with Robert Rogers and Rogers' Rangers. Rogers' Rangers were, of course, a historical reality, an independent company of colonial irregulars attached to the British army during the Seven Years' War. The unit was organized and trained by Major Robert Rogers as a rapidly deployable light infantry force tasked with reconnaissance and special operations conducted against distant targets. So effective was the unit that it became the chief scouting company of British forces in North America. In front of the Colby house at Thompson's Point lay a trail taken by Rogers and his men as they ventured north during the French and Indian War. Their mission was a reprisal for Indian raids against British settlements. After killing every man, woman, and child in an Indian village, they returned safely to Fort William Henry.

Elbridge had Bill, and, subsequently, his grandsons, read Kenneth Roberts's *Northwest Passage*, published in 1936. In the book, the young protagonist, Langdon Towne, is a Harvard graduate, an aspiring artist, an avid outdoorsman, a naturalist, a patriot—and a soldier-disciple of Robert Rogers. The villains in Towne's community are local officials who are guilty of arbitrary exercise of power, misuse of authority, and abuse of the law. The rangers in the novel assume almost mythical proportions: "Mostly they get along without sleeping, and a good part of the time they get along without eating," a Rogers' disciple told young Towne. "Sometimes they lay [*sic*] in one spot for twelve hours without moving, while the mosquitoes and the black flies chewin' 'em to pieces. Other times they run seventy-eighty miles in a day and kill a few Indians when they get where they're going. If they can go afoot, they do so; but if they can't go afoot, they go in canoes, or on rafts, or on skates or on snowshoes. . . . They're up prowling around when everybody else is a-bed." Rogers himself was, of course, a backwoods superhero—woodsman, diplomat, gentleman, a killer of men and unkillable himself.[25]

Bill Colby emerged from childhood to adolescence in the shadow of his father and his father's obsession with Rogers' Rangers and irregular warfare. But it may have been Langdon Towne as much as Robert Rogers who intrigued the Colbys. Kenneth Roberts introduced his book with the following passage: "The Northwest Passage, in the imagination of all free people, is a short cut to fame, fortune and romance—a hidden route to Golconda and the mystic East. On every side of us are men who hunt perpetually for their personal Northwest Passage, too often sacrificing health, strength and life itself to the search; and who shall say they are not happier in their vain but hopeful quest than wiser, duller folk who sit at home, venturing nothing and, with sour laughs, deriding the seekers for that fabled thoroughfare—that panacea for all the afflictions of a humdrum world." Langdon was such a man, a man Elbridge and Bill were determined to emulate.[26]

The beneficiary of some excellent schooling at home and abroad, Bill skipped a grade, graduating from Burlington High School in 1936 at the age of sixteen. He had planned to apply to West Point, following his father into the military, but he was a year too young. In the interim he was admitted to Princeton. By Christmas vacation, Bill had turned seventeen, old enough to apply to the Academy. Then, as now, candidates were nominated by their congressmen and senators, but only after passing West Point's entrance examination, which included a physical. The extremely nearsighted Bill failed the eye test. His disappointment quickly abated. "I was delighted," he later recalled, "for that one year at Princeton had disabused me of the idea of a military career."

The New Jersey school was home to the children of some of the nation's wealthiest families. The town of Princeton, population seven thousand, consisted almost entirely of students, faculty, and school employees. The Gothic architecture, set off by a wooded campus, was breathtaking. Princeton was a whites-only institution, and co-eds were still four decades in the future.[27]

   If Bill Colby was taken with Princeton, it was certainly because of its intellectual rather than its social offerings. Woodrow Wilson—who had been president of the university from 1902 to 1910—had brought the institution into the twentieth century, adding modern subjects in the social sciences to the curriculum and attracting some of the world's best thinkers to the college. He tried, but failed, to abolish Princeton's exclusive "eating clubs," which served as surrogate fraternities. Bill Colby possessed neither the money nor the social standing to be admitted. He was, financially at least, a middle-class boy at an upper-class institution. Not only did he eat at the cafeteria at Madison Hall, he also waited tables there. His social life revolved mainly around the Catholic Church and ROTC. Princeton was then still very much a Presbyterian institution, and twice-a-week chapel attendance was required; Bill was allowed to substitute by serving as an altar boy at the Catholic Church. He thrived in ROTC, rising to be cadet captain by his senior year. Throughout his life, Bill Colby would be drawn to people from working-class backgrounds with Ivy League degrees.[28]

On the Princeton campus were some of academia's leading lights, including Albert Einstein. Princeton was a traditional liberal arts institution; students were required to pass 118 hours in courses ranging from history and philosophy to foreign language, chemistry, and psychology. Like most other undergraduates, Bill's first two years were spent in survey classes. He remembered being especially caught up with anthropology. Woodrow Wilson, much enamored of Oxford and Cambridge, had introduced preceptorships at Princeton. Small groups of students, under the guidance of an individual faculty member, would pursue directed readings in a particular subject. Topping off the undergraduate experience was a comprehensive examination and a senior thesis. Colby opted to major in politics and history, ensuring that he took most of his classes during his junior and senior years in the School of Public and International Affairs. Among his favorite instructors were Edwin S. Corwin and Alpheus T. Mason, who taught constitutional law and political theory, respectively.[29]

The mid-1930s was an exciting time to be studying American politics. The administration of Franklin D. Roosevelt was attempting to pull the country out of the Great Depression through bold new experiments in political economy and social justice, including the Federal Deposit Insurance Corporation, the Works Progress Administration, the Social Security Acts, and the Agricultural Adjustment Acts. Louis Brandeis, Mason's icon, was one of the Supreme Court's minority of liberals who believed that the federal government had a right and a duty to act to regulate big business and to advance the causes of social and economic justice. In addition to teaching and writing, Corwin acted as an adviser to the Public Works Administration. Colby remembered becoming a total convert to Roosevelt's New Dealism at Princeton. His tutors certainly played a role in this conversion, but both the Colbys and the Egans had long evidenced liberal views on race, the appropriate role of government in society, and the need for social and economic justice. At the School of Public and International Affairs, Colby conducted independent research on problems such as black education, the Cuban sugar trade, and civil liberties violations in Jersey City, which was then ruled by Boss Frank Hague, one of the most corrupt machine politicians in the country.

Bill Colby's stint at Princeton also coincided with the rise of European and Japanese fascism and with a deeply divisive debate in the United States as to the nation's proper role in the looming international crisis. The peace structure established by the Treaty of Versailles was one of the shortest-lived in modern history. It took but twenty-one brief years for the world to move from one cataclysm to another, even greater one. During the 1930s, three European states emerged to challenge the status quo that Woodrow Wilson and his associates had established in the aftermath of World War I: Nazi Germany, Fascist Italy, and the Soviet Union, the world's first great experiment in Marxism-Leninism. Adolf Hitler came to power in Germany in 1933 promising to regain all the territory and power the Reich had lost in the Great War. In 1935, the führer renounced the disarmament clauses of the Versailles Treaty, and in the following year he ordered the Wehrmacht to occupy and fortify the Rhineland. Germany had given notice. Benito Mussolini and his fascist followers had seized power in Italy in 1922, ending the kaleidoscopic succession of governments that had ruled Italy since its unification. Il Duce established a one-party corporate state and declared the Mediterranean to be "mare nostrum," our sea. In 1935, Italy overran Ethiopia, strategically situated on the Horn of Africa, although Mussolini's air force and armored infantry had a difficult time with Haile Selassie's mounted spearmen. The Soviet Union, ruled iron-handedly by Joseph Stalin, had not yet made its foreign policy goals explicit, but it was no secret that Moscow intended at the first opportunity to regain the territory it had lost in Eastern Europe at the close of the Great War.

Confronting these expansionist powers were the victors of the world war: Britain and France, allied with a smaller group of states created or re-shaped by the Treaty of Versailles. The Western democracies faced two alternatives: they could confront Germany and Italy at the outset, nipping fascist aggression in the bud, or they could seek to appease Hitler and Mussolini. Enmeshed in the problems of the Great Depression and politically fractured, Paris, London, and their allies chose the latter path. One of the reasons later put forward in defense of this ill-conceived approach was the unwillingness of the United States to join with the European democracies in standing up to the dictators at that time.

In truth, isolationism was the order of the day in the United States. Americans were far too concerned with the vast economic, financial, and social crisis that followed in the wake of the Wall Street crash of 1929 to pay much attention to what was going on overseas. Presidents Herbert Hoover and Franklin D. Roosevelt were loath to embark on a risky foreign policy that could jeopardize domestic recovery. Moreover, Americans were deeply disillusioned with the results of World War I. Most had come to believe that the nation's sacrifices had been for naught, and that the United States had been tricked into participating by the wily British or by unscrupulous war profiteers. By the mid-1930s, pacifism was rampant on the nation's college campuses. At Princeton and other institutions of higher learning, a student organization—the Veterans of Future Wars—led annual class boycotts and staged protest meetings at which young men signed pledges never to participate in any foreign war. Reflecting the popular mood, Congress between 1935 and 1937 passed a series of Neutrality Acts prohibiting US citizens from loaning money to nations at war, selling arms to belligerents, and traveling to war zones.

Isolationists again carried the day when a civil war erupted in Spain in 1936. General Francisco Franco, whose Falangist Party resembled Mussolini's fascists, waged a bloody struggle to overthrow the Republican government, which included both communists and socialists. Germany and Italy supported the Falangists, supplying Franco with massive amounts of munitions, while the Loyalists (as government supporters were called) received less substantial support from the Soviet Union. The United States joined the British and French in refusing to offer assistance to either side. Americans were deeply divided over the Spanish Civil War. Many Roman Catholics, including the proto-fascist "radio priest" Father Charles E. Coughlin, strongly supported Franco, while those on the left, from liberals to members of the tiny Communist Party, supported the Republic. Over a thousand young Americans enlisted in the Abraham Lincoln Brigade that fought for the Loyalists.

Meanwhile, at Princeton, Bill Colby had decided to spend the summer prior to his senior year—that is, 1939—in France, honing his language skills and soaking up French culture. Elbridge arranged for him to live with a family in the Loire Valley. For three months, Bill bicycled through the chateau-studded countryside, stopping in various villages to sample country cuisine and converse in French. In the midst of this idyll, he and a friend ventured to the Pyrenees. There the two young men encountered a steady stream of bloody, dispossessed refugees from the Spanish Civil War raging just over the border. Just the previous semester, Bill had written an essay on propaganda in Spain, both of the right and the left, as an independent study project for the Politics Department. In it, he had anticipated a larger European conflict and lamented the excesses of both the Fascists and the Republicans. After acknowledging the right of revolution to secure popular rule, he condemned Franco for leading a "minority revolt in behalf of a reactionary and Fascist State, which the people have voted against." The Soviet Union, a totalitarian state, might be aiding the Republicans, the young undergraduate wrote, "but it frightens me not at all to learn that hitherto poverty stricken peasants are taking over acres of land which formerly went to the support of one man, or that the government and even industry are now under the control of the people."[30]

World War II erupted while Bill was in Europe. In the spring of 1939, Hitler broke his Munich pledge and overran the remainder of Czechoslovakia, annexing a state that had no cultural or historical relationship to Germany. In August, Germany invaded Poland, and Britain and France declared war. Hard on the heels of these events, Bill Colby sailed for home. The British liner on which he crossed the Atlantic was guarded by a detachment of soldiers whose duty it was to ward off attack by German submarines or surface raiders. By the time he landed on American soil, Colby had become, by his own accounts, an ardent internationalist. Indeed, he later confided to his son John that had he been old enough, he would have joined the Lincoln Brigade: "He was very proud and awed by the people who had volunteered in that struggle," John recalled.[31]

Back at Princeton, Colby chose as the subject of his senior thesis France's reaction to fascist aggression in Europe. He saw it as a case study for exploring the issue of why democracies seemed so weak in their dealings with totalitarian states. A contemporary of Colby's named John F. Kennedy was examining the same topic from the British perspective while completing his studies at Harvard. Colby was extremely critical of appeasement, coming down particularly hard on the Popular Front government in France. If the democracies had cast their lot with the Austrians and Czechs in 1938, he maintained, Hitler and Mussolini could have been stopped before they had gotten started. The young scholar abjured any sympathy for communism, however. Communism and fascism were both expansionist, imperialist, racist ideologies, and the Nazi-Soviet Pact proved that Russia could not be trusted. "I am willing to concede," he wrote in his memoir, *Honorable Men*, "my Catholicism may well have kept me from the emotional antifascism that pushed many of my time into the ranks of the Communists. . . . I was perfectly convinced—which of course many supporters of the Republican cause were not—that it was possible to be antifascist without becoming pro-Communist." Many years later he would cite George Orwell's *Homage to Catalonia* as a penetrating, authentic look at the Communist International in action.[32]

Bill Colby graduated from Princeton in the spring of 1940. Ceremonies included singing the "Cannon Song" while the new alums broke ceremonial clay pipes over the Revolutionary War cannon anchored behind Nassau Hall.[33] Within a month of his departure from Princeton, the Wehrmacht had overrun France. Three hundred and fifty thousand members of the British Expeditionary Force barely escaped with their side arms from the French port of Dunkirk. With the fall of France, the conflict between isolationists, led by the America First Committee, and interventionists, spearheaded by the Committee to Defend America by Aiding the Allies, reached a crescendo. Bill was certain, as were most liberal interventionists, that war with the Axis powers (including Imperial Japan, which had conquered Manchuria and invaded northern China) was inevitable. Although he had served as cadet captain of his ROTC unit at Princeton, Colby had not been commissioned with his classmates. He was still several months shy of his twenty-first birthday (the age of conscription did not change from twenty-one to eighteen until after the attack on Pearl Harbor).

Bill applied to Columbia Law School and was accepted. Elbridge had been assigned to army headquarters in Washington, DC, and Bill decided to spend the summer there with his parents. To pass the time and earn a little money, he landed a job pumping gas in the District of Columbia. "Gas station attendants weren't unionized," he later remembered, "and I enthusiastically joined in the effort to organize them in the best tradition of New Deal liberalism."[34]

The beginning of the fall term at Columbia brought the younger Colby's union activities to a halt. Bill moved into the law dormitory and immediately struck up a friendship with Stan Temko, who would go on to become a partner in Covington and Burlington, Secretary of State Dean Acheson's law firm. The two men would become lifelong friends. Diligent and disciplined, as always, Bill was soon named to the *Law Review*.

All was not cloistered study, however. Stan Temko later recalled a trip to Vermont that included skiing with Barnard girls. Bill subsequently met another Barnard student, Barbara Heinzen, when Temko arranged a blind date for him. "It was all very informal," Barbara later recalled, "because we were going to the Gold Rail, a local campus hangout." She was not particularly taken with the young man physically—he was of medium height, wore glasses, and seemed very conventional ("not the person to stand out in a crowd," as she put it)—but she found him to be an excellent conversationalist. The two hit it off and began dating. "We had splendid times together, racing around New York, dancing, partying, endlessly arguing politics with our friends," Bill later wrote. Those discussions generally revolved around the war in Europe and the Roosevelt administration's move from neutrality in 1939 to undeclared naval war with Germany by the winter of 1941. Bill recalled vividly that on one of their outings in early 1941, he and Barbara witnessed a communist-led demonstration on the Columbia campus. Participants paraded around with mock coffins to protest Roosevelt's decision to aid Britain. This was, of course, prior to the German invasion of the Soviet Union.[35]

In the summer of 1941, Colby applied for and received his commission in the US Army. In August, he left for basic training at Fort Bragg, North Carolina. That same month, President Roosevelt and British prime minister Winston Churchill met off the coast of Newfoundland aboard the HMS *Prince of Wales* to sign the Atlantic Charter, which outlined the two democracies' postwar aims and, more important, signified America's growing solidarity with its beleaguered ally. By November, US Navy vessels were convoying British and American transports across the Atlantic. Japan's sneak attack on Pearl Harbor on December 7 propelled the United States into the war against the Axis.

Bill Colby recalled that Pearl Harbor brought him, as well as most of the country, a sense of relief as well as horror and anger. The debate was over; at last, a united America would throw its immense weight into the fight against the Axis powers. The pressing question for Second Lieutenant Colby was how and when he would be able to enter the fray. The "day that would live in infamy" found the young officer in the artillery training program at Fort Sill, Oklahoma. To his dismay, he proved so proficient at "canon cocking" that he was detailed to the training unit as an instructor rather than being sent to a combat zone. "After six months in that job," he wrote in his memoirs, "I was afraid the war would be over before I got a chance to fight—a repetition of my father's frustration in Panama during World War I."[36]

Fate intervened, however, in the form of a notice on the post bulletin board calling for volunteers for a new type of warfare—parachuting. Colby wasn't sure what that involved, beyond jumping out of an airplane, but he noted that officers hoping to keep their best men could not obstruct those who wanted to volunteer. Like West Point, the parachute program required a vigorous physical. The nearsighted Colby was not to be foiled again. While undressing and dressing in the doctor's office, he memorized the 20/40 line—the minimum required—on the eye chart. Unfortunately, when he "read off" the numbers and letters, he reversed them. He couldn't see the 20/50 line at all. The examining physician asked the young officer if he really wanted to be a parachutist. "You're damn right I do," Colby replied. "Well I guess your eyesight is good enough for you to see the ground," the doctor replied, and passed him.[37]

It was off to Fort Benning, Georgia, where the army's new parachute school was located. Candidates had to undergo weeks of training before they were allowed their first airplane jump. Among other things, they had to leap from four 250-foot-high towers and learn how to properly pack their own chutes. Some of Colby's contemporaries remembered him as handling the whole parachuting experience with nonchalance. A combat assignment was again delayed, however, when he broke his ankle during one of the training jumps. The accident took him out of the training cycle until he could heal. After completing his training, Bill was assigned to an artillery unit within the 82nd Airborne. Unfortunately, he lacked seniority, and when the unit shipped out, Colby was left behind in the officer replacement pool. He was cooling his heels at Camp Mackall, North Carolina, when the OSS came calling.[38]

3

JEDBURGH

Like most Americans at that time, Bill Colby had never heard of the Office of Strategic Services—it had only been established in June 1942, and, for obvious reasons, its activities were closely guarded secrets. Until World War II, the United States had not had a permanent intelligence service, even though the other major nation-states of the world had possessed them for centuries. The country had its wartime spies, of course, beginning with the redoubtable Nathan Hale; but once the firing ceased, America's spies had been put on the shelf. Following World War I, Secretary of State Henry Stimson ordered the department's code-breaking unit dismantled, remarking famously: "Gentlemen do not read other gentlemen's mail."[1] The United States had to rely for its intelligence on bits of uncoordinated information provided by ambassadors, foreign correspondents, military attachés, and a small group of military-intelligence cryptography specialists. In the wake of Pearl Harbor, the men around FDR insisted that this would just not do. The Axis powers were waging war on every front, using every possible weapon, including spies, saboteurs, propaganda, and psychological warfare. The activities of fascist "fifth columnists" were already infamous.

The leading advocate of a new agency that could operate an integrated worldwide intelligence network was William Joseph Donovan. Known from his youth as "Wild Bill," Donovan had earned the Congressional Medal of Honor while leading New York's fabled Fighting 69th during World War I. An Irish-Catholic and a Hoover Republican, Donovan had gone on to build one of the most successful law practices on Wall Street. Republican though he might have been, Donovan was no isolationist. As the fascist threat emerged in Europe in the late 1930s, he had joined with those urging the administration to lend all possible aid to the Western democracies. FDR had dispatched him on fact-finding missions to Europe and the Middle East. Donovan had reported that the United Kingdom would win the Battle of Britain and thus survive, but that if the Nazis and Fascists were to be defeated, the United States would eventually have to join the war. When the inevitable happened, Donovan argued, irregular warfare would play a major role in the liberation of Axis-occupied Europe.[2]

While on his trip to Britain in 1940, Donovan had met with newly appointed prime minister Winston Churchill as well as Colonel Stewart Menzies, head of the UK intelligence service. Churchill was a longtime friend of T. E. Lawrence, the irregular war guru who had raised the Arabs in revolt against the Turks and Germans in World War I. In July 1940, Churchill authorized the creation of a new organization called the Special Operations Executive (SOE) and instructed its first director to "set Europe ablaze." Donovan returned to the United States full of enthusiasm for the creation of an American counterpart to MI-6, as Britain's Secret Intelligence Service (SIS) was called, and the SOE. Impressed by Donovan's "blend of Wall Street orthodoxy and sophisticated nationalism," as one historian of the OSS put it, Roosevelt, five months before the attack on Pearl Harbor, named him to head the newly created Office of the Coordinator of Information (COI). Six months after America entered the war, in June 1942, COI was renamed the Office of Strategic Services and placed under the US Joint Chiefs of Staff. By then, the relentlessly energetic Donovan was assembling the first of nearly twelve thousand agents who would not only gather and analyze intelligence but go into the field themselves to conduct espionage, counterespionage, propaganda, and paramilitary activities. Initial recruits featured a large number of intellectuals and relatives of influential people, many of whom had been rejected by the regular military as unfit for duty.[3]

The new intelligence agency would need a leader of Donovan's energy and audacity. From Berlin, Joseph Goebbels's minions denounced the COI/OSS as a "staff of Jewish scribblers," while in Washington a senior official at the War Department decried it as a "fly-by-night civilian outfit headed up by a wild man who was trying to horn in on the war." In private, some officers called the operatives the "east coast fagotts." But a Congressional Medal of Honor recipient who had the president's ear was hard to dismiss. Like the man in the White House, Donovan was an unconventional administrator. He welcomed, nay, demanded, new ideas. No scheme was too harebrained, no project too expensive. The OSS chief not only tolerated insubordination, but seemed to encourage it. "I'd rather have a young lieutenant with guts enough to disobey an order than a colonel too regimented to think and act for himself," he said. Although increasingly anticommunist, or at least anti-Stalinist, Donovan insisted on political diversity in the OSS. New Dealers and even communists worked alongside Willkie (moderate) Republicans. Despite the Nazi-Soviet Non-Aggression Pact, Donovan and his lieutenants had recognized that once Germany invaded Russia, as it did in 1941, communists everywhere could be counted on to fight the Axis to the death. When FBI director J. Edgar Hoover presented proof that three OSS officers were affiliated with the Communist Party of the United States and demanded their firing, Donovan replied, "I know they are communist; that's why I hired them." At the same time, Paul Mellon, the son of banker and archconservative Andrew Mellon, served as an officer of the Special Operations Branch in London; J. P. Morgan's sons were both in the OSS.[4]

In addition to Research and Analysis, the OSS was composed of two other principal branches, the Secret Intelligence Branch (SI) and the Special Operations Branch (SO). This organization mirrored Britain's MI-6, which had been conducting espionage since the early twentieth century. The SO men and women who would be dropped behind enemy lines would be charged with raising an insurrection. "The oppressed peoples must be encouraged to resist and to assist in the Axis defeat, and this can be done by inciting them[,] . . . by training and organizing them," Donovan wrote in 1941. Most important, the inhabitants of the occupied territories had to be turned into revolutionaries. Those officers who parachuted behind enemy lines were college-educated men under thirty who had grown up during the Depression. The words of the Atlantic Charter had real meaning to them. In their collective mind, they were tasked with bringing not only liberty to oppressed peoples—but democracy and social justice as well. There were, of course, exceptions.[5]

By the time Bill Colby spied the OSS recruitment poster on the bulletin board at Fort Mackall in 1943, the principal Allied leaders—Roosevelt, Churchill, and Stalin—had set in motion plans for a massive cross-channel invasion of occupied Europe. General Dwight D. Eisenhower was named commander of Supreme Headquarters, Allied Expeditionary Force (SHAEF), and D-Day was set for May 1, 1944. As the Allies began massing the men and materiel required for the assault on Nazi-occupied Europe, both the American OSS and British SOE eagerly joined in the planning. Each submitted proposals for parachuting operatives into France just before and after D-Day to help mobilize and equip the French resistance— the *maquis*—which in turn could harass the Germans from the rear as the Allied armies drove inland from the Normandy beachheads. After some difficulty, SO and SOE agreed to merge, and Operation Jedburgh was born.[6]

According to legend, Operation Jedburgh took its name from one of the training centers for its operatives situated along the Jed River in the Scots borderland of Roxburghshire. The area was known for its abbey and for "Jeddart Justice," in which the accused were hanged first and tried later. A variation on this story was that the village of Jedburgh had been the scene of guerrilla warfare during the twelfth-century conflicts between England and Scotland, and thus its name was appropriate as a moniker for an unconventional warfare operation. A French version had it that the name came from the French "J-Jour," or D-Day.[7]

Many Americans were uneasy about collaborating with the French; the resistance and, some believed, the Free French Forces headquartered in Britain were riddled with Nazi collaborators. But the need for coordination between the resistance and the invading Allied armies trumped that concern. In conjunction with the cross-channel invasion, three-man teams, each consisting of one British or American officer, one French officer, and a radioman of any nationality, would be inserted into France, where they would help organize and mobilize the maquisards. Using compact, self-powered radios, Jedburgh teams were to coordinate air drops of arms and ammunition, including heavy machine guns, bazookas, and small artillery pieces, to the resistance.[8]

In the summer of 1943, George Sharp, head of the Western European section of the OSS, set about identifying and recruiting American officers for Operation Jedburgh. Before the war, Sharp had been a partner in the prestigious Wall Street law firm of Sullivan and Cromwell, the entity that had played a major role in America's acquisition of the Panama Canal Zone and that, after World War II, would lobby intensely for a central intelligence agency. Naturally, Sharp's network concentrated on rounding up officers who already had parachute training and were fluent in French. Bill Colby matched the profile perfectly. When he and his fellow volunteers assembled at Fort Mackall, the OSS recruiter told them only that they would receive additional parachute training and that perilous missions would follow. Anyone could withdraw. Those who chose to remain were interviewed individually. Nothing specific was said to them about the Jedburgh program, but Colby and his comrades assumed they would be dropping behind enemy lines. Colby later speculated that his boredom with the officer replacement pool to which he had been assigned, and his desire not to be left out of the action, both played roles in his decision to join the OSS. "And then too, all those other influences of my youth came into play: an inclination to unorthodoxy in military service, an interest in the political aspects of war, a habit of going my own way and seeking my own band of kindred souls where money or social status, or the prep school you went to, didn't matter."[9]

In October 1943, the one hundred officers who had survived the initial selection process began arriving in Washington, DC. From Union Station they were bused across the Maryland countryside to what once had been the Congressional Country Club. Between the wars, the Congressional—with its four-story, Italianate clubhouse, 406-acre golf course, indoor swimming pool, and bowling alleys—had been the playground of the capital's elite. With the coming of the Depression, the enterprise had fallen on hard times, however, and in early 1943, with the promise of restoring the facility after the war, the OSS had acquired it as a training ground. When Colby and his mates arrived, the former country club was known simply as Training Area F. Quonset huts and tents dotted the lawn and covered the tennis courts. The fairways and greens had been turned into an obstacle course. To the north across River Road lay pistol, rifle, and machine-gun ranges.[10]

The first orders of the day were strenuous physical tests and probing psychological examinations. Those who did not pass were sent back to regular duty. Bernard Knox, who had fought in the Spanish Civil War, and who, like Colby, had volunteered for the OSS (he would go on to become a famed classicist following the war), described the kind of individuals the OSS was looking for, noting first the kind it was *not* looking for: "The problem in choosing men for such an operation, of course, is that once they are landed in enemy territory, you can no longer control them. They may do the obviously sensible thing: go to ground in a safe hiding place, do nothing to attract attention to themselves, and wait for the arrival of friendly troops." What Donovan and Menzies had in mind was quite a different type of person: "The psychological and psychiatric tests the Jeds were subjected to had one basic objective," Knox recalled—"to select men psychologically incapable of remaining quiet—troublemakers in fact."[11]

The tests were manifestly successful: "I have never known such a bunch of troublemakers in my life," Knox wrote. Colby described his compatriots as a "mixed, spectacular, and exuberant lot." Among his special friends were Knox; Stewart Alsop, who went on to a distinguished career in journalism; Lou Conein, a Franco-American who had fought with the French Army in 1941 before he was dismissed for impregnating the daughter of a high-ranking French official; Douglas Bazata, a soldier of fortune who called all of the colonels "sugar"; Hod Fuller, who had circumnavigated the globe in a small sailboat, and had fought with both the French in Europe and the First Marine Division at Guadalcanal; and Rene Dussaq, an Argentinian stuntman who had worked in a number of Hollywood movies.[12]

Training at Area F was modeled after that of British commandos. The day frequently started at dawn with a 5-mile run; continued with classes in map reading and orienteering, then instruction in hand-to-hand combat techniques, more physical training, and demolitions instruction; and ended with nighttime field exercises. The men hardened quickly, and by December, the regimen eased a bit. There was some time for cards, touch football, and weekend passes. But this was just the lull before the storm. Shortly before Christmas, the American Jeds boarded a ferry that transported them up the Hudson River to Manhattan's West Side passenger-ship terminal. There, they boarded the RMS *Queen Elizabeth*, one of the world's two largest passenger vessels, for the trip across the Atlantic.

Stripped of its luxurious fittings, the *Queen Elizabeth*, originally built in Scotland for the Cunard line in the 1930s, had been converted for military use in 1940. The ship boasted endless rows of metal or wooden bunks and could accommodate fifteen thousand men—a full division—although the vessel's lifeboats could handle only half that number. All the ship's portholes had been blacked out, the hull and superstructure had been painted a dull gray, and its decks mounted with guns and rocket launchers. Officers at the rank of captain and above—Colby had been promoted to captain—were assigned a stateroom, but instead of the two passengers usual in peacetime, the cabins were inhabited by six to eight soldiers. The passage was uneventful. The ship's speed no doubt helped—it raced along at 28 knots, more than four times faster than the rate attainable for submarines below the surface—but in any case the *Queen Elizabeth* did not encounter any Nazi subs. Once in sight of the British Isles, the massive vessel picked up a destroyer escort.[13]

Colby and his mates disembarked at Glasgow and from there were transported to an SOE training facility in western Scotland. Then it was on to Milton Hall, where the Jedburgh teams would assemble and train until D-Day. Situated 90 miles north of London near the town of Peterborough, Milton Hall, once the ancestral home of the Earl Fitzwilliam, was a rambling seventeenth-century estate; the SOE had acquired the property for temporary use. In addition to the huge Elizabethan mansion, there was a golf course, acres of woods, stables, and assorted other outbuildings. Upon their arrival, the Americans made their way up the half-mile-long driveway and were assigned quarters in the main house. The great hall had been converted into a classroom, but the trappings of British aristocracy remained, including full suits of armor standing in the corners and massive portraits adorning the walls. Then began what must have seemed like endless weeks of training. There was some duplication of the activities at Area F, but the hikes were longer—20 to 25 miles—and the night navigation courses more difficult.

None of the trainees would forget the martial arts instructor at Milton Hall, Major William Ewart Fairbain. There was nothing particularly imposing about the fifty-seven-year-old Fairbain. He stood five feet eight inches tall and weighed in at 170. The men soon learned, however, that he was the physical match of any of them. Fairbain had spent thirty years as a Shanghai policeman, subduing a population of Tong gang members, pirates, and run-of-the-mill cutthroats. He was steeped in the oriental arts of self-defense and silent killing, skills that he meticulously transferred to his students. There was also knife-fighting with a foot-long, double-edged stiletto, as well as instruction in the Fairbain instinctive shooting method: from the hip with one hand, or from a crouch with two. Everything could be turned into a weapon, the men learned, from an entrenching tool to a fountain pen (there were so many soft-tissue, vulnerable points on the human body). Field craft—the art of survival—even featured lessons in poaching. Late one afternoon while Colby and his mates were bivouacking, a truck drove up. One of the instructors rolled up the back flap and threw out a sack of flour and a live sheep. "Here's your supper," he exclaimed.[14]

For the Americans and Brits, intensive instruction in French was a priority. Pronunciation and usage would have to be perfect to escape detection by Nazi collaborators. The Yanks were taught to keep their table knives in their right hand and their forks in their left, rather than switching them, as was the custom in the New World. There were classes in tradecraft—how to tail and detect a tail, forge documents, pick locks, set up safe houses, and send encrypted messages. In weapons classes, the men were taught the workings of British, American, French, and German small arms. *The* weapon of the French resistance was the British Sten gun. It was simple, efficient, and could function for months without being oiled. Looking more like a bicycle pump than a firearm, the Sten consisted of a stock, a tube, and a short barrel with a 32-round magazine protruding from its left side. The weapon took 9x1.9 mm parabellum ammunition, the same as used in German Lugers and MP 40s. If the maquis expended the ammunition that had been dropped to them, they could find a plentiful supply in German stocks. Arguably the second most important weapons, as far as the Jedburghs and their colleagues in the resistance were concerned, were plastic explosives. The material was malleable, relatively stable, and hot-burning. The Jeds learned about Primacord (a flexible explosive detonating cord), time pencils (devices used for initiating explosions after predetermined time delays), and a variety of other fuses.[15]

Early on, those in command at Milton Hall had decided that the three-man teams to be dropped behind enemy lines would be self-selecting. To operate effectively, a Jed trio would have to be matched psychologically, physically, and temperamentally. During the endless rounds of poker and discussions of the fine points of explosives, as well as during the scant time allowed for leisure activities—which trainees largely spent sampling the charms of English girls—Colby was drawn to a French officer named Jacques Favel (his real name was Camille LeLong; all French Jedburghs used pseudonyms to protect their families). Favel hailed from the Catalan town of Perpignan, a coastal settlement at the foot of the Pyrenees near the Spanish border. He had fought against the German invasion in 1940 and then, following the armistice, migrated to North Africa. Shortly after the Allied landings in 1942, Favel joined the Free French Forces, where the OSS recruited him. Colby and Favel immediately hit it off, though

Colby observed that he was no match for the Frenchman's charisma. "He was lively and outgoing, a dazzler with the English girls, an extremely deadly poker player, tough, quick with a native intelligence and an ability to handle himself in tight places," Colby later wrote. The two agreed to an "engagement" (a trial partnership) and subsequently to a "marriage" (formalized by the command officially posting their names as a team). Louis Giry (a.k.a. Roger Villebois) joined them as radioman, and Team Bruce was born. Colby noted that though he was promoted to the rank of major five days before the Normandy invasion, it was Lieutenant Favel who was really the team leader. Immediately, the trio began participating in "schemes," two- to three-day exercises in which teams were parachuted into Wales or Scotland and told to find their way back without being detected. Authorities along the way were alerted to be on the lookout. One squad reportedly beat another back to Milton Hall by hijacking a train.[16]

As the spring of 1944 waned, those in charge of Milton Hall came to fear that their charges were overtraining; consequently, there was more time for rest and recreation. In the evenings, Colby and his mates might catch a ride into nearby Peterborough for a pint at the Bull Hotel or one of the pubs. Weekend passes to London became more frequent. Despite the ravages of the Battle of Britain, London remained one of the most vibrant cities in the world. The American Jeds took in the sights: the Tower of London, Trafalgar Square, Buckingham Palace. The streets were ablaze with the uniforms of numerous countries allied against the Nazis. For the adventurous, there were the chorus lines at the Windmill and Prince of Wales, where the showgirls wore little more than some type of military headgear. In Piccadilly Circus, prostitutes, who came to be known among the soldiers as "Piccadilly Commandos" or "Hyde Park Rangers," plied their trade. During one London outing, Colby took a breather from sightseeing and sex to visit the famous Foyle's bookstore. There he purchased a copy of T. E. Lawrence's *Seven Pillars of Wisdom*. Colby recalled in his memoirs that he read the book "voraciously for its account of how an outsider operates within the political framework of a foreign people."[17]

While a student at Oxford in the summer of 1909, Lawrence had embarked alone on a three-month walking tour of crusader castles in Ottoman Syria, during which he covered nearly 1,000 miles. After graduation, he became a field archaeologist specializing in the Middle East, working under D. G. Hogarth and R. Campbell-Thompson of the British Museum. A natural linguist, Lawrence was accomplished in French, German, Latin, Greek, Arabic, Turkish, and Syriac. Following the outbreak of World War I, he was commissioned a second lieutenant in the British Army. He was, of course, assigned to the Middle East, where the British Foreign Office was hatching plans to foment a revolt among the Arab tribes of the Arabian Peninsula and the Levant against the Ottoman Turks, Imperial Germany's ally. From 1916 through 1918, Lawrence would fight with Arab irregular troops under the command of Emir Faisal, a son of Sherif Hussein of Mecca. The insurgents tied down thousands of Turkish troops by harassing Mecca and the Hejaz Railway. In 1918, Lawrence participated in the capture of Damascus. In the newly liberated city, which the Englishman envisioned as the capital of a new Arab nation, he was instrumental in establishing a provisional Arab government under Faisal.

Seven Pillars of Wisdom, which George Bernard Shaw helped edit, was already a minor classic by the time Colby read it in 1944. The book is a combination of epic poem and guerrilla-war field manual. It is also a romance filled with a brutal enemy, heroic and feckless Arab patriots, endless desert marches, constant armed skirmishes, Arabian stallions, colorful Bedouin tents, and the search for a man on horseback who could unite the disparate tribes of the peninsula, molding them not only into a viable military force, but into a nation. It is a long paean to just war and self-sacrifice to the point of self-immolation. "We were a self-centered army without parade or gesture," Lawrence wrote, "devoted to freedom, the second of man's creeds, a purpose so ravenous that it devoured all our strength, a hope so transcendent that our earlier ambitions faded in its glare." The war became a cause, and the cause became a faith. He and his Arabs, Lawrence declared, "had surrendered, not body alone, but soul to the overmastering greed of victory. . . . The everlasting battle stripped from us care of our own lives or of others."[18]

Colby's copy of *Seven Pillars* would never be far from his reach for the rest of his professional life. As his son John later recalled, the book was his manual of operation. It was also something of a moral and religious text. In no small part, *Seven Pillars* was the story of one man's self-revelation—how willing he was to kill for his cause, to betray his friends and allies to serve his country's imperial ambitions.

After two years of intensive training, the Jedburghs were ready for action. The question confronting SHAEF was when to deploy them. If Eisenhower waited too long, the maquis, newly mobilized and armed by the Jeds, would be too late to help. If the commandos were dropped too early, details of the planned Normandy invasion might leak. Following a tense, stormy night, British, Canadian, and American troops attacked the beaches of northwestern France on the morning of June 6, 1944. The first Jedburgh teams were dropped into occupied France on June 5 and 6. Their mission was to coordinate local resistance groups with the planned Allied breakout from the Normandy beachhead. Eventually, 92 teams comprising 276 men, 83 of whom were Americans, would be inserted into occupied Europe. Not until August, however, would Team Bruce's number be called.[19]

The massive invasion of the Normandy coast—176,000 men and 1,500 tanks on the first day alone—was a success, if a bloody one. Throughout June, the Germans managed to keep the Allied forces bottled up in Brittany, but then in late July, US general George S. Patton's Third Army broke out of the envelope, driving eastward toward Brest and southwestward toward the Loire Valley. Eisenhower and his deputy, General Omar N. Bradley, became fearful that Patton was outrunning his lines of supply and dangerously exposing his flanks. Third Army intelligence asked for more OSS teams to gather information about German plans and troop movements and to galvanize the maquis to help protect Patton's exposed southern flank. The second week in August, Colby, Favel, and Giry—Team Bruce—were alerted that they were going on a mission.[20]

"On August 12, after the St. Lo breakout of Patton's Third Army, we were summoned to London," Colby remembered. "In a nondescript row house, a British officer told us we would be dropped to a maquis network led by Henri Frager, who was known as Jean Marie." The team was instructed to parachute onto the prearranged landing zone, make contact, and then do everything possible to arm and equip the members of the local resistance. "We didn't need more precise instructions; we knew the basic drill from our training, and the mission of attacking Germans to turn them away from the Allied invasion was obvious." Frager's network, or "circuit," was located in the department of Yonne southeast of Paris.[21]

Wild Bill Donovan and the men and women of the OSS who worked for him were determined to see the conflict in Europe in black and white: the Germans and all who supported them were evil and the enemy; all who opposed the Axis powers were, if not good, Allies. OSS officers in London admitted, however, that the French resistance was a "devil's brew of politics."

Within the resistance were Gaullists (conservative nationalists, followers of General Charles de Gaulle), communists, and those loyal to General Henri Giraud, commander of French forces in North Africa. Each of the factions wanted to become the dominant political force in postwar France. Some Allied officers, especially the British, had feared that the well-armed resistance groups might use the Normandy landings "to indulge themselves in a first-rate civil war." Moreover, the maquis was notoriously riddled with German agents and collaborators. And so it was with Frager's circuit, code-named "Donkeyman."[22]

Henri Frager was a veteran of World War I who had made a name for himself as an architect during the interwar period. With the outbreak of war in 1939, he found himself once again in uniform. After the fall of France, the soft-spoken, slender, prematurely gray Frager retreated to the countryside and, with the help of the SOE, began organizing the resistance in Yonne. By 1944, Donkeyman would include some five thousand fighters. Frager's right-hand man in this operation was Roger Bardet, who, in 1943, had been captured by the Abwehr, a German military intelligence organization. Under threat of torture and the death of his family, Bardet had agreed to inform for the Germans. In the months that followed, dozens of Donkeyman operatives were inexplicably captured. In February 1944, Bardet introduced Frager to a man named Hugo Bleicher, who posed as an anti-Nazi Luftwaffe officer interested in working for the British. Frager was completely taken in, sharing with Bleicher plans for his circuit's forthcoming operations in Yonne. On July 2, when Frager stepped off a train at the Montparnasse Station in Paris, Bleicher and several Abwehr agents were waiting for him. The Frenchman was executed three months later at Buchenwald.[23]

By the time of Team Bruce's briefing, none of these developments had come to light. "What should we do if we fail to make contact with Frager or his men?" Colby asked presciently. The briefer seemed taken aback, as if he had never considered such a possibility. Finally, Team Bruce was given the location of a safe house to repair to should it be unable to connect with Donkeyman. Colby and his colleagues were scheduled to take off that night from the air base at Temsford, but the weather closed in. The next day, they learned that Frager had been arrested and that the new head of the Yonne maquis was a man named Roger Bardet. He would be their contact. "We accepted the new order as simply as the first," Colby recalled, "as though our announced hostess had taken sick and was replaced by a cousin."[24]

The following evening—August 14—Team Bruce boarded a converted B-24 bomber named *Slick Chick* for a rendezvous with they knew not what. Only one thing was certain: the mission would be dangerous. Just weeks before, the German High Command had broadcast a warning to would-be saboteurs and guerrillas: "Whoever on French territory outside the zone of legal combat is captured and identified as having participated in sabotage, terrorism, or revolt is and remains a bandit or franc-tireur [guerrilla] and shall consequently be shot, whatever his nationality or uniform." In fact, the leader of one of the first Jedburgh teams to drop into Brittany, Major John Bonsal, had been stopped at a German checkpoint, identified, and executed on the spot. Of course, being shot might be the most comfortable fate awaiting captured Jedburghs.[25]

The men who delivered the Jedburgh teams to occupied France were unique, as was their equipment. The pilots—code-named "Carpetbaggers," officially the 801st Bombardment Group—were volunteers who flew into enemy territory at very low altitude with no lights. Their planes were camouflaged with nonreflective black paint, and all but two of the gun turrets, the ones in the top of the fuselage and in the tail, were removed. Inside, the bomb racks were replaced by specially designed shelves on which sat containers holding submachine guns, grenades, explosives, radios, and boots—the paraphernalia of guerrilla war. The only light inside the B-24 was a small bulb that glowed green, furnished for the navigator so that he could read his maps. Finally, ground crews covered the aperture where the belly turret had been removed with a plywood trapdoor. Colby and his mates would parachute one by one via these "Joe holes"—Joe being the name that Allied parachutists gave themselves—to be followed by the supply containers.[26]

At 12:45 hours, the pilot announced that the target area was in sight. He circled once, descended, then circled again, at 1,500 feet to make sure he was over the correct location. Satisfied, he gave Team Bruce the go-ahead signal. "The parachute snapped open with a reassuring jolt," Colby wrote in his memoirs. "We were on our own now, two Free Frenchmen and myself, floating down through the balmy August midnight into the heart of German-occupied France. And I suddenly realized that something was seriously wrong." The maquis had been instructed to set three bonfires in a triangle; the flames the parachutists saw were in a straight line. Favel thought the fires were from a burning village, but they turned out to be from a train the Allies had bombed.[27] Colby and his mates landed not in a sparsely occupied countryside, but in a town some 25 miles short of their planned drop zone in Yonne. The trio frantically manipulated their chutes to avoid chimneys and rooftops, finally coming to rest in a garden. Their landing was noisy enough, but after the men came the supply containers, which clattered down on the tiled roofs. Awakened, the residents circled around and assured the visitors that they would not be betrayed.

Team Bruce learned that it had landed in the village of Montargis. The locals informed Colby and his colleagues that there was a large German garrison in the nearest town whose soldiers would certainly be alerted by the commotion. The Jeds decided that they would not have time to gather up the supply containers before enemy troops arrived, and so they headed off to the southeast through the open fields. They had side arms, codes, maps, instructions, and 250,000 francs each; they could always radio for more equipment when they met up with Bardet and his men. The immediate task at hand was to avoid the Wehrmacht.[28]

For a time, Colby, Favel, and Giry followed the tracks of the ruined railroad, but then for security reasons they veered off. They could not have proceeded more than 5 or 6 miles when dawn began to break. By then, of course, the Germans had discovered the supply containers and guessed what was up. With the area crawling with Nazi patrols, the Jeds hid in a shallow ditch. "It was a warm summer day," Colby remembered, "the air thick with the scent of manure and wild flowers; bees and flies buzzed around us drowsily and one by one we would doze off for a few moments, each with his own private thoughts." When night fell, they set off again, using their compasses to set a course for the safe house, the location of which they had been given in London. As they journeyed through the starless, moonless night, a terrific thunderstorm blew up, drenching the men and turning the fields into a morass. For fear of becoming separated, the three tied themselves together with their pistol lanyards. A couple of hours after midnight, with lightning flashing and the rain still pouring down, Team Bruce heard voices ahead and then spied the lights of a farmhouse. It was too late for the local families to be up and about. With his comrades covering him from the shadows, Favel knocked on the door. The voices stopped. "Qui est là?" (Who is there?) "Un français," Favel replied. The door opened. At last some luck. The inhabitants were maquis, and among them was a British radio operator just arrived from London. Colby, Favel, and Giry immediately notified headquarters of their situation, and the radioman set about contacting the leadership of Donkeyman.[29]

The next day, another group of resistance operatives arrived in a battered Citroën powered by a charcoal-burning engine. For civilians in occupied France, gasoline was virtually unobtainable; during their training, the Jeds had been taught how to convert engines to run on fuels other than gasoline. From one rendezvous and hand-off to another, the Jedburghs proceeded until they arrived in the village of Sommecaise, where they were ushered into the community's only café. It was filled with heavily armed maquis. Colby, Favel, and Giry were led to a table where a thin man with coal-black hair was sitting, a bottle of red wine and a plate of food in front of him. He eyed the three for a moment and then rose and introduced himself as Roger Bardet. "Where have you been?" he asked. "We've been waiting three days. We had the signal fires ready, but no plane came."[30] After Colby explained about the missed dropped site, Bardet ordered food and drink for the new arrivals. Then Colby got down to business: "We're here to help you fight the Germans," he said, pulling out his map and spreading it on the table. Where are the Nazis? How many of them are there? How many men do you have under arms? Bardet replied that he had some five hundred members of the French Forces of the Interior (FFI) and was in contact with several other bands of approximately the same size. About the number and location of the enemy, he seemed consistently vague. If London could send arms, he said, more men could be recruited immediately.

Colby would later write that he never suspected Bardet was a German agent, but he remembered feeling from the outset that something about the man was not right. "He had the look of a minor civil servant, a petty functionary, going through the motions instead of leading," Colby wrote. In the days and weeks that followed, Colby's distaste for Bardet would only grow. The Frenchman never initiated action and always found reasons to oppose the proposals of his more daring colleagues. Colby got the feeling that Bardet's subordinates were paying him lip service out of respect for Frager's memory, but were in fact acting on their own.[31]

While Giry occupied himself with communications, Colby and Favel turned to their specialties. Bardet's men were organized into companies and squads. The Jeds trained the men on the weapons they had available before moving on to small unit tactics. The Germans were garrisoned in two nearby towns, and enemy convoys were lightly guarded. Soon the maquis were staging hit-and-run attacks on the convoys, with Colby and Favel advising them every step of the way. Bardet continued to block any larger-scale operation, insisting that London had instructed him to lay low and await word before leading a general offensive.[32]

The Jeds were soon introduced to one of the most important members of the Donkeyman network, Marguerette "Peggy" McKnight, code-named "Nicole." She had been recruited by the SOE in March 1944, when several agents had overheard her speaking near-perfect French in a London restaurant. At the time, she was working as a shorthand typist. When the SOE approached her about serving as a spy and courier in occupied France, she volunteered immediately. The British were in a desperate hurry; D-Day was fast approaching, and London needed as much information on German gun emplacements and troop movements as possible. Peggy's training was therefore short and intense. Most of her fellow recruits were allowed a minimum of four parachute jumps before being inserted. Because of bad weather, Peggy experienced only one, and that was from a basket suspended under a giant football-shaped air balloon. Some of the Jeds who had to jump from such a contraption found the experience terrifying. When leaping out of an airplane, the backwash from the propeller popped the chute open almost immediately. There was no backwash from the balloon. All but the last 150 feet of the 700-foot drop was free-fall.[33]

"Nicole" parachuted into France on the night of May 6, 1944. Leading her reception committee were Henri Frager and Roger Bardet. Over the next three months, Nicole lived on the edge. The Frager-Bardet circuit would recruit, train, raid, and spy and then disband to avoid detection and capture by the Germans. "The first time I met Roger, I took an intense dislike to him," Peggy McKnight later recalled. "He never looked you straight in the face. . . . [He] looked to me like a hunted man." There were other traitors in the midst of the Yonne-Normandy maquis. Peggy was with Frager at the village of Cezy near Sommecaise when the maquis chief confronted and shot Richard Armand Lansdell and Alain de Laroussilhe, two French collaborators who had just botched an assassination attempt on another Donkeyman leader. The twenty-one-year-old Englishwoman excelled as a courier, routinely moving through German checkpoints by automobile to deliver messages to other resistance camps. Following the Normandy landings, she acted as a liaison between Allied command posts and the maquis.[34]

After barely escaping from a German roundup, she began stowing a submachine gun in her Citroën. Peggy did not immediately confide in the members of Team Bruce concerning her suspicions about Bardet, but from the time she hooked up with Colby and his colleagues at Sommecaise, she took orders only from them. In truth, she became the fourth member of Team Bruce.

Like Lawrence during the early days of the Arab revolt, Colby was in dire need of a man on horseback, a natural leader to whom the resistance could rally. He found him in the person of "Colonel Chevrier" (Adrien Sodoul), a sixty-year-old former army officer in the French reserve who in peacetime had practiced law in Metz. At their first meeting, Chevrier imperiously informed the Jedburghs that he had been appointed by none other than Charles de Gaulle to be maquis commander for the entire Yonne district. At the time, his followers numbered no more than twenty, but that quickly changed. Where Bardet was secretive, aloof, and passive, the colonel was, in Colby's words, "flamboyant, charismatic, constantly on the move." Within days, Chevrier was in touch with all the other resistance chiefs in the department, who together commanded some two thousand fighters. Colby mediated between Bardet and Chevrier, persuading the two men to agree to rule by committee. Chevrier soon came to dominate the Yonne directorate the way de Gaulle had come to dominate the Free French National Committee (the French government-in-exile). With the Allied breakout at St. Lo in mid-April and Patton on the move, Roger Bardet had come to see the handwriting on the wall. In hopes of covering his tracks, he became one of the more active and dependable resistance leaders.[35]

Chevrier reiterated what Bardet had said when he and Colby had first met—what the resistance needed above all else were arms and ammunition. By now, Giry had received a new radio from London. Team Bruce, together with Chevrier, picked the best drop zones, generally secluded fields and pastures in the countryside. Giry would radio the coordinates of the location together with some innocuous code phrase, such as "Le vin est rouge" (The wine is red). Every evening the men of Team Bruce would listen to the BBC news broadcast to France, paying special attention to the *messages personnels* that followed the program's theme, Beethoven's Fifth Symphony. If they heard the code phrase, they knew that the drop was to be that night at that particular location. During the first two weeks of operation, Team Bruce coordinated more than a dozen drops, which provided thousands of rifles and carbines, machine guns, and bazookas to resistance fighters. Donkeyman doubled and then tripled in size. "Straight fighting job ahead," Team Bruce reported to London on August 21. "Sabotage platoon changed to heavy weapons."[36]

As Patton's Third Army advanced relentlessly toward the Third Reich, tens of thousands of German soldiers were on the move south of the Loire River in an effort to reach the fatherland ahead of the Allied armies. Only a shallow river separated the Americans and as many as 100,000 enemy soldiers. Patton was not concerned. "Forget this goddamned business of worrying about our flanks," he told his staff. "Some goddamned fool once said that flanks must be secured and since then sons-of-bitches all over the world have been going crazy guarding their flanks." When the commander of his southernmost unit expressed concern about the tens of thousands of Wehrmacht across the Loire, Patton advised, "Just ignore 'em." Patton was not as foolhardy as it seemed. The Allied code-breaking operation Ultra had revealed that the Germans south of the Loire had strict orders to extricate themselves from France as quickly as possible in order to defend their homeland.[37]

Patton may not have been worried about his right flank, but his superior, General Bradley, now commander of the Twelfth Army Group, was. In an effort to slow Patton's advance, the Wehrmacht was employing Germans who spoke perfect, Americanized English. They would talk their way into Allied camps and once there, shoot officers, blow up ammunition dumps, and in general create havoc. At Bradley's direction, Third Army intelligence sent word to Donkeyman that it needed assistance, and Colby and Favel made their way through German lines to find out exactly what the US forces required. Colby carried no identification papers, only a cyanide pill. At the first American outpost he and Favel encountered, he announced that he was Major Colby of the OSS. For his efforts, he was handcuffed and taken to headquarters. The officer in charge asked him where he had trained. "Fort Benning," Colby replied. Where was the post office, the laundry, the theater? When the correct answers were forthcoming, the handcuffs came off and the conversations began. Colby's interrogator was Lieutenant Colonel Creighton Abrams, a man who would later partner with Colby in Vietnam. Eventually, the Jeds were forwarded to Patton's headquarters, where they provided as much information as they could on enemy troop movements and promised more intelligence as well as maquis harassing actions to prevent a German attack on the Third Army's flank.[38]

Upon their return to the field, Colby and Favel had Giry radio London, asking that their region be given priority for air drops. With additional arms and equipment in hand, the maquis stepped up its attacks. On August 26, Giry reported to London: "Americans contacted and coordinating. Giving information, holding towns and acting local security. Auxerre, Avallon, Joigny, held by FFI. . . . Continually attacking groups of retreating Germans." Typical was an operation in which US troops, the maquis, and Team Bruce cooperated in assaulting a column of 1,500 German troops making its way from Montargis to Auxerre. The force was too formidable for the resistance fighters to handle alone, so Colby asked the nearest American units to help. C Troop of the 2nd United States Cavalry led the assault. As the American tanks smashed the enemy formation, the FFI lingered on the edges, picking off stragglers and providing intelligence. There was another reason, Colby recalled, for American troops to take the lead. If the Germans believed that they were dealing with the FFI, whose captured members they had systematically tortured and executed in the past, they would fight to the finish rather than surrender. When the firing stopped, only a handful of the enemy had survived, and the resistance had captured a large cache of arms, ammunition, and fuel.[39]

As the lead tank battalion of the 4th Armored Division, commanded by Lieutenant Colonel Abrams, drove east, Team Bruce had its maquis blow up one bridge after another, some to protect the Americans' flank and some to cut off retreat by elements of the Wehrmacht that had been trapped. Much of the crucial intelligence that flowed into Colby's camp and subsequently to the Third Army came from Peggy McKnight. On a typical outing, she bicycled some 40 kilometers from Gien past Briare and Cosne on the Loire, reporting back on bridges that had been destroyed, the location of enemy troops, and the state of the local resistance.[40]

As the Germans retreated, the FFI was assigned an additional job by SHAEF. Chevrier, whom the Allies had officially recognized as the principal maquis leader in Yonne, and his men were to occupy and govern the liberated towns along the Germans' escape route. On August 26, Chevrier's forces rolled into the provincial capital of the neighboring department of Auxerre. All the while, Colby and Favel moved in and out of the colonel's headquarters, advising, coordinating, supervising more air drops, and participating in an occasional firefight.[41] The liberation of Yonne and the Loire was accompanied by one continuous celebration. Joyous crowds of villagers greeted the Jeds and the maquis. They were kissed by the women, hugged by the men, showered with flowers, and treated to an endless round of banquets featuring the local cuisine, gallons of wine, and tearful, patriotic speeches.

In mid-August, French and American forces landed on France's Mediterranean coast and began making their way up the Rhone Valley. Team Bruce played a key role, transmitting information on local conditions and enemy positions as these new forces and the Third Army linked up. By September 14, the drama had all but ended. "All Germans gone from whole area," Team Bruce radioed London. "No further need of arms." After the war, Roger Bardet would be arrested and convicted of treason. Bill Colby would be awarded the Bronze Star and eventually the Croix de Guerre for his actions in France.[42]

On September 17, Team Bruce received orders to proceed to Paris and await further instructions. The Frenchmen could now use their real names. En route to the capital, Favel—that is, Camille LeLong—Colby, and Giry—Roger Villebois—took a slight detour so that Villebois could rendezvous with an old flame.

Paris was a swirl of Allied uniforms and joyous civilians. The celebrations that had awaited Team Bruce in village after village in Yonne were going nonstop in France's liberated capital. Colby managed to rendezvous with other surviving Jeds, including Robert Ansett, a fellow Columbia law student. Ansett had been part of a team that had captured fleeing French collaborators, some of whom were high-ranking officials of the now defunct Vichy regime. In the process, Ansett had come into possession of Vichy vice premier Pierre Laval's black Cadillac. Just before boarding his flight to London, Ansett bestowed the luxurious auto on his friend as a Jedburgh legacy.

In the midst of the partying, Bill found time to visit his father, Elbridge, who was then serving on the staff of General Courtney H. Hodges's First Army.[43] The colonel was immensely proud of his son's exploits, and perhaps a bit envious. There was still more fighting to come, however, and the father said goodbye to his son with a mixture of anticipation and dread.

Team Bruce was scheduled to drop into Alsace on the Franco-German border, but the Wehrmacht evacuated the area before the operation could be launched. Colby recalled that his one year of college German did not qualify him for a drop into the Reich—and so he repaired to London and requested assignment to China, where the war with Japan was still raging. It was not to be.[44]

4

A BRIDGE TOO FAR

W hen Colby arrived in London in October 1944, it appeared that the war might be over by Christmas or shortly thereafter. Allied armies were driving across France and had penetrated into Belgium and the Netherlands. But the Reich's disintegration was illusory. The führer was gathering his forces for a fight to the end. Soon the Germans had established a stable front and, unbeknownst to SHAEF, were preparing for a major counteroffensive that would eventually become known as the "Battle of the Bulge." The Allies would survive that counterthrust, but it was a near thing. Eisenhower would resume the offensive, but Allied forces would not cross the bridge at Remagen into Germany until March 8, 1945. Meanwhile, the Red Army had swept into Finland, pushing some 150,000 German soldiers into Norway. The OSS was given the task of keeping those forces bottled up in Scandinavia so they would not become a factor in the final battle for Germany. A popular uprising in Norway, such as the one that had occurred in France, was not feasible. At one time, there had been some 350,000 German troops in the country. At its largest, the Norwegian Home Force had numbered 40,000, with only half being armed.[1]

In December 1944, Gerry Miller, the OSS officer in charge of the Jedburghs, summoned Major Colby to his office. Would he be willing to take command of the OSS's Norwegian Special Operations Group (NORSO)? Miller asked. A hundred Norwegian Americans had been operating in occupied Europe and were currently out of a job; OSS wanted to turn them into Jedburghs and then drop them into Norway to sabotage the Nordland Railway—the railway over which the German High Command was planning to transport 150,000 crack ski troops to the fatherland. Colby immediately accepted. He was bored, tired of waiting for the assignment to the China-India-Burma theater. As an afterthought, Miller asked, "Do you ski?" Colby assured him that he did; as captain of the Burlington, Vermont, ski team, he had traversed the Green Mountains, skiing down its slopes and then climbing back up them with his equipment strapped to his back (this was in the days before mechanized chair lifts). Colby had no idea at the time how valuable that experience would become.[2]

Some of the NORSO volunteers were part of the larger Norwegian exile force that had fought alongside a dozen other exile units from Nazi-occupied countries. The Norwegians' leader had been the colorful and audacious Colonel Serge Obolensky, who had served in the St. Petersburg Imperial Guards and was a personal friend of Wild Bill Donovan. Others were Norwegian Americans tapped by the OSS for sabotage work in Scandinavia; they had been training since 1943, but at the time of Colby's appointment, they were resting and recuperating at Dalnaglar Castle, an ancient Scottish redoubt in the foothills of the Grampians. More than a hundred of the Norwegians and Norwegian Americans had volunteered, three times the number the operation would require. As with the Jedburghs, they would have to be weeded. They were all tough, hard men, tougher than he was, Colby would later remark. But they accepted his decisive, understated leadership. Some had gone through the course at Benning, but for those who had not, there was parachute training. On Saturday evenings, NORSO's only time off, the trainees consumed vast quantities of single-malt whiskey. Colby thanked his stars that the nearest military police station was 50 miles away. Sometimes he drank with the men; sometimes he retired to peruse his copy of *Seven Pillars*.[3]

By mid-January, Major Colby had chosen the thirty-five men who would make the long and perilous journey across Scandinavia to the far reaches of Norway. The Carpetbaggers could fly their blacked-out B-24s only during the full moon, when the planes could navigate by the light reflected off rivers and lakes. Bad weather postponed the first attempt. At February's full moon, Miller and Colby dispatched an advance team under Captain Tom Sather. It included a skilled radioman, Borge Langeland, who would help to guide the B-24 to its destination. Just as the plane neared its drop zone, however, fog set in, and the team had to turn back. Only by jettisoning every piece of equipment, indeed, everything that was not bolted down, did the B-24 manage to make it back to Harrington, its home field

in England. March's full moon found NORSO desperate. With each passing day, more German troops were moving down the rail line from Narvik
in the north to Trondheim, where they were transported by ship to the embattled Reich. Colby and his men had selected a drop site and were prepared to go when the Norwegian exile newspaper in London reported that
the area had been occupied by German troops. With the help of Herbert
Helgeson, a Norwegian resistance leader who had been smuggled out of
Norway through Sweden, NORSO arranged for another drop site. Finally,
on March 24, Gerry Miller drove out to Harrington to wish Colby and his
men bon voyage.[4]

Before climbing aboard the eight converted B-24s, Colby delivered a
final briefing to his men. He reminded them that General Eisenhower had
declared that the German forces in Norway must be kept bottled up;
SHAEF had its eye on NORSO. Operation "Rype" (*rype* is Norwegian for
ptarmigan, a bird whose feathers are white in the winter and brown in the
summer, like the parkas of the NORSOs) was crucial to the success of the
Allies' final push against the Reich.

Silently, the thirty-five commandos boarded, and the giant planes took
off into the clear midafternoon sky. The men had been divided into teams
and supplied in a manner that would allow them to operate independently
for forty days. Sitting in the bomb bay of his plane, Colby considered those
he had trained. "Their names read like heroes from some Norse saga—
Paulsen, Johansen, Iversen, Eliasen, Oistad," he wrote in his memoir. Many
had been stranded on Norwegian ships early in the war and then enlisted
in the US Army. They were typically stoic—men of the sea and the frost.
They were bred to endure and adapt. "Among this group," Colby observed,
"were men who could do anything from butchering a cow to fixing a motor
with a piece of wire, or operating on a casualty with a jackknife."[5]

The round trip from the United Kingdom to northern Norway would
stretch the range of the planes of the 801st Bombardment Group to the
limit. It would be necessary to stop for refueling at Kinloss airfield on the
bleak northeastern coast of Scotland facing across the North Sea to Scandinavia. The plan was for the Carpetbaggers to discharge their men and
materiel over Lake Jaevsjo on the Norweigan-Swedish border, which, of
course, was frozen over at the time. "The eight planes continued north,
across the North Sea, over the stark fjords and the white mountains, then
up the Norway-Sweden coast past Trondheim, Mansos—almost to the

Arctic Circle," Colby wrote. "Below, a faint mist was spreading, taking the sharpness off the rocks, but meaning trouble later." Trouble, indeed. The mist turned into fog. Three of the planes were forced to turn back. One dropped its five-man team into neutral Sweden, where the paratroopers were confronted by local police and briefly interned. Four other planes, one of which carried Major Colby, also strayed over Sweden but then discovered their mistake. Shortly after midnight the lead aircraft spotted the bonfires on the frozen lake. "Paulsen and Aanonsen pulled up the trap door," Colby related, "and I went through into the awful quiet that closes in when the engines recede. . . . Dimly, I counted the others slipping into the air— one, two, three—formation perfect, five seconds apart." At 500 feet, the parachutists could see the bonfires clearly. Colby landed, rolled, gained his feet, and tucked away his chute. He could see a tall, heavily clad figure approaching. Pistol in hand, the NORSO leader offered the pass phrase: "Is the fishing good in this lake?" Instead of the required answer, "Yes, especially in the winter," the man replied, "To tell you the truth, it's no good at all." Something kept Colby from shooting him. Fortunately, at that moment, Herbert Helgeson, the resistance liaison, appeared and vouched for the man and his companions, who had now moved out from the bonfire. The NORSO team, now fifteen in number, spent the night with their reception committee, trying to ward off the twenty-below-zero temperatures. Operation Rype was set to begin.[6]

Colby and his men spent Palm Sunday scouring the area for the containers of arms, food, and explosives that had been dropped with them. The team had not supervised the packing of the parachutes for their supplies. They should have. The materiel was scattered over a 36-mile area; some containers had not been chuted at all and had plunged deep into snow drifts. The work had to be done quickly; the arrival in the area of four-engine aircraft was sure to have been noticed, and German spotter planes would soon be roaming the area. The NORSO men gathered what they could and then, using their parachutes, built a tent camp in the woods, hoping to avoid detection by vacationing skiers and German patrols.

According to its official orders, Operation Rype was to paralyze the relevant segments of the Norwegian rail service for as long as possible. The Nordland Railway was the only north-south transportation route; the country's heavy snows rendered road travel impossible, and the Allies' Eighth Air Force made air transport too risky for the German troops. As a consequence, every kilometer of the Nordland line was heavily guarded by either fixed encampments or patrols. Convinced that he did not have enough men and explosives to successfully complete the mission, Colby decided to wait for reinforcements. He learned through the group's radio contact with London that the Liberators that had turned back would try again. As he had in France, Colby tuned in each night to the BBC and listened to the Norwegian personals to learn whether that was the night. On the sixth evening, word came that the Carpetbaggers, with their commando cargo, were on their way. Colby recalled that at the first sound of engines, the weather was perfectly clear; but then "in seconds[,] a mist out of Hamlet shrouded the lake." The three aircraft pulled up and turned around for the trip home. Two made it; the other plane crashed in the Orkney Islands, killing all thirteen men aboard, including six NORSO volunteers.[7]

Six days later, London tried again. Four B-24s departed Harrington. This time the subarctic weather proved uniformly bad, with high winds, blowing snow, and ice. The first aircraft attempted a pass over the lake but hit a nearby peak and exploded, all within earshot of the men on the ground. The three surviving aircraft turned back. A month later, with their operations complete, Colby and his men would locate the wreckage of the downed B-24 and bury the dead with full military honors. "Meanwhile," Colby later wrote, "12 days—wasted days—had gone by, and with each one, more Germans had seeped out of the trap." The NORSO team felt its failure keenly. "We decided to scrap first plans and fight our own war."[8]

The scheme that Colby, Helgeson, and Lieutenant Glen Farnsworth, NORSO's demolitions expert, came up with was a reprise of the "Great Locomotive Chase" of American Civil War fame. The team would seize a train (it was unclear whether a German troop train or a civilian transport), throw it into reverse, and blow up every bridge and tunnel it came to until the explosives ran out. The team would then derail the train and make its escape. Farnsworth was exultant; the sheer audacity of the scheme would throw the Wehrmacht off balance. If this plan fell through, Colby and his men would simply bring down a bridge, probably the one at Tangen, which was much less imposing than the one at Grana.

Shortly after Easter, the NORSO team moved into a farmhouse given up to them by a local family that sympathized with the resistance. Several days later, with six local resistance fighters added to their number, the men set off on the 100-plus-mile journey south. Each soldier carried a 50-pound pack, and team members took turns pulling one of three toboggans loaded with 60 pounds of explosives. The weather turned against them almost immediately. "Three hours after setting out we were plodding into a sleet storm, carried by the strong west wind and turning our clothing, equipment, and the snow into a sheet of ice, making it almost impossible for the skis to take hold," Colby later wrote of the experience. After only 15 miles, the team took cover in one of the unoccupied huts that dotted the Norwegian countryside. The next day Colby and his men made 25 miles before stopping. It was up one boulder-strewn, ice-covered mountain after another, with daytime temperatures frequently hovering near zero. Frostbite and broken limbs were ever-present dangers. Colby remembered worrying about a broken bone, in particular. How would he treat and evacuate an injured man? Would he have to be sacrificed to the mission? He told his men to forget their pride and sit on their skis when they felt themselves losing control. "Finally," Colby wrote, "we got to the peaks overlooking the Tangen bridge, somewhere north of Tangen, where the railroad skirts Oiingen Lake."[9]

The commandos were appalled at the scene that unfolded before them. "Picture the Hudson River," Colby wrote, "visualizing the Palisades three times their true height. Place a railroad snug against the foot of the cliffs, and then crust the whole thing with four feet of snow and six inches of wet ice."[10] The men would have to descend with their packs, their weapons, and the three explosive-laden toboggans. Helgeson, a lieutenant in the Norwegian resistance force and an expert skier, declared that the descent was impossible; the men would at the least break their skis and their legs and at the worst fall to their deaths. The team decided to sleep on a final decision, taking refuge in a large crevice in one of the peaks. By this time, Colby and Farnsworth had ditched the Great Locomotive Chase idea and settled for merely blowing up a span of the Nordland. The next day, Colby led a reconnaissance patrol to the bridge at Grana. It was more accessible than the one at Tangen, but too heavily guarded. They would have to choose the smaller, almost unguarded span at Tangen.

Upon his return, Colby dispatched additional patrols to search for a means of descent. Miraculously, one found an iced-over waterfall that descended in fairly easy stages to the lake. The team took this path and arrived at the bottom just before dawn the next day. Colby sent Captain Tom Sather and a squad to knife any German sentinels they encountered and to cut telephone and telegraph lines. Meanwhile, Helgeson had been dispatched to scout an escape route. While Farnsworth and his three non-commissioned officers set their charges along the long I-girded bridge, Colby and the rest guarded the approaches to both ends of the span. The team waited forty-eight hours hoping for the arrival of a German troop train that could be dispatched into the lake along with the bridge, but with the chances of their discovery becoming unacceptably high, Colby gave the signal.

"It is difficult to blow up steel," Colby subsequently observed. "Most often it simply bends out of shape. But the second Farnsworth touched the wires and the TNT went off, the structure vanished."[11] If the Germans did not know Colby and his men were in the area before the explosion, they did afterward. The roar from the detonation was horrific, lingering as it bounced off one mountain to another.

The NORSOs reached the woods just ahead of the pursuing Wehrmacht. What ensued was a running gun battle that lasted for more than two days and nights over ice-encrusted peaks and frozen rivers, and through woods with snow so deep that even farm animals had to wear snowshoes. The destination was neutral Sweden, some 40 miles away. Colby and his men could not pause for a moment, or the massive German force would envelop them. Spotter planes buzzed overhead, radioing their position to the pursuers. One long steep stretch the men named Benzedrine Hill for the drug that enabled them to get up it. People who reach the end of their resources and go beyond frequently hallucinate. Colby may have recalled a passage from T. E. Lawrence: "The body was too coarse to feel the utmost of our sorrows and our joys. Therefore, we abandoned it as rubbish; we left it below us to march forward, a breathing simulacrum, on its own level."[12]

With Helgeson, who would later captain the Norwegian Olympic cross-country ski team, and Hans Liermo, an experienced timber guide, breaking the path, the commandos gradually began to separate from their pursuers. At the Swedish border, they turned north, eventually reaching a hut controlled by the resistance. The men stumbled in, exhausted to the point of delirium. After some self-congratulatory banter, all fell into a deep sleep—all, that is, except Sather, who managed to shoot an elk. The beast provided a fine repast when Colby and his men finally awoke.[13]

Rested and to a degree restored, the NORSOs made their way back to base camp at Lake Jaevsjo, where they found waiting for them the five men who had been mistakenly dropped into Sweden. The authorities at the internment camp had chosen to look the other way when the contingent "escaped," taking their weapons and equipment with them. The additional men would come in handy; NORSO was not through. London informed Colby that the Germans were frantically trying to bypass the fallen bridge at Tangen, and it would be only a matter of time before the Nordland train was running again. With headquarters' approval, Colby decided to destroy an extensive stretch of rail line at Lurudal at both ends of the Plutten Tunnel. It, too, would be a dangerous mission. The Germans had more than 250 guards stationed along a 5-kilometer stretch of track. On April 22, a resupply flight dropped additional food, ammunition, cigarettes, and rail bombs, plus five uniforms for the commandos who had made it in from Sweden. "We needed the new uniforms," Colby observed sardonically, "because they [the new men] could be shot legally as spies [sans uniforms] if the enemy caught us. The remainder would have been shot illegally."[14]

On Monday, April 23, Colby once again led his men into the white wilderness, this time heading toward the Nordland rail line via Lilefjeldt and Seisjoen. That night and the next, the NORSOs broke into abandoned huts to warm themselves and sleep. The tiny structures were nowhere to be found on maps of the area, and therefore relatively secure. On the morning of the third day, Colby, accompanied by expert skier Hans Lierman and a radioman, set out to reconnoiter. After six hours of steady skiing, they reached the railroad at Lurudal. The trio surveyed the entrance and exit to the Plutten Tunnel and marked on their maps where charges should be placed. They then returned to the main force, which had remained in a hut at Skartnes.

At moonrise the following evening, the twenty-four men of NORSO separated into eight teams, each carrying 30 pounds of rail demolition charges, and set out. The weather was beginning to warm, the temperature dropping to a mere zero by nightfall.[15] To the group's amazement, the Germans were all in barracks. The commandos spread out and planted their devices along a 2.5-kilometer expanse of track on either side of the tunnel. Colby and an enlisted man took the area closest to the largest German guardhouse. At Farnsworth's signal, all of the charges were detonated simultaneously. Colby recalled that the Germans reacted like bees flying from a hive that had been violently disturbed. They rushed from their huts firing their automatic weapons and shooting off flares. As the main body of commandos headed for the woods, Sather and a rearguard kept the closest Germans pinned down. Colby and his men had to dodge a spray of bullets but managed to join the others unscathed.

With the enemy in hot pursuit, the NORSOs retreated post-haste to their hut. Colby would not let his men rest, however. They gathered their equipment and set off immediately on the sixteen-hour trip back to Lake Jaevsjo. The Germans soon gave up the chase. The Wehrmacht subsequently brought in Russian slave laborers to repair the damaged line, but the flow of troops over the Nordland slowed to a trickle, an estimated 1,000 total for the last month of the war.[16] Its Norwegian mission accomplished, Special Forces headquarters in London ordered a halt to further Carpetbagger flights. The NORSO team began to run low on food and other essentials. Then an order came dispersing all of the Rype team save Helgeson to duty elsewhere. Colby's force was cut to twenty. The snow was melting and the countryside was crawling with German patrols. At one point, a five-man enemy patrol stumbled into camp. Armed only with machine pistols, the Germans were outgunned. Colby believed he had talked them into surrendering when one raised his pistol. The Americans summarily gunned down the lot. But there would be more Germans, many more.

Before the NORSO team had set out on the Lurudal mission, a resistance figure code-named "Drama" had come to the mountains seeking a conference with the American Norwegian commandos, news of whose exploits had then spread far and wide. He proposed that NORSO begin training and equipping Norwegian volunteers for a partisan army that would operate out of Lierne, a nearby mountain redoubt.[17] At the time, the idea had appealed to Colby and his men, most of whom had had experience with the maquis in France. The second attack on the Nordland rail line had put the scheme on hold. In the days after the Lurudal operation, however, the Lierne plan seemed not only attractive but vital. NORSO was isolated and would probably not receive any help from SHAEF until the war was over. Meanwhile, it was sure to be attacked by the tens of thousands of Germans it had bottled up. Operating out of Lierne, the commandos would have access to food, shelter, and allies in their struggle to survive.

But Bill Colby had a grander scheme in mind. "I urged a political gesture," he wrote in *Honorable Men*: "let's seize the mountain redoubt of Lierne and declare it the first step of Norway's liberation, with the

NORSO Group and the friendly Norwegians who would flock to us, re-playing France's liberation." To his consternation, Special Forces headquar-ters denied permission. But Colby persisted. "I am here," he radioed back. "I know what I am doing. I know I can do it; the Resistance wants me to do it, and I intend to do it." London responded immediately. Colby and his men were to remain in hiding: "any unauthorized contact by you with enemy will subject you to immediate disciplinary action," the message said. Before matters could proceed any further, Germany surrendered. The war in Europe was over.[18]

On May 11, Colby was instructed to proceed to Snassa and accept the surrender of the large German garrison stationed there. With two of his burliest sergeants at his side and the rest of the NORSO contingent, paltry as it was, covering them, Colby approached the camp's gate and bade the commander come out. Colby recalled that the German officer in charge was almost as nervous as he was and all went well. His men would remain in their barracks, the commander declared, and observe perfect discipline. At this point, the liberated people of Snassa poured out of their houses to festoon Colby and his men with laurels and flood them with champagne. Then followed a triumphal procession to Trondheim and more celebrating. When Crown Prince Olaf arrived in the city on May 17 for an Indepen-dence Day parade, NORSO became part of his honor guard.

One last task remained. The town of Namsos, some 60 miles up the coast, had been heavily bombed in 1940 and was the home base for some 10,000 German troops. When the people of the town asked for some Al-lied presence to convince the Bosche that they were no longer conquerors but the conquered, London ordered NORSO to undertake the job. Colby and his thirty men traveled over the very railway they had worked so hard to destroy and were billeted in the homes of friendly townsfolk. Colby hoped for the best, but his men reported conspicuous shoulder brushes with German troops on the streets, together with hostile stares and assorted insults. He ordered his men to avoid confrontations and under no circum-stances try to disarm the enemy soldiers. But when the crews of five Ger-man naval vessels lined the harbor chanting, "Sieg Heil!," he realized he would have to act. Colby telephoned the commander of the German forces and informed him that at 9:00 A.M. the next day he would "inspect" each of his naval vessels. Accompanied by four NORSO soldiers, all former mariners, Colby arrived at dockside at the prescribed time. The team was escorted by each vessel's commander to his respective ship. There were sullen looks, but no open defiance. Germans and Norwegians alike had gotten the word that the war was over, and Norway was a free country.[19]

Eight days later, Colby and his team boarded a plane for Oslo. The Norwegians were treated to a hero's welcome and dispersed. Their commander and their other American colleagues then departed for London. Bill visited Elbridge, who was working at SHAEF headquarters at Versailles, and learned that the NORSO Group was to be reassembled and dispatched to the Pacific. Colby had long wanted to return to Asia and serve in the China-Burma-India theater, but there was, he believed, still some unfinished business in Europe. He asked Russell Forgan, who had succeeded David Bruce as OSS European chief, for permission to mount a Jedburgh-type operation that would drop into Spain, link up with anti-Franco partisans, and topple that country's fascist government. Absolutely not, headquarters responded. The United States was not at war with Spain and did not intend to go to war with Spain.

Colby's proposal, which was met with a combination of amusement and derision by the OSS staff, was revealing in a number of ways. The Jedburgh would later write in *Honorable Men* that as a result of the episode, he "learned that America's mission in Europe was not purely ideological."[20] In truth, Colby was only being consistent. He had thought the war was about ideas, the principles embodied in the Atlantic Charter. While in France working with the maquis, he remembered being inspired by Colonel Chevrier's "political" speeches to his comrades. By political, he meant patriotic, ideological. Like Chevrier and T. E. Lawrence, Colby believed he was acting to bring oppressed peoples freedom, self-determination, and, if possible, democracy. Unlike them, perhaps, he believed that he was facilitating the advance of social and economic justice as well. Spain, to Colby's mind, had been the original battlefield. Franco's triumph and survival would remain a blot on the honor of the Allies. Were not freedom, democracy, and individual liberty inseparable, just as totalitarianism, racism, and imperialism were inextricably linked? Actually, given the culture that Bill Donovan had encouraged in the OSS, Colby's proposal was not outrageous at all. Donovan had encouraged thinking outside the box, and if it did nothing else, the agency shunned political, military, and diplomatic orthodoxy throughout the war. In this context, what was surprising was the idea's peremptory dismissal by Forgan and his staff. Perhaps ideology was taking a backseat within the OSS, or perhaps the focus of that ideology had already begun shifting from fascism to communism.

And what of Bill Colby, the bespectacled, diminutive, twenty-five-year-old war hero? A hero he was; the citation for the Silver Star he was subsequently awarded was emphatic about that. He had engaged, endured, led, and prevailed. There seemed to be no limit to his will and determination—carrying a pack one-third of his own weight, scaling icy mountains, and fording frozen rivers. He had served as point man on the advance of every patrol and personally covered every retreat. The morale of his men had remained high even in the most desperate situations.[21] Colby's college friend Stan Temko had visited him during his Jedburgh training. How would you describe Bill Colby? he had asked another commando. "Ballsey," was the reply. His contemporaries then and later would call him fearless. No person is exempt from fear, but Colby's ability to control his was truly remarkable. Bill Colby was a warrior in the making when he arrived in Europe and a warrior in full when he left, a veteran of unconventional warfare. In many ways, that experience would mark him for life.

In this, Colby was in some ways like any other individual who fights in a war. As "the Judge," a character in Cormac McCarthy's novel *Blood Meridian*, observed "[war] endures because young men love it and old men love it in them." The Judge goes on to observe that "the world is forever after divided into those who fought and those who did not."[22] As a Jedburgh and a NORSO operative, Colby was the elite of the elite. He had experienced the intensity of relationships that come only to men who have survived combat together. For some, it would be an experience they would seek to recapture even until death. Moreover, Colby had fought in the "Good War," against the real Axis of evil. His experiences had not compromised his morality, but confirmed it. In some ways, the young soldier was still the naive adolescent, a captive of Elbridge's outsized expectations.

Shortly after his return from the European theater he wrote an account of his NORSO experiences entitled "Skis and Daggers." It was a precursor of the World War II genre books for adolescents such as *Dave Dawson over Burma*. Just as Dave's sidekick consumes a whole cherry pie before flying off to shoot down Jap Zeroes, the men of NORSO engage in delirious horseplay after their return from Tangen. Helgeson sends his comrades into a fit of mirth by demanding "a dish of pineapple," while Sather calls Colby a "Trojan Norse."[23]

War, of course, is a dangerous business, for body and soul. Decisions of life and death, of what shall be and what shall not be, generally eclipse questions of right and wrong. For the men and women who served as Jedburghs and NORSO commandos, this was doubly true. Not only were they deciders of life and death, as all soldiers are, but they were agents of revolution, molders of societies, and purveyors of ideals, however small the scale. Donovan's people worked outside of traditional political, diplomatic, and military channels; that free agency could be intoxicating. Bill Colby was a good man, a good Catholic, fighting a just war. And yet, in that righteous conflict, in the very triumph over the fascist empires, there lurked danger for the man and for his country. As the Judge in *Blood Meridian* says to a former priest turned Indian fighter (the novel takes place in the 1850s' American West), "For the priest has put by the robes of his craft and taken up the tools of that higher calling which all men honor [war]. The priest also would be no god-server but a god himself."[24] Colby may not have been the archetypal Nietzschean superman Cormac McCarthy was referencing, but he had allowed his patriotism and his religion to take the fine edges off the horrors of war. For the vast majority of men and women who served in World War II, the experience would be unforgettable, but temporary and eventually fleeting. For a few, it would determine the course of the rest of their lives, and they in turn would shape the future of the nation. William Egan Colby was one of those few. No conscript crusader he, but a professional, a lifer.

Following the operation in occupied France, most of the Jedburghs were reassigned to the Far East, dropping behind Japanese lines in China or Indochina to rally, train, and equip the native resistance movements. NORSO had not been intended as a substitute for service in the Pacific theater, only a detour. Accordingly, when Colby arrived in London from Oslo, he was informed that he would take ship for America and, after a brief shore leave, depart for the other war, probably to be stationed in Indochina because of his French.

Rejection of his proposal to overthrow the Franco regime in Spain notwithstanding, Colby was pleased. The ensuing transatlantic voyage was slow but uneventful—there were no Nazi wolf packs to dodge. Colby remembered sailing into New York Harbor past a huge banner that read "WELCOME HOME—WELL DONE." Almost the first thing the young hero did was to call Barbara Heinzen, the Barnard co-ed he had dated while he was at Columbia. Whether it was love or lust—the family later would joke that John, the eldest child, was born nine months and one minute after Bill landed in New York—the couple became engaged just two weeks after they were reunited. But Bill and Barbara did not set a date for the wedding. He recalled that he did not want to leave a war widow, and she probably did not want to become one.[25]

In the Pacific, the Allies had turned the tide. General Douglas MacArthur had returned to the liberated Philippines in the fall of 1944, and early the next year the US Marines, supported by the army and navy, began their island-hopping march northward toward the Japanese homeland islands. By the summer of 1945, the Japanese had lost all of their carriers and most of their air force, but the assumption among MacArthur's staff was that the enemy would fight to the bitter end. The battles for Iwo Jima and Okinawa had been the bloodiest of the war. Then, as Colby was packing his bags and mentally girding his loins, word came of the atomic bombing of Hiroshima on August 6. The Soviet Union invaded Manchuria on August 8, and Nagasaki was bombed the next day. On August 14, 1945, Japan surrendered unconditionally. World War II was over. On September 15, Bill and Barbara were married in St. Patrick's Cathedral in Washington, DC. "I stopped in advance at a quiet Catholic church to confess the lively bachelor life I had lived as a paratrooper for three years," Bill wrote in *Honorable Men*.[26]

The OSS recommended Major Colby for Command and General Staff College in Fort Leavenworth, Kansas, and he was accepted. With his war record and education, the twenty-five-year-old officer could look forward to rapid advancement in the postwar military, but it was not to be. Colby recalled that he admired and respected the army in which his father had made a career, but that it was not for him. The regular military was too confining and rigid. Colby had spent the war in an organization that encouraged innovative thinking, individual initiative, and self-reliance. The men and women of the OSS with whom he had associated were intelligent, educated, daring, and immensely stimulating. The former Jedburgh did not quietly suffer fools, or even average people. "Generally admirable," his OSS evaluation for 1945 read, "but critical of the incompetents in the higher positions." Colby liked adventure, but he did not want to be told what to live and die for by people less intelligent than himself. His father had had to live with that ever since he had joined the military. No, Bill Colby decided, he wanted to return to Columbia and earn his law degree, make a nice living, serve the cause of New Deal liberalism, and raise a family.[27]

Pressure on the Truman administration—FDR had died of a massive heart attack on April 12, 1945—to demobilize the armed forces was intense, but America's international responsibilities had grown immeasurably as a result of the war. Its strategic and economic interests were vast and in need of protection. The War Department came up with a point system to govern release from the service based on time in service and merit. Colby had been in uniform since before Pearl Harbor; he had earned the Bronze Star, the Silver Star, the Croix de Guerre, and the Medal of St. Olaf. He received his discharge and immediately entrained for New York, where Columbia's registrar told him that he would be admitted if he could start classes the following Monday. Colby rushed back to Washington to tell Barbara.

Before the young couple departed to begin their new life, there was a final gathering of OSS eagles. On the evening of September 28, Wild Bill Donovan presided over a reunion at the Riverside Skating Rink near where Washington's Rock Creek Park meets the Potomac River.[28] The research and analysis people were there, but it was the Jedburghs and their counterparts in the Far East who were the stars. Before addressing his followers, Donovan lined up those who had most recently been decorated and pinned their medals on them. When he reached Colby, Donovan expressed regret that he himself had never earned the Silver Star. Yes, Colby replied diplomatically, it would have been a nice complement to the Congressional Medal of Honor.

Wild Bill's remarks were brief and to the point. "Within a few days, each one of us will be going on to new tasks, whether in civilian life or in government service," he said. "You can go with the assurance that only by decisions of national policy based upon accurate information can we have a chance of a peace that will endure."[29]

THE AGENCY

As early as 1943, in the midst of World War II, Bill Donovan had proclaimed the need for a peacetime intelligence agency capable of gathering, collating, and analyzing all information affecting the US national security as well as conducting espionage and supervising covert operations overseas.

Espionage and counterespionage had existed as the "dark side" of diplomacy since the formation of the nation-state system. So had black propaganda (the deliberate spreading of misinformation), psychological warfare, and covert operations. General George Washington, building on his experience as a British officer during the French and Indian War in which he had utilized Indian informants, was America's first spymaster. In a letter to his subordinates on July 26, 1777, he wrote: "The necessity of procuring good intelligence is apparent & need not be further urged." The Revolution produced the new nation's first intelligence "mole"—Dr. Benjamin Church, who posed as a Boston patriot while secretly providing intelligence about American rebel activities to British general Thomas Gage. Church's treachery was uncovered by America's first cryptanalyst, the Reverend Samuel West, who was hired by Washington to decipher one of Church's letters.

In the years between the American Revolutionary War and the Civil War, the nation, absorbed with domestic matters, saw no need to engage in international espionage or defend against it. But in the early stages of the Civil War, Lincoln, like Washington, acted as his own spymaster. He soon turned to professionals in his search for information on the machinations of the Confederacy. Two rival organizations, one headed by the famous detective Allan Pinkerton and the other by Lafayette Baker, filled the void, but they frequently worked at cross purposes. In 1885, President Grover Cleveland called for assignments of military attachés to foreign countries to gather information. During the Spanish-American War, the US Secret Service ran espionage and counterespionage operations. Before and during American participation in World War I, Secret Service and FBI agents were successful in ferreting out German agents and saboteurs operating within the United States, but between the two world wars, American intelligence once again fell into abeyance.

In November 1944, Donovan wrote to President Roosevelt, an old Columbia Law School classmate, proposing the establishment of a central authority directly under White House control that would coordinate the other intelligence bureaucracies in the federal government (naval intelligence and the intelligence division of the State Department, for example) and collect its own information through a network of spies and counterspies that it would recruit, train, and deploy. The new entity, reporting directly to the president, would gather, evaluate, and disseminate all intelligence relating "to national planning and security in peace and war, and the advancement of broad national policy." This supreme intelligence organization, with its own independent budget, would be authorized to conduct "subversive operations abroad" and perform such other functions related to intelligence as the president should direct. The agency, Donovan made clear, would be strictly prohibited from conducting domestic operations.[1]

There was every indication that Roosevelt planned to approve the Donovan plan for a central intelligence agency, but his death on April 12, 1945, intervened. Donovan lacked a personal relationship with Harry S. Truman. Indeed, the new president regarded the postwar avalanche of OSS glamour stories as nothing more than a campaign of self-aggrandizement by what Truman called that "Black Republican leprechaun." When Donovan eventually gained access to the White House and presented Truman with a copy of his intelligence memo, the president tore it in two and handed it back to him.[2]

On September 20, 1945, Truman issued an executive order officially disbanding the OSS. Its two principal functions were delegated to other agencies, the researchers and analysts to the State Department, and the clandestine operatives—the spymasters and counterspies—to the War Department. The paramilitary types, the parachutists and guerrilla fighters like Colby, were left to go home. Donovan announced that he was abandoning public life to return to his New York law firm.[3]

Despite his distaste for Donovan, Truman was not unsympathetic to the notion of an overarching intelligence authority. Presidential aide Clark Clifford remembered being in the Oval Office one afternoon in late August 1945, just after the termination of hostilities. Referring to Ambassador to Japan Joseph Grew's 1941 cables to the State Department, Truman declared, "You go back and read Joe Grew and then you come in here and tell me how anybody could have read those cables and not know there was an attack coming." Grew had reported rumors circulating in Tokyo predicting the exact timing and nature of the attack on Pearl Harbor weeks before it occurred. "If we had had some central repository for information and somebody to look at it and fit all the pieces together, there never would have been a Pearl Harbor."[4]

On January 22, 1946, Truman, by executive order, directed the establishment of a new National Intelligence Authority. It would comprise the secretaries of state, war, and the navy, and would have as its operating arm the Central Intelligence Group (CIG). In a White House ceremony, Truman named his old friend Rear Admiral Sidney Souers as the first head of the CIG, presenting him with a black cloak and wooden dagger and pronouncing him "director of centralized snooping." The director of the CIG would have no money and no authority of his own. Asked by a reporter several weeks after his appointment what he wanted to do, the first director replied, "I want to go home." The operatives of the new agency moved into a string of temporary buildings—built for the OSS during the war—located along the Reflecting Pool in front of the Lincoln Memorial. They were shabby structures, poorly cooled and heated, one OSS officer recalled. This central intelligence entity might have remained the empty shell it was except for one thing—the onset of the Cold War.[5]

During his first year and a half in office, Harry Truman alternated between conciliation and rhetorical confrontation in his dealings with the Soviet Union. The thrust of his policy, however, was to have the United States live up to the letter and spirit of the Yalta Accords—the agreements entered into by the Allied nations dividing liberated Europe into occupation zones—and to insist that the Kremlin do likewise. Gradually, however, the administration's attitude toward Moscow hardened. On February 22, 1946, the American chargé d'affaires in Moscow, George F. Kennan,

responding to a request from the State Department for an analysis of Soviet policy, penned his "Long Telegram." Neither friendship nor war with
the Soviets was conceivable, Kennan declared. The Kremlin held a "neu-
rotic" view of the world and was "committed fanatically to the belief that
with [the] U.S. there can be no permanent modus vivendi." The Marxist-
Leninist fear of capitalist encirclement and traditional Russian fears of an
attack through Eastern Europe by another Napoleon or Hitler were mutually reinforcing. It was imperative that the United States rebuild and secure the industrial strong points of the noncommunist world, that is,
Western Europe and Japan. Through alliances and economic aid, Kennan
wrote, America should seek to contain communism until it collapsed as a
result of its own internal contradictions. In March 1946, with Truman on
the dais, former British prime minister Winston Churchill delivered his
famous Iron Curtain speech: The Soviet Union and its satellites would
not rest until all of Europe and eventually the entire world were communist, he said. The only thing standing between Western Europe, gravely
weakened by World War II, and the five hundred Soviet divisions stationed in Eastern Europe was the United States. Churchill's warning came
as no surprise to Truman. His administration had already come to the
conclusion that British and American strategic interests in Europe were
more or less identical.

In his Long Telegram, Kennan, who would go on to head the Policy
Planning Staff in the State Department, had warned that the Soviet threat
was all the more terrifying because, in addition to its vast internal resources,
Russia had at its disposal "an elaborate and far-flung apparatus for exertion
of its influence in other countries, an apparatus of amazing flexibility and
versatility managed by people whose experience and skill in underground
methods are presumably without parallel in history." Kennan was referring
to the Communist Party of the Soviet Union (CPSU) and the scores of
communist parties operating in countries around the world that had, until
1943, been directed and coordinated by the Communist International.
There was also the Soviet Union's People's Commissariat for Internal Affairs, or NKVD, which, despite its name, was heavily involved in overseas
espionage, counterespionage, propaganda, covert action, and subversion.
Like the Communist Party itself, every individual communist was an evan-
gelist of the proletariat and as such a potential spy, saboteur, political operative, or counterspy. Each and every Communist Party member was a

revolutionary with a license to subvert. Because of their openness, Western societies were especially vulnerable. As Kennan had noted in his 1946 missive to the State Department, the United States and its fellow democracies featured a "wide variety of national associations or bodies which can be dominated or influenced by such penetration," including "labor unions, youth leagues, women's organizations, racial societies, religious societies, social organizations, cultural groups, liberal magazines [and] publishing houses."[6]

As it was mobilizing diplomatically against the Soviet threat in 1946–1947, the Truman administration was also debating how to organize internally—how to create bureaucracies capable of meeting the new challenge. Out of those debates came the National Security Act of 1947, which effectively created the national security state. The measure brought into being a unified military establishment by setting up a cabinet-level Department of Defense. Another new body, the National Security Council (NSC)—composed of the president; vice president; secretaries of defense, state, and Treasury; and the chief of intelligence—would meet regularly to oversee the nation's strategic well-being. The Joint Chiefs of Staff (JCS), established in reponse to the crisis of World War II, would become permanent. Finally, the National Intelligence Authority and the CIG were transformed into a new bureau, the Central Intelligence Agency. Both the OSS's chief European spymaster, Allen Dulles, and General Dwight Eisenhower testified before Congress in favor of a central intelligence authority. "A small but elite corps of men with a passion for anonymity and a willingness to stick to the job," is how Dulles described the individuals who would staff the new agency.[7]

It seems that the creators of the CIA originally intended that it limit itself to intelligence gathering and analysis. The agency's first director, Admiral Roscoe H. Hillenkoetter, was not an ambitious man, either for himself or his bureaucracy. He discouraged all talk of psychological warfare, black propaganda, and covert political and military operations. All of this did not sit well with Donovan and the corporate lawyers who had created and run the OSS. These so-called "Park Avenue cowboys" had reveled in the guerrilla and paramilitary operations of the service. In tacit alliance with them were the hardline anticommunists, or "determined interventionists," who were increasingly asserting themselves within the foreign policy establishment, men like future ambassador to the USSR Charles "Chip" Bohlen, former ambassador to the Soviet Union W. Averell Harriman, and George Kennan. In December 1947, the activists won their first victory when the NSC directed Hillenkoetter to undertake "covert psychological operations" against the Soviet Union. Subsequently, CIA operatives intervened in the 1948 Italian parliamentary elections to prevent a communist victory. Then, on May 4, 1948, in the midst of the Berlin Blockade crisis, Kennan's Policy Planning Staff recommended "the inauguration of organized political warfare." What Kennan had in mind was the creation of a new "covert political warfare operations directorate within the Government."[8] American officials had to realize that the boundaries between war and peace had virtually evaporated, he declared. The British had long recognized the fact; the Soviets were currently the world's leading practitioners of political warfare and covert operations.

Kennan's arguments carried the day, and the result was a new body, the Office of Policy Coordination (OPC)—Cold War agency names and operation code-names were meant to conceal rather than reveal—which would be housed within the CIA. The OPC would in effect become the third leg of the intelligence stool, along with analysis and espionage. Kennan approached Allen Dulles about heading covert operations, but he declined, thinking that he would become director of central intelligence in the Republican administration that he believed would surely come to power in the fall. So Kennan turned to the hard-driving Frank Wisner, former OSS head of Eastern European operations. Wisner in turn set about bringing back into government service those men and women who had served the OSS as guerrillas, paratroopers, and covert operatives.[9]

Meanwhile, Bill and Barbara Colby had settled into the rather drab but intense lives of law student and spouse. The couple rented "a rather dark and dingy" apartment on Manhattan's Upper West Side. Bill's $80 a month from the GI Bill paid the rent, while Barbara's salary as editor of the New York State Department of Labor's official publications took care of the rest of the couple's expenses. Bill toiled away at his studies, making law review. He was aware of the burgeoning Cold War and had an inkling of Donovan's struggles to see a free-standing intelligence authority established. The Jedburghs gathered periodically for merriment and nostalgia. Occasionally, the Colbys were guests of the Donovans for a Columbia football game or for dinner at the latter's Sutton Place apartment. Then, when Bill graduated in February 1947, the Donovan law firm hired him.

Donovan, Leisure, Newton, Lumbard, and Irvine occupied three floors of the office building at No. 2 Wall Street and "exuded the successful air of brilliant legal minds working on the great corporate problems of the day," Colby wrote in his memoir. As a junior member of the firm, he took depositions, recorded minutes of the partners' meetings, and ran errands; he quickly began learning the ins and outs of antitrust, corporate, and tax law. Donovan and most of his partners were Republicans, but they not only tolerated but encouraged political diversity. It was good business to have friends and contacts across the political spectrum. New Dealer to the core, Colby joined the hidebound New York Young Democratic Club and the more activist Robert B. Blaikie Regular Democratic Association of the 7th Assembly District. He rang doorbells for Harry Truman and celebrated his upset victory on election night, 1948.[10]

American liberals were then in the process of choosing sides in the Cold War. During the 1930s, many progressive Americans had come to admire the Soviet experiment, Stalin's horrendous purges notwithstanding. A few joined the Communist Party of the United States (CPUSA), but most, like former vice president Henry Wallace, contented themselves with warning the United States not to become the cat's paw of British imperialism and calling for postwar foreign policy based on Soviet-American friendship. Historian Arthur Schlesinger Jr., Minneapolis mayor Hubert Humphrey, and other Cold War liberals set about distancing themselves from the Wallacites by forming the Americans for Democratic Action (ADA), a group committed equally to New Deal/Fair Deal reforms and to combating the menace of Soviet communism. Although he was not a member of the ADA, Colby was certainly of this ilk.

In late 1946, Bill received a call from Mickey Boerner of the American Veterans Committee (AVC). The organization had been established as an alternative home for US service personnel who were too liberal for the American Legion. The CPUSA hoped to establish a presence in the veterans movement and, not surprisingly, concentrated on the AVC rather than the conservative Legion. Communist rank-and-file members were going to try to seize control of the group, and Boerner asked Colby, whose name had been given to him by a law-school friend, to come to the next meeting of Manhattan Chapter No. 1. Colby arrived, paid his dues, and immediately plunged into the ensuing debate regarding the Veteran Committee's proper attitude toward the Greek revolution, which pitted communist insurgents against the pro-Western government. The communists touted a resolution endorsing the struggle of "democratic forces" against the "fascist-dominated" government. Colby and like-minded veterans appreciated the role that the communist insurgents in Greece had played in the resistance against the Nazis, but they did not want to see Greece become another Soviet satellite. The war of words stretched long into the night, with the liberals finally managing to block the communist resolution. It was his first taste, Colby remembered, of the focus and discipline of Marxist-Leninists. The debate over the Greek Civil War, as it turned out, was a foretaste of things to come.[11]

On May 16, 1948, the body of George Polk Jr., overseas correspondent for CBS, washed ashore on Salonika Bay in Greece. His hands and legs were bound and the back of his skull had been blown away by a bullet fired at point-blank range. Polk, a protégé of Edward R. Murrow, the pioneering broadcast journalist, was a decorated World War II veteran, having served as a navy pilot during the battle for Guadalcanal. He had been assigned to Greece to cover the civil war.

The thirty-four-year-old reporter was aggressive, ambitious, and dogged. His focus was the corrupt, graft-ridden government supported by the Royalists, the military, and the scions of the banking, shipping, and trading houses. On May 6, following the assassination of the minister of justice, the Greek government had summarily shot forty-four suspected communists. It seemed, Polk reported on CBS, that the rule of law was going by the boards in Athens. (At the same time, the American journalist was reporting on the *pedomazoma*, the campaign by the communist provisional government that controlled much of the mountainous countryside to collect every child between the ages of three and fifteen and send them to live in "people's democracies" behind the Iron Curtain.) The Greek government and the American embassy, which in the wake of the Truman Doctrine was lending unquestioning support to the regime in Athens, viewed the young journalist's broadcasts with increasing alarm. Indeed, Polk had written Ed Murrow that relations between certain foreign correspondents and Greek and American officials had reached the point that "somebody was likely to get hurt." Polk had been scheduled to return to the United States to accept a Neiman Fellowship, but before leaving he wanted to make contact with the leaders of the Greek National Liberation Front (ELAS, using the Greek acronym, and EAM, its military wing) to get their take on the conflict. It was for that purpose that he had flown to Salonika.[12]

As George Polk was being buried in Athens, the Overseas Writers Association was setting up a special committee, chaired by the renowned columnist Walter Lippmann, to investigate the murder. To lead the investigation, the committee chose Wild Bill Donovan. Lippmann believed that the founder of the OSS was perfect for the job: utilizing the OSS's connections with the former Greek resistance, both communist and noncommunist, Donovan would be able to get to the bottom of the matter. Ever the adventurer, Donovan eagerly accepted. In the months that followed, he put together a small team of former Greek OSSers and made several trips to Athens and Salonika. In July, Donovan's principal investigator, James Kellis, an OSS veteran who had worked closely with the Greek underground, made his report. Polk had tried to make contact with the Greek communists but failed; they would not have had access to his itinerary. In any event, Polk's increasingly antigovernment reports would have attracted rather than alienated ELAS. It was the Greek security forces and their British advisers who had knowledge of his movements, had access to him, and had the motive to do away with him. After reading the report, Donovan removed Kellis from the case. Writing after his retirement from the CIA in 1977, Kellis recalled, "While I was in Greece, I often heard the statement that national interest had to be given a higher priority than discovering the real murderers of George Polk."[13]

In its search for a scapegoat, the Greek government focused on Polk's twenty-year-old widow, Rhea, a Greek airline stewardess whom George had met and married some eight months earlier, and the couple's closest friend. Authorities implied a love triangle or a paid assassination. What made Rhea Polk such a compelling target was that at the time, she was telling anyone who would listen that it was the state security forces and not the communists who had murdered her husband. In June, Donovan spirited Rhea Polk out of Greece, either to protect her from the government or to keep her and her stories out of the public venue, or both. The person assigned to the feeding and care of the young widow was Bill Colby.[14]

Bill and Barbara put up Polk's widow in their apartment until she could find her own place to live. Eventually, Barbara would help Rhea enroll at Barnard, her alma mater. In the first few weeks of her sojourn in the United

States, Rhea Polk was not often out of Bill Colby's sight. He debriefed her and delivered written reports to Donovan. He counseled her on the realities of the Cold War, urging her to look to her own future and not tilt at windmills, no matter how great the injustice done to her and her husband. During their conversations, Rhea told the former Jedburgh that before George had departed for Salonika, he had had a stormy session with the Greek foreign minister, Constantine Tsaldaris. He had discovered, George told the Greek politician, a secret $25,000 bank account in a Chase branch in New York. It was American aid money, and it was traceable to Tsaldaris; news of it was sure to come out. Subsequently, Tsaldaris's son, in New York City on United Nations business, physically and verbally assaulted Rhea, telling her to keep her mouth shut.[15]

Colby dutifully reported all of this to his boss; none of that information was ever passed on to the Lippmann committee. On April 21, 1949, a Greek journalist with ties to ELAS was sentenced to life imprisonment for complicity in the murder of George Polk. Shortly thereafter, Bill Colby made the decision to leave the Donovan law firm.[16]

In his memoirs, Colby recalled that the reasons for his departure were personal and political. Though Donovan and his partners were tolerant, even encouraging of his liberal activism, the fact remained that they were pillars of the Republican Party. Bill observed that he did not want to spend his time in the service of the corporate elite, and he and Barbara did not want to raise their children (John and Catherine by then) in Scarsdale or some other affluent suburb of New York. Years later, Bill told John that he had received a lucrative offer from American Can Company, but had decided that he did not want a future in the container business.

Colby also may have been troubled by the Polk affair, believing, with James Kellis, that it was unacceptable for the United States to "support national interests by disregarding moral principles."[17] Bill Colby was a true believer, but he was not an automaton. Anticommunist though it may have been, the government in Athens was proto-fascist, much like the Franco regime that Major Colby had wanted America to fight in 1945. His heart had not been in the advice he had given Rhea Polk to turn the other cheek. Here was the classic Cold War conundrum. To what lengths could a country justifying itself in terms of natural rights philosophy and the Judeo-Christian ethic go in fighting perceived evil? Catholic though he was, Colby was enough of a Niebuhrian to be conflicted. The Polk case involved traps that were more than moral, however. Colby was familiar enough with spycraft to know that Donovan had in effect made him an accomplice to murder and could blackmail him if he tried to blow the whistle. There was an old rule in the trade: never trust patriotism; always have a backup to coerce loyalty should it become necessary.

By the fall of 1949, the United States was in the grip of a mounting anticommunist hysteria. The Russians and East Germans had called off the Berlin Blockade, but that same year, Mao Tse-tung and the Chinese communists had driven Chiang Kai-shek and the Chinese Nationalists off the mainland and onto the nearby island of Formosa. The world's most populist nation was in the hands of the enemy. If that were not enough, word came that the Soviets had exploded their own atomic device, years ahead of predictions by American atomic experts. Those hundreds of divisions of Red Army troops were still stationed in Eastern Europe. Some Americans, unaware that Stalin could not properly feed and house this multitude, were convinced that they were there as a prelude to an armed invasion of Western Europe.

In addition, it seemed as if the enemy was not only at the gate but within the walls. In 1947, the House Un-American Activities Committee (HUAC), populated primarily by conservative super-patriots, had opened hearings on an alleged plot by domestic communists to take control of the motion picture industry. When HUAC subsequently turned its attention to the federal government, Truman issued an executive order mandating a loyalty investigation of all federal job applicants. In February 1950, Great Britain announced the arrest of noted scientist Klaus Fuchs for betraying atomic secrets to the Soviets. Shortly thereafter, in the United States, Harry Gold, David Greenglass, and Julius and Ethel Rosenberg were arrested as atomic spies.

The Cold War and its newly formed instrument, the CIA, were waiting for Bill Colby, but there would be a brief interregnum. Even before he officially parted company with the Donovan firm, Colby had applied for and accepted a job with the National Labor Relations Board (NLRB) in Washington. Given his interests and liberal values, it was a natural—if temporarily impoverishing—move. In his memoir, Colby gave no other reason for his decision other than to expand his credentials as a New Deal/Fair Deal labor lawyer. During his yearlong stint with the NLRB, he helped represent Philadelphia garment workers who were trying to unionize, and wrote briefs in a case in which agribusinesses in California were illegally breaking strikes by their migrant grape pickers. But Colby was well aware of the evolution of the OSS into the CIA—in 1949, he had accompanied Donovan to Norway for a memorial service commemorating those who had died in Operation Rype—and he wanted to be at hand if an opportunity arose.

Sure enough, just weeks after the Colbys moved to Washington, Bill got a call from Gerry Miller, his old London chief from OSS days. Would Colby meet him for lunch? Miller asked. During the meal, Miller told his former Jedburgh that he had left a promising banking career to join the CIA. He was appropriately vague about his duties, but he made it clear that in Soviet communism, the nation was facing a threat as dire as that posed by Nazism. He finished by asking Colby to come work for him.

Bill was intrigued, but he put off his old boss. He wanted very much to come on board. "Given my OSS experience," he later wrote, "given my special political interests, given my taste for adventure, the CIA was the answer." But full-time employment would have to wait, he told Miller. For him to leave his new job so quickly would not be fair to those at the NLRB who had hired him. Moreover, two moves in such a short time would not look good on his résumé. But, Colby said, he was willing to consult for the Agency on matters in which he had some expertise. Why not go ahead and run the necessary security check and hire him as a consultant? Miller readily agreed.[18]

There things stood until the outbreak of the Korean War in June 1950. Colby and many in the US foreign policy establishment assumed that the North Korean invasion marked the opening shot in a Sino-Soviet campaign to conquer the free world. The Truman administration authorized a massive expansion of the CIA, and Colby quit his job to go to work for Miller, who headed the Western European Division of the Office of Policy Coordination under Frank Wisner. Patriotism and a sense of duty were no doubt important factors in this decision, but, as Colby later commented to a friend, "I was just bored out of my mind."[19]

COVERT OPERATIONS ON THE PERIPHERY OF THE COLD WAR

B ill Colby's attitudes toward the Cold War were shaped by his religion, by his education—formal and informal—by his and his father's romanticism, and by his experiences in the "Good War." From his birth until his second marriage in 1984, he was a practicing Catholic. For his father, the church was a discipline; for his mother, it was a comfort. Neither parent was a religious fanatic; Colby wasn't, either. Instead, like his parents, he was a social and political liberal, prizing the faith for its values of compassion, forgiveness, tolerance, and good works, not for self-righteousness or exclusiveness.

Catholicism was a moral and cultural frame of reference for Bill Colby. Faith and reason were mutually reinforcing, not mutually exclusive.[1] Like the Jesuits, he valued a classical education. He had taken Latin in high school and college, and he studied Greek on his own as an adult. And, like the Jesuits, Colby was more concerned with action than with matters of doctrine. Princeton's motto was "In the nation's service," and he would have wholeheartedly agreed with that sentiment. Unlike the Jesuits, Colby was not in thrall to Christianity, but dedicated to his country, and eventually to the CIA. But he was Jesuitical in the ways he served them: he loved a cause and reveled in taking action in behalf of that cause.

Colby's son John recalled that his father's favorite period in history was the world of the Middle Ages with its fictional stories of chivalrous knights and King Arthur's roundtable. Chivalry was a code of honor enforced by an elite class with swords; King Arthur acted in the name of the people, beholden to them but above them, paternalistic—but liberal. In Asia, Colby would have been the idealized mandarin. Like his father, Bill was a romantic in the tradition of Kipling, Baden-Powell, and Lawrence, an agent of good in a dangerous world. But he never let his romanticism eclipse his realism: like the Jesuits, Colby was well aware of the moral pitfalls of his calling. Carl Colby recalled his father repeating Harry Lime's famous speech in *The Third Man*. The Italians, Lime declared, have had five hundred years of torture, war, the Borgias, the Medicis; they had also had Michelangelo, Da Vinci, and Botticelli; the Swiss, on the other hand, could boast of five hundred years of the cuckoo clock.[2]

Colby avoided fanaticism not only in religion but also in politics. In the war against communism, Colby was a soldier, not an ideologue. "My father wasn't a vehement anticommunist," son Carl recalled. "He wasn't always talking about getting rid of the communists. He did not talk about them as if he were a football announcer." Bill remembered with pride that when he was with the NLRB, he had helped write a brief for the American Civil Liberties Union in a Supreme Court case involving the harassment of a left-wing California group that had protested the Marshall Plan. In his memoir, he recalled, also with pride, that he and the young activists who constituted the Office of Policy Coordination (the division devoted to secret political and paramilitary operations) were anticommunist but rejected "the right-wing hysterical demagogy of the likes of Joseph McCarthy."[3]

Bill Colby was opposed to communism because it placed the welfare of the state above the welfare of the individual, because it was undemocratic, and because it was determined to extend itself through coercion. "My dislike of Soviet Communism dated back to my college days, to my studies of the Spanish Civil War, to my reading of Lenin, to my awareness of the Stalinist purge trials, to my disgust with the Hitler-Stalin Pact," he wrote in *Honorable Men*. He had heard from fellow Jedburghs about the French communists' efforts to seize control of southern France by force as the Allied armies were advancing. World War II and the Cold War, communism and National Socialism, Sino-Soviet imperialism and Axis aggression were all part of the same seamless threat. It was his duty as an American, a Christian, and a liberal to answer the call to duty. He would later compare the CIA to "an order of Knights Templars [established] to save Western freedom from Communist darkness—and from war." But as the Judge in *Blood Meridian* observed, war and religion are a dangerous mix.[4]

In 1950, the year Bill Colby joined the CIA, the nation was in thrall to the Agency. In the popular mind, America faced a mortal danger both from within—in the form of a communist fifth column—and without—in the form of the five hundred Red Army divisions in Eastern Europe and the hordes of Chinese in Mao's People's Liberation Army. For the most part, the country had shed its fears about an American Gestapo and embraced the Agency as its first line of defense against the clandestine communist menace. The Office of Foreign Intelligence would conduct espionage abroad, while its counterintelligence division would act as a barrier to block communist spying and sabotage in the United States. The research and analysis division would collate and summarize intelligence for decision-makers in the foreign policy establishment. Frank Wisner and his troops in the Office of Policy Coordination would conduct spoiling operations— in effect, try to beat the enemy at his own game. New York publishing houses and Hollywood studios teemed with scripts featuring heroic American agents and counteragents battling an insidious and merciless enemy. Intellectuals were drawn to British writer George Orwell's antitotalitarian novels *Animal Farm*, published in 1945, and *1984*, published in 1949. Despite the extremes of McCarthyism, the vast majority of Americans looked to a coalition of liberal anticommunists and conservative interventionists to lead them in this new crusade.

Colby reveled in his new fraternity, his "band of brothers." The Agency, he wrote, "attracted what nowadays we would call the best and the brightest, the politically liberal young men and women from the finest Ivy League campuses and with the most impeccable social and establishment backgrounds, young people with 'vigor' and adventuresome spirits who believed fervently that the Communist threat had to be met aggressively, innovatively and courageously."[5] Colby's description of the CIA at its inception not only mirrored popular enthusiasms but also highlighted a significant personality trait: he may have been a liberal, but he was also an elitist— there are no more elitist institutions in America than academia and the military. He did not necessarily think of himself as better than other people—and like his mother, he did possess true compassion—but he believed he had been born to and trained for responsibility.

In those early days, Colby's cover was thin. He would carpool with non-Agency people into downtown Washington from the housing development in the Southeast District where he, Barbara, Catherine, and John lived. The carpool driver would drop him off at Fourth and Independence in front of the Labor Department building, just as he had when he worked for the National Labor Relations Board. But as soon as the car was out of sight, Colby would hop a bus to the Reflecting Pool and the collection of huts that served as CIA headquarters. Soon, he was advised by his superiors at the Agency to inform those who inquired that he had left the NLRB to take a new job in government having to do with defense and foreign policy. None of his acquaintances believed him. Washington was a small town, and it was assumed that his vague responses meant that he was now an intelligence operative fighting the good fight. His friends not only did not press Colby, they sought at social gatherings to protect him from more aggressive questioners. They were proud to be the friend of a secret agent.[6]

Barbara, Colby recalled, acted the good soldier, too. Bill was as vague with his wife as he was with his non-Agency friends about what he did. She knew that he was in intelligence and defense and that he was a cold warrior, but little more. She must have extrapolated from his OSS past that there would be some danger involved, but the war against communist totalitarianism appealed to her as much as it did to him. She, too, was a liberal Catholic with a strong social conscience. A future "Dame of the Order of Malta"—that is, a member of a lay religious order of the Catholic Church dedicated to humanitarian work—Barbara would become far more involved with the social and fraternal side of Catholicism than her husband. Catholicism and anticommunism were part of her makeup. She insisted on only one thing—that her husband have a life outside of his work.

Bill recalled that life in the CIA was different from his experience in the OSS. As a Jedburgh and NORSO, he had associated exclusively with fellow operatives; they were a close-knit band of men who laughed and drank together, lived and died together, an exclusive fraternity that existed within its own world. But as a CIA agent with a wife and children, Colby was forced to live a double life. He was both secret agent and school parent, the husband of an outgoing, socially active woman. He reveled in the double existence, drawing strength and balance from his non-Agency acquaintances. Some, Colby recalled, did not make the transition successfully. They associated only with fellow officers and their families so their defenses would not always have to be up. They dined together, worshipped together, and married and divorced each other. They became insular, sometimes withdrawn even from others in the Agency beyond their immediate circle, and eventually formed societies within a society, perceiving themselves as elites within an elite. It was such operatives, Colby recalled, who would give rise to the term "cult of intelligence." For them, the art of intelligence was "above the normal processes of society, with its own rationale and justification, beyond the restraints of the Constitution," he wrote.[7]

The three divisions of the CIA were tightly compartmentalized and, dating from the time of the OSS, those who served in them were often jealous—at times even suspicious—of one another. Colby recalled that in the days immediately following the war, when the OSS was broken up— with the research and analysis scholars sent to the State Department, and the clandestine operatives (spies) to the War Department—the split had worsened, with the two groups "often hostile or contemptuous of each other." But neither had any use for the paramilitary types, the "knuckle-draggers" like Colby, who had been sent home. When the latter group was resurrected under Frank Wisner as the OPC, that antagonism became even sharper, especially for the espionage and counterespionage people who had to rub elbows with the covert operatives in the field. As Colby put it, "the spymasters and counterspies feared that the high-risk, flamboyant operations of the 'cowboys' jeopardized the security and cover of their carefully constructed clandestine networks."[8]

In November 1950, when he became a full-fledged employee of the CIA, Colby was aware of these schisms, but he was part of the A-team, part of the "Mighty Wurlitzer," as Wisner (one of the few non–Ivy Leaguers at the top rungs of the Agency) referred to the OPC. To Colby's and Wisner's generation, the term "Wurlitzer" (from the Rudolph Wurlitzer Company, maker of musical instruments) conjured up images not only of jukeboxes but also of giant theater organs, such as the one at Radio City Music Hall. It was, as its designers intended, a "one-man orchestra." It seemed as if there were as many keys in Wisner's instrument as there were in a Wurlitzer organ. The OPC's mandate was to duplicate what the Soviets were doing and beat them at their own game. This meant boosting anti-communist propaganda in countries at risk, with the CIA subsidizing pro-Western newspapers and exploiting sympathetic American correspondents.

It meant Radio Free Europe and Voice of America, CIA-funded broadcast networks whose messages were designed to sow the seeds of unrest
behind the Iron and Bamboo Curtains. It meant paramilitary actions intended to block communist ascents to power in Third World countries
and, occasionally, to subvert communist governments already established
there. It meant, especially in the 1950s, the creation of "front" organizations that would fight communist activists for control of women's and
veterans' organizations, labor unions, youth groups, lawyers' associations,
and cultural organizations. In 1949, the OPC employed some three hundred officers with a budget of $4.7 million. By 1952, those numbers had
grown to 2,812 and $82 million, respectively. This was Wisner's "Mighty
Wurlitzer."[9]

Colby had assumed that he would be assigned to the "Far East," as East
Asia was then called, because of his Chinese-language skills, but Gerry
Miller had hired him, and Miller headed the Western European Division
of the OPC. Soon after Colby began reporting to the Reflecting Pool huts,
Miller told his newest recruit that he was being assigned to the Scandinavian Division. The NORSO experience had trumped Tientsin.
    Among its myriad tasks, the CIA in 1950 was planning for a possible
Soviet invasion and occupation of Norway, Denmark, and Sweden. Those
who had run Jedburgh and NORSO during World War II concluded that
it would be far easier and more efficient to recruit, fund, equip, and train
an underground resistance force before a particular country was overrun
than afterward. Parachuting in men, money, and equipment after the fact
was not the ideal way to raise a partisan resistance. The Agency wanted
trained, equipped, and well-led anticommunist guerrilla forces at the ready
even before the Red Army arrived. Colby's assignment was to use his
knowledge of the area and its people to set up these "stay-behind nets," as
they were called. To prepare for his new post, he was given a desk in the
middle of one of the busiest corridors in the OPC building.
    While he mulled over the current intelligence from Scandinavia, Colby
had to learn to become a spy. His duties with the OPC would only slightly
resemble those he had performed for the OSS. The first order of business
was to sign a secrecy agreement, a lifetime pledge not to reveal any classified
information relating to the activities of the CIA. Because of his background, Colby was spared "fluttering," the Agency term for a lie-detector

test. Neither did he have to undergo parachute training—which the new DCI, General Walter Bedell Smith, had ordered for all new recruits so there would be no macho pecking order. Colby was also spared paramilitary training at "The Farm," the special CIA training facility that had been set up at Camp Peary, about 100 miles south of Washington. But he did have to learn "tradecraft," as the skills of intelligence were referred to in the West. The Russians called these skills the "rules of conspiracy," but the basic concepts were the same.[10]

Colby received instruction on how to pass messages by way of dead-letter drops (where the message is left by one spy in a secret location, and picked up later by another) and cut-out agents (intermediaries), how to set up clandestine meetings, and how to handle safe houses, manipulate the chemicals used in invisible writing, shake tails, and use miniature cameras and other James Bond–type equipment. Then there was tutelage on the complicated and extremely important process of recruiting agents in an assigned country. The CIA officer, operating undercover as a diplomatic or military official attached to the American embassy, would scour the population for potential agents, usually beginning with government officials of the host country encountered at cocktail parties and receptions. Anticommunist sympathies were the best indicators of a prospective informant, but personal peccadilloes or a simple lust for money would do in a pinch. The CIA recruiter would then have the Agency run an extensive background check on the mark. If he or she passed, a third party would be brought in to make the pitch; if something went wrong, the CIA officer stationed in-country would be protected. Once an agent had been recruited, his case officer would test him by assigning him to collect information on something the Agency had already investigated. If the information checked out, the recruit was in. He was then asked to sign a document connecting him to the CIA so he could be blackmailed if he got cold feet. If the information did not check out, however, the recruit was assumed to be either a con man or an agent of the Soviet or East European security services. According to Victor Marchetti, a former CIA operative who wrote the classic exposé *The Cult of Intelligence*, a good case officer had to "combine the qualities of a master spy, a psychiatrist, and a father confessor."[11]

Of the relationship between handler and recruit, there were two prevailing philosophies within the Agency. In the "buddy" system, the handler developed a close personal relationship with his mark, convincing him that they were working together on a common goal and invoking personal loyalty as the risks and doubts mounted. Critics of this approach argued that it made the handler emotionally vulnerable. In their view, the best relationship was a purely detached one in which the handler treated the recruit as a commodity to be used, getting the most out of him as possible, and then discarding him. Colby claimed to have preferred the former and to have been "distressed" by the latter: "[T]rust and friendship . . . were the keys to successful secret collaboration," he wrote. Yet trust and friendship were not always in the offing, and success was relative. He would recruit and use men and women throughout his career, relying on friendship and appeals to altruism, and then send some to their deaths in Soviet-occupied Eastern Europe and communist North Vietnam. If the enemy was to be defeated, the heroes would have to adopt some of the methods of the antiheroes. In his novel *Harlot's Ghost*, in which he explored the world of espionage, Norman Mailer has one character remark, "If a good man is not ready to imperil his conscience, then the battlefield will belong to those who manipulate history for base ends."There were certainly limits on how far the CIA would go in using the methods of its adversary, however; if an agent backed out on the NKVD [the Soviet intelligence apparatus], it might very well kill his family.[12]

What Colby would find most challenging was leading a double life in the field. There was his existence as a spy, an agent provocateur, a clandestine operative. He was engaged in work vital to America and the entire free world, battling an enemy without scruple and in command of vast human, industrial, and natural resources. The world of officer and agent was a shadowy one where things were often not what they seemed. And yet, he was also a family man, a churchgoing Catholic trying to lead a normal life with normal relationships. He was a man of integrity, and yet his job was rife with deception and manipulation. In the tumult, it was sometimes easy to become disoriented. As reality is to dream, so one life was to the other, but which was which? Bill Colby did not despair; he was confident of his own internal moral compass, and he trusted his self-discipline and sense of duty. He was a man who could distinguish between illusion and reality. Or so he convinced himself.

Early in 1951, Gerry Miller called Colby in and told him that he was being sent to Stockholm, Sweden, to build an OPC presence. The first order of business was to establish a cover, a particularly difficult part of the job for American intelligence officers. In totalitarian societies, where the state controlled all bureaucracies, public and private, the left hand was used to not knowing what the right was up to. The NKVD, for example, could order any Soviet government agency or corporation to provide cover and support for its operatives. In a sense, the entire governmental apparatus and society were extensions of Soviet intelligence. In Western democracies, establishing cover was a bit more difficult. The United States, in particular, was a remarkably open society with no history of institutionalized peacetime intelligence. CIA personnel attached to embassies as cultural attachés or assigned to work for corporations overseas were bound to stick out if they underperformed or performed in an unusual manner. Their peers were bound to talk. It was decided that Colby's public job would be the Foreign Service; he was to be attached to the American embassy in Stockholm as a junior political officer in the Foreign Service reserve, a category established for bureaucrats from agencies other than State who were temporarily working abroad. In April, Bill, Barbara, John, Catherine, and baby Carl deplaned for Sweden.[13]

As a Cold War battlefield, Scandinavia was particularly complex. Denmark and Norway were part of the North Atlantic Treaty Organization (NATO), firmly in the Western camp. Sweden clung to its official and traditional neutrality, a stance that had sheltered it during two world wars. Because of its proximity to the Soviet Union, Finland had to defer in its foreign policy to its huge neighbor. Denmark and Norway could, with CIA help and advice, build their own stay-behind nets, but in Sweden the process would have to go on without official government cooperation. Finland was generally considered too risky an environment for covert networks. Colby had expected to be sent to Norway, but Sweden was more centrally located and a more difficult assignment. In his instructions, Miller had stressed the need for absolute secrecy. If the OPC's activities in Denmark and Norway were revealed, questions would arise concerning state sovereignty. Moreover, one possible interpretation of the construction of the stay-behind nets was that NATO had given up on Scandinavia as a lost cause in the event of a Soviet invasion. The problems in Sweden were more obvious. Colby's efforts to develop stay-behind nets throughout Scandinavia, if made public, would be seen as a threat to Swedish neutrality. In all three—Sweden, Denmark, and Norway—the governments in question would have to disavow the Agency's efforts to build an anti-Soviet resistance if they became known. The region was fertile ground for Soviet espionage: Finland and Sweden hosted large Soviet embassies, and all of Scandinavia was rife with communist front organizations.[14]

Colby later recalled that he got on well with his Office of Special Operations (OSO) counterpart in Stockholm, mainly because he generally deferred to him. But the relationship between the spies (OSO) and the covert operatives (OPC) was strained nonetheless. Scandinavia, and especially Sweden, teemed with exiles from the three Baltic states that the Soviet Union had annexed following World War II. Harry Rositzke, chief of the OSO's Soviet Bloc Division, mounted a major operation to insert agents into the former states of Estonia, Latvia, and Lithuania and from there into Russia. In each of these new Soviet republics, there were active, well-organized partisan movements clamoring for help from the United States and its allies. Covert operations belonged to the OPC, Wisner and Miller argued, but the OSO resisted, fearing that the knuckle-draggers and cowboys would blow their cover. If matters were not complicated enough, there was also the British Secret Intelligence Service (SIS, or MI-6). Harry Lambton Carr, controller of the northern area for MI-6, had his own network of spies and operatives. In April, just before moving his family to Stockholm, Colby had accompanied Rositzke on a trip to London to coordinate CIA operations with the British and other relevant members of NATO.[15]

In October 1950, after the CIA failed to predict the outbreak of hostilities on the Korean peninsula, Roscoe Hillenkoetter had been replaced as director of the CIA by General Walter Bedell Smith, former ambassador to the Soviet Union and General Eisenhower's chief of staff during World War II. Nicknamed "Beatle," Smith was an intense, demanding individual, his naturally gruff demeanor exacerbated by acute stomach ulcers. "His temperament is even," remarked a subordinate. "He is always angry." Smith was a plain-spoken midwesterner who resented the empire being built by Frank Wisner and his upper-class, Ivy League friends. He had never put much stock in psychological warfare, unconventional warfare, or covert operations of any sort. The Agency's second director was determined that it stick to intelligence collection and analysis. "If you send me one more project with goddamned balloons," he once yelled at a subordinate, using his synonym for any type of gadgetry, "I'll throw you out of here." The new DCI much preferred the more modest and reserved officers of the OSO to the men of the OPC. In August 1952, Smith announced that he was merging the OPC and the OSO to form a new division, the Directorate of Plans. To head the new entity, he brought on board Allen Dulles, a former OSS spymaster in Europe and a member of one of the most powerful clans in America. Wisner would report to Dulles, as would his counterpart, Richard Helms, newly appointed head of what had been the OSO. For Wisner, this amounted to a "severe double demotion."[16]

Colby's first priority in Stockholm was to establish his cover. In this Barbara, with her outgoing personality and social skills, proved an able ally. She immediately became active in the cultural and charitable work of the American community and established friendships with Swedish women at all social levels, from the Royal Court on down. Consistent with his cover job as a political officer, Bill wrote reports on Swedish political development. Meanwhile, at the endless rounds of receptions, cocktail parties, and lunches that typified the existence of a junior diplomat, Colby began spotting and recruiting Swedes, Danes, and Norwegians to be leaders and organizers of stay-behind nets. Some were government officials, some military officers, and some ordinary businesspeople. Having been recruited and then checked out, these partisans of the future generally had no more contact with Colby. Either the Agency sent over additional officers under separate cover, or Colby recruited members of the American community in Scandinavia to interact with the stay-behind nets, leaving instructions, maps, and cash in dead drops or meeting clandestinely in safe houses. Frequently Colby, undetected, would observe the contacts to make sure matters were proceeding smoothly. "The perfect operator in such operations is the traditional gray man, so inconspicuous that he can never catch the waiter's eye in a restaurant," Colby later observed. And he prided himself that he was just such a man.[17]

It was in Scandinavia that Colby began a practice that endured through most of his career—using his family as cover. In Denmark, he identified a group of anticommunists who agreed to form the nucleus of a stay-behind net. The Agency subsequently dispatched a trainer to work with the cell. Meanwhile, Colby had received a shipment of the special crystal-powered miniature radios then favored by spies and saboteurs. He announced to Barbara and John that they were going to take a tour of Denmark's glorious historical castles. Colby recalled that the trunk of their car was so heavily

laden with radios that it barely cleared the ground. He held his breath as
Swedish customs inspectors aboard the ferry connecting Sweden and Denmark eyed the car, but his diplomatic passport got the vehicle through without inspection. Driving between sights, Colby abruptly turned off on a dirt
road leading into the woods. There he rendezvoused with the CIA trainer.
Barbara and John took a stroll while the resistance novices unloaded the radios. John remembered that on Sundays in Stockholm, the family would go
to church at the French embassy, one of the few places where Catholic services were held. "The Russian Orthodox priests there, monks, would serve
us hot chocolate after Mass," he recalled, "and the old man would go upstairs." The wait seemed endless. "He was running nets out of there."[18]

As he had been warned, Colby found Sweden an incomparably more
difficult place in which to work than Norway and Denmark. The country's
institutionalized neutrality was the most formidable obstacle, but there
were others. Anticommunists inside and outside of the Swedish government, some of them in the national intelligence service, had formed their
own underground, and Colby had to be careful not to step on toes. And
then there was the pro-fascist organization Sveaborg, which had collabo-
rated with the Nazis during the war. Its members were more than happy
to join a stay-behind net, but Colby avoided them because of their disdain
for constitutional government, not to mention the bad publicity that would
ensue should it become known that the CIA was hobnobbing with fascists.
The decision was prescient: Shortly after Colby left for his next post, the
Swedish government arrested and tried the head of the Sveaborg operation,
Otto Halburg, for plotting a right-wing revolution. These difficulties
notwithstanding, Sweden's stay-behind network grew to anywhere from
1,000 to 2,000 operatives during the time Colby worked in Stockholm.[19]

In the early 1950s, Sweden teemed with emigrants from countries overrun
by the Soviets, especially the Baltic states, Poland, Hungary, and Romania.
Colby cultivated this community assiduously, hoping to gain useful bits of
information on life behind the Iron Curtain. "I found it an exhilarating experience to develop friendships with exiled East European cabinet ministers, dissident intellectuals, and would-be political leaders," he later
recalled.[20] But there was more to the contacts than mutual admiration. In
each of the countries and regions in question, there were various resistance

and dissident groups. The CIA used the exiles to communicate with and encourage these anti-Soviet elements, sometimes with tragic results.

Soon after Colby arrived in Stockholm, he began cultivating a promising source, a Romanian expatriate. One evening in the spring of 1952, he paid a visit to the man in his high-rise apartment. The conversation seemed routine, but later, as Colby was getting into his car to leave, he heard a loud thud behind him. The Romanian had jumped out of his upper-level window, killing himself. Communist agents had learned of his contacts with the CIA and were threatening to liquidate family members he had left behind the Iron Curtain.[21]

Because of his experience as a Jedburgh, Colby was asked to help the Soviet Bloc Division and MI-6 recruit and train East European exiles who were to be dropped into Lithuania, Latvia, and Estonia. There they would link up with anti-Soviet resistance networks and engage in acts of espionage and sabotage. The 1950s were the heyday of covert operations, even after Bedell Smith merged the OPC and the OSO. Following the outbreak of the Korean War, paramilitary teams had been dropped behind North Korean and Chinese lines to organize attacks on enemy formations and installations. CIA agents worked closely with Chiang Kai-shek's forces to train and insert guerrilla fighters into mainland China. In the Philippines, the soon-to-be-famous Edward Lansdale was advising President Raymond Magsaysay as he put down the communist-led Hukbalahap rebellion. In Vietnam, the Agency ran two stations, one collaborating with the French, the country's colonial ruler, and the other with a Catholic nationalist named Ngo Dinh Diem. In 1953, the CIA would help overthrow left-leaning governments in Guatemala and Iran.[22]

Colby's piece of the paramilitary war on communism proved to be a disaster. Virtually every dissident and paramilitary group behind the Iron Curtain had been penetrated by the NKVD or the security apparatus of the communist East European government in question. Colby found himself in charge of a four-man team of Latvians who had escaped into West Germany and then made their way to Sweden. After being given the entire Jedburgh treatment, the team was dropped into Latvia only to be immediately rolled up. In the fall of 1952, Max Klose, a German under contract to the CIA, inserted a four-man team into Lithuania by boat and was subsequently able to extract only a single agent. Unbeknownst to him and

Colby, all four were communist operatives. "I went down to the airfield each time an agent team was about to be inserted into a target country to do a final check of their equipment and to wish them good luck," recalled an army officer assigned to Colby's operation. "[N]one of those I was responsible for made contact [with their CIA handlers] after being inserted."[23]

It was not as if Colby and his colleagues did not know what to expect. During his stint in Sweden, an Estonian exile, a female journalist, pointed out to the former Jedburgh that there were vast differences between the Nazi and Soviet occupations. In their obsession with the notion of a master race, the Germans had not been interested in converting the subjugated. What the Nazi occupying authorities required was that the subject populations not challenge authority and that they perform the jobs assigned to them to support the war economy. By contrast, the Soviets and their satellite governments were profoundly ideological. They were determined to control every aspect of peoples' lives, even their thoughts. Each citizen behind the Iron Curtain was called upon to spy on his or her neighbors, reporting any suspicious activity to the state police. Those CIA-trained agents who parachuted into communist nations could not count on a receptive population ready to welcome them and rise up in revolt. States like Estonia, Poland, and North Vietnam became known as "denied areas." One US intelligence officer labeled them "counterintelligence states" because of their overriding attention to internal security and population control. Colby found this picture "chilling," he wrote in his memoirs, and he remembered wondering at the time whether "we had to think in new and revolutionary terms."[24]

In his actions in Scandinavia and subsequently in Italy and Vietnam, Colby gave no indication that he had fallen out of love with the Jedburgh model, however. He would have agreed with Paul Hartman, a Riga-born CIA officer, who, when challenged over the sacrifice of so many brave men and women, commented, "It's all part of our mission."[25]

POLITICAL ACTION AND LA DOLCE VITA

D espite its proximity to the Soviet Union and Eastern Europe, Stockholm was still a sideshow in Cold War Europe. The real action was in Berlin, Rome, and Vienna. Thus, when Gerry Miller, relegated to Rome station chief after the consolidation of the OPC and the OSO, offered Colby a position on the Italian front in the summer of 1953, he promptly accepted.

It would be difficult to exaggerate Italy's importance in the thinking of US strategists and policymakers during the decade following World War II. The architects of the anticommunist alliance perceived Italy— strategically located athwart the Mediterranean Basin and a historic crossroads connecting Europe with the Middle East and Asia—to be the keystone in NATO's southern arch. If the nation succumbed to the forces of international communism, the rest of Western Europe would be in grave peril.

Two years after the end of World War II, the Christian Democrats of Italian prime minister Alcide De Gasperi headed a tenuous coalition government that included representatives of all Italian factions, including the Italian Communist Party (PCI). The key to the political and strategic situation was Italy's near economic collapse. The country's industrial heart in the north had survived the war relatively unscathed, but it was starved of the raw materials it needed to operate. Axis and Allied bombing had devastated Italy's highways and railroads and sunk its merchant marine. De Gasperi's government faced a deficit of some 600 billion lire. An economically distraught Italy would continue to be vulnerable to a communist takeover and unable to shoulder its responsibilities as a future member of NATO even if it remained in the Western camp.[1]

In the spring of 1947, under intense pressure from the United States, De Gasperi kicked the Communists out of his coalition. In September, Palmiro Togliatti, a founding member of the PCI who had spent the war in exile in Moscow, announced to his followers in Modena that if the other parties continued to reject the Communists as a partner, they might have to take up arms against the government. American intelligence estimated that the Communist resistance in Italy could call on up to 50,000 well-armed and seasoned fighters who could be supplied and reinforced by Josef Broz Tito's Communist regime in neighboring Yugoslavia. Meanwhile, the Truman administration threatened military intervention in case of a Communist insurrection. Thus did Italy's national elections of 1948 take on enormous significance. The PCI had every reason to feel confident. By the end of 1945, the party could count 1,760,000 members. By the end of the following year, membership stood at 2,166,000. Posters of Stalin, affectionately known as *Baffone* ("Walrus moustache"), could be seen in factories and on city walls all over Italy.[2]

On April 18, 1948, the centrist parties handed the left a clear electoral defeat. The Christian Democrats won an absolute majority in parliament and, with the support of the Liberals and the Social Democrats under Giuseppe Saragat, formed a relatively stable government. The Communists, and the Italian Socialist Party (PSI), under Pietro Nenni, were shut out of power. But 1948 would prove to be a mere prologue to the real drama.

Despite his inflammatory rhetoric, Togliatti made the decision to keep the struggle in Italy within constitutional bounds, to establish Communist Party control through the electoral process rather than by force of arms. This approach was not universally popular with his compatriots. In the summer of 1948, Togliatti survived an assassination attempt by militants within the PCI who were disgusted with his pacifism. His near martyrdom, his continuing commitment to electoral politics, and Italians' growing resentment at America's increasingly heavy-handed intervention in Italy proved very advantageous to the PCI. Meanwhile, De Gasperi was proving to be an irresolute and ineffective leader. Despite Marshall Plan aid, Italy continued to wallow in the economic doldrums. Amid poor economic reports and evidence of widespread government corruption, the Social Democrats quit the governing coalition, while on the right monarchists and neo-fascists stepped up their attacks on De Gasperi, demanding, among other things, that he outlaw the PCI.[3]

In the meantime, a major shift in US policy toward Italy had taken place. In 1951 the newly established Psychological Strategy Board declared that the communist threats in Italy and France were more than just a matter of political extremism flourishing in climates of social and economic unrest; the communist parties there were part of a Sino-Soviet threat to subvert free governments everywhere. The United States would have to move beyond mere economic and military aid and fight the enemy on its own terms, making full use of the dark arts—espionage, propaganda, misinformation, front organizations, and *agents provocateur*. The creation of the CIA's Mighty Wurlitzer was in no small part a response to the situation in Italy. In this, as in other foreign policy matters, there was more continuity than discontinuity between the Truman and Eisenhower administrations. NSC 5411, a policy document that President Eisenhower approved in 1953, called "for all practicable means" to reduce the strength and effectiveness of the PCI. To implement this policy, Eisenhower selected Clare Boothe Luce—actress, playwright, former congresswoman, and wife of Time/Life publisher Henry Luce—as ambassador to Italy.[4]

The glamorous Mrs. Luce, "La Signora," as she was subsequently dubbed by the press, hit the Italian political and social scene with primal force. Some commentators observed that Europe had not experienced an American envoy of her celebrity since Benjamin Franklin took Paris by storm. Because of her fame and the Luces' status within the Republican Party, she—unlike other ambassadors—enjoyed direct access to the White House. The new ambassador arrived in Rome just weeks before the 1953 Italian national election. Her selection had not been universally applauded. In the United States, some Protestant leaders had expressed fears that her fervent Catholicism would make her a tool of the Vatican. In Italy, one observer commented that Italian feminism had not matured sufficiently to accommodate her. Clare Luce was not deterred. Blonde, beautiful, elegant, bright, and majestically egotistical, she set about implementing the Eisenhower administration's policies with a vengeance.

The results of the 1953 election proved disappointing to Washington. The four-party coalition headed by the Christian Democrats failed to obtain an absolute majority. The Communist/Socialist tally held steady at around 35 percent. Only the Monarchists and Fascists gained any ground.

Such was the political situation when Bill Colby and his family arrived in Rome in the autumn of 1953.[5]

In the midst of the poverty and hopelessness of southern Italy and the factionalism and cutthroat politics of the north, Rome stood as a shining jewel in the Italian commonwealth with its majestic monuments—the Coliseum and statue of Victor Immanuel II—its Renaissance art and architectural treasures, its fabulous restaurants and beautiful people. Indeed, by the early 1950s Rome had become a mecca for hedonists from around the world; funded by the super-rich and adorned by movie stars, the city's nightlife was incomparable. After the blandness and cold of Scandinavia, the Colbys—Bill, Barbara, John, Catherine, and Carl—found the Eternal City intoxicating.

Colby rented an apartment near the Coliseum. "On one side of us lived the grandson of Garibaldi," Carl recalled, "and on the other an American race-car driver named Masten Gregory."[6] Gregory boasted a beautiful wife, three daughters, and a trophy signifying his triumph at Le Mans. Behind the Colbys lived the Italian actress Claudia Cardinale, who graciously made her pool available to the children. Barbara immediately enrolled in an Italian language class, the better to immerse herself in Rome's social life. After Bill was promoted in his Foreign Service capacity from special assistant to the ambassador to first secretary, barely an evening passed without him hosting or attending a banquet or reception.

Colby's position as second-ranking political officer in the embassy dovetailed perfectly with his CIA assignment. Working under Gerry Miller, he was to head up the political action side of the station, working as a coequal with the head of the regular intelligence operation. As Colby described it, his job "was to prevent Italy from being taken over by the Communists in the next—1958—elections and thus prevent the NATO military defenses from being circumvented politically by a subversive fifth column, the Partito Communista Italiano [PCI]."[7]

The CIA estimated that by 1953 Moscow was pouring $50 million a year into Italy. Some of the aid was funneled through the party-owned import-export firms that had been set up to monopolize trade with various Eastern European companies. But much of the money was "black-bagged," that is, delivered directly to the PCI by Soviet and East European embassies. Most of these funds were in the form of nontraceable US dollars.

The Red dollars went to support a kaleidoscope of front organizations, including groups for women, youth, labor, artists, farmers, and veterans. Each organization had a journal propagandizing on behalf of the communist way. Every region of the country boasted a party office with paid organizers and propagandists. The country was plastered with pro-PCI posters and its people deluged with leaflets, newspaper articles, and pamphlets. Colby was tasked with matching this effort, and he set about his work with relish.[8]

The only apparatus in Italy that could match the PCI for money and organization was the Roman Catholic Church. From Italy to the United States to Vietnam, the church acted as the cutting edge of anticommunism. The Vatican saw Bolshevism, rooted as it was in atheism, as the greatest threat to Catholicism since the Protestant Reformation. There was more than ideology and spirituality at stake; the church had benefited for centuries from alliances with landed and financial elites, and the Vatican was one of the biggest landholding and richest entities in the world. Pope Pius XII made no bones about the Vatican's attitude toward the PCI: as of 1949, all Italian Communists were, by definition, excommunicated. Every parish and every priest in Italy was in service to the anticommunist cause. Catholic Action, the church's political wing, had 3 million members.[9]

Colby reveled not only in Rome's culture but in its Catholicism. He remembered the thrill of "being at the center of world Catholicism, with the rich ritual of the Vatican and the earnest seminarians of every race and nation showing the depth of our religion over the centuries and its breadth over the continents." From the outset, the CIA had been laden with Catholics. Their anticommunism was unquestioned and they were, as one observer put it, "good brawlers." In 1944, Pius had decorated Wild Bill Donovan with the Grand Cross of the Order of Saint Sylvester. Several future directors of the Agency would be Knights of Malta. Both Clare Luce and Barbara Colby belonged to Knights' women's affiliate, the Dames of Malta. Bill declined an offer to join the order—"I'm a little lower key," he confessed—but he was more than happy to exploit his Catholicism in the performance of his duties to the nation.[10]

Colby's mandate was to provide support—principally cash—to the centrist political parties in Italy. For this purpose he was provided with approximately $30 million a year. He and his associate, Tom McCoy, would deliver the funds directly to members of the Christian Democratic, Liberal, and Republican Party hierarchies or shower money on newspapers and magazines friendly to them. The parties, in turn, used the money to finance leaflets, posters, congresses, and voter registration drives—the usual activities engaged in by political organizations. But this particular organ in the Wurlitzer family also attempted to mirror what the Soviets and PCI were doing by stimulating and supporting anticommunist front organizations within the powerful labor movement and various cultural organizations.

As Colby readily admitted in his memoir, interference by one country in the political affairs of another was clearly illegal; most nations, including the United States and Italy, had laws against it. Yet, given the massive Soviet effort in Italy, what choice did the United States have? Espionage was also illegal, but since the founding of the nation-state system, governments had justified it on the grounds of national survival. Was it not so with US political action and paramilitary operations? Still, Colby had to go to great lengths to cover his tracks. US interference in Italy's domestic politics, if made public, would leave nationalists no choice but to turn against America.[11]

As had been the case in Scandinavia, after initial contacts, regular CIA personnel did not rendezvous directly with Italian anticommunists except at the highest levels. The Agency dispatched "outside officers" who had no traceable connection to the CIA or to the American embassy. If they were apprehended, American authorities would be able to renounce them with "plausible deniability." The handful of officers that Colby and McCoy ran found it easy to secure cover in *dolce vita* Italy. At any given time, some ten thousand American tourists, businesspeople, and officials of labor and cultural organizations could be found in Rome or the other major Italian cities. There were some sour notes coming out of the Italian Wurlitzer, however. One of Colby's outside agents was jailed for beating up his wife's lover, and another was discovered padding the books. The principal problem facing the station, according to Tom McCoy, was finding bags and car trunks large enough to hold the sheer bulk of lire involved in the payoffs.[12]

Bill Colby loved fieldwork and found it hard to resist even as he moved up in the Agency hierarchy. His son John remembered that every Sunday, the family would attend Mass at one of the Catholic churches situated in the Plaza Del Populo. There were no pews in Roman churches then; congregations would stand until they received communion. John remembered that the women were always in the front ranks, with the men milling about in the rear. After services, the males would move out into the plaza, don red scarves, and talk politics. John recalled his father saying that "the women were all Catholics and the men were all communists." Bill would mix with the crowd, gauging its mood and gleaning bits of information. It seemed that here, as elsewhere, he found the enemy more interesting than the ally. It was from the communists that he would learn the means and methods to defeat the communists. As Colby proudly recalled in *Honorable Men*, the political action program he headed was the largest ever undertaken in the history of the CIA. But his was only part of a larger effort.[13]

For some reason, Colby was not selected to head the huge stay-behind, paramilitary operation the CIA ran in Italy. Though covert operations were the former Jedburgh's proven area of expertise, Gerry Miller decided to run "Project Gladio" himself (the name was an allusion to the short sword that was ubiquitous in the Roman legions of old). Like the stay-behind nets in Scandinavia, Gladio originated with the so-called "secret anti-Communist NATO protocols" that committed alliance members and their security services to preventing a communist seizure of power within their own borders and those of their allies "by any means." Compared to Colby's Scandinavian nets, Gladio was far more extensive and more ideologically conservative. Miller's agents found willing operatives among former followers of Benito Mussolini and among archconservative Catholics. By 1958, Gladio comprised hundreds of cells operating throughout the country and dozens of strategically located arms caches, including both small arms and heavy weapons. The Italian stay-behind operation was hardly unique. In West Germany, the CIA built its espionage and stay-behind operations around former Nazi general Reinhard Gehlen. The Italian network would remain active for the rest of the Cold War and would be linked to a series of rightwing terrorist attacks in the 1970s.[14]

Colby made no mention of Gladio in his memoir, but he did state that "a very deliberate and conscious policy was made both in Washington and in Rome that no help of any kind go to the Neo-Fascists or Monarchists." He was speaking of political action, his operation, but even in this he was being disingenuous. Colby's job was to control matters so that Washington would not have to choose between a centrist government and a regime of neo-fascists. But if push came to shove, there was no doubt as to the choice the Eisenhower administration would make. NSC 5411/2, the Eisenhower administration's primary policy document on postwar Italy, declared that "an extreme rightist government," though "almost certainly authoritarian, probably ultra-nationalist," would be "far less dangerous than a Communist regime." Moreover, Clare Boothe Luce, who oversaw every aspect of the Agency's activities in Italy, was not nearly as fastidious as Colby. And it was her approach, not Colby's, that would dominate the Eisenhower administration's foreign policy.[15]

In 1954, Eisenhower had convened a panel chaired by General James Doolittle to report on the state of American intelligence. Its conclusion for the CIA was unequivocal: "It is now clear that we are facing an implacable enemy whose avowed objective is world domination by whatever means and at whatever cost." In the looming contest between Sino-Soviet communism and the free world, there could be no rules. If the West was to prevail, it would have to discard notions of "fair play" and Judeo-Christian ethics. "We must develop effective espionage and counterespionage services and must learn to subvert, sabotage and destroy our enemies by more clever, more sophisticated and more effective methods than those used against us," declared the report. But Colby continued to believe that ends did not always justify means. From 1954 until 1956, he and Clare Luce would clash repeatedly over whether the United States should support an opening to the left or the right as part of the effort to shore up the Italian political center. At the same time, rumor had it, the ambassador and the spy found each other personally congenial enough to conduct an affair.[16]

The failure of the Christian Democrats to gain a clear majority in the 1953 elections had marked the end of De Gasperi's political career. His successors as prime minister, Guiseppe Pella and Mario Scelba, were forced to turn either to the right—to the neo-fascists and monarchists—or to the left—the socialists (PSI)—in order to fashion and sustain a parliamentary majority. At this point, the United States faced a crucial choice in its Italian policy. In Rome, the debate played out chiefly between Colby and Luce. Colby later recalled that every Tuesday, the ambassador presided over a brainstorming session in her ornate office in the embassy, the former residence of Queen Mother Margherita of Savoy. The setting, Colby later recalled, "wonderfully and somewhat theatrically set off [Luce's] blond hair, the pastel colors she favored in her clothing and her regal bearing." One journalist referred to her as "that poised, coiffed, Rhinemaiden of conservatives."[17] She and Colby butted heads initially over tactics. He, on the one hand, had been pressing for yearly budgets of US aid for Italy's noncommunist parties in order to enable them to build strong, durable infrastructures. She, on the other, wanted to hold the CIA money hostage in order to compel America's erstwhile allies to toe the anticommunist line. She had been annoyed, for example, when the Christian Democrats refused to support national legislation outlawing the PCI in the wake of the 1953 elections. She increasingly perceived Pella and Scelba as prevaricators who, while appeasing the communists, continually badgered the United States for more handouts.

In 1954, La Signora brokered a deal between Italy and Yugoslavia that brought the long-disputed city of Trieste into the Italian polity, much to the delight of the country's nationalists. She began to dream of a new ruling coalition composed of the conservative wing of the Christian Democrats, the business-oriented Liberal Party, neo-fascists who supported the constitution, and monarchists. Colby argued long and hard against this strategy. Instead, he maintained, the United States should support an opening to the left, to try to split the Socialists off from the Communists. If this could be accomplished, the PCI would be reduced to a mere 20 percent of the electorate. Colby did not say so in front of the ambassador, but he observed to McCoy and others that only a left-center coalition would pursue social and economic policies capable of attracting and holding the masses.[18]

In her tilt to the right, Clare Luce enjoyed the support of a powerful ally within the CIA: James Jesus Angleton, head of the Agency's counterintelligence division and, for much of his career in the CIA, Colby's bête noir. Jim was the son of James Hugh Angleton and Carmen Mercedes Moreno—the elder Angleton had met his Mexican bride in Nogales while serving as a cavalry officer in 1917—and had spent his youth in Rome, where his father had run the National Cash Register franchise. In 1933, Jim had been shipped off to England to attend Malvern College in Worcestershire. In 1940, his father moved the family to New York, and the following year Jim enrolled at Yale. It was there that he began acquiring his reputation as an eccentric. "He was quite British in his ways," recalled poet Reed Whittemore, his close friend. "He was a mixture of pixiness and earnestness, very much at home in Italian literature, especially Dante, as well as the fine points of handicapping horses."[19]

Jim's intellect was wide-ranging, inquisitive, and eclectic. Many of his classmates found him less than attractive, however. Angleton never slept, and he was never wrong. "Collapsing into bed late at night," remembered his roommate, William Wick, "I would often arise next morning to find Jim still reading or furiously writing, ashtrays stuffed with cigarette butts, and the room littered with library books." With Whittemore, Angleton edited the literary magazine *Furioso*, whose contributors would eventually include T. S. Eliot, e. e. cummings, William Carlos Williams, and Ezra Pound. Angleton had met Pound in 1938, while summer vacationing with his family in Rapallo, and the two subsequently became fast friends.[20]

In 1943, Jim was inducted into the US Army and assigned to the Italian division of the OSS. His first stop was London, where he went to work for the Italian desk of X-2, OSS's counterintelligence branch (the component tasked with preventing or ferreting out enemy penetration of Allied intelligence operations). Angleton fell in love with the world of counterintelligence; it would be his home during the remainder of his CIA career. It was also in London that Angleton became part of an exclusive club that had access to the high-level enemy radio and teletype communications collected in the "Ultra" decryption project. Both Churchill and Eisenhower later remarked that Ultra, which deciphered the "Enigma" codes of the Germans, was key to the Allied victory. Because its work was so important, X-2 operated in an atmosphere of absolute secrecy and security. It had its own overseas stations separate from regular OSS offices, a dedicated communications channel, and independent liaison with British intelligence. X-2 could veto OSS espionage and paramilitary operations without explanation. Angleton was also privy to the Allied Double Cross operation launched in support of the Normandy invasion, in which captured Nazi intelligence operatives were fed false information to transmit back to Berlin. It was at this point that Angleton became convinced of the primacy of counterintelligence in national security operations and the absolute efficacy of "need-to-know."[21]

In 1944, Angleton and his lifelong deputy, Ray Rocca, moved their operation to Italy; following V-E Day, they stayed on, working for the OSS's successor agencies. Angleton was an anticommunist true believer. In his view, Moscow was at the head of a monolithic communist threat bent on world domination by any means and at whatever cost. Angleton helped the Carabinieri, the Italian military police, develop a counterintelligence unit and recruited spies that penetrated the PCI, the PSI, and the Vatican. He reputedly paid a Vatican code clerk $100 a week for copies of the Holy

See's worldwide intelligence reports. Angleton's office was at 22 Via Sicilia, in the fashionable hotel district just off the Via Veneto and only three blocks from the US embassy. One of Angleton's missions was to gather evidence for the Nuremburg Trials of alleged Nazi war criminals. In the process, he made contact with members of the Zionist underground in Italy and in refugee camps elsewhere. He cultivated those contacts and helped key individuals make their way from Europe to Palestine. Angleton became an ardent supporter of Israel, personally running the Israeli desk within the CIA from 1952 through 1974 while simultaneously heading counterintelligence. Among other things, he anticipated that the Soviet Jews who would flood into the new state would provide an excellent and ongoing source of intelligence on Russian affairs.[22]

In 1948, Angleton returned to the United States as an army major. He resigned his commission and immediately joined the CIA, serving Bedell Smith as chief of foreign intelligence operations. When Allen Dulles came on board as DCI following the 1952 presidential election, Angleton was made head of a powerful new unit named the Counterintelligence (CI) Staff. He had been chosen personally by the new director. For the next eight years, Angleton would enjoy unprecedented access to Dulles—he was the only staff member with permission to enter the director's office unannounced. He and the DCI would drive home together at the end of each workday.[23]

By tradition, responsibility for internal security had rested with the FBI. With the advent of the CIA, the two agencies proceeded in uneasy partnership. In theory, the FBI had responsibility for subversive activities within the United States, and the CI Staff handled communist espionage abroad. In reality, the CIA retained control of all operations designed to penetrate opposition intelligence services, domestic or foreign. Whereas the FBI historically simply arrested and deported enemy spies, the CIA attempted to "turn" them, that is, to convert them into double agents. Attached to virtually every overseas CIA station were one or more counterintelligence officers whose duty it was to monitor US espionage and covert action operations to ensure that they had not been penetrated by the KGB. Successful "moles" would be in a position to feed false information to CIA officers and disrupt carefully planned operations.

Beyond monitoring the activities of their own intelligence community, counterintelligence personnel were tasked with penetrating the KGB and other communist intelligence services. Because Marxist-Leninist societies were so tightly controlled, recruitment of double agents behind the Iron and Bamboo Curtains proved extremely difficult. Counterintelligence's primary targets were KGB and GRU (Soviet military intelligence) agents, the only Russians empowered to move freely about the world. In the United States, counterintelligence concentrated on preventing KGB penetration of the Agency itself and, if penetration occurred, on ferreting it out. "As practiced by the CIA and the KGB," Victor Marchetti wrote in *The CIA and the Cult of Intelligence*, "counterespionage is a highly complex and devious activity. It depends on cunning entrapments, agents provocateur, spies and counterspies, double and triple crosses. It is the stuff that spy novels are made of, with limitless possibilities for deceptions and turns of plot."[24]

From the perspective of the CI Staff, every Agency employee was a potential Soviet spy or "mole." According to some reports, the chief of CI maintained a list of the fifty or so key positions in the CIA that were most likely to be targeted for penetration and kept the individuals occupying those positions under constant surveillance. Angleton was convinced that mole hunting was absolutely crucial to any and every successful intelligence operation. "If you control counterintelligence, you control the intelligence service," he was quoted as saying. Compared to totalitarian societies, the Western democracies, with their characteristic emphasis on openness, individualism, and privacy, as well as their suspicion of authority and secrecy, were particularly vulnerable to penetration by the KGB and the GRU. Moreover, as America's spy handlers cast their net for new agents, they were bound to land a bad fish from time to time. By penetrating the CIA and other Western services, the Soviets could do far more than spy on them, Angleton pointed out: they could also serve as agents of influence, creating deceptions that would enable Moscow to manipulate those services and, by extension, their governments. The goal of the opposition, he wrote, was to create "a wilderness of mirrors"—a phrase borrowed from T. S. Eliot. The "wilderness" consisted of the "myriad of stratagems, deceptions, artifices, and all the other devices of disinformation which the Soviet Bloc and its coordinated intelligence services use to confuse and spilt the West . . . producing an ever-fluid landscape where fact and illusion merge."[25]

As Jim Angleton well knew, the intelligence labyrinths in which Moscow hoped to trap Western intelligence were historical realities. In the early

1920s, Lenin and his first intelligence chief, Felix Dzerzhinsky, had devised an elaborate counterespionage apparatus named "the Trust." Agents of the Trust spread out across Europe to make contact with White Russian refugees, portraying themselves and their organization as an anticommunist network operating within the Soviet Union. They fed the émigrés false information, saying, in effect, that communism was failing and that the Bolshevik regime was about to be overthrown by the Russian people. The émigrés, in turn, sold these mutually reinforcing bits of information to Western security forces, with the result that they halted plans for military landings, economic blockades, and other forms of coercion. Then there was the Rote Kapelle (Red Orchestra), the highly effective Soviet military intelligence network that spied on Germany during World War II. Its agents successfully penetrated Nazi occupation authorities in France, Belgium, and the Netherlands as well as in Nazi Germany itself. Because of "Venona"—the US-UK operation that broke the Soviet intelligence code during World War II—the CIA, and Angleton in particular, was intimately familiar with the Rote Kapelle. Indeed, he subsequently used it as a teaching tool for training his operatives.[26]

Angleton himself had once been victimized by a Soviet "double game." While working in London for X-2, he had made the acquaintance of Harold Adrian Russell "Kim" Philby. The son of the famous British Arabist St. John Philby, Kim, who was nicknamed after the boy spy in Rudyard Kipling's novel, was a top-level operative in Britain's SIS. A handsome, charming man, Philby seemed a stereotypical member of the British aristocracy, complete with tweed jacket and pipe. Before Angleton had departed for Italy, Philby had acted as something of a dark arts tutor to the young American. The friendship began anew in Washington in 1949, when Philby was posted there as SIS liaison with the FBI and the CIA. For two years, the men would meet every week at Harvey's restaurant—J. Edgar Hoover's favorite—for lobster, martinis, and wide-ranging discussions of the worldwide Anglo-American intelligence effort. All the while, Angleton was unaware that in 1934 Philby had been recruited into a Soviet spy ring along with fellow Cambridge students Guy Burgess, Donald MacLean, and Anthony Blunt. During World War II, MacLean had provided the Kremlin with copies of top-secret British and American documents, including correspondence between Churchill and Truman. In Washington, as an official of the British embassy, Burgess lived in Philby's basement, where he worked transmitting copies of secret documents to his Russian handlers. In 1951, Burgess and MacLean, fearing that they were about to be exposed, fled to the USSR. Philby was recalled to London, interrogated, and dismissed from the SIS; there was not enough evidence to prosecute him, however. In 1963, Philby himself would flee to Moscow, where he subsequently revealed all. Philby, Burgess, MacLean, and Blunt eventually became known as the Cambridge Four; some allege the involvement of a fifth man, John Cairncross, making them the Cambridge Five. "We shall never know how many agents were killed or tortured as a result of Philby's work as a double agent," Lord Birkenhead observed at the time, "and how many operations failed." For the rest of his days, Angleton would be haunted by memories of those candid lunchtime conversations.[27]

In 1955, Pietro Nenni and the Italian Socialists began the long, slow process of separating from Togliatti and the PCI. Colby saw the development as a breakthrough in the campaign for *apetura alla sisistra*, or "opening to the left." In 1956, he recommended to his superiors in Washington that the Rome station be authorized to open a dialogue with Nenni; facilitating a Socialist switch from the Communists to the center coalition "would be desirable from the viewpoint of both Italian and US interests." The United States must be pragmatic, he said: "Under present circumstances, we cannot afford to be guided by likes or dislikes, moral approval or disapproval."[28]

Like Clare Luce and the Catholic hierarchy, Jim Angleton viewed the Nenni-led PSI as nothing more than a Trojan horse to help Togliatti and the Communists penetrate the ruling coalition. He was not going to stand idly by and allow liberals like Colby to open the door to a fifth column. One day in 1956, Gerry Miller, chief of the West European Division of the Office of Plans, summoned Colby to his office. There was a very special American agent operating in Rome, a "singleton" who observed and reported independently to CIA headquarters and the State Department. Miller told Colby that he wanted him to "handle" the agent, whose code name was "Charlie." The simplicity of the code name belied the complexity of the personality, Colby soon learned. Miller, Colby, and Charlie subsequently rendezvoused at a suburban café for a cappuccino and a get-acquainted session. The new man on the block had been part of the OSS team that had come to Italy during the last stages of World War II and the onset of the Cold War to help the Italians put together a new government. Charlie was Catholic, sophisticated, cosmopolitan, and incredibly well-connected in

Italy's political and social circles. "Well-educated and widely read," Colby said of him, "he could discourse with ease on medieval philosophy and the Pope's social encyclicals." In truth, Miller was having trouble keeping Charlie in his loop, and even more trouble gaining access to Charlie's loop.[29]

Charlie was, of course, working for Angleton, the two having become acquainted in postwar Italy. Through Charlie, Angleton kept in touch with Italians in the police force and government whom he had recruited in the late forties. Colby soon discovered that Charlie's independent communiqués to Washington were arguing against an opening to the left, taking the Luce-Angleton position that Nenni was just a stalking horse for Togliatti and, by association, Moscow. "The professional intelligence operators who managed him," Colby wrote in his memoir, "to ensure that this direct truth reached policy levels, had arranged that his reports be forwarded in their raw form in sealed envelopes to Washington and laid on the desks of senior policy-level officials as the real story direct from the source." According to one account, on one of Charlie's visits to Washington, John Foster Dulles's limousine rather melodramatically picked him up on a street corner so he could brief the secretary of state in private.[30]

In typical Colby fashion, Bill cultivated Charlie, flattered him, and deferred to him. They became friends. For Charlie, however, the station's political action chief seemed increasingly omnipresent. Could he see Charlie's latest dispatch? Who was he going to talk to next? Colby began to insist that Charlie's product was so important that it had to be disseminated more widely, beginning with the ambassador and the embassy's other political officer, then with the CIA station chief, and subsequently with the analytical staffs of the CIA's Directorate of Intelligence in Washington. "Charlie's material then reached all its proper readers," Colby said, "but arrived without a special aura of mystery, and was put in proper proportion in the jigsaw puzzle collection of information needed to understand the variegated Italian political scene."[31] Angleton was annoyed, but there was little he could do. Colby could hardly be accused of suppressing Charlie's reports. The former Jedburgh understood that nothing was more dangerous in intelligence than allowing one person's views and information to be left unjuxtaposed against others. This would not be the last time Colby turned "need-to-know" against itself.

The conflict between Luce and Colby, civilized though it was, was fundamental. Colby spoke for liberal cold warriors who wanted to undercut the PCI's appeal by growing center-left political coalitions that pursued social and economic reforms, which would in turn improve the lot of the working classes. Luce represented those Americans who equated socialism with communism, who insisted that the only viable economic model was free enterprise rooted in the private ownership of property. "She was extremely reactionary," Senator J. William Fulbright, who had served in the House with Luce, later remarked. "Sort of like what you would associate with Louis XVI." In 1955 and 1956, two successive Christian Democrat prime ministers, Giovanni Gronchi and Amintore Fanfani, threw their support behind the so-called Vanoni Plan, named for budget minister Ezio Vanoni. The scheme, based on the assumption that private industry and finance in Italy was too weak to generate sufficient economic growth, called for a vast expansion of public investments in housing and public works and the nationalization of some sectors of the economy. In his reports to Washington, Colby lauded the Vanoni Plan as a vehicle for the promotion of social and economic justice in Italy, absolutely vital to creating a lasting noncommunist majority. Luce could not have disagreed more. The Vanoni Plan, she declared, was actually a scheme to build a bridge between the Christian Democrats and the "pro-Communist socialists."[32]

Soviet premier Nikita Khrushchev's February 1956 speech to the Central Committee of the Communist Party of the Soviet Union (CPSU) attacked the "crimes of the Stalin era." It seemed to herald the beginning of a reformist movement behind the Iron Curtain, possibly involving growing tolerance for dissent, respect for law, and even national self-determination. The speech was supposedly "secret," intended only for the Kremlin's inner circle. By April, however, the CIA had managed to obtain not one but two copies of the potentially explosive address. Angleton acquired one through his network of Soviet émigré Jews, while Ray Cline, head of the Agency's research and analysis division, obtained one separately through a paid informant in Eastern Europe.[33]

Cline and Frank Wisner, Angleton's immediate superior, differed drastically on what to do with the purloined documents. During the 1952 presidential campaign, Secretary of State Dulles and leading Republicans had promised to "roll back" communism rather than just contain it, as Truman and the Democrats had advocated. Wisner and Angleton were enthusiastic supporters of roll-back; Cline and others in the foreign policy establishment were more cautious, arguing that overt US support for uprisings in Soviet-bloc countries could easily lead to World War III. Angleton would later argue that he and Wisner wanted to delay publication of Khrushchev's speech until "secret armies" of anticommunist émigrés could be trained in West Germany to be unleashed at the appropriate moment. If it was not delayed, they said, the speech should be edited to create maximum consternation among the communist parties of Europe. Bill Colby was certainly not against rolling back the Iron Curtain, but his first priority was to save Western Europe from a communist takeover. He had become a convert to political action. He and like-minded figures within the CIA and the State Department wanted the speech published in full as a means to promote democracy in Italy, to commit Nenni and the Socialists—and perhaps even Togliatti and the PCI—to the democratic process and the rule of law. The liberals won this particular battle; CIA director Allen Dulles delivered a copy of the full text to the State Department, which in turn released it to the *New York Times*.[34]

The ultimate test of roll-back versus containment came in the fall of 1956. Nationalist and democratic elements in Poland and Hungary, in part inspired by the Khrushchev speech, began pressuring Soviet authorities for more autonomy and multiparty elections. The Kremlin managed to placate the Poles, but events in Hungary soon got out of hand. Roving bands of militant students and workers attacked government buildings, defaced symbols of Soviet power, and retaliated against members of the communist secret police. In the midst of this turmoil, the CIA-controlled Radio Free Europe broadcast calls to arms to the people of Hungary and implied that help was on the way. Emboldened by these promises of support, Hungarian nationalist leader Imre Nagy announced not only the formation of a coalition government, but also Hungary's intention to withdraw from the Warsaw Pact, the Soviet–East European alliance system. Faced with the collapse of their Eastern European empire—Americans were not the only ones who believed in the domino theory—Khrushchev and his generals acted. On November 4, Soviet tanks rolled into Budapest; during the fighting that ensued, some thirty thousand Hungarians and seven thousand Russians died. Newsreels showed freedom fighters in Budapest launching futile attacks against Soviet tanks with Molotov cocktails and small arms and then being cut down in the streets. To the end, the revolutionaries sent out urgent pleas for help.

Colby later wrote that Frank Wisner was ready to intervene in Hungary with arms, communications equipment, air resupply, and even exile fighters—"this was exactly the end for which the Agency's paramilitary capability was designed"—but the White House was unequivocal in its opposition. "Starkly," Colby observed, "we demonstrated that 'liberation' was not our policy when the chips were down in Eastern Europe as the price might have been World War III."[35] In truth, the CIA's so-called "secret armies" would have made no difference whatsoever: only full-scale military intervention by NATO could have forced the Soviets to withdraw. With French and British troops tied down by the Suez crisis, there was little support in the alliance for such a move; as Eisenhower was to observe afterward, there was about as much chance of assembling and inserting a major multinational force into Hungary as there was of sending in the military to aid Tibet.

Frank Wisner was one of the casualties of the uprising. He happened to be on an inspection tour of European CIA stations at the time. As the fighting in Budapest intensified, he rushed first to West Germany and then to Austria, where he stood at the border watching helplessly as Hungarian refugees flooded across. Some had been wounded. Indeed, "people [were] killed by the Russians as he stood there, in his sight," recalled a colleague. "It was a profound shock." Wisner rushed back to the embassy and frantically phoned Washington, pleading with the White House to commit troops. It was all to no avail. Later, in Rome, as the fighting continued to rage in Budapest, Wisner, a close friend of Clare Luce, made a point of attending Mass with Hungarian refugees. The ambassador recalled that he regularly returned from these outings dead drunk. By the time the maestro of the Mighty Wurlitzer returned to the United States, he was a nervous wreck and sick with hepatitis from eating tainted clams. He was, recalled a friend, "rambling and raving . . . totally out of control." Three years later, Wisner was eased out as deputy director of plans, and in 1965 he took his own life, a victim of the delusion of roll-back.[36]

Appalled though he was by the Hungarian debacle, Colby moved immediately to make propaganda hay out of it. By 1956, the United States Information Service (USIS) employed a staff of 50 Americans and 250 Italians who labored in offices throughout the country writing newspaper articles, designing posters, and co-opting Italian journalists. Colby's operation worked hand-in-glove with the USIS. The cruel suppression of the

Hungarian uprising exposed the Soviets for what they were, ruthless imperialists rather than selfless sponsors of workers' paradises, proclaimed the anticommunist media in Italy. The Agency also arranged care for the refugees who poured across the border, as well as memorial services for fallen freedom fighters.[37]

The Hungarian uprising created turmoil within the communist and socialist parties in Western Europe, and in Italy it facilitated the efforts of those urging an opening to the left. Within the PSI, pressure mounted on Nenni and his followers to throw in their lot with the Christian Democrats and abandon the PCI now tainted even more than before by its association with Moscow, and through it, suppression of the Hungarian uprising. Clare Luce remained as adamant as ever, but a bizarre series of events sidelined her. In 1955, she had fallen ill, and she remained so. Her weekly meetings with Miller and Colby were transferred from her office to her equally ornate bedroom in the Villa Taverna, her residence. When she still did not improve, the ambassador's doctors ordered her home for tests and treatment. Suspecting foul play by the KGB or operatives of the PCI, Miller ordered a thorough investigation. The culprit turned out to be not a communist assassin but lead from paint chips that had fallen into her food during meals at the residence. She returned to Rome, but departed for good in December 1957.[38]

In April 1958, with the next round of national elections looming in Italy, Colby again pressed the issue of an opening to the left. "It is essential that dynamic and effective democratic government be possible in Italy," he wrote to Washington. "This can hardly be the case if a powerful Communist Party is able to maintain its hold over the PSI. It is more than ever necessary to break this hold, splitting the PSI in such a way as to insure the maximum accession of strength to the forces of Democratic Socialism." To his delight, Colby found that the tide was shifting. The new ambassador, James David Zellerbach, authorized direct talks with members of the Nenni wing of the PSI. The 1958 elections were indecisive, however, and it was not until 1963, during the Kennedy administration, that the opening to the left occurred. In that year, the PSI was admitted to the ruling coalition, and Pietro Nenni was named deputy prime minister.[39]

By 1958, Bill Colby was ready to move on. He had, he observed, been in Italy for five years—"long enough to have become knowledgeable about the country, but not long enough to have become more oriented to it than to United States interests." He was extremely proud of the political action operation he had headed. He believed fervently that in its struggle with the forces of international communism, Washington must do more than just damage its enemies; it must help its friends. US intervention in Italian political life may have been extralegal, but in his opinion, it was eminently moral. The Italian campaign, he wrote, "showed that the United States can conduct such a struggle on a political level rather than wait until it must be confronted on a military one."[40]

Colby's Italian tour came to an end as a Cold War consensus was emerging within the United States. On the right were conservatives like Henry Luce, former isolationists who had decided that if the United States could not hide from the world, it must control it. They argued that the only way America could be safe in a hostile world was through a network of alliances and overseas military bases as well as through possession of the largest nuclear arsenal in the world. On the left were liberal internationalists like Arthur Schlesinger Jr. and Senators J. William Fulbright and Hubert Humphrey, public intellectuals and political reformers who saw America's welfare as being tied to that of the other members of the international community. To a degree, they supported alliances and military aid, but in addition, they wanted to eliminate the social turmoil and economic deprivation that they perceived to be a breeding ground for Marxism-Leninism and an invitation to Sino-Soviet imperialism.

The CIA mirrored that division no less than the American polity as a whole. In 1949, Arthur Schlesinger, a former OSSer, published *The Vital Center*, which subsequently became the bible of anticommunist liberals. Schlesinger, who was as strongly anti-McCarthy as he was anti-Stalin, was in regular contact with senior officers of the CIA. At the other end of the ideological spectrum was James Burnham, a former Trotskyite turned fervent anticommunist. In *The Struggle for the World*, published in 1947, he depicted international communism as a conspiratorial movement bent on worldwide domination. His subsequent *Containment or Liberation?* was the definitive call for roll-back. During the late 1940s and early 1950s, Burnham worked for the Office of Policy Coordination as a full-time consultant. Within the CIA, Colby was the personification of liberal internationalism, whereas Jim Angleton embodied the hardline, uncompromising approach of Burnham and the conservatives.[41]

8

COLD WAR COCKPIT

Because of his experiences in China and his passing familiarity with the language, Bill Colby had assumed that the OSS would assign him to the Far East. Instead he had gone to France and then Norway. As he readily admitted, he had been fascinated with Asia ever since his romantic sojourn in Tientsin as a child. In 1956, while he was still in Italy, CIA headquarters had offered him Edward Lansdale's just-vacated post in the Philippines, but Colby opted to remain in Rome through the 1958 elections. In his subsequent application for transfer, he specified Asia, and the request was duly passed on to Desmond FitzGerald, who headed the Far East Division of the Directorate of Plans.

As a young army officer during World War II, FitzGerald had served in Burma and then in China as liaison officer to the Chinese Nationalist Sixth Army. After joining the CIA in 1950, he served successively in Korea and Japan, where he supervised espionage and sabotage activities directed against China. He had also been posted to the Philippines for a time, working the political action desk of the Manila station. Colby's application immediately caught his attention. By this point, the former Jedburgh had credentialed himself in the fields of both covert political action and paramilitary operations. There were the intangibles as well. FitzGerald, whose first military assignment had been command of an African American company, noted Elbridge's service with the 24th Infantry Division with satisfaction. Finally, FitzGerald and Colby had had a passing acquaintance after the war when their respective law firms shared the same building. There were two spots open, one in Malaya, where the British were fighting off a communist-led insurgency among the ethnic Chinese, and the other in

South Vietnam, where President Ngo Dinh Diem was gearing up for a campaign against a Viet Minh rebellion still in its infancy. Colby's fluency in French was the deciding factor. Vietnam it was to be, as deputy chief of station. "And so it was," Colby observed in his memoir, "that I began more than a decade and a half of intense involvement in what was to be one of the most traumatic and tragic experiences in modern American history, the Vietnam War."[1]

From the last quarter of the nineteenth century until the outbreak of World War II, Vietnam had been part of French Indochina, a tightly controlled colonial federation. The French had ruled Vietnam with an iron hand, exploiting it economically and crushing any sign of indigenous opposition. In 1940 and 1941, Japan, with the aid of its ally Germany, forced the French to cede control of the area, and from 1941 to 1945 Vietnam was a Japanese protectorate with the French still nominally in power. In 1941, Ho Chi Minh, a cofounder of both the French and Vietnamese communist parties, established the Viet Minh, a communist-led but broadly based insurgent movement whose goal was to rid Vietnam of foreign control, whether Japanese or French. At first, American operatives in the China-Burma-India theater supported Ho and the Viet Minh and opposed French reinfiltration. But with President Franklin D. Roosevelt's death, the onset of the Cold War, and the perceived need to shore up metropolitan France as a bastion against Soviet aggression, the United States decided to tacitly aid France's efforts to regain control of its lost colony.

In 1945, from Hanoi in the north of Vietnam, Ho and his colleagues in the Viet Minh proclaimed the establishment of the Democratic Republic of Vietnam (DRV). The following year, France and the Viet Minh went to war in a conflict that would last eight bloody years. In 1950, in order to dispel notions that it was fighting a purely colonial war, Paris recognized the State of Vietnam as an autonomous state within the French Union and brought deposed emperor Bao Dai out of exile to rule the new entity. Despite massive amounts of US aid—military and nonmilitary—France gradually wilted in the face of a war, both conventional and guerrilla, waged by the Viet Minh's commanding general, Vo Nguyen Giap. In 1954, following the disastrous French defeat at Dien Bien Phu, the United Kingdom, the Soviet Union, France, the People's Republic of China, Laos, Cambodia, and the Democratic Republic of Vietnam signed the Geneva Accords, dividing Vietnam temporarily at the seventeenth parallel, with the Viet Minh compelled to withdraw to the north and the French and their Vietnamese allies to the south. National elections for a government to rule a unified Vietnam were scheduled for 1956.

John Foster Dulles and the Republican Party viewed the Geneva Accords as something of a sellout, however, and the Eisenhower administration set its face against the reunification provisions of the agreements. From 1954 until 1961, Eisenhower and Dulles labored tirelessly to build a viable noncommunist republic south of the seventeenth parallel. One of the principal instruments they wielded in this task was the CIA.

There were in Saigon in the summer of 1954 not one but two CIA stations. The first was to gather intelligence and establish a liaison with the government of South Vietnam as soon as it was established. The other, called the Saigon Military Mission (SMM), was headed by Colonel Edward Lansdale, who had helped put down the communist-led Hukbalahap insurrection in the Philippines. Lansdale, quite simply, was DCI Allen Dulles's man in Vietnam, reporting only to him and operating with complete autonomy. In June 1954, when ordering Lansdale to Saigon, Dulles had instructed him to "find another Magsaysay," that is, a charismatic leader capable of building a viable economic and political system and rallying noncommunist nationalists. The "Quiet American," to use the title of Graham Greene's fictionalized account, believed he had found such a figure in Ngo Dinh Diem, the newly named prime minister of South Vietnam.[2]

When France granted unconditional recognition to Bao Dai's government in June, the former emperor had turned to Diem, who had a long history as a nationalist but anticommunist figure in Vietnam, as the natural choice to run his government. Diem, who would dominate South Vietnamese political life for nearly a decade, was part mandarin, part monk. He was a devout Catholic, remaining celibate throughout his adult life, and a Confucian, agreeing with its emphasis on hierarchy, respect for authority, and noblesse oblige paternalism. Diem was honest, patriotic, and sincere, but he was no democrat and had absolutely no patience with the give-and-take of Western-style politics. He and his brother Ngo Dinh Nhu, who would serve as presidential counselor and later minister of the interior, embraced "personalism," a philosophy espoused by an obscure twentieth-century French Catholic intellectual, Emmanuel Mounier.[3] Personalism placed equal emphasis on the value of the individual and the duty of each citizen to make sacrifices for the community. Diem and Nhu saw in it a means to reconcile the modernist, Western notion of individualism with Vietnam's Confucian traditions.

Diem, who would oust the playboy-emperor Bao Dai in 1955 to become president of a newly created republic, faced a host of problems during his first two years in office. The colonial economy was in shambles; the bureaucracy was filled with sycophants who had catered alternately to the French and the Japanese; and the large French community lurked in the background, waiting to pick up the pieces if Diem and the Americans faltered.

Within days of his arrival in Saigon, Ed Lansdale had obtained an interview with Diem, and in the weeks that followed, he positioned himself as the prime minister's adviser and confidant. The quiet American had two things to offer: the first was an insurgency in the north intended to keep Ho and the Viet Minh off balance, and the second was a constituency that could serve as the beginning of a political base in the south. Within weeks, Lansdale had assembled a colorful team of operatives. The SMM was supposedly part of the Military Assistance and Advisory Group (MAAG), which had been put in place in 1950 by the Truman administration to help build a viable South Vietnamese Army, but Lansdale and company, clad in khaki shorts, knee-length socks, and pith helmets, operated completely independently.

Perhaps the most conspicuous member of Lansdale's lot was a prototypical knuckle-dragger named Lucien Conein. Born in Paris in 1919, Conein had been raised by an aunt in Kansas after his father, a French Army veteran, died. In 1941, he enlisted in the US Army and graduated from Officer Candidate School at Fort Benning two years later. Like Colby, he and the OSS seemed made for each other. The two men first crossed paths at Area F, the Congressional Country Club, where Conein was an instructor. He made the trip with Colby and the other OSS operatives to the United Kingdom and then served as an instructor at Milton Hall from January to May 1944. In August of that year, Conein parachuted into occupied France just ahead of Operation Anvil. He and Colby subsequently spent time together in London haunting its many nightclubs and bordellos. In March 1945, Conein was transferred to the Pacific. There he joined up with a group of Vichy French who had escaped the Japanese; from their base in China, these irregulars waged guerrilla warfare against Japanese positions in Vietnam. After V-J Day, Conein was sent back to Europe to work with the OSS and its subsequent iterations, running saboteurs and spies into Eastern Europe from West Germany. During his stints in France and in Germany, Conein established strong links with the Corsican Brotherhood, an underworld organization allied first with the anti-Nazi resistance and then employed as contract workers for the Western intelligence services in their struggle with the NKVD. Joining the CIA shortly after its formation, Conein was a natural for Lansdale's team.[4]

Lansdale and his cohorts were instrumental in helping the Diem regime survive its first great crisis, the so-called sect wars of 1955. The Vietnamese Army that the French had left behind was little more than a shell, more a police force than a conventional fighting force. In the countryside, the government had to compete with two religious sects, the Cao Dai and the Hoa Hao, which had been nurtured by the Japanese. The Cao Dai sought to combine the best of the religious and secular worlds. Its adherents worshipped a pantheon of figures that included Jesus, Buddha, Victor Hugo, Joan of Arc, and Sun Yat-sen (the founder of the Chinese Nationalist Party) at colorful rococo temples and a giant cathedral at Tay Ninh, north of Saigon. By 1954, the sect could count more than 2 million adherents and boasted a paramilitary force of 20,000. The Hoa Hao, named for a village in the Mekong Delta, emerged by the eve of World War II as a sort of reform Buddhism whose driving force was a faith healer named Huynh Phu So. The Hoa Hao appealed particularly to the tens of thousands of Cambodians who lived in the western delta. By 1954, it could claim a membership of some 1 million and an army estimated at 15,000. Finally, there was the Binh Xuyen, a Vietnamese mafia operating prostitution rings, opium dens, protection rackets, and a black market in and around Saigon. A large portion of the metropolitan police was in the pay of this group.

The Cao Dai, Hoa Hao, and Binh Xuyen each demanded virtual autonomy in its zone of operation. Utilizing Lansdale and his deputy, Rufus Phillips, Diem negotiated with the first two, but he refused to have anything to do with the Xuyen. In the fall of 1955, the three sects banded together; in and around Saigon, fighting erupted between their paramilitary forces and government troops. With the fate of the House of Ngo hanging in the balance, Lansdale and Phillips journeyed deep into the forests near the Cambodian border to make contact with the Cao Dai leaders at their hideout on Black Lady Mountain. The Americans succeeded in bribing them with cash and promises of high office. With the Cao Dai now fighting by their side, government troops routed the Binh Xuyen; the Hoa Hao withdrew to its delta strongholds and subsequently negotiated its own deal with the government in Saigon. Diem's victory in the sect wars was key: whatever opposition there was to him in Washington melted away, and from 1955 onward, the Eisenhower administration proved an unflagging ally.[5]

Lansdale himself did not survive the events of 1955–1956. Washington's envoy to Saigon, J. Lawton Collins, a World War II general and chum of General Paul Ely, head of the French military mission, detested the quiet American and distrusted the Ngo brothers. Indeed, he had been in Washington pressing for the withdrawal of US support for Diem when the sect wars erupted. In addition, the regular CIA mission in Saigon had deluged headquarters with a steady stream of complaints about its rogue rival. Diem, having read too many reports in the American press of Lansdale's influence over his government, had himself tired of the American. Whatever the cause, by the end of 1956 Ed Lansdale and the SMM were gone, and all CIA functions in South Vietnam were being carried out by the regular station.

Despite his recall, Lansdale's name would become synonymous with pacification and counterinsurgency in Vietnam. As with the Filipinos, he told a colleague, his objective with the Vietnamese was to help them achieve the goals they set for themselves. But he was convinced that communism was not one of those goals, that any people with the freedom to choose would reject totalitarianism and embrace democracy. During his first two years in Vietnam, Lansdale had worked tirelessly to convince the Diem regime that the key to securing the countryside, to filling the political and military vacuum there before the Viet Minh did, was to win the hearts and minds of the peasantry. He made little headway. Diem perceived the primary threat to his country to be the North Vietnamese Army (NVA) and insisted that his military should concentrate on preparing to meet an invasion. Nhu's secret police could deal with any insurgency in the south. Diem did not say so, but he believed it was demeaning for a ruler to ask for support from his subjects.[6]

From 1955 to 1961, the United States poured more than $1.4 billion into South Vietnam; by the end of that period there were 1,500 American civilians and just under 700 uniformed personnel advising the South Vietnamese government. In 1956, Diem and Nhu launched their Anti-Communist Denunciation Campaign, which was designed to root out the 10,000 to 15,000 cadres the Viet Minh had left behind as they departed for the north. In June of that year, Diem sought to tighten his control over the peasantry by replacing locally elected village councils with committees appointed by his province and district chiefs. Soon, local authorities were focusing almost exclusively on rooting out and jailing subversives in their respective communities. Efforts to organize the peasantry politically and win them over through health, education, and economic development programs went by the boards. The result of the denunciation campaign, according to Chester Cooper, another Agency expert on Vietnam, was "innumerable crimes and absolutely senseless acts of suppression against both real and suspected Communists and sympathizing villagers. . . . Efficiency took the form of brutality and a total disregard for the difference between determined foes and potential friends."[7]

Meanwhile, the national legislature became a rubber stamp while the Ngo family exercised total control over the executive. In addition to Diem as president and Nhu as counselor/minister, there was Ngo Dinh Can, governor and warlord of central Vietnam, and Ngo Dinh Thuc, the Catholic archbishop of Hue and primate of Vietnam. Nhu established the Can Lao (Workers) Party, modeled on the communist parties of Asia and Europe. Clandestine cells of three to five people each penetrated political parties, the highest reaches of the military, and every echelon of the bureaucracy. Those who dared voice dissatisfaction with the government were dealt with quickly and harshly.

If there had been no communist insurgency in the south, Diem's increasingly repressive policies would have created one. Initially, the ruling Politburo in Hanoi had ordered the stay-behinds in the south to abjure violence and concentrate on political organization. But with the demise of reunification elections and the success of the Anti-Communist Denunciation Campaign, Hanoi changed direction in 1959, authorizing the Viet Minh in the south to arm and defend themselves. The level of violence increased dramatically, with assassinations of South Vietnamese government officials ballooning from 700 in 1958 to 2,800 in 1960.

The North Vietnamese Army's corps of engineers began working in 1959 to improve the network of jungle trails leading from the north into the south through Laos and Cambodia; these became the precursor of the famed Ho Chi Minh Trail. In December 1960, at Hanoi's direction, southern revolutionaries founded the National Liberation Front (NLF), a broad coalition of groups, factions, sects, and individuals opposed to the House of Ngo, but in fact directed and controlled by the Lao Dong (Vietnamese Communist Party). The NLF's military wing was named the People's Army of Vietnam (PAVN) (subsequently dubbed the Viet Cong by the South Vietnamese and Americans). The Diemists and communists found themselves caught up in a never-ending cycle of provocation and reprisal. On May 6, 1959, Diem promulgated Law 10/59, which created special military courts to hear charges against individuals accused of plotting or committing crimes against the state, whether political, economic, or military in nature. Those found guilty were to be summarily guillotined.

The Colbys arrived in Saigon on February 8, 1959; it was Tet, Vietnam's most revered holiday, the first day of the New Year. Tan Son Nhut Airport was one of the few operations in the country open for business. Bill, Barbara, John, Catherine, Carl, and Paul, the newest addition, were overwhelmed by the tropical heat as soon as they stepped off the plane. It was midwinter, but Saigon lay only ten degrees north of the equator, and the terminal did not yet have air conditioning. Bill's diplomatic passport enabled the family to hurry through customs. Colby recalled that the officials were focused on a Chinese-Vietnamese woman whom they suspected of smuggling gold in her packages of silk and transistor radios. "The heat, the ritualism, the suspicion of contraband was my introduction [to Vietnam]," Colby wrote.

The mission had sent an automobile to pick up the new CIA deputy chief of station. Tan Son Nhut lay north of the city, and the trip allowed the family to get a long look at their new home. The residential outskirts consisted of streets and alleyways densely packed with squalid shanties, which were interrupted periodically by high-walled French villas, oases in a desert of poverty. The road they traveled was named for Ngo Dinh Khoi, Diem and Nhu's elder brother, who had been executed by the communists in 1930. Soon, however, the little motorcade entered Saigon proper; its Chinese district, Cholon, lay just to the west. The family was charmed. "The city itself," Colby later recalled, "was shaded by tall trees spaced evenly along the streets, with gracious white and cream-colored tropical houses behind walls giving both privacy and security. The sight evoked memories of provincial towns in the south of France."[8]

Saigon, the "Paris of the Orient," with its wide boulevards and plastered villas, had been built by the French to rival Singapore in colonial charm and culture. The city of some 2 million was situated on the west bank of the Saigon River some 25 miles inland from the South China Sea. An additional 700,000 ethnic Chinese lived in Cholon. As in a typical European city, the boulevards of Saigon were periodically intersected by traffic roundabouts with island centers; most of these were adorned with monuments to a fallen Vietnamese—or, more rarely, French—hero. As in Paris, there were large parks, archipelagos of greenery that set off the vivid orange blossoms of the tamarind trees. The principal street, at least as far as Europeans were concerned, was Tu Do. It ran from the Catholic Cathedral in the heart of Saigon east to the Hotel Majestic overlooking the Saigon River. Tu Do was lined on both sides with shops featuring clothing, wine, furniture, raw silk, tobacco, and other consumer items affordable only to the elite. In addition to the Majestic, Europeans could find air-conditioned rooms, fashionable bars, and fine restaurants at the Continental at 132 Tu Do, and at the Caravelle, just a block over at 23 Place Lam Son. The Continental, situated in the heart of the city, was the favorite haunt of journalists and writers. The American journalist Robert Shaplen had a permanent room booked there, as did British novelist Graham Greene.

Saigon was known for its cuisine—Indian, Chinese, and French, as well as Vietnamese. Colby would later claim that the Arc-en-Ciel in Cholon served the finest Chinese food in the world. For Europeans, Americans, and upper-class Vietnamese, there was the Golf Club de Saigon and the equestrian-themed Cercle Hippique Saigonnais. By far the most popular club, however, was the Cercle Sportif Saigonnais, situated near the Presidential Palace in the heart of the city. There, members could swim, dine, play tennis, indulge in cards or chess, and, of course, drink. It was in Saigon's hotels, clubs, and restaurants that contacts were made and deals discussed, whether having to do with diplomacy, espionage, black marketeering, or romance. Aficionados of Hollywood could see films at the Alhambra Theater.

Western influences did not extend to the narrow, crowded side streets where Vietnamese families occupied single rooms behind and over shops. One place where Saigonese of all social classes could be found was the central market, the Marché Central Saigonnais. Under one vast roof were hundreds of stalls packed tightly together. Shoppers could buy fish, meats, vegetables, fruits, fabrics, chopsticks, candleholders, straw placemats, and a thousand other items.[9]

By 1959, the French diplomatic and military presence in Vietnam had been greatly reduced, but the Corsicans still dominated the social and economic life of South Vietnam's principal city. They were among the first European settlers, having come out to escape a life of poverty and discrimination. The Corsicans owned and operated many of the city's eateries, ran the police department, operated the city's vast smuggling operation, and, along with remnants of the Binh Xuyen, provided private muscle to various individuals, factions, and secret societies.[10]

The Colbys moved first into a French colonial villa near the cathedral, "a lovely, old-fashioned one," Barbara recalled fondly. Their second house, occupied after Bill was promoted to station chief, was more modern, verging on art deco. It was situated on Alexandre de Rhodes, one of the two streets bordering the park in front of the Presidential Palace, a sprawling stone edifice that faintly recalled Versailles. The Colby residence was the second house on the right as one faced the palace. The first order of business for an American family assigned to Saigon was to hire a staff of servants. For a family of the Colbys' status, that meant a cook, a boy or *boyesse* (a French term for a female servant) to clean and serve meals, a laundress, a gardener, and an *amah*, or nanny, for the small children. One could employ either Vietnamese or Chinese, but not both in the same household. Tuberculosis was an ever-present threat, so families were advised to have potential employees' chest's X-rayed. "Servants were plentiful, loyal, and friendly," Colby wrote in his memoirs, "freeing my wife, Barbara, for a busy schedule of gatherings with wives of senior Vietnamese and other diplomats." As in any tropical, semideveloped country, health problems were a concern. Malaria was under control in Saigon but not in the countryside. When the government inaugurated a DDT-spraying campaign in the provinces, the sprayers were immediately targeted by communist insurgents. Neither water nor food was safe to ingest without processing. The former had to be boiled for at least ten minutes. Because crops were fertilized with feces, both animal and human, fruits and vegetables needed to be peeled and preferably also cooked before being eaten.[11]

Barbara and Bill put the boys in a French Catholic school, but when they learned that the curriculum would be taught in Vietnamese rather than French, they transferred them to the American Community School. "We didn't speak French or Vietnamese," Carl later recalled of his first school. "The only other Caucasian was my brother." If that were not bad enough, the monks would constantly rap Carl on the knuckles with a ruler—he was left-handed, and left-handedness was still seen as the sign of the devil in many Catholic schools worldwide. Catherine was enrolled in a convent school for girls where the language of instruction was French. Almost as soon as they were settled, Bill took Barbara and the children to visit the gravesite of Roger Villebois, his Team Bruce partner who had been killed in Vietnam during the First Indochinese War.[12]

In those days, the First Indochinese War was a fading memory and the Second a faint cloud on the horizon. One could move about the city day or night by taxi, pedicab, or motorbike. Except at military installations, there were no checkpoints or guardhouses. The children, Carl remembered, had free rein in both Saigon and Cholon. "Noon frequently meant a family gathering at the Cercle Sportif," Bill recalled, "where a fine French lunch was served during the two-hour midday break." It was terrifically hot and humid; the Colbys learned to limit their physical movements during the middle of the day, and the bedrooms of Europeans were generally air-conditioned.[13]

Bill Colby did not arrive in Vietnam in 1959 unprepared. He had spent nearly six months at Agency headquarters in Washington reading in-house histories of Vietnam and the increasingly dense cable traffic between the American mission and its bureaucratic partners in Washington. He was aware of the role the United States had played in the First Indochinese War—that the Eisenhower administration had limited aid to money, materiel, and advice, stopping at the water's edge during the siege of Dien Bien Phu. He was aware of Diem's rocky first two years, when he'd had to battle both the sects and the French who backed them in hopes of controlling Vietnam indirectly. He knew of the dueling CIA stations, and he knew of Lansdale's philosophy of basing policy on winning hearts and minds, an approach with which he sympathized to a degree. The former Jedburgh was aware of both Diem's patriotism and his penchant for autocracy. By the time he arrived in Saigon, the government's anticommunist denunciation campaign had caused the north to begin openly aiding communists in the south. In addition, Hanoi had started funneling some of the ninety thousand Southern Viet Minh who had gone north in 1954 back into the south, with orders to eat away at Diem's political base through agitation, terror, and socioeconomic reform. But one of Bill Colby's enduring characteristics was an awareness of his own limitations. There was still much to learn, and he knew it. Before the lesson could begin, however, the Saigon Military Mission's newest arrival was forced to deal with a "flap"—the CIA word for crisis—of major proportions.

Only months before, Cambodia's neutralist ruler, Prince Norodom Sihanouk, had formally recognized the government of the People's Republic of China and followed up the announcement with a state visit. Cambodia was a large, populous, but almost defenseless country, its army more virtual than real. Sihanouk was not a communist and did not want to become an instrument of Sino-Soviet foreign policy, but neither did he want his country to become a Western protectorate. As the South Vietnamese and Thai governments saw it, however, Sihanouk was opening the door to the communists, paving the way for his country to become a staging ground for North Vietnamese and Chinese incursions. As the Colbys approached the US embassy on their journey in from the airport, the wife of the officer driving them had flagged down their automobile on the street to inform them that Sihanouk had just announced that he had thwarted a coup against him organized by the Thai and South Vietnamese governments with the help of the CIA.

There had indeed been a plot. It was headed by General Dap Chhuon, a rightwing warlord who had been encouraged and supplied by Saigon and Bangkok. Moreover, the agents whom Sihanouk had sent to capture Chhuon and his coconspirators had found in their midst one Victor M. Matsui, a CIA agent who had been keeping headquarters abreast of events by radio. Colby would claim that Matsui was there merely to monitor the situation for the Agency, and that the thrust of US advice to the coup plotters had been to cease and desist. Sihanouk was convinced otherwise, however, and publicly denounced the CIA specifically and the United States in general. Disinterested observers noted that the US ambassador to Thailand at the time was John E. Peurifoy, who had overseen the 1954 coup that ousted a leftist regime in Guatemala. Colby was detailed to secure Matsui's release, which, after much negotiating, he did. Chhuon was subsequently killed while trying to escape. The lesson to be learned from all this, Colby wrote in his memoir, was that the Agency would be identified and blamed for any activity it was found to be in contact with, no matter its role or motives. There was a second lesson to be learned as well: the United States, despite being a burgeoning presence, had and would have remarkably little control over events in Southeast Asia. With Matsui safely extracted from Cambodia, Colby was at last able to look about him and get his bearings.[14]

Heading the US Mission, which encompassed the various bureaucracies—civilian and military—accredited to the Diem government, was Elbridge Durbrow. Colby had come to know Durbrow while serving as Clare Luce's deputy in Rome. Head of the Military Assistance and Advisory Group was General Samuel "Hanging Sam" Williams, a spit-and-polish career officer who jealously guarded the military's prerogatives. He aggressively resisted Durbrow's efforts to put military, political, and economic matters under one umbrella, insisting on communicating directly to Washington through the commander in chief of the US Pacific Command (CINCPAC). The US Agency for International Development (USAID) chief in Saigon upon Colby's arrival was Arthur Gardiner, who was much more perspicacious than many of his colleagues but no less determined to protect and enhance his agency's turf.[15]

CIA chief of station was Nick Natsios, a veteran operative who had served with the OSS in Italy and the CIA in Greece during that country's civil war. Natsios was a tough-minded individual who evoked fierce loyalty from his team of some forty members. The head of station in Saigon needed to be a strong personality: there was the usual handful of academic types—quiet students of the Orient—on the staff, but the majority were colorful swashbucklers like Conein. They were not only accustomed to danger and adventure, but eager for it. Some had been born and raised in China as members of missionary or business families and had played a role in the communist-nationalist civil war and the subsequent Taiwan Strait crises. Some had been in the Philippines fighting the Huk, while others had participated in the failed 1958 uprising against Sukarno in Indonesia. These were men who were used to living at the edges of civilization and authority; most had been through the coups and countercoups that had wracked Thailand, Laos, and Burma since World War II. They lived in a world of conspiracy and violence, both overt and covert; were equally comfortable dealing with established governments and the Orient's innumerable secret societies; experienced in the ways of the authoritarian regimes so typical of underdeveloped nations; and equally adept at working through military and civilian channels.[16]

The CIA station in Saigon was not divided, as other stations were, into foreign intelligence and covert action, but rather into "liaison" and "unilateral"

operations. The liaison officers focused on partnering with Vietnamese intelligence and police to gather as much information on communist activities as possible. This involved interviewing refugees from North Vietnam,
recruiting double agents, and infiltrating operatives into the north. Given
the division of Vietnam after 1954 and America's recognition of the Diem
regime as the sole political authority throughout the country, liaison agents
required little cover. Not so for the unilateral personnel, whose job it was
to cultivate ties with the whole array of political factions working openly
or covertly in South Vietnam. This included everything from the Cao Dai
and the Binh Xuyen before its demise to the old noncommunist nationalist
parties, such as Nguyen Ton Hoan's Dai Viet Quoc Dan Dang (Nationalist
Party of Greater Vietnam) and the Viet Nam Quoc Dan Dang (VNQDD,
Vietnamese Nationalist Party). These operatives worked under deep cover
as members of MAAG; USAID; private charitable entities, such as the
Catholic Relief Organization; or the American business community. They
recruited and ran Vietnamese agents from the organizations they were assigned to keep tabs on. They did not necessarily share their contacts or the
information they gathered with the Vietnamese government.[17]

Diem and Nhu's attitude toward the growing American presence in
Vietnam was, not surprisingly, ambivalent. They needed US guns and
money; they were not sure they needed American advice, but that seemed
to come with the territory. The Ngo brothers were authentic nationalists
fully aware that their own positions depended on their ability to ensure
that the Americans remained in a subordinate position. To this end, Diem
pursued the divide-and-conquer approach that the Chinese and French
had used so effectively against Vietnam. The brothers dealt with Ambassador Durbrow and General Williams formally, while behind the scenes
they nurtured ties with as many American bureaucracies and nongovern-
mental organizations as possible, seeking their guidance and playing up
to their host organizations back in Washington. At the same time, Diem
maintained contact with Francis Cardinal Spellman, Senator Mike Mansfield, the Kennedy brothers, and other powerful individuals who had befriended him during his stay in the United States. "Diem's style," Colby
observed, "was that of the traditional mandarin, assuming the legitimacy
of his position to be beyond challenge and manipulating the currents of
the distant imperial court (now in Washington) to ensure the continued
support necessary to his mission."[18] Because Diem and Nhu perceived the

CIA to be above both politics and the law in the United States, and because they knew the Agency had probably penetrated every faction, sect, and secret society in Vietnam, the Ngo brothers singled it out for special attention.

During the summer of Colby's first year in Vietnam, 1959, Chief of Station Natsios returned to the United States for his annual leave. In his absence the deputy chief of station began a series of weekly meetings with Ngo Dinh Nhu that would continue for nearly three years. To many Vietnamese and French, Nhu was Vietnam's Rasputin. From 1954, the year of Diem's return, until his fall in 1963, Nhu held the position of counselor to the president, but he was clearly the second most powerful figure in South Vietnam—some said the most powerful. He personally controlled not only the Can Lao (the government's party apparatus), but also the Army of the Republic of Vietnam (ARVN) Special Forces, which existed not to combat a communist insurgency directly but to act as a palace guard and supply political muscle for the House of Ngo. Nhu was as corrupt as Diem was uncorrupt. A lifelong opium user, the counselor to the president used his connections with international drug-smuggling rings to enrich himself and his extended family.

Colby knew all of this, but it was his duty, as he perceived it, to take what was available and do the best he could with it. Just before leaving for his vacation, Natsios had escorted his second to Independence Palace to meet Nhu. They entered through the back gate, turned left to the West Wing, and went upstairs to the small office inhabited by the presidential counselor. Following a short wait, Nhu entered. "He was . . . thinner than his brother, delicately handsome, informally clad in a white sport shirt, and very soft-spoken, giving the impression of being extremely shy," Colby recalled of that first encounter.[19] The meeting, conducted in French, stretched over some four hours and covered a variety of subjects. At this and subsequent conferences, Colby quickly learned that the Ngo brothers did business in a most un-Western way. The American came prepared with a list of topics, talking points, and options. Nhu would listen quietly and then break in, discoursing at length on a subject of interest to him—the travails of the House of Ngo before Dien Bien Phu, the evils committed by the French-trained bureaucracy that still remained in place, the machinations of the French themselves, the irrelevancy of the noncommunist political critics of the government, and the relevancy of Mounier's philosophy of personalism, not only to Catholics but to all Vietnamese. Nhu smoked constantly, and servants moved in and out serving tea and emptying ashtrays. Diem's brother struck Colby one minute as a man of the Enlightenment—his reasoning precise, rife with Cartesian logic—and the next as a mystic, with every argument and scheme cast in spiritual terms. Nhu expressed his devotion to Diem but confided to Colby that his brother was somewhat naïve. Vietnamese leaders could no longer command respect simply by virtue of the position they held. Nhu observed that the president thought of modernity only in technical, concrete terms—highways, schools, bridges, hospitals—assuming that if these were provided, the people would follow. In this he was mistaken, Nhu said. To Colby's great satisfaction, Nhu seemed to appreciate the need for a political base, particularly in the countryside.

Desperately, Colby searched for common ground with the Saigon regime. He sensed that Nhu was the key. During his less frequent meetings with Diem, which also lasted at least four hours, there were no discussions of political models and theories, but rather an endless monologue, in which the president expounded with great enthusiasm and even greater detail on his infrastructure programs. There was his Agroville Program in the delta, where, typically, the population lived dispersed and isolated, scattered along the banks of the endless network of canals. In this project, peasants would be clustered in communities large enough to support schools, hospitals, and proper marketplaces. There were new cash crops to raise the living standards of the peasants; light industries, such as textiles, for the cities; and a national Institute of Administration to train bureaucrats and free the country of the Francophile bureaucrats who then ran it. All fine and good, thought Colby and Nhu, but the people were not a formless mass waiting to be shaped. The government swam in a sea of sects, secret societies, political factions, and ethnic groups that were ambitious, more or less organized, and sometimes armed. And, of course, there were the communists.

"I sympathized with Nhu's insistence that Vietnam needed to discover and develop a new political identity around which its people could rally if the competing Communist appeal for change and for nationalism was to be defeated," Colby later wrote. But what identity? That was the rub. Like the pope, the Ngos wanted to be both loved and obeyed, but if they could not have love, they were certainly going to have obedience. The difference between the pope and the Ngos, who claimed to be acting in his name, was that the former resorted to excommunication to compel conformity, whereas the latter were willing to use imprisonment, torture, and execution. Colby decided that for the time being, that was going to have to do. "The task in South Vietnam required strong leadership," he wrote, "and Diem's messianic dedication seemed more appropriate for it than did the confusion and indecision that could come from overly precise application of the American doctrine of the separation of powers."[20] From the very beginning of his tour in Vietnam, Colby faced the quintessential Cold War dilemma. In the war against the forces of international communism, what were acceptable levels of tyranny and corruption? Would his and the Agency's tolerance exceed that of the American public? In this regard, was it the CIA's duty to lead or to follow? Should it advise, or merely inform the political powers that were?

As with any imperial government, there was a court. Chief among the courtesans was Nguyen Dinh Thuan, secretary of state for the presidency, and Tran Kim Tuyen, chief of the Service d'Etudes Politiques et Sociales (SEPES, Bureau of Political and Social Research), the government's intelligence and security service. Thuan oversaw the vast bureaucracy upon which the Ngo brothers depended to rule. He was also the principal interpreter of the regime to the American mission. Soft-spoken and fluent in English, he listened far more than he talked. US officials like Colby could sound out an idea with Nhu and Diem through Thuan before formally broaching it. Tuyen, who occupied the French governor general's servants' quarters, was a tiny man, less than five feet tall and tipping the scales at a hundred pounds. "He projected the quiet and shy air of the Confucian scholar," Colby wrote, "the long and carefully tended nail on the little finger of his left hand certifying his status," an affectation left over from the Chinese tradition intended to signify freedom from physical labor. Tuyen's manner and stature, of course, belied a ruthlessness and cruelty that were the necessary qualifications for his job.[21]

In July 1959, less than six months after the Colbys' arrival in Vietnam, the first American military casualties occurred when two servicemen died in a communist attack on a MAAG billet outside Bien Hoa. The US Mission was alarmed but did not know what to make of the incident. The level of violence in the countryside was low, and as late as 1958, Hanoi had once again made overtures to the Diem regime about holding nationwide elections. Saigon had rejected that initiative and scheduled parliamentary elections for the south on August 30, 1959. Still, Ho Chi Minh and the Politburo clung to hopes for a political settlement: communist cadres in the south received instructions to have their supporters vote for left-leaning candidates as a step toward influencing political life, at least indirectly. Privy to this information, Nhu and the Can Lao rigged the elections so that the government won 121 out of the 123 contested seats. Not satisfied, the Saigon government indicted the two non–Can Lao candidates on fraud charges and refused to seat them. On August 31, Cambodia's Prince Sihanouk, whom Saigon viewed as a communist dupe, barely survived an assassination attempt by Nhu's agents. On Nhu's orders, two suitcases had been delivered to Sihanouk's palace, one addressed to the prince and the other to his chief of protocol, Prince Vakrivan. Sihanouk's was filled with explosives, and Vakrivan's was not, but, following protocol, the latter opened both suitcases and was blown to bits. A shaken Sihanouk issued a communiqué blaming the Ngo brothers and the CIA. There was no hope of a political solution, Hanoi concluded, and in early 1960 it began work on what would become the Ho Chi Minh Trail.[22]

Undeterred by this gathering storm, the Colbys set about exploring their environs. Vietnam, according to a local saying, resembled two rice baskets hanging from the ends of a farmer's carrying pole. Stretching more than 1,000 miles from north to south, the country was 400 miles across at its widest in the north and less than 35 miles across in the center, the pole between the baskets. The northwest was mountainous, forested, and thinly populated; the northeast, featuring the Red River Delta, was heavily populated and included the twin cities of Hanoi and Hai Phong. Along the western flank of the country, from the northern highlands to just north of Saigon, ran the Annamite Range, the site of the Central Highlands and home to many of the country's forty-three ethnic minorities. Between the mountains and the sea ran a strip of incredibly fertile, densely populated land that produced, along with the Mekong Delta to the south, much of the nation's food staple—rice. The southern basket on the pole, with Saigon as its gateway, was the vast Mekong Delta, featuring thousands of miles of mangrove swamps, which had largely been reclaimed and turned into rice paddies. Villages were widely dispersed, running along the canals that provided irrigation and transportation. To the interior toward the Cambodian border lay the dense and mysterious U-Minh Forest.

Ever restless, Colby got out of Saigon at every opportunity. He traveled to the Central Highlands with a legislative delegation to witness the inauguration of a government-sponsored settlement to accommodate northern immigrants and surplus population from the coastal lowlands. He did not realize at the time that what he was seeing was a phenomenon similar to the displacement of Native Americans by white settlers. He journeyed to the far south of the country to visit one of Diem's agrovilles in the Ca Mau peninsula. In that province, his hosts told him, there were now some forty elementary and secondary schools, whereas before 1954 there had been but four. In truth, Ca Mau was one of the most insecure regions in South Vietnam; the Agency reported to the State Department in April 1959 that entire districts were under communist control.[23]

During his first three-year stint in Vietnam, Colby showed no reluctance in traveling to all parts of South Vietnam with his family. There was a Sunday outing to see the multicolored tile and ceramic Cao Dai cathedral at Tay Ninh. The family journeyed farther south, to the coast, and hired a fishing boat to ferry them to the island of Phu Quoc, a refuge for the leaders of the Tay Son Rebellion of the 1770s and onetime home to Alexandre de Rhodes, the Portuguese missionary who had published the first Portuguese-Latin-Vietnamese dictionary. Colby's son Carl remembered two things from the trip: a shark larger than the fishing boat, and the incredible smell from the bins of fermenting fish destined to become *nuoc mam*, the ubiquitous fish sauce of Vietnamese cuisine. Bill remembered "the main roads of the Mekong . . . filled with multicolored, rickety buses hurtling through bucolic villages to teeming market centers."[24] On another outing, Bill and his oldest son, John, took a train north from Saigon to Hue, the old imperial capital situated at the mouth of the Perfume River and home to many of the country's most influential intellectuals and revolutionaries. From Hue the two traveled by automobile to the Ben Hai River which bisected the Demilitarized Zone separating North Vietnam from South. From this vantage point they could see the North Vietnamese flag flying from a military outpost. It was then on to Khe Sanh by way of Highway 9. All along the route were burned-out French villas and tiny forts and guard towers manned in the past, usually with disastrous results, by the French and their Vietnamese collaborators. The Colby family loved to visit Dalat, the exotic mountain resort town where, at 5,000 feet, Americans, Europeans, and members of the Vietnamese elite could escape the heat and humidity of Saigon and its environs.

Somehow, Bill found time to head up a Boy Scout troop during his stint in Vietnam, where the Scouts were immensely popular. The upper echelons of the Viet Minh, the military force that had defeated the French in the First Indochinese War, had been filled with former Scouts. Carl remembered on one occasion being flown with the rest of his troop for an outing near Dalat by an air force colonel named Nguyen Cao Ky. Finally, Vietnam was home to some of the most beautiful beaches in the world. Europeans and Americans favored two resorts—Cape St. Jacques, only 60 miles from Saigon, and Nha Trang, an overnight train ride from the capital. During a return trip from one of their weekends at the beach, the Colbys' train shuttered violently to a stop. Shrouded in darkness, huddled in their compartment, Barbara and the children, including baby Christine, born in Saigon in 1960, waited while Bill went to investigate. It turned out that a squad of communist insurgents had dynamited a rail bridge, taking the locomotive and the first couple of cars down with it. With a single ARVN guard at each end of the surviving string of coaches, the passengers were forced to wait in suspense until dawn brought a relief train from Saigon.[25]

As 1959 turned into 1960, Bill Colby became increasingly convinced that the Diem regime, supported by the American mission, was pursuing policies that were not only irrelevant to effective nation-building but counterproductive. The Agroville Program, designed to concentrate scattered peasant settlements into larger communities where the ARVN could provide security, was a case in point. The Vietnamese practiced ancestor worship, which included annual ritual visitations to their gravesites. To induce the rural population to move far from their ancestors' tombs, the government promised schools, hospitals, and market facilities. But when the uprooted arrived at their new villages, they found that they were expected to build their own homes and community facilities without compensation. Everyone agreed that land reform was essential to pacifying rural Vietnam. A large percentage of the arable land had historically been owned and operated by large absentee landholders who exploited tenants and agricultural laborers unmercifully. Writer Duong Van Mai Elliott, who had lived in Hanoi during the period when the Viet Minh came to power, recalled that the single most important move Ho and his colleagues made was to dispossess French and Vietnamese landlords and distribute their holdings among the peasantry. Diem and Nhu were committed to agrarian reform in name, but when push came to shove, the national government exempted all holdings smaller than 250 acres. Colby recalled that "we went to Diem at one point saying, 'Well, you know, you've really got to cut this down and make it smaller, because there were still landlords.' He said, 'You don't understand. I cannot eliminate my middle class.'"[26]

Most important, Colby believed, was the absence of any viable political movement in the countryside. Diem was firmly of the opinion that South Vietnam's only enemies were colonialism, feudalism, and communism. With the first two defeated, the sole task remaining was to hold North Vietnam at bay while crushing the insurgency in South Vietnam. The Ministry of Information had created a "mass political organization," the National Revolutionary Movement, in October 1955; failure to support the party was interpreted as sympathy for the communists. All reform came from the top down. This was true in North Vietnam as well, but there at least some reform was genuine. "The sole political function expected of the citizenry," Colby later wrote, "was to assemble later in well-ordered lines in the hot sun to greet visiting delegations of foreigners or officials from Saigon, to wave the national flag with its three red stripes on a yellow field, and to cheer 'Muon Nam!' ('A Thousand Years!') at mention of President Diem's leadership."[27] There was political dissent in Saigon and Hue, but it consisted primarily of educated and wealthy cliques that resented being shut out of power by the Ngo family and had no connection with the 90 percent of the population living in the countryside. The Cao Dai and Hoa Hao, South Vietnam's largest religious sects, were thoroughly penetrated by the Can Lao, Nhu's political apparatus.

Meanwhile, the Lao Dong, the communist party of North Vietnam, and, after its formation in December 1960, the National Liberation Front, designed a strategy—a "people's war"—that would exploit the political void and the peasant resentment that Diem's policies were creating. The key to victory over the "American Diemists," Hanoi believed, was to disperse armed political cadres throughout South Vietnam and convince the rural populace that it was the communists—the former Viet Minh who had defeated the French and the Japanese—who held out the best chance for social and economic justice. Drawn from the southerners in the Viet Minh who had regrouped to the north in 1954 and headed south in 1959, as well as Viet Minh still hiding in the south, these cadres would wage a war of terror against Diemist officials to create fear and demonstrate their powerlessness, propagandize and organize disaffected peasants, and, in areas where government control was weak, establish shadow hamlet and even district governments capable of levying taxes and instituting land reforms. As the official history of the CIA in Vietnam put it, "the movement's anticolonialist legacy, its land reform policy, its egalitarian style and offer of opportunities for the ambitious among the rural poor, together with the assiduous personal attention devoted to even low-level candidates for recruitment, stood in stark contrast to Diem's mandarism, which had 'dried the grass' of peasant resentment into incendiary opposition." The Saigon government was not without its supporters. There were thousands of Catholics, Hoa Hao, and Montagnards (tribespeople of the Central Highlands) who for various reasons were anticommunist, but they were the minority.[28]

To make matters worse, the US Mission was deeply divided. The embassy under Durbrow wanted to condition US aid on Western-style democratic reforms; this was especially true following the election of John F. Kennedy. American diplomats in Vietnam urged the Ngo brothers to stop persecuting their noncommunist opponents, to name some Dai Viet and VNQDD personalities to ministerial posts, and to restore self-government at the local level. With the support of the Pentagon, General Williams and MAAG resisted any attempt to tie political reform to military aid. At mission meetings, he and Durbrow were openly hostile to each other. Williams took the position that military matters were beyond the comprehension of civilians. The bulk of US military aid went to the ARVN in anticipation of it having to fight a Korean-style war, a conventional invasion from the north. Diem was most happy with this arrangement, not least because the Americans were simultaneously providing him with a formidable armed force that he could use against his enemies whether they were the North Vietnamese Army, the Viet Cong, or some noncommunist ethnic or sectarian force. Colby noted with dismay that virtually no aid went to the local territorials of the "Self-Defense Forces"—village-level troops organized in platoons to protect local communities—or to the Civil Guard, the company-level force at the disposal of province chiefs. "Little wonder that their morale was abysmal, and that their nightly maneuver was limited to closing the barbed wire around their pathetic fort and waiting for morning in hopes that Communist guerrillas would ignore them as they went about the organization, exhortation, and direction of their fellow villagers," Colby wrote.[29]

Colby thought both the soldiers and the diplomats were wrong. The US Mission was convinced that if physical security could be established in the countryside, the peasants—innately anticommunist—would rally to the government in Saigon. Diem and the American leadership in South Vietnam assumed that whatever support for the communists there was among the peasantry was coerced. Colby gave the communists more credit than that. In a people's war, the focus would not be on traditional military encounters. The enemy would employ violence to discredit the government and intimidate the population, but it would also bring a degree of social and economic justice to the countryside. Conventional battles would serve no purpose and indeed would be counterproductive, in that they would turn large portions of the rural population into alienated refugees. Nor were Western-style democratic forms and the empowerment of well-meaning intellectual elites in Saigon the answer. Empowerment would have to be authentic, to come from below. A solution, rooted in Colby's philosophy, background, and reading of the situation on the ground, was taking shape in his mind. As fate would have it, that perspective would be made all the more significant by Colby's elevation to chief of station in June 1960. But before he could act, he would have to deal with a situation that threatened to bring down the whole South Vietnamese house of cards.

On the evening of November 10, 1960, Bill and Barbara, clad in formal dress, attended the annual Marine Birthday Ball at the US embassy. Only a select few were invited, and the Colbys felt fortunate to be included. In a ceremony repeated at Marine outposts around the world, the youngest and oldest soldiers present cut the birthday cake. Before retiring for the evening, the Colbys and Durbrows stopped at a popular restaurant barge on the Saigon River for a nightcap. At around 3 A.M., Bill and his family were awakened by thunder, or so they thought. Looking out his bedroom window, Colby saw red and blue tracers arcing across the night sky. The Presidential Palace at the end of their street was under attack.

Bill's immediate thoughts were for the safety of his family. As bullets thudded into the exterior walls of the house, he built an impromptu fortress of bookcases and furniture and loaded his weapons. "My father herded us into the middle of the house on the theory that stray bullets would have a harder time hitting us," Paul, the youngest son, recalled. "I remember him going back and forth to a phone that was in a more exposed place."[30] Finally,

Colby pulled out the voice-activated radio he kept in a closet for emergencies and got in touch with the embassy. Peering out an upstairs window, he soon saw that the site of the fighting was the palace; his family was exposed only to collateral damage. As Colby soon discovered, the Ngo brothers were under siege from a renegade army parachute unit.

At dawn, a young American diplomat, John Helbe, appeared at the Colbys' back door. He had been dispatched by the embassy to monitor the siege, and the Colbys' house, at 16 Rue de Rhodes, offered the perfect vantage point. Colby drafted Helbe to do double duty—look after Barbara and the kids and report what he saw to the embassy over the radio. Bill then left for the office.

In midmorning, the embassy informed Helbe that it was safe to move the family to a more secure location farther from the fighting. "At some point when it was quiet," Paul recalled, "we filtered out the back of the house away from the action. I remember seeing armed men there. They had no interest in us."[31] Barbara, with kids in tow, walked five blocks to the house of another US Mission family, and then the next day moved still farther from the scene of action to the home of friends in Cholon. Nevertheless, it was a near thing. As the family left the house, they noted that baby Christine's bed had been crushed by falling debris.

With his family safe, the CIA chief was able to give his full attention to the coup.

Colby spearheaded the station's liaison team, keeping in constant touch by radio with the Ngo brothers as their Philippine-trained Palace Guard fended off the paratroops. One operative, Russ Miller, monitored senior police and military officials, while another, George Carver, kept in close touch with the insurgents. By the afternoon of the 11th, noncommunist political figures, led by Phan Quang Dan, had gathered at the house of a paratroop officer killed early in the fighting. "Dr. Dan," as he was known to his American admirers, was a Harvard-educated physician who had been one of the two non–Can Lo Party members elected to the National Assembly in 1959 but barred from taking office on trumped-up charges. Energetic, honest, and charismatic, Dan began issuing proclamations intended to give political purpose to the uprising.[32]

Throughout the crisis, Durbrow communicated to Nhu by radio that the position of the United States was not to take sides. The US Mission did not in fact align itself with either the government or the insurgents, but that was due more to lack of consensus than to the absence of opinion. The CIA station was of three minds. One group, led by Carver, held that the authoritarianism and ruthlessness that had allowed the Ngo brothers to survive earlier crises were no longer relevant and were in fact counterproductive. For Carver, Diem had become "a boil to be lanced." Colby was of the opinion that the Diem regime was still a work in progress and that there were signs that Nhu was ready to embrace the notion of a "rice-roots" political movement that would connect the government with the countryside. Carver later observed that Colby seemed "mesmerized" by the president's brother. Russ Miller, who was connected to high-ranking police and military officers, reflected their view that although the Ngo brothers were problematical, there was no viable alternative to them at hand. Indeed, if the House of Ngo should fall, a military dictatorship, Dr. Dan notwithstanding, was a virtual certainty. The situation in South Vietnam was unlike those Colby had confronted in Italy; Colby, the Agency, and the United States were being forced to choose between two forms of totalitarianism. As yet, there was no vital center in South Vietnam.[33]

At the outset of the fighting, Diem's military aide, General Nguyen Khanh, had climbed the rear wall of the presidential compound and set off to rally outlying military units to the government's side. Meanwhile, the beleaguered Ngo brothers played for time. Colby ordered Carver to urge Dan and the paratroop leaders to open negotiations with Diem. Carver argued that the United States was wasting a golden opportunity to effect a much-needed regime change. "I bitched and moaned and explained why I thought my orders were stupid," he later recalled. Colby was not to be deterred, however. "George, I know your position," he told his subordinate. "I don't agree with you and we haven't got time to discuss it right now." Carver persuaded the coup leaders to order a cease-fire and send a delegation to the palace for talks. Meanwhile, Khanh had succeeded in persuading Colonel Nguyen Van Thieu, commander of the Fifth Division of the ARVN, to move up from My Tho and rescue the government. Within twenty-four hours, the insurgent paratroopers were themselves surrounded, and the coup attempt collapsed. The highest-ranking rebel officers fled to Tan Son Nhut Airport, where they persuaded the head of the Vietnamese Air Transport Command, Colonel Nguyen Cao Ky, to provide them with a C-47, which they subsequently used to flee to Cambodia. Dr. Dan and the civilians were not so lucky: Nhu's secret police rounded them up and threw

them in the Chi Hoa prison, home to several generations of Vietnamese
who dared rise against the French. They would remain there until the government's demise in 1963.[34]

Diem and Nhu were not at all happy with the role the US Mission had
played in the coup. Tuyen's intelligence agents had discovered that Carver
was with the coup plotters throughout the crisis and was perhaps more
than a neutral observer. Colby tried to explain that the station's objective
was to stay informed as much as possible about the activities of all individuals and groups in a position to affect the security of the country or the
political status quo. Nhu was not mollified. "All nations conduct espionage,
and this is not a matter to get upset about," he said. "But what no nation
can accept, and our Government no less, is interference with its political
authority and processes."[35] The president's brother informed Colby that
Carver was persona non grata. The chief of station replied that the person
in question was a USAID worker and that the Mission had no reason to
send him home.

Shortly thereafter, Carver received a letter ostensibly from coup participants still in hiding. They rebuked him for encouraging and then abandoning them, and threatened Carver and his family with retribution. Colby
and Carver recognized the paper and typeface: the letter had come from
Tuyen's headquarters. It was time to end the confrontation. The station
chief went to see Nhu and told him that Carver was being threatened by
unnamed individuals and had to be taken out of the country. Nhu nodded
gravely and ordered his security services to guard the Carver family until
it could safely depart. While this was going on, Carver's principal contact
with the insurgents—a lawyer named Hoang Co Thuy—presented himself
at the embassy. Thuy was a paid agent of the CIA working for Carver; if
he were captured, Tuyen would make short work of him. Colby arranged
for Thuy to be sequestered in an Agency safe house, and he was eventually
smuggled out of the country in a large mail sack.[36]

9

FIGHTING A
PEOPLE'S WAR

Bill Colby spent most of his first year in Vietnam putting out fires—
and keeping himself and his family from getting burned. The official
charge to the station was to gather information on everything that happened of any import in South Vietnam, and, if possible, in the Democratic
Republic of Vietnam in the north as well. But Colby's assignment to Vietnam and his quick promotion to station chief indicated that Langley had
another priority—nation-building. Colby's background was not in intelligence per se but in covert operations, and especially in political action, an
area in which he had been spectacularly successful in Italy.

The former Jedburgh spent his first months in-country learning about
Vietnamese society and politics and trying to master the bureaucratic jungle that was the US Mission. By the close of 1960, he had come to the conclusion that the House of Ngo's approach was flawed. Economic and
technical progress in the countryside à la Diem was not enough; Nhu understood the need to win hearts and minds, but he did not seem to know
how to go about it. Colby did not insist on democracy for South Vietnam,
but he did believe the government would have to be responsive to the needs
of the people and foster local empowerment. Specifically, South Vietnam's
villagers would have to be armed and encouraged to defend their communities. In this, Colby believed, was the key not only to rural security but to
nation-building as well. The advent of a new president in the United States
seemed to set the stage for the program that was beginning to take shape
in Colby's mind.

A week before the failed coup attempt, the American people had elected an old friend of Diem's as president of the United States. In a 1956 speech, while he was still a US senator, John F. Kennedy had declared that "Vietnam represents the cornerstone of the Free World in Southeast Asia, the keystone in the arch, the finger in the dike." If the "red tide of communism" should pour over it, he said, much of the rest of Asia would be threatened. Vietnam, he insisted, was "our offspring; we cannot abandon it; we cannot ignore its needs."[1] Although initially he was concerned more with the communist threats in Laos and Cuba, Kennedy as president had no intention of backing down on his pledge. His inaugural address was a call to arms. According to Carl Colby, he and his father listened intently to the radio as the new president called upon the American people to pay any price and bear any burden to defend democracy and freedom at home and abroad. Kennedy and his secretary of defense, Robert McNamara, were determined to combat the forces of international communism on every front. The new administration poured billions of dollars into the US Air Force and its nuclear arsenal and vastly expanded the nation's conventional forces. At the same time, Kennedy and his foreign policy team believed that the real struggle would be in "the countryside of the world," to anticipate Chinese minister of defense Lin Piao's phrase.

The new president had long been concerned about the threat of communist-supported insurgencies and was especially alarmed by a speech Soviet premier Nikita Khrushchev delivered in 1961 entitled, "For New Victories of the World Communist Movement." In it Khrushchev pledged to support "just wars of liberation," making it clear that he believed these conflicts would serve as a prelude to the collapse of the West. Kennedy distributed copies of Khrushchev's speech at the inaugural meeting of his National Security Council and suggested that his colleagues read the writings of Mao Tse-tung and Che Guevara on guerrilla warfare. He had already read them, the president said. "We are opposed around the world by a monolithic and ruthless conspiracy that relies primarily on covert means for expanding its sphere of influence," the new president declared, "on infiltration instead of invasion, on subversion instead of elections, on intimidation instead of free choice, on guerrillas by night instead of armies by day." Following the meeting, Kennedy directed McNamara to develop a counterinsurgency capability. An instrument was already at hand.[2]

The US military had long struggled—and not very successfully—with the concept of unconventional warfare. By its very nature, the US Army was a hide-bound, traditional institution. Instances of organized violence that did not seem to fit under the term "war" were labeled aberrations or quarrels. In conventional conflicts, the role of soldiers, acting as agents of the state, was to apply force and violence—"to kill people and break things," as Thomas K. Adams, a former director of intelligence and special operations at the US Army's Peacekeeping Institute, put it. Wars were to be fought between armies whose goal was to destroy each other. But military scientists seemed to assume that armed conflicts took place in a void. In the years immediately after World War II, OSS veterans, including Colby, began urging the US military to train soldiers to live among and mobilize foreign populations threatened by a common enemy. They argued for the institutionalization of *un*conventional warfare, conflict in "the gray area where violence has entered the practice of politics but the struggle has not yet reached the level of conventional warfare," Adams wrote.[3]

The Truman Doctrine's commitment to aid peoples of the world threatened not only by overt aggression but also by internal subversion provided further impetus to the creation of a corps of unconventional warriors. Ranger companies served in Korea, but they were more shock troops than counterinsurgency operatives. In 1952, the Office of the Chief of Psychological Warfare authorized the creation of a Special Forces Division. An OSS veteran, Colonel Aaron Bank, was recruited to head the 10th Special Forces Group headquartered at Fort Bragg, North Carolina. Unlike main force units, the Special Forces were not concerned primarily with destroying the enemy's army, at least directly, or even with occupying and holding territory. As Adams, who was the SF's principal historian, put it: "Its terrain is symbolic and lies in the minds of the population. . . . In most forms of unconventional warfare the objective is the allegiance of the people around whom, and presumably on whose behalf, the conflict is taking place."[4]

In the spring of 1961, President Kennedy and his brother Robert, who was then serving as US attorney general, paid a visit to Fort Bragg to view the Special Forces soldiers in action. Colonel William Yarborough, the commander of the Special Warfare Center, did not disappoint them. The center put on a show that included hand-to-hand combat, the scaling of an obstacle course, and the use of weapons ranging from bow and arrow to exotic rifles. The finale featured a soldier flying past the grandstand propelled by a futuristic rocket belt.[5] During the Kennedy administration, the Special Forces—more popularly known as the Green Berets—increased from some one thousand personnel to more than twelve thousand. In January 1962, the White House created the 303 Committee Special Group (counterinsurgency) chaired by General Maxwell Taylor and including Robert Kennedy. (The 303 Committee was the successor to Eisenhower's 5412 Committee.) The Taylor committee saw the Special Forces not only as a paramilitary unit capable of sabotage and counterterrorism, but also as a progressive political and social force that would assist local governments in winning the hearts and minds of indigenous peoples—a sort of Peace Corps with guns.

For Colby, the advent of the Kennedy administration—with its obvious awareness of the role that propaganda, political action, counterinsurgency, and covert operations were to play in the Cold War—was like a dream come true. And, in fact, Vietnam was to become the primary laboratory for testing America's new commitment to unconventional warfare. But the CIA and the new administration wanted to do more than just defeat the communist insurgency in South Vietnam; they wanted, initially at least, to take the fight to the enemy.

When Colby arrived in Saigon, he had discovered two locked safes left behind by Lansdale and his team. They contained information on Vietnamese Catholics the French had recruited in 1954 to stay behind and report on doings within the DRV. Then there was some information on the twenty or so spies and saboteurs Lou Conein had recruited during his brief stay in North Vietnam. After 1959, the CIA station in Saigon had come under increasing pressure to provide information on what the communists called the Truong Son Route and the Americans called the Ho Chi Minh Trail. After all, the principal threat to stability in South Vietnam would come from the ninety thousand former Viet Minh who were returning to their home provinces. The NVA went to great lengths to keep the route secret and conceal the identity of the infiltrators, clothing them in peasant garb and equipping them with captured French weapons. Colby had recruited some Europeans and Vietnamese to go to Tchepone, a Laotian town adjacent to the communist transportation network, but they provided little useful information.[6]

The Eisenhower administration had demonstrated a penchant for paramilitary operations, helping to overthrow suspected pro-communist regimes in Guatemala and Iran and then planning the Bay of Pigs operation in Cuba. In late 1960, the National Security Council, with DCI Allen Dulles's enthusiastic concurrence, had directed the Saigon station to accelerate its penetration of North Vietnam and add sabotage and resistance-building to its list of duties. By the end of the year, Colby had nine CIA officers on the project, plus several others acting as liaison with South Vietnamese police and intelligence. Russell Miller was in charge. In Danang, US Navy SEALs (sea-air-land naval commandoes) began training ships' crews to land secret agents in the north; they also organized a civilian raiding force, the Sea Commandos, for hit-and-run coastal attacks.[7]

On March 9, 1961, President Kennedy approved NSAM 52, a National Security Action Memorandum explicitly endorsing covert action against North Vietnam. To come up with specific initiatives, McNamara created a policy review group under Deputy Secretary of Defense Roswell Gilpatric. Allen Dulles recalled Colby from Vietnam to participate in the meetings. "One of the questions came up very soon," Colby recalled: "Why don't we do to them what they do to us, in North Vietnam. And we went back to our World War II experience of dropping people in by parachute." The ensuing report to JFK recommended that measures to be taken "include penetration of the Vietnamese Communist mechanism, dispatch of agents to North Vietnam and strengthening South Vietnamese internal security services."[8]

Kennedy authorized use of American personnel to penetrate North Vietnam—a revival of the World War II Carpetbaggers and Jedburghs—but expressed a preference for Vietnamese and foreign nationals, especially agents of the Chinese Nationalist government. It should be noted that Kennedy's order was accompanied by an intense debate as to the objectives of the penetration effort. To do what the North Vietnamese were doing to South Vietnam meant to subvert and eventually bring down Ho's government. The CIA and State Department argued that a successful armed uprising against the communist regime in Hanoi was highly unlikely. Ho was popular, and a quarter million Chinese troops lurked just over North Vietnam's border. In 1958, the Agency had turned down requests for arms and other supplies from anticommunist guerrillas scattered along North Vietnam's Chinese border and from the king of the Black Thais, who offered to send three thousand French-trained soldiers to fight against the DRV.[9] Langley and Foggy Bottom saw operations in North Vietnam by clandestine operatives as a means to convince the North Vietnamese Politburo that there was more internal opposition in the north than there actually was, and hopefully to compel it to agree to coexistence with South Vietnam. The Kennedy brothers took note of these arguments, but in the spring of 1961, at least, US policy included clandestine efforts to not only harass but also overthrow the communist regime in Hanoi.

One overcast evening in February 1961, a 38-foot fishing junk threaded its way through the towering limestone islands that lay off the coast of North Vietnam. Such vessels—wooden, hand-built, two-masted, with a small rectangular wheelhouse on the aft deck—had sailed the waters of the South China Sea and the Gulf of Tonkin for hundreds of years. This particular junk bore blood-red sails to identify it with the communist Democratic Republic of Vietnam. The captain and crew had selected what was the monsoon season in the north because it reduced the chance of being stopped by a government patrol boat. But it was not Diem's navy they were worried about; it was North Vietnam's. Despite the hue of its sails, the ship had been built in Vung Tau, South Vietnam, some 800 miles to the south. The crew members were North Vietnamese who had fled south in 1954. They had subsequently been recruited to use their knowledge of the North Vietnamese coastline to insert agents capable of gathering intelligence on Ho's Vietnam; the agents would then radio that information to Colby and his subordinates. As the junk neared the seaside village of Cam Pha, a slight, middle-aged man named Pham Chuyen came from below decks and was lowered into the water in a basket boat. It was loaded with a crystal-powered radio and provisions sufficient to support him for several weeks. Chuyen, code-named "Ares," would be the CIA's first long-term North Vietnam–based operative.[10]

Shortly thereafter, Colonel Nguyen Cao Ky, the slender, mustached commander of Tan Son Nhut Air Base, was summoned by the air force chief of staff. "We've been working on new plans with the American CIA to drop specially trained agents into key positions in North Vietnam," he said. "What we need now from you is a highly trained group of flyers to drop the right men at the right spot." The mission would involve flying unmarked, blacked-out C-47s deep into enemy territory at treetop level. The thirty-year-old pilot smiled and replied, "When do we start?" The code name given to the overflight and insertion operation was Project Tiger.[11]

Ky selected twenty of his best pilots for the operation and developed the fundamentals of the project. His C-47s would fly northward and enter the DRV where one of its rivers emptied into the sea. The planes would fly as low as possible and carry two navigators, one to calculate time and distance and the other to maintain visual contact with the ground. The CIA provided Air America (the private airline owned and operated by the CIA) personnel to help train Ky's aviators. The men practiced by flying night missions through tight mountain passes near Dalat. Upon returning from one of these training runs, Ky found a slight, bespectacled American waiting for him. It was Colby. "I remember thinking he looked like a student of philosophy," he wrote in his memoirs. From this point on, the Saigon station chief would personally supervise Project Tiger.[12]

Colby arranged for Ky and his men to move to a detached, guarded villa within the Tan Son Nhut compound to better maintain security. In defiance of protocol, Ky insisted on commanding the inaugural flight himself. "I'm the commander; I'll fly the first mission," Colby recalled him saying. The first team to be dropped, four in number, was code-named Castor. The night before its scheduled flight, Colby, Ky, passengers, and crew gathered at a Chinese restaurant in Danang for dinner. Noting that their number was thirteen, one of the Vietnamese offered to retire, but Ky would have none of it. The next evening they reassembled, with the Vietnamese clad in the pajama-like clothing—cotton died indigo blue—typical of Vietnamese peasants. Each carried $100 in currency and a cyanide pill. While Ky and his team waited on the tarmac with the plane's engines running, Colby and his communications officer tried desperately to secure a final go-ahead from the 303 Committee in Washington. When their "Immediate" cable received no response, they sent a "flash," a cable of the highest priority. Within minutes the go-ahead was received, and Colby gave Ky thumbs up.[13]

To the CIA chief's relief, the first Tiger flight reported in as the C-47 turned inland from the Gulf of Tonkin. All aboard the aircraft were northerners, and it was with some excitement and nostalgia that they flew over their former homes. Ky recalled sighting a battlefield where he had fought the French when he was with the Viet Minh. At approximately 1:30 A.M., Team Castor was parachuted into the mountains west of Hanoi in Son La

Province. The plan was to stay away from the more densely populated areas, at least at first. "I think there was the idea that if you could live in the mountains you'd be safer than if you'd tried to live in a highly controlled structured society," Colby later told one interviewer. "The idea was, I think, to build up a base or bases from which you could then penetrate the lowlands." The C-47's return trip through Laos proved uneventful, and Ky put his wheels down at Tan Son Nhut around 6:00 A.M. To his delight, Colby was there to greet him and his crew with a case of champagne.[14]

Ky was scheduled to pilot the second team, code-named Atlas, but was persuaded by one of his recruits, Lieutenant Phan Thanh Van, to allow him to fly instead. The C-47 carrying Team Atlas was hit by antiaircraft fire crossing into North Vietnam and crash-landed. Three months later, Hanoi held a much publicized trial of the survivors. "Hanoi issued a press release," Colby recalled, "containing confessions by the crew and team that they had been trained by Americans and sent by South Vietnam. No plausible denial there." Things quickly went from bad to worse. Team Castor went off the air and its members were presumed captured. Three more teams—Dido, Echo, and Tarzan—were inserted. After one of the operators included a code word indicating that he had been turned, that is, compelled to become a double agent, Saigon operated under the assumption that all of the teams had been turned and began feeding them false information. Another seven-man team was lost over North Vietnam on May 16, 1962. By the end of 1963, only four teams and one singleton were thought still to be operating inside North Vietnam. The rest of the infiltrators were dead, in prison, or had been doubled. By the time he left South Vietnam in 1962, Colby had become disillusioned. The encrypted code word sent by the radio operator warning that his team had been captured had included more than one message, he subsequently told an interviewer. "The message sent to me," he said, "was that the thing wouldn't work."[15]

Not only was North Vietnam a denied area, but Project Tiger had been penetrated by the communists at the outset. Pham Chuyen—Ares—was either a North Vietnamese agent who had been sent south for the sole purpose of being recruited into the US–South Vietnamese scheme, or he had been captured and turned. He had lured at least one junk to its destruction. Captain Do Van Thien, deputy chief of the South Vietnamese unit cooperating with the CIA on Tiger, was also a North Vietnamese intelligence officer; he fed Hanoi a continuous stream of information on the air and sea insertions. In truth, a number of CIA operations that took place during Colby's tenure as station chief had been compromised. "It is clear . . . operations [under William Colby] were thoroughly penetrated by the Communists from the start," counterintelligence operative Russell Holmes later recalled. "By this, I mean they had penetrated the South Vietnamese and because we were not even looking at them from a CI [counterintelligence] point of view; we inherited their penetration." Holmes did not know the half of it. Tran Kim Tuyen's most trusted deputy at SEPES, South Vietnam's intelligence and internal security apparatus, was the famous North Vietnamese spymaster Pham Xuan An.

In Washington, Colby's nemesis, Jim Angleton, smelled blood. From the beginning, he and his colleagues in counterintelligence had viewed covert operations and nation-building as extraneous to the mission of the CIA. According to Ray Cline, Angleton considered Colby to be "just a paratrooper."[17] The intelligence operation Colby presided over in Vietnam was Swiss cheese, he declared, and he persuaded Allen Dulles to allow him to send a counterintelligence team to investigate and, if possible, clean up the mess. No one was beyond suspicion, even Colby himself. To Angleton's delight, his men uncovered a friendship between the station chief and a French doctor. Vincent Gregoire (a pseudonym, as it turned out) had been or would be recruited by the National Liberation Front and was later caught passing documents to the Russians. Angleton decided not to confront Colby. He would keep that nugget tucked away for later use.

Colby was aware of some communist penetrations and unaware of others. He was vastly annoyed by Angleton's meddling. He did not believe that the kind of counterintelligence security Angleton sought for the United States was possible in South Vietnam. Some Vietnamese nationalists were willing to work with Hanoi, or at least with the NLF. Both communists and anticommunists had once been brothers-in-arms against the French. Family ties were strong, even transcendent. Many members of Diem's government and military had brothers, sisters, uncles, or cousins who served the communists. If the United States was not to supplant the South Vietnamese government with a colonial regime, it would have to work with the existing authorities, penetrated or not.[18] Colby had come to believe that, except for monitoring traffic on the Ho Chi Minh Trail, the spy game—intelligence gathering and analysis—was of secondary importance. The communists made no secret of what they intended to do. The task at hand was to beat them at their own game, to build a nation before the Lao Dong (the Communist Party of North Vietnam) and the NLF could.

Upon his arrival in Saigon, Colby had been struck by the absence of any political or paramilitary initiative on the part of the US Mission. "I had come to Vietnam from Italy," he later recalled, "where, apart from our cooperation with the Italian intelligence services, the CIA had conducted major programs to support the Italian center democratic parties against the Communist effort to subvert Italy through political means." It seemed to him that both the embassy and the Military Assistance and Advisory Group were missing the point. General Samuel Williams and his successors believed that the primary threat came from an invasion by North Vietnam, and so they concentrated on converting the ARVN into a mirror image of the US Army. MAAG did provide some assistance to the Civil Guard, the 68,000-man rural force, but viewed it primarily as static defense to protect lines of communication and supply depots while main force units conducted massive sweeps through the countryside. For his part, Ambassador Elbridge Durbrow believed that stability and security would flow from Western-style democratic reforms and processes. The embassy continued to press Diem to take noncommunist nationalists into his cabinet and to conduct US-style congressional investigations to root out corruption. "More influenced by the growing discussion in those days of doctrines of counterinsurgency, coming from the post-mortems on the French failures in Vietnam and Algeria and the British success in Malaya," Colby wrote in his memoir, "I soon found that I didn't agree with either the military or the diplomats."[19]

Neither did President Kennedy. While still president-elect, Kennedy had dispatched Ed Lansdale, then assigned to the Pentagon as its expert on counterinsurgency, to Vietnam to investigate and report. Colby knew of Lansdale and his work in the Philippines. "Lansdale . . . developed warm and personal relations with Asians and sought to understand their cultures and yearnings and not just the texts of their political and propaganda statements," he later observed. Colby arranged for his section chiefs to brief the man behind Magsaysay and then accompanied him into the field. During the tour, the two compared and contrasted the Philippine experience with

Malaya, Algeria, and Vietnam. Lansdale returned to Washington to report that the situation in the countryside was deteriorating. The communist insurgency was accelerating at an alarming pace. At Lansdale's suggestion, Durbrow was replaced as ambassador by Frederick Nolting, a less assertive Foreign Service Officer who was not likely to insist that American aid be conditioned upon reforms within the Diem regime. Then came NSAM 52 in March 1961, in which Kennedy authorized a "program for covert actions to be carried out by the Central Intelligence Agency which would precede and remain in force after any commitment of US forces to South Vietnam."[20]

"Uniquely in the American bureaucracy, the CIA understood the necessity to combine political, psychological, and paramilitary tools to carry out a strategic concept of pressure on an enemy or to strengthen an incumbent," Colby wrote in his 1989 book *Lost Victory*.[21] Fundamental to his thoughts on nation-building was that there was an essential link between political and paramilitary action. That is, in defending themselves from a communist insurgency or a predatory government, individuals in a community experienced a sense of empowerment and entitlement. In the American and French Revolutions, the armies of the rebellions had become agents of nationalism and nation-building, both symbols of and advocates for new regimes that would be responsive and responsible to the people. Colby remembered the effect that Colonel Chevrier (Adrien Sodoul) had had on villagers in occupied France as his patriotic speeches rallied them to the resistance. The problem was to come up with a model that was appropriate to Vietnam.

Low-intensity conflict had been part of warfare since men had first taken up arms against each other. But following the emergence of nation-states in the thirteenth and fourteenth centuries, individuals or small groups that committed acts of violence against the state were considered bandits or criminals rather than legitimate combatants. Kings commanded their armies in set-piece battles disconnected both strategically and politically from their respective populations. With the coming of the Napoleonic Wars, that began to change. Indeed, the term "guerrilla"—derived from the Spanish term for "small wars"—originated with the Peninsular Campaign of 1808, in which Wellington's sixty-thousand-man army, together with a much smaller Spanish force and Spanish *guerrilleros*, tied down a quarter million French soldiers. More important, Napoleon, building on the experience of the French Revolution and its armies, combined the people, the army, and the government into what Carl von Clausewitz had termed a "remarkable trinity." The true author of "the people's war," however, was Mao Tse-tung. Unlike Napoleon, Mao viewed the populace not as an effective adjunct to war, but the principal weapon. In its simultaneous struggle against the Japanese and the Nationalists, the Communist Party under Mao had focused on building a "unity of spirit" between soldiers and the local populace. "Be neither selfish nor unjust," read the third of Mao's "Three Rules."[22]

There were two ways open to those who would put down revolutions through counterinsurgency—one with many variations, and the other with none. The first was an extension of Antoine-Henri Jomini's nineteenth-century dictum, "Annihilate the enemy's force in the field and you will win the war." The operative word here was "annihilate."[23] Modern sensibilities made such a course much more difficult than in the past, as public outcry in the United States had demonstrated during General Valeriano Weyler's "reconcentration" campaign in the Spanish-American War in 1898 and the subsequent and equally barbaric struggle against guerrilla forces in the Philippine-American War from 1899 to 1902. Nevertheless, such an approach still had its advocates in the 1960s. The other stratagem was to "win the hearts and minds" of the populace in which the rebellion was being fomented, that is, to counter the communist insurgency by doing what the insurgents were doing. In this approach, military action was to be subjugated to political maneuvers. With friendly outside powers advising and supplying it, the anticommunist central government would build trust among the people, if not through democratic reforms, then through responsive and responsible government.

By 1961, a kind of counterinsurgency think tank had emerged in Saigon. There was Colby with his OSS experiences, Lansdale in and out of country, and Colonel Francis Philip "Ted" Serong, the Australian counterinsurgency expert retained by the Diem regime as a temporary adviser. In September 1961, Sir Robert Thompson, the United Kingdom's best-known counterinsurgency expert, was appointed head of the British Advisory Mission in Vietnam. Each of these individuals had read Clausewitz, Jomini, Mao, Sun Tzu, and Che Guevera. Each had as great an understanding of unconventional warfare as anyone in the West at that time. Each was aware of the dictums of insurgency and counterinsurgency. The task at hand was to adapt and apply them to Vietnam, with its religious diversity, ethnic minorities, colonial heritage, and strategic realities. Colby and his colleagues set about learning all they could about Vietnam, Laos, and Cambodia and then coming up with a plan.

Colby was particularly influenced by the experiences of Marshal Louis Hubert Gonzalve Lyautey, who had served as French resident general in Morocco from 1912 to 1925. His principal task, he knew, was to put down an anticolonial insurgency, which he proceeded to do by means of "peaceful penetration" and the "oil-spot theory," or, in French, the *tache d'huile*. This was Lyautey's term for his method of influencing a region, named after the way an oil spot slowly spreads out on a dry surface. Military force was secondary in Lyautey's scheme, used primarily to intimidate the enemy by its presence. By working through existing authorities and structures and demonstrating respect for Islam and Moroccan culture, the resident general, who had also been a member of the French Academy, succeeded in decreasing anti-French feeling and deflating the nationalist insurgency. The idea was to work in the safest areas first, winning hearts and minds through projects of economic development, education, and public health. Gradually, these loyal, secure areas would spread and link up until eventually the entire country was pacified. Lyautey actually strengthened the authority of the sultan. Not only was the armed uprising defeated, but Lyautey's reforms contributed to the emergence of modern Morocco. One of France's most respected military intellectuals, Lyautey had been a contemporary influence on T. E. Lawrence. Colby applauded Lyautey for recognizing that the employment of a massive conventional force in guerrilla warfare was counterproductive. "My line has always been that you could conduct a strategic offensive through defensive tactics," he would later say.[24]

Colby believed that Robert Thompson, probably the dominant counterinsurgency voice in South Vietnam in the early 1960s, could have profited from a closer study of Lyautey. An advocate of "clear and hold," Thompson, like Lansdale, gave great weight to physically separating the peasantry from communist insurgents. Small and medium-sized indigenous forces trained by Western military advisers would expel guerrillas from a discrete area and then establish and maintain a defensive perimeter. Colby had familiarized himself with the British counterinsurgency experience, especially in Malay, even before Thompson's arrival. "I had studied enough of the Malayan Emergency to have gained great respect for the priority the British had given there to the local-level struggle, in which they used only 80,000 troops and 60,000 police but some 400,000 home guard," he wrote in *Honorable Men*. Like other British colonial officials, Thompson gave great weight to the training and deployment of local police forces. With this, Colby the lawyer also agreed. Freedom from crime and arbitrary justice—a mechanism to settle disputes fairly—was crucial to pacification. Thompson and the British sought to impose firm but fair discipline on the villagers as they cut them off from the insurgency. But Malaya was different from Vietnam. It was ethnic Chinese who launched the Malay Communist Party in the early 1930s, and the Chinese who dominated it. The Malays were never really interested in communism and tended to remain loyal to the British. What was missing with Thompson's approach, Colby believed, was a political or ideological dimension. In his discussions with Nhu, Colby emphasized that the peasantry must be motivated rather than simply directed to organize self-defense forces. They had to feel truly empowered and look upon the national government as a source of that empowerment. "[In Vietnam] we had to enlist the active participation of the community in a program to improve its security and welfare on the local level," Colby observed, "building cohesion from the bottom up rather than imposing it from the top down."[25]

As CIA station chief, Colby's two most important counterinsurgency assets were a Political Action Section and a Military Action Section, the latter headed by Colonel Gilbert "Chink" Layton. Layton, who arrived in Saigon in 1959, was one of Colby's favorites. Part Native American, Layton had grown up in Iowa, raised by his grandmother. He was an excellent athlete and a fine student with a passion for history. Because of his high cheekbones and narrow eyes, his fellow high-school students had nicknamed him Chink. Layton had served with distinction in Patton's Third Army, participating in the relief of Bastogne, Belgium, during the Battle of the Bulge. He joined the Agency in 1950, serving first in West Germany, and was then in the Pacific on the island of Saipan. There he trained Chinese Nationalists and South Koreans in the art of guerrilla warfare. A stickler for detail, Layton constructed entire villages for liberation or capture and taught his charges the fundamentals of small-unit tactics.[26]

While Colby was deputy chief of station from 1959 to 1960, Layton's principal duty was to advise and train the commando teams of South Vietnam's 1st Observation Group. The outfit was part of the South Vietnamese Special Forces, which were commanded by Colonel Le Quang Tung; its assignment was to cross into Laos and Cambodia and stage hit-and-run attacks against the Ho Chi Minh Trail then being built. During these early years, the 1st Observation Group was the CIA's most important source of information on the burgeoning network of paths and roads that the North Vietnamese Army was expanding and improving. He also helped train the singletons and teams that Russ Miller was inserting into North Vietnam. "You would have a field day if you were here," Layton wrote a friend. "It's just like War Planning! You write a plan, go find some people, train 'em, equip 'em, deploy 'em, fight 'em, rescue 'em, furlough 'em, catch 'em, make another plan and start all over again."[27]

In 1960, Layton and Miller, who were nominally assigned to MAAG, established the Combined Studies Division as a front for their clandestine activities. After Colby became station chief, he called in Layton and told him, "Gil, there's something going on out there; find out what it is and see what we can do about it." By "something going on," Colby meant the growing insurgency, and by "out there," he meant the Central Highlands and the lower delta, both of which the South Vietnamese government had virtually abandoned. During his subsequent gamboling in the Highlands, Layton ran into an International Volunteer Services (IVS) worker named David Nuttle who was living among one of the Montagnard tribes, the Rhade. It would prove to be an auspicious encounter.[28]

IVS was part of the "Tom Dooley phenomenon" that swept the United States during the 1950s and early 1960s. Thomas Anthony Dooley III was the idealistic (some said self-seeking) US Navy doctor who became a celebrity in Vietnam and in the United States when, in 1954, as part of Operation Passage to Freedom, in which the navy transported more than 300,000 Vietnamese from North Vietnam to South Vietnam following the partition of the country, he risked his life treating refugees with type IV malaria and other serious diseases. Dooley subsequently appeared on the popular television show *This Is Your Life* and wrote a bestselling book about his experiences. Inspired in part by Dooley, Nuttle arranged for and passed a telephone interview, and IVS sent him a one-way ticket to Saigon. The young midwesterner wound up in Darlac Province in the Central Highlands, where he introduced new seed strains and programs focusing on irrigation, animal husbandry, and the use of simple farm machinery. His hosts were the Rhade, the largest of numerous aboriginal tribes living in the Highlands. Within a year, the Rhade, concentrated around the provincial capital of Ban Me Thuot, had accepted Nuttle as a friend.[29]

At the time of his arrival, the insurgency was heating up in the Highlands. The Viet Cong were quick to recognize that the persecution of minorities by the Diem regime and its efforts to settle Catholic refugees and Vietnamese lowlanders in the Rhade's midst made them ripe for recruiting. Nuttle traveled about the countryside on a BMW motorcycle that had been muffled. "If you kept at about seventy miles an hour," he recalled, "you could run right through an ambush."[30]

An incident in early 1960 demonstrated the heavy price to be paid for the continuing divide between the indigenous people of the Central Highlands and the government of South Vietnam. Nuttle learned that a team of officials was coming out to inspect an agricultural project in a village some miles from Ban Me Thuot. A friend, Y-Cha, warned the American that the group would be ambushed by the local Viet Cong. The IVS worker tried to warn the province chief—an ethnic Vietnamese—that the site was remote and the danger great. The chief responded by adding more security guards. Nuttle wisely contrived an excuse not to go. In the midst of its journey, the Vietnamese officials and their guards were indeed ambushed. The Viet Cong felled two large trees at either end of the column. Guerrillas popped out of spider holes on one side of the group, peppering it with fire. The officials and their guards exited their vehicles on the other side only to be greeted by fire from another row of spider holes. Thirty-six of the thirty-seven-man party died, with one spared to tell the tale.[31]

It was at this point that Gil Layton appeared on the scene. After encountering Nuttle during a tour of the Highlands, he asked the IVS worker to visit whenever he was in Saigon. He did, and the two men struck up an ongoing conversation about the situation of the Rhade.[32] The animosity between the ethnic Vietnamese and the people of the Highlands, whom the Vietnamese referred to as *moi* (savages), was so great that it was unlikely the tribe, or other Montagnards of the region, would ever take up arms against the communists on behalf of the government in Saigon. The two men agreed, however, that the aboriginals would fight to defend their homes and families. The tribesmen were fiercely independent, and, after all, the Viet Cong themselves were mostly ethnic Vietnamese. Nuttle recalled that the French had singled out the Montagnard tribes for special attention, providing them with health care, education, and farming equipment. The Highlanders had responded positively, and during the First Indochinese War had acted as a counterweight to the Viet Minh. One thing was certain: the Rhade and the other tribes were going to be crushed between the ARVN and the Viet Cong if they did not have some means to defend themselves.

On May 5, 1961, Layton sent a memo to Colby requesting that he approve a program to recruit as many as a thousand tribesmen to "operate in the guerrilla-infested areas bordering on northern Cambodia and southern Laos." Layton introduced Nuttle to Colby, and one discussion led to another. The Montagnards seemed the perfect guinea pigs to try out Lyautey's, Thompson's, and Serong's ideas, not to mention Colby's own. "We . . . decided that we should start small and make the case for a program by a successful experiment, rather than try to sell a massive panacea and arouse all possible objections before we had any experience with the idea," Colby later wrote.[33]

The first task was to sell Nhu on the concept, and Colby reserved that job for himself. In truth, Colby had been trying to point Nhu toward his particular vision of counterinsurgency and pacification since their first meeting in 1959. The station chief was careful to express sympathy with the counselor's criticism of his brother's essentially military and developmental approach. Both men agreed on the necessity of building political support for the regime among Vietnam's vast peasantry. Diem and Nhu both realized that these efforts could backfire, fostering antigovernment insurgencies among noncommunist peasant communities. Nowhere was this irony more likely than among the Montagnards. Colby would recruit some trustworthy Vietnamese to monitor the program; this, together with the promise that Vietnamese Special Forces would be designated to train the Montagnard self-defense forces, did the trick.[34]

Next, Colby and Layton had to persuade the larger US Mission, especially the Military Assistance and Advisory Group, to embrace the idea of a Montagnard self-defense force. The former Jedburgh was all too aware that the regular military had historically taken a dim view of unconventional warfare. The Joint Chiefs had approved the creation of Special Forces in the army and air force and the US Navy SEALs, but only very reluctantly. The brass believed that violence was violence and on any scale could be handled by conventional military. MAAG also suspected that the unconventional forces would drain off the best and the brightest from regular units. Political action was completely beyond the pale for the US military in the early 1960s. Civil action companies in the army were in their infancy and tended to be dumping grounds for the inept and incompetent. General Williams and his replacement, General Lionel C. McGarr, believed that the conflict in Vietnam was military in nature and that they were there to provide a military solution. The issue of a viable, responsible political culture was of purely secondary importance. More significant, as a result of events halfway around the world, covert operations and the CIA had suddenly fallen out of favor with the Kennedy administration and the American people.

In the spring of 1960, the Eisenhower administration approved a plan to bring down the Cuban regime of Fidel Castro, a plan to which President Kennedy subsequently gave the go-ahead despite deep divisions among his advisers.[35] Early on the morning of April 17, 1961, the Cuban Exile Brigade, comprising some 1,450 anti-Castro fighters who had been trained in Guatemala by the CIA, landed at the Bay of Pigs on the southern tip of Cuba. The invaders established two of three beachheads, fought well, and inflicted substantial casualties on Castro's forces, which soon numbered more than 20,000. But the exiles soon ran out of ammunition. A tiny rebel air force, flying outdated B-26s, had failed to destroy Castro's planes in an April 15 attack; as a result, Cuba's defenders enjoyed air superiority. Cuban planes sank an exile freighter loaded with ammunition and communications equipment. The anti-Castro forces and their CIA handlers pleaded for US military intervention, but President Kennedy refused. On the second day of the operation, with ammunition running out and casualties mounting, the exiles surrendered.

For Jack Kennedy, who publicly accepted responsibility for the Cuban fiasco, the whole affair was a humiliation. "We looked like fools to our friends, rascals to our enemies, and incompetents to the rest," declared the *New York Times*. The White House blamed the CIA: indeed, Kennedy was so angry that he considered dismantling the Agency on the spot— "to scatter CIA to the winds," as he put it. Instead, he appointed Maxwell Taylor to head a committee charged with rooting out the causes for the Bay of Pigs disaster and notified Allen Dulles that he would be retired from public service after a respectable interlude. From April 1961 on,

Colby and his team would have to operate under the shadow of the failed Cuban operation.[36]

The second week in May, David Nuttle received an urgent message from IVS headquarters: Ambassador Nolting wanted to see him in his office the following day. The aid worker jumped on his motorbike and set off on the "Frontier Highway," the main north-south route connecting Saigon to the Central Highlands. "I arrived in Saigon about an hour after dark," Nuttle wrote in his unpublished memoir, "having flipped over after hitting a big wild hog that ran out of the jungle into my path."[37] Nuttle showered and dropped by the Layton villa to see Bonnie Layton, Gil's daughter. The elder Layton intercepted him at the door. "Listen," he said, "all I want to do is make sure that you got the message about your meeting with the Ambassador."

"How do you know about that?" Nuttle asked.

"I have my sources," was Layton's terse reply.

As it turned out, Colby and Layton had arranged a meeting of the US Mission to discuss the situation in the Highlands with Nuttle present.

At 2:00 the next afternoon, Nuttle walked through the front door of the US embassy and was directed to the ambassador's conference room. As he waited at the long mahogany table, others began to file in: General Lionel C. McGarr, head of the US military mission, and his deputy; USAID director Arthur Gardiner; Colby; Vietnam expert Douglas Pike; and then the ambassador himself. MAAG presented its solution to the threat of a communist takeover in the Highlands. Essentially, McGarr supported the Diem regime's plan to concentrate the tribal population in secured reservations while the ARVN conducted massive sweeps to root out and kill the Viet Cong. It was a makeover of the reconcentration tactic the Spanish had used in Cuba from 1895 through 1898 and that was adopted by US forces in their war against Philippine insurgents—in both cases with disastrous results.

When McGarr finished stating his view, Nolting asked Nuttle to respond. "I ripped into the 'reservation plan' by focusing on all the obvious negatives," Nuttle recalled. The Montagnards would resist being relocated. It would be impossible to keep them from slipping away at night into the dense jungle, which was honeycombed with hunting trails. Once there, they would become fodder for the Viet Cong. With McGarr clearly irritated,

Colby interceded, asking Nuttle whether there was an alternative. There was, Nuttle said: "Mr. Colby, if the GVN [government of South Vietnam] will begin to bring the Montagnard into the social and economic mainstream, there will be some motivational basis for a security program." The Diem government could make a good beginning by stopping the bombing of aboriginal villages. If arms were provided to the Highlanders, and they were allowed to defend themselves, there was a chance that further communist inroads could be stopped.[38]

Nuttle had played the role that Colby, Layton, and Nolting had hoped he would. By this point Nolting and Colby had bonded. "Colby became not only a friend," Nolting later recalled, "but one of my most trusted advisers." When it became clear that Colby had cleared away any objection the House of Ngo might have, Nolting, with the approval of the 303 Committee, gave the go-ahead for a small, experimental counterinsurgency/ pacification program focused on the Rhade.[39]

In 1962, the Rhade numbered between 100,000 and 115,000. Residents of the high plateau that formed the heart of the Central Highlands, the tribe had migrated southwestward from China and Mongolia centuries earlier, dependent on slash-and-burn agriculture for its subsistence. The Rhade had a matrilineal society with the eldest woman in the family owning the house, property, and livestock. Members of an extended family resided in a bamboo longhouse sometimes reaching 400 feet in length. Male and female roles were traditional, with the males hunting, clearing the land, building the houses, burying the dead, conducting business, and preparing the rice wine. The women drew water, collected firewood, cooked, cleaned, washed the clothes, and wove the traditional red, black, yellow, and blue cotton cloth of the Rhade. The average Rhade male was about five feet five inches tall, with a brown complexion and broad shoulders. Healing was the responsibility of shamans or witch-doctors. The religion was animist, but included a god (Ae Die) and a devil (Tang Lie).

Nuttle signed on as a contract agent with the CIA on October 4, 1961. His assignment was to survey the tribes around Ban Me Thuot and identify those willing to participate in a self-defense and development program. Colby arranged for a Special Forces medic, Sergeant Paul Campbell, to assist Nuttle. Accompanied by a Captain Phu from Thuy's Presidential Survey Office (PSO, the South Vietnamese government's version of the CIA) and Nuttle's man Friday, Y-Rit, the team set up shop in Ban Me Thuot. Nuttle recalled that before departing for the bush, they took stock: Rhade villages were being attacked by the ARVN and bombed by the Vietnamese Air Force when they were suspected of supporting the Viet Cong. For their part, the communists were using terrorism to extort rice, livestock, and manpower from the Rhade villages. Native lands had been taken without compensation by the government in Saigon for resettlement of refugees from North Vietnam.[40]

The team found tribal elders initially suspicious and reluctant to cooperate, but "Mr. Dave" and "Dr. Paul" persisted, with Campbell conducting sick call at each village and Nuttle sounding out the leadership about a possible cooperative effort. The tribesmen hated the South Vietnamese government, but they were afraid of the Viet Cong. In one village, insurgents had captured the sister of a Rhade who had been working with the IVS; they took her into the village and eviscerated her, "filling the cavity with odds and ends[,] and gave propaganda lectures to the assembled observers while the girl was engaged in dying," according to a CIA report.[41] Eventually, Colby and his colleagues settled on the village of Buon Enao, only 6 miles from the provincial capital of Ban Me Thuot, for their first operation. During October, the team visited Buon Enao every day for three weeks. Its proposals were minimal: a perimeter fence for defense and a dispensary.

Layton and Colby made frequent visits to the site, and the team grew to include more Agency personnel, USAID workers, and the first Special Forces A-Team under Captain Lawrence Arritola. Everything was subject to extended debate: the Rhade said the fence would provoke the ARVN; the Americans promised they would secure a letter of approval from the province chief; the Rhade said the fence would elicit a Viet Cong assault; the Americans said they would arm the Rhade and teach them to shoot; the Rhade said they had no bamboo for the fence; the Americans replied that they would go into the jungle and cut it for them. Gradually, the elders' resistance began to melt. In a Hollywood touch, Campbell, working in conjunction with the village shaman, was able to cure the village chief's daughter of a serious illness.[42]

In early November, work on the defensive perimeter began, with some 50 residents of Buon Enao and another 125 people from surrounding villages performing the labor at 35 piasters (50 cents) a day. When building materials ran low, Campbell led nocturnal expeditions to steal what was needed. The scavengers commandeered sand from a Vietnamese landowner's riverbed and crushed rock from a highway construction project. Vietnamese who had been resettled in the area would cut bamboo by day, and Campbell would confiscate it by night. The Rhade were delighted. And indeed, the scavenging raids were more about demonstrating that the Americans were not dupes of the government than about any real logistical necessity.[43]

Although work on Buon Enao's defensive perimeter and dispensary was completed in early December, there was nothing to defend the perimeter with. Layton and Colby arranged a quick visit from some of Thuy's people at the Presidential Survey Office. They certified that the Rhade had lived up to their end of the bargain: the village chief had arranged for signs on the fence declaring the Viet Cong persona non grata and had personally vouched for each of his people. PSO authorized the arming of thirty of Buon Enao's residents. Layton requisitioned the necessary number of carbines from MAAG, and the Special Forces began training. By this time Colby had come up with a name for the Buon Enao experiment—Civilian Irregular Defense Groups (CIDGs)—descriptive and nondescript at the same time.

Military action was to be purely defensive. Buon Enao and villages that were subsequently brought into the program were connected by radio. Platoon-sized strike forces conducted long-range patrols and were on call to come to the aid of a village under attack. The patrols were scouting enterprises to gather intelligence on the whereabouts of marauding Viet Cong. By July 1962, the strike force at Buon Enao had about 650 armed and trained men deployed in support of 3,600 unpaid village defenders; Layton's people were recruiting among the Jarai, Sedang, and Bahnar in the neighboring provinces of Kontum and Pleiku.[44]

As the CIDGs evolved, Combined Studies and Special Forces personnel became deeply involved in health and economic development projects. By July 1962, Campbell and his cohorts had set up dispensaries in eighty-eight Rhade villages around Ban Me Thuot. Widespread application of the insecticide DDT began to bring malaria under control. The Americans wanted desperately to improve living standards among the Highlanders, but other than paying the construction workers and members of the strike force, there was no way to directly introduce money into the economy. Recognizing the dangers posed by the nonmilitary side of the CIDG project, the Viet Cong began targeting health workers and those who aided them. In two cases, they executed villagers, one an old man and the other a small boy, for warning Layton's people of an impending ambush.[45]

As the number of fortified villages and strike forces multiplied, the Viet Cong stepped up their campaign of terrorism. The communists decided to make an example of one particularly effective strike-team commander. An informant came into the captain's village and told him that the Viet Cong were setting up an ambush some kilometers into the jungle. That evening the officer took his platoon out to investigate. While he and his men were absent, a Viet Cong squad entered the village and ordered the people to assemble. They dragged the strike-force commander's wife and infant son out of their hut, decapitated the woman, placed her head on a stake, and then bayoneted the baby. These were the fruits of cooperating with the South Vietnamese government, the Viet Cong cadre declared.[46]

The more engagements the Rhade irregulars fought, however, the more confident they became. In 1960, Buon Enao defenders alone killed more than 200 Viet Cong and captured another 460. During CIDG's heyday—from 1960 through 1962—the US Air Force established an operation entitled "Farmgate" to provide tactical air support for ground operations. Flying prop-driven trainers and substituting cowboy boots for combat footgear, Farmgate pilots provided close support to Rhade villages under attack. Indeed, for several months, Farmgate acted as the unofficial air force of the CIDGs.[47]

There was no political or ideological dimension to the Civilian Irregular Defense Group program, at least in the form of propaganda or organization. Colby recognized that in the act of self-defense, the Montagnards would experience a sense of empowerment, but beyond that, it was the medical care, new clothing, improved agriculture, and animal husbandry that would gain and hold the Highlanders' loyalty. In truth, as between the Montagnards and the ethnic Vietnamese, all one could really hope for was peaceful coexistence. And as with the CIA station's other operations, there was little or no security or counterintelligence. "In my shop, and most of the Agency shops," Layton said, "you assumed [your South Vietnamese counterparts] were penetrated. . . . When I started recruiting all these people, somebody said, aren't you afraid there might be some Viet Cong in there[?] . . . I said, we figure on about ten percent but then we outnumber them nine to one." Colby and Layton insisted that information be shared on a strictly need-to-know basis and limited to the mission at hand.[48]

In December 1961, Colby had persuaded Nhu to pay a visit to Buon Enao. So impressed was he, that he not only okayed expanding the project to other tribes in the Highlands but also approved it for the lower Mekong Delta. The problem that had plagued the Agroville program—namely, the remote and dispersed nature of the rural population living amidst a maze of canals and dikes—still remained. Colby and Layton had enjoyed some success in the delta, but the South Vietnamese government had so neglected the Buddhist and Confucian Vietnamese of the coastal lowlands and the delta that Colby and Layton felt they had even less traction with them than they did with the Montagnards. Nevertheless, the threat of a communist takeover in the south was great and had to be addressed. The Viet Cong had turned the Agroville program against the government, and CIA intelligence reports indicated that the communists regarded the Ca Mau peninsula as one of its strongholds. Indeed, the U-Minh Forest would subsequently become home to PAVN's famous U-Minh Battalion. During the 1950s, the station had cooperated with Diem's intelligence apparatus in creating stay-behind nets in the south composed of indigenous Catholics and Vietnamese who had fled from the north in 1954. In 1961, Colby decided to try to create an archipelago of anticommunist islands—starting with the Catholic villages—in the Mekong.

The principal locus of what the CIA termed "the clerical paramilitary program" was a network headed by Father Nguyen Loc Hoa. In truth, Father Hoa was Chinese and had only adopted a Vietnamese name in 1951 when he led his flock of three hundred from southern China through northern Vietnam and Cambodia and all the way to the Ca Mau peninsula. Neither the French nor the South Vietnamese government dared venture south of Ca Mau city, and in 1959 Diem created a special district there, called Hai Yen, for Hao and his parishioners. From this stronghold, Father Hoa was able to contend with the communists for control of an area stretching from the ninth parallel to the tip of the peninsula. In 1960, the Viet Cong launched a frontal assault on Father Hoa's headquarters, but were repulsed with a loss of 174 men.

Father Hoa—Colby referred to him as the "dynamic Pastor from the North"—became a frequent visitor to Layton's house in Saigon. "At dinner at our house, he didn't dress as a priest," Dora Layton, Gil's wife, re-called. In 1961, Colby and Layton dubbed Father Hoa's army the Sea Swallows. In early January 1962, Layton and Colby coordinated a Seabee (US Navy Construction Battalion) effort to construct a landing strip near Father Hoa's headquarters, and weapons, uniforms, medicine, and other supplies began flowing in. Shortly thereafter, Father Hoa began recruiting ethnic Chinese from Cholon. By the fall of 1962, ten Special Forces A-Teams were working in the lower delta, and by the end of the year more than 4,500 armed and trained Catholic youth had joined the "Fighting Fathers."[49]

By mid-1962, Gil Layton, loosely supervised by Bill Colby, found himself in command of a clandestine paramilitary force numbering more than 36,000, trained and reinforced by three dozen Special Forces A-Teams. "Gil ran the war by night from our compound in Saigon," Dora Layton recalled. The Layton's house was a spacious, two-story white stucco of French colonial design. It featured a roof garden and a high cement-and-steel picket fence surrounding a small yard. Large iron gates could close the driveway and seal the compound in case of a security threat. And security threats there were. In January 1963, Dora Layton wrote a friend in the States: "They came yesterday to measure for barbed wire all around the place. We have our guns freshly cleaned and loaded in our room, and a whole arsenal in our bathroom." Just outside the main living quarters, within the walled villa, was a communications shack with a Vietnamese radio operator on duty twenty-four hours a day. From that vantage point Gil Layton could direct strike forces and call in air support for operations all across the country.[50]

In comparison to the Laytons, the Colbys lived a rather humdrum existence. Colleagues remembered Bill attending Mass regularly, sometimes at the cathedral and sometimes at a Benedictine chapel in Cholon. He left childrearing to Barbara and the Catholic Church. Each morning, a van would pick up Carl and his brother Paul and take them to school. Carl recalled that he and his friends had the run of the city when they were not in class. "I would sometimes sleep over at my friend Billy Shepherd's house (his father worked for the United States Information Service) for two days in a row. My parents would not know where I was." In the evenings, Bill

and Barbara would often give the kids a kiss and leave for one of their continuous rounds of parties. Carl and his friends would then call a cab to
drive them to Cholon. He was eleven.[51]

In August 1960, when he was fourteen, John was shipped off to the
States to attend Portsmouth Priory, a Catholic boarding school in Rhode
Island. Barbara put him on a plane in Saigon, and Elbridge picked him up
at the airport in Washington, where the young man, already intensely
homesick, spent time with his grandparents until school opened. On the
day the term was to begin, Elbridge drove John to the Benedictine school
his parents had picked out for him. The brother in charge told Elbridge
that Hurricane Dora had torn the roofs off of several buildings; the opening
of school would have to be delayed. John recalled Elbridge's retort: "Well,
I've done my duty; his father instructed me to deposit him and here he is."
He then got in the car and drove off.

By the next spring, John was depressed and getting fatter by the day. He
would call Elbridge and Margaret collect; sometimes his grandfather
wouldn't accept the charges. When Bill returned to Washington that fall
to testify before the Senate Foreign Relations Committee, John flew to
Washington to meet him. Following a pleasant weekend, John boarded his
plane for the return trip. When it landed, and the youngster saw the school
bus waiting for him, something snapped. He told the flight attendants he
was sick and wanted to go back to Washington. As that happened to be
the aircraft's return destination, he was allowed to stay on board. From
the terminal, John called Bill to come and get him. Father and son argued
until three in the morning in the basement of Elbridge and Margaret's
house. John was homesick, lonely, disgusted with Elbridge, and tired of
the harsh New England climate. Boarding school was his duty, Bill replied;
he needed to buck up and be somebody. John implied that, like Elbridge,
his father was hard-hearted and self-absorbed and did not care about his
family. The message had the desired effect. Angry though he was, Bill
agreed that if John would finish the term in Rhode Island, he could then
move to Florida, where his maternal grandparents lived, and go to school
there.[52]

The Civilian Irregular Defense Groups in the Central Highlands and Father Hoa's Catholic Youth in the Ca Mau peninsula were promising starts
in the emerging counterinsurgency/pacification initiative envisioned by Bill

Colby and his colleagues, but they did not address the political core of Vietnam—the Buddhist-Confucian majority. At one point, Nhu pleaded with Colby to provide a step-by-step plan to build a stable democracy in Vietnam; the trouble was, he said, that the communists had a plan, and the "Free World" did not. A charismatic strongman like his brother would serve only as a temporary stopgap. The West expected underdeveloped countries to move from colonialism to democracy in one step, he complained.[53]

Nhu and Diem, it will be recalled, had very different ideas about how best to mobilize the Vietnamese-Buddhist peasantry, with Nhu committed to an essentially political stratagem and Diem to an economic-military one. Colby, of course, discreetly sided with Nhu. In October 1961, the counselor to the president convened a meeting of province chiefs and informed them that he wanted to launch a "social revolution . . . in which a new hierarchy should be established, not based on wealth or position." The most important people in a village would be the model anticommunist fighters. The losers, he said, would be the "notables and gentry," many of whom had been "lackeys of the imperialists and colonialists."[54]

Shortly thereafter, Colby persuaded Nhu to try going national with the CIDG model, adding a political component. The counselor was receptive, but his brother was not. Diem's prime minister, Tran Van Huong, told Colby that weapons delivered to villagers could easily find their way into the hands of the Viet Cong. Colby replied that arms were not the primary issue; the real enemy was communist propaganda and political action. Huong did not say so, but what he and Diem were really afraid of was that weapons furnished to peasant groups could be used to fuel a noncommunist uprising against the regime.[55]

In late 1961, the South Vietnamese president decided to hire his own counterinsurgency expert—Sir Robert Thompson. As usual, Colby adapted to the situation. As plans for what became known as the Strategic Hamlet Program evolved, it became clear that the main difference between Nhu and Colby, on the one hand, and Diem and Thompson, on the other, was that the American wanted development and political indoctrination—"winning hearts and minds"—to come first, and physical security to follow. Thompson, whom Nhu regarded as nothing more than a colonial administrator, favored fences, moats, guard towers, self-defense forces, and police first, and political and economic development second. Colby and Nhu eventually conceded the point, and the Strategic Hamlet Program was born. In February 1962, Diem announced an interministerial committee to manage it and named Nhu its chairman.[56]

Colby got behind the Strategic Hamlet Program with a vengeance. In theory, it had everything—local self-defense, economic development, health care, and education—all leading to a sense of empowerment. It had been child's play, Colby wrote, for a few armed communist cadres to enter a village at night, terrorize and propagandize the population, recruit soldiers, and impose taxes. Not so anymore. There were failures, fraud, and fakeries, he admitted, but the program marked the beginning of the first nationwide response to the Viet Cong. And, by Hanoi's own later admission, the sheer volume of the military and economic activity of the program eliminated the Viet Cong presence from hundreds of villages, even in those where the local populace was hostile to the South Vietnamese government.[57]

On the whole, however, the Strategic Hamlet operation was a failure, and, like the Agroville initiative, largely counterproductive. At Nhu's insistence, arms were not given to village defense forces, but merely "loaned" for a period of six months. The provincial leadership, itself rich and well-educated, was supposed to support a new system that accorded no special status to wealth, social position, or education. That did not happen. There was no meaningful land reform. The assumption that the South Vietnamese peasantry was either anticommunist or neutral was erroneous. In some villages, there were families that had supported the Viet Minh and its successors for three generations. Finally, the man Nhu relied on to implement the program was Colonel Pham Ngoc Thao, a Catholic and a favorite of the Ngo family. He was also a communist agent. Thao used his position to see that as many strategic hamlets were built in communist strongholds as possible, thus exposing the settlements to maximum external attack and internal subversion.[58]

Colby later recalled his first meeting with Thao:

> I arose at 4:00 A.M. one morning to meet National Assemblywoman Pauline Nguyen Van Tho, a graduate of Bowdoin College in Maine, and drive south with her to her constituency in Kien Hoa province, historically a redoubt of the Communists in the war against the French and once again beginning to stir with revolutionary fever. We were met there by the new province chief, Colonel Pham Ngoc Thao, who combined strong Catholic credentials with an active role in the

Viet Minh rebellion against the French. . . . After describing the benefits of concentrated economic and social development programs in building up the villages, and then providing these viable communities with local security forces, he took us on a tour by motorboat. We went through the canals to an arm of the Mekong, meandering through the delta on its way to the sea, and stopped at a small village. The inhabitants greeted Colonel Thao as a frequent visitor, and I was further impressed by the fact that he needed no guards for himself or his Saigon visitors.[59]

During his first two years as station chief, Colby had made a significant start toward his goal of seeing South Vietnam and the United States partner in an effort to win the support of the rural population. The CIA's efforts—the CIDGs, the Fighting Fathers, and so on—were small and sporadic, and the Saigon government's nationwide effort—the Strategic Hamlet Program—ended up with more failures than successes; but at least there were signs that some in authority were beginning to recognize that the conflict in South Vietnam was a "people's war" rather than a conventional conflict. The events of 1962 and 1963 would conspire to sidetrack the pacification/counterinsurgency train with—to Colby's mind at least—near disastrous results.

THE MILITARY ASCENDANT

B ill Colby had a love-hate relationship with the military. He was a warrior and had immense respect for soldiers, but he did not trust the military as an institution. Though it was free of corruption, and for the most part apolitical, the US military was hidebound and inflexible. As an institution, it lacked agility, the ability to adapt to changing circumstances. And if there was ever a time and a place for pragmatism and imagination, it was the Cold War in the developing world. The Vietnamese military suffered from the same rigidities, but it was also in many places and at many levels incompetent and corrupt. One of the reasons Colby continued to support the House of Ngo was that it transcended the Army of the Republic of Vietnam. But then, in 1962–1963, to Colby's great dismay, and to the detriment of the counterinsurgency/pacification effort, the military captured the flag in both Washington and Saigon.

Early on the morning of February 15, 1962, the residents of Saigon were again awakened by the thud of bombs and the rattle of machine-gun fire. Stanley Karnow, an American journalist, recalled the scene: "Rushing to my hotel room window, I peered across the city to see smoke billowing above the presidential palace, nine or ten blocks away. I pulled on my clothes, ran downstairs, and sprinted up Tu Do . . . to the Boulevard Norodom, a handsome avenue that opened onto the palace, an imposing structure that dated back to French colonial days. It was now a flaming shambles. Overhead, beneath a low cloud cover, two fighter aircraft were circling in an almost leisurely racetrack pattern."[1]

Bill Colby was preparing to head for the office when he heard the roar of aircraft overhead, followed by explosions at the palace. "I quickly went to the porch to see another airplane coming in low and aimed at us," he wrote in *Lost Victory*. "I saw its rockets release. I ducked into the house and herded the family and servants into a protected area under the stairs while some of the rockets detonated in the trees in front of the house." Carl Colby was already at school when the assault began. Naturally, the students were sent home, but that decision, with the Colby residence three doors down from the presidential residence, meant the child would be deposited into the heart of the battle. Government tanks and personnel carriers clogged the streets. "I was picking up shrapnel because I thought I could use it in show and tell," Carl remembered. "Then I walked into the house and there was glass and some plaster on the floor. My heart sank. Then my father stuck his head around the door of the kitchen and said, 'Sit down, sport. We're having lunch.'"[2]

The attack on the palace was not the harbinger of a coup but an attempt to assassinate Diem and Nhu by two South Vietnamese Air Force pilots. They had turned back from a combat mission against the Viet Cong and dropped their ordnance on the palace because they had been passed over for promotion and believed that the government was not prosecuting the war with sufficient vigor. One was shot down over the Saigon River; the other escaped to Cambodia. The Ngo brothers, their paranoia increasing, chose to view the attack as part of a multifaceted plot to oust them. This fear, coupled with the Bay of Pigs fiasco, spelled trouble for the Civilian Irregular Defense Group program as well as counterinsurgency and pacification in general.

From its inception, Colby's initiative with the Rhade had been plagued by hostility and jealousy on the part of the South Vietnamese military and the provincial governors. Even as it complained about American usurpation, the ARVN refused to supply the officers that Combined Studies had asked for. Layton later described the role of South Vietnamese government officials in the program as one of "obstructionism, jealousy, suspicion and continual concerted drive to get their hands in the till." In the spring of 1962, two Viet Cong companies attacked the village of Buon Trap. With the defenders under siege, a strike-force relief unit had to fight its way through a large ambush before it could relieve them. While the battle raged, a company of ARVN marines sat on a hill overlooking the village and did nothing. Dave Nuttle, who was a CIDG adviser, subsequently learned that they were cheering for the Rhade and Viet Cong to kill each other.[3]

Beginning in June 1962, Nhu started pressuring Combined Studies to turn over CIDG villages to local ARVN commanders. That same month, Colonel Le Quang Tung's Special Forces began moving in and disarming the Rhade. The government then drafted strike-force members into the regular army and sent them to the Cambodian-Laotian border to guard the frontier. The Highlanders were, of course, interested in protecting their homes and families, not the Vietnamese, and they melted away into the jungle. As far as the Montagnards were concerned, the government in Saigon and the Americans had violated both the letter and the spirit of their original agreements. During the Vietnamese takeover, two Montagnard representatives petitioned Layton. Why have you abandoned us? they asked. "Mr. Dave" had come to the villagers and promised them that the weapons they were being given would belong forever to the Rhade. Without arms, the villagers would once again be at the mercy of the Vietnamese; it mattered not whether they were from the South Vietnamese government or the Viet Cong. Their appeals fell on deaf ears. In truth, the CIA was in the process of being pushed out of the paramilitary business in Vietnam.[4]

If distrust and antagonism from Saigon were not enough, the CIDGs and other CIA-run covert operations in Vietnam were coming under attack from Washington. In October 1961, Chairman of the Joint Chiefs Maxwell Taylor and Deputy National Security Adviser Walt Rostow arrived in South Vietnam to conduct a fact-finding mission for President Kennedy. Colby almost missed them; he had been summoned to Baguio, in the Philippines, together with other Far Eastern heads of station, to meet with newly appointed DCI John A. McCone. He arrived back in Saigon just as Taylor and Rostow were preparing to leave. "I had the chance for no more than a hurried exchange with Taylor and Rostow at the end of their visit," he wrote in his account of the Vietnam conflict, "certainly not enough to give the rationale for our approach and to interest them in its potential."

Upon his return to Washington, Taylor advised the White House and the 303 Committee that the CIA was not adequately staffed or organized to carry out any but the smallest paramilitary operations. Robert McNamara, the Joint Chiefs of Staff, and MAAG smelled blood. Unlike the regular military, McNamara did not disdain unconventional warfare—he had vocally seconded Robert and Jack Kennedy's enthusiasm for special forces—but he believed that any and all paramilitary operations should be controlled by the Department of Defense (DOD). The new DCI was not one to swim against the tide. On June 28, 1962, the 303 Committee met to consider the Agency's request for a $10 million supplemental to support the CIDGs, the Sea Swallows (Father Hoa's Catholic Youth), and other paramilitary operations. McCone spoke up: "It may be advisable for DOD to take the lead in CIA counterinsurgency programs, with the CIA in support, rather than the reverse situation." Thus was "Operation Switchback" born. It would have a profound impact on America's struggle to contain communism in Southeast Asia.[5]

Colby would have an opportunity to monitor and, he hoped, influence Switchback directly. In the summer of 1962, Desmond FitzGerald, who had been named head of the Division of Far Eastern Affairs in the Directorate of Plans, summoned the former Jedburgh to Washington and asked him to become his deputy. Colby recognized a promotion when he saw one, but he asked FitzGerald for another year in Vietnam to see his various projects through to maturity. FitzGerald said no—and so the Colbys bid a fond farewell to Vietnam. Before leaving, in company with General Nguyen Khanh, Diem's military aide, and General Tran Van Don, from whose father-in-law the Colbys had rented their second house, the station chief toured the Highlands. Bill accepted a tiger skin from the Corps Commander, General Ton That Dinh; visited Father Hoa in Ca Mau; and then met Barbara and the children (sans baby Catherine and the newly independent John) as they emerged from a drive over the picturesque Hai Van Pass separating Hue and Danang. The entire family attended an exit interview with President Diem. Smoking cigarette after cigarette, Diem reminisced from early afternoon until dusk. Finally, Bill interjected: "Mr. President, we would like to continue this conversation as long as you would like, but we are expected for dinner at the ambassador's and your brother will be there." Diem apologized and called in the photographer.[6]

Colby was well-satisfied with his work in Vietnam: "For one thing, I could feel that CIA had played a key role in helping to find a proper strategy by which to fight the war," he wrote. "Moreover, the station had contacts and influence throughout Vietnam, from the front and rear doors of the Palace, to the rural communities, among the civilian opponents of the regime and the commanders of all the key military units."[7] Following a leisurely trip halfway around the world that included stops to see the Taj Mahal in India, Jerusalem, Greece, Rome, Lourdes, and the bull rings of Spain, the Colbys arrived back in Washington in the summer of 1962. To Barbara's delight, Bill bought a house in suburban Bethesda, Maryland, and equipped her with a station wagon.

Colby found the atmosphere in Washington very different from when he had last worked there in 1951. The CIA was in turmoil on several levels. Throughout the 1950s, Americans had viewed their spooks and spies as unadulterated heroes. Even, and sometimes especially, to those on the political left, the Agency was exemplary. Had not Joe McCarthy himself targeted the CIA for a purge? "After all," Colby wrote, "we were the derring-do boys who parachuted behind enemy lines, the cream of the academic and social aristocracy, devoted to the nation's service, the point men and women in the fight against totalitarian aggression, matching fire with fire in an endless round of thrilling adventures like those of the scenarios of James Bond films." In those halcyon days there had been no journalistic exposés or congressional investigations. The press accorded the Agency a privileged position, heeding its call to refrain from reporting on its activities in the name of national security and even allowing operatives to use jobs in the print and broadcast media as cover. Congressional oversight was superficial, at best. The CIA director consulted periodically and vaguely with the chairmen of the Armed Services and Appropriations Committees as well as with a subcommittee of the latter that supervised the process by which the CIA's budget was hidden among those of other agencies. The senators and congressmen, typified by Senator Richard Russell of Georgia, were patriotic, anticommunist, and discreet. All agreed that in the intelligence business, the need for secrecy trumped both the press and the public's need to know. Russell told the director that though he was entitled to detailed information about the Agency's activities, he didn't want it "except in the rarest of cases."[8]

But the Bay of Pigs had tarnished the CIA's image and opened a Pandora's Box. Virtually every literate American became aware of the CIA, and not in a positive way. The botched invasion of Cuba made the Agency appear callous, incapable of secrecy, and, worst of all, inept. Contempt and respect are mutually exclusive. America's James Bond had become a character out of Laurel and Hardy. Media coverage of the nation's intelligence community intensified. News stories appeared on the CIA's failed attempt to oust Sukarno in Indonesia, its use of ex-Nazis to build the West German intelligence service, the Gary Powers U-2 fiasco, and other failures.

No one was angrier at the CIA and its humiliation of the president over the botched Bay of Pigs operation than Robert Kennedy, JFK's alter ego and guardian angel (or devil, as some would say). The attorney general, with the White House's approval, had decided to seize control of the intelligence community and do what it had not been able to do—get rid of Castro. JFK had wanted to appoint his brother DCI, but Bobby felt the White House needed to distance itself from covert operations. After six months, the Kennedys had settled on McCone, a deeply conservative Catholic from California who had made a fortune in the shipbuilding business. He had served in both the Truman and Eisenhower Defense Departments and as head of the Atomic Energy Commission. Robert Kennedy and McCone immediately bonded; the attorney general's Hickory Hill home was adjacent to the brand-new CIA headquarters compound at Langley, Virginia, and he would often stop by to visit with McCone on his way to the Justice Department in downtown Washington.

The 303 Committee continued its supervisory role over covert operations, but the Kennedy brothers created a supercommittee, the Special Group (augmented), to oversee the plan, code-named Mongoose, to kill Castro and overthrow Cuba's communist government. Just before McCone's swearing in, the Kennedy brothers summoned him to the White House and introduced him to Brigadier General Edward Lansdale, who would be chief of operations for "Project Cuba" (subsequently renamed Operation Mongoose). McCone promised to make Richard Helms, the newly appointed deputy director of plans, and all of his assets available for the war against Castro. Over the next few months, Lansdale devised more than thirty anti-Castro schemes; psychological warfare, sabotage, the raising of a guerrilla force within Cuba, disruption of the Cuban economy, and assassination of Castro himself and his chief lieutenants were all on the drawing board. The more outrageous assassination plots involved the use of exploding cigars, a lethal hypodermic needle disguised as a pen, a bacteria-infected wetsuit, and exploding seashells. To implement Mongoose, Helms selected William King Harvey, a pop-eyed, potbellied veteran of the Berlin spy wars of the 1950s. Over the winter of 1961–1962, Harvey, the only CIA officer to openly carry a gun, assembled a team that included some 600 CIA operatives with some 4,000 to 5,000 contract personnel at their disposal. There were those in the Agency who decried Mongoose. Samuel Halpern, deputy chief of the Cuban desk, informed Helms that the Agency had only a few agents on the island, and they were rarely heard from. There was no evidence at all of a meaningful guerrilla movement. "Some people believed Ed [Lansdale] was a kind of magician," Halpern later observed. "But I'll tell you what he was. He was basically a con man."[9]

The Cuban Missile Crisis, culminating in October 1962, derailed any invasion plans, but after the dust settled, Bobby Kennedy ordered the men and women of Mongoose to redouble their efforts to wreak havoc on the island. Why, he kept asking, was it not possible for commandos to blow up Cuba's power plants, sugar mills, and factories?[10] In early 1963, the Kennedy brothers, disgusted with the lack of results in the Cuban operation, fired Harvey, sidelined Lansdale, and brought Des FitzGerald on board to head the team. Bill Colby would replace FitzGerald as head of the Far East Division.

Perhaps the most important change Colby found upon his return to Washington from Saigon was an altered culture at CIA headquarters. During one of his first interviews with President Kennedy, McCone had observed that the CIA could not continue to be seen "as a 'cloak and dagger' outfit . . . designed to overthrow governments, assassinate heads of state, [and] involve itself in political affairs of foreign states." The primary task of the Agency should be to gather intelligence from its agents and from all intelligence agencies within the government, analyze it, and present its findings to the president. McCone would establish a Division of Science and Technology within the CIA to build on the successes of the U-2 and the Discover Spy Satellites. He did not say it, but McCone believed that the DCI should be one of the chief executive's principal advisers on foreign policy. Significantly, McCone chose Dick Helms, who came from the Foreign Intelligence (espionage) branch of the Agency, to head the Directorate of Plans. During their first year in office, McCone and Helms fired more than a hundred clandestine operatives. "It was clear that the FI culture was in the ascendancy and CA [covert action] no longer had the glamorous advantage it once had," Colby wrote. Rumor had it that there would be no more large-scale paramilitary operations. Funding was cut for Colby's political action initiative in Italy and for Frank Wisner's innumerable front operations.[11]

The irony was that nobody was more committed to covert action as a means to combat communism and realize the foreign policy objectives of the United States than the Kennedy brothers. Because of its unique position, only the CIA could operate behind the scenes to plan and fund covert paramilitary and political action operations, avoiding, as Colby put it, "diplomatic and political complications."[12] In the eyes of the Kennedy brothers, the CIA had been able to redeem itself in part through its actions during the Cuban Missile Crisis. U-2 overflights and reports from agents on the ground in Cuba had provided absolutely vital information on the presence and placement of Soviet missiles. In 1963, the White House would okay the continuation of covert operations in Laos and dozens of other hotspots around the world, but this turn of events was not in time to halt Operation Switchback in Vietnam.

The assumption between May 1962 and November 1963 of all paramilitary operations in Vietnam by the Department of Defense dealt a major blow to the counterinsurgency/pacification operations begun by Ed Lansdale and revived by Bill Colby and his colleagues. Colby's successor as Saigon station chief, John "Jocko" Richardson, quickly came to see the struggle between the South Vietnamese government and the National Liberation Front purely in military terms. Events in the field seemed to confirm the wisdom of that view. On December 6, 1962, the Politburo of the North Vietnamese Communist Party (Lao Dong) voted to "dispatch combat forces to South Vietnam to build our mobile main force army and our combat arms and combat support units."[13] In January 1963, only 40 miles from Saigon, a small contingent of Viet Cong mauled a division-sized ARVN force near the village of Ap Bac. Sixty-one South Vietnamese soldiers were killed, a hundred were wounded, and five helicopters were shot down; only three Viet Cong bodies were found at the site at the end of the battle. Ap Bac would become grist for the mill of US journalists, many of whom were becoming increasingly disillusioned with the Diem regime; but neither John Richardson nor General Paul Harkins, the head of Military Assistance Command, Vietnam (MACV, the successor to MAAG), seemed to blame the government in Saigon. Harkins geared up for the war the US military had always wanted to fight, and Richardson continued to heap praise on the Ngo brothers, particularly Nhu. In the Highlands, Gil

Layton and Combined Studies reluctantly began to turn over control of the CIDG program to the South Vietnamese Army and US Special Forces. Surprisingly, given their training, Special Forces personnel seemed deaf and dumb to the need to build political consciousness and self-determination among the Rhade and other tribesmen.

By early 1963, Diem and MACV were increasingly obsessed with the Ho Chi Minh Trail and communist sanctuaries in Cambodia and Laos. Those CIDG strike forces that Colonel Tung and his men did not disarm and disband were organized into regiment-sized units by the Special Forces and moved to the border to conduct intelligence and harassing operations against the Viet Cong and Pathet Lao (Laotian communists) across Vietnam's western borders. Meanwhile, in the Highlands, Tung replaced strike-force leaders with "haughty, cocky Vietnamese, who 'intend[ed] to ride hard on the Rhade,'" according to one of the few remaining Combined Studies officers. The result was low morale and numerous desertions; the number of personnel enrolled in the CIDGs shrank from 38,500 in January 1963 to about 19,000 in January 1964. By early 1963, in fact, the Montagnards were on the verge of open revolt.[14]

Meanwhile, in Washington, Colby, as deputy and then head of the Far East Division, was trying to accommodate himself to Switchback. In February 1963, he advised the DCI that there was no alternative to the Agency relinquishing full control of paramilitary operations to the military. MACV and the ARVN might turn to Combined Studies when they needed advice and liaison on political matters, but there were no guarantees. Colby was not optimistic. He understood that in Vietnam, the military had from time immemorial been the enemy of the peasant: "Throughout history the army has been tax collector, oppressor and representative of 'outside' authority and control," he observed in a report to the National Security Council. Colby had experienced MAAG and MACV's tunnel vision during his tour as station chief; political action was, in their view, not only irrelevant but counterproductive. As often as not, the US military mission believed, political action threatened the regime in Saigon, and in wartime, political "stability" was a must. General Harkins paid lip service to the need to win the support of the countryside, but he would never admit to the need to subsume military measures to a political and social program, much less to the idea that large-scale military operations might be damaging to an effort to win hearts and minds. In these views, Colby would later write, the military was complicit in the Ngo brothers' growing tendency toward authoritarianism and insularity.[15]

In meetings at US Pacific Command headquarters in Honolulu in May and November 1963—the latter held two days before JFK's assassination—McNamara outlined the Pentagon's increasingly grandiose plans for counterinsurgency and pacification in Vietnam. Special Forces would continue to train and arm irregular units in the Highlands, the delta, and the Central Lowlands, but they would be used in support of traditional military operations, in gathering intelligence, and in harassing the Viet Cong and the North Vietnamese Army. The secretary of defense unveiled Operational Plan 34A (OPLAN 34A), which would see the US military take over and expand the remnants of Project Tiger, the effort to insert spies and saboteurs into North Vietnam. Under the supervision of a new, top-secret unit—the Studies and Observation Group, or MACV-SOG—the Pentagon's unconventional warriors would, in Clausewitzian terms, attack North Vietnam's "centers of gravity."[16] The first target would be Hanoi's internal security. SOG would continue to smuggle agents into North Vietnam—this time primarily through maritime operations—to spy, harass, and sabotage. It would create a resistance movement in North Vietnam to do what the communists were doing in South Vietnam. McNamara expressed confidence that a massive covert effort could wreak havoc inside the Democratic Republic of Vietnam and cause Ho Chi Minh to stop supporting the insurgency in South Vietnam. The second target was the Ho Chi Minh Trail. SOG would coordinate the Special Forces border operations and attempt to launch strikes into Laos and Cambodia that would interdict North Vietnamese Army and Viet Cong traffic.

Following his return to the States, Colby found himself in the thick of the Vietnam policymaking process, especially after he became head of the Far East Division in January 1963. He frequently accompanied McCone to National Security Council meetings and sometimes made the Agency's presentations himself. What he had seen of McNamara, he did not like. "In so many briefings," he wrote, "I saw him furiously scribbling notes about the number of weapons, trainees, and equipment being supplied to Vietnam rather than standing aside and considering how to adjust our style of war to the one being conducted from the North." During the discussions of OPLAN 34A and SOG in Hawaii in November, Colby finally had enough. Taking his career in his hands, the former Jedburgh stood up and said, "Mr. Secretary, it won't work," referring to the stepped-up plan to insert espionage and sabotage agents into North Vietnam. The DRV was a denied area. As had been the case in Eastern Europe and Communist China, the inserted personnel would be killed or turned and used against the United States and its allies. McNamara ignored him. Following the group's return to Washington from Honolulu, President Kennedy approved NSAM 273, which gave the go-ahead for OPLAN 34A. Operation Switchback would prove to be a disaster, Robert Myers, Colby's deputy, later recalled. McNamara, Myers said, succeeded in "increasing American and South Vietnamese failures by a factor of ten."[17]

In his plans for Vietnam, Bill Colby had placed his trust in two things: first, a CIA-controlled counterinsurgency/pacification program, and second, the House of Ngo. One had fallen prey to the military, and now the other was enduring the same fate. The November 1963 coup that would oust Diem and Nhu from power would be an excruciating experience for Bill Colby. The pair were clearly flawed, but not to the degree of some other anticommunist leaders with whom the United States had chosen to work. The Ngos wanted to do the right thing, but just did not know how, Colby believed. Like the Kennedy foreign policy establishment as a whole, the CIA would split as to the wisdom of a coup. Diem's supporters would lose out; to make matters worse, once the decision was made, Colby, as Far East Division head, would be compelled to do everything in his power to facilitate a change of government.

By 1963, the Ngo brothers felt the political and military walls closing in on them. The National Liberation Front had grown to some 300,000, and its military wing, the PAVN, or Viet Cong, as the Americans and South Vietnamese called it, was able to launch regiment-sized attacks on ARVN and regional forces. A large majority of the Strategic Hamlets had either been abandoned by their disgruntled inhabitants or overrun by the Viet Cong. In order to convince the Americans and the rest of the international community that Saigon was prevailing, Nhu's subordinates simply incorporated communist-dominated districts, and even some provinces, into government-controlled ones. The Montagnards had staged a bloody, unsuccessful uprising against the government in Saigon earlier in the year.

A number of noncommunist, non-Catholic dissidents were still in jail, and their followers were becoming increasingly restive and vocal, especially against the Can Lao (the Ngo brothers' personal political party) and a National Assembly that rubber-stamped every presidential decree. Elements of the military were on the verge of open rebellion, infuriated by Diem's habits of promoting the loyal rather than the competent and interfering in military operations down to the company level.[18]

There were still members of the French Sûreté (secret police) around who were conspiring with every possible group to overthrow the Diem regime. As early as 1962, Nhu began to suspect that the Americans were complicit in various coup plots. Nhu and Diem even managed to get into a dispute with their brother Ngo Dinh Can, warlord over central South Vietnam. Angry that Diem and Nhu had not cut him in on their lucrative counterinsurgency deal with the CIA, he moved forward with not only his own version of Project Tiger but also a counterinsurgency/pacification organization named the Force Populaire (which was actually fairly effective). And then there were the Buddhists, who made up a large majority of South Vietnam's population. They resented being ruled by a Catholic minority that constituted no more than one-tenth of the whole. So offensive was Diem and Nhu's method of ruling that it brought a certain degree of cohesion to a religious group historically devoid of a political agenda. The largest and best organized of the rapidly galvanizing Buddhist groups was the General Association of Buddhists of Vietnam, which, at its strongest, spoke for nearly five thousand pagodas and corresponding lay organizations. Their leader, operating out of Hue, was the charismatic and enigmatic Thich Tri Quang.

Although there had been protests and demonstrations led by monks and carried out by Buddhist youths before 1963 in South Vietnam's largest cities, they had been sporadic. But then, during Vesak, the celebration of Gautama Buddha's birth, an incident occurred that brought South Vietnam to the verge of civil war. On May 8, the Buddhist community in Hue staged a public celebration, ignoring a previous order by the provincial government banning the display of religious flags. The Buddhists were indignant that only a few days earlier, Catholics had flown Vatican flags during a ceremony honoring Archbishop Ngo Dinh Thuc. Police and local civil guards surrounded the Buddhists and ordered them to disperse. When they refused, the deputy province chief, a Catholic, ordered the police and troops to open

Young Bill Colby in Tientsin in native garb
(The Colby Family Collection)

15th Regiment on parade
(The Colby Family Collection)

Guardians of American interests in China
(The Colby Family Collection)

Members of the 15th Regiment in training
(The Colby Family Collection)

Colby, the newly minted paratrooper
(The Colby Family Collection)

(above) Jumpmaster for a training drop *(The Colby Family Collection)*

(left) Colby with NORSO commandos *(The Colby Family Collection)*

NORSOs depart to blow a bridge on the Northland Railway
(The Colby Family Collection)

Saluting NORSO crash victims
(The Colby Family Collection)

Colby and Herbert Helgerson, Norway, 1945
(The Colby Family Collection)

Liberating Namsos, Norway, 1945
(The Colby Family Collection)

fire. When the smoke cleared, nine celebrators, including children, lay dead, with scores more wounded. Diem immediately issued a statement blaming the carnage on a Viet Cong hand grenade.

More than ten thousand people participated in a protest demonstration in Hue on May 10. Prominent monks signed a manifesto demanding legal equality with Catholics, an end to official persecutions, and indemnification of the victims of the May 8 shootings and their families. On June 10, a Buddhist monk named Thich Quang Duc sat down in the middle of a busy Saigon intersection and set himself on fire. His colleagues at the local pagoda had invited members of the media, and soon images of the protesting monk engulfed in flames appeared on front pages and television screens across the world. From that point, the Buddhist protests grew into a powerful, deeply rooted movement with broad support among students, intellectuals, and even some in the Catholic community. Aware that unrest had spread to the military and that certain officers were planning a coup, Nhu hatched a byzantine plan to crush the Buddhist movement, blame the military, and seize control of the government from Diem. He had concluded that his brother had become too weak to rule. "I don't give a damn about my brother," Nhu exclaimed to CIA station chief John Richardson in June. "If a government is incapable of applying the law, it should fall." The regime, he said, was incurably "mandarin and feudal."[19]

In a gesture of goodwill toward the United States, Diem permitted his flag officers to attend a Fourth of July reception at the US embassy. Afterward, CIA operative Lou Conein joined the men, nearly all of whom he had known since his OSS days in 1945, for drinks at a downtown hotel. There, General Tran Van Don informed Conein that he and fellow officers were going to remove Diem and Nhu from power. Conein duly passed this information on to Richardson, who, with the approval of the ambassador, told the former legionnaire to maintain his contacts.

On the evening of August 18, the coup plotters met and decided to ask the president to approve imposition of martial law. They would argue to Nhu and Diem at a subsequent meeting two days later that the decree was needed to enable the military to disperse Buddhist crowds in the nation's cities. It was clear, they said, that the communists had co-opted the protest movement, a charge Diem was only too ready to believe. Their real purpose, however, was to use martial law to position troops strategically in and around Saigon.

But Nhu had other plans. On the night of August 21, with Ambassador Nolting out of the country, Colonel Tung's Special Forces, dressed in regular ARVN uniforms, attacked pagodas all across the country. Armed with pistols, submachine guns, and clubs, they flattened the gates of Xa Loi Pagoda in Saigon and began beating monks and nuns with clubs and pistol butts. They then vandalized the main altar and seized the intact heart of the martyred Thich Quang Duc. In Hue, the violence was even worse. At Tu Dam Pagoda, the temple of protest leader Thich Tri Quang, Nhu's Special Forces soldiers ransacked the building before blowing it up. At Dieu De Pagoda, a Buddhist crowd fought back but was eventually overwhelmed, with 30 dead and 200 wounded. The total number of people killed in the raids nationwide was never confirmed, but estimates ranged into the hundreds. More than 1,400 monks, academics, and other protest leaders were arrested and jailed indefinitely. Nhu knew that the raids would further outrage the Vietnamese and Americans, and he hoped that ire would be directed at the regular military, thus undercutting support for a possible coup. He miscalculated.[20]

As it happened, at the time of the raids, outgoing ambassador Nolting and incoming ambassador Henry Cabot Lodge Jr. were meeting in Honolulu with Admiral Harry Felt, commander of US forces in the Pacific. Bill Colby was there representing the CIA. At that point, the Agency had ruled out Nhu as head of government no matter what transpired in Vietnam. McCone had not made up his mind on Diem, but he tended to agree with Colby, who would subsequently note the danger of discarding a bird in the hand before knowing the "birds in bush, or songs they may sing." Nolting reiterated his view that the Diem regime was the best choice available and that its overthrow would lead to a communist victory. Colby observed that the best that could be hoped for from a military coup was that the United States and anticommunist elements in South Vietnam would work through "a Naguib first phase" while waiting for the emergence of a "Vietnamese Nasser." The references were to Muhammed Naguib and Gamal Abdel Nasser. The former was the popular nonpolitical general who had become the first president of Egypt after the antimonarchist uprising of 1953. He was a front man for a younger, nationalist, and politically ambitious group of officers headed by Nasser. Lodge kept his counsel, but in fact he had already set his face against the House of Ngo.[21]

Washington, DC, unbearably hot and humid, was typically nearly empty in August. Thus it was that on the Saturday following the pagoda raids, a rump of the foreign policy establishment gathered to decide how to respond to the embassy's request for guidance. Present were Undersecretary of State George Ball; Roger Hilsman, the State Department's Vietnam expert; Michael Forrestal, an aide to NSC director McGeorge Bundy; and W. Averell Harriman, the veteran diplomat who was then serving as undersecretary of state for political affairs. To a man, the four believed that Diem and Nhu were morally and politically bankrupt and that the United States must abandon them. They prepared a cable instructing Lodge to seize the opportunity to rid himself of Nhu; if the president refused to jettison his brother, "the U.S. must face the possibility that Diem cannot be preserved." Lodge was also to make clear to the generals that Washington would provide them with direct support during the period between the breakdown of the present government and the establishment of a new one. The cable was cleared with President Kennedy, who was vacationing at Hyannisport in Massachusetts. On Sunday, a copy was circulated to the relevant agencies. As soon as he read it, Colby realized that a major change of policy was in the offing. He phoned McCone, who was vacationing at his palatial home in California. At the DCI's request, Colby borrowed one of the CIA's small jets and flew out to brief his boss. McCone, according to Colby, was furious and returned to Washington with him Sunday evening.[22]

On the following day, August 26, with the full team back in Washington, JFK presided over a stormy NSC meeting. McNamara and Maxwell Taylor, chairman of the Joint Chiefs of Staff, together with the DCI and Vice President Lyndon B. Johnson, declared their support for Diem and accused Harriman and Ball of blindsiding them. Kennedy wavered, but in the end he instructed Lodge, at his discretion, to publicly announce a reduction of American military and economic aid to Diem's government, the signal the rebellious generals had asked for. From late August on, the United States was firmly committed to a coup. As Colby noted in *Lost Victory*, "there was an almost total absence of consideration and evaluation of the personalities who might succeed Diem[,] beyond generalized references to 'the military.'"[23]

The day following the NSC meeting, Colby instructed Richardson in Saigon to begin casting about for a replacement if Diem could not be saved. The chief of station did not trust the generals. If and when they came to power, he told Colby, "the Ngos would be lucky to get out of the country alive." He wanted to see Vice President Nguyen Ngoc Tho succeed to the presidency and the constitution preserved. Don't be absurd, Colby replied. The "U.S. must win this affair if it goes into it, and it has already decided to do just that. . . . We are confident you will keep [your] eye on this main ball rather than [the] window dressing of civilian leadership." He wanted, he said, ideas on a "man, team, or false face behind which we can mobilize the necessary effort to continue the main war against the Viet Cong." Colby had such a person in mind, although he saw him as more of a Nasser than a Naguib. Before leaving Saigon, Colby had suggested to Langley General Nguyen Khanh as a possible replacement for Diem. Both former parachutists, Colby and Khanh had become personal friends during the former's tour as chief of station. Colby was drawn to Khanh because of his skill at maneuvering between the palace and various generals as well as among the political factions that constantly roiled the waters in Saigon. The general had expressed understanding of, and sympathy for, Colby's ideas on counterinsurgency and pacification. Last but not least, he had not demonstrated the racism toward the Montagnards that was characteristic of so many of his fellow Vietnamese.[24]

Policymakers in Washington and Saigon anticipated a coup before the week was over, but on August 30, General Tran Thien Khiem, chief of staff of the South Vietnamese Army, informed General Harkins that he and his colleagues did not have sufficient forces in and around Saigon and did not feel ready to proceed. "This particular coup is finished," Richardson cabled headquarters.[25] The fundamentals of the situation had not changed, however. The Buddhists may have been intimidated, but they were no less resentful of the regime, and the military would never trust the House of Ngo again. The White House was wracked with angst, but Kennedy insisted on leaving the matter in Lodge's hands. Thus it was that the newly arrived ambassador would be the American who held the fate of South Vietnam's ruling family in his hands.

In 1953, when Lodge was serving as Eisenhower's ambassador to the United Nations, a crucial vote on the Korean War had come before the Security Council. The State Department advised the New Englander to vote yes. When Robert Murphy, head of the International Organizations section in State, read the next day that Lodge had voted no, he cabled him: "Apparently, our instructions failed to reach you," he wrote. The ambassador replied, "Instructions? I am not bound by instructions from the State Department. I am a member of the President's cabinet, and accept instructions only from him." Ten years later, nothing had changed.[26]

Lodge, according to Colby, was a disaster as an ambassador. "He had no concept of running a mission," Colby later told an interviewer. "He was a total lone wolf, and couldn't waste his time on administration. He took an instant dislike to Diem."[27] In truth, Lodge came to Vietnam not to manage and coordinate, but to rule. He brought with him a military and a civilian aide, Lieutenant Colonel John Michael Dunn and Frederick Flott, respectively, both junior in rank but both entrusted with his personal mandate. Together they ran roughshod over the rest of the mission—or tried to. Lodge did not believe in delegating authority. He anointed himself as sole spokesman to the press for the entire US Mission and insisted on the right to fire and hire any member of the team, including the CIA chief of station. The ambassador had patience neither for the palace intrigues that swirled around the Ngo brothers nor for the bureaucratic maneuverings within his own camp.

President Kennedy knew who and what Cabot Lodge was and had selected him deliberately. As historian Jane Blair has pointed out, JFK saw Vietnam in 1963 as primarily a political problem. His goal was to keep the South Vietnamese ship of state afloat while shielding his administration from excessive criticism. Lodge, a Republican presidential aspirant, would protect his Vietnam policy from partisan attacks. Above all, however, JFK wanted Lodge to deflect a crescendo of criticism coming from a group of young American newspapermen in Saigon. Beginning with the disastrous battle of Ap Bac, this pack of ambitious journalists, led by David Halberstam of the *New York Times* and Neil Sheehan of United Press International, had led an assault on US support for the Diem regime. They made the Buddhist crisis their own, writing scathing reports about the perfidious Ngo family and the outrages committed by Tung's Special Forces. Indeed, these young media turks wrote about the situation in South Vietnam with the deliberate intention of promoting a coup. JFK demanded of Halberstam's editors that they reassign the young reporter, but at the same time he made it clear to Lodge that he wanted him to get Diem and Nhu to clean up their act. Colby certainly thought that the American press corps and the Buddhists' manipulation of it were crucial. "When that picture of the burning bonze [monk] appeared in *Life* magazine," he told an interviewer, "the party was almost over in terms of the imagery that was affecting American opinion. That put enormous pressure on President Kennedy."[28]

It was not until four days after he landed in Saigon that Lodge deigned to meet with Diem. He arrived at the palace dressed in a white sharkskin suit and accompanied by twelve aides. The ambassador urged his host to appease the Buddhists and tone down Madame Nhu—Nhu's outspoken wife, who was considered the First Lady of South Vietnam because Diem had never married, and who had caused a stir by offering matches and fuel if any monks planned future self-immolations. Diem listened to Lodge and then launched into a two-hour diatribe, during which he chain-smoked two packs of cigarettes. The Buddhist protesters represented a small minority of the total population of South Vietnam, he declared. What he expected of Lodge was that he put an end to interference in the internal affairs of South Vietnam by representatives of various US agencies. Lodge feigned ignorance. This would be the last face-to-face meeting between the two men for nine tension-filled weeks. On September 2, Nhu's English-language mouthpiece, the *Times of Vietnam*, sported the banner headline "CIA Financing Planned Coup d'Etat."[29]

Meanwhile, Nhu had begun openly consorting with the National Liberation Front and the North Vietnamese. There had been rumors of secret contacts between the South Vietnamese government and the communists before, but the palace had steadfastly denied them. With the French encouraging and facilitating him, Nhu had recently entered into tentative discussions with North Vietnamese representatives concerning the possibility of a cease-fire and a neutralization scheme that would be similar to the 1962 Geneva Accords on Laos. Word of the contacts spread quickly. On September 4, Conein was summoned by Brigadier General Ton That Dinh, the military governor of Saigon, which was then under martial law. Dinh's direct command of troops in the capital area made him indispensable to the success of a coup. Conein found him "exultant, ranting, raving," flanked by bodyguards who kept their submachine guns pointed at Conein even during the luncheon phase of their four-hour session. Dinh declared himself the man of the hour who would save Vietnam from communism and who could kill or kidnap anyone in Saigon, including—should there be a move to accommodate the communists—Nhu himself.[30]

By this point, Lodge had taken Lou Conein and Rufus Phillips—the Lansdale protégé who had stayed on in South Vietnam to advise the government on its Strategic Hamlet Program—into his inner circle. Phillips had turned sharply against the Ngo brothers, as had Conein. On September 13, Lodge cabled Secretary of State Dean Rusk, asking that Chief of Station Richardson be replaced by Ed Lansdale. Richardson, it seemed, had disobeyed Lodge's orders to cease all contact with Nhu. The State Department and the CIA had no intention of allowing a free radical like Lansdale back into the picture. Nevertheless, McCone, angry though he was, had no choice but to reassign Richardson. In the meantime, Deputy Chief of Station David Smith became acting chief.[31]

Colby had been monitoring these developments from afar with a growing sense of unease. Diem was apparently in Lodge's sights, with the Kennedy administration divided and adrift. "Diem might be difficult," Colby wrote in his memoirs, "but he was the best—and only—leader South Vietnam had." The Agency's Far Eastern chief was generally dismissive of the Buddhists. During one of his frequent visits to Vietnam, Colby had attempted to come to grips with Buddhism as a political movement. "I invited one of the leading bonzes to tea one afternoon," he later recalled. "Resplendent in his yellow robe, he arrived in a polished limousine equipped with immaculate white cotton seat coverings, precisely as one of Diem's ministers would have." Their conversation, Colby said, resembled two ships passing in the night. "Not only could I not understand what he was trying to say, I was inwardly convinced that he did not know what he wanted to say," he wrote in *Lost Victory*. Luminaries such as Thich Tri Quang were adept at rallying crowds and stirring protests, Colby believed, but they had no idea what to do with the political power that flowed therefrom.[32]

Colby's response to the Buddhist crisis is somewhat puzzling. He repeatedly equated it with the sect wars of 1955 in which the South Vietnamese government had subdued the Cao Dai, Hoa Hao, and Binh Xuyen. Rather than placing Buddhism on the same level as Christianity (i.e., Catholicism), as one of the world's great religions, he seemed to have been relegating it to the status of a sect. There was certainly hard information on the General Association of Buddhists and its goals and organization: CIA dossiers, based on material gathered in July and August, included data on the leaders of the association and their complaints of discrimination by the government in favor of the Catholics as well as conclusive evidence that the movement was free of communist infiltration. Unlike Nolting and Lodge, Colby did not buy the notion that the Buddhist uprising was communist inspired and communist dominated. But he did share his countrymen's belief that Buddhism was a "soft" religion lacking the discipline and will of the Catholic communion. More important, Colby refused to acknowledge that by the late summer of 1963, Diem had become completely eclipsed by Nhu and that both brothers had lost the support of the military. Those who differed with Colby whispered that it was because the Ngos were Catholic. Colby's most telling argument was that Lodge and his supporters in Washington—Harriman, Hilsman, and Forrestal—had given no consideration whatsoever to what would follow politically in the wake of the fall of the House of Ngo.[33]

To make matters worse, it looked as if the ambassador intended to make the CIA his tool in facilitating the fall of the House of Ngo. "There was a clear inconsistency between John McCone's and my opposition to the move against Diem and Lodge's use of our subordinates [Conein] to carry out the action we opposed," he wrote. But, as he noted, the CIA was not supposed to be a policymaking body, and the president's deferral to Lodge made the Agency available to him to use as he wished.[34]

On September 23, President Kennedy ordered McNamara and Taylor to South Vietnam to assess the situation. Colby was part of the team. By then, the long trip from Washington to Vietnam—a twenty-four-hour flight in a windowless KC-135 from Andrews Air Force Base, to Anchorage, Alaska, for refueling, and thence to Tan Son Nhut—had become somewhat routine. Lodge was prepared to allow the Taylor-McNamara mission to gather all the information it desired as long as it did not come from the House of Ngo. Knowing of Colby's close relationship with Nhu and Diem, the ambassador forbade him from calling at the palace or having any contact with high-ranking members of the government. "He did not want the palace to gain any false impression that [the Taylor-McNamara group] offered a potential way around his declared policy of waiting for Diem to come to him with the concessions Lodge thought necessary," Colby later wrote. The former Jedburgh was outraged, and he sensed that McNamara was displeased, but Kennedy's Republican proconsul was still in charge. Colby realized that if he could not contact Nhu and Diem, he could not talk with other Vietnamese either, as it would give the Ngo brothers the impression that he was plotting against them. Little did he know that they already had that impression. As the Taylor-McNamara mission was leaving Vietnam, Diem's chief of special police was reporting that the United States had targeted the president for elimination. According to an Agency informant, the police chief told Diem that "an assistant to the chief of the American CIA [Colby] and about fifty sabotage and assassination experts had been in Saigon for over three months."[35]

On October 2, Lou Conein and General Tran Van Don bumped into each other at the Saigon airport; Don asked the CIA operative to visit him at Nha Trang. From this point on, Conein was the mission's sole contact with the coup plotters. Both the station and the embassy would have preferred someone else; as Bob Myers, Colby's lieutenant, put it, Conein was one of the "sitting around the bar people," a relic from an earlier age. Indeed, "Luigi," who was usually in some stage of inebriation, was notorious. On one occasion when Taylor was ambassador, Conein had become enraged at the airport when his car would not start, pulled out his .45, and blasted away at the engine. Taylor sent him out of the country for a time. Later, during one of Saigon's rooftop parties, Conein attempted to get the attention of a pal entering the hotel by dropping a flowerpot off the roof. The missile just missed hitting Ambassador Nolting on the head. But the mission had little choice. The generals had made it clear that Conein would be their only acceptable interlocutor. David Smith ordered his operative to go on the wagon for the duration.[36]

During the first week of October, USAID announced that it was suspending payments to the South Vietnamese government, and the CIA withdrew financial support from the Vietnam Special Forces. Diem and Nhu had Tung draw his 5,000-man force more tightly around the palace. General Don, speaking for the conspirators, told Conein to expect a coup no later than November 2. On October 27, he told him that the conspirators now believed that "the entire Ngo family had to be eliminated from the political scene in Vietnam." The question of what exactly "elimination" meant had already come up at the CIA. Smith had recommended to Lodge that "we not set ourselves irrevocably against the assassination [of the Ngo brothers], since the other two alternatives mean either a bloodbath in Saigon or a protracted struggle which could rip the Army and the country asunder." McCone and Colby immediately ordered Smith to stand down; the Agency could not condone assassination without ultimately being saddled with responsibility for it.[37]

Also on October 27, Diem finally approached Lodge, inviting him to come to the presidential mountaintop retreat at Dalat to discuss Vietnamese-American differences. During the ensuing meeting, the ambassador reiterated his demands that Diem's government release the Buddhist prisoners from jail, cease its discrimination against the religious majority, and reopen schools and universities. Vietnam was becoming a public relations nightmare for President Kennedy, he declared, citing as an example Madame Nhu's offer to furnish matches and fuel for the Buddhist self-immolations and Nhu's public threat to have his father-in-law (a critic) killed. Diem listened in stony-faced silence and then replied that his government would continue to deal firmly with any disorder so that it could successfully prosecute the war against the communists.[38]

Shortly thereafter, Bill Colby briefed President Kennedy and the NSC on the situation in South Vietnam. A coup attempt seemed inevitable unless Washington intervened, he said, but the outcome was uncertain. Loyalist and insurgent forces were about equal in strength. JFK's team remained as divided as ever, with Robert Kennedy joining McCone in declaring that one coup would just lead to another. Harriman observed that support for the Diem regime in Vietnam was continuing to decline, and that there was no way the present government could deal with the communist insurgency. From Saigon, Lodge cabled that the coming coup would succeed, and that the United States could not delay or discourage it. President Kennedy remained on the fence. The day following, Colby proposed to McCone that Ngo Dinh Nhu be installed in his brother's place. Despite his shortcomings, which included a philosophy with "fascist overtones," he was a "strong, reasonably well oriented and efficient potential successor." Colby seemed oblivious to the fact that it was Nhu's crushing of the Buddhists and his wife's shenanigans that had precipitated the decision in Washington in late August to let matters take their course in Saigon. McCone did not even bother to bring his subordinate's suggestion before the president and the NSC. At JFK's direction, Rusk instructed Lodge not to provide direct aid to the coup plotters, but observed that "once a coup under responsible leadership has begun . . . it is in the interest of the U.S. Government that it should succeed."[39]

Nhu was aware of the plotting against the regime, although confusion among the generals made the waters murky even to the best informed. What Nhu did not know was that Ton That Dinh, a devout Catholic and heretofore staunch Diem loyalist, was among the conspirators. Desperate, Nhu came up with an outlandish scheme, code-named Bravo, to save the House of Ngo. Loyalist troops under Colonel Tung would stage a fake coup, vandalizing the capital. In the ensuing chaos, assassination teams organized by Tung would do away with the principal coup plotters—Generals Duong Van "Big" Minh, Tran Van Don, and Le Van Kim—and possibly key Americans, such as Conein and even Lodge. The brothers would then flee to Vung Tau on the coast some 60 miles from Saigon. Finally, another group of loyalist officers organized by Tung would "arrest" the fake coup leaders and call for a restoration of the Diem government. Ton That Dinh was placed in charge of the fake coup. He persuaded Tung to disperse his Special Forces to the provinces and summoned the ARVN's 7th Division to the capital.[40]

The morning of November 1, Lodge escorted Admiral Harry Felt to the palace for a courtesy call. At the end of the meeting, Diem asked Lodge, who was due to depart for a long-scheduled trip to Washington the next day, to stay behind for a few minutes. Alluding to rumors of a coup, the president asked Lodge to inform JFK that "I am a good and a frank ally, that I would rather be frank and settle questions now than talk about them after we have lost everything." Ask Mr. Colby about brother Nhu, he said. It was Colby who had suggested that brother Nhu climb down out of his ivory tower and get out among the people. He was prepared to make changes in his government, Diem said, but it was a question of timing. He was not interested in power but only solutions. Lodge assured the president that rumors of assassination plots directed against him (Lodge) had not in any way "affected my feeling of admiration and personal friendship for him [Diem] or for Vietnam." Shortly before his meeting with Diem, Lodge had told Conein that if the coup did not go off soon, he would see that the CIA operative would never again work for the US government.[41]

While the ambassador was at the palace, the station reported to Langley that the city was quieter—"more normal"—than at any time since the first Buddhist demonstration. Then at 13:30 hours, it sent a flash cable reporting "red neckerchief troops pouring into Saigon from direction Bien Hoa, presumably marines." With the Special Forces out of the capital, Diem and Nhu had only the Palace Guard to fight for them. As Conein looked on, General Ton That Dinh called Nhu, cursing and threatening him. Initially, the counselor to the president believed this was all part of the fake coup, but then he realized the game was up. Meanwhile, the coup leaders had summoned Colonel Tung to military headquarters on a pretext. Shortly after his arrival, he was taken outside and shot. Colby would view the killing as barbaric and unnecessary, describing Tung, Nhu's instrument in the brutal August pagoda raids, as "a very mild, straightforward, decent guy." With the palace under full assault, Diem called Lodge to inquire about the American position. Lodge told him that the embassy was not well enough informed to have an opinion. Exasperated, Diem responded, "You must have some general ideas. After all, I am a Chief of State. I have tried to do my duty." No one could question that, Lodge said, and then noted that the rebels had offered the brothers safe conduct out of the country. "I am trying to reestablish order," Diem exclaimed, and hung up.[42]

At 20:00 hours, the brothers escaped the palace by way of a secret underground tunnel. They emerged in a wooded park in Cholon and were whisked away to a safe house that Nhu's agents had prepared. Using a telephone line that ran directly to the palace, the brothers negotiated futilely with the plotters. Thinking that Diem and Nhu were still inside, Big Minh ordered a final assault on the building. By dawn, the 5th Division under the command of Colonel Nguyen Van Thieu had killed or captured the last of the Palace Guards.

The next morning—November 2—the brothers sought asylum in a Catholic church in Cholon and notified the coup leaders that they were prepared to accept the offer of safe passage. Minh sent an armored personnel carrier to pick them up. During the ride to headquarters, Nhu and one of the men guarding him, Captain Nguyen Van Nhung, got into a shouting match, insulting each other. The other guard, Major Duong Hieu Nghia, later recalled what happened next: "[Nhung] lunged at Nhu with a bayonet and stabbed him again and again, maybe fifteen or twenty times. Still in a rage, he turned to Diem, took out his revolver, and shot him in the head. Then he looked back at Nhu, who was lying on the floor, twitching. He put a bullet into his head too." Minh is reported to have told an American confidant some months later, "We had no alternative. They had to be killed." Diem was too popular with the Catholics and refugees, and Nhu posed a threat through the Can Lao Party and the Special Forces.[43]

In Washington, the National Security Council met again on the morning of November 2. By that time, Kennedy had been informed of the brothers' deaths; he had blanched and left the room at the news. He could not know that his own date with the assassin was but twenty days away. On his way to the meeting, Colby had stopped off at the Catholic church where Barbara attended Mass every weekday morning at 8:00. He told her of Nhu's and

Diem's deaths and asked that she say a special prayer for the departed. Colby found the mood at the White House sober—even somber. Only Rusk seemed to share Lodge's enthusiasm; the ambassador had cabled that the coup had been "a remarkable performance in all respects." But Colby recalled that there were no recriminations. The NSC turned to face the cold, hard truth that a group of generals, about whom they knew very little, was now in charge of South Vietnam. By this point, Colby had convinced McCone that Washington could no longer continue to treat Lodge with kid gloves. The Military Revolutionary Council, the temporary ruling body that Big Minh and his colleagues had set up in the wake of the coup, was already asking the CIA station for guidance in setting up a new, permanent government.[44]

Following the NSC meeting, McCone took Colby by the arm and proceeded to the Oval Office. In his usual direct manner, the DCI requested an immediate audience with the president. The two CIA men were duly ushered in. Colby remembers that Kennedy was stricken but composed. "Mr. President, you remember Mr. Colby," McCone said. JFK smiled and nodded. "In view of the confusion in Saigon, I would like to send him immediately to Saigon to make contact with the generals there and assess the situation on the basis of his close connections with them and his knowledge of the country. I would also like to be able to say that he is going on your authority." JFK and Colby knew what McCone was talking about: the imperial Lodge. "Certainly," Kennedy replied.[45]

Colby was anxious to make the trip, although he was somewhat apprehensive about how he would be received by the coup leaders, given his well-known intimacy with Diem and Nhu. That evening, the Colbys kept a long-standing dinner engagement with the Noltings and Richardsons. It was probably the only wake held for the House of Ngo, Colby later recalled.[46]

The CIA was in South Vietnam to gather intelligence and to combat the communist insurgency. Bill Colby saw the first function as primarily a handmaiden to the second. His context, as always, was the Cold War. He may have been "mesmerized" by Nhu, as one of his colleagues claimed, and he considered himself Diem's friend, but personal relationships were a means to an end, and that end was the military defeat of the Viet Cong and the political defeat of the National Liberation Front. Colby clung to Diem and then, at the last moment, to Nhu because he saw no alternative. He considered the Buddhists to be self-serving publicity seekers, mystics, or both. Perhaps the Ngos had mishandled the Buddhist crisis, but Washington would just have to live with it. A military government was not the answer, especially in Vietnam, where, since time immemorial, soldiers of the central power had been associated in the mind of the peasantry with oppression and exploitation. At least Diem and Nhu had recognized the need for economic development and political action, even if their philosophy was tinged with fascism. It was true that Nhu and Tung were ruthless, but the communists were nothing if not ruthless. What kind of conflict did Harriman and Hilsman think the United States and its ally were involved in? Roosevelt and Churchill had embraced Stalin. How much more compromised could the Western democracies be?

Colby had briefly considered resigning in protest over America's decision to abandon Diem and Nhu, but he quickly rejected the idea. "In the early 1960s," he wrote, "we had not yet reached that national state of mind that considered any difference from one's own views as based on immorality or arrant stupidity and justifying the most extreme denunciations and rejection of authority."[47] Colby consoled himself with the thought that he was but an instrument to be wielded by the forces of good in the Cold War. But, in truth, neither he nor the Agency saw themselves as passive instruments. Lodge, the Bay of Pigs, and Switchback had emasculated the CIA in South Vietnam, but Colby and his colleagues were hardly resigned.

The chilly reception Colby anticipated from Lodge and the Vietnamese generals did not materialize. The ambassador was effusive in his praise for the Agency, and for Acting CIA Chief of Station David Smith in particular. Lodge had obviously gotten the message that the head of the Far Eastern Division was JFK's personal representative. Then it was time to huddle with the junta. Colby was somewhat taken aback when the members greeted him as an old and wise friend. Tran Van Don joked about having been his landlord. Tran Van Kim recalled their work together on the Mountain Scout program. Even the usually reticent Big Minh came around. They barraged him with questions concerning politics, national security, and the US Constitution. General Ton That Dinh did request the immediate recall of Gil Layton, the head of the CIA's covert operations in Vietnam, who had been the murdered Le Quang Tung's opposite number and close friend.

Colby met twice with Colonel Pham Ngoc Thao, South Vietnam's counterinsurgency/pacification guru, who was also a communist agent. He also journeyed to Dalat to call on General Nguyen Khanh, who had been the first to advise the CIA that serious planning for a coup was underway. Khanh, who had not been named to the ruling Military Revolutionary Council (MRC), gave a rather pessimistic view of the generals' ability to solve the problems facing South Vietnam. Colby asked about the beginnings of a beard that Khanh was sporting. He would continue to grow it, Khanh said, until he was convinced that the new leaders were on the "right path."[48]

Colby was due in Honolulu for the fateful conference with McNamara that would endorse Switchback and OPLAN 34A, so he had to leave after only a few days in Vietnam. Before departing, he prepared a report for McCone outlining the enormous tasks—political, administrative, and military—facing the generals, all of whom had grown to maturity during the heyday of French colonialism. Though the junta was actively seeking guidance from the US Mission, he said, Lodge was insisting that it remain detached. Many in the Mission regarded Big Minh as a feckless opportunist and the MRC as a Trojan horse for National Liberation Front and French neutralization schemes.[49]

As the generals isolated themselves within their respective compounds waiting for the future to define itself, the situation in the countryside continued to deteriorate. In an effort to court the Military Revolutionary Council, the National Liberation Front had ordered the Viet Cong to reduce the level of violence, but that was hardly necessary. The fall of the House of Ngo revealed that the South Vietnam government's counterinsurgency/pacification statistics had been a sham. Hamlets and villages listed as secure either had no government presence or were ruled by shadow communist administrations. Strategic Hamlets had either fallen prey to their discontented inhabitants or been overrun by the Viet Cong. Long An Province, barely 40 miles south of Saigon, was a communist hotbed. Because the Strategic Hamlet program was identified with Diem and Nhu, the generals lent it no support whatsoever. Meanwhile, the leadership in Hanoi decided that the time was ripe for it to take a direct hand in the conflict. At the Central Committee's Ninth Plenum, held in December 1963, the Politburo decided to throw regular units of the North Vietnamese Army into the fray in South Vietnam.[50]

Meanwhile, in Honolulu, Colby argued fruitlessly against Operation Switchback. He objected particularly to McNamara's plans to expand

Project Tiger to include the insertion of more agents in the north, maritime raids along North Vietnam's coast, the establishment of a fake resistance movement, and covert bombing raids by unmarked South Vietnamese planes. When it became clear that the Department of Defense would carry the day, Colby, ever the good soldier, agreed to cooperate in developing OPLAN 34A.

Only days later, Colby and his deputy, Bob Myers, sat in the former's office, listening to radio reports on the assassination of President Kennedy. JFK's vacillation on Vietnam, especially his willingness to let Henry Cabot Lodge call the shots in the last days of the Diem regime, had dismayed Colby. There was also the disastrous Bay of Pigs operation—arguably the White House's responsibility—that had so sullied the reputation of the CIA. But Colby admired JFK's idealism and his activist foreign policy. Had Kennedy lived, Colby wrote in *Lost Victory*, "I am convinced that his sensitivity to the political aspects of the war waged by the Communists would have led him to insist on a strategy on our side to match them."[51] There certainly would not have been the massive buildup of troops and indiscriminate use of firepower that occurred under the succeeding administration, Colby believed. How Kennedy would have dealt with the almost certain collapse of South Vietnam in 1964—a product of the South Vietnamese government's own weakness and North Vietnamese Army infiltration—was a question Colby left unanswered.

Like most Americans at the time, Colby did not know what to make of Lyndon B. Johnson. He knew that he was a political operator par excellence and had been a Diem supporter. But Colby and many others believed the new president to be inexperienced and uninformed on foreign policy matters. Colby applauded Johnson's dismissal of Roger Hilsman (for his role in the ouster of the Ngo brothers), but he questioned the wisdom of keeping on the rest of JFK's foreign policy team, fearing that Johnson would become the victim rather than the master of events.[52]

Johnson was in fact in basic agreement with the foreign policies of the Kennedy administration: military preparedness and realistic diplomacy, he believed, would contain communism within its existing bounds. To keep up morale among America's allies and satisfy hardline anticommunists at home, the United States must continue to hold fast in Berlin, oppose the admission of Communist China to the United Nations, and continue to confront and blockade Cuba. He was aware of the growing split between the Soviet Union and China, and of the possibilities inherent in it for dividing the communist world. He also took a flexible, even hopeful, view of the Soviet Union and its leader, Nikita Khrushchev. It was just possible, he believed, that Russia was becoming a status quo power, and as such would be a force for stability rather than chaos in the world. The United States must continue its "flexible response" of military aid, economic assistance, and technical and political advice in response to the threat of communist expansion in the developing world. However, there was nothing wrong with negotiation with the Soviets, in the meantime, in an effort to reduce tensions. Insofar as Latin America was concerned, Johnson was an enthusiastic supporter of the Alliance for Progress. As a progressive Democrat, he was drawn to historian Arthur Schlesinger's stratagem of appealing to the vital center at home and abroad while pursuing openings to the left, as Bill Colby had done in Italy. At the outset of his administration, it appeared that the new president did not buy into the myth of a monolithic communist threat. To all appearances, then, Johnson was a cold warrior, but a flexible, pragmatic one.

Nevertheless, LBJ was no more ready than his predecessor had been to unilaterally withdraw from South Vietnam; nor was he interested in seeking a negotiated settlement that would lead to neutralization of the area south of the 17th parallel. On November 24, 1963, he instructed Ambassador Lodge to tell the generals who had overthrown Ngo Dinh Diem that they had the full support of the US government. Two days later, the National Security Council incorporated his pledge into policy, affirming that it was "the central objective of the United States" to assist the "people and Government of South Vietnam to win their contest against the externally directed and supported communist conspiracy."[53]

Frustrated, and angry with Lodge because of his refusal to allow the Agency to do its job in South Vietnam, McCone and Colby were determined to rein in the ambassador. Shortly after Johnson became president, McCone paid a visit to the Oval Office. There could never be a working relationship between the embassy and the Agency in South Vietnam as long as the New Englander was ambassador, he told Johnson. "Lodge would destroy [the new station chief] if he opposed his assignment or did not like him," McCone declared. "Lodge was absolutely unconscionable in matters of this kind and he had resorted to trickery time and time again during the Eisenhower administration. . . . He never failed to use the newspapers in order to expose an individual or block an action."[54] Johnson assured McCone that he understood how poor a manager Lodge was. He had seen that for himself. But it was impossible to recall the man at that point. The junta would take it as a repudiation of the coup and an invitation to the Diemists to return to power. Moreover, replacing Lodge would remove the political cover that the administration had enjoyed over Vietnam. Lodge needed to come home; one could only hope that he would decide to throw his hat in the ring for the 1964 GOP presidential nomination. Nevertheless, McCone and Colby could have their own man as CIA station chief, the president declared, and he would make it work.

Colby already had that man in mind—Hong Kong station chief Peer de Silva. De Silva was a fellow graduate of Columbia and one of the most experienced field operators the Agency possessed. Colby vetted him with McCone and the president, and both men gave their approval. The Far East Division chief and his boss decided to beard Henry Cabot Lodge in his den.[55]

In mid-December, McCone, Colby, de Silva, and their aides boarded a C-135 bound for Saigon. There, McCone was to link up with McNamara, who was leading yet another fact-finding mission. The day following their arrival, Lodge hosted a luncheon at the embassy for the CIA men. The issue of who was to be station chief soon came up. Lodge made it clear that he was perfectly happy with David Smith. Mr. Smith was a fine young officer, McCone declared, but the sensitive post required someone with more experience, namely, de Silva. He added, with a tight smile, that the appointment would proceed unless Lodge had some specific objection. It was clear that whoever became chief of station, it would not be Smith. De Silva later recalled that he, Smith, and Colby spent a lot of time staring at the ceiling until, mercifully, the luncheon came to an end.[56]

Shortly thereafter, the ambassador received a cable from the White House. "It is of the first importance," LBJ declared, "that there be the most complete understanding and cooperation between you and him [de Silva]. . . . I am concerned not only to sustain effective cooperation, but to avoid any mutterings in the press. . . . I cannot overemphasize the importance which I personally attach to correcting the situation which has existed in Saigon in the past, and which I saw myself when I was out there." Lodge was vastly annoyed, but after de Silva agreed to give up the oversized black limousine that John Richardson had used, the two men began to get on rather well. Indeed, during one of the first meetings between the revamped CIA team and the ambassador, David Smith let it be known that he had anticipated the naming of a more experienced man as chief of station all along. "Do you think I give a damn about you?" Lodge sneered. For the time being, however, the ambassador continued to block the station from having direct contact with the Military Revolutionary Council.[57]

Upon his return from Saigon, McCone reported to the president that because of ongoing tensions and rivalries within the military junta, the disconnect between the central government and the provinces, and stepped-up Viet Cong activity in the countryside, the prognosis was not good. "It is abundantly clear," he wrote, "that [Vietnamese] statistics received over the past year or more . . . on which we gauged the trend of the war were grossly in error."[58]

With the MRC fiddling and South Vietnam burning, a new generation of coup plotters stepped forward. First among these was General Nguyen Khanh, Colby's favorite to replace Diem. A professional soldier, Khanh had fought with the Viet Minh and then rallied to Diem after he came to power. As deputy chief of staff of the Vietnamese Army, he had parlayed with the rebellious paratroopers during the 1960 coup long enough for loyalist units to move up from the south. He had subsequently joined the circle of generals who overthrew the House of Ngo. In December 1963, to his vast annoyance, however, the MRC had assigned him to be commander of IV Corps, the military region furthest from Saigon. In conversations with CIA personnel in January 1964, Khanh complained that members of the MRC were plotting with various Frenchmen to bring about the neutralization of South Vietnam. This he could not permit.

Early on the morning of January 30, Khanh and his fellow conspirator, General Tran Thien Khiem, overthrew the junta that had ousted Diem. South Vietnam's new leader elevated Big Minh to the figurehead position of chief of staff and sent five leading members of the MRC, including Tran Van Don and Le Van Kim, off to Dalat, where they were placed under house arrest. Colby believed that Khanh, in addition to satisfying his own ambition, was avenging the deaths of Diem and Nhu. In his memoir, Colby cited a statement attributed to Diem before his assassination: "Tell Nguyen

Khanh that I have great affection for him, and he should avenge me." And in fact, the only casualty of the second coup was Captain Nguyen Van Nhung, the officer who had gunned down the Ngo brothers. Khanh had him shot.[59]

The new regime faced truly staggering problems. Military operations and the Strategic Hamlet Program had come to a complete standstill. The government's authority was nonexistent throughout much of the countryside, and the nation's cities were sliding into anarchy. Increasingly, the Buddhists viewed the Khanh regime as a reincarnation of the House of Ngo. At the same time, Khanh's foreign minister was confiding to the American embassy that his chief had "possible Communist or neutralist connections."[60] A new wave of protests swept the capital, accompanied by armed clashes between Buddhist and Catholic street gangs. General William Westmoreland, whom Johnson had named to replace Harkins as head of the US military mission in the spring of 1964, wrote that Saigon looked like a city under siege. Concertina wire and military checkpoints were omnipresent.

Colby made another one of his frequent trips to Vietnam in May 1964 to survey the situation. There was one bit of painful business to take care of. Though both were CIA operatives, Lou Conein and Gil Layton were bitter rivals. Like Colby, Layton, who had survived the MRC's attempts to remove him, was a Diem loyalist, whereas the francophile Conein had worked to bring about the downfall of the House of Ngo. In the wake of the coup, Conein had decided that Vietnam was not big enough for the two of them—and Conein had the ear of both Lodge and Khanh. Before the 1963 coup and his death, Colonel Tung, Layton's counterpart in Vietnamese intelligence and security, had confided to his friend that if the limousine that came to pick up Layton every morning contained individuals other than the driver, he should not get in it. The extra person meant that he had been targeted for elimination. During the spring of 1964, Gil and his wife, Dora, began noticing that they were gradually being frozen out of parties and receptions. Then one morning the limousine showed up with an unidentified man in the backseat. Layton stayed home. The person in charge of training Khanh's security force—in effect, Tung's replacement—was Lou Conein. After Colby landed in Saigon, Layton confronted him. Tell Conein and his Vietnamese friends to back off or there would be blood. Colby said he would take care of it, but there was nothing he could do to keep Layton on the team. He offered his old comrade a post in Thailand, but Layton refused.[61]

From Saigon, Colby moved on to Honolulu for yet another summit meeting on Vietnam, where McNamara continued to extol the virtues of OPLAN 34A. He reveled in listing trucks destroyed, ammunition dumps blown up, and North Vietnamese paranoia stimulated. McCone and Colby were not impressed. "If we go into North Vietnam," McCone declared, "we should go in hard and not limit ourselves to pinpricks."[62]

On the way from Saigon to Honolulu, Colby had prepared a report and recommendations for the White House. The Khanh regime was making progress, he declared, but not fast enough. The government was particularly ineffective at the grassroots level. He recommended making province chiefs the key officials in the pacification effort, with their American counterparts as the sole commanders of every US activity within their province. The South Vietnamese Army should concentrate on clearing and holding, in line with the "oil-spot theory," and cease and desist from random sweeps and artillery bombardments.[63]

On June 6, after the US contingent had returned from Honolulu, McGeorge Bundy took John McCone aside and asked if the CIA was ready to reenter Vietnam in an active role: that is, to reverse Operation Switchback. "If the president so desires and the Pentagon and Embassy were supportive," the DCI said. He did and they were, primarily because McNamara and the Joint Chiefs of Staff were increasingly preoccupied with planning a major escalation of the war.[64]

The spring and summer of 1964 found Lyndon Johnson an intensely frustrated man. Military intelligence provided evidence of the first main force units of the North Vietnamese Army coming down the Ho Chi Minh Trail and entering South Vietnam. The prospect of a broad-based, responsive government in South Vietnam seemed as remote as ever. General Harkins declared that victory over the communists was just months away, but Lodge warned that South Vietnam was teetering on the verge of collapse. Johnson had repeatedly told his foreign policy advisers that it was up to the Vietnamese themselves to get their political and military house in order. Meanwhile, Khanh and the government of South Vietnam initiated a public campaign in support of "marching North." Hot on the campaign trail, GOP presidential hopeful Barry Goldwater suggested the use of "low-yield atomic weapons" against the communists in Vietnam.

Hardliners within the Joint Chiefs of Staff, notably Air Force chief of staff Curtis LeMay and Marine Corps commandant Wallace Greene, insisted that "operations in Vietnam should be extended and expanded immediately." But it wasn't just politicians like Goldwater and hawkish generals like "Bombs Away" LeMay who were sounding the alarm. In Washington, the CIA's George Allen, and in Saigon, Peer de Silva, advised McCone that without the commitment of US troops, South Vietnam would fall to the communists in a matter of months, if not weeks. McCone relayed that information to the president and the NSC. McCone did not dispute his subordinates' dire warnings, but he expressed doubt that the effort was worth it. "I think we are . . . starting on a track which involves ground force operations [that will mean] an ever-increasing commitment of U.S. personnel without materially improving the chances of victory," he told the president. "In effect, we will find ourselves mired in combat in the jungle in a military effort that we cannot win, and from which we will have extreme difficulty in extracting ourselves."[65]

The angst coming from the West Wing was palpable. "Let's get some more of something, my friend," the president told McNamara in late May, "because I'm going to have a heart attack if you don't get me something. . . . Let's get somebody that wants to do something besides drop a bomb, that can go in and go after these damn fellows and run them back where they belong." Later, in conversation with Senator Richard Russell, LBJ said, "I don't think the people of the country know much about Vietnam and I think they care a hell of a lot less." But if he were to lose Vietnam to the communists, he admitted, there was not a doubt in his mind that Congress would impeach him.[66]

Mercifully, Henry Cabot Lodge resigned his post in June, returning to the United States to challenge Goldwater for the Republican presidential nomination. To replace him, Johnson chose General Maxwell Taylor, perhaps the military's best-known intellectual and a Kennedy family intimate. Still, he was a career officer and tended to see things in military terms. Taylor was distinctly unimpressed with Nguyen Khanh—and with the entire upper echelon of the ARVN officer corps, for that matter. Quite simply, he believed, South Vietnam's new leaders did not know what they were doing. At the end of May, he arranged for the "Dalat" generals—Don, Dinh, Xuan, and Kim—to be released from house arrest. When rumors of a coup began to circulate, Taylor summoned the suspected plotters and dressed them down. If the senior officer corps could not behave with a degree of maturity and responsibility, the United States would have to rethink its economic and military aid program, the ambassador declared.[67]

With a massive expansion of the Ho Chi Minh Trail underway and North Vietnamese Army regulars trickling into South Vietnam, pressure began to mount within the Johnson foreign policy establishment for air strikes against North Vietnam. As contingency planning for a possible bombardment, blockade, or invasion got underway in Washington, military intelligence began gathering information on a network of antiaircraft missiles and radar stations that had been installed by the Soviets on the bays and islands of the Tonkin Gulf. MACV enlisted South Vietnamese commandos to harass the enemy radar transmitters, thereby activating them, so that American electronic intelligence vessels cruising in the gulf could chart their locations and frequencies. These operations were, of course, in addition to the infiltration and harassment excursions already being carried out under Switchback. On August 2, North Vietnamese patrol boats attacked the USS *Maddox*, and the Gulf of Tonkin incident was underway. There followed a congressional resolution authorizing the president to take military action in Vietnam to protect US and allied forces. It was somewhat ironic that OPLAN 34A triggered the decision to escalate.

Meanwhile, the political situation in South Vietnam continued to deteriorate. Widespread fear among ARVN officers that the Gulf of Tonkin air strikes would provoke retaliation, even invasion, by North Vietnam provided Khanh with the excuse to decree a state of emergency, which gave him and his associates on the MRC all but absolute power. The government severely curtailed civil liberties, imposed strict censorship on the media, and moved against pro–Dai Viet generals who had been plotting against him. The Dai Viet Party (or Brotherhood) had been formed in the late 1920s by Nguyen Thai Hoc. It took its name from the Vietnamese kingdom that had broken away from China in A.D. 939. Politically conservative, and heavily dominated by nationalist mandarins, the Dai Viet had staged an unsuccessful uprising against the French in Tonkin in the 1930s. Afterward, a number of Dai Viet had sought refuge and military training with Chiang Kai-shek's army in Nationalist China. The Dai Viet were pro-Japanese during World War II. Following the partition of Vietnam in 1954, the society was banned in the communist north but continued to play an active role in the south. Those who fled from the north

following partition tended to be pro-American, and the indigenous southern branch was more pro-French.[68]

Instead of enabling Khanh to tighten his grip on South Vietnam, his
state of emergency decree and the attempted purge of the Dai Viet weakened it. On August 24, 1964, the Buddhists and their student allies took
to the streets, staging massive demonstrations. Caught between the Buddhists and the pro–Dai Viet generals, Khanh sought to appease the former.
He promised Buddhist leader Tri Quang constitutional reform, early elections, and freedom of both religion and speech. Catholic youth then rioted,
and the dissident generals moved in for the kill. In February 1965, Nguyen
Khanh resigned and accepted a post as roving ambassador.

As Saigon writhed in the coils of palace intrigue, political theater, and
coup plots, the CIA station, with Colby monitoring and encouraging it,
proceeded with a series of counterinsurgency/pacification incubators in the
countryside.[69]

In the aftermath of the 1963 coup that toppled the Diem regime, Lodge
and one of his counterinsurgency officers, Everett Bumgardner, had sent a
young United States Information Service officer named Frank Scotton into
Long An Province, only 40 miles south of Saigon. Long An was a Viet
Cong hotbed, despite its proximity to the capital, and Scotton's task was
to survey the situation and come up with a counterinsurgency initiative to
combat the communists. To this end, he recruited a handful of Americans
to go with him to live among the peasants, and they created "armed propaganda teams," essentially to do what the Viet Cong were doing—fighting
by night and recruiting followers by day. With the Long An experiment
up and running, Saigon dispatched Scotton and Captain Robert Kelly to
Quang Ngai Province on the Central Coast and instructed them to replicate the armed propaganda teams. Impressed by Scotton's work in Long
An, Colby and de Silva decided to adopt the program, hoping that it could
eventually be applied throughout South Vietnam. From that point on,
Scotton and his comrades had access to CIA money and CIA-operated
warehouses containing arms, food, medicine, and building supplies.[70]

De Silva also ordered that aid and advice be given to Nguyen Van Buu,
a Catholic businessman who exercised a virtual monopoly on the shrimp
and cinnamon trade in the south. The CIA station helped train more than
five hundred "shrimp and cinnamon soldiers," who, in turn, were largely
responsible for keeping the highway from Saigon to the port of Vung Tau

open.[71] Another CIA-sponsored operative, ARVN lieutenant colonel Do Van Dien, established armed defense teams in, among other places, a Catholic convent and a leper colony situated in the communist-infested Zone D north of Saigon. By far the most significant initiative supported by the station, however, was Major Tran Ngoc Chau's comprehensive pacification program in Kien Hoa Province, another Viet Cong hotbed located southeast of Long An. Chau, a former Viet Minh who had rallied to Diem, but had grown increasingly disillusioned with Saigon's repressive policies, had become province chief in 1962.

The situation in Kien Hoa when Chau assumed control was bleak. Station officers who overflew the province in early 1964 had noticed that where once there had been sizable strategic hamlets, there was now nothing left but bare earth. The Viet Cong had dispersed the population and taken everything else. At this point, military activity against the communists consisted of ARVN sweeps coupled with harassing air and artillery bombardment. There was no concerted effort to carry the war to the enemy, to identify Viet Cong cadres and installations, or to infiltrate their safe areas in order to harass and destroy. De Silva dispatched Stuart Methven, a CIA operations officer, to act as adviser to Chau.

What Methven and Chau came up with were Counter-Terror (CT) Teams trained and armed by the US Special Forces. The first fifteen-man units were, Chau admitted, drawn from "deserters and small time crooks, currently in refuge with one of the district chiefs." Once they were well armed (and well paid), the CT Teams proved fairly effective and surprisingly loyal. Indeed, Viet Cong leaflets offered 15,000 piasters for the killing of a US adviser or South Vietnamese district chief; 20,000 piasters for an ARVN officer; and 40,000 piasters for a CT cadre. The war in Kien Hoa became quite personal and specific. A Viet Cong sniper assassinated the US adviser to the ARVN Ranger unit in the province, and communist propaganda lionized the shooter. This could not stand, Chau decided, and a CT Team, after pinpointing the man's location, grenaded his hut, killing him and his family.[72]

The objective in Kien Hoa, de Silva wrote to Colby, was to "increase results to a level at which they [are] not merely psychological but actually affect [Viet Cong] military and political effectiveness."[73] More significant, Chau developed and implemented what he dubbed the "Census-Grievance Program." Members of his counterinsurgency force would move throughout the province conducting a thorough census, and in the process they would encourage villagers to list their grievances against both the Viet Cong and the government. Chau and his men made it clear that they understood that before the people could be expected to support their government and its soldiers, they would have to show themselves to be nurturers rather than exploiters.

In November, de Silva visited Quang Ngai and was electrified by what he found. The experiment initiated by Frank Scotton and Robert Kelly and supported by the resident CIA officer was flourishing. Quang Ngai, in Military Region IV, was the southernmost province of Vietnam. (The military regime in Saigon had divided South Vietnam into four military regions, with I being the northernmost and IV the southernmost.) It was a gorgeous area, with the Annamite Range descending from the west to the coastal lowlands and the South China Sea. The area had been a Viet Minh stronghold since World War II but was also the redoubt of one of Vietnam's oldest noncommunist, nationalist parties, the Viet Nam Quoc Dan Dang. The province chief was a VNQDD member and a strong supporter of the CIA-funded counterinsurgency/pacification incubator. The small, armed propaganda teams that Scotton and Kelly had started with had morphed into 40-man units that, while putting on pro–South Vietnamese government plays and building village infrastructure, were inflicting heavy casualties on the local Viet Cong. The teams elected their own leaders and had no fixed installations. According to the provincial MACV adviser, between June and October these units, now named People's Action Teams (PATs), had killed 167 of the enemy and captured 236 others along with large caches of weapons. PAT losses were 6 killed and 22 wounded with no desertions. The PATs would move through the province, living in a particular village for three days while dispensing medicine, giving out seed, helping with various construction projects, and gathering information on the Viet Cong. Then they would move on until the entire province had been covered. The following year, a PAT unit in Binh Son District of Quang Ngai Province provided intelligence and scouting services to a US Marine battalion that led to the destruction of more than 600 enemy troops. According to Stu Methven, de Silva returned to Saigon looking "as if he had found God." The chief of station was now a committed convert to the Colby cause, but he soon found himself butting his head against the same wall as his predecessor.[74]

When de Silva presented the PATs as the solution to the counterinsurgency/pacification program to the US Mission Council, he found Westmoreland "less than enthusiastic," as he put it. The general's staff saw the chief of station's recommendations as an indictment of the military's efforts in the field and just another power grab by the Agency, another attempt to build its own private army. In frustration, de Silva appealed to headquarters. The PATs were the solution to the problem, he wrote to Colby. If the rapidly growing Viet Cong penetration and domination of the rural population were not halted and reversed, it would not matter how well trained and well equipped the ARVN was. The suppression of the Viet Cong had to be seen as a "psychological, political, and spiritual war which distinguishes the war here from classical war, and which I am convinced is susceptible to solution by civil and civic actions spawned in the local populations." This from a West Point graduate and former army colonel.[75]

This was all music to Colby's ears, and he made a forceful presentation to McCone and Helms. Headquarters gave the go-ahead to de Silva to expand the PAT program, and during his February 1965 visit to Vietnam, McGeorge Bundy provided the NSC's stamp of approval. MACV reluctantly acquiesced on the condition that the program not drain off the military's best and brightest. Plans were developed to apply the PAT concept in Binh Dinh and Phu Yen Provinces, and Westmoreland paid the program the compliment of asking Frank Scotton to raise up local self-defense forces in the districts around Saigon.

Although Colby was enthusiastic about the People's Action Team program, he was the first to see its limitations. De Silva conceived of counterinsurgency and pacification much as Ed Lansdale had a decade earlier. If the South Vietnamese government and its American advisers could deny the enemy access to the masses of peasants who inhabited the countryside, the Viet Cong would wither on the vine. In this, de Silva assumed that South Vietnam's peasants were innately anticommunist and that the Viet Cong held sway principally through the use of terror. Not so, Colby observed to McCone and Helms. The South Vietnamese government and its friends had to fill the void with something positive. There had to be programs of social and economic justice—permanent programs—and a degree of self-determination at the village level. In other words, there had to be something positive for the local people to fight for. Also, who would defend the villagers when the PATs moved on? But the PATs were a start, and Colby limited his criticisms to the inner circle at Langley.[76]

Unfortunately for counterinsurgency and pacification, South Vietnam was on the verge of collapse by early 1965. A newly constituted Military Revolutionary Council, dominated by ARVN chief of staff Nguyen Van Thieu and Air Force marshal Nguyen Cao Ky, had replaced Khanh. Paying lip service to civilian control of the government, the generals named Phan Huy Quat, a prominent Dai Viet politician, to the post of prime minister. These comings and goings in Saigon were accompanied by a sharply deteriorating security situation in the countryside. On February 7, 1965, the Viet Cong attacked the US air base at Pleiku in the Central Highlands, killing eight Americans and destroying a number of aircraft. National Security adviser McGeorge Bundy, then in-country, rushed to witness the carnage and sent an emotional report to the White House calling for direct American action. The Viet Cong followed up with a bombing of the US military barracks at Qui Nhon, killing twenty-three more GIs. On February 28, the CIA station in Saigon reported "an alarmingly rapid erosion of the GVN [South Vietnamese government] position" in Military Region II: "Provincial capitals and district towns have been progressively isolated (in some cases abandoned)—ARVN Regional and Popular Force units have been decimated in increasingly large scale actions. Finally, the Viet Cong have assumed effective control over more and more hamlets in the countryside." Privately, CIA and Foreign Service officers in Saigon began discussing their next assignments.[77]

On March 2, the United States replaced its earlier ad hoc retaliatory raids against the north with a sustained bombing campaign known as Operation Rolling Thunder. Anticipating Viet Cong attacks against US air bases in retaliation for the aerial assault, Westmoreland urgently requested two Marine landing teams to protect the air base at Danang. President Johnson reluctantly approved, and on March 8, two battalions of Marines, fitted out in full battle dress, with tanks and 8-inch howitzers, splashed ashore near Danang, where they were welcomed by South Vietnamese officials and a bevy of local beauties passing out leis of flowers. Neither Rolling Thunder nor the Marine landing did anything to stop the deteriorating situation in the countryside, however, and in mid-March, MACV requested two army divisions—one to be committed to the Central Highlands and the other to the Saigon area. These were to be main force units capable of taking on the battalion-sized echelons the communists were now deploying.

On April 6, President Johnson authorized US ground forces to undertake offensive operations in Vietnam. In May, the Army's 173rd Airborne Brigade arrived in Central Vietnam; the 4th Marine Regiment then landed farther up the coast. The White House approved an additional 50,000 troops to be placed at Westmoreland's disposal and promised 50,000 more before the end of the year. The first major engagement took place in November when a brigade of the 1st Cavalry Division battled three North Vietnamese regiments in the Ia Drang Valley in the mountains of Military Region II.

Bill Colby understood the necessity of the United States sticking "its finger in the dike," as Westmoreland had put it, but what then? "The main problem Washington faced was strategic," he later wrote, "—its effort to fight its kind of war, a soldiers' war instead of the people's war the enemy was fighting." The Johnson administration would soon discover, he feared, that main force units, artillery and air bombardment, and large-scale sweeps were irrelevant, even counterproductive. "The finger of Death [would point] too often at the very people who should have been our allies, not our enemies," he later wrote. The war would be won or lost in the bush, at the village, even at the individual level. Following a particularly intense White House meeting on Vietnam, Colby approached McGeorge Bundy and asked for a word in private. He recommended that instead of fine-tuning the bombing of the north or discussing the next increment of US combat forces to be sent to the south, the foreign policy establishment focus on the real problem: how to meet the communist challenge at the village level. Bundy replied, "You may be right, Bill, but the structure of the American Government probably won't permit it."[78]

As 1965 progressed, Colby found himself more and more peripheral to Vietnam policy discussions in Washington. In April, John McCone resigned as DCI. His imperiousness and flip-flopping on Vietnam had alienated Johnson. In 1964, he had been a leading advocate of the bombing of North Vietnam, but in 1965, as the bombing was getting underway, he had warned that Rolling Thunder might very well bring Communist China into the war. The DCI began to complain that LBJ was not giving him enough face-time. And so the two agreed to a parting of the ways. Johnson replaced McCone with Rear Admiral William F. "Red" Raborn Jr., a blue-water sailor with almost no experience in intelligence. Raborn, a native Texan, had publicly campaigned for Johnson in his victory over Goldwater in the 1964 presidential election. Colby's power cord, McCone, was gone. The former Jedburgh would be front and center on Vietnam again, but not for more than a year.[79]

SECRET ARMIES

Vietnam was but one hotspot in the "arc of crisis" that demanded Bill Colby's attention when he was head of the Far East Division. Although Switchback and the 1965 decisions to escalate US military involvement in Vietnam temporarily blunted the CIA's initiatives in Vietnam, the mid-1960s witnessed a dramatic expansion of covert operations around the world. Between 1964 and 1967, the US government increased the funds available for political action and paramilitary operations by 60 percent. A quarter of these monies went to support secret armies or to pay for covert arms transfers to established military forces. The Directorate of Plans employed 6,000 people—two-thirds engaged in espionage and counterespionage activity and one-third in paramilitary operations—a quarter of whom worked for Colby. The Directorate of Plans spent 58 percent of the Agency's annual budget of $750 million.

The CIA's clandestine operations were fundamental to the nation's Cold War strategy. The United States could not fight more than one Korean or Vietnam War at a time. Colby viewed the CIA's covert operations as more than just necessary, however; to him they were far preferable to the type of main force conflict that was developing in Vietnam. The so-called "secret wars," like the one the CIA was sponsoring in Laos, cost fewer lives, ran less risk of a nationalist backlash against US interference, put the onus of defending themselves against communist invasion and subversion on the people of the country in question, and helped to keep antiwar, anti-imperial sentiment at home to a minimum. Indeed, Colby would tout the secret war in Laos as a model for fighting the Cold War in the developing world.[1]

Even with all its assets, however, the Far East Division confronted a number of crises that it lacked the means to deal with. In such cases, the Agency had to resort to cruder methods and hope for a bit of luck. The most glaring example was Indonesia. The archipelago nation, extending more than 1,000 miles from east to west and comprising more than 1,000 inhabited islands, boasted a population of almost 80 million. The predominantly Muslim country was the world's fifth-largest nation in the 1960s. Indonesia had gained its independence from the Dutch in 1949, following Japanese occupation during World War II and a two-year war against returning Dutch colonialists. The leader of the independence movement was Kusno Sosrodihardjo, known popularly as Sukarno. Well educated, charismatic, and thoroughly modern, Sukarno espoused a political philosophy rooted in nationalism, racial tolerance, socialism, "guided democracy," and religious faith. He would be Indonesia's first and only president, ruling from 1950 through 1965.[2]

Sukarno first came to the attention of the Eisenhower administration in 1953, when the CIA reported that the island nation, sitting atop perhaps 20 billion barrels of untapped crude oil, also boasted a thriving communist party, the PKI, and a leader who was unwilling to align himself with the United States. According to former director of plans Richard Bissell, the CIA seriously considered assassinating Sukarno in the spring of 1955, going so far as to identify an "asset [assassin]," but the scheme never came to fruition. Later that year, Sukarno convened a meeting of nonaligned Asian, African, and Arab nations in Bandung. The conference was intended to establish a neutralist bloc that would be able to fend off the advances of the superpowers. The Dulles brothers—Secretary of State John Foster and CIA director Allen—did not believe in neutrality: if a nation was not with the free world in its struggle with the forces of international communism, then it was against it. Nineteen days after the Bandung Conference, the White House ordered the CIA to use all means at its disposal—monetary, political, and paramilitary—to keep Indonesia from following the Marxist-Leninist path. The Agency set to the task, but it made little headway. In Indonesia's national parliamentary elections in 1955 and then again in 1957, Sukarno's Indonesian National Party came in first, the Muslim Majumi Party second, and the PKI a strong third.[3]

By the time Lyndon Johnson was sworn in, Indonesia was involved in a war with Malaysia. Sukarno was growing weaker politically as well as physically, and intelligence reports indicated that he was relying more and more on the PKI, which by then numbered some 3.5 million, making it the largest communist party worldwide outside the Soviet Union and China. At an NSC meeting on January 7, 1964, Bill Colby listened as Secretary of State Dean Rusk railed against Sukarno, declaring him "the least responsible leader of any modern State."[4]

In the months that followed, the Indonesian president continued to move steadily closer to the PKI. He initiated a communist-supervised land reform program, included PKI leaders in his government, and made threatening noises toward foreign capital, including $500 million worth of US-controlled petroleum properties. Then, on August 17, 1964, during his Independence Day address, Sukarno declared the United States to be the number one enemy of anticolonialist nationalism, not only in Indonesia but in all of Asia. He announced his intention to form an anti-imperialist alliance with Communist China, virtually daring the military to stop him. "The current combination of Sukarno's tough dictatorship," Colby reported to his superiors, "coupled with an increasingly effective brainwashing of all local population elements, plus the skilled PKI exploitation of legitimate Indonesian nationalism, and lastly the inbred Javanese tradition of acquiescence before authority, will surely result in elimination of the remaining barriers between communists . . . and those who would resist them." Two months later, Colby presented the 303 Committee with a blueprint for covert action in Indonesia that would have as its objective "agitation and the instigation of internal strife between communist and non-communist elements."[5]

Colby's man in Jakarta was Bernardo Hugh Tovar, a Colombian-born Harvard graduate who had parachuted into Laos with the OSS in 1945. Following a tour of duty with Lansdale in the Philippines, he joined the CIA. Low-key, intelligent, and staunchly anticommunist, Tovar was one of Colby's favorites, and the compliment was returned. That the two were practicing Catholics did not hurt their relationship. Despite the growing seriousness of the situation in Indonesia, however, the station remained small and surprisingly ineffective. As of 1964 the Agency's sole success had been to recruit Adam Malik, a forty-eight-year-old disillusioned ex-Marxist who had served as Sukarno's ambassador to Moscow and his minister of trade. Back in Washington, Assistant Secretary of State William Bundy asked Bill Colby why operations to counter communist influence in Indonesia were so meager. "We just don't have the assets," the Far East Division chief replied.[6]

On the morning of October 1, 1965, a group of junior army officers assassinated six of the seven members of the Indonesian military's high command—executing three of them in their own homes and the other three in an open field near Jakarta's Halim Air Force Base. All six of the bodies were thrown down an abandoned well. Only General Abdul Haris Nasution, the minister of defense, managed to escape.[7] Apparently, the killings were the result of long-held grievances by the junior officer corps, which was resentful over the lack of promotions and conspicuous corruption on the part of their superiors.

At this point, Nasution, Malik, and the commander of the Armed Forces Strategic Reserve, General Suharto (most Indonesians go by only one name), stepped forward to fill the void. Suharto declared that he was taking command of the armed forces and ordered all uniformed personnel to barracks. The triumvirate then announced the formation of a new political organization, the 30 September Movement, which would exercise temporary political control and protect President Sukarno from his enemies. From that point on, Sukarno was nothing more than a pawn. A week later, the new regime, fully backed by the armed forces, launched a major propaganda campaign against the PKI that, among other things, blamed the communists for the assassinations. The leaders of the PKI were hunted down and killed. Then followed a bloodbath of horrendous proportions, with the military and rightwing Muslim gangs murdering every PKI or suspected PKI member that could be found. The victims were shot or beheaded in Japanese samurai style. Municipal officials complained to the army that the rivers running to the city of Surabaya were so clogged with bodies that commerce had ground to a halt. The killings continued sporadically until 1969. Best estimates were that more than 500,000 Indonesians lost their lives at the hands of Suharto's henchmen.[8]

Hugh Tovar would later claim that the coup and countercoup of 1965 took the station completely by surprise. Assistant Secretary of State Bill Bundy confirmed that assessment. In a 1967 interview, Bundy was asked whether the United States had played a role in the Indonesian drama. "No," he replied, "we just lucked out." But Washington certainly welcomed developments. Bill Colby flew into Indonesia immediately following the coup, landing at the same airfield where the generals had been murdered. With Colby camping out on his office couch, Ambassador Marshall Green provided words of encouragement to the new government and arranged for the transfer of radio equipment and small arms to troops in the field. American approval extended as well to the rural massacres that followed. Green's deputy told a high-ranking Indonesian army officer "that the embassy and the USG [US government] were generally sympathetic with and admiring of what the army was doing." Indeed, in 1990, American journalist Kathy Kadane charged that the CIA station in Jakarta had provided Suharto and his minions with a list of 5,000 alleged PKI members. In a subsequent interview, Tovar denied that there was a list. He said he had heard that someone in the embassy had given the government twenty or thirty names, but none that could not have been gleaned from the newspapers.[9]

But of course there was a list. The CIA maintained extensive files on communists and communist sympathizers all across the arc of crisis in Asia. That was its job. Lansdale's Vietnam card files—passed down through the years and expanded—included tens of thousands of names. "I don't suppose that certain people would forgive what we did," Bill Bundy said later, "but I thought that it was eminently justified."[10] What is surprising is that the CIA did not do more in Indonesia, much more. It was a nation of 80 million people, rich in petroleum and other mineral resources. Strategically situated astride Asia's seaborne trading routes, it had been the principal prize of Japanese imperialism during World War II. It also had the third-largest communist party in the world. Indeed, in his recommendations to the 303 Committee in 1964 recommending a modest program of covert action in Indonesia, Colby had observed that if the PKI was not thwarted, even a clear-cut victory in Vietnam would mean nothing. What was the Johnson foreign policy establishment thinking? It may have been that the CIA knew that the Indonesian military would never tolerate a communist takeover. It may have been that Sukarno did not seem to pose a threat until 1965. It also may have been that by 1965, Bill Colby and his Far East Division were completely consumed with the secret war then raging in Laos.

Once a substantial power on the Indochinese peninsula, the Kingdom of Laos had collapsed in the eighteenth century, splintering into three petty principalities that survived by appeasing their stronger Vietnamese and

Thai neighbors. The French reassembled the country when they imposed a protectorate in 1893 and ruled it until 1953. Elections to a parliamentary-style government were held in 1955, and in 1957 Prince Souvanna Phouma formed the first coalition government. By mid-1954, the communist Pathet Lao (PL), claiming to speak for the exploited peasantry and Laotian nationalists who had struggled against the French and their collaborators, had taken over de facto control of the two northernmost provinces—Phon Saly and Sam Neua. Backed—and essentially controlled—by the Viet Minh, the PL soon dominated parts of other provinces as well. From the fervently anticommunist perspective of 1954, vulnerable Laos appeared to Washington to represent a potential domino that, if toppled by North Vietnam and China, could fall on any or all of its four noncommunist neighbors.

Laos was the quaintest of dominoes. Shaped like an upside-down gourd, the broad northern part of the country consisted of hills and mountains surrounding the 500-square-mile Plain of Jars. The area derived its name from the presence of dozens of huge, lipped bowls carved from solid stone, standing as high as a man's head, placed there either as storage bins or funeral urns by some ancient civilization. The Mekong River flowed south along the western edge of the panhandle, forming the boundary between Thailand and Laos, with the land rising in the east toward the Annamite Range on the Laotian-Vietnamese border. The river valley and lowlands were occupied by ethnic Lao, who also constituted a large part of the population of adjacent Thailand. Most were rural-dwelling rice farmers living in longhouses raised on stilts. Vientiane, the largest city and modern capital of Laos, was exotic in a laid-back sort of way. Buddhist monks dressed in saffron robes gamboled along the tree-lined French colonial boulevards. Two open-air markets and a series of Western-style shops made up the commercial district. Portraits of the king adorned nearly every public wall. The Forces Armées Royales (FAR) had never missed a meal or won a battle.[11]

The Geneva Accords of July 1954, which recognized Viet Minh control of North Vietnam, also provided for a neutralized Laos under a regime to be safeguarded by the International Control Commission. The United States did not sign the accords but promised not to use force to alter them. The Pathet Lao had refused to lay down its arms and entrenched itself in the north. Then, in November 1957, the newly named prime minister,

Souvanna Phouma, reached a short-lived agreement with the Pathet Lao.[12]

Washington did not approve of Souvanna Phouma's collaboration with the communists—dalliances with the devil never turned out well, John Foster Dulles believed. In 1959 General Phoumi Novasan proposed to the CIA that he and the Laotian military "engineer" the next round of parliamentary elections to produce an anticommunist majority. This would be followed by "directed democracy," a system that observed constitutional, parliamentary forms but excluded "masses too ignorant for normal democracy."[13] The National Assembly's mandate duly ran out in December 1959, and King Sri Savang Vatthana authorized the military to supervise the ensuing elections. The PL was virtually shut out of the new assembly, and General Phoumi Novasan assumed the post of minister of defense in Souvanna Phouma's new government.

On August 9, 1960, the twenty-six-year-old commander of the elite 2nd Parachute Battalion, Captain Kong Le, staged a mutiny that quickly blossomed into a full-fledged coup. Kong Le was an able, patriotic man dismayed by a corrupt government, an entrenched privileged class, the heavy US hand in Laos, and the interminable internecine warfare between the Pathet Lao and the Royal Laotian Government (RLG). Souvanna Phouma and most of his ministers fled Vientiane for Bangkok, Thailand, but Phoumi Novasan took up residence at Savannakhet, in the Laotian panhandle, where he appealed to the Americans for help in driving the insurgents out of the capital. The embassy, including its CIA station, demurred; Kong Le had evidenced no pro-communist leanings. At this point the king accepted the coup and called on Souvanna Phouma to return to Vientiane and set up a new government that would include communists, neutralists, and rightists.

During the next few weeks, the State Department became convinced that under a government headed by Souvanna Phouma, and including the PL and Kong Le, Laos would soon go communist. Undersecretary of State Douglas Dillon now described the paratroop commander as "a Castro communist-type individual." But Washington was unwilling to unleash Phoumi Novasan for fear of bringing North Vietnam into the conflict on one side and South Vietnam and Thailand in on the other. Washington did agree to continue paying and supplying troops loyal to Phoumi Novasan, however. At this point Souvanna Phouma fled to Cambodia. Kong

Le's troops still held Vientiane, but Phoumi Novasan's forces reached the outskirts of the city on December 13. The insurgents chose to abandon the city, retreating to the north. Thereupon, Phoumi Novasan, Laos's self-appointed dictator, occupied the capital.[14]

On December 21, the crew of an Air America Beechcraft photographed a twin-engine Soviet supply aircraft dropping supplies to Kong Le's columns. On New Year's Day 1961, Kong Le's soldiers, allied with Pathet Lao forces, drove the unprepared Royal Laotian defenders from the strategically and economically vital Plain of Jars. Soviet supply aircraft subsequently began landing at the military airfield that had been built there by the French. The Laotian imbroglio left the Eisenhower administration few options. The US embassy continued to report that the RLG could not be counted on. The Lao, he informed Foggy Bottom, "suffered from disorganization and lack of common purpose within the government, the Army, and the society generally." On January 3, at a meeting with his foreign policy advisers, Eisenhower declared that "if the communists establish a strong position in Laos, the West is finished in the whole southeast Asian area." As a stopgap measure, the 303 Committee authorized the CIA to organize and arm the indigenous peoples of the north, who, it was believed, wanted to preserve their independence and way of life.[15]

Except for concentrations of Lao on the Plain of Jars and in some valleys, northeastern Laos was inhabited by tribes driven up from the lowlands over the centuries by more numerous and better-organized rivals. As of 1961 they inhabited a succession of mountain ranges (the highest peak rising to 10,000 feet). The largest and most cohesive was the Hmong. Animists without a written language, they practiced slash-and-burn agriculture on the high ridges and plateaus of the mountains overlooking the Plain of Jars. The Hmong were originally Chinese—hill people from Yunan—who, like the ethnic Vietnamese, had been pushed south by the Han Dynasty. They had borrowed the Lao language, but had otherwise refused to assimilate. In Xieng Khouang Province, they created a thriving economy based on silver mining and cattle-raising. The Hmong were content to live and work at higher altitudes in part because they did not possess the lowlanders' inherited immunity to the bite of the anopheles mosquito, which can carry a deadly strain of malaria. Dutch missionaries introduced the Hmong to steel knives and flintlock muskets, and every village boasted a family of metalworkers who hammered scrap into weapons and jewelry. Most important, as far as the CIA was concerned, the Hmong were fierce warriors who would fight to the death to protect their families and way of life. In 1959 and 1960, the US Mission in Vientiane delivered 2,000 light weapons to the tribespeople to help them protect their villages from the Pathet Lao and the North Vietnamese Army. True to form, the CIA looked for a Laotian Magsaysay, a charismatic but sensitive leader who could unify and mobilize the Hmong.[16]

The leading candidate was the newly promoted commander of the Royal Laotian Army contingent in Xieng Khouang Province, a young Hmong major named Vang Pao. Life in the Laotian Army was not demanding, and Vang Pao was left free to politic among the Hmong communities of northern Laos. A fiery orator and ardent Hmong nationalist, he soon attracted a wide following. During the coups and countercoups of the 1950s, Vang Pao had sided with Phoumi Novasan and the rightists, not out of ideology, but because the North Vietnamese and their Pathet Lao clients were his people's mortal enemies. When Kong Le revolted, fled to the Plain of Jars, and allied with the Pathet Lao, Vang Pao, still in command of a Forces Armées Royales battalion, had his tribesmen retreat into the heavily forested mountains to bide their time. "This is the man we have been looking for," the CIA team in Vientiane concluded.[17]

By this point, Stuart Methven, a paramilitary expert attached to the Saigon station, was the CIA's point man for dealing with Laos's version of the Montagnards. He epitomized the OSS-CIA operative—a cultivated man who jumped out of airplanes and spoke several languages. "After he moved to Saigon," journalist Zalin Grant recalled, "he lived in a large villa with a duck-eating boa constrictor as a pet. Many would come to see him as a smoother version of Lou Conein."[18]

Methven arranged for a rendezvous with Vang Pao for himself and his deputy, Bill Lair, at the Laotian's bivouac site. Lair was a fifth-generation Texan who had been recruited out of Texas A&M by the CIA. His first assignment in 1951 was Thailand, where the Agency was trying to build up guerrilla forces to contain China's southern flank, should fighting from the Korean War spread. Following the 1953 armistice, Lair convinced his superiors in Washington, along with the Thai government, to allow him to organize an elite paramilitary group named the Police Aerial Resupply Unit, or PARU for short. The Thais commissioned him a major in the Thai Army, and the Agency picked a wife for him—the sister of the Thai foreign minister at the time. She and Lair would remain wedded for twenty-five years. Methven and Gordon Jorgenson, the CIA station chief in Vientiane, decided that Lair and his PARU would be perfect for training a Hmong guerrilla force commanded by Vang Pao.[19]

Flying in on an H-34 helicopter operated by Bird & Sons Airlines—another CIA front—Lair and Methven met with Vang Pao at Muong Om on a bank high above the River Sane. Lair was immediately struck by the Hmong chieftain's appearance and presence. Five foot five, but sturdily built, with a rounded face; even, white teeth; and narrow, intense eyes, Vang Pao exuded charisma—and ruthlessness.[20] He and his people could either flee to the west or stay and fight, he told the Americans; if the Hmong chose to stay, Methven said, the Agency would equip and feed them. The Hmong leader nodded and declared that he could recruit ten thousand fighters; adequately armed and trained, they would be able to hold the mountains in most of Xieng Khouang and even Sam Neua Province, harassing enemy traffic along the mountain roads and valleys.

Vang Pao confided in Methven about his people's fear of being abandoned by the Americans as they had been by the French in 1954. Would the United States stay the course, once it began supplying and arming the Hmong, or was there a risk that at some point it would leave him and his people to the tender mercies of the North Vietnamese? Methven assured the Hmong chieftain that an American commitment would be honored as long as his people were threatened by the communists. The CIA men voiced their own concerns. What were the Hmong's long-range plans, Lair asked? Did his people ultimately seek independence? Vang Pao acknowledged a history of mistrust between the Hmong and the ethnic Lao, but he observed that the Lao had not, like the Chinese and the North Vietnamese, tried to forcibly assimilate the Hmong. The National Assembly had a Hmong member, Touby Lyfoung; his people had no separatist aspirations, Vang Pao declared.[21]

The Hmong were fine marksmen with their homemade flintlock rifles, and a few had been trained as militia by the French, but they would have to master new weapons and at least the basics of guerrilla tactics. Vang Pao proposed to bring the first three hundred volunteers to Ban Pa Dong, a tiny Hmong hamlet about 8 miles south of the Plain of Jars; the training would take place under the very noses of the enemy.[22] Ban Pa Dong, 4,500 feet above sea level, typified the beautiful and dangerous terrain in which the CIA operatives and their Hmong soldiers were to operate. With neighboring peaks hidden behind towers of cumulus clouds, the village stood in crystalline air on a ridgeline that sloped, first gradually and then precipitously, until it disappeared in the stratus clouds that concealed the valley below. During the rainy season, thunderstorms swept the valleys, and those perched in their mountain villages could observe the lightning and torrential rains from above. The thin air would make it difficult for the H-34 transport and resupply helicopters to take off and land. But at this point, Washington saw the Hmong irregulars as a temporary expedient, a stopgap force that would hold off the neutralists and Pathet Lao until the FAR could get its act together.

On February 8, 1961, President Kennedy authorized the arming and training of up to five thousand Hmong tribesmen. Weapons were prepackaged on wooden pallets and flown in to Ban Pa Dong from a CIA warehouse on Okinawa. Unfortunately, Phoumi Novasan's army—its commander more a petty warlord than an authentic leader—reverted to its customary indolence following the capture of Vientiane. Meanwhile, Prince Souvanna Phouma bided his time in Phnom Penh, while the Soviets and North Vietnamese continued their air drops to the Kong Le–Pathet Lao forces ensconced on the Plain of Jars. The CIA personnel in Laos were well aware that the fortunes of war had not placed them and their country on the side of the angels. Many anticommunist Lao regarded Phoumi Novasan as a "crook." Kong Le, in the CIA's own judgment, was a "highly competent professional soldier," an essentially apolitical "born leader" whose motivation, when he launched the August 1960 coup, was hostility toward the admittedly "corrupt bureaucracy" of his own government.[23]

Methven and Lair were in constant touch with Colby (then still Saigon station chief) and their other CIA colleagues in Saigon. Both men would look upon Colby's rapidly evolving Civilian Irregular Defense Group operation among the Montagnards as something of a model. The Americans wanted to run Operation Momentum, as the Laotian project was codenamed, through the Hmong leadership structure. They were determined to keep the number of white westerners to an absolute minimum; in this regard, the Thai trainers of PARU were a blessing. Operation Momentum's first field operative was Anthony Alexander Poshepny, or Tony Poe, as he called himself. Poe was a balding paramilitary specialist who carried all of his belongings in a duffel bag. He spent his spare time devising homemade explosive devices. Poe had run behind-the-lines operations in Korea and subsequently trained Tibetan Khampa tribesmen for a projected rebellion against the mainland Chinese. Poe's assignment in Laos was to open up dirt airstrips north and northeast of the Plain of Jars. Moving from site to site, recruiting Hmong soldier-laborers as he went, he would drink himself into a stupor every night and then rise at 5 A.M. to train local militia and supervise construction. As he had done in Korea, Tony Poe had his Hmong patrols prove their victories by turning in the enemy's ears threaded on a lanyard. Poe would eventually become the model for Colonel Kurtz in the film *Apocalypse Now*.

Kong Le's soldiers rarely attacked the Hmong, but the Pathet Lao immediately began trying to encircle Ban Pa Dong. Vang Pao's irregulars not only repulsed them but began conducting successful night ambushes up to the very edge of the Plain of Jars situated but two ridgelines away. The Hmong proved to be natural guerrilla warriors. Their strategy was to control the high ground, and they did by means of speed and endurance. Living off the land and carrying heavy loads of weapons and ammunition, they would descend to strike the enemy and then withdraw to higher elevations where their foe found it very difficult to follow. By mid-April, operating out of their high-elevation bases, Vang Pao's soldiers had blocked all the exit routes from the Plain of Jars. The next step was to take the offensive.[24]

The Americans found life in Ban Pa Dong beyond exotic. The village was an old opium-trading base with a grass landing strip and a few wooden buildings. The Hmong fighters were inevitably accompanied by their wives and children; as a result, scores of thatched huts sprang up virtually overnight. Vang Pao hosted a dinner every evening for thirty to thirty-five tribal leaders, visiting Americans, and Thai. His newest wife, a seventeen-year-old beauty from the Moua clan, nicknamed "Field Wife" by Lair and Methven, cooked daily meals for the guests. One evening, the visiting CIA men—they were under strict orders not to get captured or killed in combat—were awakened by volleys of gunfire. They ran out of their tents to find Hmong—men, women, and children—shooting at the moon, which was then being eclipsed. "What's happening?" Lair shouted to a nearby woman. "The frog is eating the moon! The frog is eating the moon!" she cried.[25]

As of 1961, the communists and neutralists still controlled the all-important Plain of Jars; besides being relatively populous and agriculturally productive, it served as the nexus for the road system of northern Laos. Nevertheless, the Kennedy administration on March 23 endorsed the British proposal for a cease-fire and the reconvening of the 1954 Geneva Conference. The object of the exercise was to establish a stable, neutralist government in Laos.

As the date for the conclave approached, hardliners within the Kennedy administration insisted that, at the very least, the United States must assist the FAR and Vang Pao's forces in taking the Plain of Jars. Admiral Arleigh Burke, chief of naval operations, declared that unless the United States was prepared to intervene militarily in Laos, all of Southeast Asia would be lost. Secretary of Defense Robert McNamara seconded him: it was essential that Laos not become another link in the "present Soviet chain of successes." Assistant Secretary of State for Far Eastern Affairs Averell Harriman, who had been placed in charge of the American delegation to the Geneva Conference scheduled for mid-May, vigorously dissented; pressed, the JCS admitted that successful intervention in the land of the "Million Elephants and White Parasol" might require sixty thousand troops. When, on May 1, Kong Le and the Pathet Lao suddenly proposed a cease-fire, the Kennedy administration dropped any immediate plans for a US military intervention.[26]

The cease-fire, as it turned out, was honored more in the breach than the observance. The first week in June 1961, as Kennedy was having his famous encounter with Nikita Khrushchev in Vienna, elements of the Pathet Lao overran Vang Pao's base at Ban Pa Dong. The Hmong called for a new infusion of American aid, including air support, to retake Pa Dong, but Washington demurred. Frustrated, Vang Pao established a new headquarters at Long Tieng, some 12 miles to the west.[27]

Meanwhile, in the southern Laotian panhandle, which bordered the northern part of South Vietnam, Hanoi's special engineering battalion, Group 559, had started improving the network of jungle trails that came to be known as the Ho Chi Minh Trail. The increasingly isolated and oppressive regime of Ngo Dinh Diem was losing control of the South Vietnamese countryside, which made it even easier for the communists to dominate the border with Laos. The CIA proposed organizing a force of a thousand Hmong guerrillas to gather intelligence and harass Group 559, but from Geneva, Harriman blocked the plan. The Soviets had promised him that they would "keep communist forces in line in Laos" and end the infiltration through Laos into South Vietnam. In return, the United States would have to comply, "spirit and letter," with the pact that was being hammered out.[28]

In July 1962, the Geneva conferees finally signed a comprehensive agreement regarding Laos—a "good bad deal," as Harriman subsequently described it to President Kennedy. Prince Souvanna Phouma would head a coalition government that included neutralists (Kong Le), Pathet Lao, and Royal Laotian Government representatives. All foreign military personnel—US, Soviet, and North Vietnamese—were to leave the country. A revived International Control Commission (ICC) would police the arrangement. At this point, there were approximately nine thousand North Vietnamese troops in Laos; Vang Pao had eleven thousand tribesmen under arms.[29]

There was a schizophrenic quality to American policy toward Laos. Harriman and his aide, and subsequent ambassador to Laos, William Sullivan, were absolutely committed to living up to the letter of the Geneva Accords. They would, until presented with irrefutable proof, deny the continued presence of North Vietnamese troops in Laos. The CIA, with the approval of the National Security Council, would continue to supply and advise the Hmong guerrilla force.

In the wake of the Geneva settlement, Vang Pao and his tribal leaders needed reassuring. Lair and Methven helicoptered into Long Tieng for a powwow. Joining the communists in a coalition "was like going to bed with a tiger," one of Vang Pao's lieutenants observed. "Everyone would have to stay awake all night." The Hmong leader predicted that any government headed by Souvanna Phouma would quickly fall under communist control. The Americans declared that they would not desert the Hmong. Stay armed, gather intelligence, hold your ground, and we will continue to supply you with arms and rice, the Hmong were told. If worse came to worst, the nomadic Hmong could settle in western Thailand. Resignedly, Vang Pao assented, and his tribal elders voted to stand by him.[30]

Bill Colby arrived in Washington to take up his new post as head of the Far East Division just as the ink was drying on the 1962 Geneva Accords on Laos. For the next five years, he would oversee all CIA operations from Indonesia to Japan. The secret war in Laos would be his pride and joy.

Like South Vietnam, Laos was not a denied area. Large portions of the population were determined to resist communist tyranny. In both countries, but especially in Laos, with its weak central government, there would be abundant opportunity for the Agency to conduct paramilitary operations. Colby would kick against Harriman, Sullivan, and the Geneva Accords on one level, but on another he would welcome them. As long as the United States kept its uniformed personnel out of Laos and concealed its aid to the Hmong tribal army, the Soviet Union was content to look the other way. Moscow even kept its embassy in Vientiane open. In violation of the "ground rules" established by the Geneva agreements, North Vietnam would increase its forces in Laos from nine thousand to seventy thousand over the next ten years. As Colby later wrote, "the CIA's capabilities for covert action became the key to our position with respect to Laos. Since its activities were officially secret, they could be conducted without official exposure or admission to the world. As a result, the Soviets could officially ignore them." And, in fact, Colby observed, the secret war in Laos was exactly the model that the United States should employ in fighting communism throughout the developing world. The Far East Division chief would view the subsequent decisions by the Kennedy and Johnson administrations to put main force military units in South Vietnam with dismay. The United States was not a traditional imperial power, he observed. America's goal, as it had been in the Philippines, was to help indigenous peoples become economically, militarily, and politically strong enough to stand on their own feet and assume the principal burden of resisting communist aggression.[31]

"The Crocodile," as Harriman was dubbed by his associates—in recognition not only of his weathered, craggy features but also his toughness and snappishness—would not be easy to deal with. Harriman had been "present at the creation," that is, at the time of the new international order that emerged following World War II, and he never let his colleagues forget it. Colby and DCI John McCone were made to understand that all CIA operations in Laos would have to be cleared with the ambassador-at-large. Initially, the Far East chief had to journey to Foggy Bottom and beg for every arms drop to the increasingly beleaguered Hmong. "During some of our weekly meetings," Colby recalled, Harriman "would ostentatiously turn off his hearing aid in the middle of my arguments, or bait me mercilessly until we engaged in a shouting match."[32] Two of the Agency's top field men in Laos, Colby said, were reporting that the communists were overrunning Hmong villages, beheading Hmong elders, and killing all the young men. Only after several of these encounters did Harriman agree to a single 100-ton ammunition drop.

One of the operatives Colby brought up in his conversations with the Crocodile was Tony Poe; the other was a young Ivy Leaguer named James Vinton Lawrence, who would become a protégé of Colby's and one of the Agency's most trusted operatives in Laos. Like Colby, Lawrence was a Princeton graduate; he had been recruited during his senior year by Dean Oliver Lippincott IV, the CIA's on-campus spotter.[33] In February 1962, Lawrence departed for Vientiane and his first assignment. Bill Lair immediately took him under his wing. Lawrence was bright and inquisitive— his pleasure reading included Friedrich Nietzsche, Arnold Toynbee, Oliver Wendell Holmes, and Barbara Tuchman. He wanted to learn as much as he could about the Hmong and Lao as quickly as possible. Nothing gets done by ordering these people around, Lair told him. Personal relationships made things happen. Control your emotions. Do not threaten. And, above all, patience.

A few days later, the novice flew upcountry and met with Vang Pao. Like Tony Poe, with whom he was to partner, Lawrence was to coordinate supply drops to the Hmong, help train new militiamen, and supervise the building and maintenance of airstrips. His radio kept him in touch with the Hmong command structure and with Bill Colby in Washington. "It is true that Tony Poe was the Kurtz [the antihero of Francis Ford Coppola's *Apocalypse Now*, Colonel Kurtz was a US Army officer who has gone native, gone mad, and become a savage] and I was the anti-Kurtz," Lawrence later recalled. "We shared this hut at the end of the runway at Long Tieng. It got cold up there. He would drink himself into a stupor by the fire while I wrote my reports and read Nietzsche and Tolstoy. I would have to haul him to his bunk without dropping him in the fire. But he was up at 5:30 ready to train the Hmong recruits how to fire, maneuver, and fight hand-to-hand."[34]

Lawrence was entranced by the physical beauty of northern Laos. Ensconced in a trench dug out of orange laterite, he could look down on the blue-green verdancy of the mountainsides as they fell away to the valleys below. And he was intrigued with Vang Pao. The Agency had instructed Lawrence to eat, sleep, and live with him. The Hmong leader was "strategically simple-minded but tactically brilliant," Lawrence reported. Years later, he told an interviewer, "He thought I was a prince in my own country. . . . He thought I was a prince because I didn't fuck the local girls and because I wasn't a drunk like Tony." (Lawrence was following Lair's requirement that upcountry operatives remain celibate in order to avoid entanglement in local rivalries and jealousies.) "We had a wonderful joking relationship, and one in which rank was rarely pulled. In some ways there was no rank to be pulled. The choice of operations was his. He could pull rank on me, but I could cut off his money. The trade-off was that I never tried to influence [him] except in the large issues[,] . . . and he never bothered me when I was poking my nose around trying to find out what was going on within the Meo [Hmong] community."[35]

Lawrence succeeded because, like the famous Englishman with whom he shared a surname, T. E. Lawrence, he showed respect. He would sit for hours with individual tribesmen, listening to them talk about their lineage and learning their language. He collected and cataloged specimen plants from an ancient female herbal healer. He asked the local shamans, who would jump up and down for hours in their trances, chanting and clanging cymbals, why they "rode so hard." The medicine men explained that this helped them better communicate with the spirit world. "Relationships explained everything," he said. "Family relationships explained why some Hmong turned communist and some did not. . . . In order to get anything done . . . you had to know who is related to who and the history. . . . If you don't respect it, you won't know even what questions to ask, never mind the answers." Lawrence's awareness and the knowledge he gained as a result enriched his detailed reports to Colby on the course of military operations. The content of those reports, however, grew increasingly ominous.[36]

Armed with Lawrence's specific, on-the-ground observations, Colby kept at Averell Harriman to approve increased aid to Vang Pao's army. Initially, the Crocodile had feared that the CIA would train and deliver a Hmong army to General Phoumi Novasan, who would then use it to oust the neutralist Souvanna Phouma and establish a rightwing military dictatorship. First, Colby set about convincing Harriman that the Agency viewed him and him alone as the administration's point man on Laos. And second, he repeated the assurances that Vang Pao had given regarding the Hmong's willingness to remain loyal to the government in Vientiane. At his direction, Colby told Harriman, Lawrence had set up a powerful radio station, named The Union of the Lao Races, to communicate with and hopefully unify the Hmong, Lao, and other ethnic groups. Helping

Colby's cause was the defection of Kong Le from his alliance with the Pathet Lao, and the departure of Prince Souphanouvong, a half-brother to Prince Souvanna Phouma and the chief Pathet Lao figure in the coalition government. These developments, coupled with International Control Commission reports of North Vietnamese Army–Pathet Lao violations of the cease-fire, led Souvanna Phouma to tacitly endorse the CIA's private war. As a result of all this, Harriman authorized larger and larger supply drops to Vang Pao's forces. In addition, dozens of the CIA's best operatives flooded into Long Tieng. By April 1963, full-scale fighting had returned to Laos.[37]

Despite the fact that 4,500 Hmong irregulars were now allied with Kong Le and his forces dug in on the Plain of Jars, the military situation deteriorated sharply throughout the spring, so much so that by late June, the Kennedy administration was once again giving serious consideration to direct US military intervention in Southeast Asia. In late April, Colby and McCone reported to the NSC that the Pathet Lao and North Vietnamese Army forces possessed a two-to-one military advantage in northern Laos. If the communists overran the plain, they would be able to control the upper panhandle as well. Secretary of State Dean Rusk agreed that the insertion of US military forces in northern South Vietnam might be necessary, and with the president's approval, the chairman of the Joint Chiefs of Staff ordered a naval task force, including a carrier and a Marine battalion landing team, to sail from Subic Bay in the Philippines to the Gulf of Tonkin. There the situation rested until late June, when JFK gave the go-ahead to a three-phase operation designed to salvage the situation in Laos and, by extension, in South Vietnam.[38]

Bill Colby, as Far East Division head, played a key role in drafting NSAM 249 of April 1963, which essentially established the framework for the Second Indochinese War. In phase one, the Pentagon and the CIA would dramatically escalate their aid to the Royal Laotian Army and the Hmong irregulars, to include howitzers, heavy mortars, and T-28 propeller-driven aircraft. The T-28's slower speed was suited to the tactical strafing and bombing missions called for in Laos. The CIA would build its paramilitary force to a total of 23,000 men, which, with the Royal Laotian Army, would try to link up zones of influence in a soon-to-be-familiar ink-spot pattern. To Colby's delight, the Agency was authorized to spread the concept of CIDGs and Strategic Hamlets to the upper Laotian panhandle.

A network of villages organized for economic self-sufficiency and local defense would act as a counter to the proselytizing activities of the Pathet Lao and North Vietnamese Army cadre.

In the second phase—approved only on a contingency basis—US Air Force units operating out of Thailand would fly reconnaissance and close support missions for Vang Pao and FAR, while the US Navy would permanently station a task force in the South China Sea. If these steps did not deter the communists, the third phase—to include a bombing campaign against North Vietnam and a US-allied invasion of North Vietnam and Laos—would go into effect.[39] The bombing of North Vietnam would in fact occur. In 1965, the Johnson administration would deem it necessary to Americanize the conflict in South Vietnam, but the struggle in Laos would change only in scale, with Colby overseeing a burgeoning secret war and pacification program.

In 1963, Vang Pao began recruiting men who would make up the Special Guerrilla Units (SGUs), which became the core of the Hmong force. Following their training in Thailand, they would enable the Hmong to take the war to the enemy. Platoon-sized at first, with about 30 men, the SGUs were by 1965 operating at battalion strength, with up to 350 men. In April 1963, Averell Harriman, promoted to undersecretary of state for political affairs, was replaced by Roger Hilsman as the State Department's point man on Laos. Colby found Hilsman, a veteran of the Pacific war, to be much more amenable than Harriman had been to requests for air support, supplies, and increased personnel. Air America and Bird & Sons began flying almost without restriction, transporting Hmong, Royal Laotian soldiers, arms, ammunition, food, and—adhering to a "don't ask, don't tell" policy—quantities of opium acquired clandestinely by Lao officials. Long Tieng, initially a hamlet of thatched huts nestled in a picturesque valley interspersed with formations of limestone karst, became a small city of 20,000, including some 300 CIA operatives. An Agency lie-detector expert who visited the settlement after its growth spurt recalled: "The cast of [American] characters at Long Tieng was something the likes of which I had never seen. They were a composite of Robin Hood's merry men, Hogan's Heroes, the A-Team, the Magnificent Seven, and the Dirty Dozen. Most were contract employees who had been hired to work in Laos. Many were former Special Forces sergeants, and some were former smoke jumpers who had worked for the U.S. Forest Service. All were adventurers."

All of this activity, a clear violation of the Geneva Accords, was still, officially, a secret.[40]

In January 1964, King Sri Savang Vatthana made an unprecedented trip
to the Hmong base at Sam Thong to express his appreciation. Vang Pao
was promoted to general and named a Commander of the Order of the
Million Elephants. The Hmong leader was then at the pinnacle of his
power, mediating among rival personalities and clans, receiving—Solomon-
like—individual supplicants on almost a daily basis. Methven noted that
"the finesse and ease with which [he] handles men vanishes when confronted with sobbing women. Every woman on speaking with him bursts
spontaneously into tears as if the word on how to handle him had gotten
around." Vang Pao had his less gentle side, however. Prisoners were rare in
the secret war; those Pathet Lao and North Vietnamese soldiers that he
did not order shot were packed into 50-gallon drums with just their heads
protruding and left to die.[41]

Most of the CIA operatives, at Colby's insistence, demonstrated deference to Hmong culture. At his direction, field personnel were to do their
best to bring Western health care and modern agricultural techniques to
the Hmong while doing minimal damage to their traditions. Initially, the
tribesmen had resisted bathing, believing that washing would remove one
of the body's thirty-two souls. But eventually, on their own, they came to
see the benefits of personal hygiene. American medics plied their trade but
did so in concert with healing ceremonies conducted by the shamans.
Buildings and runways were constructed so as not to disturb ancestral spirits or sacred animals inhabiting the forests. Colby, recalling the abandonment of the Burmese minorities after the OSS had armed and employed
them against the Japanese in World War II, worried constantly that the
United States might be setting the Hmong up for a fall.[42]

By May 1964, the conflict in Laos had risen to the top of the Johnson
administration's foreign affairs priority list. "The political and diplomatic
course of action with respect to Laos is probably still the most immediate
possible trigger of larger decisions," National Security Adviser McGeorge
Bundy wrote to President Johnson.[43] Unarmed US reconnaissance flights
out of Thailand, Hmong road-watch teams, and White Star US Special
Forces probes had revealed continued construction on the Ho Chi Minh
Trail, much of which ran through Laos, and larger and larger truck convoys
carrying men and materiel into Laos and South Vietnam.

McCone and Colby attended a series of tense NSC meetings at the White House in May and June. The CIA and the Pentagon disagreed sharply as to the proper course to follow. On June 6, a US Navy jet on an aerial photography mission was shot down over Ban Ban. As the pilot parachuted to the ground, he was surrounded and captured by the Pathet Lao. McNamara and the US Air Force chief of staff called not only for armed escorts for future reconnaissance flights, but also a retaliatory raid on the antiaircraft battery that had shot down the navy plane. America's toughness, its very credibility, was at stake, they declared. The CIA, still smarting from Switchback, the US military's takeover of all paramilitary operations in Vietnam in 1962–1963, objected. What the Pentagon proposed was a precipitous, dangerous step, taken not as part of any rational plan to salvage the situation, but out of a desire for revenge. LBJ tended to agree. "The President then said that he questioned whether we had thought through where we are going," Colby's notes of the meeting read. "Specifically, he said, 'and what comes next?'" That question—the most important question raised in the meeting—remained unanswered. McNamara was infuriated. It wasn't LBJ's fault, he declared, but the administration was increasingly being perceived as talking tough and doing nothing. There were risks in attacking the Pathet Lao and North Vietnamese Army's antiaircraft battery, but they were worth it. Reluctantly, Johnson gave the go-ahead, but it was clear that he favored the tactics being employed by the CIA. The Agency subsequently secured permission to expand the scope of its operations in Laos.[44]

In August 1964, Vint Lawrence returned to Southeast Asia from the States, where he had been recovering from a bout with hepatitis. He arrived just in time. Tony Poe, who had replaced Lawrence as chief CIA liaison with Vang Pao, had proved to be a disaster in that position. Poe had refused to turn a blind eye to what he perceived to be the Hmong leader's corruption. Vang Pao would pay his tribal leaders and soldiers only part of the money he received from the CIA for wages, keeping a substantial portion for himself. It seemed not to matter to Poe that the Hmong commander used the slush fund to provide food, clothing, and shelter to war widows and tribal chieftains, whose mountain families faced intermittent starvation. When Vang Pao seemed to dally in getting his Special Guerrilla Units into action, Poe, usually drunk, confronted him. The last straw came when Poe married a Hmong woman whom the Hmong chieftain had his eye on.

Poe's description of the ceremony said it all. "I was clean," he recalled of the wedding. "Loaded to the gills with lao-lao [Laotian rice wine]. Normal fighting clothes. Wore my .357 Magnum, like always. But that day I didn't have any hand-grenades on. . . . And after that, Vint never had to carry me home when I drank. My family did." Lawrence inserted himself between Poe and Vang Pao, and the crisis passed. Colby could have gotten rid of Tony Poe, but he demonstrated his usual weakness for knuckle-draggers.[45]

Indeed, as Far East Division chief, Colby was, by all accounts, a good shepherd. As much as possible, he gave his station chiefs free rein, encouraging innovation and delegating authority. He was famously tolerant of dissent, sometimes permitting high-risk activities among his overseas operators if they served a purpose. "One, for example," he wrote in *Honorable Men*, his memoir, "rigged himself with a microphone and tape recorder to report his conversation with his close drinking buddy, the chief of state, in precise detail." He did insist that the stations reporting to him be more discriminating in the intelligence they submitted to headquarters, going so far as to set up a grading system—"A" for information secured through the most sophisticated and reliable means, and "F" for what amounted to little more than newspaper summaries. At one point, he admonished his officers to spend less time spying on America's friends and more time spying on its enemies. The felt need to maintain close personal contact with his station chiefs dovetailed with Colby's love of travel. "There were sips of rice wine in tribal-village ceremonies," he remembered, "sophisticated finger-game contests with cultured Chinese officials, late-night discussions of Indonesian revolutionary theory, drinks at the Selangor Club in the Somerset Maugham atmosphere of Kuala Lumpur." In 1965, Peer de Silva was seriously injured, blinded in one eye by a Viet Cong bomb that took the life of one of his secretaries. After meeting de Silva's plane at Andrews Air Force Base outside Washington, Colby proposed a rotation system for CIA officers serving in Southeast Asia, telling John McCone that he wanted to distribute the burden of high-risk postings more evenly among his officers. No, Colby remembered McCone responding. The president wants only our very best men assigned to Asia, and that is what the Agency will give him.[46]

When Colby returned to Langley, his duel with counterintelligence chief James Angleton had resumed. The Saigon bombing that had so grievously wounded de Silva brought the security issue to the fore once again. With proper counterespionage work, the incident could have been prevented, Angleton declared. He demanded that the counterintelligence detail in Saigon be beefed up and that, among other things, every Vietnamese employee at the US Mission undergo a background check and take a lie-detector test. Colby objected. The goal in Vietnam was to win the trust and cooperation of the South Vietnamese government. A massive counterintelligence operation would be counterproductive of that goal. Angleton then tried an end run. He summoned John Mertz, a counterintelligence veteran, and dispatched him to Saigon to set up a counterespionage operation outside the regular station, a Vietnam version of the vest pocket operation Angleton had run in Italy. Mertz's men would have US military cover and report directly to Angleton, bypassing both the station and the Far East Division. Colby got wind of the plot and called a showdown meeting in the DCI's office. McCone backed his Far East chief, and Angleton's scheme died aborning.[47]

Throughout the remainder of 1964 and 1965, the battle for Laos ebbed and flowed. As usual, the Pathet Lao and the North Vietnamese Army took the offensive during the dry season, with the Hmong and Kong Le regaining lost territory during the rainy period. With the infiltration of North Vietnamese troops into South Vietnam, the launching of Rolling Thunder on March 2, 1965, and the introduction of the first US combat troops that summer, the stakes in the struggle for Laos began to rise dramatically.

Ambassador William Sullivan arrived in Vientiane in November 1964. Caught between his desire to preserve the Geneva Accords of 1962 and to keep Laos from being overrun by the communists, he fended off pressure from Military Assistance Command, Vietnam, to expand the ground war from South Vietnam into Laos, while at the same time giving freer rein to the CIA to conduct secret bombing operations in Laos. Code-named Barrel Roll in the north and Steel Tiger in the south, these clandestine air operations were run out of the burgeoning American air bases in Thailand.[48]

At the same time, the village defense program, designed to better secure the eastern edge of the panhandle and modeled after Colby's CIDGs, was accelerated. The Laotian version was called Mu Ban Samaki. The CIA provided support for the "covert or semi-covert" aspects of the program, including weapons, radios, and militia pay, while the US Agency for International Development and the US Information Service designed and funded the accompanying economic and social programs. Sullivan, Colby, and the CIA station chief in Laos, Douglas Blaufarb, were able to keep much of this activity secret from Laotian prime minister Souvanna Phouma. Paramilitary and political activities among upland tribal peoples were no less suspect in the eyes of the dominant ethnic group in Laos than they had been in Vietnam. CIA officials in Vientiane and Washington feared that Souvanna Phouma would give in to his chronic urge to accommodate his half-brother, Prince Souphanouvong, the titular head of the Pathet Lao, and reveal details of the operation to the communists, or at least demand that the programs be turned over to the Royal Laotian Army.[49]

As chief of the Far East Division, Colby made semiannual tours of Southeast Asia, including Laos. His December 1965 to January 1966 tour was one of the most memorable. After paying his respects to Sullivan and visiting with station chief Blaufarb in Vientiane, Colby flew to Long Tieng. His drip-dry suit, bow tie, and polished shoes were a stark contrast to the fatigues and Hawaiian shirts of the resident Americans. Lair and Lawrence met the man from Langley at the landing strip. Colby had read Lawrence's long, literate, and insightful reports. He had been impressed with his fellow Princetonian's combination of toughness and sensitivity, his thirst for knowledge about the Hmong culture, and his care for the welfare of the people. Colby asked the young man to act as his guide and interpreter.

Following a long and cordial meeting with Vang Pao, Colby and Lawrence visited over drinks. He had served two two-year tours in Laos and intended to complete another, Lawrence confided, but to his surprise, Colby discouraged him. "You'll never come home," he said. Lawrence at first thought the Far East chief meant that he would die in an air crash, as had five other CIA operatives in Laos. But he soon realized that he was being warned not to "go native," a seduction always present for counterinsurgency operatives like Lawrence and Lair, whose effectiveness depended in no small part on their ability to submerge themselves in the local culture. In Langley's view, once the line was crossed, the operative lost his or her usefulness. Colby said he wanted to talk to him about returning to the States and beginning his ascent up the Agency hierarchy, but that that conversation could wait. Colby wanted to visit Phou Fa, a Hmong outpost in the mountains surrounding the Plain of Jars, to really get out in the field.[50]

The method of transportation for CIA operatives in the bush in Laos was the Helio-Courier STOL (short takeoff and landing) aircraft. Without this remarkable plane, which could take off on a runway 100 yards long and land at an airspeed of 35 miles an hour, the secret war in Laos could not have gone forward. Utilizing the Helios, CIA personnel and Vang Pao's cadres could reach the remotest Hmong base. In addition to people, the aircraft carried medicine, radios, and payrolls. Many of the tiny airstrips followed ridgelines that featured a precipice at one end and a nearly vertical mountainside rising at the other. Landings were always made going uphill, and the approach had to be correct the first time; if an unanticipated downdraft or other event forced the pilot to break off, he would lack the airspeed to rise up from the precipice or turn away from the mountain.

The landing area at Phou Fa was typical. The strip there followed a sharply sloping ridgeline near the summit of the mountain. It also tilted to one side near the downhill end. The Hmong had tried to reduce the angle by building a log retaining wall and filling earth in behind it. The result was something that resembled a ski jump. Though the Helio-Courier that carried Bill Colby was piloted by an experienced man, he misjudged his approach that day. The plane skittered off the side of the strip—the uphill side, fortunately—and the plane overturned. Both men extricated themselves and escaped before the plane's fuel had a chance to ignite. Once in the village, Colby recalled the strictures imposed on Americans operating upcountry to avoid too close contact with the local culture, "including politely tasting but not ingesting the locally fermented rice 'wine,' keeping clear of the ritual bull-baiting that preceded feasts and tactfully turning down the maiden offered by the local chief to ease the strain of a mountain village visit." The exhilarated Colby was later evacuated by an H-34 helicopter.[51]

Back in Long Tieng, the chief of the Far East Division paused briefly to regroup and then flew southeastward to the panhandle to inspect the Laotian version of the Strategic Hamlet Program. The approaches in the south were sometimes as hazardous as the mountain landings in the north. Colby recalled rocking along "from side to side during a ten-foot altitude approach along the Mekong under a morning fog bank, twisting and turning to avoid the islands in the river."[52] There, in the fortified villages struggling to achieve modernity, was where Colby's heart lay. Indeed, the sight of villagers beginning to prosper and cooperating in their own defense was what Bill Colby had come to the bush for.

In some respects, Colby was never able to break free of his experiences as a Jedburgh and NORSO operative during World War II. Parachuting in, linking up with anti-Axis partisans, and facilitating their efforts to overthrow the occupying power or its collaborators had made a deep impression on him. He subsequently witnessed these partisans coming to power in Italy and other European countries, and helping the noncommunist factions defeat those controlled by the Kremlin. He had sponsored agent drops behind enemy lines in the Baltic and subsequently in North Vietnam in Project Tiger. Colby reluctantly concluded that these two operations had been dry holes, but he continued to believe in the efficacy of covert action behind enemy lines. Consequently, in 1964–1965, the head of the Far East Division began to press for the CIA to organize and arm the Hmong who lived in the mountains of western North Vietnam so that they could act as a fifth column behind enemy lines. Doug Blaufarb, station chief in Vientiane, was aghast. Proponents of such tribal resistance, he opined to Langley, were being "carried away by visions derived from [World War II] experience and [were] thinking of an approach that would inevitably end in disaster unless [the] United States were serious about seeking a complete victory over [North Vietnam]." Ambassador Sullivan, who feared that such a move would lead to an escalation of the war in Laos, agreed. Finally, there was something that Colby seemed unaware of, namely, that the 303 Committee had already decided not to undertake any efforts to subvert the government in Hanoi (in fact, only a handful of people were privy to the decision). On May 18, 1964, Sullivan wrote William Bundy, who headed Far Eastern Affairs at the State Department, saying that it was his understanding that "to nurture the seeds of internal resistance" on North Vietnamese soil would undermine Washington's ongoing attempt to assure Hanoi that any peace agreement would respect absolutely the integrity of North Vietnam. And there were the Hmong themselves. "It would be immensely cruel and counterproductive to develop such a movement and then bargain it away as part of a political counter."53

Colby remained unconvinced. The CIA and its allies could not operate in areas where the local population was not committed to supporting them. The Agency and its Hmong allies would not even be able to gather intelligence, much less take effective action to interdict the flow of men and supplies down the Ho Chi Minh Trail, without counterinsurgency bases supported by pacification programs on both sides of the Laotian–North

Vietnamese border. In short—and this was true throughout the conflicts in Southeast Asia—Colby wanted to do to the enemy and its clients what it was doing to the United States and its allies.

In November 1965, US forces fought a pitched battle with the North Vietnamese Army in the Ia Drang Valley in northern South Vietnam. Each side bloodied the other, but the communists withdrew to bases in Laos. To MACV it was simply unthinkable to allow Hanoi a quasi-sanctuary through which to supply its soldiers, now engaged in bloody combat with American troops. The Joint Chiefs of Staff proposed an amphibious landing on the coast of North Vietnam at Vin and a subsequent drive inland that would sever the country at the 17th parallel and block the Ho Chi Minh Trail at its source. Concerned about possible Communist Chinese intervention, President Johnson and his advisers rejected the proposal, however. Then let us cut the trail by other means, the military said, through covert action by US and South Vietnamese commandos and clandestine bombing raids.

In early 1965, LBJ had appointed Averell Harriman ambassador-at-large with a twofold mission: to build international support for the war effort in South Vietnam, and to pave the way for peace talks with North Vietnam. As part of this effort, Sullivan, Harriman's protégé, refused to permit the US Air Force to conduct unrestricted bombing of the Ho Chi Minh Trail; he also opposed significant ground operations. They would, he feared, bring down Souvanna Phouma's government in Vientiane and destroy the Geneva Accords. Sullivan finally agreed, however reluctantly, to Operation Shining Brass, in which twelve-man teams, composed of three US Special Forces personnel and nine Nung Chinese each, would penetrate from South Vietnam into Laos to conduct intelligence and interdiction activities. The incursions were limited to 12 miles of the border, however. Privately, the ambassador referred to Shining Brass as "an Eagle Scout program." For his part, General William Westmoreland, MACV commander, accused Sullivan of "fiddling while Rome burned." The Special Forces began referring to the Ho Chi Minh Trail as the Averell Harriman Memorial Highway.[54]

In mid-1966, Colby dispatched a new CIA station chief to Vientiane. Theodore Shackley had been recruited by the Agency in 1951. Fluent in Polish (from his mother, a Polish immigrant), he was first assigned to Berlin, where he had worked under Lou Conein. In April 1962, CIA officer

William Harvey summoned Shackley to head Operation Mongoose, the Kennedy brothers' scheme to assassinate Fidel Castro. Harvey had known Shackley in Berlin, where Harvey had been in charge of constructing a secret underground spy corridor beneath the Berlin Wall. In Operation Mongoose, it was Shackley and the Cuban exiles he supervised who would wield poison pills, poison dart guns, exploding cigars, and more conventional means in an effort to do away with the charismatic Castro.[55]

Ted Shackley was an ambitious, intelligent, and rather ruthless company man. He was not interested in native cultures, or in nation-building, for that matter. The winners in Washington's bureaucratic sweepstakes were those officials who fit into the larger plan, and the larger plan was containing communism and stopping the advance of Sino-Soviet imperialism. By the time Shackley joined the country team in Laos, the 303 Committee had made it clear to Langley that operations in Laos were to be subsumed into the burgeoning conflict in Vietnam. Washington wanted two things from the Laos operation: first, complete and timely intelligence on communist traffic on the Ho Chi Minh Trail, and second, a much higher level of resistance to that traffic. One can only assume that Colby made the choice to name Shackley to head the Vientiane station under pressure from his superiors; he made no mention of Shackley in *Lost Victory*. The pressure from the Pentagon to assume control of military operations in the panhandle was intense, Colby and Bill Bundy told the new man. The message he was to take to his CIA colleagues was, "If we don't do it, the Army will."[56]

The Hmong operation was then being directed out of Udorn Air Base in Thailand by Bill Lair and Pat Landry, with Vint Lawrence—and Tony Poe before he was shot in the hip on an operation he should not have been on—acting as liaison with Vang Pao at Long Tieng. Shortly after he arrived in Vientiane, Shackley flew to Thailand to meet with Lair and Landry. He first made it clear that this would be his last trip to Udorn; in the future, they would come to him in Vientiane. They had been running a country store, he declared; he was going to turn it into a supermarket. There would be many more CIA personnel arriving in-country; there would be dozens of T-28 fighter bombers and B-24 bombers. American airpower would be used to support the Hmong, who would now be expected to fight the North Vietnamese and Pathet Lao in battalion and even larger-sized units. Lair and Landry received this news in glum silence. They rather liked their country store. Thus far the operation had been effective for the very reason that it was low key. There were very few white men to stir anti-Western prejudices among the Hmong and the Lao. The hit-and-run guerrilla tactics employed against the communists had kept the North Vietnamese Army from moving in with division force and crushing the CIA's secret army. And there was the salient fact that the Hmong were not suited, by experience or temperament, to fighting large-scale battles and defending fixed positions. But Lair and Landry kept their counsel. The handwriting was on the wall.[57]

Ambassador Sullivan was pleased with the new arrangement. The only alternative to escalating the secret war was direct US military intervention, and with it the final collapse of Laotian neutrality. For these same reasons, Souvanna Phouma proved compliant. During the period that followed, from 1965 through 1968, Sullivan and Shackley were left largely to their own devices. "We got practically no instructions from Washington," the ambassador later recalled. "In a way the assignment was intoxicating." One of his lieutenants said it best: "It was great fun. You sit in the Ambassador's office, deal with leaders of the Lao government, arrange for Thai artillery strikes, map out strategy, decide what moves Vang Pao's army should make, send orders to field commanders. It had everything." Clearly, Colby had been sidelined in the secret war in Laos, a conflict in which he had once taken so much pride.[58]

Shackley began by establishing a standard road-watch team, giving it a chief and a deputy, a radioman, a medic, and six riflemen. Within six weeks, seventy of these teams were operating along the Ho Chi Minh Trail. At the same time, the chief of station ordered his field officers to begin forming battalion-sized units in the panhandle. To conserve and focus resources, he ended CIA support for the village defense program, a move that must have been particularly galling for Colby. For Shackley, the CIA was in Laos to win the war in Vietnam, not to build a nation.[59]

With the North Vietnamese Army still streaming down the trail, and the Pentagon continuing to lobby for a larger role in the Laotian theater, LBJ, in February 1967, approved a vast expansion of Operation Shining Brass, to include company-strength incursions. It was the Studies and Observation Group, or SOG, that would implement the expanded operation. Created in the wake of Operation Switchback, SOG consisted of Special Forces teams that trained and led South Vietnamese commandos on top-secret missions into Laos. Initially, the SOG teams dropped in; called in

airstrikes on the trail, its convoys, and supply and maintenance barracks;
and then were extracted. Soon, however, these highly decorated warriors
were engaging much larger North Vietnamese forces in close combat and
then calling in airstrikes on their own positions. During one six-month
period, the American contingent of the SOG teams suffered 100 percent
casualties. Shackley coordinated Shining Brass raids first with Colonel Don
Blackburn and then Colonel John Singlaub. By 1967, SOG comprised
2,000 Americans and 8,000 Indochinese.[60]

The first Shining Brass incursion—the first of thousands—would be
typical. The commander of SOG in 1965 was already legendary. During
the Bataan Death March of World War II, Blackburn and a fellow soldier
had escaped into the hills, where they had linked up with Filipino partisans.
Dodging Japanese patrols, Blackburn and his compatriots had established
jungle training camps to train Igorot tribesmen—notorious headhunters
during the nineteenth century—in guerrilla tactics. In 1944, when General
Douglas MacArthur's forces returned to the Philippines, "Blackburn's
Headhunters" emerged from the jungle to scout for the Americans, act as
spotters for aircraft and artillery, and rescue downed fliers.[61]

The Shining Brass teams—which were Blackburn's idea—consisted of
two or three Special Forces noncommissioned officers and nine indigenous
people, usually either Nung (ethnic Chinese tribespeople who were generally anticommunist and supplied mercenaries to the US military and
CIA) or Montagnards. The teams would be inserted into and removed
from Laos by H-34 Kingbee helicopters, powered by 32-cylinder engines
and capable of hovering on slopes with one wheel on the ground. When it
was too dangerous to land—which was often—the Shining Brass teams,
or what was left of them, harnessed up and were snatched from the ground
by skyhooks attached to the aircraft. Commanding each team was a Green
Beret, with the code number "One-Zero." These men, who were responsible for leading their tiny forces against far superior odds, inflicting as many
casualties as possible, calling in airstrikes on what remained, and then assembling at a prearranged landing zone, would become legendary in Laos
and Vietnam.

The One-Zero for SOG's first cross-border operation was Master Sergeant Charles "Slats" Petry. The entire team was "sterile," meaning that its
members wore no rank or unit insignia. They carried Swedish K submachine guns and Belgian-made Browning 9 mm pistols, both of which had

been acquired clandestinely. If captured, "RT Iowa," as the team was code-named, was to recite a flimsy story about how it had accidentally strayed across the border looking for the crew of a downed C-123. If team members were killed or captured, the US government would deny knowledge of them. RT Iowa's landing zone would be a slash-and-burn area that looked like an old logging clear-cut in the Pacific Northwest. The team dropped in at dusk and proceeded through the rain-soaked jungle to their target area, a camouflaged North Vietnamese fire base that had been shelling US facilities near Danang. The area was dense with trails and campsites, and crawling with enemy troops. For three days, the team engaged and then maneuvered away from enemy patrols, waiting for the weather to ease so that they could summon airstrikes. Finally, the clouds lifted, and RT Iowa called in thirty-seven sorties by F-105 Thunderchief fighter bombers. The team was successfully extracted, with one missing in action and one killed. Petry returned soon thereafter with a forward air controller and called in fifty-one additional sorties, whose bombs and cannon fire touched off numerous secondary explosions.[62]

These Special Forces teams had been consciously modeled on the Jedburghs. Colby had worked with the Green Berets closely, beginning with the CIDG operation, and he subsequently supported and advised SOG. Colonel John Singlaub, who replaced Blackburn in 1966 as SOG chief, was himself an old Jedburgh. Shining Brass was Colby's kind of warfare—individual, heroic, low-level, with maximum gain for minimum effort.

With money and arms pouring in from the CIA, and with US close air support, Vang Pao managed to reach the high-water mark of his territorial conquests in the late summer of 1966. The focus of military operations was in northern Laos in the mountains ringing the Plain of Jars. After repulsing a major communist thrust at Nakhang, his forces controlled not only that town, near the Xieng Khouang border with Sam Neua, but also Phou Pha Thi, only 25 miles west of Sam Neua. And each of these strongpoints served as a base for operations threatening key communist enclaves. In July and August, Colby made another one of his semiannual inspection tours. "I found the situation in Laos exhilarating," he subsequently reported to headquarters. Not only had Vang Pao recovered 90 percent of the territory lost around the Plain of Jars during the previous dry season, but the Hmong and elements of the Royal Laotian Army were taking the offensive in the southern panhandle. Operating with "courage, energy and a high degree of professionalism," Hmong–Forces Armées Royales units and village security teams had secured Saravane and opened the road between there and Pakse. From these secure areas, road-watch teams and saboteurs were operating effectively against the Ho Chi Minh Trail. Seemingly oblivious to Shackley's termination of CIA aid to local security forces, Colby reported: "The most important point of a review of the Lao situation is the clear effect of a smoothly working country team under a forceful Ambassador and the strength that results from patient adherence to a balanced program of building popular participation in local security forces."[63]

In truth, Shackley did not have a completely free hand in Laos. Bill Colby, like Stu Methven and Bill Lair, remained committed to the marriage of pacification and counterinsurgency. The first without the second would leave a political void and ensure that a self-sustaining, self-reliant, anti-communist entity would never emerge in Laos. In his July 1967 report following another survey of the situation in the field, Colby noted that in 1963–1964, the Pathet Lao and North Vietnamese Army were on the verge of establishing a foothold on the all-important Bolovens Plateau in southern Laos. But then, building on the Civilian Irregular Defense Group experience in the Highlands of Vietnam, CIA personnel had organized self-defense units, armed them, and implemented social and economic programs. In the north, "from its positions dominating all of North Laos some years ago," Colby reported to Washington, "the Viet Minh / Pathet Lao enemy has been pushed back to holding a thin edge of North Laos, with a single substantial salient into the Plaine des Jares." Most important, he continued, US aid was promoting the integration of the Hmong into the larger Lao society, keeping it from acting as "a centrifugal force." In the process, he boasted, "Meo [Hmong] school registration has risen from 3,000 in 1962 to 12,000 in 1967, settled agriculture is replacing mountain village slash and burn farming, an elected Meo sits in the national assembly . . . and seventy Meo attend the top lyceum of Laos where only 10 were present in 1962."[64]

By then Colby's stature in the foreign policy establishment had grown to the point where his memos were being submitted directly to President Johnson. The Far East Division chief continued to worry that the brutal war being fought in South Vietnam would spill over into Laos. He noted in a July 1967 memo to the president that Westmoreland wanted to move beyond the SOG operations and outfit regular ARVN battalions, complete with American advisers, and unleash them on the trail. Colby observed to Johnson that the harassment and interdiction of Pathet Lao and North Vietnamese Army traffic along the corridor was the best that could be hoped for. An intrusion in force might bring Souvanna Phouma's government down, provoke a massive North Vietnamese offensive in Laos, and eventually threaten the security of Thailand. "The most serious policy question . . . would seem to be the degree to which the U.S. wishes to contemplate increased commitment of U.S. forces in active operations in Southeast Asia," Colby told Johnson. "The contest in Laos has been by proxy, engaging minimal U.S. prestige, tying down no U.S. forces and involving few casualties."[65] Johnson concurred, and the Pentagon's drive to expand the land war into the Laotian panhandle was thwarted. But the flow of men and supplies down the Ho Chi Minh Trail continued to increase inexorably. If American main force units were to be kept out of Laos, Shackley would have to be allowed to go ahead and prepare the Hmong to engage battalion-sized Pathet Lao and North Vietnamese units.

By late 1967, it was obvious that the enemy viewed Laos as a major front in its war of liberation and unification. In the spring of 1968, combined Pathet Lao and North Vietnamese forces, now numbering some 110,000, captured twenty-seven Hmong outposts and airstrips. The fighting created an estimated 10,000 refugees. Vang Pao fought on, but by 1969, observers reported an increasing number of adolescents in the ranks of his warriors. Reading Colby's book *Lost Victory*, one would never know that the secret war in Laos ended in disaster for Vang Pao and his fellow Hmong. "The enemy was fought to a standstill," Colby wrote. "After ten years the battle lines in Laos were approximately where they were at the start, although the North Vietnamese forces had increased from 7,000 to 70,000." By the time the denouement began, Bill Colby was out of the CIA (ostensibly) and back in Vietnam as second in command of the largest and most successful counterinsurgency/pacification program in American history.[66]

12

LAUNCHING THE
OTHER WAR

Colby had to accept the subordination of the secret war in Laos to the conflict in Vietnam, but he did not and would not accept the subordination of counterinsurgency and pacification to the main force, search-and-destroy operations that General Westmoreland was running. In Colby's view, the United States was fighting one war in South Vietnam—largely irrelevant and even counterproductive—and the communists another—relevant and generally effective. If the United States and its allies did not meet the enemy on its own terms and fight a people's war, it would surely lose. Physical security was important, but so were political accountability, a reliable justice system, educational opportunity, and at least a modicum of economic and social security. US and South Vietnamese forces could kill communist soldiers until the coming of the next ice age, and it would make no difference if South Vietnam did not evolve into a viable society. He believed that military action should be subsumed to nation-building, not substituted for it. He dreamed of an integrated civilian/military operation that would train and equip the Vietnamese to defend themselves at the local level, build better lives for the majority of Vietnamese who lived in the countryside, and bridge the political and cultural gap between Saigon and the villages and hamlets of South Vietnam.

During late 1965 and 1966, the tide began to turn in Colby's favor. On the ground in Vietnam, a team of counterinsurgency/pacification officials—men with time and experience in the bush—began putting together a plan they called "Harnessing the Revolution," a strategy for fighting a people's war. In Washington, Colby, joined by unconventional war converts in the Pentagon, began lobbying the White House to approve a change of course in South Vietnam. Lyndon Johnson, the architect of the Great Society, responded with enthusiasm, and "the other war" was launched.

In the summer and fall of 1965, the Johnson administration poured more than 200,000 troops into Vietnam. These, together with ARVN units, succeeded in blunting communist military operations in the south. The CIA matched the military buildup, increasing its in-country staff from some 200 to 6,000 and employing more than 400 contract personnel, many of them retired military, especially Special Forces. By early 1966, there were CIA officers on duty in each of South Vietnam's 44 provinces and 242 districts. Agency operatives gathered intelligence, advised the South Vietnamese government and its provincial and district security forces, and supervised a variety of paramilitary operations. As of September 1965, nearly 15,000 Vietnamese cadres—men and women—were deployed across South Vietnam in Political Action Teams (PATs) and Advanced Political Action (APA) Teams. Counter-Terror (CT) Teams comprised 1,900 members, and Tran Ngoc Chau's Census Grievance (C-G) Program was in the process of going national. (Chau was province chief in Kien Hoa and South Vietnam's leading expert on counterinsurgency and pacification.) C-G personnel conducted 350,000 interviews, while medics attached to the Advanced Pacification Program treated more than 200,000 patients. US Navy Construction Battalion engineers built and repaired roads, dug wells, and maintained bridges. Frank Scotton, the USIS officer who had fathered the armed propaganda teams in Long An Province, moved to Saigon, where, with Westmoreland's imprimatur, he organized combined Political Action–Counter-Terror Teams in the six districts around the capital.[1]

Counterterror activities were particularly effective, leading to collection of dossiers on thousands of suspected Viet Cong cadres and the killing of some 3,100. An operation in Quang Tin Province, in September 1964, was illustrative. Twenty-five-man teams followed in the wake of a conventional ARVN sweep. Dressed in civilian clothes, they stayed behind after government forces departed and assassinated 83 Viet Cong who emerged from hiding. CT Teams also engaged in so-called "black ops," posing, for example, as Viet Cong tax collectors and occasionally staging a killing and blaming it on the communists. Colby proudly circulated captured Viet Cong documents to the State Department and the White House that lamented the damage done by CT black ops.[2]

Throughout 1965, however, US-sponsored counterinsurgency/pacification efforts remained localized and compartmentalized. Even down to the district level, Agency personnel operated almost as free agents. There was no central clearinghouse for intelligence acquired or for the management of either civil or military programs. The South Vietnamese government did not take advantage of the Political Action and Advanced Pacification Teams to build a political network in the countryside. In some cases, the US military authorities cooperated with counterinsurgency/pacification initiatives, and in others they did not. IV Corps adviser Colonel Jasper Wilson, General Nguyen Khanh's former coconspirator, was so hostile to the CIA that he forbade his subordinates from cooperating in any way with the programs. But the obvious successes of the CIA's initiatives did attract one disciple: Henry Cabot Lodge. The proconsul returned to South Vietnam as ambassador again in August 1965, with Ed Lansdale in tow as his personal pacification adviser.[3]

As Lodge was making his return to Saigon, the military junta was dispensing with Prime Minister Phan Huy Quat and the vestiges of civilian leadership. Nguyen Van Thieu, a southerner and head of the Military Revolutionary Council, assumed the largely ceremonial post of chief of state, while Nguyen Cao Ky, a northerner, became prime minister. In September, Thieu asked Gordon Jorgenson, the new chief of station in Saigon, to stop by the palace and discuss counterinsurgency operations. At this point, the regime was anticipating a negotiated settlement with the National Liberation Front and Hanoi, and it viewed the Political Action, Advanced Political Action, and Counter-Terror Teams as means for combating renewed infiltration, subversion, and political organization by the communists. Ky and Thieu declared pacification to be at the top of their priority list and assigned the task of overseeing nation-building to the Ministry of Rural Reconstruction under the energetic, pragmatic, and generally capable General Nguyen Duc Thang. At a meeting in November, Thang pledged to Jorgenson and his assistant, Tom Donohue, that CIA-sponsored programs would become the core of the government's pacification effort. The process would take two or three years, however. In a "personal judgment which he could not express officially," Thang observed that an immediate government takeover of the programs would destroy them. Thieu's paranoia about possible rivals would see to that.[4]

The most visible manifestation of this mini-renaissance in counterinsurgency/pacification was the National Training Center for Revolutionary Development Cadre at Vung Tau, the former seaside resort of Cape St. Jacques. A result of a partnering effort between the CIA and General Thang's Ministry of Rural Development, the center was to train cadres who would work in Frank Scotton's armed propaganda teams, or in Tran Ngoc Chau's Census Grievance Program, or in counterterror initiatives then on the drawing board. The curriculum at Vung Tau was the creation of Tran Ngoc Chau, whom Thang had recruited to head the ministry's cadre program. In December 1965, Chau produced a two-volume pacification plan that was to become a model for both US and Vietnamese counterinsurgency/pacification personnel. The document was the product of Chau's experiences as a Viet Minh, as a government officer, and then as province chief of Kien Hoa. It was also the product of extended talks with John Paul Vann—who was then a US provincial adviser in Hau Nghia—along with Frank Scotton, Ev Bumgardner, and, especially, Bill Colby. "Colby and I had had many long conversations during his visits to Kien Hoa," Chau recalled in his memoir. "I felt Colby had a much better insight [than other US personnel] into Vietnam in general, and the pacification process in particular."[5]

In postcolonial Vietnam, Chau wrote, the rural population was divided into three groups by the government: those who supported the government—the police, civil servants, military personnel; those who were Viet Cong or their active sympathizers; and the great silent mass in between. During the 1940s and 1950s, the vast majority of peasants had rallied to the Viet Minh and fought against the French and their Vietnamese puppets. The Saigon regime and its representatives viewed anyone who had been affiliated with the Viet Minh as communists or communist sympathizers. Nothing could have been further from the truth, Chau wrote. Ninety percent of the villagers in Kien Hoa were nationalists, not communists. It was this group to whom the South Vietnamese government and their American allies must appeal. Through the Census Grievance process, authorities would learn what the people wanted and who was abusing and who was respecting them. It was simple; as Chau's friend Ed Lansdale had put it: find out what the people want and give it to them.[6]

The first Revolutionary (or Reconstruction, as the South Vietnamese government preferred) Cadre teams graduated from the National Training Center on May 21, 1966, with Prime Minister Ky delivering the graduation address. The fifty-nine-man teams were recruited from districts and villages around South Vietnam, trained, and then returned to their homes to work. In this way it was hoped that the counterinsurgency/pacification effort would not be seen as the initiative of an absentee government operating out of Saigon. The teams would provide local security; conduct Census Grievance surveys; help with medical, agricultural, and infrastructure initiatives; and, significantly, oversee elections for local officials. Separately, the counterterror squads, now named Provincial Reconnaissance Units (PRUs), sometimes with a contingent of US Navy SEALs embedded, would roam the countryside gathering information on Viet Cong cadres and either turning or killing them. The province chiefs had no control over resident ARVN units: "They wanted some [military] force that they could use for a local purpose and we supported that," Colby said. In some regions, the PRUs acted as effective—if brutal—adversaries of the Viet Cong; in others, they operated as the enforcement arm of corrupt province chiefs. All of these programs belonged ultimately to Bill Colby. He examined them minutely in theory and in practice, signed off on them, and touted them to the director of central intelligence and the White House.[7]

In Vietnam, as elsewhere, the CIA operated in a legal and moral world of its own making. The only controls were internal. CIA director Richard Helms (Red Raborn had lasted less than a year); George Carver, the DCI's special adviser on Vietnam (SAVA); and Colby reported in executive session to select congressional committees that were populated with Cold War hawks who wanted only to be briefed in general terms. By its own definition, the CIA existed to operate outside of boxes, whether political, bureaucratic, legal, or moral; the only operations and schemes Bill Colby ever rejected were the ones that he considered counterproductive of long-range policy goals. Like the soldier-priests who came to Southeast Asia in the fifteenth and sixteenth centuries and embraced the world with all of its flaws to win it for Christianity, Colby was willing to employ virtually any means to achieve the end of containing and then defeating the forces of international communism. His pragmatism, coupled with his political liberalism, impelled him to advocate openings to the left to create a vital noncommunist center. This was as true in Vietnam as it had been in Italy.

Colby's ideological flexibility was one of the reasons he was relatively unconcerned with Viet Cong penetration of the civil and military bureaucracies in South Vietnam. Many of those recruited into the Rural Development Cadre and the PRUs were former Viet Minh, and a significant number were turncoat Viet Cong. Colby had no illusions about the CT Teams and PRUs. "They were tough nuts, there's no question about it," he later observed to an interviewer. "The key was that that was a period in which there was an enormous amount of anarchy and confusion and chaos, and a lot of bad things went on on both sides."[8] Some worried about the age-old question: if a protagonist adopted the tactics and techniques of its antagonist, would it not become morally, politically, and ideologically undifferentiated from the enemy? It was not a question that bothered the head of the CIA's Far East Division. The Cold War was a war, and in warfare rules were made to be broken, boundaries overstepped.

Despite emergence of the National Training Center at Vung Tau, most of South Vietnam remained unpacified through 1965 and 1966. There were two types of villages: those in which there was a vacuum, with neither communists nor the South Vietnamese government showing an appreciable presence, and those that were occupied and administered by the Viet Cong, such as the villages in the provinces of Hau Nghia, Long An, An Giang, Binh Ainh, and Quang Ngai. In these latter communities, "the task was not so much to resist an insurgent threat to Saigon's authority as it was to replace Viet Cong rule with that of the [South Vietnamese government]," Colby noted. The province chief in Hau Nghia told one American official that 200,000 of his 220,000 constituents were under the control of the Viet Cong: "I am not a province chief, I am a hamlet chief," he said. In June 1965, John Paul Vann, the US representative in Hau Nghia, was ambushed in broad daylight.[9]

In those provinces where there was an opportunity for the South Vietnamese government to take control, Ky and his subordinates seemed clueless. In a sense, little had changed since Diem and Nhu. The Ky-Thieu regime did not even pretend to adhere to a political philosophy. There was no notion of local empowerment. As one US embassy official observed: "Vietnamese officials do not visualize the program [counterinsurgency/pacification] as essentially revolutionary," but as an "opportunity for economic development and a channel for the injection of large quantities of American aid." And, though he did not say it, an opportunity for personal enrichment.[10]

By early 1966, the Johnson administration was ready to turn its attention to "the other war," as the president termed it. It was never LBJ's intention to win the conflict in Southeast Asia in conventional military terms; rather, he intended to temporarily interpose American military power between the communists and noncommunists in Vietnam until the South Vietnamese were strong enough to triumph on their own. Indeed, in terms of building a viable society in South Vietnam capable of governing and defending itself, a clear-cut American "victory" would have been counterproductive. Vietnamization, a term Richard Nixon would claim as his own, was always America's policy; the line separating intervention from imperialism was extremely fine, but the White House believed initially that it could be walked. In truth, the concept of nation-building lay at the very core of the Johnsonian vision: at home, the president's Great Society itself, especially the Second Reconstruction, was nothing if not an experiment in social engineering. The speech LBJ delivered to a joint session of Congress on November 27, 1963, immediately following the Kennedy assassination was meant to evoke memories of JFK, but it was pure LBJ. "We will carry on the fight against poverty and misery, and disease and ignorance, in other lands and in our own," he declared.[11]

At the outset of his administration, Johnson disavowed any intention to replicate America overseas. But once the exigencies of the Cold War seemed to demand intervention in Vietnam, his mind turned naturally to internationalizing the Great Society. There was, in his philosophy, the assumption that human beings everywhere, especially at the individual and family levels, were the same. "For what do the people of North Viet-Nam want?" he asked rhetorically in his speech at Johns Hopkins University in 1965. "They want what their neighbors also desire: food for their hunger; health for their bodies; a chance to learn; progress for their country; and an end to the bondage of material misery."[12]

Throughout the 1950s and early 1960s the views of American counterinsurgency/pacification enthusiasts such as Ed Lansdale, Rufe Phillips, Ev Bumgardner, and Frank Scotton had percolated up through the US foreign policy bureaucracy. Indeed, one of the reasons the Pentagon and the State Department had opposed Lansdale as ambassador during the Kennedy administration, and subsequently worked to circumscribe him, after he returned to Saigon with Lodge in 1965, was that they thought he had too much clout. But no actor in the South Vietnamese theater created a greater impact in this arena than the iconic John Paul Vann. The subject of journalist Neil Sheehan's *Bright Shining Lie*, which won the Pulitzer Prize for nonfiction in 1989, Vann would come to represent "the other war" in Vietnam with all its promise and its pitfalls. He would become its prickly advocate, first in Vietnam and then in Washington. After counterinsurgency and pacification got underway in a national, coordinated way, he would become its symbol in Vietnam, a hero, almost an avatar, to the men and women who labored in the vineyard, including Bill Colby.

John Paul Vann was a professional soldier who had distinguished himself during the Korean War, leading his ranger unit on reconnaissance missions behind enemy lines. Following the requisite stint at the US Army Command and General Staff College, Vann was promoted to lieutenant colonel and then, in 1961, earned a master's degree in business administration from Syracuse University. In 1962, Vann arrived in Vietnam and was assigned as military adviser to the ARVN Seventh Division in IV Corps. At the disastrous battle of Ap Bac, he earned the Distinguished Flying Cross for his bravery in directing the South Vietnamese effort from a bullet-riddled spotter plane. By that point, he had made the acquaintance of *New York Times* reporter David Halberstam and UPI's Neil Sheehan. He was their chief source as they produced article after article indicting both the inept and cowardly ARVN commander at Ap Bac and the ever-optimistic MACV chief General Paul Harkins. Not surprisingly, Vann was forced out of his adviser position, and he resigned from the army a few months later. Tiring of civilian life, he returned to Vietnam as an employee of USAID and subsequently became the chief US pacification officer in Hau Nghia.[13]

A short, muscular, athletic man, Vann was brilliant, if a bit undereducated. He was also ambitious, hyperactive, and egotistical. Like Frank Scotton, Vann was determined to live and work with the Vietnamese, whom he was supposed to help toward political and economic self-sufficiency, rather than hailing them from the nearest safe enclave. He deliberately drove around one of the most insecure provinces in Vietnam—night and day—in his International Harvester truck, armed with a carbine and a .45. His duty, as he saw it, was not to kill the Viet Cong, although he reacted with a vengeance when attacked, but to compete with them. If he and his comrades could build more schools, irrigate more crops, and cure more diseases while containing ARVN and South Vietnamese government corruption, then the struggle for the countryside just might be won.

Vann spoke only a few words of Vietnamese, but that did not keep him from attempting to have sex with every Vietnamese girl he encountered. Indeed, rumor had it that he was drummed out of the military as much for seducing a fifteen-year-old as for criticizing his superiors. Vann would show up at district and village outposts at any and all hours demanding an accounting from his American and Vietnamese staff. The recalcitrant were often invited to take a nighttime ride through the district of Cu Chi, which was laced with Viet Cong tunnels. Vann would come to know anyone who was anyone in Vietnam, but he became particularly close to Tran Ngoc Chau.

Following his return to Vietnam as an USAID employee, Vann would drive into Saigon from the provinces on almost a weekly basis for drinks, dinner, and long conversations with Frank Scotton, Ev Bumgardner, and, after his arrival in August 1965 as part of the Lansdale team, Daniel Ellsberg. When they were in-country, David Halberstam and Neil Sheehan joined the group. For these men, able as they were to move about the country at will interacting with whomever they pleased, Vietnam would be the greatest adventure of their lives. "While Vietnam was a tragedy for many," Scotton later recalled, "I would not trade all of the wealth in the world for the experiences I had there." After dinner with the group at a restaurant in Cholon, Patricia Marx, who would later marry Ellsberg, described its members as "desperate men" in the sense that they were detached from family; most of them were single or divorced and were willing to die for what interested them, she observed. There was nothing to keep Vann and his cronies from living a foreign, colonial-type existence in Vietnam, and they loved it. Indeed, Halberstam wanted Sheehan to entitle the book he was planning on Vietnam *The Last Frontier*. It was "the last place to have fun, to fool around with somebody else's country," Halberstam told his friend.[14]

Like Colby, the group understood that American troops were needed to prevent the collapse of South Vietnam, but they were deeply frustrated with General Westmoreland's war of attrition. It was a rigid, unwieldy strategy that did not permit adaptation to varying local conditions, ignored the Maoist roots of the Viet Cong's tactics, led to a great deal of collateral damage, and failed to take into account the complex political and cultural divisions in Vietnam. According to the Vann group's math, the North Vietnamese could reproduce and conscript soldiers at a faster rate than the

Americans and their ARVN allies could kill them. Moreover, the enemy had captured the flag. "They are imbued with an almost sacred sense of mission," Scotton observed. "This is the generation [in its own view] that is going to unify the country and expel the foreign presence."[15]

Indeed, the ongoing refusal of the US Mission to acknowledge that a communist could be an authentic nationalist was as great a problem as Westmoreland's obsession with conventional warfare. Typical was a MACV report asserting that "VC reservoir of strength can be found in intimidated farmers and villagers; anti-government dissidents; isolationists; kidnapped persons who have been brainwashed; various sorts of malcontents throughout the country; and those who believe that the VC will prevail." On the document, Vann scribbled, "The one kind of person no American can imagine joining the VC is a patriotic Vietnamese who wants to kick the foreigners and those who serve them out of his country." Something had to be done.[16]

During the summer of 1965, Vann, Scotton, Bumgardner, and Ellsberg put together their position paper, "Harnessing the Revolution." The National Liberation Front and the Viet Cong were winning the war because their program promised a better life for the average Vietnamese, they wrote. Until and unless Washington and Saigon seized control of the revolution and used it for their own purposes, there could be no progress. The paper called for a different kind of government in South Vietnam, "a national government . . . responsive to the dynamics of the social revolution," a regime that the masses would fight and die for and that would survive the inevitable American withdrawal.[17] The ongoing fears of some Americans that their country was slipping into imperialism was nonsense; the United States did not want to convert Vietnam into a colony, but it was going to have to interfere in the political and military life of the country to the extent necessary to end corruption and warlordism and establish a responsive, if not democratic, government. Vann and his colleagues called for placing all military and civilian authority in the hands of carefully selected province chiefs. Combat had to take a backseat to conversion. MACV and the ARVN must be utilized as a tool to facilitate counterinsurgency and pacification.

In Saigon, Henry Cabot Lodge read "Harnessing the Revolution" and endorsed it. That Westmoreland had reservations only solidified the ambassador's support. Indeed, the relationship between MACV and the embassy under Lodge was almost as bad as that between MACV and the CIA. Shortly after Westmoreland had arrived in Saigon in 1964, he attended a dinner Lodge was hosting. When the general began to sing "I Want to Be an Airborne Ranger," Lodge turned to Mike Dunn, his military aide, and said, none too quietly, "Oh dear. First they send us Paul Harkins, and now they send us this fellow, Westmoreland. You know Mike, we just might not make it this time."[18] The ambassador's relationship with Vann was the antithesis of that with Westmoreland—cordial and trusting. It did not hurt that during his time in the States, Vann had actively and conspicuously campaigned for Lodge when he was running for the Republican presidential nomination.

Colby also read "Harnessing the Revolution" eagerly—he had been apprised of the paper's existence while it was in gestation—and enthusiastically recommended it to Richard Helms. But powerful forces from expected quarters arrayed against it. Some in the military failed or refused to grasp its significance. "Pacification . . . depends upon the degree of security in the countryside," Maxwell Taylor—at the time supposedly the military's foremost intellectual—observed. "We found that in our frontier days we couldn't plant the corn outside the stockade if the Indians were still around. Well, that's what we've been trying to do in Viet Nam. We planted a lot of corn with the Indians still around. . . . As security becomes greater . . . pacification will move along much better."[19]

Westmoreland expressed a similar if somewhat more sophisticated view. "Pacification could not be the objective—eliminate the enemy and all the rest falls into place," he declared in a postwar interview. He acknowledged the contributions made by the Rural Development Cadre, the Popular Forces, and the Provincial Reconnaissance Units, but he saw them as merely auxiliary forces, not the building blocks of a new nation. Hawks in the diplomatic establishment were equally dismissive of the notion that mobilizing the countryside was the key to victory. "I don't think this war is going to end by pacification of most of the country," Walt Rostow, McGeorge Bundy's successor as national security adviser, wrote to the president in a memo. In his opinion, attrition of the enemy's forces in the south, bombing the north, interdicting the Ho Chi Minh Trail, and establishing a stable regime in Saigon were the keys.[20]

Nevertheless, the Vann group had its supporters—not only Colby, Lodge, and Lansdale, but also Army Chief of Staff Harold K. Johnson and

Westmoreland's deputy, General Creighton Abrams. Just as important were Halberstam, Sheehan, and the *New York Times*. After Vann had been forced out of the military in 1963, it was Halberstam who had rescued him from oblivion, praising him extensively in a long profile in *Esquire* magazine and in his 1964 book, *The Making of a Quagmire*. At lunch at the Harvard Club in late 1964, Halberstam briefed Dan Ellsberg on the war and on John Paul Vann. Thus, when Ellsberg came to Saigon in August 1965 as part of the Lansdale team, he was already a Vann fan and acted as a link between his boss and the proconsul of Hau Nghia Province.[21]

In February 1966, President Johnson called an impromptu summit meeting in Honolulu. Following the formal opening session, LBJ retired to the King Kalakauau Suite in the Royal Hawaiian Hotel for private talks with Prime Minister Ky and President Thieu. He pointed out that 85 percent of the South Vietnamese were peasants who had suffered terribly from the ravages of war during the previous ten years. That must stop, and the regime must earn the support of the people. At the conference's close, the two sides issued the Declaration of Honolulu, in which the United States and South Vietnam pledged to keep fighting until an honorable peace could be negotiated and to launch immediately an accelerated program of social, economic, and political reform. Before they departed Honolulu, LBJ informed Ky that there would be another meeting somewhere in the Pacific in three to six months "to evaluate the progress toward social justice and democracy that had been made in South Vietnam." Johnson was realistic. "He [Ky] certainly knows how to talk," LBJ subsequently observed. "Whether he knows how to do as well as he knows how to talk is different."[22]

In 1966, as it would throughout the remainder of the Second Indochinese War, the United States faced a choice—whether to fight a war of search and destroy or of counterinsurgency and pacification. Was physical security paramount, or should building a society based on social and economic justice take priority? There was no question that the generals in control of the South Vietnamese government favored the first option in both cases. In the eyes of the regime in Saigon, the Vann group was profoundly subversive. Its members were seen as revolutionaries no less dangerous than those of the National Liberation Front and the Viet Cong. The Americans threatened the existing order—a kind of militarized Confucianism in which the Military Revolutionary Council and its extended families controlled the guns and money in South Vietnam. The Ky-Thieu regime tolerated counterintelligence and pacification only as means to defeat the Viet Cong and to "pacify"—in the infantile sense—the rural population. As the Saigon generals had proven in their attitude toward the Civilian Irregular Defense Groups program, and would demonstrate again in their attitude toward the Rural Development initiative at Vung Tau, they did not view local self-defense and community development as sources of popular empowerment, the building blocks of a vital and independent nation. Reconstruction, not revolution, was their watchword. Vann, Scotton, and company wanted to harness the revolution, but the regime in Saigon was profoundly counterrevolutionary.

Colby understood this and attempted to confront the dilemma. "If . . . the American position supports the reactionary trends which a new sense of nationalism is attempting to shake off," he wrote to Michael Forrestal, Rusk's special assistant for Vietnam, "can we hope to maintain a position in these new emerging nations[?] Even with the use of considerable force as in Vietnam, can we hope to have other than a discouraging stalemate with an aggressive communist movement which aligns itself with the aspirations of the young and arising leadership and repudiates us along with the old and colonialist leadership?"[23] Citing Ed Lansdale's 1964 article in *Foreign Affairs* entitled "Do We Understand Revolution?" Colby in his memo pointed to the overwhelming irony of the American position in Vietnam. The United States was the product of the most successful revolution in history—success defined as participation of the electorate, the guarantee of personal freedoms, the rule of law, and the steady (if uneven) economic betterment of the populace. Why was it that the United States was losing out to the National Liberation Front and the Viet Cong in the struggle for hearts and minds?

Colby did not say so, but the answer was clear: in Vietnam, as in other Cold War battlegrounds, the United States was consistently aligning itself with the forces of reaction. This was so sometimes because ideological conservatives controlled the foreign policy agenda, but more often because of the institutional mechanisms that emerged with the founding of the nation-state system. Perhaps, as McGeorge Bundy had remarked to Colby, there was no institutional means by which the United States could nurture a "rice-roots" revolution that would bring to Vietnam the same blessings that Americans enjoyed. The United States could apply diplomatic and economic leverage to a friendly government—even support coups against it—but it did not possess the means or the will to foment revolutions that would change the social and political equation in other countries. This seemed particularly true in South Vietnam. For the most part, the South Vietnamese Army, one of MACV's principal tools in the war with the communists, was one of the most counterrevolutionary entities in South Vietnam. If things did not change, Colby told Forrestal, the United States was going to lose the fight against the forces of international communism. His people on the ground were urging a policy shift whereby the United States would seek out rising young leaders even if they had joined the National Liberation Front. This would mean working with "dynamic young men" in the trade unions, in peasant organizations, in veterans groups, and on college campuses.[24]

Throughout 1965 and 1966, the Johnson administration operated on the assumption that it did not have to make a choice, that it could pursue counterinsurgency and pacification vigorously in the countryside without repudiating the Ky-Thieu regime. If the United States just refocused and redoubled its efforts, victory was still in reach. The picture of the nation-building effort in South Vietnam painted for President Johnson in 1966 was not compelling. "[I] don't think there's a single area pacified," McNamara reported on January 11, following one of his many fact-finding trips to Vietnam. Returning from a similar mission in August, Henry Kissinger, an unofficial adviser to the State Department, observed that eighteen months after the Marines landed at Danang, one could not go outside the city at night without running the risk of being shot. Traveling by helicopter, he had observed numerous Viet Cong roadblocks across some of South Vietnam's principal highways. There was not a moment to be lost, the president decided, and ordered his advisers to draft a plan to pursue the "other war."[25]

Would-be architects of a comprehensive counterinsurgency/pacification program were struck first by the huge advantage the communists held in the field of command and control. Department of Defense analyst Townsend Hoopes wrote, "For the enemy the war remained fundamentally . . . a seamless web of political-military-psychological factors to be manipulated by a highly centralized command authority that never took its eye off the political goal of ultimate control in the South." By contrast, the United States was fighting three very loosely connected conflicts: the large-scale conventional war on the ground, the air war over North Vietnam, and the counterinsurgency effort in the countryside. The counterinsurgency campaign was just as bureaucratically splintered in 1966 as it had been when Lansdale had left Vietnam for the first time. Lodge insisted on absolute authority and overall command, but he was lazy, leaving the military, USAID, USIS, the Joint US Public Affairs Office (JUSPAO), and the CIA to go their own ways in the provinces. As a consequence, dozens of counterinsurgency/pacification operations unfolded without any interaction whatsoever between them. Matters were further complicated by the always complex relationship between the South Vietnamese and the Americans, from the US Mission and the government in Saigon down to the village-level advisers. As one pacification official later observed of the struggle in the countryside: "It was everybody's business and nobody's."[26]

As early as 1964, Bill Colby had recommended the appointment of a counterinsurgency/pacification "czar" to oversee the "other war" in South Vietnam, but his suggestion had gotten lost in the turmoil of escalation. Nevertheless, he had been heard, especially by McGeorge Bundy. In early 1966, the national security adviser arranged for a conference on pacification to be held at Airlie House, the CIA retreat near Warrenton, Virginia. The State Department was represented by Leonard Unger and William Porter. Colby headed the Agency delegation, with Chester Cooper, an assistant to Bundy, representing the White House. Lansdale was there as well. After much pulling and tugging, the group decided to recommend to the president that he appoint a deputy ambassador for pacification. LBJ did just that at the Honolulu Conference in February, naming Porter to the post and gently nudging Lodge to get on board. LBJ followed up on March 28 by naming Robert Komer, a National Security Council staffer, to the post of special assistant to the president for pacification and rural reconstruction. In doing so, he took the first major step toward shutting the bureaucratic Pandora's Box.

Colby had known Komer since his days with the CIA in the early 1950s. A short, bespectacled, intense man, the new presidential assistant for counterinsurgency and pacification was a Harvard graduate and fervent Democrat who had joined with Colby in advocating an "opening to the left" in Italian politics during the 1950s. He subsequently became a member of Kennedy's NSC staff and earned his spurs as a Middle East expert. Impressed with Komer's energy and initiative, Johnson and Bundy subsequently asked him to concentrate on Vietnam, which he did.[27]

Komer came to his new post determined to bring the apparatchiks and even the politicos like Lodge to heel. His primary task, however, was to keep the president converted. What followed was a series of trips to Vietnam during which Komer would thoroughly irritate the civilian members of the US Mission while deluging LBJ with reports and recommendations. The United States had no choice but to work with and through the South Vietnamese government, he declared. "Suggestions that we must take over Vietnam miss the very purpose of the exercise," he observed to Johnson. Lodge had proved incapable of coordinating the military and civilian sides of pacification. The military's efforts to secure the country in the short term through free-fire zones and the deliberate creation of refugees was doing more to lose hearts and minds than win them. "We can spur a socio-economic revolution in a non-country even during wartime," he told the president, "but it won't be easy at best." Although he was at pains to keep the fact secret, Komer's chief inspiration and mentor was the iconoclastic Vann. In a letter to a friend in which he reminisced about crucial influences, Komer wrote, "And above all [there was] the incomparable John Paul Vann—whose role in counseling me during 1966–1968 had never been told."[28]

"Blowtorch Bob," as Komer would be nicknamed by the US contingent in Vietnam, was long on action and short on thought. For example, he was initially determined to make the struggle for the control of the countryside primarily an ARVN operation. John Paul Vann, for one, was appalled. It was his experience that the South Vietnamese Army was frequently a greater threat to counterinsurgency and pacification than the Viet Cong. "Night before last," he wrote a friend, "a group of ARVN soldiers became drunk at the town's [Bao Trai's] only eatery . . . got into a fight with security officials who tried to stop them—then began shooting up the town—to include ricocheting about twenty rounds off the side of my house." This all occurred within yards of the province chief's house and the quarters of the local military command. "You can imagine how much respect the population must have for the allegedly constituted authority when it can't control its own soldiers—or—how ridiculous it is that soldiers who will not seek out the enemy will nevertheless terrorize an entire civilian community."[29]

Many in the CIA thought Komer a rank amateur. When one of his reports was circulated through the foreign affairs bureaucracy, Special Adviser for Vietnam Affairs George Carver wrote Helms: "Surface features such as its 'gee whiz style,' fondness for the perpendicular pronoun, and breezy bandying of first names ('Westy') are irritating but relatively unimportant. What is important is its tone of activist omniscience which masks some fundamental misconceptions about the nature of the war in Vietnam." For Komer, it was all about the organization and allocation of resources. If military security could be provided and rural reconstruction undertaken, all would be well, he seemed to think. What then would happen when the United States pulled out? Carver asked. Pacification meant more than that. Echoing Colby, he declared that there had to be a "doctrine," an ideology, something for the people to fight for. As Helms (via Colby) subsequently put it to Komer, "engagement of the population in a pacification effort, to secure its collaboration in expunging the communist fish from the popular sea, must come as a result of a motivated population, not merely an administered one."[30]

For his part, Lodge did not know whether Komer was an expert or an amateur on pacification; he did think him a pain in the ass. The ambassador did not respond well to having arrangements imposed upon him. He had accepted Porter as deputy for pacification and then assigned him most of the embassy's administrative duties. When Porter was able to give time to the "other war," he showed himself to be a conciliator rather than a whipcracker, and he wanted to be left alone. "I am frankly non-plussed by the tone of our recent exchanges," Komer wrote to Porter in late July, "which from your end seems almost to suggest either that the real war is between Washington and Saigon or that you wish we'd stop bothering you."[31]

If these philosophical, personal, and bureaucratic issues were not enough, Komer's decision in the fall of 1966 to recommend that counterinsurgency and pacification be put under Westmoreland and MACV, with himself as civilian deputy in charge, threatened to blow matters completely apart. Surveying the bureaucratic landscape in Saigon, Blowtorch Bob came to the conclusion that only the US military, with 80 percent of the money and personnel in Vietnam, was big enough to take on the other war. Whether or not MACV was the organization best equipped by experience to assume the task—and clearly, with the exception of the Marine Corps, it was not— the counterinsurgency/pacification effort was going to remain a stepchild as long as the US military was not invested in it. But there were signs that the Pentagon was ready to get on board.[32]

By 1966, Secretary of Defense McNamara was coming around to the idea that pacification was crucial. In part, this had to do with his growing disillusionment with the war itself. In the spring of that year, the Pentagon chief had shocked LBJ by observing that, in his estimation, the United States had no better than a one-in-three chance of winning in Vietnam, and that Washington should consider openings to the National Liberation Front, even to the point of including its representatives in a coalition government. He was, he said, ready to accept responsibility for counterinsurgency and pacification. "McNamara feels it is inevitable that I be given executive responsibility for American support of the Revolutionary Development program," Westmoreland recorded in his diary. "He is convinced that the State Department officials do not have the executive and managerial abilities to handle a program of such magnitude and complexity. I told McNamara I was not volunteering for the job, yet I would undertake it if the President wished me to do so." The president tended toward the Komer-McNamara solution, but he did not want to ride roughshod over Rusk and Lodge, who were adamant in their opposition to a military takeover of pacification. The CIA was not only opposed to a MACV takeover, it was ready to cite legal and constitutional arguments—whatever those might have been—to block administration of Agency funds and operations by another bureaucratic entity. The stalemate in Washington continued through the winter of 1966, while counterinsurgency and pacification remained at a standstill in South Vietnam. In November, LBJ wrote to Lodge saying that the civilian sector had four months to get its pacification act together.[33]

In *Lost Victory*, Colby painted a favorable portrait of Bob Komer. "As chief of the CIA's operations in the Far East," he wrote, "I came directly under Komer's gun—and loved it. Finally, I had found someone who understood the need for a pacification strategy and who had the clout to push the Washington agencies. . . . He understood what the CIA Station was trying to do in its various experimental programs in the countryside. Insisting only that more be done, he provided the policy approval we needed to do it." To some extent, Colby was right. Following his April 1966 visit to Vietnam, the Blowtorch reported to LBJ that although the Rural Development program had some "questionable aspects," it looked like "the most promising approach yet developed."[34]

In truth, the thousands of Vietnamese who passed through the Vung Tau training center were a microcosm of the society, a reflection of its many ambiguities and contradictions. Some of the trainees, indeed many, were former Viet Cong. "Every effort was made to convert VC sympathizers (and even those who engaged in guerrilla activities)," South Vietnamese pacification expert Tran Ngoc Chau wrote, "by helping to solve their personal and family problems, usually created by local authorities and troops. . . . If these efforts did not succeed, we tried compromising the individuals in various ways so that they would either have to work with us, or at a minimum be less effective for the other side." A few of the trainees were Viet Cong cadres themselves and remained so, clandestinely organizing and recruiting agents who would sabotage pacification efforts once the trainees graduated and went into the field. Many of the recruits brought their families with them to Vung Tau to protect them from communist retaliation. Security was hardly absolute, however; periodically, the Viet Cong units active in the Vung Tau area would shell one of the camps. The South Vietnamese government had its own agents in the barracks and classrooms. Ky clearly did not trust Chau, who became camp commander in 1966; the whole census-grievance methodology, with all its revolutionary implications, was anathema. As was true of South Vietnam in general, loyalties at the training camps were unclear and constantly shifting; intrigue and conspiracy were everywhere. Chau and his successor, Major Nguyen Be, an exceptionally able and outspoken officer who had been running pacification in Binh Dinh Province, labored constantly to create a higher loyalty, but they were only partially successful.[35]

As Far East Division head, Bill Colby kept close tabs on developments at Vung Tau. He thought Chau able and energetic, but a bit too independent, a bit too much "the mandarin," as he once put it. He expressed support for Be, but observed that although he was an exceptionally talented pacification planner, he was possessed of "ingrained xenophobia and hypersensitive nationalism." For Colby, Chau and Be were a means to an end; at this point, however, that end remained obscure. Colby and Carver would criticize those who would seize control of counterinsurgency and pacification, including Komer, for not having a "doctrine," for neglecting the political approach, for seeking to manipulate rather than engage the population. In their own way, however, they were as vague and mystical as the activist Mahayana Buddhists of whom they were so dismissive. Yet another CIA review of the Vietnam situation, vetted in February 1967, and in all probability written by Colby, declared that neither the military nor the civilian roles and mission statements provided "a clear-cut definition of the fundamentally political objective of the pacification task, which is to align the people against the Viet Cong and on the side of the GVN [South Vietnamese government]. All other aims and goals—security, social development, administrative control, democracy, economic development, etc.,—are really subordinate to the basic political objective of turning the people against the VC and gaining their support for the GVN."[36]

One thing was clear—that Bill Colby and the CIA were not averse to dallying with the devil—in this case, the Vietnamese communists. Neither was Lyndon Johnson, but his room for political maneuver was shrinking. Archrival Robert Kennedy had come out in favor of negotiation with the National Liberation Front, raising a firestorm among supporters of the war, both Democratic and Republican. The president had to publicly disavow any intention of allowing the communists into whatever political tent might be erected, but what he said behind the scenes was another matter. As noted earlier, in 1966 LBJ named Averell Harriman his "ambassador for peace." Most wrote off the appointment as a stunt to undercut the mushrooming antiwar movement in the United States, but they were only partially correct. There was some real hope in the State Department that the United States could find exploitable issues between the National Liberation Front and its northern sponsors, and in the summer of 1965, Bill Bundy asked the CIA to explore this possibility. Nguyen Khanh, then in exile in the United States, met secretly with a CIA operative, offering himself as an intermediary in talks with the NLF.[37]

Meanwhile, the Komer juggernaut was about to pick up steam. Despite the Rural Development Cadre program, pacification continued to proceed at only a modest pace. The CIA estimated that during all of 1966, 400 villages were brought under South Vietnamese control, for a total of 4,400 out of 11,250. These less than impressive numbers were due in part to enemy countermeasures. The NLF's Liberation Radio on April 3 broadcast a warning that "the enemy is concentrating great efforts on training a group of lackeys, the so-called Pacification . . . Cadres, and organizing them into groups to follow the rebel forces to deceive and repress our population." Accordingly, the communists called for "great attention to the destruction of US-Rebel Pacification Groups."[38]

In March 1967, LBJ appointed Komer deputy for pacification to the US military commander, William Westmoreland. All pacification activities would be placed under his supervision, whether they were civilian or military. At the same time that Johnson named Komer to assume control of the pacification effort, he created a new, more comprehensive organization for him to head. National Security Action Memorandum 362 established CORDS—Civil Operations and Revolutionary Development Support.[39] Leaving no question regarding his authority, the Blowtorch descended on Saigon and ordered the biggest, blackest limousine he could find. He had it adorned with a four-star flag indicating that he was the equal of Westmoreland's other three deputies. In the days and weeks that followed, Komer ran roughshod over anyone and everyone who got in his way except Westmoreland, to whom he was relentlessly obsequious. But Komer was only the first member of a new American team that would put the "other war" front and center.

By the close of 1966, it was clear that Henry Cabot Lodge's days in Saigon were numbered, politics or no politics. In December, John Roche, special assistant to the president, reported on his trip to Vietnam: "I discovered on arriving that—with the elections [to a constituent assembly] a mere ten days off—Ambassador Lodge was off on vacation in Thailand," he wrote. "Deputy Ambassador Porter has been virtually forbidden by the chief of Mission to deal with Thieu and Ky—the Kys talk only to Lodges. And Lodge doesn't talk to anybody—in Saigon at least."[40]

Mercifully, in February 1967, the ambassador announced his desire to return to the States and resume civilian life. To Colby's delight, LBJ chose veteran diplomat Ellsworth Bunker to replace him. A tall, regal aristocrat, Bunker had made his fortune with the United Fruit Company and assorted banking and investment firms. He had served as ambassador to Brazil, Italy, and India, and most significantly, as far as LBJ was concerned, as his troubleshooter during the 1965 Dominican crisis. Vigorous despite his seventy years, Bunker had recently married the US ambassador to Nepal. "The president emphasized the fact that he wanted to see the training of the Vietnamese accelerated and speeded up to enable us to more quickly turn the war over to them," Bunker later recalled of his appointment. After stopping off at Guam in March for yet another Vietnam summit conference, he arrived in Saigon on April 22.[41]

Then in May, General Creighton Abrams—who had welcomed Colby in out of the field in France in 1944—arrived to assume the post of liaison between the US and South Vietnamese militaries. A West Point graduate, Abrams had distinguished himself in both World War II and the Korean conflict. Although he could be gruff and profane, the cigar-chomping Abrams was, as Colby put it, "more the Eisenhower than the MacArthur or the Patton."[42] Indeed, JFK had thought him sufficiently enlightened and diplomatic to place him in command of federal troops during the Mississippi integration crisis. A connoisseur of classical music, Abrams was a convert to the "other war," indeed, a not-so-secret agent in the campaign to subsume conventional military operations to counterinsurgency and pacification.

At the Guam Conference in March, Johnson had touted democracy and told Prime Minister Nguyen Cao Ky that his birthday was in August—and the best present he could possibly receive would be national elections. Dutifully, Ky returned home and announced that elections for president, vice president, and delegates to the National Legislature would be held in the fall of 1967. Here, if ever, was the opportunity for Colby, perhaps the Agency's preeminent theoretician and practitioner of political action, to apply the lessons he had learned in Italy to Vietnam.

In April, a "Political Development Working Group" convened at CIA headquarters to decide how best to facilitate the elections. Several participants argued, in line with the February report, that the CIA must do all in its power to help establish a broad-based political movement that could serve as the rallying point for noncommunist nationalists and compete with the National Liberation Front and Viet Cong. To everyone's consternation, Colby objected. There was no time to grow a rice-roots movement, he insisted. The best alternative was to develop a list of acceptable candidates and provide them with surreptitious support.[43] For all his talk about local empowerment and his subordinates' repeated calls for a rice-roots revolution, Colby was not able to shed the Agency's penchant for men on horseback. Vietnam was not Italy with its Western-style parliamentary institutions, legal system, class system, and educational infrastructure. But neither was it a political void. Nevertheless, Colby's only frame of reference seemed to be Lansdale, Diem, and the sect wars of 1954–1955. The Agency should continue to search for another Diem-Magsaysay and then use its money and influence to align Vietnam's various factions behind him.

Shortly after Ky set the date for national elections, he declared his candidacy for the presidency. Chief of Station John Hart and the station assumed that a military ticket would win; indeed, at that point they preferred such an outcome. Ky sent his police chief, General Nguyen Ngoc Loan, to the embassy to solicit campaign funds, which Bunker instructed Hart to provide, but the Americans did insist that the military admit legitimate candidates to the field and that it maintain at least the appearance of honesty. In June, urged on by his ambitious wife, Nguyen Van Thieu threw his beret into the ring. Fearing that a split in the military would lead to a civilian and perhaps pro-neutralist victory in September, the Military Revolutionary Council met in emergency session on June 30. Following three days of wrangling, the generals announced that Ky had agreed to run on a Thieu-Ky ticket as vice president. In the weeks that followed, the station worked to persuade various labor, student, and religious organizations to throw their support behind the sure winners. The Thieu-Ky ticket did indeed triumph in September, but with only 35 percent of the vote, a testimony to the relative fairness of the electoral contest.[44]

Meanwhile, Langley was rife with anxiety that the CIA's counterinsurgency/pacification operations would be swallowed by the Komer operation. The Agency was willing to cooperate, but only to a degree. It was not just a matter of bureaucratic ego, but of protection of the Agency's ever-sacred methods and sources. If those were opened up to outsiders, the CIA would no longer be the CIA. In July, Helms dispatched Colby to Vietnam to survey the Agency's operations, especially its liaison with CORDS, and report back.

Driving into Saigon from Tan Son Nhut, Colby reflected on how much the city had changed since Diem's time. The airport itself had become one of the largest and busiest in the world, home to a constant stream of military and civilian aircraft ferrying in troops and supplies. Another air base of similar size had been established at Bien Hoa, just 17 kilometers away. One entire corner of Tan Son Nhut was given over to Air America and its secret missions. Madame Nhu was gone; bars and nightclubs were everywhere and open for business twenty-four hours a day. The streets were filled with GI's, both American and Vietnamese, with pedicabs, food vendors, and black marketers hawking their goods and services on every street corner. Merchandise, much of it still bearing PX markings, was displayed in shop windows and sidewalk stalls. Luxury items from Europe were plentiful. People frequented restaurants, hotel bars, and cabarets far into the night. The aroma of barbequed ribs and hamburgers was now as common in some areas of the city as that of *cha gio* (egg rolls) and *pho* (beef soup with noodles and spicy vegetables). It seemed that everything and everybody was for sale. The outskirts of the city had changed little, still consisting of an endless network of warrens, hutches, and tents housing the city's indigent masses. To make matters worse, Saigon was swollen with refugees, nearly a million since 1963. Rock music blended with traditional Vietnamese melodies, forming a backdrop for the intermittent automatic weapon and artillery fire coming from the perimeter of the city.

One thing had not changed—Saigon's incredibly attractive women. David Lilienthal, whom LBJ had charged with devising a plan for the postwar reconstruction of Vietnam, visited the city about the same time as Colby. Never, he wrote in his diary, had he seen the like. "Along every street, in the open half-plaza, crowded and noisy, these fluttering birds—butterflies?—with the incredibly tiny waists, the silken, long, brilliantly white 'pants' with the dark panels fluttering fore and aft, half concealing and half not the long silken legs." There was no contrived shyness, but rather a boldness without calculation. These were not the bar girls, but the working young women of Saigon.[45]

Colby paid his respects at the embassy and huddled with Hart and his colleagues. He drove the 60 kilometers to Vung Tau and subsequently visited a delta hamlet of some 160 families where the Rural Development Cadre had been active; six months earlier, the area had been home to a mere twelve families, all under Viet Cong control.

Colby was adamantly opposed to the use of Rural Development Cadre or local militia in offensive military operations against the Viet Cong, but that did not mean that his view of pacification was pacifist. Beginning with Lansdale's initial mission to Vietnam, the Agency had compiled names of suspected communists who were active in South Vietnam. The General had carted his burgeoning file trays with him everywhere he went. Colby decided to build on this database, making it more systematic and comprehensive. By the time he arrived in Saigon in 1967, the station had set up several Provincial Interrogation Centers (PICs), where suspected Viet Cong, apprehended primarily by the South Vietnamese counterterror units, were brought for questioning. Colby took time to inspect a couple of the detention centers, which were supervised by a CIA officer but operated by the South Vietnamese government's Special Branch. Whether or not he saw any blood on the walls is unclear, but he did note with pride that the

Agency was churning out seven thousand reports a month, including the identity, location, and function of members of the Viet Cong Infrastructure. Before leaving, he huddled with Komer, who declared that the team that he was part of along with Bunker and Abrams was well on its way to making the "other war" the only war. Upon his return, Colby submitted a comprehensive and generally positive report to Helms, who in turn passed it on to LBJ.[46]

By 1967 the war had spawned a bitter, divisive debate within the United States. On the right were those who insisted that the administration was not doing enough. Goldwater Republicans and conservative Democrats, most of them southerners, were the hawks. For them, communism was an unmitigated evil, the regime in Hanoi was an extension of Sino-Soviet imperialism, and Vietnam was the keystone in a regional arch that they believed would collapse if America lost its nerve. Led by Richard Russell of Georgia and John Stennis of Mississippi in the Senate, and Mendel Rivers in the House, these super-patriots enjoyed close ties to the Joint Chiefs of Staff and the entire military-industrial complex. They chafed under the restrictions imposed on the war by Lyndon Johnson, who would not allow American troops to invade North Vietnam or the US Air Force to bomb communist sanctuaries in Cambodia. The hawks demanded that the United States do whatever was necessary to win a military victory.

Acting as a counterpoint was a diverse collection of individuals and groups opposed to the war, viewing it variously as immoral, illogical, or counterproductive. The antiwar coalition included establishment figures, such as Senators J. William Fulbright (D-Arkansas), George McGovern (D-South Dakota), and Wayne Morse (D-Oregon), but it gradually drew in figures who were not professional politicians or policymakers, such as civil rights leader Martin Luther King Jr., pediatrician and author Dr. Benjamin Spock, and heavyweight boxing champion Cassius Clay. There was, of course, much more to the antiwar movement than celebrity personalities. The doves even managed to invade the Colby household.

Bill Colby not only tolerated but encouraged dissent within his family. Carl, Catherine, and to a lesser extent Paul, who was only twelve in 1967, sided with most of their peers in opposing the war. Catherine, an epileptic with a severe identity crisis, and Carl, who had, to grandfather Elbridge's enragement, dropped out of ROTC, periodically harangued their father on the evils of the conflict in Vietnam. Paul recalled especially one stormy dinner just after his father had returned from Vietnam. The war was not only counterproductive of US interests, they declared, it was also manifestly immoral. Wasn't it true that the CIA supervised secret operations that tortured and killed people? For the only time in his memory, Paul later recalled, Bill lost his temper. Red-faced, he shouted that war was brutal—it brutalized everyone who came into contact with it—but sometimes there was no alternative. He himself, he admitted, had killed men in war, even with his bare hands.[47]

CORDS: A PEACE CORPS WITH GUNS

By the close of 1967, the CIA had come to symbolize for many Americans all that was wrong with the US government—its values, its policies, its practices. For doves, the Agency was the evil empire, a secret society in thrall to the radical right, Wall Street, and the military-industrial complex. It would become the Great Satan in the Cold War passion play penned by liberals and radicals.

In March of that year, an article appeared in a small, muckraking California magazine—*Ramparts*—documenting a relationship between the CIA and the National Student Association. The student association acted as a bridge between US college students and their compatriots abroad. To Langley's consternation, the *Times* and the *Washington Post* followed with their own exposés, revealing CIA links to the AFL-CIO and the American Newspaper Guild. Americans read how the Agency had used the Ford Foundation to funnel funds to the Asia Society, and learned that the Voice of America and Radio Free Europe were nothing more than CIA mouthpieces. The orgy or revelation climaxed on March 13, when future *60 Minutes* television reporter Mike Wallace stood before a large diagram depicting the flow of covert subsidies to various front organizations as part of an hour-long CBS documentary entitled "In the Pay of the CIA: An American Dilemma."[1]

In the weeks that followed, syndicated columnist Jack Anderson repeated rumors that the Agency had plotted to assassinate Fidel Castro. Outraged congressmen and senators, virtually all of them opponents of the war in Vietnam, wrote to LBJ protesting the CIA's corruption of democratic institutions and its reckless violation of the law. The president was properly outraged and announced the formation of an investigatory body. Helms ordered his own internal investigation, and Colby was part of the team. If there were any plots to liquidate foreign leaders, Helms said, he wanted to know about them. The Far East Division head was able to report that the Agency had played no direct part in the Diem coup, or at least in the deaths of the president and his brother. News brought by Colby's compatriots was more ominous. There was Operation Mongoose, as well as Agency involvement in the assassination of Dominican dictator Rafael Trujillo. Helms ordered the results of the probe locked away as far from public and congressional sight as possible.

Much as Frank Wisner had been a victim of the Hungarian uprising, Desmond FitzGerald, deputy director for plans, was to be a victim of the *Ramparts* revelations. In addition to overseeing CIA political and psychological operations and manipulation of various cultural oganizations, he was also deeply complicit in the anti-Castro operation; indeed, on the day that Jack Kennedy was assassinated, FitzGerald had been in Paris meeting with a would-be assassin to hand over instructions and weapons. FitzGerald—bird-watcher, poetry-lover—was an enormously social animal. Richard Helms once remarked that he believed that the DDP knew everyone on the New York and Washington social registers personally.[2] During the summer of 1967, FitzGerald's friends noted his unusual despondency, his sudden self-absorption, and his rundown physical appearance. On September 13, while playing mixed doubles with the British ambassador and his wife, FitzGerald collapsed and died of a massive coronary. Like Frank Wisner, Des FitzGerald was fifty-six years old when his life ended.

Helms had the president award FitzGerald the National Security Medal posthumously and then began the search for a successor. Colby was a candidate, or believed that he was. In June 1965, when Helms had been promoted to deputy director, he had launched a search for his own successor as DDP. At the time, he had called Colby in and told him, "Your time will come later." Colby now seemed to be a likely candidate to replace FitzGerald. There was his Jedburgh pedigree; he was an Ivy Leaguer (if a liberal, middle-class one), had worked political action in Italy, had served as station chief in Saigon, and then, as Far East Division head, had run the Agency's many complex paramilitary operations throughout Asia. But he was not foreign intelligence (espionage), and Helms was. Helms was a traditionalist, believing that the primary functions of the CIA were to spy on the enemy, to gather intelligence from every possible source, and to provide that information to policymakers. In 1967, he chose as deputy director of plans not Colby but Thomas Karamessines, a Greek American with impeccable foreign intelligence credentials. He had opened the CIA's station in Athens and then overseen its activities in Vienna. Most recently, he had served as FitzGerald's chief of operations. Helms never even discussed the DDP position with Colby. Instead, in September 1967, he summoned him to his office and suggested that he take over the Soviet and East European Division.[3]

Colby tried to put the best face on the offer, choosing to view it as a move by Helms to provide him with the credentials to advance, to "shuck my stereotype as strictly a political and paramilitary operator."[4] Although he had spent the last eight years obsessed with Southeast Asia, Colby believed he had no choice but to accept. The new post would offer an opportunity to move against the "hard targets," the military and civilian officials who held the secrets of the Soviet empire.

Years later, Colby recalled that as he prepared for his new duties, he became aware of two separate and often conflicting cultures within the Agency regarding Russia and its satellites, one in the division he was to head, and another in counterintelligence, Angleton's CI Staff. Colby's Soviet and East European Division was charged with developing sources behind the Iron Curtain, identifying and encouraging defectors, and coordinating with allied espionage operations. The CI Staff was devoted to protecting the Agency against penetration and disinformation operations by the KGB. Colby soon discovered that in its obsession with uncovering a Soviet mole, counterintelligence was not only overshadowing, but also undermining, the Soviet and East European Division.

Theoretically, CI was just another component of the clandestine services supervised by the deputy director of plans. In reality, by the mid-1960s, Angleton and his staff had evolved into an autonomous fiefdom operating outside of regular channels, reporting to the DCI only. Helms was as enamored of Angleton as Allen Dulles had been. "Do you know what I worried about the most as Director of the CIA?" he asked Ben Bradlee of the *Washington Post* several years after his retirement. "The CIA is the only intelligence service in the Western world which has never been penetrated by the KGB," the former DCI said. "That's what I worried about."[5] Angleton was the shield that Helms thought indispensable. The CI director, who was also sole manager of the Israeli desk, was a legend by the time

Helms took over. He would provide invaluable intelligence to the DCI, and through him to the White House, on the 1967 Arab-Israeli Conflict.

Counterintelligence itself was perceived to be an esoteric undertaking involving unique expertise and Jesuitical dedication. It required, or so its practitioners would have others believe, the cerebral acuity of Lord Peter Wimsy and the ruthlessness of Rasputin. Personally, Angleton delighted in his eccentricities, among which were fly-fishing, orchid-raising—a hobby requiring infinite patience—and drinking. He continued to patronize La Niçoise on Wisconsin Avenue, where lunches would frequently last from noon to 3 P.M. Though no Bill Harvey—he of the Berlin tunnel and Bay of Pigs fame, whose alcohol consumption was legendary—Angleton would sandwich a martini or two between bourbons. Shortly after he became counterintelligence chief in 1954, Angleton set up the Special Investigation Group to look into the possibility that the Agency itself had been penetrated. He succeeded in converting his subordinates into a devoted, even fanatical band of followers not only because of ideological affinity, but also because he understood the isolation and loneliness of counterintelligence; only he was able to recognize and reward his underlings' sacrifices.[6]

Angleton's office at Langley reflected the man and his trade. There was a large inner chamber, its windows covered with venetian blinds that were permanently closed when the doctor was in. Angleton perched in a high-backed leather chair behind a large, executive-style wooden desk that dominated the room. "When a visitor entered Angleton's office," his biographer wrote, "it was almost impossible to see the head of CI. His long, thin frame would be stoop-hunched behind a Berlin wall of files. Since the blinds were firmly closed, the room was always dark, like a poolroom at midday. The only light came from the tip of Angleton's inevitable cigarette and . . . his desk lamp, permanently wreathed by nicotine clouds." The outer office featured several large black iron safes, and across the hall was a specially reinforced vault with a combination lock and an electronic keypad. Only Angleton and his secretary possessed the combinations. Here were stored the millions and millions of pages of intelligence that Angleton and his staff had gathered on KGB spies and suspected turncoats in the CIA.[7]

The Soviet Union and its satellites were dedicated to the destruction of the West, Angleton continued to believe. The KGB, the largest and most imposing security and intelligence apparatus the world had ever seen, was determined to penetrate Western intelligence agencies to gather crucial data and spread destructive disinformation. Rumors of a Sino-Soviet split had been planted by the KGB to sow confusion in the ranks of its enemies. An "integrated and purposeful Socialist Bloc," Angleton wrote in 1966, sought to foster false stories of "splits, evolution, power struggles, economic disasters, [and] good and bad Communism" to ensnare America and its allies in a "wilderness of mirrors." The object of the communist initiative was to splinter Western solidarity and pick off the Free World nations one by one. The only protection the United States and its friends had was the counterintelligence service. Literally, Angleton believed that he and his team held the fate of Western civilization in their hands. Always in the back of Angleton's mind was the traitorous Kim Philby, the ultimate mole, his former friend and confidant.[8]

Just as the fictional James Bond had a license to kill, Jim Angleton, it seemed, had a license to cast suspicion. From the beginning of Helms's tenure, he had given the CI chief free rein, tolerating his secret trips abroad and his end runs around Karamessines. Like so many others, Helms seemed in thrall to Angleton. Howard Osborne, director of security, recalled "how Helms never turned [Angleton] down on anything." Even if everyone in a meeting opposed Angleton's view, Helms always decided in favor of his CI chief. "It never failed," Osborne declared, "no matter how senior [Angleton's] opponent."[9]

By the mid-1960s, Angleton's obsession and Helms's tacit support of it had hamstrung the Soviet and East European Division's efforts to conduct espionage within the Soviet bloc, especially by recruiting defectors. To Angleton and his team, every defector was a KGB plant charged with spreading disinformation. By extension, every Soviet and East European Division officer who sought to provide bona fides for defectors was a willing or unwilling tool of the KGB. Bolstering this view were the cases of two Soviet defectors, Yuri Nosenko and Anatoliy Golitsin.

Late in 1961, Golitsin, a KGB officer, had surrendered himself to CIA agents in Finland. He was vetted by Britain's MI-6 and officers of Angleton's CI division. America's counterspy personally endorsed Golitsin's bona fides and from that point on treated everything the defector said as the gospel truth. Angleton subsequently gave him the keys to the kingdom, that is, access to the vault. Using the material within, Golitsin began casting suspicion on various CIA operatives, especially in the Soviet–East European division. The Agency was riddled with moles, he told Angleton. Expect the KGB to send false defectors to spread disinformation.

Just as Golitsin had suspected he would, Angleton exulted. Almost on cue, Soviet KGB officer Yuri Nosenko contacted American embassy officials in Geneva in June 1962, offering to sell information. The deal was sealed, and for the next two years Nosenko fed the CIA intelligence on KGB activities inside and outside the Soviet bloc. In 1964, feeling the hot breath of the Kremlin's security apparatus on his neck, Nosenko himself defected.

From the outset, Angleton and others on his CI team were suspicious of Nosenko. He was just too good to be true. When the Russian insisted that the KGB had shunned Lee Harvey Oswald repeatedly during the assassin's time in the Soviet Union, and in fact had been "horrified" by the killing of the president, Angleton became convinced that he was a double agent. Golitsin had warned him that Nosenko's appearance just three months after JFK's assassination, and his news that Oswald was not a KGB hit man, seemed too coincidental. Angleton bullied the head of the Soviet and East European Division at that time into agreeing with him, and for the next two years Nosenko was intermittently confined and interrogated in a CIA safe house in Clinton, Maryland. During the first year and a half, his home was a ten-by-ten-foot concrete cell with an iron bed bolted to the floor. He was put on a diet of little more than bread and water and subjected to sensory deprivation. Throughout, Nosenko refused to confess. In 1966, Helms ordered his release, but the case was still pending when the director asked Bill Colby to take over the Soviet and East European Division. Nosenko's plight was symptomatic.[10]

By the time Colby arrived on the scene in the fall of 1967, Angleton had so paralyzed the Soviet and East European Division that the Agency was producing virtually no human intelligence (HUMINT) on its most fearsome opponent. "Indeed," he later observed, "we seemed to be putting more emphasis on the KGB as the CIA's adversary than on the Soviet Union as the United States' adversary." Colby hoped to avoid a clash with Angleton, but if that was what the situation required, so be it. A sudden turn of events, however, postponed the confrontation.[11]

One afternoon in November, Richard Helms summoned Colby to his office. Bob Komer had pulled a fast one on him, he complained. During the most recent of LBJ's famous "Tuesday lunches," the president had turned to Helms and said that Komer had asked that Colby be dispatched to Saigon to act as his deputy in running CORDS. Johnson had made it plain that this was not to be considered a request, but an order. Would he think it over? Helms asked Colby. Of course, the former Jedburgh replied.

Colby later wrote in *Honorable Men* that he was at first shocked by the sudden assignment change, but upon reflection, he decided that it made sense. He had been deeply involved in Vietnam for almost a decade; Komer was embarking on a course that Colby had been advocating for years. The assignment would interrupt his career path within the CIA, but hopefully he could get back on track when the war was over. His departure would impose a hardship on Barbara and the children, but he had ordered numerous CIA and Foreign Service Officers to make the same sacrifice. During a lengthy discussion with his wife, Colby convinced her that the family would have to do what was best for the country. The temptation "to move toward the sound of the guns" was irresistible, and both knew it. Informed of the decision the next morning, Helms thanked Colby and assured him that he would be welcomed back to the Agency at the close of his assignment.[12]

From a bureaucratic perspective, Colby's appointment as CORDS deputy was essential. The CIA was already running the Rural Development Cadre program, the counterterror teams, and the Provincial Interrogation Centers. It would have to assume a central role in any assault on the infrastructure of the enemy in South Vietnam, the omnipresent Viet Cong cadre. The Agency was not about to allow Komer and CORDS to gain control over Agency operations and funds. Having a CIA man as Blowtorch Bob's deputy was a solution to the problem. Nevertheless, in his memoir, Helms accused Colby of conspiring with Komer behind his back. "In his book, Colby notes that the appointment came as news to him," Helms wrote. "This I must doubt. I've been around Washington too long to believe that a senior officer of one agency might be transferred across town to another agency, and offered the prospect of ambassadorial rank, without ever having been asked if he might so much as consider the proposition." He added, "It is probably just as well that Colby was assigned to Saigon. His lack of understanding of counterintelligence, and his unwillingness to absorb its precepts, would not have been compatible with the Soviet responsibility, and would surely have put him at loggerheads with Jim Angleton."[13]

Helms's reaction to Colby's reassignment is fraught with possible hidden meanings. One explanation is that he felt insulted: the Soviet division was a plum, and Colby had rejected his offer of it. Another is that Helms was setting Colby up for a showdown with Angleton, a confrontation in which he was sure Angleton would prevail. In truth, Helms was much closer to Angleton than Colby; he came out of the espionage and counterespionage side of the organization. Political action and covert operations had never excited him, although he was willing to bend with the wind when counterinsurgency and pacification became popular at the White House. The sound of guns aside, by accepting the CORDS position (even possibly having arranged to be offered it), Colby might have been escaping the trap that was being set for him. But the former Jedburgh had another reason for wanting an assignment in South Vietnam. By 1967, he had become completely alienated from Barbara.

According to one source, Bill had told Bob Myers, his old friend and former deputy, that he knew two weeks after his marriage that he had made a dreadful mistake. Barbara Heinzen came from money and had attended Barnard College, but her adolescence and early womanhood had not been particularly happy. Following a nervous breakdown and subsequent illness, her father died during her freshman year in college. Her mother was a fashionista, a social butterfly, and not particularly nurturing. Bill Colby was just one of several boys she dated. After Bill left for the service, she became engaged to a young man who was subsequently killed in action. Bill would later confide to his second wife that when he was home on leave awaiting orders for the Pacific, he got out his little black book and began calling girls he had dated before the war. Barbara was the fifth or sixth, not the first, as he would claim in his memoir.[14] They got married because that was what returning veterans and the girls who waited at home did. The couple had five children not because they were Catholic—both Bill and Barbara were only children—but because this was typical in the 1950s: couples during that decade had four offspring, on average.

As the years passed, Barbara became more and more garrulous, talking at times nonstop about nothing in particular. "She was completely effervescent, talked all the time, going from one thing to another. Sometimes she would come back to what the hell she was talking about and sometimes she wouldn't," family friend Stan Temko later observed. "They [Bill and Barbara] were completely in a way different personalities." Barbara loved cocktail parties and small talk; he hated both. Bill loathed suburban life; Barbara thrived on it. The task of raising five children with her husband absent for long stretches of time created a rising tide of resentment. To make matters worse, one, Catherine, had medical problems. She suffered from epilepsy all her life, her grand mal seizures only moderated by medication. Redheaded, plump, insecure, Catherine adored her father. She wanted desperately to please him, for him to be to her what Bill's mother had been to him. When he was with his daughter, Bill largely filled the bill. There were shared interests and an intimacy that sometimes seemed lacking in Bill's relationships with other members of his family. The problem was that father and daughter were too often separated.[15]

Increasingly, to Barbara's intense frustration, her husband shut her out, even from the family arguments that periodically raged after Carl and Catherine began flirting with the antiwar movement. She would sometimes join them, trying to take the moral high ground. Bill generally ignored her. "Their marriage was unbelievable," Susan Colby, John's wife, recalled. "I've never seen anything like it. They fought all the time, about the war, when he was going to come home, you name it. . . . There would be these endless dinners."[16]

Several times after returning from trips, Colby would pull up in front of the house in Bethesda and be unable to get out of the taxi. When rumors of a Saigon affair drifted back to Barbara, she denied the possibility. "We have a contract," she declared. By the time Bill was assigned to CORDS, families were not allowed to accompany military and government personnel assigned to Vietnam. "I had one friend, a wife, who said why don't you come to Bangkok," Barbara recalled. "But I had five children, and Cathy wasn't well. I couldn't go to Bangkok or the Philippines. I wouldn't have seen that much of him anyway, and I would have had a whole new deal with schools."[17] Her husband was, no doubt, greatly relieved. Bill Colby agreed to go to Vietnam to become second in command at CORDS because he wanted to serve his country and save himself. For him, freedom had become a personal as well as a political cause.

It would be three months, however, before Colby could actually take his leave of the Agency and depart for Saigon. He was still tasked with finding his replacement as head of the Far East Division, and he had to get his personal life in order. Feeling some guilt over leaving Catherine and Paul, who was just entering adolescence, Colby spent as much time as he could with his children. While skating on a frozen portion of the Chesapeake and Ohio Canal that runs through Georgetown, he fell and broke his ankle. During his brief convalescence, Colby talked with his children about the future. Catherine had become vastly enamored of Vietnam, though she had been a small child during the family's years there. What he intended to do, he assured her, was to help the Vietnamese help themselves, to build on the CIDG program and raise up self-sufficient, politically active communities throughout the countryside that could put South Vietnam on the road to self-determination and a prosperous, noncommunist future.[18]

In the privacy of his own thoughts, Colby was moderately optimistic. The team being assembled in Vietnam—Komer, Bunker, and Abrams—promised a coordination and cooperation that had not hitherto existed within the US Mission. The Johnson administration had declared that the "other war" would take precedence, that the regular military would be the tail and counterinsurgency and pacification the dog. Colby was enthusiastic about a CORDS in which civilians reported to military and military to civilians, though he was never able to rid himself of a lingering distrust of the Pentagon.[19] He had been heartened when, on November 27, the White House announced that Robert McNamara was stepping down as secretary of defense to become president of the World Bank. Colby speculated that the original whiz kid had become disillusioned with the war when he realized, finally, that success or failure could not be measured in numbers. In truth, McNamara's views on the war were driven by the Kennedy family. When Jack and Bobby were hawks, he was a hawk. By 1966, Bobby had begun to turn against the war, partly out of conviction and partly out of his determination to offer an alternative to the hated LBJ and deny him the Democratic nomination in 1968. Whatever the case, a major obstacle to fighting the other war had been removed. Hopefully, Westmoreland would soon follow McNamara to the exit.

On the afternoon of January 29, 1968, Langley received a flash message from the Saigon station. It was 3 A.M. in South Vietnam. A team of Viet Cong sappers was in the process of blasting a large hole in the wall surrounding the US embassy and infiltrating the courtyard of the compound. Colby, still nominally Far East Division head, flashed back the gratuitous advice that the Communications Center should button up its steel doors.[20] The sappers were unable to penetrate the heavy doors at the main entrance to the embassy building and so retreated to the courtyard to take cover behind large concrete flowerpots. They raked the building with rockets and automatic weapons fire. A small detachment of Marines and Military Police (MPs) kept the Viet Cong pinned down until reinforcements arrived and killed all nineteen of them.

The attack on the US embassy was but a small part of the Tet Offensive, a massive, coordinated communist assault against the largest urban areas of South Vietnam. In all, the Viet Cong struck 36 of 64 provincial capitals, 5 of 6 major cities, 64 district capitals, and 50 hamlets. In addition to the embassy, enemy units assaulted Saigon's Tan Son Nhut Airport, the Presidential Palace, and the headquarters of South Vietnam's general staff. In Hue, 7,500 Viet Cong and North Vietnamese troops stormed and eventually took control of the ancient Citadel, the interior city that had been home to the emperors of Vietnam.

The US Mission had once again been caught off guard. The CIA and military intelligence had reported increased activity in and around South Vietnam's major population centers, but MACV's attention had been focused on the siege of Khe Sanh.

In the midst of Tet, the Agency panicked. On February 2, 1968, Colby, George Carver, and John Hart, Langley's onsite Vietnam experts—nicknamed "the brethren"—prepared a memorandum entitled "Operation Shock." "Tet," the trio declared, "demonstrated that the Thieu-Ky regime clearly lacked the attributes of a national government" and could not "defend its frontiers" without the help of a half million American troops. The GVN [South Vietnamese government] continued to resist pressure to clean up corruption, generate broad-based political support, and prosecute the war in an aggressive, competent style. If Thieu did not demonstrate significant progress toward achieving these goals within a hundred days, the United States should "reserve its position" in regard to future aid. Incredibly, given the public prominence of the Thieu-Ky feud, the brethren envisioned a key role for the vice president in any reform effort. Ky should personally head a team that would ferret out and punish incompetence and corruption among military and civilian officials. He should also be charged with organizing a national political front uniting all noncommunist elements in a "massive rallying of the entire population . . . to develop the country and free it of Viet Cong terror." If, after the hundred-day interregnum, there was no significant progress, Washington should replace Thieu and consider halting the bombing of North Vietnam, seeking direct negotiations with

Hanoi, and begin treating the National Liberation Front as a legitimate negotiating partner.[21]

Colby and his mates were jumping the gun. American and South Vietnamese forces quickly rallied. Within days, US and South Vietnamese soldiers had cleared Saigon, and in the weeks that followed they drove the communists from virtually every other city and town they had occupied, forcing them deep into the countryside and inflicting massive casualties. In Hue, the occupying forces held out for three weeks. Allied forces pounded the ancient city into rubble and then cleared what remained of the enemy in house-to-house fighting. Estimates of communist troops killed in action in that battle alone ran to 5,000. The liberators of Hue uncovered the graves of 2,800 government officials, police, and soldiers massacred by the communists. In fact, Tet constituted the worst single defeat ever suffered by the fighting forces of North Vietnam and the National Liberation Front. More than 40,000 communist soldiers were killed or wounded, one-fifth of the enemy's military strength. As a result of Tet—and two smaller offensives in March and August that cost the enemy another 66,000 casualties—the Viet Cong lost much of its ability to conduct offensive operations.[22]

But public, media, and congressional opinion in the United States reflected Langley's initial pessimism—and continued to do so. Americans had been led to believe, by Westmoreland's optimistic accounts, that victory was in sight. How could that be when the Viet Cong could wreak havoc in virtually every major city and town in South Vietnam? "What the hell is going on?" demanded the respected CBS television news anchor Walter Cronkite. "I thought we were winning the war."[23]

The long plane ride over the Pacific provided Colby with an opportunity to take stock. The dimensions of the MACV-ARVN victory on the ground, along with the paradoxical wave of disillusionment sweeping America in the wake of the Tet Offensive, were just becoming apparent. The blow dealt to the Viet Cong, coupled with the emergence of a new team in Saigon devoted to prosecuting the war for the countryside to the maximum, had created a window of opportunity, but that window would not stay open forever. Americans were not an imperial people in the traditional sense. They did not have the patience to fight a war of indefinite duration for indeterminate ends. "Our results had to be so effective that they would receive support at home for our efforts. If not, they had to so put the enemy in trouble and so strengthen the Government that it could survive with a major reduction in American assistance," Colby wrote in his memoirs. He failed to mention his role in contributing to the burgeoning disillusionment.[24]

As the Pan American jetliner dove steeply into Tan Son Nhut—to fend off possible ground fire—Colby spotted a South Vietnamese Air Force plane off the right wing on a bombing mission. During the drive into Saigon he could hear gunfire coming from the ongoing battle for the suburbs. He was where he should be.

By the time Bill Colby arrived in South Vietnam on March 2, 1968, "Blowtorch Bob" Komer and CORDS had been in operation for nearly ten months. Despite the flow of optimistic reports from the deputy commander of CORDS (DEPCORDS)—Komer's official title—the results were spotty. There was a CORDS deputy for each of the four corps areas, with the inimitable John Paul Vann in charge of III Corps, which included his old stomping ground Hau Nghia. Under the deputies were province and district senior advisers, with US personnel eventually stationed at the village and hamlet levels. Overlaying this organizational structure were the various functions assigned to CORDS: the Rural Development Cadre program out of Vung Tau; Chieu Hoi, or "Open Arms," a program to encourage defection from communist ranks; Census Grievance (C-G); the Hamlet Evaluation System (HES), which involved questionnaires designed to determine if a province or district was controlled by friend or foe; and a program called Phoenix, which aimed to identify and eliminate members of the Viet Cong. MACV, the CIA, USAID, the State Department, and the Joint United States Public Affairs Office (JUSPAO) were in charge of or shared responsibility for these initiatives.[25]

Belatedly, the Johnson administration had recognized the need for Vietnamese-language training for Americans if counterinsurgency and pacification were going to succeed. The United States Vietnam Training Center was established in early 1967. Classes were held initially in an airless garage in Arlington, Virginia. The Foreign Service imported a number of Vietnamese-English speakers from Vietnam to serve as instructors. The trainees would attend class for five to six hours a day and then take home reel-to-reel tapes of the day's lessons to study at night. "The key to almost anything I did in Vietnam was the language," CORDS officer Mike Hacker later recalled. "Going to a war zone without knowing the language . . . was unthinkable to me. Suicidal." There was some instruction on Vietnamese culture. Toward the end of the cycle, the students were shipped to "the Farm," the CIA's paramilitary training facility at Camp Peary, Virginia. Later in the program there was a brief stint at the army's unconventional warfare school at Fort Benning, Georgia. At the Farm, the Foreign Service Officers were taught the rudiments of hand-to-hand combat. "For some reason they taught us to blow up automobiles," Bruce Kinsey recalled with a laugh. Upon graduation, each officer was expected to procure his own sidearm. At President Johnson's direction, from 1967 onward all incoming unmarried Foreign Service Officers were to serve one tour in Vietnam.[26]

The leadership of CORDS was well aware of the ongoing need for local security, even in the wake of Tet. In addition to ARVN units, the average province boasted 20 Regional Forces (RF) companies and 100 Popular Forces (PF) platoons. But they had not been provided with modern weaponry, and most lacked US advisers. The Rural Development Cadre program was tasked with turning out 46,000 graduates a year, but desertion rates for 1967 ran as high as 35 percent. General Thang, the minister for rural development, confided that South Vietnamese corps commanders were "basically hostile to the program." Major Nguyen Be, who then supervised the program at Vung Tau, was more explicit. As long as the majority of South Vietnamese military and civilian officials at the provincial and district levels remained corrupt, incompetent, and antidemocratic, he declared, the Rural Development Cadre program would make little headway. The CIA repudiated Be when he attempted to revise the curriculum and called for a new national leadership, drawn from elected district and provincial officials, to replace the Thieu-Ky regime. But he continued to name names as part of his clean government campaign. Frank Scotton finally had to smuggle him out of South Vietnam in an Air America plane to prevent his assassination. Because the RFs and PFs moved in and out of villages, the security they provided was transitory. Left on their own, the RD cadres were terrorized by the local Viet Cong. The ARVN and MACV were still hostile to arming villagers, a step that Bill Colby considered essential, not only for security, but for nation-building as well. Saigon's opposition to a rice-roots revolution continued unabated.[27]

The so-called Viet Cong Infrastructure (VCI) constituted the heart of the communist insurgency in South Vietnam. With Ed Lansdale's help, Diem and Nhu had identified a number of these individuals and killed or captured them during the notorious anticommunist campaign of the late 1950s. Many within the US Mission assumed at the time that the back of the organized insurgency had been broken. Then came the 1963 coup and subsequent revelations that, despite all that Nhu's Special Forces and the Can Lao had done, the VCI still existed and in some areas was flourishing. In 1963 and 1964, the CIA station, under Colby's successors, had begun to try to pick up the trail and put together an organization that could identify Viet Cong cadres and either turn or kill them. All they had to go on were the dozens of file-card trays that Lansdale and his people had accumulated over the years containing the names, occupations, and locations of suspected communists. Much of this information had come from the Hamlet Informant Program, in which the station subsidized police payments to casual and usually untrained informants. MACV had its own extensive intelligence mechanism, but it focused on the enemy order of battle rather than on the VCI.[28]

In 1964 and 1965, Chief of Station Peer de Silva developed an analytical unit within the Saigon Station to coordinate intelligence activity against the communists. To gather information, the CIA turned to the South Vietnamese Police Special Branch—a descendent of the old French Sûreté, the internal security arm of the French colonial government—and subsequently to the South Vietnamese government's newly created Central Intelligence Organization (CIO). With CIA encouragement, the Special Branch began developing a system of Provincial Interrogation Centers nationwide. By mid-1966 there were twenty-two in existence. The Sûreté had been notorious for torturing its detainees, and that culture carried over to the Special Branch. An Agency officer who toured all of the existing PICs in 1966 found two in the Mekong Delta that were exemplary, but elsewhere, the facilities were "absolutely appalling," with prisoners being interrogated in the presence of other prisoners, clerks, and janitorial staff. Suspected members of the Viet Cong Infrastructure were often housed in a common detention room, which guaranteed collusion and facilitated intimidation of the weak by the hard core. Interrogators seemed not to know the difference between a criminal investigation and an intelligence debriefing. The South Vietnamese, who were aware of the American aversion to torture, reacted not by refraining from it, but by hiding it. Nevertheless, several CIA inspectors remembered seeing blood-spattered walls, batteries and wires, and assorted cudgels and restraints.[29]

When Bob Komer arrived in South Vietnam in the spring of 1967, he had set about institutionalizing the war on the communist cadre. What he wanted was a national intelligence clearinghouse to collect and analyze information gathered from detainees at the PICs. To this end, he established, in the words of Agency historian Thomas L. Ahern Jr., a "new VC infrastructure intelligence collection and exploitation staff (ICEX) system reaching from [the CIA] station down through corps, province, and district levels." The CIA would continue to supervise the PICs and the Special Branch efforts in the field. Finally, the decision was made to assign the Provincial Reconnaissance Units—South Vietnam's counterterror shock troops—to the war on the VCI. The 303 Committee stipulated that these strike forces would remain under the sole supervision of the CIA. The PRUs gave teeth to the ICEX program, providing it with a heavily armed force capable of acting on the intelligence that was gathered. In December 1967, the figurehead prime minister, Nguyen Van Loc, renamed ICEX "Phung Hoang" after a mythical Vietnamese bird endowed with extraordinary powers. Komer came up with what he believed was the closest English equivalent—Phoenix. The name Phung Hoang was ironic. "The Phung Hoang," according to one source, "does not show itself except in times of peace and it hides at the slightest sign of trouble." Komer's bird, however, was frequently the harbinger of imprisonment, torture, and death.[30]

According to Tom Martin, the CORDS district adviser in the Mekong Delta, the Provincial Reconnaissance Units were notorious by the time they were incorporated into the Phoenix program. Because the PRUs and their SEAL advisers wore civilian clothes and operated at night, they were invisible, at least to the other Americans in the area. "These were sort of like the Dirty Dozen," Martin recalled. "They were recruited from jails and deserters; they were real killers. The PRUs were a very deadly force; they were the ones who started giving rewards for enemy ears and noses and stuff like that." In January 1967, the station reported that an "overzealous" PRU contingent in Long An Province had decapitated several Viet Cong after killing them in a pitched battle. In many districts, the campaign against the communist infrastructure turned into a duel between the local

Banh-anh-ninh—the terrorism, espionage, and assassination arm of the Viet Cong province committees—and the PRU. In Tan An, the capital of Long An, a former head of the communist assassination unit who had defected in 1966 learned the whereabouts and itinerary of the current Banh-anh-ninh chief. He passed it on to the PRU, which mounted an ambush in which the Viet Cong unit leader and his bodyguard were killed. At this point, the Banh-anh-ninh had lost seven chiefs at PRU hands, while communists had managed to kill three PRU commanders in three months. In the delta, a Viet Cong "avenger unit" had killed the mother of one defector after he rallied to South Vietnam; he swore revenge on the perpetrators, whose identities he knew. Leading his five-man team into Viet Cong territory, the defector discovered the unit's hideout, and in the ensuing attack all eight of the enemy were killed. Found in the hideout was an outboard motor of a Special Forces lieutenant who had been ambushed and shot to death while patrolling a nearby canal a week earlier. In many ways, then, the CIA-supervised PRUs operated as combat units fighting an enemy asking no more quarter than it gave, rather than as a police force constrained by law and procedure. For the period from May through September 1967, the PRUs registered 1,500 Viet Cong killed and 960 captured. Counter-terror team losses were 99 dead. Nevertheless, the stated objective of the PRU campaign was to capture and interrogate; killing was a last resort.[31]

Still ensconced in Langley, Colby had viewed the evolution of the war on the Viet Cong Infrastructure with mixed feelings. He approved of the campaign in principle, even of its organized violence. Every effort should be made to lure members of the communist cadre to switch sides through indoctrination, persuasion, or blackmail. Failing that, however, the PRUs should take "direct action to capture or arrest" members of the infrastructure; "on occasion casualties will result from efforts by the Viet Cong to escape arrest or capture." Colby wanted the PRUs to be incorporated into the South Vietnamese National Police. He was, as he would later claim, concerned about due process and ethical treatment of prisoners, but he had another reason. If there should be a cease-fire and negotiations, the PRUs, as part of the police rather than the ARVN, would be able to continue the struggle against the Viet Cong.[32]

The former Jedburgh quickly settled into his new job as chief deputy to Komer. He was to be Blowtorch Bob's alter ego, knowledgeable about every aspect of CORDS and thus able to stand in for his boss. Technically, Colby was on leave from the CIA, but he had full access to the station and CIA operations. He could go places where Komer could not. Indeed, that was one of the reasons for his selection. Becoming bogged down in the CORDS-MACV bureaucracy was an ever-present danger. As he had when he was station chief, Colby got out into the field whenever possible. "I saw as the real purpose of my being in Vietnam to spend as many nights as possible in the provinces," he wrote in *Lost Victory*.[33] Initially, the new DEPCORDS deputy limited his forays to the weekends. He would put in a half-day at the office on Saturday and then helicopter out in the afternoon to spend the night with a district or province advisory team. Colby did not give advance notice of his arrival. Dinner with the Americans and Vietnamese, an inspection tour the next morning, and then a flight back to Saigon Sunday afternoon in time for a swim and dinner at the Cercle Sportif.

Tet had dealt a major blow to the Viet Cong, but that did not mean the countryside was secure. Excluding communist military forces, the VCI still numbered some 82,000 nationwide. The South Vietnamese government, anxious about protecting its urban constituencies, reverted to its habitual passiveness, redeploying ARVN and even Regional and Popular Forces troops around the country's major population centers. On a visit to the provincial capital of Vinh Long, Colby's helicopter had to descend rapidly in a tight circle to avoid enemy ground fire from the outskirts of the city. A trip to Ban Me Thuot, near his old stomping grounds of Buon Enao, was enlivened by a Viet Cong mortar attack. As the barrage marched up the main thoroughfare, Colby and his cohorts retreated to their compound and, fully armed, sat up all night waiting for a ground attack that never came.[34]

During his weekend visits to the countryside, Colby, to his dismay, discovered that CORDS would have to spend much of 1968 simply rebuilding South Vietnam. Destruction from the fighting was widespread; virtually every town and village had suffered damage to its infrastructure. Before the 1 million refugees created by Tet could return home, there would have to be homes for them to return to. Colby understood that the vacuum in the countryside would have to be filled before nation-building could begin once again.

What Komer needed above all else were energetic, effective CORDS personnel in the field. His model was John Paul Vann. One of Colby's first forays out of Saigon was to visit with the already legendary proconsul, then

DEPCORDS for II Corps. The two men had met only once, in Washington, when Colby was Far East Division head. Vann had paid a visit to Langley to inform him that the members of the Rural Development Cadre of which the Agency was so proud were spending more time huddled in their compounds protecting themselves than proselytizing among the peasants. With characteristic diplomacy, Colby had observed that he and his colleagues realized that the Vung Tau graduates were a work in progress. Vann remembered the exchange and, mindful of his job security, had expressed some concern to Komer that his new deputy might bear a grudge. One of the reasons for Colby's visit was to assure Vann that this was not the case.

Vann had done his homework and knew where Colby's predilections lay. Their first night together, he took his guest to visit a nearby village whose chief had armed his young men with spears fashioned out of straightened and sharpened car springs. Still hobbled by his skating accident, Colby inspected the ranks with cane in hand and promised the chief real weapons. "The important result of the evening," Colby observed in *Lost Victory*, "was a clear understanding between Vann and myself that the real way we should be fighting the war was by building communities such as the ones we visited, and gradually pressing the Communists away from the population."[35]

Vann and Colby would become allies, if not friends. Colby's depiction of Vann in *Lost Victory* conformed to the image that so many of the counterinsurgency/pacification personnel laboring in the vineyard had of him: an almost fearless man absolutely committed to empowering the rural Vietnamese to take control of their communities and defend them simultaneously against the communists, the Saigonese, and, when necessary, inept Americans. Vann's personal shortcomings, so relentlessly portrayed in Neil Sheehan's *Bright Shining Lie*, were overstated and largely irrelevant, Colby wrote.

There was no doubt about John Paul Vann's bravery, his commitment to the villagers of South Vietnam, or his determination to speak out against injustice and ineptitude, but he was often all sail and no anchor—intelligent, undereducated, and intensely ambitious. Part of the Ellsberg-Scotton-Bumgardner coterie, indeed its titular head, Vann had largely traded in the ideas of others. In truth, Vann's views on the conflict in Vietnam were contradictory, even paradoxical. Like Colby, he was opposed to large-scale US military operations. The further American main force units were kept from his area of responsibility, the easier his job would be. Unlike Colby, he was opposed to forced relocation programs like the Strategic Hamlet initiative because he thought they tore the fabric of Vietnamese society.[36]

Vann could be pessimistic, even cynical, about the war. He remained a great friend of Dan Ellsberg even after the latter turned against the conflict and became one of its most vocal critics. "John Paul Vann was just the first among many who served in Hau Nghia who came slowly to believe that we were on the wrong side," declared Vann's friend Colonel Carl Bernard. "[He and I believed] that the better, and most conscientious persons in Hau Nghia—with just a few exceptions—were working for the Viet Cong." Bernard recalled that he and Vann often likened themselves to "bankruptcy referees," that is, individuals dedicated to limiting the damage being done by both sides. The two men, Bernard claimed, had read Ferdinand Otto Miksche's *Secret Forces: The Technique of Underground Movements*, the principal conclusion of which was that once revolutionaries succeeded in implanting an infrastructure, they had won. Yet Vann remained an uncompromising hawk throughout his time in Vietnam. He never reached the point where he believed that too many Vietnamese and Americans were dying. "John Vann never considered that the Vietnamese war might have demanded more, in terms of lives, money, and effort, than it was worth," Bernard recalled. "No price would have been too great. Vann felt that since America had committed herself to the war effort, she should make the best of it." On the second if not the first assumption, Colby and Vann saw eye to eye.[37]

Vann's popularity with the counterinsurgency/pacification people stemmed in no small part from his willingness to speak truth to power. There was his famous exchange with Walt Rostow, LBJ's relentlessly hawkish national security adviser, in December 1967. Buoyed by Westmoreland's optimistic reports, Rostow predicted that there would be a great victory in the coming summer. "Oh, hell no, Mr. Rostow," Vann replied. "I'm a born optimist; I think we can hold out longer than that."[38] He and another CORDS deputy, Colonel Wilbur Wilson, were openly contemptuous of Westmoreland and his search-and-destroy strategy. At the same time, Vann obsequiously cultivated patrons who could protect him, such as General Bruce Palmer, deputy commander of the US Army in Vietnam from 1967 to 1968 and vice chief of staff of the army from 1968 to 1972. Vann was deferential to Komer, as well as to Ellsworth Bunker, who had a reputation for firing those who bucked him. Vann was a prolific letter-writer, treating public figures with whom he had only a passing acquaintance—Henry Kissinger, for example—as confidants.

Colby became somewhat addicted to touring the countryside of South Vietnam with Vann. Risk-taking was something the two men had in common, though Colby was somewhat less flamboyant about it. Periodically, Vann would decide to motor about the provinces under his supervision to "find out who owned what." Inevitably these trips were through territory that was contested. Vann would tell every adviser who came under his command that they must get out in the villages and rice paddies and see for themselves what conditions were like; they needed to visit with village elders and show friend and foe alike that they were not afraid.[39]

In some ways, the two men were very different. Vann's sexual appetites were legendary, a trait he shared with Ellsberg. Bernard recalled that when he was stateside, Vann would make it a point to visit Ellsberg in Santa Monica for an orgy. In Vietnam, Vann at one point lived near a girls' orphanage and reputedly spent a lot of time there. "His approach to sex was strictly physical," Bernard observed. "It was something to be done quickly and as often as possible." Colby professed ignorance of these activities. He would later tell his second wife, Sally, that he and Vann would venture out into the countryside in a jeep or in the latter's International Harvester Scout on Saturday nights in order to "avoid temptation." Colby was dissembling; he could not have helped knowing about Vann's exploits—the man was an exhibitionist. Nor was Colby pristine in sexual matters; he had come to Vietnam in part to escape from what for him was a loveless marriage. There were reports of other women, but Colby, unlike Vann, was the soul of discretion.[40]

Three weeks after his arrival in Vietnam, Colby tuned in with other members of the US Mission to listen to LBJ's March 31 speech to the American people on Vietnam. Everyone sensed that a turning point in the war was afoot.

In the weeks following the Tet Offensive, former administration supporters in the media, including the *New York Times* editorial board, had advised the president to negotiate a withdrawal from Vietnam. The "Wise Men"—a group of veteran diplomats called together by LBJ to advise him on the war in Vietnam—which included such Cold War luminaries as former secretary of state Dean Acheson and Secretary of Defense Robert Lovett—called for the "gradual disengagement" of the United States from the war.

The military, however, took a different lesson from Tet. Sensing that the time was right for a knockout blow, Westmoreland and the Joint Chiefs asked for an additional 205,000 troops, approval for an amphibious landing north of the 17th parallel, and permission to attack North Vietnamese sanctuaries in Cambodia and Laos. Lyndon Johnson was, to say the least, conflicted. "I feel like a hitchhiker caught in a hailstorm on a Texas highway," he remarked to an aide. "I can't run, I can't hide. And I can't make it stop."[41] After conferring with Clark Clifford, the new secretary of defense, Johnson rebuffed his military commanders. He approved an additional 22,000 men, chiefly to help lift the siege of Khe Sanh, and ordered Ambassador Bunker to make a "highly forceful" approach to Thieu and Ky to get their house in order.

In his March 31 speech, President Johnson announced that henceforward the bombing of North Vietnam would be limited to the area just above the demilitarized zone, and he declared that the United States was ready for peace talks anytime, anywhere, anyplace. In the event the enemy responded positively and such talks opened, LBJ said, Averell Harriman would serve as head of the US delegation. Then came the bombshell: "I shall not seek, and I will not accept, the nomination of my party for another term as president."[42] Johnson had come to the conclusion that much of the divisive debate at home centered on him personally. The prospect of new leadership, he concluded, might lead to reconciliation both in the United States and abroad.

The "Operation Shock" memo from Colby and his colleagues had played a key role in the decision to deny the request for a major escalation from Westmoreland and the Joint Chiefs. It had been the substance of George Carver's presentation to the Wise Men and their subsequent advice to the president that he throw in the towel in Vietnam. On March 27, LBJ demanded and received the same briefing from Carver. Vice President Hubert Humphrey subsequently wrote to Carver to thank him for his "brutally frank and forthright analysis." The president's speech of March 31, Humphrey declared, "indicated that your briefings had a profound effect on the course of U.S. policy on Vietnam."[43] The irony of the "Operation

Shock" memo was heavy indeed. Tet would provide Bill Colby and his fellow advocates of the "other war" with their greatest opportunity, but the backlash from that initial pessimistic evaluation would constitute their greatest obstacle.

After a great deal of back-and-forth concerning the location and composition of delegations, preliminary peace talks opened in Paris on May 13, 1968. Colby recalled a visit by the new secretary of defense and his chief of international security affairs, Paul Warnke, in the spring of 1968. Neither man seemed at all interested in the military's optimistic reports or the presentations put on by CORDS. "The two visitors departed," Colby wrote in *Lost Victory*, "with no successful contradiction of their attitude on arrival—to wit, the United States was deep in a quagmire, and the sooner it withdrew, the better."[44]

Though the Paris talks immediately deadlocked, those on the ground in Vietnam—both Americans and Vietnamese—assumed that a cease-fire was possible. In that eventuality, the two adversaries would have to continue the struggle by other means. Indeed, much of the war after March 1968 was built around this premise, and this gave the CORDS mission of counterinsurgency, pacification, and nation-building a special urgency. "Having failed in their bid for conquest in the Tet attacks, the communists were now laying the groundwork for a claim to political power, or at least participation, and for an effort to negotiate a compromise political solution with the Americans over the heads of the Vietnamese Government," Colby later observed. "Clearly the response of the Vietnamese Government and its American ally had to be political: to establish legitimate local authority to counter the claims of the Communists and their fronts."[45]

What was clear to Bill Colby was not so clear to President Nguyen Van Thieu. In the wake of Tet, the national government abolished village elections and once again began sending Saigon appointees to rule the countryside. Pressed for a timetable to return South Vietnam to civilian rule, Thieu declared that Americans must understand that "the army could not be removed from politics overnight." The army was not only "his major political supporter," but "the only cohesive force holding the country together."[46]

In terms of counterinsurgency and pacification, however, the ARVN continued to be the problem rather than the solution. General Thang, the South Vietnamese minister of reconstruction, confided to his American contacts that, in his opinion, ARVN corps commanders were actively sabotaging pacification. Indeed, the entire South Vietnamese performance was marked by "corruption in the provinces and districts, inefficiency at corps, and incompetence in Saigon." In the fall of 1968, none other than the director-general of the South Vietnamese National Police, Colonel Tran Van Hai, outlined, in a confidential report to the CIA station, five South Vietnamese weaknesses that, if not remedied, would lead to a communist victory. First was the government's inability to control the hamlets and villages, an ever-increasing number of which contained a liberation committee. Indeed, by one count, the number of communist-administered villages grew from 397 in September 1968 to 3,367 in mid-January 1969. Second was the government's failure to secure any support in the nation's schools and universities. "The best and most dedicated students are also dedicated Communists," Hai reported; their role models among teachers and professors were "invariably Marxists." Third was the arrogance of the South Vietnamese leaders and their representatives. In the post-Tet refugee centers, procommunist students and cadres were winning over refugees, while government relief officials "walked around in white shirts, looked down on the refugees and, in some cases, profited from relief supplies." Fourth, Tri Quang and the Buddhists remained firm in their opposition to the Thieu-Ky regime. Finally, whatever the theoretical merits of democracy, what the government was offering could not compete with the communists, who possessed precisely the "discipline and cohesiveness which the democratic forces lack."[47]

Colby was aware of these weaknesses even before Hai's report made them explicit. The Johnson administration had been persuaded by the "Operation Shock" memo and eroding domestic support for the war to freeze troop levels, limit the bombing campaign against North Vietnam, and initiate peace talks, but the White House proved unwilling to abandon Thieu. In part, harkening back to McGeorge Bundy's observation to Colby, there was no institutional way for the United States to avoid dealing with whatever national government existed in South Vietnam. So Colby, undaunted, continued his campaign to build a nation beginning at the village level.

During a visit to Washington in August 1968, the deputy chief of CORDS presented his plan for a "People's War" in South Vietnam. It was to be based on the "Three Selfs": Self-Help, Self-Defense, and Self-Government. White House aides could not decide whether Colby was mimicking Sun Yat-sen or Mao Tse-tung. First, as always, was local self-defense. "Experience had shown that a disarmed village community could be entered and dominated by a five-man enemy squad," Colby wrote. "If they met no opposition, they could assemble and harangue the population with their message, collect taxes and supplies, and conscript or recruit some of the local youths into the Communist forces." Even the most modest local self-defense forces could discourage such activities. In the three years that followed, Colby saw to it that some 500,000 weapons—mostly of World War II vintage, harvested from the Ruff-Puffs (a nickname for the RFs and PFs), who had been supplied at last with M-16 rifles—went to village defense squads. The Rural Development Cadre would be freed of security duties and allowed to focus on economic development and political indoctrination.[48]

By this point, Bob Komer had become a prisoner of the Hamlet Evaluation System and numbers in general. The CORDS chief was losing patience, and what Colby was advocating—essentially emulating the techniques of the communists—required patience. What he proposed was an Accelerated Pacification Campaign (APC) aiming to convert 1,000 hamlets from a "contested" to a relatively "secure" state under the HES ranking system.[49] For the APC—and pacification in general—to work, they would have to have the explicit support of the new MACV commander, General Creighton Abrams. Komer had reason to be hopeful.

Westmoreland's replacement was a career soldier loyal to his superiors, but his misgivings about search and destroy were well known. "The military . . . have a little problem," Abrams told his commanders in one briefing, "an institutional problem." The army could recognize and react to organized violence, he said. "But this trouble [the activities of the liberation committees and the Banh-anh-ninh] that nobody can see, and nobody can hear . . . is just meaner than hell—just going around collecting taxes, quietly snatching somebody and taking him off and shooting him." He understood the implications of the Paris Peace Talks (though he believed that Harriman and company were giving away too much too soon)—that in the event of a cease-fire, the Americans and South Vietnamese would have to switch to a completely political/guerrilla war. Abrams acknowledged that the operations of US main force units often created more problems for counterinsurgency and pacification than they solved. He deeply resented that the course of the war in Southeast Asia was tied to the vicissitudes of American domestic politics, but, like a good soldier, he was determined to work around the problem. Finally, he appreciated the enemy he was fighting. "The fellows that are running the show up there [in North Vietnam] have been at this a long time," he observed in another commanders' meeting. "They've been down this road before. They've stood right on the precipice and stared hell right straight in the face—and, and, and took it—and took it—and won."[50]

In September, Colby, Komer, and Vann made a pacification presentation to Abrams and his corps commanders. Ambassador Bunker was also in attendance. Colby led off. He described the evolution of North Vietnam and the National Liberation Front from the original Indochinese Communist Party and discussed the activities of the liberation committees, tracing their proliferation on a map. He then outlined the methods and targets of the Accelerated Pacification Campaign. All the military needed to do, he said, was to keep the North Vietnamese Army and what remained of the Viet Cong off-balance and away from areas being pacified. As always, Colby emphasized that there would have to be a political dimension to the APC: "By establishing democratic legitimacy in the villages through local officials, [the APC] would provide a non-Communist structure to counter the claims of the Liberation Committees." Colby remembered that Abrams listened intently and, at the conclusion of the briefing, thanked Colby warmly. Abrams then gave Komer the go-ahead to work out the details of Accelerated Pacification with President Thieu.[51]

Urged on by Joint General Staff Chairman General Cao Van Vien, Thieu signed off on the Advanced Pacification Campaign, and the launch date was set for November 1. Then, suddenly, just as the program was to get underway, Komer was named ambassador to Turkey. He departed South Vietnam without ceremony on November 6. "I accompanied Komer to the small Air Force jet that would take him to Hong Kong for the connection to Washington and thanked him for all he had done to get pacification finally launched as a major strategy of the war," Colby wrote in *Lost Victory*. "I thanked him also for arranging for me to succeed him in the job of making it work." Komer had worn out his welcome. Obsequious though he had been with Bunker and Abrams, he was aggressive and abrasive with everyone else. His tendency to see pacification in terms of the Hamlet Evaluation System had created a multitude of enemies in the field and especially within the CIA station in Saigon. To some he had become absurd. On one occasion he arrived at a party in Saigon following a trip to the provinces clad in a shiny, starched fatigue uniform. A CIA officer standing within earshot of Komer inquired, "Who is that silly-looking twerp?"[52]

Komer apparently saw the Accelerated Pacification Campaign almost entirely in military terms, as an opportunity for him to do what Westmoreland and the military had not been allowed to do—take the offensive following Tet. "We can and must achieve victory," he declared to Washington. "By Tet 69 [that is, 1969, just before the scheduled end of the first phase of the APC], we can make it clear that the enemy has been defeated." In his hurry to move 1,000 hamlets from the "theirs" to "ours" column, he was willing to abandon the painstaking Rural Development approach designed to demonstrate the South Vietnamese government's benevolence and attract peasant loyalty. On a Colby memo declaring that the Rural Development Cadre must be the "major political instrument available to confront the VC political apparatus," Komer had scribbled, "Baloney."[53]

Thus it was that Bill Colby assumed command of CORDS in November 1968 with the personal rank of ambassador. He was now one of the three most powerful Americans in Vietnam. Komer had indeed recommended Colby to replace him, but the former Jedburgh's main supporters were Abrams and Bunker. The counterinsurgency/pacification struggle was his to win or lose, he believed.[54]

Colby decreed that although the APC was nominally a nationwide effort, it should focus on the Mekong Delta. The region contained a disproportionate percentage of the rural population, some 6 million in all, and was the nation's rice basket. He persuaded Vann to abandon his beloved Hau Nghia and move down to head up the CORDS operation in the delta. While MACV and the ARVN attempted to push communist main force units to the periphery, local security was provided by the mobile Ruff-Puff units and Colby's village militia. To Thieu's dismay, CORDS insisted on funneling development funds—up to 1 million piasters per village—directly into the hands of hamlet and village chiefs. Preference was given to the communities that were quickest to hold elections. One village chief, upon hearing that he would be able to expend funds without clearance from national officials, broke down and wept. Vung Tau continued to turn out Rural Development Cadre teams, now slimmed down from fifty-nine to forty men, but also added a six-week training program for village chiefs. Each graduation ceremony was attended by President Thieu and relevant government ministers. In accordance with Marshal Lyautey's "oil-spot"

theory, the APC was to focus on the most populated, most secure settlements first and then spread out to more contested areas.[55]

"The Accelerated Pacification Program was a great success," Colby
wrote in *Lost Victory*. In his cables to Washington, Bunker fully concurred:
the South Vietnamese government was able to establish a presence in an
additional 1,350 hamlets, he reported. According to the ambassador, by the
spring of 1969 the percentage of the population controlled by the Viet
Cong nationwide had dropped to 13.3 percent, a new low. The People's
Self-Defense Force claimed 500,000 members, and between November
1968 and January 1969, 17,000 additional weapons were delivered to their
keeping. Conflicted though he was, Thieu, in June 1969, authorized Phase
II of the new pacification program, which was basically a continuation of
the methods and structure of the APC into the indefinite future. The South
Vietnamese president was willing to support the program as long as the
Americans threw money at it, it succeeded in rooting out Viet Cong cadres,
and it did not threaten his political position.[56]

By the end of 1970, CORDS comprised more than 1,000 civilians and
5,000 American military personnel spread across the villages and hamlets
of South Vietnam. The civilians were graduates of the Vietnam Training
Center in Washington, meaning that all had come to Vietnam able to function in spoken and written Vietnamese. Some were State Department officers, some were from the US Agency for International Development, and
some were from the United States Information Service. A few came from
the CIA and the Defense Intelligence Agency. Many of them were extremely bright and motivated individuals, graduates of some of the best
universities in the country. A few had previous experience in the Peace
Corps. They were independent thinkers, committed but critical. Some had
used their days off from the training center to march in antiwar demonstrations. Mike Hacker had joined the Peace Corps in 1962, completing a
stint in Bolivia. "I was one of the thousands of young people who at the
time were caught up in the Kennedy fever," he recalled. "We were in college,
but we were bored, and along came this idea that just struck the right chord.
That we could make a difference." His first assignment was Vinh Binh
Province in the delta.[57]

Vinh Binh was one of the most insecure provinces in South Vietnam,
at one point ranking forty-fourth out of forty-four in terms of the level of
Viet Cong activity. Hacker moved into a house with three other Americans,

one USIS and the other two military, who acted as advisers to the armed propaganda teams. Hacker and his compatriots employed every tactic imaginable to persuade Viet Cong to defect and villagers in contested areas to relocate to the Chieu Hoi camps in and around Vinh Binh's capital city. Chieu Hoi operatives offered cash incentives for defections as well as for any weapons the defectors were able to bring with them. The armed propaganda team members were all former Viet Cong cadres who were carefully screened. Together with their American advisers, they went out into the villages and talked to the people about the benefits of coming over to the government side. There were leaflets for those who could read, and for those who could not, plays extolling the virtues of democracy and capitalism and the vices of communism. Once in the Chieu Hoi camps, villagers were presented with more information in special classes. The instructors were all Vietnamese. Hacker's job was to go into the camps and converse with as many people as he could, but in particular with former Viet Cong. "I talked to them about their families, their economic situation, their experiences with the VC and the government," he later recalled. "Many had seen battle with the communist forces. The most reliable converts were those who had been pressed into service, but there were hard-core VC who had been wronged or become disillusioned."[58]

The Americans stationed in Vinh Binh operated under no illusions about the strength of the Viet Cong. Travel was absolutely forbidden at night. Every road offered the possibility, if not the probability, of death through mines or ambush. Hacker recalled that the enemy would regularly mortar the Chieu Hoi compound, killing mostly women and children, as a means to discourage defection. A favorite tactic was to blow up a bus, killing thirty or forty people. Americans and their Vietnamese counterparts would rush to the scene only to be ambushed. "The carnage of a mine going off under a vehicle the size of one of our yellow American school buses was just unbelievable," Hacker said. "Arms and legs and heads were scattered everywhere. They counted on the horror to paralyze us and throw us off guard."[59]

Hacker remembered Colby periodically visiting Vinh Binh. "He was the right guy at the right time . . . very cool. I could not imagine Colby sweating." Vann was omnipresent. One either loved or hated Vann, Hacker recalled. He loved him. "If you worked for CORDS and believed in counterinsurgency/pacification, Vann was your hero," said Hacker. He showed no weakness or ambivalence, but led by example. Both Vann and Colby knew that the war was going to be a protracted struggle, Hacker said, and they believed that only pacification could win it. Colby was the brains, Vann the brawn and the inspiration. Even more striking than these two Americans were the Vietnamese peasants themselves, Hacker remembered: "Nine hundred years of Chinese domination, one hundred years of French, and now the Americans were pounding the hell out of them." And yet, whenever the Chieu Hoi teams stopped to ask directions, the locals would invariably invite them for a meal. They were swarmed by smiling children. "They had this innate decency about them," Hacker said.[60]

After Abrams, Komer, and Colby arrived on the scene, and John Vann was transferred to the delta, the US military began to recede into the background there. Rural Development teams were paired effectively with CORDS staff and the ablest village leaders. In the wake of Tet, the liberation committees began to step up their pressure on the rural population, demanding more money and more recruits and sowing terror when they were not forthcoming. Slowly, trust began to shift. Bruce Kinsey, who headed the pacification effort in Long An Province, recalled that villagers became increasingly willing to finger Viet Cong tax collectors and members of the Banh-anh-ninh. Kinsey became aware that, over time, local leaders in the delta had worked out accommodations with the Viet Cong. The two sides agreed unofficially on a division of territory: you take everything between here and the river, for example, and we will control everything between here and the marketplace. Kinsey discovered the existence of these clandestine arrangements during one of his first forays into the countryside. He asked for and received a tour, but when his party approached a particular footbridge, the chief halted and forbade Kinsey to go any further. Over time, he and his colleagues began to push the boundaries to expand their work into communist-controlled territory. Vann's idea, Kinsey recalled, "was that the VC do not wear seven league boots and that they are just as scared as we are and a lot of this war is psychological." Thus the constant jeep rides through contested territory night and day. Kinsey recalled that the morning after a local official was beheaded in a remote, contested village, Vann declared, "Those people need to know who their friends are." Vann loaded Kinsey and two of his compatriots into his jeep and, armed to the teeth, they made their way to the village to pay their respects to the dead leader's family.[61]

Despite the depredations of the Viet Cong, ongoing government corruption, and other problems, there was progress in Long An. As chief civilian officer for CORDS in the province, Kinsey had an abundance of resources at his disposal: a Construction Battalion (Seabee) team, a battalion of Army Corps of Engineers, road-building equipment, a contingent of nurses and medics, a civil affairs platoon, and a steady flow of unrestricted funds. By the time he left in 1970, things were happening that had not been seen in years: mail delivered, small electrical grids, Kubota tractors in the rice paddies, and roads open day and night. "That did not happen all over the country," he said, "but it happened over most of the Mekong Delta, and that's where 65 percent of the people lived."[62]

Virtually all CORDS personnel involved in reconstruction, development, and local self-empowerment wanted American main force units to be kept as far away from their areas of operation as possible. The battalion- and division-level sweeps and free-fire zones were, to say the least, counterproductive of what Colby's outfit was trying to accomplish. But there was a special evil, "Operation Speedy Express," that unfolded from December 1968 through May 1969.

Speedy Express was the code name for a massive American search-and-destroy offensive against Viet Cong and North Vietnamese forces in the Mekong Delta; in charge was Lieutenant General Julian Ewell, commander of the Ninth Infantry Division. Ewell, later dubbed by one journalist "The Butcher of the Delta," was obsessed with body count, and he was determined that Speedy Express set a record for number of enemy killed; to this end, he applied relentless pressure on his brigade and battalion commanders. Lieutenant Colonel William Taylor recalled a visit from Ewell. "What the fuck are you people doing down here; sitting on your ass? The rest of the brigades are coming up with a fine body count and you people aren't producing. . . . If you can't get out there and beat 'em out of the bushes, then I'll relieve you and get somebody down here who will."[63]

Ewell was not above faking numbers, but he much preferred dead bodies. It was his Ninth Division that pioneered nighttime hunter-killer operations. Cobra gunships would fly over "enemy" terrain, spotlighting anything that moved and raining down fire from their miniguns. Vann, who at the time was DEPCORDS for the delta region, began to hear reports of hundreds of dead and wounded civilians. The division claimed 10,899 Viet Cong and North Vietnamese soldiers killed but could produce only 788 weapons. Vann forwarded the information to Colby, who asked him to investigate. The practices and procedures the Ninth was using were unprofessional, Vann subsequently reported. The First Air Cavalry did not count an enemy dead until one of its number had "put a foot on 'em." Eventually, Vann confronted Ewell. How could he account for the disparity between body count and captured weapons? The enemy was crafty, Ewell responded. Frequently, his men got to the Viet Cong only after they had conducted an operation and hidden their weapons. During a trip to Washington, Vann briefed Westmoreland, then army chief of staff, on what Ewell was doing. Vann's senior advisers in the provinces and districts were up in arms. They were trying to pacify villagers while Ewell was killing them. Westmoreland feigned surprise, Vann recalled. In truth, the person responsible for Julian Ewell was Creighton Abrams. Ewell was one of his top commanders; Abrams had to know about the excesses committed by the Ninth Infantry. In 1972, the army inspector general would estimate that between 5,000 and 7,000 civilians were killed by Speedy Express.[64]

Colby saw the armed components of CORDS as a police force, not as a military contingent. Ewell and Speedy Express might not have been typical, but they were a byproduct of the military mentality. The CORDS effort, Colby later wrote to a military historian, "was an ad hoc instrument to provide a non-military and primarily political function." What he envisioned was a police model based on the British constabulary, aiming to protect and serve, not the American model, which was primarily military— "us vs. them, Wyatt Earp at the OK Corral." The United States had had a brief experience with the constabulary model in the Philippines at the turn of the century, Colby observed, but had apparently forgotten it. The object should be to control and convert enemy guerrillas; killing them should be a last resort. The goal was to engage the population, not impose upon it.[65]

CORDS men in the field were not merely instruments of Colby's intellect, however; they were individuals through which he could once again live his Lawrence of Arabia, Baden-Powell, Robert Rogers dream. Kinsey and Hacker—these were Colby's people. CORDS was his ideal; its concept and practice were his seven pillars of wisdom all in one. It was the dream of Vann, Scotton, and Bumgardner, and, before his defection, Ellsberg, too. Colby's real contribution, as Bruce Kinsey observed, was to make it all work.[66] Prior to 1968, the US effort in Vietnam had been a jungle of competing bureaucracies and clashing personalities. Wielding the authority provided by Abrams and Bunker, Colby somehow got everyone working together, something Komer could never do. Instead of acting like rivals, the State Department, USAID, MACV, and even to some extent the CIA began functioning as a team. The notion that America could produce an organization that blended military and civilian authority would previously have been considered impossible. Indeed, it was antithetical to the writings of the Founding Fathers, who were sharply aware that military power had been an impediment to liberty and self-determination as often as it had been its protector. Only Colby, with his peculiar combination of will, ego, and humility rooted in perceived service to a higher cause, could have presided over an operation like CORDS. The idea that it was possible to fight tyranny and preserve a civil, democratic society went to the root of the man's beliefs. It was a bold and perhaps unrealistic assumption, but it underlay much of America's Cold War effort in the developing world.

14

BIRDS OF PEACE
AND BIRDS OF WAR

While Colby's CORDS programs were making progress in South Vietnam, new actors appeared on the American political stage; indeed, a new play was about to unfold. The bloodletting at the Democratic National Convention in Chicago in August 1968 had ended with the nomination of Hubert H. Humphrey, Johnson's vice president. Though he had been "loyal as a beagle," as LBJ put it, Humphrey had begun to have doubts about the conflict in Vietnam. After the convention rejected an antiwar plank in its platform, however, Humphrey could not avoid association with the increasingly unpopular war. The Republicans, meantime, had nominated Richard M. Nixon, Eisenhower's vice president, a politician with impeccable anticommunist—some said red-baiting—credentials. During the campaign, he announced that he had a "secret plan" for ending the war in Vietnam.

Democratic Party leaders pleaded with the Johnson White House for a dramatic peace initiative to boost Humphrey, who lagged well behind Nixon in the early polls. Over the next few weeks, Harriman, in Paris, carefully negotiated an "understanding" with the North Vietnamese. The United States would halt its bombing unilaterally, but in return Washington would expect cessation of communist rocket and mortar attacks in South Vietnam and a limit on the infiltration of men and supplies. Hanoi agreed, and the two sides declared that meaningful peace talks would begin four days after the bombing halted.

The problem was that President Thieu refused to go along. Ky and other South Vietnamese hardliners, including virtually the entire Catholic community, warned him against an American sellout. Henry Kissinger—a Harvard government professor who had served in the Johnson administration as an unofficial envoy, but now smelled a Republican victory—informed Nixon that Johnson was planning an election-eve end to the bombing. Using Anna Chennault, the widow of Lieutenant General Claire Chennault and a prominent member of the conservative China Lobby, as an intermediary, the Nixon camp urged Thieu to hold out; he was certain to get better treatment from a Republican administration, Madame Chennault assured him. Thereupon, Thieu informed the Americans that Hanoi would have to agree to negotiate directly with the government of Vietnam; he proclaimed that his administration was not "a car that can be hitched to a locomotive." He knew that North Vietnam would never extend to the south the de facto recognition such negotiations would entail.

Thieu's opposition notwithstanding, Johnson announced a bombing halt on November 1, four days before the general election in the United States. Polls showed Humphrey and Nixon in a dead heat. But without South Vietnamese participation, the US delegation to the Paris Peace Talks felt that it could not proceed with negotiations. Nixon won by a hair, and two weeks later, Thieu agreed to send representatives to Paris. By that time, however, the Johnson administration had run out of time.

Prior to taking office in January 1969, Nixon, along with Kissinger, who would become Nixon's national security adviser, vigorously defended the American commitment in Vietnam. Indeed, during the campaign, the Republican candidate had criticized the Johnson administration for not putting more military pressure on North Vietnam. The presence of American troops in Southeast Asia, he declared, was necessary to contain Communist China. Kissinger admitted privately that the strategic assumptions that had led to escalation might have been flawed, but he believed that America's prestige was now on the line, and it must persevere. In truth, Vietnam was but a pawn in the larger game that the two men had in mind. They envisioned a US-led new world order that would be based on great-power negotiation and accommodation of strategic and economic interests. At the heart of this plan were openings to Communist China and the Soviet Union. For these things to occur, there would have to be peace in Vietnam. But it would have to be "peace with honor," as Nixon put it, that is, there would have to be no hint of defeat.

The president and his national security adviser decided to gamble. They would intensify the bombing campaign against North Vietnam and communist positions in the south, and authorize a joint MACV-ARVN incursion to wipe out the communist sanctuaries in Cambodia and Laos. At the same time, to undercut the antiwar movement at home, the administration would order a gradual US stand-down in South Vietnam. Perhaps North Vietnam and the National Liberation Front would feel pressured enough to negotiate with the Thieu regime, and the United States could quietly repair to the sidelines. "We were clearly on our way out of Vietnam by negotiation if possible, by unilateral withdrawal if necessary," Kissinger declared in his memoirs.[1]

The White House was playing a dangerous game, however. What if none of the parties involved—Hanoi, the NLF, Saigon—cooperated? The CIA warned the White House that the ARVN could not hold out against the Viet Cong and the North Vietnamese Army without US help. Even after plans for modernization of the South Vietnamese military were completed in 1972, government forces were "simply . . . not capable of attaining the level of self-sufficiency and overwhelming force superiority that would be required to counter combined Viet Cong insurgency and North Vietnamese Army main force offensives," said Abrams.[2]

In March 1969, Nixon dispatched Secretary of Defense Melvin Laird to Saigon to notify Abrams that a gradual drawdown of American combat forces was at hand. MACV, backed by the CIA, expressed strong reservations. Laird subsequently reported that in his opinion, the US military mission was being too pessimistic. Once freed from the stifling presence of the huge American expeditionary force, the ARVN would be able to hold its own against all comers. The secretary of defense, a former power in the House of Representatives and still a force in the Republican Party, would become a relentless advocate for military withdrawal.

The following month, Vice President Ky came to Washington to prowl the corridors of power. During one meeting, Laird made it clear that the role of the United States henceforward would be to enable the South Vietnamese to choose their own form of government, whatever that might be. How did the South Vietnamese government like the term "Vietnamization"? Just fine, Ky replied gloomily. On June 8, Presidents Nixon and Thieu met at Midway Island, where Nixon announced that 25,000 US combat troops (out of a total of 542,000) would be out of Vietnam by August. On November 3, in a major address to the American people, he outlined his plan for turning the war over to the South Vietnamese. After seeming to appease opponents of the conflict, he lashed out at them in the same speech. Antiwar protesters were irrational and irresponsible. He openly appealed for the support of "the great silent majority" and then concluded with a melodramatic warning: "North Vietnam cannot humiliate the United States. Only Americans can do that."[3] Lest the communists think that he was throwing in the towel, Nixon ordered the air force and the navy to conduct top-secret saturation bombing raids against communist sanctuaries in Cambodia.

Meanwhile, in Hanoi, representatives of the NLF and other front organizations announced the formation of a Provisional Revolutionary Government (PRG) for South Vietnam. This would be the capstone for the village and hamlet liberation committees and give form and structure to the communists' subsequent claims to be the legitimate government of South Vietnam. At the same time, the Central Committee of the Lao Dong, the Communist Party of Vietnam, instructed communist operatives in the south to focus once again on political organization and small-scale guerrilla warfare. In effect, Colby, Abrams, and Bunker had been put on notice by Washington and indirectly by Hanoi. The other war had become the only war, and they had a very limited amount of time to win it.[4]

Colby and Abrams decided that the quickest and most effective way to secure victory was to break the back of the Viet Cong. "That infrastructure is just vital," Abrams proclaimed to his staff, "absolutely critical to the success of either the VC military or . . . political [effort]. You wipe that part out and goddamn it, if he's got 50 divisions it's not going to do him any good." Colby could not have agreed more. The CORDS chief now believed that Phoenix, the war against the Viet Cong Infrastructure, must receive top priority. "You'd have a village election, and the VC would come in and chop off the village chief's head in front of his family and the villagers and then shoot his family. You are not going to have much community development in that environment." Colby continued to insist that the communist cadres were imposing their will on the rural population rather than winning their support through appeals to nationalist sentiment and promises of social and economic justice. The enemy had "a wonderful cadre machine, absolutely magnificent cadre machine," Colby observed at a MACV commanders' meeting, "but it hasn't turned into mass political support." The CORDS chief was probably correct, but his observation was largely irrelevant. Vietnamization was in full swing, but for the villager it was all about not burning bridges with the winning side. One did not have to show political support for the communists, merely to stay out of the way, turning a blind eye when they beheaded the district chief.[5]

The Provincial Reconnaissance Units continued to be the heart of Phoenix. This collection of ARVN deserters, Viet Cong turncoats, common criminals, and Nung tribesmen was funded and supervised by the CIA through early 1970. The Agency provided weapons and training and paid the salaries of the strike team members, salaries that averaged three times what was paid to regular ARVN soldiers. Bounties were available for information, captured weapons, prisoners, and, in some cases, dead bodies. Because the Agency's funds were hidden within the regular budgets of other government entities, an accurate accounting is impossible; estimates of the amount the United States spent on Phoenix ranged from $7 million to $15 million a year. The CIA vastly improved its purchasing power by buying South Vietnamese piasters on the black market, which was illegal under both Vietnamese and US law.[6]

Colby would insist throughout the life of the Phoenix program that the primary objective of the operation was capture and interrogation, not assassination. Indeed, he deeply resented the term "assassination." What the PRUs and US Navy SEALs were doing was both legal and justified. The South Vietnamese National Assembly had passed legislation in 1967 that forbade "any activity designed to publicize or carry out Communism." Those convicted under the law were guilty of treason. Moreover, according to historian Guenter Lewy, between 1957 and 1972 the Banh-anh-ninh— the terror, security, and espionage branch of the Viet Cong—carried out 36,725 targeted killings and abducted another 58,499 South Vietnamese. If there were deaths associated with Phoenix, Colby insisted, they came about as part of a normal and appropriate reaction by the PRUs when Viet Cong cadres fought back or tried to run. A US Information Service officer working with CORDS developed a set of posters with the names and photos of suspected members of the local Viet Cong Infrastructure emblazoned on them. "In a significant contrast to the old Western posters offering a reward for the subject 'dead or alive,'" Colby recalled with pride, "a statement at the bottom of the poster conveyed the word to those described that the amnesty program would receive them without punishment for whatever they had done."[7]

Frank Snepp, a CIA operative who came to Vietnam in 1969 and who spent a lot of time with the PRUs and at the Provincial Interrogation Centers that housed the people they apprehended, identified a continuing problem, however, one that eventually placed a premium on killing rather than capture. The Phoenix operatives would conduct a successful "snatch" operation and deliver their captives to the PICs. Following interrogation, they were jailed. The more incorrigible were housed in Chi Hoa prison in Saigon—a facility that CORDS officer Gage McAfee described as looking like something out of *Midnight Express*—and on Con Son Island on the southern coast of South Vietnam, soon to be notorious for its "tiger cages." (The "tiger cages" were tiny bamboo cells used to house Viet Cong and North Vietnamese Army prisoners.) But most were released within six months. The strike team members were not going to risk life and limb to capture the same person over and over. "Let's say you're a Tucker Gougleman [the CIA man in charge of overseeing Phoenix] or a SEAL guy running a PRU team," McAfee said. "You go out and you're targeting some fairly high-level VC infrastructure guy. You pick him up. It's harder to capture a guy than kill him. You run the snatch operation correctly. You bring him in with some evidence against him. Six months later the guy is out. He knows the province chief's brother. So the PRU team is not going to risk its collective life. Next time they are going to shoot him." Frank Snepp recalled: "Several times, I said, 'I'm going with you [the PRU] to make sure you capture this guy.' . . . What they would do was to take me to the edge of the hamlet, and I would lie low. They would go zipping in and come back empty-handed. What happened to our guy? I would inquire. 'Oh, he tried to escape.'"[8]

Corruption was also an ongoing problem for Phoenix. It was not unusual, especially in the northern part of South Vietnam, for the provincial or district power structure to treat the PRUs as their private armies, extorting protection money, intimidating rivals, and suppressing dissent. Sometimes one reconnaissance unit would be pitted against another in local vendettas. It was relatively easy for the well-to-do to buy their way out of a PIC, and some people were imprisoned there just so they would.

"The VCI blacklist eventually became corrupted," said PRU adviser Mike Walsh. "It became a place to put the names of these corrupt senior officers' enemies, to avoid repayment of debt or even to settle a score." Underpaid provincial and district province chiefs would frequently rake money off the top of funds that were given to them to provide for their prisoners' care.[9]

Finally, there were rumors of atrocities by the PRUs and even by the Americans. On the night of February 25, 1969, Team One of SEAL Platoon Delta, under the command of Lieutenant Robert Kerry (the future senator from Nebraska), infiltrated the village of Thanh Phong. Its mission was to capture the National Liberation Front district committee chief, who, according to intelligence, was supposed to be sleeping there. To conceal their presence, "Kerry's Raiders," as they called themselves, murdered villagers on their way in. Thinking they were under fire from the Viet Cong, they then killed more villagers as they retreated. When the smoke cleared, Kerry's Raiders had twenty-one dead civilians to their credit, with not a Viet Cong cadre among them. Word of these and other misdeeds inevitably percolated up to headquarters. In August 1969, Colby asked MACV to require that all American Phoenix advisers attend lectures at Vung Tau on South Vietnamese police procedures.[10]

In the fall of 1969, Colby hired a young lawyer named Gage McAfee as MACV-CORDS legal adviser. McAfee, who spoke both French and Vietnamese, was to put together a team that would bring accepted police practices and the rule of law to the Phoenix program. In 1968, the Vietnamese officials working with Phung Hoang (the Vietnamese name for Phoenix) had three categories in which detainees were to be placed: there were class "A" offenders, who were communist cadres working at the district level and up; class "B" offenders, who were active in the communist infrastructure as tax collectors, terrorists, or propagandists, or performing any other function on behalf of the NLF; and class "C" offenders, individuals who had not done anything concrete to benefit the Viet Cong but were suspected sympathizers. Those arrested were tried by a Province Security Committee, but the proceeding was considered extrajudicial, and there was no appeal. The suspect had no right to counsel, no right to see his dossier, and no right to testify, confront accusers, or question the prosecution. Security forces could hold a detainee for a total of forty-six days while they gathered evidence. At trial, three pieces of evidence were sufficient for conviction, and acceptable evidence ranged from allegations to confessions under duress to actual captured documents.[11] McAfee and his team preached Western legal methods to the South Vietnamese—consistent procedures, rules of evidence, a detainee's right to legal defense, the requirement that there be a new piece of hard evidence every year to keep a dossier alive—but much of this fell on deaf ears. Characteristically, the Thieu regime saw the anti-VCI campaign not only as an instrument with which to combat the communists but also as one to stifle noncommunist dissent.

In addition to introducing proper legal procedures into the Phoenix program, McAfee was also charged with looking into abuses. The problem was that it was very difficult for outsiders to gain entrance to the Provincial Interrogation Centers. The attitude of the Special Branch—a division of SEPES, the South Vietnamese intelligence and internal security apparatus—which ran the PICs, was that if the Americans did not like coercive interrogations, then they wouldn't let them see any. In this the CIA was complicit. McAfee recalled that during a trip into a really dangerous part of the Mekong Delta, he first contacted the principal American adviser for Phoenix, who happened to be a US Army officer. "I want to tour the nearest PIC," McAfee said. "I don't know," the officer replied. McAfee asked if he had ever been inside of one. "No," the officer said. McAfee, talking about the incident years later, said, "Here is a guy who is running the Phoenix program who hasn't even been to the PIC." Describing what happened next, he said, "We went to the CIA place, which was this ratted out, dusty, sand-bagged hooch full of radios. The CIA guy looked like the Ohio State football coach. You know, shaved head . . . tough guy wearing a Chicom pistol. He said to me, 'You can't go to the PIC.' I said, 'That's my job, and I'm going to the PIC whether you like it or not.'" The Woody Hayes lookalike called headquarters and was told that McAfee worked for Bill Colby. "Okay, you can go," he announced, "but not the Phoenix guy." Later, Frank Snepp complained to Station Chief Tom Polgar about a prisoner whom Snepp found beaten nearly to death by the South Vietnamese. "Wait a minute," Polgar responded. "You want me to go to the South Vietnamese with 140,000 North Vietnamese in their country and say to them you've got to ease up on the bad guys because we think it is wrong?" McAfee labored long and hard to have the Geneva Convention on treatment of prisoners applied to Phoenix detainees, but to no avail.[12]

Estimates are that during its existence—roughly from 1968 through 1972—the Phoenix program was responsible for neutralizing—that is, killing, capturing, or turning—between 19,000 and 20,000 Viet Cong cadre. The ratio of captured to killed ran about 2:1. During one ten-month period from mid-1968 through the spring of 1969, the PRUs ran 50,770 missions and tallied 7,408 captured and 4,406 killed.[13]

In March 1969, the South Vietnamese government decreed that the PRUs be absorbed into the National Police. From that point on, Vietnamese province chiefs appointed PRU commanders, but the CIA continued to advise and fund the units. After the war, North Vietnamese officials termed Phoenix the most effective program the Americans and South Vietnamese had mounted against the Viet Cong. Colby's appraisal was more negative. Though he was proud of Phoenix, he regarded it as a failure. "You know our special program on the VCI, General," he reported to Abrams in July 1969. "This, frankly we can't report any great success on. Figures of those neutralized seemed fairly impressive standing by themselves. But they represented a reduction of only one and one-half percent of the total VCI strength each month." That would amount to 20 percent by the end of the year. "And they can probably replace a good part of that," he said. "The standard version was that they were all being abused, killed," Gage McAfee said. "From our perspective, the problem was that they were all being freed." Indeed, Colby estimated that during the life of the Phoenix program, the South Vietnamese government released some 100,000 "communist offenders" from its correction centers.[14]

Phoenix became one of the seemingly endless ironies plaguing the American effort in Vietnam. Colby and Abrams placed increased emphasis on the campaign against the Viet Cong Infrastructure in 1969 and 1970 out of a recognition that time was running out, that US opinion was turning against the war. But by the beginning of 1970, news reporting on Phoenix—always identified as a CIA program in the American media— had become one of the principal factors contributing to public disillusionment. In story after story, the word "assassination" was used to describe the CIA's war on the Viet Cong.[15]

Colby understood the impact that bad press could have, not only on Phoenix but on CORDS in general. In October 1969, he issued a directive through MACV that Americans working with Phoenix should have nothing to do with targeted killings, that they should observe the rules of war when conducting operations, and that they should promptly report questionable activities by the PRUs to their superiors. But what would Phoenix be without at least the threat of violence? Colby's directive ended by allowing for "reasonable military force . . . as necessary."[16] Whatever effect Colby's order had on American opinion was vitiated when, on November 13, 1969, journalist Seymour Hersh reported in the *New York Times* that US Army troops at a village called My Lai had massacred hundreds of Vietnamese civilians eighteen months earlier. Lieutenant William Calley and his Americal Division soldiers were not attached to Phoenix, but most Americans did not or would not differentiate.

In February 1970, the Senate Foreign Relations Committee, under the direction of its powerful chairman, J. William Fulbright (D-AR), held four days of hearings on pacification in Vietnam. Colby returned to Washington to testify, bringing with him a CORDS team that included John Paul Vann. By this time Fulbright had become the symbol of establishment disillusionment with the war. In 1967, he had published *The Arrogance of Power*, in which he charged that in its mindless pursuit of communist enemies, the United States was supporting dictatorships abroad and suppressing civil liberties at home. In so doing, it was violating the very principles for which it claimed to be fighting.

During the hearings, Colby combined lawyer like adroitness with McNamara-style statistics to demonstrate how the joint US–South Vietnamese pacification effort would bring 90 percent of South Vietnamese villages into the secure category by 1971. An entire day was devoted to Phoenix, with testimony being given in executive session. Fortunately for Colby, Fulbright used the term "execution" rather than "assassination" when asking questions about Phoenix. "There has been no one legally executed," Colby testified. "You have not had convictions of members of the enemy apparatus in which executions followed." In another exchange, New Jersey senator Clifford Case demanded that Colby "swear by all that is holy" that Phoenix was not a counterterror program. At this point Colby's emotions uncharacteristically got the better of him. "I have already taken an oath," he answered with some heat. "There was a counter-terror program, but it has been discarded as a concept." Of course, nothing could have been further from the truth. In its war on the Banh-anh-ninh, Phoenix was nothing if not a counterterror program. Colby's failure to defend the program on its own merits is striking.[17]

"The only two things that the Fulbright Committee was interested in, and most of Washington, really . . . were Phoenix and the Chau case,"

Colby told Abrams and his staff upon his return from Washington.[18] The arrest and trial of Tran Ngoc Chau, the father of Vietnamese pacification, was rooted in Vietnamese national politics and went to the heart of Bill Colby's nation-building philosophy. The official American reaction to the Chau case would in many ways determine whether there would ever be a connection between the "rice-roots" revolution building in the countryside and the government in Saigon. Since 1962, men like Colby, Lansdale, Scotton, Bumgardner, Ellsberg, and Vann had been trying to foster self-determination and political self-consciousness among the peasantry. If the rice-roots revolution was going to succeed, however, it would have to be manifested at the national level. Some, like Colby, believed that Nguyen Van Thieu was capable of making the connection, and some did not. The naysayers saw in Tran Ngoc Chau an alternative to the venal, grasping, and autocratic generals who continued to hold the keys to power.

Two themes dominated post-Tet politics in Saigon: fear that the United States was going to broker a deal with the communists behind its ally's back, and the ongoing Thieu-Ky rivalry.

In the wake of Tet, the US Mission had briefly thrown its money and influence behind a nonpartisan political movement headed by the former general Tran Van Don, now a senator. Designed to meld South Vietnam's myriad of parties and factions into one noncommunist whole, Don's organization took the name National Salvation Front. Thieu's suspicions were immediately aroused. The new organization was obviously an instrument that the Americans intended to use to generate support for a coalition government that would include the National Liberation Front, he proclaimed to his friend Lieutenant General Le Nguyen Khang, commander of III Corps. During this same conversation, Thieu asked whether there was any evidence the United States had assisted the Viet Cong during the Tet Offensive. Fear of a betrayal continued to accelerate through 1968 as the Paris Peace Talks got underway. LBJ had announced a unilateral US bombing halt on October 31, and then Secretary of Defense Clifford had declared on December 15 that the United States felt completely free to discuss military matters, including troop withdrawals, unilaterally with the North Vietnamese. The Nixon administration subsequently embraced Vietnamization. Thieu's fears were, then, not without foundation.[19]

The hidden heart of South Vietnamese politics continued to be the corps commander system. Between 1966 and 1968, these warlords acquired the power to appoint all the key civil and military officials in their zones, including division and regimental commanders and province and district chiefs. These positions generally went to the highest bidders. Utilizing intermediaries—that is, wives, aides, and staff assistants—the corps commander and the aspiring candidate would work out a lump-sum down payment and the monthly tribute that was to follow. These payoffs were made possible by the corruption that came with the post. The key money-collecting official in the system was the province chief, who earned huge sums by raking off funds from various public works projects and payoffs from businessmen for favors and protection. According to Ed Lansdale, who reappeared on the Vietnam scene in the mid-1960s as an adviser to the ambassador, the corps commander system was much more the control mechanism for the South Vietnamese government and the ARVN than the ministries and channels of authority listed in the official organizational charts. In a system in which extortion and payoffs needed to be overseen by intermediaries, a coterie of corrupt subordinates grew up around each of the five warlords (the region around Saigon had been declared a separate corps area). Frequently, these networks became power centers and self-sustaining entities in themselves that continued to operate as various generals came and went. On the rare occasion that a new province chief arrived on the scene determined to eliminate corruption, key subordinates would quietly oppose his efforts at every turn, working to discredit him with his superiors. Significantly, the head of this snake was General Tran Thien Khiem, minister of the interior and subsequently prime minister, whose wife and brother-in-law oversaw a drug ring that sold heroin to all comers, including American GIs.[20]

Along with Bunker, Colby, as deputy commander of CORDS, had direct responsibility for the war against corruption and for overseeing the creation of a responsible, responsive government. He installed a permanent liaison officer in the prime minister's office—Jean Sauvageot, a US Army officer who was detailed to CORDS in part because of his fluency in Vietnamese—and paid personal visits to Huong, and subsequently Khiem, several times a week when he was in Saigon. On one level, he came across as a champion of a rice-roots revolution. In a February 1969 letter to Thieu, Colby urged the president to make the Pacification and Development Plan the cornerstone of his nation-building effort. "It should call upon all to share the burden and at the same time it would provide all a share of the power," he wrote.[21]

Yet, in 1967, when he was chief of the Far East Division, Colby had reported to Helms: "On the Ambassador's behalf we are developing discreet relationships and covert assets that can be manipulated to sponsor the emergence of what appears to the outside world as genuinely Vietnamese political initiatives, constitutional provisions, and electoral platforms." Colby was, of course, a pragmatist. In a note to Bob Komer about the South Vietnamese government, he wrote, "While I certainly concur in its many flaws I am somewhat inclined to believe that this is part of the 'given' of any problem such as this and that we should find a similarly flawed instrument almost wherever we looked." The real solution to this sort of dilemma was the "patient collaboration" the United States was providing to Thieu but had denied to Diem. One day, Frank Scotton, then on special assignment to CORDS, was having lunch with Colby at the latter's house. "You know," Scotton said, "does it strike you as strange that we are maintaining these files and presenting cases for removal to one of the half dozen most corrupt officials from one of the most corrupt families in South Vietnam [Khiem]?" Colby just laughed and said, "Well, that's the most we can do right now." There came a point, however, when Bill Colby could no longer temporize.[22]

On February 26, 1970, Tran Ngoc Chau, secretary-general of the lower house of the National Assembly, was arrested in his office and forcibly removed by a squad of plainclothes policemen. Days before, he had been convicted in absentia by a military tribunal of collaborating with the enemy. Chau was confined in an eight-by-ten-foot cell and informed that he had been sentenced to twenty years of hard labor. During the mid-1960s, as province chief in Kien Hoa and then director of the Rural Development Cadre center at Vung Tau, Chau had become the darling of American counterinsurgency/pacification enthusiasts. The creator of the Census-Grievance Program, Chau had authored a two-volume work on the dos and don'ts of nation-building in South Vietnam. Vann, Scotton, and Ellsberg considered him a mentor and a friend. In 1967, frustrated with the corps commander system, Chau had resigned from the military and run successfully for the National Assembly. He became the representative from Kien Hoa, where he had built a noncommunist political coalition that included Catholics, Buddhists, Cao Dai, and members of various ethnic minorities. He and Thieu had been classmates and friends at the South Vietnamese military academy at Dalat. Initially, like Colby, Chau had viewed Thieu as a pragmatic, patriotic leader who might be induced to put together an authentic national political organization that included all of the major noncommunist factions, religious groups, and ethnic minorities. He watched approvingly as Thieu gradually moved Ky and the northerners to the edge of the South Vietnamese political stage, but he steadfastly refused to join the growing coterie of Thieu loyalists in the National Assembly. Repeatedly, Chau pleaded with Thieu to broaden his political base, and, in particular, to reach out to the Buddhists. "How can I compromise with them," the president had replied. "Their leaders are at least pro-Communist, if not outright Communists." Ridiculous, Chau retorted. Marxism-Leninism called for the eradication of all religions. What the Buddhists wanted was a clean, responsive government in Saigon.[23]

Chau had long believed that those who had fought with the Viet Minh were nationalists first and communists second, turning to Marxism-Leninism only because they believed it was the only alternative for achieving unification and freedom from foreign domination. In 1964, he had informed the CIA station in Saigon that he had been in contact with "some high ranking officials from Hanoi" who wanted to discuss a possible compromise peace settlement. He asked for an interview with Ambassador Taylor to get his advice, but was rebuffed. The contact, as it turned out, was Chau's brother, Tran Ngoc Hien, an agent of the North Vietnamese government. Hien and Chau would meet periodically at the house of their parents. In Vietnam, family generally trumped ideology. In 1967, Chau finally identified Hien as his communist interlocutor. The Saigon station, then under the direction of Far East Division head Colby, told Chau that he needed to bring Hien in. He refused. The following year, in the wake of Tet, Hien did his best to persuade Chau to defect, promising him any position within the National Liberation Front that he might desire. Chau refused. He could not buy into a system that would always sacrifice the interests of the individual to those of the state.[24]

In the fall of 1968, Chau moved to create a national political movement that would be built on the rice-roots political revolution that Vann, Scotton, Bumgardner, and Colby had been touting since 1964. He asked the CIA for help; Bill Kohlman, Chau's CIA contact, replied that help would be available only if Chau and his movement made a commitment in advance to support President Thieu and his policies. Chan demurred. In January 1969, the soldier turned politician announced his peace plan. The National Liberation Front would be asked to designate a certain number of delegates to the National Assembly, as long as they were not communists. The NLF would be permitted to participate in the 1971 presidential elections. Saigon and Hanoi would enter into direct negotiations. Significantly, there was no mention of the United States. Chau later claimed that he recognized immediately that Nixon and Kissinger intended to abandon South Vietnam at the first opportunity. Shortly thereafter, Hien was captured, and in July he was convicted of being an enemy agent. His relationship to Chau was widely touted by the Thieu regime and its captive newspapers. Ominously, Scotton, Bumgardner, and Vann were ordered by Ambassador Bunker to sever all ties with their comrade.[25]

Knowing that Jean Sauvageot was also an old friend of Chau's, Colby told him to keep his distance. Sauvageot could not. One day he snuck out of the Presidential Palace, where he had a desk in the prime minister's office, and rode his bicycle to the house where Chau was hiding. The two men talked for a while, the American urging Chau to do what was best for him and his family. Upon his return to the palace, Sauvageot found a note from Colby waiting. "I warned you not to see that man," it read. A CIA acquaintance later told Sauvageot that Colby had a transcript of their conversation on his desk before Sauvageot returned to his post.[26]

Chau's arrest, conviction, and imprisonment caused a major flap in the United States. Fulbright had his staff investigate and subsequently incorporated the case in his indictment of both the Thieu regime and the US war effort. Vann and Ellsberg were furious at the US Mission's abandonment of Chau. "It wasn't hard to get Vann pissed," Scotton recalled, "but I had never seen him that mad before or after." The real villain in the whole affair, in the eyes of Chau's American supporters, was not Colby, but Ted Shackley, the CIA station chief. "Shackley told Bunker that 'We had documentary proof' that Chau was a communist," Scotton said. "That was an absolute lie." Frank Snepp agreed. "Ted Shackley did his best to destroy Chau," he said. "He had this fixation on Chau. Shackley was a political animal to the core." In fact, the head of the Vietnamese Special Forces had contacted Shackley before he arrested Chau. The chief of station assured him that he had no interest in the man and no objection to Saigon taking legal action against him.[27]

If Vann was infuriated, Daniel Ellsberg was devastated. By 1970, he was back in the United States, working as a consultant for the Rand Corporation. Following Chau's arrest he arranged an interview with former undersecretary of state Nicholas Katzenbach to plead for US intervention. The State Department asked Bunker to look into the affair, but that was as far as it went. "Chau and [Nguyen] Be and Hien were all part of a group who Ellsberg, Vann, Bumgardner, and I thought, if South Vietnam could make it through the next decade, through the Thieus, the Viens, the Khiems—this would be the leadership for a new Vietnam," Scotton later said. "We thought if they do in Chau, and we allow it, then what hope was there?" For Ellsberg, Chau's arrest and America's official indifference was a turning point. "The single most important person in Dan's thinking about the war, the sociology of it, was Tran Ngoc Chau," Frank Scotton said. "Vann was committed to staying in the war with this smoldering resentment at what had happened; Ellsberg was not. I was in Washington when he was preparing the [Pentagon] papers for release. The Chau case was unfolding at the time and was crucial to his decision."[28]

That Colby could have saved Chau is doubtful. What is clear is that he did not try. It was true that, on one level, it was structurally difficult, if not impossible, for the United States to aid and abet a change of government that would profoundly alter the social and economic structure of the country in question. Colby may have recalled McGeorge Bundy's observation in 1965 when he had told him that fostering such change might be desirable, but was institutionally impossible—that is, under time-honored diplomatic rules, Washington interacted with established governments, not revolutionary movements (not unless they were anticommunist). A coup was a different matter. Usually, it was a family affair, involving the exchange of one group of elites for another. The nations of Latin America had labored long and hard to persuade the United States to recognize the juridical equality of all states and not, à la Woodrow Wilson, to apply ideological and other standards to a new regime when considering recognition. And, of course, there was the Cold War prism through which the United States still tended to view every foreign regime and international situation. Colby would remark to Jean Sauvageot, his liaison to the prime minister's office, that Chau's trial and imprisonment were "very unfortunate but . . . we had our relations with the Vietnamese government to consider and had to be very careful." In subsequent remarks he was not nearly so sensitive. "He

[Chau] was an officer, and he was a province chief and a good one," Colby said in an oral history, "but he had been contacted by his brother who was a North Vietnamese officer. He had not reported it, and in time of war I really can't get very much cranked up about punishing somebody who plays that game."[29]

The arrest and trial of Tran Ngoc Chau showed the CIA in Vietnam in its true colors, and when push came to shove, Bill Colby was CIA to the core. In the developing world during the Cold War, picking the right side was everything. In 1963, during the coup that overthrew the House of Ngo, the Agency had cultivated each faction, waiting to see who would come out on top, and then, just before the climax, threw in with the victor. This was the classic realist approach to counterinsurgency. Colby was a realist first, an idealist second. He was no doubt sincere in his efforts to empower the Rhade, the Hmong, and the Vietnamese peasantry in general, but neither he nor the Agency was going to lead a revolution. In this they were reflecting American Cold War policy. In the end, Chau and Thieu, like Diem, Khanh, and Ky, were merely pawns. Chau, Scotton, Ellsberg, and to a degree Vann were subversives; unconventional Colby might have been, but there were lines beyond which he would not go.

Life for Bill Colby in South Vietnam was not all reports, briefings, and overnight trips to contested villages. He lived alone in his villa in downtown Saigon. Much to the admiration of his subordinates, the former Jedburgh drove himself around Saigon without escort day and night. This was in contrast to Shackley, who traveled about ostentatiously in his armored black limousine with armed outliers. When in town, Colby was a frequent attendee at the endless round of cocktail parties and dinners. One of his aides, Tony Cistaro, remembered being at a private dinner when Colby, unaware that any other CORDS people were invited, showed up with a beautiful Vietnamese woman on his arm. Colby was on leave from the CIA, but he was still CIA, and the Agency personnel who worked the PRUs and PICs were under his command. If Colby wanted to hobnob with the Vietnamese and French elite, there was the Cercle Sportif. If he wanted American, and especially CIA, company, there was the Duc Hotel. Situated at 14 Tran Qui at the corner of Cong Le, the Duc was only a block from the Presidential Palace and four blocks from the US embassy. The CIA leased the entire five-story hotel to serve as a residence for new arrivals until they completed in-country processing and received their assignments.

The rooftop swimming pool was nicknamed "The Bay of Pigs." Sundays at the Duc were reserved for socializing. The day started with Bloody Marys and brunch, then continued with swimming, sunbathing, and conversation. Besides the restaurant, bar, and swimming pool, there was a small theater, a liquor store, and a recreation room. Behind the pool was a poker room where a high-stakes game was almost always in session. Nung Chinese guarded the front and rear gates with unloaded weapons. The family that rented the hotel to the CIA had twelve children, one of whom was an officer in the North Vietnamese Army.[30]

Colby was always surrounded by a coterie of admiring protégés. In addition to Gage McAfee, there was Steve Young. Colby had known Young's father, Kenneth, who had been Kennedy's ambassador to Thailand. Steve had met Colby for the first time when the CORDS chief came to Vinh Long for one of his inspections. Young was a USAID officer and happened to be assigned to give the briefing that day. The topic was energizing village governments. A week or so later, Young got a call on the radio ordering him to report to Saigon. He asked why, but received no answer. Dutifully, he caught a ride on a C-134. After landing at Tan Son Nhut, he reported to CORDS headquarters and was directed to a Mr. Aubrey Elliott, "a very prim and proper senior aide with a starched white shirt and a bow tie," he recalled. Young introduced himself, and Elliott told him to be ready to report for work the following Monday. "The hell I am," Young said. "I don't know if you've noticed, but there is a war going on and it's not happening in Saigon." You have your orders, was the reply. At that point, Young had not lost his idealism. He had volunteered for Vietnam; he had come to make a difference. He thought, "I'll call Ambassador Colby and he'll get me out of this." Colby's secretary put Young through at once.

"Yes, this is Bill Colby."

"Mr. Ambassador, I am sorry to disturb you, but some son of a bitch is trying to pull me out of the provinces and bring me to Saigon. I need your help."

"Oh, Steve, I thought you would be very good in that job."

(Pause)

"Was that nine o'clock on Monday morning?"[31]

Like McAfee, Young found Colby to be selfless, unassuming, committed, and always open to criticism and new ideas. "You are a leader whom we would follow anywhere," Young would write as his boss was about to depart Vietnam, "because we believe that with you we can finish the job, any job." Years later, Paul Colby, Bill's youngest son, observed: "In many ways my father was more intimate with his protégés—Stephen Young and Gage McAfee—than with his children. He was, after all, responsible for his children—discipline, preparation for life and all that."[32]

In March 1970, Richard Nixon announced the phased withdrawal of 150,000 troops over the next year. He hoped, as he later observed in his memoirs, that this would "drop a bombshell on the gathering spring storm of anti-war protest." But the move caused him serious problems with the military. Abrams pleaded with the White House to avoid setting fixed timetables and instead tie withdrawals to advances in pacification and modernization of the ARVN. Nixon and Kissinger refused. General Alexander Haig, one of Kissinger's deputies and a White House errand boy, visited MACV. One of Abrams's lieutenants blurted out, "We have two of your messages. One of them says 'go get 'em' and the other one says 'hurry up and get out.'" Haig replied, "Well, it's 'go get 'em' until the end of the period."[33]

The same month that Nixon made his troop withdrawal announcement, Cambodia's Prince Sihanouk was overthrown by a pro-American clique headed by General Lon Nol. On March 12, the new government issued a decree ordering all Viet Cong and North Vietnamese troops to be out of the country within three days. The US Mission in Saigon was overjoyed. Not only had Sihanouk tolerated communist sanctuaries along the border with South Vietnam, he had also turned a blind eye as North Vietnam funneled thousands of tons of arms and other supplies through the port of Sihanoukville. The Nixon administration quickly extended diplomatic recognition to the new regime in Phnom Penh and launched a major aid program. The president subsequently endorsed a plan whereby a combined US-ARVN force would invade and clean out two enemy troop concentrations in Cambodia just west and north of Saigon. Chances were that the Cambodian incursion would reignite the antiwar movement in the United States, the president realized, but it would also appease MACV and the Thieu regime and, more substantively, buy time for Vietnamization. This was vintage Nixon: alternately appease and attack the doves, and placate the hawks, all the while pursuing an irreversible course of de-escalation.

The Nixon administration claimed a great victory in the wake of the Cambodian incursion: 2,000 of the enemy killed, 800 bunkers destroyed, and the Central Office for South Vietnam, the "nerve center" of North Vietnamese operations in the south, dispersed. In truth, forewarned, the communists had retreated further into the interior. The incursion had little impact on the enemy's war-making capacity. As the White House had anticipated, Cambodia galvanized the antiwar movement. In May, six students were killed at Kent State and Jackson State, and more than 100,000 protesters gathered in Washington. In June, the Senate voted to repeal the Gulf of Tonkin Resolution. An amendment sponsored by Senators George McGovern (D-SD) and Mark Hatfield (R-OR), subsequently defeated, would have required the administration to pull all US troops out of South Vietnam by the close of 1971. Nixon, infuriated, approved the "Huston Plan," which authorized the intelligence services to open mail, employ electronic surveillance devices, and even burglarize to gather evidence against domestic enemies of the administration.

In early 1971, again over the protests of General Abrams, the White House announced the withdrawal of 100,000 additional troops by the end of the year, leaving 175,000 in-country, only 75,000 of whom were combat soldiers. In February, Nixon approved a major ground operation in Laos whose objective was the same as in Cambodia—to buy time for Vietnamization. This time, the North Vietnamese and the Pathet Lao were ready. They repelled the offensive, inflicting a 50 percent casualty rate on the invading ARVN.

Throughout 1970 and 1971, Bill Colby, well aware that he and Abrams were in a race against time, set a consistently upbeat tone in his reports to the US Mission and to those in the American media who were still taking an interest in Vietnam. "By year's end," he wrote in his memoir, speaking of 1969, "I was staying overnight in areas that had been 'Indian country' the year before, driving on local roads or going up canals where prudence had dictated no penetration earlier." To demonstrate that change had truly come to the countryside, he motored 100 miles along Route 4, the road leading south from Saigon through the heart of the Mekong Delta. He encountered the remains of blown bridges and mine craters newly filled with dirt, but no one shot at him. Then, during the 1971 Tet holiday, Colby and John Paul Vann embarked on a much-publicized motorcycle trip across the delta, from Can Tho near the South China Sea to the Cambodian border. "By late 1971," Colby would later write, "the war in the Delta essentially had been won. Security was so improved that there remained only a residual level of violence, such as the pop-pop of an AK-47 firing at our helicopter as we flew over the mangrove swamp along the sea in a distant southern district." Robert Kaiser, a reporter for the *Washington Post* who covered CORDS, dubbed Colby the spokesman for "the new optimists."[34]

Many observers believed that the DEPCORDS was helping to create a false reality. James Nach, a high-level political analyst in the US embassy in Saigon and a student of Vietnamese history, likened the situation in the Mekong to that which had existed in Hau Nghia province. While American and ARVN troops swarmed the surface, the Viet Cong and their sympathizers had withdrawn. But the latter were operating their own society belowground in the tunnels of Cu Chi northwest of Saigon. Vann and Colby had literally taken the "high road" during their famous motorcycle trip. If Vann had taken his boss down the muddy side roads that led away from Highway 4, however, he would have found that the area was less pacific than he thought. Perhaps the level of violence had declined, but history and the populace's memory of it remained. Since the late nineteenth century, the rural population in the upper delta had suffered at the hands of landlords and French colonial officials. The communists had begun organizing in Long An and western Dinh Tuon in the 1930s. The flag of the Democratic Republic of Vietnam (North Vietnam), a yellow star on a red field, was designed and first flew in the delta. Officially "pacified" by 1971, the amoeba-like Viet Cong Infrastructure had separated, reformed, and returned. In 1972, the whole area would blow up once again, leaving the Americans and the South Vietnamese in possession of Highway 4 and little else.[35]

Vietnamization affected all aspects of the US effort in Vietnam, including the Phoenix program. The PRU teams were Vietnamese, and they were led by Vietnamese officers, but until mid-1970 the South Vietnamese government had not spent a piaster on the program. In July, the US Mission began shifting responsibility for Phuong Huong (the Phoenix program) to the government. Thieu ordered it placed under the Directorate of National Police and canceled draft deferrals for interpreters, those who had constituted the vital link between the PRUs and their American advisers. Shackley, arriving in Vietnam with instructions from Helms to abjure nation-building and counterterrorism and concentrate on traditional intelligence gathering, was anxious to break the CIA-Phoenix link. In 1971, Abrams ordered his staff not to fill the spots in Phoenix that were being left vacant by officers rotating home. During a December 1970 visit to Washington, Colby found a distinct lack of interest in the entire pacification effort on the part of the administration. As would soon become evident to many within the US Mission, Nixon and Kissinger wanted to deliver a series of face-saving blows to the enemy and then get the hell out of Vietnam.[36]

Colby consoled himself with the belief that the battle had been won. He and Vann agreed that there would not be another Tet; the possibility of a communist takeover in South Vietnam by means of guerrilla warfare and a popular uprising was gone. The focus of the war would henceforth be on the northern provinces, which would come under increasing pressure from North Vietnamese main force units. Vann asked to be transferred back to II Corps, but this time with supreme authority over all military as well as civilian personnel. It was an audacious request even for a man who had made a career out of being audacious. But after Colby had managed to deflect Bunker's direct order to fire Vann for insubordination, the gadfly had toned down his criticism of the US military and the South Vietnamese government. Abrams probably figured that by the time Vann was in the saddle, there would be very few US troops for the former lieutenant colonel to command. Consequently, he acceded to Colby's request and agreed to make Vann proconsul.[37]

During this period, Colby appeared to be unwavering in his support of Nguyen Van Thieu. The president had embraced pacification in all its forms, Colby reported to MACV—land reform, village elections, the rule of law, a curb on corruption, and national elections open to all comers.[38] He clung to the belief that America's greatest mistake of the war had been to abandon Ngo Dinh Diem. Its greatest accomplishment, perhaps, was to show continuing patience with Thieu, whom Colby believed to be endowed with the same virtues as Diem, but fewer of the vices. Whatever the case, President Thieu required a lot of patience.

In 1969, a joint operation run by the CIA and South Vietnam's Police Special Branch had discovered that the president's top intelligence adviser, Huynh Van Trong, was a communist agent. When Thieu was confronted with the information, he wanted to sweep the matter under the rug. The US Mission insisted, however, that Trong be arrested and publicly denounced. But Trong was just the tip of the proverbial iceberg. In 1970, CIA analyst Sam Adams reported to his superiors that the entire government and ARVN superstructure was Swiss cheese. He and his colleagues estimated that the communists had infiltrated between twenty thousand and thirty thousand operatives into the officer corps and civil bureaucracy. Then there was Thieu's ongoing contempt for the westernized politicians in Saigon and, in George Carver's words, the "alien institutional toys they call political parties." The president continued to insist that the South Vietnamese were "not interested in [political doctrine]" but simply "wanted to lead better and more prosperous lives without being afraid." Thieu seemed, Diemlike, unwilling or unable to comprehend that constitutional procedures and the rule of law were a means to that end. In this sense, his views were diametrically opposed to those of Bill Colby.[39]

National elections were due in October 1971; Thieu and his wife wanted another term. The US Mission was more than happy for the president to stay in power—what Nixon and Kissinger wanted was someone who would maintain order while the United States withdrew—but it wanted the election to be contested. Thieu announced his candidacy on July 24. At that point, Ambassador Bunker paid a clandestine visit to General Duong Van "Big" Minh and offered him as much as $3 million to challenge Thieu. Minh, whose CIA handler affectionately described him as having "the body of an elephant and the brain of a mouse," agreed to throw his hat into the ring. Vice President Ky then declared his candidacy for the highest office in the land but was disqualified by the Supreme Court. On August 20, Minh withdrew from the race. President Thieu went on to win, with 91.5 percent of the vote.[40]

All the while, Bill Colby kept up his weekly visits to Prime Minister Khiem and President Thieu, discussing the course of pacification and proposing various anticorruption measures. The Presidential Palace never for a moment believed that Colby had severed his ties with the Agency. Thieu, egged on by Khiem, was already convinced the CIA was trying to pressure him into negotiating a shameful peace with the communists, or even to bring about his overthrow. "I don't think he [Colby] was naïve about what was going on in the Presidential Palace," Frank Snepp later said. "There was just no other place to go. He kept looking for ways to jerry-build the system. That's what you do when you're fighting the devil incarnate, and Bill Colby believed that the communists were the devil incarnate."[41]

Like Frank Scotton, John Paul Vann, Ev Bumgardner, and Dan Ellsberg, Bill Colby had fallen in love with Vietnam. Individual liaisons aside, he reveled in the manners and customs of the people, the tropical climate, the physical beauty of the place, his postcolonial life in Saigon, and the excitement and adventure of nation-building. "Wear the Arab kit," T. E. Lawrence had advised young British Foreign Service Officers destined for the Middle East. "Learn all you can. Get to know their families, clans and tribes, friends and enemies, wells, hills and roads . . . speak their dialect of Arabic . . . acquire their trust and intimacy. . . . You will be like an actor in a foreign theater." There was a saying among old Vietnam hands about those whose final tour was up: "They had to leave their loved ones to return to their families."[42]

By this point, Bill and Barbara's marriage was a shell; he dreaded returning home, but by the summer of 1971, he decided, grudgingly, that there was no choice. His eldest daughter, Catherine, was in dire straits. During Bill's rare and brief trips home, Barbara had tried to tell him that the family needed him, but she did not try very hard. Her husband had long ago made it clear that he was doing important, even heroic work, and that he expected his wife and family to do their duty and take care of themselves. Eventually, however, some of the family's friends in the CIA became concerned; an informal delegation approached Colby in Saigon and told him it was time to return to Washington. He could not do it, he said; his country needed him. Finally, Barbara asked thirteen-year-old Paul to intervene. During Bill's last trip home as deputy commander of CORDS in June, Paul met him in the parking lot of the Little Flower Church after one of the interminable meetings his father seemed always to be attending. He told him that he absolutely had to come home. Grudgingly, Colby agreed.[43]

15

THE FAMILY JEWELS

B ill Colby would adamantly deny that his role in Vietnam in general, and in the Phoenix program in particular, had anything to do with his daughter's illness. Catherine may not have blamed her father, but the negative publicity surrounding the war on the Viet Cong Infrastructure could not have eased her mind. Indeed, almost as soon as he stepped off the plane from Saigon, Colby was under assault for what one publication would label "The Phoenix Murders."[1]

In mid-July, a subcommittee of the House Committee on Government Operations opened hearings on the USAID program in Vietnam. On the committee were two outspoken critics of Phuong Huong, Ogden Reid (R-NY) and Pete McCloskey (R-CA). Reid, who, like Colby, was a graduate of Columbia Law School, was concerned with the alleged illegal and extraconstitutional aspects of Phoenix. McCloskey, a fierce opponent of the Nixon administration, had previously visited Vietnam. He had been appalled by the conditions he had found at the Provincial Interrogation Centers. Colby appeared on the 19th, and the questioning focused on Phoenix exclusively. "The Phoenix program is not a program of assassination," the former CORDS chief declared.

> "Can you state categorically that Phoenix has never perpetrated the premeditated killing of a civilian in a noncombat situation?" Reid asked.
>
> "No," Colby replied, "I could not say that, but I do not think it happens often. . . . Individual members of it, subordinate people in it, may have done it. But as a program, it is not designed to do that."

"Did Phoenix personnel resort to torture?" McCloskey asked. There were incidents, Colby replied, and they were treated as an "un-justifiable offense."

"If you want to get bad intelligence you use bad interrogation methods," Colby explained. "If you want to get good intelligence you had better use good interrogation methods."

"Did Phoenix meet legal standards for due process?" Reid asked. Not always, Colby said, but as DEPCORDS, he had turned every effort toward seeing that it did.[2]

A day later, K. Barton Osborn, a US Army intelligence operative, testified that he had witnessed widespread abuses, including beatings, electrocution, and both the threat and reality of dropping an accused Viet Cong member out of a helicopter. The Colby and Barton testimony made front-page headlines all across the country. "My refusal to say under oath that no one had been wrongly killed in Vietnam," Colby later wrote, "was headlined as an admission of assassinations."[3]

Colby's failure to get into what "wrongly killed" meant in a guerrilla conflict was puzzling, especially for a lawyer. Perhaps he realized that in their disenchantment with the war, Congress and the American people were unwilling or unable to differentiate between what Julian Ewell was doing in Operation Speedy Express and what the SEALs and PRUs were doing in their Phoenix operations. Much less could they differentiate between Phoenix operations and the terrorist activities of the Banh-anh-ninh. Colby's operatives were targeting Viet Cong based on received intelligence and either killed or captured them. Like Ewell, the Banh-anh-ninh killed combatants along with noncombatants just to terrorize the population.

The Phoenix hearings, along with My Lai, leaks of the Pentagon Papers in the press, ongoing Senate Foreign Relations Committee hearings on the war, Cambodia, and Kent State, were grist for the antiwar mill. Mocking a technique used by Phoenix personnel early on, opponents of the war tacked up "Wanted" posters all around Washington, with Colby's face superimposed on the ace of spades. The former Jedburgh was harassed on the streets, jeered at public venues, and peppered with death threats. "There was one guy who would call regularly at 5:00 A.M.," Gage McAfee recalled, "calling him a murderer, a war criminal, and other things." Instead of getting upset about it, Colby used the jangling phone as an alarm clock.[4]

The overriding problem Colby faced upon his return from Vietnam was finding a job. He made an appointment to see DCI Richard Helms; the Director received Colby at his regular table at the Occidental and expressed sympathy for an old comrade-in-arms. "In my heart," Colby wrote in *Honorable Men*, "what I had been secretly hoping for was the post of Deputy Director for Plans, to complete my career as the head of CIA's clandestine operations. But, in my head, I was perfectly aware that that was a vain hope for now." The deputy for plans was Thomas Karamessines, an able spy and a Helms loyalist. The job the DCI offered Colby was that of executive director/comptroller. Colby, until days ago one of the three most powerful Americans in Vietnam, was crestfallen. On the organizational chart, the executive director was the third-ranking officer in the CIA, just below the DCI and the deputy director of central intelligence. But in reality it was a staff position, a glorified clerical job. No one got between the director and his four division heads, the deputy directors for plans, analysis, technology, and supply. Colby told Helms that he would have to think about it. During the next few days, he consulted associates and had a brief chat with Barbara. In the end, he decided to accept Helms's offer. Intelligence was what he knew; the CIA was his home. He looked up the definition of "comptroller" in the dictionary and asked Secretary of Health, Education, and Welfare Elliott Richardson to allow his budget team to educate him on the complexities of fiscal management.[5]

The Agency he returned to had changed, Colby soon discovered. Technology reigned supreme. The U-2 spy plane, radar, electronic sensors, infrared photography, and especially the Key Hole 11 spy satellite just then coming online gave the Agency an unparalleled ability to spy on enemies and allies alike. These new devices "produced exquisitely detailed reports of secret test centers and experiments deep in Asia; of truck parks and barracks for armored divisions in Eastern Europe, permitting a stunningly accurate reading of foreign military forces," Colby said. The intelligence community could monitor virtually any type of communication, learning about everything from coup plots to plans for ever more advanced missile systems. The second change that Colby noticed was an acceleration of a trend that had begun following the Bay of Pigs and that had continued under the Helms directorate: a de-emphasis on covert and political action. Whereas covert action had consumed up to 50 percent of the CIA's budget in the 1950s and 1960s, it absorbed only around 5 percent in 1971. Ever since the 1967 *Ramparts* article exposing the CIA's role in the National Students Association had appeared, the Agency had been withdrawing from it and other front organizations such as the Voice of America and Radio Free Europe. Colby decided that, for the time being, he would just have to accommodate.

As he familiarized himself with the ins and outs of his new position, Colby came to realize what his colleagues at Langley already knew— Richard Nixon did not like or trust the CIA. Kissinger later wrote that the president believed that the Agency was "a refuge for Ivy League intellectuals opposed to him."[6] Aside from the fact that Nixon thought the CIA, like the State Department, consisted of men and women who considered him their educational and social inferior, he blamed Langley for his defeat in the 1960 presidential election. The CIA, he was convinced, had created false data showing that the Soviet Union had gained strategic nuclear superiority over the United States—the so-called "missile gap." In addition, Nixon and his men believed that the analytical branch's consistently pessimistic reports on the course of the war in Vietnam—the bombing was not working; pacification was largely an illusion; the military governments in Saigon were incorrigible; enemy strength would grow no matter what the United States did, short of annihilating North Vietnam—proved that the Agency was full of antiwar liberals. Despite all this, however, Nixon had asked Helms to stay on as DCI. LBJ had recommended him as nonpartisan and disinterested, and Nixon was aware of the respect Helms commanded in Congress on both sides of the aisle.

Helms had heard rumors of Nixon's attitude toward the Agency, and his suspicions were soon confirmed. Word came to him that the president did not like and therefore did not read the "Daily Briefings" that had provided primary intelligence sustenance to presidents since Harry Truman. Shortly after it was announced that Helms would stay on, Kissinger called him in and told him that all intelligence would pass through the national security adviser to the president. Moreover, in a break with precedent, Helms was to present the Agency's summary report to the National Security Council and then retire. Melvin Laird subsequently intervened to bring the DCI back into the inner circle, but Helms would continue to feel like an outsider. And in truth, he was.

The struggle between the White House and the CIA's analytical branch that had developed in the wake of *Sputnik*—Nixon blamed his loss in 1960 on the "missile gap" that he believed the CIA had fabricated—continued after Nixon became president, but this time, ironically, he charged the Agency's brain trust with underestimating rather than overestimating Soviet strategic capability. By 1969 the Soviet Union had developed a new intercontinental ballistic missile (ICBM), the SS-9, whose payload, American intelligence suspected, was equipped with the first multiple independent reentry vehicles (MIRVs). The Defense Department and the White House declared that the ability of the enemy to unleash up to sixty warheads per rocket, independently targeted, gave Moscow strategic superiority and the ability to deliver a "first strike," a knockout blow that would leave the United States defenseless. Nixon and Kissinger had Laird go to Congress and request billions of dollars for an antiballistic missile (ABM) system. In the hearings that followed, the CIA refused to back the administration. The Agency said the Soviets clearly did not possess the technology to provide each warhead with a guidance system. Moscow was not planning a first strike; the enemy's so-called "hardened silos" were not, as the Pentagon claimed, impervious to existing US missiles. Laird was furious. "Where," he demanded, "did CIA get off contradicting Nixon's policy?" Kissinger was equally outraged. The Agency was undercutting his efforts to create a giant bargaining chip—an ABM system—for use in the forthcoming Strategic Arms Limitation Treaty (SALT) negotiations with Moscow. Helms recalled of Nixon, "He would constantly, in National Security Council meetings, pick on the Agency for not having properly judged what the Soviets were going to do with various kinds of weaponry. He would make nasty remarks about this and say this had to be sharpened up."[7]

Nixon and Kissinger denigrated covert operations—unless they were operations that they initiated and controlled. Soon after his return from Vietnam, Colby began to hear rumors of a major top-secret campaign controlled and directed by the White House but carried out by the CIA to prevent the election of Salvador Allende Gossens to the presidency of Chile. Many of Colby's friends and colleagues were involved in the operation, and the situation in Chile seemed in some ways to parallel that of Italy during the 1950s. Fearing the spread of Castro-style communism to the mineral-rich Andean nation, the United States had funneled aid to noncommunist political parties throughout the 1960s. In 1964, the Agency provided some $3 million to secure the election of President Eduardo Frei and his fellow Christian Democrats. Unlike many other Latin American nations, Chile's modern history was characterized by respect for constitutional processes and an apolitical military.

During his generally successful six years in office, Frei worked to ameliorate the plight of the poor and bring about a greater degree of economic and social justice. Nevertheless, by 1970 there was still a wide gap between rich and poor, and Chile's economy continued to be dominated by US corporations such as International Telephone and Telegraph (ITT), Anaconda Copper, and General Motors. Chile's 1970 presidential election, with Frei ineligible for another term, evolved into a three-cornered affair featuring National Party candidate Jorge Alessandri Rodriguez on the right, Radomiro Tomic Romero representing the left wing of the Christian Democrats, and Salvador Allende, the candidate of the Marxists and similar factions, on the left. In the midst of the campaign, the Agency produced a National Intelligence Estimate (NIE) on Chile warning that if Allende was elected, he could "take Chile a long way down the Marxist-Socialist road . . . [creating] a Chilean version of a Soviet-style East European state."[8] His opposition to capitalism was implacable, and his regime would certainly move to nationalize major foreign businesses. There were, in addition, rumors that Allende would consider leasing a Chilean port to Cuba as a base for its navy. Helms warned Kissinger, who as national security adviser chaired the 303 Committee, that if Allende was going to be stopped, the Agency would have to be given the green light to aid noncommunist candidates. The DCI recalled that neither Kissinger nor Nixon displayed much interest at that point.

On September 4, Allende won the election with a razor-thin margin—39,000 out of 3 million votes cast. He garnered 36.3 percent of the vote, with his nearest rival, Alessandri, polling 34.9 percent.[9] Suddenly Chile had the White House's attention. Nixon was angry and a bit frightened, Helms recalled. It was all the CIA's fault, he groused to Kissinger, who agreed with him but argued that there was still time. Because Allende had received a plurality rather than a majority, he would have to have the approval of the Chilean Congress.

On September 15, Nixon summoned Helms. "In a conversation lasting less than 15 minutes," Kissinger recalled, "Nixon told Helms that he wanted a major effort to see what could be done to prevent Allende's accession to power. If there were one chance in ten of getting rid of Allende, we should try it; if Helms needed $10 million he would approve it. Aid programs to Chile should be cut; its economy should be squeezed until it 'screamed.' Helms should bypass [US ambassador Edward] Kory and report directly to the White House." The no-holds-barred effort to prevent Allende from taking and holding office—known as Track II—was to be kept secret not only from the State Department but also from the Defense Department and the 40 Committee (the new name for the 303 Committee). Helms later claimed that he was dubious all along about the chances of stopping Allende—and the wisdom of even trying. The record shows little hesitancy, however. "If I ever carried a marshal's baton in my knapsack out of the Oval Office, it was that day," Colby remembered him saying. "All of us were aware," one participant later observed, "that in such a short period of time, no matter what other techniques we might try, what we were talking about, basically, was a military coup." There was not a moment to be lost. The Chilean Congress would vote on October 24.[10]

Helms set up a Track II task force at Langley. Agency-generated propaganda subsequently appeared throughout Latin America and in a number of European countries comparing the situation in Chile with the communist takeover of Czechoslovakia in 1948. A Track II team member journeyed to New York to enlist ITT's aid in destabilizing the Chilean economy. Four undercover agents arrived in Santiago and established contact with known anti-Allende officers in the military. Chief among these was Brigadier General Roberto Viaux, who had been retired following an abortive coup attempt against Frei in 1969. He asked for money and guns, receiving some of both, and a coup was scheduled for October 9 and 10. The takeover was called off by the Agency, however, because it seemed to have no prospect of success. It is clear that the United States dissociated itself from Viaux not because it considered him unfit, which he probably was, but because it thought he could not succeed. "It is a firm and continuing policy that Allende be overthrown by a coup," Deputy Director of Plans Tom Karamessines cabled Henry Hecksher, chief of station in Santiago.[11]

Increasingly, anti-Allende forces within Chile saw General René Schneider, army chief of staff, as the principal obstacle to a successful coup. The men around Viaux informed Agency operatives that they intended to kidnap Schneider. On October 22, Viaux's men tried to seize the army chief; he was wounded trying to escape. On October 24, Salvador Allende received 153 of the 195 votes cast in the Chilean Congress. Schneider died the next day, and on the day after that, President Frei and president-elect Allende stood side by side at the general's funeral. Allende assumed office on November 3, but the CIA would continue its efforts to undermine him.[12]

"Track II, of course, was well in the past by the time I became Executive Director," Colby later wrote, "and indeed for a considerable time I knew nothing of it in accordance with the President's directive that it be handled in the utmost secrecy."[13] But Colby, as comptroller, oversaw the budget, and it was hard to keep secrets in the gossip-ridden halls of Langley. Eventually Colby learned of the Chilean operation, and in general he approved. He would later write that Agency money went overwhelmingly to centrist parties, and that Allende's faction was clearly Marxist-Leninist and pro-Castro. He passed over Schneider's death as a casualty of war, collateral damage that the CIA would have avoided if it could have. Colby and the CIA as a whole had become supersensitive to the charge of assassination. In 1967, in the wake of the *Ramparts* article, Jack Anderson had reported rumors of a CIA plot against Castro's life. Colby, as Far East Division chief, had been part of the internal investigation ordered by the White House into rumors that the Agency had been complicit in the deaths of the Ngo brothers. He had duly certified that the Agency had had no role in the killing of Diem and Nhu. When Colby returned from Vietnam to become executive director in 1971, assassination was again a hot topic, something he learned firsthand during the Phoenix hearings. Despite the fact that the killing of enemy operatives, political and military, lay at the very heart of terrorism and counterterrorism, Colby had convinced himself that no component of CORDS, including the CIA-run PRUs, had engaged in assassination as a policy.

In late 1971, *Parade* magazine, read by millions of Americans as an insert in their Sunday newspaper, declared that the CIA was the only agency of the US government authorized to carry out assassinations. Colby was incensed. "I knew from personal experience that the Agency was not engaged in assassinations in Vietnam," he wrote in his memoir. "Indeed, quite to the contrary, it had been my specific directive as head of CORDS that, for both moral and practical reasons, assassinations were strictly prohibited."[14] He decided to write a sweeping rebuttal, but then hesitated. Perhaps there were activities that he was not aware of. Angleton's counterintelligence division was a little shop of horrors, and there might be others in the highly compartmentalized CIA. He began to check around. Castro was still alive, but that did not mean that there had not been a conspiracy to eliminate him. Gradually, the details of Operation Mongoose began to emerge. A compatriot on the African desk assured Colby that the Agency was not involved in the killing of Congolese nationalist Patrice Lumumba, at least not directly. Colby learned that the Kennedy administration had very much wanted Dominican dictator Rafael Trujillo out of the way, but his death in 1962, like General Schneider's in 1970, had not been at the hands of CIA agents. Instead of issuing the flat denial to *Parade* that he originally planned, Colby decided to slam the proverbial barn door. He prepared a directive to all CIA personnel stating that "CIA would not now or in the future engage in, stimulate or support assassinations in any way." Helms duly signed it.[15]

In the fall of 1971, White House aide John Ehrlichman asked the DCI for documents on the Bay of Pigs, the Diem assassination, and the death of Trujillo. President Nixon, it seemed, wanted to use them to smear the Democratic Party in general and the Kennedy administration in particular. In October, Helms duly delivered the material, but he warned that its publication could open a can of worms that would gnaw away at more than one administration. The White House held off, but in the meantime Colby and Helms issued their backside-covering directive.[16]

According to Colby's memoir, by late 1971 younger officers in the CIA were increasingly concerned about the reputation of the Agency. The CIA had become the whipping boy of not only the antiwar left but also the mainstream media. Every conceivable evil was laid at Langley's door. In 1964, investigative journalist David Wise had published his widely read *Invisible Government*. Thus was born what would become America's favorite conspiracy theory: the comings and goings of presidents and congressmen, the nominating conventions and their platforms, the public debates over foreign and domestic policy, the very edifice of national government was just a front behind which a coterie of powerful and unscrupulous men pulled the levers of power, manipulating politicians, bureaucrats, and journalists at will. They protected their secrets at all costs, Wise wrote. The young men and women who came to Bill Colby in confidence told him that the notion of a secret surveillance state run by the CIA and FBI might not be so far from the truth. "Young analysts, computer operators and operations officers," Colby recalled, "were all aware that a most secret project was lodged in that most secret of Agency crannies, the Counterintelligence Staff, and that it had a great deal to do with the antiwar movement."[17]

When the CIA was established in 1947, its supporters had had to overcome widespread fears that the new Agency would become an American Gestapo, prying into the lives of American citizens. Consequently, the CIA's charter forbade it from "police, subpoena, law-enforcement powers or internal security functions."[18] But the Doolittle Report, commissioned by Eisenhower and issued in 1954, had warned that the United States faced a ruthless enemy that would stop at nothing to undermine the Western democracies. If Washington and its allies did not fight fire with fire, it would lose the Cold War.

In 1952, during the waning days of the Truman administration, the CIA had begun secretly opening and examining all mail postings between the United States and the Soviet Union. At La Guardia, and subsequently at a secure vault at Federal Building 111 at JFK International Airport in New York, every piece of mail passing between the two countries was examined for bits of information that would aid in the war on communism. The super-secret mail-intercept program was run first by the Directorate of Plans, but in 1955 was transferred to Angleton's CI shop. The move was a logical one, given Angleton's philosophy. Every Soviet citizen—whether student, scientist, journalist, or diplomat—was fully vetted by the KGB. Indeed, many Russian students who studied in the United States later returned as professional spies. Every Soviet citizen resident in or visiting the United States was, in the view of counterintelligence, a KGB agent by definition. In the beginning, that was true. In 1954, Allen Dulles and his deputy director for plans, Frank Wisner, briefed the incoming Eisenhower administration on the mail-intercept operation, and that process was repeated through the Kennedy, Johnson, and Nixon presidencies. Colby was aware of the existence of the program; he believed that the potential for revelation and scandal outweighed the program's value to intelligence and counterintelligence operations, and in his usual low-key manner he had said so. All to no avail.[19]

In 1967, the CIA got into the domestic spying business in a big way. The antiwar protests and urban rioting that wracked the country were driving President Johnson to distraction. He could understand neither the Vietnam protest nor the Black Power movement. Didn't the nation's youth, both black and white, understand that he was one of them, the author of the 1964 and 1965 Civil Rights Acts, federal aid to education, national health care, and the war on poverty? The violence sweeping the nation's ghettoes was indeed appalling. Between 1964 and 1967, 75 separate urban riots had erupted across the nation from Detroit to New York to Los Angeles, resulting in 88 deaths and property damage estimated at $664.5 million. This chaos had to be the work of subversive elements. "I'm not going to let the Communists take this government and they're doing it right now," Johnson declared in one of his periodic rants. "I've got my belly full of seeing these people put on a Communist plane and shipped all over this country," he exclaimed to Rusk, McNamara, and Helms at a White House meeting on November 4. Johnson directed the DCI to obtain proof positive that the violent antiwar protests and urban violence were the work of foreign agents. Helms warned the president that investigation of domestic dissident groups was a potential violation of the CIA's charter. "I'm quite aware of that," Helms recalled LBJ saying. "What I want is for you to pursue this matter, and to do what is necessary to track down the foreign communists who are behind this intolerable interference in our domestic affairs."[20]

Having expressed his reservations, Helms became an enthusiastic supporter of the operation code-named MH/Chaos. "I established the unit," the DCI later told an interviewer, "because it seemed to me that since this was a high priority in the eyes of the President, it should be a high priority in the Agency." In his view, the CIA was an instrument of the executive branch, a tool that the president could wield at his discretion. If challenged, Helms could quote the clause in the 1947 National Security Act that stated that the director of central intelligence could perform "such additional functions and duties related to intelligence affecting the national security as the national security council may direct."[21]

In response to the president's order, Helms set up a Special Operations Group (SOG) with Richard Ober, one of Angleton's lieutenants, as its head. Ober was classic CIA, "a tall, levelheaded Harvard alumnus and third-generation oar on a winning crew," as Helms described him. Helms put Operation MH/Chaos in counterintelligence, Colby later wrote, "so that it could be conducted with maximum compartmentation [*sic*] and secrecy."

SOG was to be free of the normal processes of review of its finances, records, and methodology.[22]

Nixon proved no less desirous than Johnson of uncovering evidence of foreign influence on domestic dissent. By 1971, Ober's operation comprised 36 full-time staff members, which were housed not at Langley but in a Washington office complex situated some two blocks from the White House. Collaborating closely with J. Edgar Hoover's FBI, Ober's operation eventually opened files on some 7,200 American citizens and 6,000 organizations. In November 1967, SOG produced its first product, "International Connections of the U.S. Peace Movement." Its findings were essentially that there were none. A second report, "Restless Youth," was a thoroughgoing exploration of the roots of domestic dissent; it was clearly outside the Agency's purview but tended to prove again that the peace and Black Power movements were not extensions of the international communist conspiracy. So dissatisfied with the reports was the White House that it had Hoover dispatch a number of FBI agents overseas to find the missing link between domestic dissent and international communism.[23]

Whatever its intent, the activities of the SOG within counterintelligence at times crossed the line. In order to credential their recruits as peace activists, Agency case officers infiltrated them into domestic peace organizations before sending them abroad to gather evidence of foreign influence. They inevitably reported on activities of antiwar and Black Power activists that had nothing to do with foreign influence.[24]

With the accession of Richard Nixon to the presidency, the boundary between foreign and domestic subversive activities became even more blurred. In the summer of 1970, in the wake of the demonstrations against the incursion into Cambodia, an embittered President Nixon declared virtual war on those he considered his enemies: the "madmen" on Capitol Hill, the "liberal" press, and particularly antiwar peace activists. But he did more than rant. That spring, the Weathermen faction of the Students for a Democratic Society (SDS) had bombed the New York headquarters of three major US corporations, including the Bank of America. White House aide Thomas Charles Huston subsequently told H. R. Haldeman, Nixon's chief of staff, that not only was the SDS determined to overthrow the government by force; it was also fully capable of doing so. In response to his aide's hysteria, the president authorized Huston to assemble a team of "countersubversives" who would ferret out and neutralize enemies of the Republic and of Nixon—and in Nixon's view, the two were interchangeable. In addition, under what became known as the "Huston Plan," intelligence agencies were directed to install wiretaps, open mail, and even break and enter to gather information that could be used to thwart opponents of the administration. In December, White House counsel John Dean set up the Intelligence Evaluation Committee (IEC) to coordinate CIA, National Security Agency (NSA), Defense Intelligence Agency (DIA), and FBI activates carried out under the Huston Plan.[25]

Affiliated with the interagency countersubversive team were the so-called "Plumbers," a team of former FBI and CIA agents who would identify and stop "leaks" of information the White House considered damaging. It was the Plumbers, including former CIA operative G. Gordon Liddy, who broke into Daniel Ellsberg's office at the Rand Corporation following release of the Pentagon Papers. In late July 1971, E. Howard Hunt, another former CIA man who had become one of the Plumbers, suggested to White House aide Charles Colson that the administration put together a psychological profile of Ellsberg that would help "destroy his public image and credibility." As part of this effort, Hunt suggested that the CIA be asked to prepare a psychological assessment-evaluation. David Young, White House assistant for security, told CIA representatives that "the Ellsberg study had the highest priority and had been requested by Mr. Ehrlichman and Dr. Kissinger." On July 29, Helms approved the request, and the Agency's chief of medical services was directed to comply. Subsequently, a contingent of Plumbers, headed by Hunt, replete with a disguise furnished by the CIA, would break into Ellsberg's psychiatrist's office. In 1972, at the behest of the interagency task force, Richard Ober's staff at the CIA prepared a special report: "Potential Disruptions at the 1972 Republican National Convention."[26]

Despite the best efforts of Angleton and Helms, the existence and activities of the Ober group were generally known within the CIA by the time Colby became executive director. Consequently, he was in a position to respond to the concerns of the younger generation of CIA officers who were worried that the Agency was spying on the domestic antiwar movement. In truth, he shared their alarm. The avalanche of criticism, the invariable suspicion with which nearly all Americans then viewed the Agency, could not be ignored. "The CIA, it seemed obvious to me, was in very real danger of ultimately being crippled as an effective weapon in the defense of the nation's security if not in fact threatened with being destroyed outright," he later wrote. The only alternative, he remembered thinking, "was to lift as much as possible that thick cloak of secrecy that had traditionally veiled the Agency and its operations from the scrutiny . . . of the public at large."[27] Perhaps Bill Colby experienced an epiphany as early as 1972; perhaps not. What is clear is that he had long believed that the culture of super-secrecy and compartmentalization that pervaded the Agency, the culture of Jim Angleton and to a degree Richard Helms—*The Man Who Kept the Secrets*, as he was later called in a book title—was counterproductive of the CIA's overriding mission: to win the Cold War. But in 1971–1972, Colby, hovering on the fringes of power, had to tread lightly.[28]

On March 12, 1972, a copy of a book-length manuscript entitled *The CIA and the Cult of Intelligence* turned up at Langley. The author was a sixteen-year veteran of the Agency named Victor Marchetti. He had resigned in 1969, having become increasingly disenchanted with the CIA's unaccountability, with covert operations that in fact were secret wars, with Angleton's counterintelligence empire, and with MH/Chaos. He had already published *The Rope Dancer*, a novel mildly critical of the Agency. Langley paid little mind. A number of former Agency officers, from Allen Dulles to E. Howard Hunt, had written books centering on US intelligence, and no harm had been done. But *The CIA and the Cult of Intelligence* was a concise, thorough, nonfiction description of the CIA and its activities. It even included a detailed description of "The Farm," the Agency's training facility at Camp Peary, Virginia.

Immediately, Helms summoned his top advisers. Colby and General Counsel Lawrence Summers advised against seeking criminal prosecution of Marchetti and his coauthor, John Marks, a disillusioned intelligence officer in the State Department. True, Marchetti and Marks, like all intelligence personnel, had signed an agreement to keep secret any and all classified information they encountered in their jobs. But a trial would force disclosure of secrets beyond their knowledge and generate a tidal wave of bad publicity. What Colby and Huston suggested—the course that was eventually followed—was that the CIA enforce in civil court that part of the secrecy agreement that compelled employees to allow the Agency to vet articles and books before their publication to ensure that they did not include official secrets. Marchetti and his publisher, Alfred A. Knopf, refused, and the case went to trial. At John Ehrlichman's direction, the Justice Department pitched in to help. The CIA won on appeal and secured 168 deletions from the manuscript. Knopf went to press with the resulting product, marked by heavy black redactions showing where and how much material the Agency had suppressed.[29] Colby was for more transparency and accountability, but he did insist that the CIA had an unconditional right to keep secret its "sources and methods"—accounts of specific cases and the names of the operatives involved. When Philip Agee, acting from the juridical safety of the United Kingdom, published an account of his days in Latin America as a CIA officer in which he described cases and named names, Colby denounced him as a traitor.

On June 10, 1972, Colby learned that John Paul Vann had been killed in a helicopter crash in Vietnam. While carrying out his duties as executive director, Colby had kept an eye on the seemingly endless conflict in Southeast Asia, and he continued to sit on the Agency's Vietnam task force. His decision to recommend Vann to Abrams as the overall US authority in II Corps had paid off in spades. On March 30, 1972, 200,000 North Vietnamese soldiers, supported by tanks and artillery, had crossed the demilitarized zone. The communists laid siege to Quang Tri City in I Corps, and within a month, it fell. As one column moved on to Hue, another advanced on Kon Tum in the Central Highlands. If the North Vietnamese could capture Kon Tum, Plieku and the entire Highlands would fall, and South Vietnam would be cut in two. Defending Kon Tum were the 22nd and 23rd ARVN Divisions under Lieutenant General Ngo Dzu, a particularly inept officer. As the North Vietnamese Army advanced, Dzu froze, unable to even give orders to fire on the enemy. Vann assumed command and rallied the South Vietnamese in a successful defense of the city. He emerged as the chief American hero in the so-called Easter offensive, hailed by both Americans and South Vietnamese as a decisive victory. His death came shortly after the campaign ended, during a routine helicopter flight from Pleiku to Kon Tum. Colby took the news hard. His son, Paul, remembered him watching TV accounts of Vann's life while getting quietly drunk.[30]

John Vann was buried with full military honors at Arlington National Cemetery on June 16, 1972. The red brick chapel near the entrance was the site of a gathering of eagles—establishment journalist Joe Alsop, Edward Lansdale, Senator Ted Kennedy, and a host of other soldiers and public figures. At the insistence of Vann's widow, Daniel Ellsberg, now considered a turncoat by many in the room, was seated with the family. The front doors of the chapel swung open, and the flag-draped coffin bearing Vann's body entered, flanked by eight official pallbearers, four soldiers, and four civilians. Among them were Generals William Westmoreland and Bruce Palmer. Bill Colby and Bob Komer headed up the civilian contingent. Komer delivered the eulogy. "I've never met one among the thousands of men who served with or under John who didn't admire him," Komer proclaimed. "He educated and inspired a whole wartime generation of Vietnamese and Americans—as our teacher, our colleague, our institutional memory, our hair-shirt, and our friend."[31] It was a wrenching experience for Colby. He had thought Vann headstrong, at times his own worst enemy, but his devotion to Vietnam, his bravery, and especially his commitment to the "other war" were unquestioned. Colby thought his friend too impatient with the military governments that came and went in Saigon—indeed, too impatient to be a decent imperialist. In truth, Colby valued others who worked for him—such as Frank Scotton and Ev Bumgardner—more than he did Vann. But Vann could say what Colby could not, especially to the US military and to American journalists like David Halberstam and Neil Sheehan, regarding the shortcomings of the South Vietnamese government and military.

On June 17, 1972, the day following Vann's funeral, Colby was abruptly shaken from his reveries about his friend and the ongoing drama in Southeast Asia by news that five men had been caught red-handed burglarizing the Watergate headquarters of the Democratic National Committee. All five had ties to the CIA.

In late 1971, G. Gordon Liddy, a former Agency operative and member of the Plumbers team that had broken into Ellsberg's psychiatrist's office, joined the Committee to Reelect the President (CREEP) as counsel to its finance committee. In January 1972, in the office of Attorney General John Mitchell, with White House counsel John Dean present, Liddy had proposed a fantastic scheme of harassment against the Democratic Party, including wiretaps, kidnappings, and hijackings. Mitchell rejected the scheme—not because it was illegal and unethical, but because it was too expensive; the estimated price tag was $1 million. But in late March, Mitchell, who had stepped down from his post at the Justice Department to head CREEP, approved a plan for bugging the Democratic National Committee (DNC), providing Liddy with $10,000 to finance the operation. CREEP, and probably President Nixon, wanted to be privy to DNC chairman Larry O'Brien's campaign strategy.

In April 1972, Liddy hired E. Howard Hunt and James W. McCord Jr., two former CIA agents who had been part of the Plumbers, to spy on the opposition. They, in turn, retained several Cuban exiles, veterans of the Bay of Pigs and subsequently Agency operatives within the Cuban exile community. Hunt, who had been chief of station in Uruguay in the 1950s, was a Cold War romantic and the author of several mediocre spy novels, a man whose reach frequently exceeded his grasp. Following several bungled attempts, the team succeeded in bugging O'Brien's office. When one of the devices failed, the burglars returned to replace it.[32]

Early on the morning of June 17, 1972, Frank Wills, a night watchman at the Watergate office and apartment building, made his usual rounds. Upon finding the door lock to the office of the DNC taped shut, he alerted the police, who arrived in time to apprehend McCord and four of the Cubans. Among the items found on the suspects was a check to McCord signed by Howard Hunt.[33] Hunt, who was monitoring the break-in from a nearby motel room, notified Liddy at CREEP headquarters. In a panic, Liddy began shredding documents, but the damage had been done. That evening, Richard Helms's phone rang. It was Howard Osborn, the CIA chief of security. He told the DCI of the break-in; the five burglars all had ties to the Agency. Helms knew, of course, that Hunt had gone to work for the White House as a "security consultant" a year earlier.

"Is there any indication that we could be involved in this?" Helms asked.

"None whatsoever," Osborn replied.

It was significant that Helms had to ask the question. The DCI recalled in his memoir that he immediately contacted L. Patrick Gray, acting director of the FBI, who had been nominated by Nixon to be Hoover's permanent replacement. Helms assured the acting director that despite the burglars' past ties to the Agency, Langley had had nothing to do with the break-in. "You might want to look into the relationship of John Ehrlichman, the President's domestic policy advisor, with McCord and Hunt," Helms remembered saying. "He'll be familiar with the circumstances in which Howard Hunt was hired for work at the White House and with McCord's job on the Committee to Re-elect the President as well." Gray,

Helms recalled, seemed "unresponsive." His antennae aquiver, the DCI on the Monday following the break-in appointed Colby to head the effort to keep the Agency's skirts clean.[34]

Colby later recalled that he knew he was headed for dangerous waters. Who to trust? The media was in a CIA feeding frenzy, with Congress waiting in the wings. The White House was another shark-infested body of water. And then there were Angleton and Helms. The CIA director would later claim that Angleton had nothing to do with MH/Chaos. That was a lie, and Colby knew it. Angleton's worldview, his KGB paranoia, would have made him most amenable to spying on dissidents, foreign connections or not. Helms had authorized Chaos and represented the CIA on the IEC, the White House–created interagency committee to investigate foreign links to domestic radicals. In 1971, he had personally signed off on a CIA medical evaluation of Ellsberg.

Then, shortly after Colby received his marching orders from Helms, Karl Wagner, the executive assistant to the deputy director, drew him aside and said that he had some information that might be useful. He recalled that about a year earlier, Hunt had contacted General Robert Cushman, who was then deputy director of the CIA, and asked him for Agency assistance in an operation he was working on. Shortly thereafter, Ehrlichman had called Cushman and told him that the White House expected full cooperation from the Agency. In the days that followed, Hunt requisitioned, among other things, false identification papers, a wig, and a camera hidden in a tobacco pouch. All of these devices were subsequently utilized in the Plumbers' break-in into the offices of Dr. Lewis J. Fielding, Daniel Ellsberg's psychiatrist. As far as the Nixon White House was concerned, Cushman, a retired Marine officer—like General Vernon Walters, who replaced him—was its man in the CIA. Ehrlichman had had no compunction about contacting him directly. But Cushman had sense enough to activate the telephone recording machine in his office. When Hunt's demands escalated—he told Cushman to have his former secretary transferred from her job in the Paris station and placed at his disposal—the deputy director went to Helms, and Hunt was rebuffed. Or at least that was the story Helms told. Again, he had authorized the medical profile of Ellsberg and was an active member of the IEC. Dick Ober's countersubversive team was still in full operating mode. In the end, Colby decided he had no choice but to trust his boss.[35]

When Wagner was finished with his tale, Colby escorted him to the director's office. After Wagner told Helms what he knew, the three decided to keep the information to themselves. A decision was necessary because on the Monday following the Watergate break-in, the Alexandria, Virginia, office of the FBI had begun peppering Colby with questions about links between the burglars and the Agency. Colby might not have to volunteer the Cushman-Hunt encounter, but he did have to explain what had already been revealed—that Hunt and McCord were former employees, and that one of the second-story men, Eugenio Martinez, was then on a $100-a-month Agency retainer to report on the activities of Cuban exiles. In addition, Colby confirmed that the Mullen Company, which Hunt was using as cover, was a public relations firm that in the past had put CIA overseas operatives on its payroll. Shortly thereafter, articles on Martinez and the Mullen Company, described as "a CIA front," appeared in the national press. With the Alexandria office leaking like a sieve, Colby decided that in the future he should communicate directly with FBI headquarters in Washington.[36]

Throughout the Watergate affair, the FBI would prove to be much more a foe than a friend to Colby and the CIA. Hardly a surprise. J. Edgar Hoover had been opposed to the very creation of the Agency, demanding of President Truman in 1946 that if there absolutely had to be a central intelligence entity, it be attached to the Bureau. Truman not only turned Hoover down, but the following year ordered the FBI to surrender its Latin American operation to the CIA. Rather than comply, the director had his agents burn their files and dismiss their informants. Hoover subsequently supplied Senator Joseph McCarthy with ammunition for attacks on the Agency. Allen Dulles felt it necessary to assign his inspector general, Lyman Kirkpatrick, the task of making sure Hoover-McCarthy loyalists did not penetrate the Agency. Hoover harbored the secret belief that the Dulles brothers, like Eleanor Roosevelt, were agents of international communism. In Richard Helms he found no improvement. According to journalist Andrew St. George, the director hated the CIA even more than he did long-haired hippies, Black Panthers, communists, and Dr. Martin Luther King Jr. "He thought of it as a viperine lair of liars and high-domed intellectuals," St. George wrote, "of insolent Yalies who sneered at Fordham's finest, of rich young ne'er-do-wells who dabbled in spy work because they could not be trusted to run the family business, of wily 'Princeton Ought-Ought' himself,

'Dickie' Helms, who spun his tweedy web from an . . . enclave up the river in Virginia." In February 1970, Hoover forbade all contacts with the CIA that he did not personally approve.[37]

Nixon and Hoover's shared animosity toward the CIA was not sufficient to overcome their mutual distrust, however. Hoover was far too independent for the president and Kissinger—and as far as the FBI director was concerned, the White House was full of amateurs like Thomas Charles Huston. Then, on May 2, 1972, Hoover died. Nixon picked L. Patrick Gray, then assistant attorney general and a known Nixon loyalist, to succeed to the directorship.

With Gray awaiting Senate confirmation but nevertheless in charge of the FBI, Nixon, on June 23, approved the idea of using the CIA to block the FBI investigation of the Watergate break-in. At a White House meeting that morning, Haldeman complained that Gray wanted to do the right thing but couldn't. "[T]he FBI is not under control," he said, "because Gray doesn't exactly know how to control them." But John Dean had come up with what he thought was a perfect plan. He and Ehrlichman would call in Helms and Deputy Director Vernon Walters and order Walters to tell Gray to back off Watergate because national security was involved. "[J]ust say, 'Stay the hell out of this . . . we're set up beautifully to do it.'" Would Gray go along? Nixon asked. Absolutely, Haldeman replied. It should work, the president observed, because "we protected Helms from one hell of a lot of things." As they had during the Chilean imbroglio in 1970, Nixon and Kissinger continued to believe that they could use Mongoose and the rumored CIA roles in the assassinations of Diem, Lumumba, and Trujillo as weapons to fend off Democratic-led investigations of executive wrongdoings.[38]

That afternoon, Helms and Walters were summoned to the White House for a top-secret meeting on Watergate. This was the first time the DCI had ever been directed to bring along his deputy. A veteran of bureaucratic in-fighting and West Wing maneuverings, Helms smelled something fishy. No sooner had Helms, Walters, and Ehrlichman squeezed around a table in a small conference room than Bob Haldeman strode in and took charge of the meeting. The chief of staff observed that the Watergate break-in was causing a great deal of trouble, and the FBI investigation was threatening a "lot of important people."[39]

He then turned to the DCI and asked "very formally," according to Helms, what role the CIA might have played in the burglary.

"The CIA had no connection whatever with Watergate," Helms declared.

Haldeman seemed not to have heard. The FBI had traced money paid to the Plumbers by the Committee to Re-elect the President to a laundering operation in Mexico City.

"It has been decided to have General Walters go to see Pat Gray and tell him that further investigation in Mexico could lead to the exposure of certain Agency assets and channels for handling money."

Helms protested that he had told the acting FBI director that the Agency had nothing to do with Watergate; it had been two years since any of the burglars had worked for Langley. Again Haldeman ignored him. Walters was to see Gray and convey the message. He added for good measure that if the FBI was not stymied, its investigation would lead to revelations concerning the CIA's role in the Bay of Pigs affair. At this point, Helms exploded: "The Bay of Pigs hasn't got a damned thing to do with this," he said. "And what's more, there's nothing about the Bay of Pigs that's not already in the public domain."[40]

Not true, of course; Nixon and Haldeman probably had in mind Langley's dalliance with the Mafia during the course of Operation Mongoose. At this point, Helms could have ordered Walters to ignore the White House directive to see Gray and invoke CIA operations in Mexico, but he did not. Such a move would have led to his immediate dismissal, he suspected. During a conversation in the White House parking lot, Helms told Walters to have his meeting with Gray and remind him of the long-standing agreement between the FBI and the CIA, which was that if one agency's operations threatened to cross lines with the other, the latter would be notified immediately.

The next day during his meeting with Gray, Walters delivered both messages: the FBI and the CIA had an agreement to keep their lines clear, and the White House had directed him to say that the FBI's investigation was endangering CIA activities in Mexico. Upon his return from this conflab, the deputy director asked Colby to investigate: Were there Agency activities in Mexico that might be threatened by an FBI investigation? Colby checked and reported that such an eventuality was extremely unlikely.[41]

On Monday, June 26, Walters received a call from White House counsel John Dean asking him to come to 1600 Pennsylvania Avenue for further talks on the Watergate matter. Dean informed Walters that he was heading up the Watergate affair for the president. The FBI was proceeding with three hypotheses: that the Republican National Committee, or the CIA, or some other party was behind the break-in. Of one thing he was certain, Walters replied, the Agency was not involved. "It must have been," Dean said. "These people all used to work for the CIA." Perhaps this went on without the leadership at Langley knowing anything about it. Perhaps, Walters replied, but he had investigated, and that was not the case. Dean turned plaintive. Couldn't the Agency accept some of the blame? Not without destroying itself, Walters replied.[42]

Three days later, Dean again summoned Walters to the White House. Could the Agency see its way to paying bail for the burglars? Walters was noncommittal. Absolutely not, Helms declared in their subsequent meeting. The Agency had unvouchered funds, but it would not expend them for such purposes without congressional approval.[43]

Helms, Colby, and Walters thought they had put this little White House plot to bed, but on July 5, Walters received a call from Gray. Unless he received a written statement from the CIA saying that the FBI investigation was threatening its overseas operations, he was going to have to proceed. There would be no request, oral or written, Walters replied, for the simple reason that the FBI probe did not endanger any Agency operation.[44]

They were on their own, Helms and Colby realized. The Nixon White House would frame the Agency for Watergate if it could. In July, James McCord, a former CIA agent and a member of the team that had broken into Watergate, got word to Helms that the president's men had offered him a pardon if he would testify under oath that the Watergate break-in was a CIA operation. In 1972, the American press and public were ready to believe the CIA capable of virtually any wrongdoing. But if the leadership at Langley confronted the White House directly and revealed what it knew of the unfolding conspiracy, Nixon would simply sweep the fourth-floor corridors clean and install a coterie of lackeys ready to do his bidding. The Agency must do everything in its power to "distance" itself from Watergate, Helms told his lieutenants. He wanted, he said, "no freewheeling exposition of hypotheses or any effort made to conjecture about responsibility or likely objectives of the Watergate intrusion." All well and good, but by 1973, not only the Justice Department but two separate congressional committees were investigating the Watergate break-in. The simple fact was that the CIA had partial knowledge that the White House had engaged in a conspiracy to obstruct justice. As a lawyer trained in constitutional law, Colby understood the precipice upon which the nation and the Agency stood. He chose to follow Helms's orders.[45]

Watergate came too late to affect the 1972 presidential election. The Watergate burglars' trial did not get underway until January 1973, and it would be two more months before the Senate Special Committee on Presidential Campaign Activities, the "Watergate Committee" under the chairmanship of Senator Sam Ervin, came into being. The Democratic nominee, George McGovern, attempted to make an issue of CREEP and its misdeeds, but he found the American people unresponsive. Promises of more money for social programs, amnesty for Vietnam-era draft-dodgers and deserters, and his "rainbow coalition" of minorities, young people, and union supporters found no purchase either. Kissinger declared that "peace was at hand" in Vietnam, and the White House dismissed the Watergate break-in as a "third-rate burglary." The incumbent's 47.1 million popular votes and 520 electoral tallies made him the most successful GOP candidate ever.

On November 20, some two weeks after the election, Helms received a routine message that Nixon wanted to meet with him at Camp David. The DCI assumed that the topic of discussion would be the Agency's budget for the upcoming year. Shortly after his electoral triumph, Nixon had assembled his cabinet and asked for its collective resignation as well as those of all political appointees. Traditionally, decisions to appoint and dismiss DCIs were private matters handled in a nonpartisan fashion. Republican DCIs had served Democrats and vice versa. Helms had been tapped by Johnson to head the CIA in 1966, and Nixon had asked him to stay on. Over lunch on Election Day, General Alexander Haig, Kissinger's deputy, had hinted to Helms that he would be allowed to set his own retirement date. Helms knew that he was no favorite of Haldeman and Ehrlichman, but he felt he had survived tougher adversaries than them.

After his helicopter landed at Camp David, Helms walked to Aspen House, where he was met—not "greeted," he noted in his memoir—by Haldeman. Nixon told him what a good job he had done as director, but then declared that he wanted a change of leadership at the Agency. What did Helms think? He served at the pleasure of the president, Helms said. Could he be allowed to stay on until the CIA's official retirement age of sixty, which would be in a few months? he asked. Certainly, the president replied. Would he be interested in becoming ambassador to the Soviet

Union? Nixon asked. He did not think the Russians would appreciate that, Helms observed. What would he like? Iran, perhaps, Helms said. And the meeting was over.[46]

There were all kind of reasons, legitimate and illegitimate, for Nixon wanting to get rid of Helms as DCI. First and foremost was his refusal to cooperate on the Watergate matter. Colby, for one, thought this was the crux of the matter. Noting with pride that none other than the *Washington Post* had singled out the CIA as the only agency in town to say no to the White House, Colby later observed that "Dick Helms paid the price for that 'No.'" Nixon had entered office viewing the Agency as an adversary. Subsequent events, Watergate not included, had done nothing to change his mind. There was Langley's apostasy over the antiballistic missile debate, and the constant negativity on Vietnam from the Agency's analysts. The CIA had failed utterly to uncover the fact that Sihanoukville had for years been a principal entrepôt for North Vietnam as it funneled arms into Cambodia, Laos, and South Vietnam. But it seems that Nixon had just been waiting for an excuse to change leaders at Langley. Haldeman's notes of a September White House meeting on goals for the second administration read: "Helms has got to go. Get rid of the clowns—cut personnel 40 percent. Its info worthless."[47]

Later, Daniel Patrick Moynihan asked Henry Kissinger why Helms had been fired. "I didn't do it," Henry replied. "The Germans did it."[48] Nixon would not even allow Helms the dignity of retiring. On February 2, 1973, the president swore in several new members of his administration; among them was James R. Schlesinger as DCI.

Schlesinger's term as director would be the shortest in the Agency's history—roughly four months—but he was to have a major impact on the CIA. A native New Yorker some ten years Colby's junior, Schlesinger, like Kissinger, had begun his career as an academic. He had earned a Ph.D. in economics from Harvard and had gone to work for the Rand Corporation in the early 1960s, rising to become chief of its strategic studies program. With a McNamara-like reputation for expertise in management efficiency and solid conservative, anticommunist credentials, Schlesinger was tapped first to be assistant director of what became the Office of Management and Budget and then to become head of the Atomic Energy Commission (AEC). It was Schlesinger who, at Nixon's direction, had authored a 1971 study advocating consolidation of the various elements of the intelligence community under the DCI. Schlesinger arrived at Langley "running, his shirt tails flying, determined, with that bulldog, abrasive temperament of his," as Colby put it, determined not only to consolidate the various intelligence services but also to impose major reforms on the CIA.[49]

Soon after he was picked to succeed Helms, but before his Senate confirmation, Schlesinger began meeting with Colby at his AEC offices in Germantown, Maryland, sometimes for six hours at a time. Schlesinger made it clear that he wanted to continue de-emphasizing covert operations, but he said he also intended to dismantle the analytical wing of the Agency. The emphasis should be on gathering intelligence on communist "hard-targets" such as the Soviet Union and Communist China, with CIA personnel complementing the sophisticated technology developed largely by the military. But even beyond that, Schlesinger told Colby, he wanted to change the whole meaning and culture of "intelligence" at Langley. The super-secretiveness and severe compartmentalization that had emerged over the years had hamstrung the Agency, he said. Under the aegis of its spies and counterspies, the CIA had become bloated and complacent. He referred scathingly to "the good old boys" as "deadwood" that had to go. In this spirit, Schlesinger ordered a green-and-white highway sign reading "Central Intelligence Agency" erected on the parkway. When Langley had been built, there had at first been such a sign, but Bobby Kennedy thought it ridiculous for an intelligence agency to advertise its whereabouts and ordered the sign replaced with one reading "Bureau of Public Roads."[50]

Much of what Schlesinger said was music to Colby's ears. While in Vietnam, he had come to admire the analytical branch's courage, if not its wisdom. The constant negativity seemed to fly in the face of the facts. "I had come to wonder," he later wrote, "whether some of the analysts' opinions had not become too firmly fixed and whether their objectivity had not come to reflect academia's bias that our programs in Vietnam just could not succeed." Even more encouraging, Schlesinger seemed to share his doubts about Angleton and the whole thrust of counterintelligence. Upon his return to Langley from Vietnam, Colby had once again been struck by the dampening effect the counterintelligence culture was having on intelligence gathering as a whole. Intelligence and counterintelligence were missing the forest for the trees, spending endless effort and time on "turning" minor functionaries within communist embassies, for example. Angleton's obsession with moles continued to paralyze the Soviet and East

European Division in its efforts to identify and recruit defectors. Schlesinger's pillorying of the cult of intelligence, Colby hoped, would lead at last to an end to Angleton and the CI Staff's chokehold on the clandestine services. The former Jedburgh continued to believe in the efficacy of covert action, especially as an alternative to full-scale war, but dared to hope that with the blooming of détente—the ongoing US effort to achieve peaceful coexistence with the communist superpowers—there would not be as much need for the knuckle-draggers.[51]

Colby had long coveted the job of deputy director of plans, head of the clandestine services. Tom Karamessines, a Helms loyalist, had retired with the departure of his boss. "Look," Colby told Schlesinger, "where you are going to have your biggest troubles is with the clandestine crowd downstairs. I'm one of them. I grew up with them. I know them. Let me go down there and take care of that for you." Schlesinger proved amenable, but what would he do about the executive director position Colby had been filling? Schlesinger said he would need either an executive director or a chief of staff. Colby did not think so, but he agreed to serve as ad hoc chair of a management committee that consisted of the other deputies. Thus was his dream of becoming deputy director of plans fulfilled.[52]

As Langley soon learned, Schlesinger had a mandate from the White House to make changes, and he intended to do just that. He began actively chairing the United States Intelligence Board, which included representatives from all US intelligence entities, and had some success in asserting control over the intelligence community. The new director quickly backed off his war against the analysts, however, deciding to encourage participation by the younger members of the staff in the preparation of National Intelligence Estimates. Of John Heisinger, head of the Office of National Estimates, Schlesinger said, "I am not going to have it said of me that I fired the smartest man in the CIA." Schlesinger was, however, relentless in his drive to cut clandestine services. As deputy director for plans, Colby became his hatchet man.[53]

Colby began his tenure by renaming the Directorate of Plans. It would now be the Directorate of Operations to more accurately describe what the branch did. He established a committee under Cord Meyer, his deputy, to come up with the best method for achieving the personnel cuts Schlesinger wanted. At that time clandestine services employed 6,000 to 7,000 of the Agency's total of 17,000 officers; no less than 85 percent of its officers had been on the job for more than twenty years. Colby began with the oldest, arranging for retirements, or, if that was not possible, demotions. But soon there was no choice but to fire. "It wasn't long," Colby recalled in his memoir, "before a phone call from me cast a chill over any recipient." Those affected attempted to push back. Senior people leaked stories to the press. Schlesinger was hauled before the House Armed Services CIA subcommittee and asked if he was trying to destroy the very agency he commanded. At one point the DCI summoned rebellious staff members to his office and in their presence phoned Nixon. The firings were going to cause a public flap and bad publicity; there might even be lawsuits, he told the president. Nixon made it clear that Schlesinger had his full support. From that point on, organized opposition to the purge began to die down. When the dust had cleared, Schlesinger and Colby had pared somewhere between 1,000 and 1,800 individuals from the Agency's staff, between 7 and 10 percent.[54]

One person whom Colby expected to go but did not was James Jesus Angleton. Colby made no secret of the fact that he thought Angleton's super-secret mode of operating; his huge, invasive staff; and his obsession with communist moles were drags on the Agency. He recommended to the DCI that the longtime head of counterintelligence be eased out. But Schlesinger refused. Like his predecessors, the new director was intrigued with Angleton's "undoubted brilliance," as Colby put it. And he did not want to be the first DCI caught with a major mole in his operation. There was also a shared hardline anticommunism between the two. Schlesinger would not agree to ground Angleton, but he allowed Colby to clip his wings. During the Schlesinger-Colby purge, CI lost 80 percent of its staff. The team that ran MH/Chaos was gutted. Angleton was stripped of his role as liaison with the FBI. And then there was the super-secret mail-intercept program. Colby claimed in his memoir that neither he nor Schlesinger knew about the program until shortly after Colby became head of plans, when the postal inspector informed Langley that he would not continue what was clearly an illegal activity without a presidential directive. Colby visited the law library and, assured that the CIA's opening of correspondence between the Soviet Union and the United States was indeed a violation of the law, went to Schlesinger and recommended that the program be terminated. This, in turn, led to a confrontation with Angleton in the director's office. Since the inception of the mail-intercept program, CI had been the sole recipient of the information it produced. Appeal to Nixon, Angleton demanded; obtain the presidential order. Schlesinger refused, but with a view to saving a portion of Angleton's face, he decreed that the program be "suspended" rather than terminated.[55]

In mid-April 1973, Catherine Colby died. She was twenty-three years old. Upon his return from Vietnam, Colby had bought a house on Briley Place off of Massachusetts Avenue in Bethesda. "It exuded suburbia," his daughter-in-law, Susan, recalled, "that parochial mentality that is so Catholic middle class. It was next to a church and he could park his family there." The backyard was encircled with a chain-link fence; Bill bought Barbara a dog to patrol it. Catherine had actually seemed to be making some progress. The Phoenix hearings and the public slander that followed had been hard on her, but the anorexia that had set in after a trip to Israel had begun to abate. She had gained some weight, and in March she had signed up to take the civil service exam. To calm her nerves, Catherine took medication the night before the test. Carl, two years younger, heard commotion in her room and rushed in to find that his sister had choked on her own vomit. He gave her CPR, but without success. At that point, Bill appeared. There was nothing either man could do. John Colby recalled that his father was weeping when he telephoned to break the news. Nixon sent a letter of condolence, and Schlesinger kept company with Bill and Barbara the entire day of the funeral.[56]

A tour of the Agency's overseas outposts offered some distraction from the tragedy of Catherine's death. Colby met the Middle East station chiefs in Athens, journeyed through Austria and West Germany to check on Agency operations there, and traveled to Bangkok to see old friends from the Far East (now East Asian) Division. While in Bangkok, Colby read in the newspaper that during Daniel Ellsberg's trial on theft and conspiracy charges for revealing the Pentagon Papers, it had come to light that E. Howard Hunt, using equipment borrowed from the CIA, had broken into the offices of Ellsberg's Los Angeles–based psychiatrist. Hunt and his fellow Plumbers had been after damaging material that could be furnished to Langley's medical branch as it prepared its "psychiatric profile" of Ellsberg. Colby recalled that when the FBI had inquired about Hunt's relationship with the Agency during the Watergate investigation, he had seen prints of some film Hunt had given to Langley's technicians to develop. They were grainy but

Rural spy rendezvous with family cover, Sweden, 1950s
(The Colby Family Collection)

Clare Booth Luce, US Ambassador
to Italy and WEC intimate
(The Colby Family Collection)

In St. Peter's Square, Rome, 1950s
(The Colby Family Collection)

Barbara and Clare Luce, Rome
(The Colby Family Collection)

Barbara and other members of Saigon's elite, Cercle Sportif, Saigon, 1960
(The Colby Family Collection)

1960 Coup, Saigon, from the Colbys' upstairs window
(The Colby Family Collection)

The Colby family's farewell to President Ngo Dinh Diem, Saigon, 1962
(The Colby Family Collection)

Colby goes native?
(The Colby Family Collection)

Colby, the American proconsul
(The Colby Family Collection)

Colleagues
(The Colby Family Collection)

Ambassador Colby, DEPCORDS
(The Colby Family Collection)

Colby wanted poster, Washington, DC, 1972
(CIA Library)

Colby presents to the Ford foreign policy team
(Gerald R. Ford Library)

showed the exterior of offices with the names of two physicians etched on a plaque. Colby had ordered the film turned over to the FBI, but he did not realize its significance until he read the account of the Ellsberg trial.

Back at Langley, Colby went immediately to see Schlesinger. He had assured the DCI that he had told him everything about the Agency's involvement or noninvolvement with Watergate. To Colby's relief, Schlesinger declared that he assumed that Colby was as much in the dark on the burglary of the psychiatrist's office as he was. Nevertheless, the DCI was in one of his cold rages. What other ticking time bombs were being concealed within the clandestine services? They would tear the place apart and "fire everybody if necessary" to find out. At Schlesinger's direction, Colby drafted a memo to all officers, ordering them to reveal any knowledge of activities that were illegal, beyond the scope of the CIA's charter, or both. In a separate communication, Colby, also at the DCI's direction, invited ex-employees to come forward as well.[57] Schlesinger's insensitivity to the simple dictates of politics and psychology was never more apparent than in this particular move. A letter from Colby, the man who wielded the axe, inviting them to confess any sins of the past! What were the chances that some ex-officers were going to volunteer any information they had to the press as well as to the Agency? The DCI asked Colby to supervise the compilation of wrongdoings, putting the inspector general and his staff at his disposal.

Colby had to tread a fine line. He was part of the past himself, a CIA old-timer. He did not want to appear disloyal to Helms, but he did not want to be associated with previous misdeeds, or with efforts to sweep them under the rug. Colby was in due course told about the letters from James McCord to the Agency warning that the White House staff, led by Charles Colson, had embarked on a campaign to blame Watergate on the CIA, arguing that it was part of an Agency plot to do in President Nixon. Before Colby could notify Schlesinger, another of his lieutenants told him of the McCord missives. The DCI was furious: "His anger had to be experienced to be believed," Colby later recalled. "For the first—and only—time I feared that Schlesinger had become suspicious that I too, as an old Agency hand, was trying to keep secrets from him." But Colby was allowed to get on with his assigned task.[58]

By the time the last officer had come forward, the inspector general had compiled a list of "potential flap activities" that ran to 693 pages. The "family jewels," as one wag would term them, included domestic spying via MH/Chaos; the mail-intercept program; the Agency's contacts with Hunt and the other members of the Plumbers team; its cooperation in the scheme to frame Daniel Ellsberg; surveillance of journalists as part of the effort to identify the source of leaks within the government; experiments with mind-altering drugs, which had led to the suicide of one CIA officer; and various assassination plots in which the CIA was directly or tangentially involved.[59] Colby remembered thinking that the list, covering the entire twenty-five years of the Agency's existence, wasn't really so bad, especially in light of what he knew about the NKVD, MI-6, and other intelligence shops. Indeed, the White House had found the CIA so uncooperative in its campaign of dirty tricks that it had had to form its own "intelligence group," the Plumbers. But the United States, unlike the United Kingdom, had no Official Secrets Act. The public mood, recently so enamored of James Bond, 007, with a license to kill, was in an ugly and unforgiving mood. Colby concluded—and Schlesinger concurred—that for the sake of the American intelligence community, the family jewels should be kept locked away.

16

ASCENSION

O n May 9, 1973, Colby received an unexpected call from Alexander Haig, who had replaced Haldeman—at last a casualty of Watergate—as White House chief of staff. There was going to be a cabinet reshuffle. Attorney General Richard Kleindienst was going to have to resign because of Watergate, and President Nixon intended to replace him with Secretary of Defense Elliott Richardson. James Schlesinger would move to the Pentagon. "And the President wants you to take over as Director of the CIA, Bill," Haig concluded.[1]

Colby was stunned. He had thought heading the clandestine services would mark the culmination of his career in the Agency. He had met Nixon only once, and that was in Vietnam during a formal occasion. True, his son John had been roommates at Princeton with Edward Cox, the young man who had married Nixon's daughter Patricia, and each would serve as a groomsman in the other's wedding, but that was hardly sufficient to explain the decision to tap Colby for DCI. Whatever the case, Colby finally blurted out that he was honored and promised to do his very best.[2]

On one level, Nixon respected Colby. Bill had conducted himself as a professional in Vietnam, showing no hint of partisanship. Nixon had not only sent a letter of condolence to Colby following Catherine's death but had also written him a personal note on February 20, 1973, on the occasion of the return of American prisoners of war from North Vietnam. "As I saw our POWs come off the plane at Clark Field," the president wrote, "I was never so proud to be an American. This would not have been possible had it not been for those—like you—who served America with such dedication." Most important, perhaps, the White House needed an apolitical figure who could pass muster with Congress without causing a major partisan flap. Finally, Schlesinger and others had assured the White House that Colby would be a good fit.[3]

But at bottom, Nixon and Kissinger considered Colby a bureaucrat, a political nonentity who could be easily controlled and from whom they had nothing to fear. Colby had absolutely no constituency outside of the CIA, an entity on which the White House had declared war. They must have known that selecting the former Jedburgh would be controversial within the Agency, given his relative lack of experience with the intelligence side and the fact that he had acted as hatchet man for Schlesinger and the White House, but they did not care. Nixon and Kissinger wanted someone who would carry out orders even when they went against his principles. Colby would be to Nixon what Colin Powell would be to George W. Bush, Suffolk to Henry VIII. As for Kissinger, his mentors, Klemens von Metternich and Otto von Bismarck, had been their own spymasters. He would never trust someone he could not control. "In retrospect, I must admit, there was something disconcertingly casual in the process of elevating me to the top CIA job," Colby wrote in *Honorable Men*.

Colby, along with Schlesinger and Richardson, attended the next scheduled cabinet meeting, where their nominations were to be announced. Just before the names were read, the president leaned over and spoke to Haig. The chief of staff scribbled on a piece of paper and passed it to Colby. "Did you have any connections with Watergate that might raise problems?" it read. Colby looked at Haig and shook his head no. What the hell was that about? Colby thought. If the president had doubts, he should have raised them earlier. What if Colby had said yes? Was there some kind of implied threat in the query? Perhaps Nixon still went through periods of actually believing that Watergate was some sort of CIA plot to get him. Shortly thereafter, a group of Bill's friends sent him a telegram: "Congratulations, one of ours finally made it. [Signed] Nell Gwyn." Nell Gwyn had been an illiterate prostitute, the mistress of Charles II—a sordid commoner who had made good.[4]

The four-month interregnum between Colby's nomination and his swearing-in was awkward, to say the least. As DCI-designate, Colby was recognized as the decisionmaker, but he did not yet hold the title of director. In Washington, titles were everything, Colby later observed. Fortunately, the acting director was Vernon Walters, who had an easygoing personality and no further ambitions in the intelligence field.

There was unfinished business to attend to. Colby and Schlesinger had decided that the family jewels had best be kept locked in a safe. But they did feel compelled to consult with the Agency's congressional watchdogs. Led by Senators J. William Fulbright and Mike Mansfield (D-MT), a group in Congress had since the mid-1960s been trying to wrest control of CIA oversight from the southern hawks who had traditionally dominated the process. In the Senate, Richard Russell and John Stennis and in the House, F. Edward Hebert (D-LA) and L. Mendel Rivers (D-SC) had fought them tooth and nail. But with the coming of the Second Reconstruction and the tidal wave of disillusionment that swept the country in the course of Vietnam and Watergate, protectors of the national security state had been placed on the defensive. Members of the Senate Foreign Relations Committee were admitted to the CIA oversight body, while in the House, Hebert had appointed Lucien Nedzi, a liberal Democrat from Michigan, to chair the intelligence subcommittee. The DCI-designate duly made the rounds.

Unlike the other solons Colby visited, Nedzi was not so sure that skeletons should be kept in the closet. Wouldn't most of the secrets come out eventually, he asked Colby? Wouldn't it be better for the Agency to come clean voluntarily sooner than to be forced to fess up later? Colby was not unsympathetic. He recognized that the days when Langley could go about its business without any outside accountability were over. The mood of the country had changed. Many in the media and Congress saw the CIA more as a potential threat to civil liberties than a protector. Colby recalled that he was more than just resigned to a new era of accountability. "I considered it correct in our Constitutional democracy," he wrote. But he pleaded with Nedzi to let the past bury the past and the future deal with the future. "The shock effect of an exposure of the 'family jewels,' I urged, could, in the climate of 1973, inflict mortal wounds on the CIA and deprive the nation of all the good the Agency could do in the future." Nedzi agreed, and Colby, breathing a sigh of relief, hoped that the matter had been closed.[5]

The problem was that the Watergate scandal was just beginning to gather steam in 1973, and as long as the break-in continued to be the subject of daily headlines and televised hearings, the CIA was going to be dragged through the mud. The trial of the Watergate Seven got underway in January 1973. Five of the defendants pleaded guilty; two underwent a jury trial and were convicted. On March 23, the day scheduled for sentencing, presiding judge John J. Sirica read a letter from James McCord admitting that he had been acting on orders from the White House and that he and the others had been pressured to keep quiet. During the months that followed, federal prosecutors, Judge Sirica, and the Senate Watergate Committee worked in tacit alliance. Meanwhile, journalists Bob Woodward and Carl Bernstein, fed information by FBI official W. Mark Felt—known to the public at that time only by the moniker "Deep Throat"—kept the public abreast of events in the pages of the *Washington Post*. All the while, Nixon continued to approve the payment of hush money to Hunt and the other Plumbers.

Then on the advice of his lawyer, White House counsel John Dean came clean before the Watergate Committee, admitting to and describing the cover-up. On April 30, the president went on national television to announce that there had indeed been a conspiracy to conceal the facts about Watergate, but that he was in no way involved. Then followed Nixon's firing of Ehrlichman, Haldeman, and Dean. As a condition of his confirmation, Attorney General–designate Elliott Richardson was forced to name a special prosecutor to investigate Watergate. When Dean revealed the existence of a secret taping system in the Oval Office, a yearlong battle ensued between the White House and the Watergate Committee over control of the potentially incriminating recordings.

Colby's confirmation hearings got underway in late July 1973. As soon as the Senate began hearing witnesses, the old "Wanted" posters featuring a photo of the DCI-designate imposed on the ace of spades began popping up around Washington, especially at construction sites for the new metro. The phone calls to the Colby household also recommenced. One caller told his daughter Christine, who was then thirteen, "We'll get your daddy." Colby, who prided himself on being able to take a punch, ordered his lieutenants at the Agency not to try to find out who was behind the posters and calls; if word got out, it would only make matters worse. Colby consoled himself in part with the knowledge that Catherine did not have to endure this latest round of vilification. Eventually, a particular caller got to the DCI-designate, an individual who would call at all hours and then stay on the line saying nothing. Colby asked his clandestine people to track the call. The next time the phone rang, and Colby realized it was the phantom, he called him by name. There was a gasp, and the line went dead.[6]

Meanwhile, in the Senate, Stuart Symington (D-MO) led the nominee through a series of public questions that provided him with the opportunity to assure the Senate Armed Services Committee that the Agency's estimates would remain free of policy and political considerations. Colby promised that under his direction, the Agency would collect only "foreign intelligence," and that he would resign if asked to undertake any illegal activity. The going got tougher when the committee went into executive session. A number of hostile witnesses associated with Phoenix had testified against Colby's confirmation. Senator Edward Kennedy (D-MA) took up where they had left off. Mirroring the about-face on Vietnam that his brother Bobby had made before his assassination, Ted was now a relentless dove. For nearly four hours he questioned Colby about assassination squads and American-supported terror in Vietnam. He then turned to Watergate, accusing the Agency, Colby included, of being part of the cover-up. Colby denied it. When the dust had settled, Kennedy was one of only thirteen senators voting nay; 83 approved.[7]

The confirmation vote on August 1 should have eased Colby's mind, but it didn't; the White House seemed to have forgotten that he needed to be sworn in. Walters, who was still acting director, had to remind the president, and Colby was finally called to 1600 Pennsylvania Avenue on September 4. Nixon praised his professionalism and emphasized Colby's role as director of counterinsurgency and pacification in Vietnam.[8]

Press reactions to Colby's appointment had been mixed. Which Bill Colby would he prove to be? David Wise asked in a July 1973 article. Was America's new super-spook the mild-mannered suburban dweller, the devout Roman Catholic who regularly attended Mass at the Little Flower Roman Catholic Church in Bethesda, the father of four, and a former Boy Scout troop leader? Or was he the ultimate product of the "super-secret Directorate of Operations, sometimes known as the 'Department of Dirty Tricks?'" Deliberately uncharismatic and self-effacing Colby may have been, but he was a product of the culture that had overthrown Mohammed Mossadeq in Iran and Jacobo Arbenz Guzmán in Guatemala. It had conducted the abortive Bay of Pigs invasion. Colby himself had run the secret war in Laos and the infamous Phoenix program. The new director may not have talked like the proverbial duck, but he certainly walked like one. Neil Sheehan also suggested a Jekyll and Hyde personality. "Colby's office is a light-filled and airy one," the journalist observed after an interview with the soon-to-be DCI. "There is a picture window that runs along the entire right side of the office as you come in. . . . Through it you can see other buildings of the CIA complex and the trees surrounding it. Looking out on the scene from this pleasant office, you would never think that such dark things have been discussed and ordered from such a light and airy place." Sheehan found Colby to be an enlightened observer of contemporary and historical events and a good listener. But there was something behind the eyes, something of the fanatic. Could this be America's Felix Dzerzhinsky, the brutal head of the Soviet Union's first intelligence and internal security apparatus?[9]

Within the Agency, Colby's ascension met with mixed reviews. "Colby never became a member of CIA's inner club of mandarins," Agency historian Harold Ford later wrote. CIA officers Richard Helms, Tracy Barnes, John Bross, Kermit Roosevelt, James Angleton, and Bronson Tweedy were of the elite, comfortable on the Georgetown cocktail circuit, connected socially and politically. Bill Colby was a middle-class Ivy Leaguer and a loner. Spying and counterspying—those were the coins of the realm in the Agency—but Colby was a doer, impatient with the caution and painstaking procedures of intelligence collection. In addition, his experience was in East Asia, while the primary preoccupation of the CIA was the Soviet Union and the East European bloc. To some, his colorlessness and lack of charisma were off-putting. "Slight of build, with pale, dull eyes, Colby appeared to be almost anything rather than soldier or intelligence chief," David Phillips later wrote. Although most junior officers loved him, some of his senior colleagues found him rigid and closed-minded. "I just have a feeling about Bill Colby that he is quite lacking in the qualities that enable most of us to be introspective about our behavior," one critic stated. "He had a total incapacity to compromise."[10]

In 1977, Phillips, then a Directorate of Operations officer, took a poll of some eleven senior CIA alumni who had worked closely with one or more of five DCIs. He found that when asked which director one would want as an effective companion in a perilous situation on a desert island, all either chose Colby, Richard Helms, or John McCone, with no votes for Red Raborn or Allen Dulles. Given a comfortable, nonthreatening situation, however, where one would want an easy, stimulating companion on a desert island, six chose Dulles, five Helms, and one McCone—with no votes for Raborn or Colby. Phillips expanded on why he had selected

Colby for the first category. "He would get us both off that island," he wrote. "Certainly he would never entertain the notion of building a boat for one or, if he did reach that point, he would later stand in the surf and wave goodbye—a faint smile on his thin lips—after pushing me out to sea."[11]

It fell to Colby—after his nomination but before his swearing-in—to preside over the final battle in the Nixon administration's war with Salvador Allende. The Chilean Constitution limited its presidents to one six-year term. If Allende was to implement *La via chilena al socialismo*, Chile's Path to Socialism, he was going to have to hurry. The government issued decrees nationalizing large-scale industries, including the American-owned Anaconda Copper and ITT, and confiscating all landholdings larger than 80 hectares. The vote was extended to eighteen-year-olds and illiterates. Massive public works projects provided employment for hundreds of thousands of poor Chileans. Spending on housing, public health, and education skyrocketed. In 1971, Chile, along with Mexico and Canada, extended diplomatic recognition to Castro's Cuba. Fidel himself declared his enduring friendship for both Chile and Allende and made a highly publicized tour of the country. Unfortunately for the socialists, the bottom fell out of the copper market; this, together with a massive increase in government spending, led to runaway inflation. By 1972, in part as the result of economic boycotts imposed by the United States and strikes in the copper and service industries, Chile was experiencing a severe shortage of consumer goods. Opposition to Allende's rule grew apace in Chile's National Congress, which was controlled by the Christian Democrats and the military. There was no doubt that Allende had received support from the KGB during the 1970 electoral campaign—some $400,000—and continued to do so thereafter. He promised to provide whatever information Soviet intelligence might require, and in 1972, Moscow awarded him the Lenin Peace Prize.

Nixon and Kissinger watched these developments with growing alarm. The Track I and, to an extent, Track II campaigns to destabilize Chile politically and economically continued. In August 1972, the 40 Committee approved another $1 million for Chile's opposition parties, bringing the total for the Allende period to $6.5 million.[12]

New coup plots began to materialize by the end of 1972. The CIA station in Santiago kept in close touch with all anti-Allende factions, including the military, but there was no effort to provide aid or even promises of US support. The consensus within the 40 Committee was that the Chilean military would launch a coup sometime in the near future and that it did not need help from the CIA to succeed. On September 10, 1973, an emissary from a group of high-ranking military officers appeared at CIA offices in Santiago. He informed the station chief that an assault on the Presidential Palace would take place the next day and asked for US support. After checking with headquarters, the chief of station informed the coup emissary that the United States would not interfere in what was a purely internal Chilean matter. With Agency personnel limiting themselves to reporting events, the attack on the palace got underway, as predicted, on the 11th. Presidential guards, who, incidentally, had been trained by the Cubans, fought fiercely, but they were quickly overwhelmed. Allende refused offers of safe passage and, following an eleventh-hour radio broadcast from the palace, allegedly placed a rifle under his chin and blew off the top of his head.[13]

Chilean leftists claimed that the military fabricated this account, and that Allende had actually been assassinated with the assistance of the CIA. But the coup plotters who were present stuck to their story. Allende's death has been a subject of controversy ever since. The Nixon administration and the CIA insisted the United States had nothing to do with Allende's demise. In any case, democracy would not return to Chile for more than twenty years. The military regime that took control following the coup, under General Augusto Pinochet, would become one of the most notorious rightwing dictatorships in a region where rightwing dictatorships were standard fare. The new government suspended the National Congress, outlawed labor unions and political parties, and established one of the most feared secret police organizations in the world—the Dirección de Inteligencia Nacional, or DINA. Thousands of leftists were imprisoned indefinitely, interrogated, and tortured. "Methods employed," according to an International Commission of Jurists report in 1974, "included electric shock, blows, beatings, burning with acid or cigarettes, prolonged standing, prolonged hooding and isolation in solitary confinement, extraction of nails, crushing of testicles, sexual assaults, immersion in water, hanging, simulated executions . . . and compelling attendance at the torture of others." Those considered most subversive disappeared entirely.[14]

Colby would have preferred a different outcome—the election of someone like Frei, for example. But he believed that anything was better than Allende. "If you support some authoritarian leader against a Communist threat," he later remarked to an interviewer, "you leave the option that the authoritarian state could become democratic in the future. With the Communists, the future offers no hope. . . . Pinochet is not going to conquer the world. Nobody is worried about Pinochet." Colby's experiences with the "closed societies" he had encountered following the outbreak of the Cold War had led him to believe that communism was the worst of all totalitarian systems. For the most part, his fellow Americans shared that view. But they were less and less willing for the United States to intervene in a Third World country to stop communism's spread. An October 29, 1973, Harris Poll reported that fully 60 percent of the American people believed that the CIA should not have tried to destabilize the Chilean government; only 18 percent approved.[15]

Bill Colby may never have expected to be named DCI, but, like every other senior officer in the CIA, he had thought extensively about the role of the office of director—its mission, methods, and responsibilities. The philosophy that Colby brought to the fourth floor at Langley was an extension of the philosophy he had embraced as a Jedburgh, political officer in Italy, chief of station in Saigon, Far East Division chief, and DEPCORDS. He was still a true believer. People joined the CIA, he observed in a 1976 oral history, because they were patriots. The Agency, like the armed services and the US Foreign Service, was dedicated to the safety and welfare of the country.[16]

It was fitting that as Colby took the reins at Langley, preparations were being made to raise a statue of Nathan Hale in the courtyard. Although he was American intelligence's first martyr, Hale was certainly not a role model for future spooks, Colby observed in his maiden speech to Agency personnel. He had volunteered for espionage duty at the last minute; he had a very weak cover story; he had little training and no secret writing or other gimmicks; and when he was captured, his reports were in his shoe. Not only was he apprehended by the British, but the information he sought—where on Manhattan Island General Howe planned to land—had already reached his superiors by another route. But Hale was to be valued not for his expertise or his success, the new DCI declared, but for his motives, his courage, and his willingness to sacrifice for his country. "We may not, God willing, need to demonstrate physical courage," Colby told his comrades, "but in the intelligence profession we will be required to show moral and intellectual courage."[17]

But patriotism was a hard thing to define in an era that featured the Sino-Soviet split, Washington's openings to Moscow and Beijing, and spreading American disillusionment with its government in the wake of Vietnam and Watergate. Colby, like George Kennan, Harry Truman, Dwight Eisenhower, Jack Kennedy, and Lyndon Johnson, wanted to contain communism until it either collapsed from its own internal contradictions or evolved into something nonthreatening to the rest of the world. He continued to believe that the best way to fight Sino-Soviet imperialism was to subsidize the anticommunist left. He would dispatch John F. Devlin, deputy director of political research at the CIA, to the 1974 American Historical Association Conference to recruit. In his pitch, Devlin made it clear that all were welcome, including Marxists. Of course, Colby still believed that the best defense was a good offense. He may have abandoned the notion that the Western democracies could train and equip freedom fighters within communist hard targets to overthrow their respective governments, but he was still committed to covert action, both military and political, in disputed areas. In terms of the Soviet Union, Colby viewed intelligence gathering in much the same way the advocates of mutually assured destruction viewed the arms race. There was his telling comment to Soviet leader Leonid Brezhnev during his June 1973 visit to Washington: "The more we know of each other the safer we both can be."[18]

As it had in the past, Colby's approach put him on a collision course with the men who kept the secrets—Helms, Angleton, and the whole counterintelligence culture. The extreme compartmentalization that had characterized the CIA under his predecessors, Colby believed, had visited a number of evils on the Agency. It had crippled the CIA's ability to fight the Cold War. It had kept Langley from producing the best, most informed, most integrated intelligence products for the nation's policymakers. There was only one component of the CIA charged with an unconditional need-to-know, and that was CI. This had given primacy to the mole hunters, defining the Cold War as the CIA vs. the KGB rather than the United States and its allies versus Moscow, Beijing, and their allies. The obsession had been with protecting against penetration rather than with penetrating.

Ideologically, this meant that the Agency had sometimes been dominated by anticommunist hardliners, conservatives who preferred monarchists and fascists not only to communists, but to socialists as well. Compartmentalization had also led to the abuses, mild though they were in Colby's eyes, that were in the process of destroying what was left of Congress's and the American public's confidence in the CIA.

Colby longed for an Official Secrets Act similar to the one in Britain that made it a crime to reveal classified information and that protected MI-6. He continued to battle Victor Marchetti and Philip Agee—the former CIA officers who were attempting to out the Agency in print—working through the courts to censor their publications in order to protect sources and methods as well as publicly denouncing their disloyalty. If Agee were a member of a foreign service, there was no doubt what would happen to him, Colby told an interviewer; "He'd be shot." But he was not going to have a US Official Secrets Act, and he knew it. The CIA was an American intelligence agency, Colby told a college audience, not MI-6, not the KGB, not the Chinese communist apparatus. But what did that mean? It was no small question. Upon how he answered it might hinge the very existence of the Agency and the security of the country.[19]

Colby soon came to recognize that the National Security Act of 1947 and constitutional requirements aside, the world of 1974 was very different from the world of 1947. From the time of his return from Vietnam to become executive director, he had cultivated close ties with rising young officers in the Agency. That trend would continue when he became DCI. "We make no effort to get out in front of Congress," one of his protégés wrote him in a memo during the spring of 1974. "We concentrate on trying to preserve what we have, and as a consequence look what we are becoming. Twenty-five years have been devoted to immunizing and insulating CIA as an institution, and its population as individuals, from the evolutionary and riotous changes that have engulfed the society at large. . . . We don't look for ways to make change, we search exhaustively for ways to prevent it. . . . Maybe intelligence shouldn't serve the Executive Branch exclusively. . . . Maybe the principle of separation of powers shouldn't apply to intelligence." Colby agreed—with the first part, at least. If the CIA was to weather the gathering storm, there would have to be sweeping reforms.[20]

What the new DCI envisioned was an integrated team that would turn out the best possible intelligence product and report frankly to Congress on its activities, excluding sources and methods. Indeed, he promised as much in his confirmation hearings: if the Agency were to survive, "it has to conform with [*sic*] the laws, the standards, and the customs of our country," he proclaimed. "It has to retain the confidence of the American government and the American people." The family jewels were missteps of the past; under Schlesinger, and then on his own, he had issued edicts prohibiting any and all Watergate-type actions, assassinations, and other wrongdoing. Perhaps most important, the CIA would no longer keep secrets from itself. "The way to solve the problem of the baronies and the separate lives of the different elements of the Agency," he told an interviewer, "is more and more to pull the experts in their different fields into direct contact with each other. Don't scare them by having them feel that he [*sic*] can't possibly talk to somebody in another Directorate because it is a little bit worse than talking to the KGB."[21]

What Colby was suggesting was revolutionary, subversive, and absolutely counter to the culture of secrecy that pervaded intelligence operations across nations and across time. Compartmentalization equaled security. Limiting information to those with a need-to-know kept it out of the hands of moles, those who could be compromised, the careless, or those with a personal grudge against an individual or an agency. Not only Angleton but the vast majority of spooks trusted only those they had to—and then very reluctantly. Colby's timing may have been necessary, but for the keepers of the secrets, it could not have been worse. With leaks springing up everywhere, the DCI was getting ready to call for more disclosure.

Ever the liberal, Colby began his tenure as DCI by signaling a new openness, a new sense of collegiality. "When I was abroad, at various stations, when I was Chief of Station and then when I was Chief of the Division," he told an interviewer, "I spent a great deal of time worrying about the individual members of the organization that I was part of; I tried to step in and help them with their problems. I tried to correct them and encourage them to solve their problems rather than to discipline them as a way of getting changes made." His office, in deliberate contrast to Angleton's, was open and light-filled; his assistant, Jenonne Walker, and the division heads were free to come and go. "Senior people from across the Agency felt very comfortable coming up—they would check with his secretary—and would walk in," Walker recalled. Colby made a point of lunching in the general mess and sitting with junior officers. He launched an

equal opportunity program to bring more blacks into one of the most seg-
regated agencies in Washington and to help female employees break the
glass ceiling. Not all was wine and roses; he had spent much of the previous
year firing people, and that trend, at the insistence of the White House,
would continue.[22]

In truth, despite his goodwill and good intentions, Bill Colby—driven
in part by events but in part also by his personal prejudices—would do
more to divide and demoralize the CIA than any of his predecessors. One
of the few things the former Jedburgh had in common with the Nixon
White House was a prejudice against the Directorate of Intelligence. Colby
had no experience on the analytical side; his time had been spent in the
clandestine services. To remedy this imbalance, he named Jenonne Walker
as his assistant. Walker was a ten-year veteran of the Office of National
Estimates, specializing in Western Europe. Colby then proceeded to do
away with the venerable Board of National Estimates, whose reports (National Intelligence Estimates) had been the coin of the intelligence realm
for twenty-five years. The board, Colby later wrote, had developed a certain
"ivory tower mentality" and had become even more isolated in reaction to
the denigration of its product by the Pentagon and the Nixon-Kissinger
foreign policy team. Colby wanted to be the funnel through which intelligence flowed to policymakers. It was he who had to participate in top-level
meetings, conduct briefings, and take responsibility. The NIE process took
place independently of the DCI. Abolition of the board freed up twelve
senior-level positions in the Agency. Colby used those slots to create twelve
national intelligence officers (NIOs) who would report directly to him on
the major issues the country faced, whether it was China, arms control,
Vietnam, or the Middle East. Each officer was limited to one assistant and
one secretary "so that they could identify totally with my position and not
develop a role of their own," as Colby later put it. He saw the special assistant for Vietnamese affairs as a model, comparing it favorably with other
arrangements where he had been faced by a whole "roomful of China experts" when he would have preferred to have dealt with one individual.[23]

John Huizenga, chairman of the board, fought Colby, arguing that abolition of the Board of National Estimates, which comprised individuals
from within and without the Agency, would compromise the independence of the intelligence product. But Colby insisted, and Huizenga retired. Colby later recalled that he could not have done without the new

national intelligence officers, particularly as he spent more and more time testifying before congressional committees. "They would call me late in the evening or show up at my desk early in the morning with some development they had plucked out of the reams of material flowing through Langley and say that it presented an unforeseen danger or a novel aspect of a complex problem."[24]

As coordinator of the NIOs, Colby selected George Carver, his former case officer in Saigon, who had risen to become the DCI's special assistant for Vietnam (SAVA). The analysts were appalled. Like Colby, Carver had very little experience on the espionage or analytical side. "Carver was a true believer," Jenonne Walker observed, "and more important, he was an operator, not an analyst. It is just human nature that if you are working your heart out twenty hours a day on a policy that you believe passionately is essential to the national interest, you will believe it will succeed because it must succeed." In the early days, the analysts engaged in a lot of self-censorship, telling the DCI, and through him, the White House, what they thought he wanted to hear. Walker would assure them that Colby did not want them to pull their punches, but they would say, "Yeah, he says that, but he fired John Heisinger [the longtime and very distinguished head of the analytical branch] and promoted George Carver. That tells us what he really wants." Colby himself addressed the problem during a question-and-answer session with top management. "There is much confusion over the two words, 'policy support,'" he said. "Our mission is to support the policy makers, not the policy of the makers." But here was the crux of the problem. He had appointed a man, George Carver, who, like himself, was an operative, a person who was used to committing completely to whatever project he was involved in, emotionally and psychologically; it was frequently impossible for such a man to stand back and question the assumptions upon which their operations were based. How much more difficult to do so working for men like Nixon and Kissinger.[25]

Colby wanted the CIA's product to matter, and for that to happen, he believed, the Agency's daily intelligence reports had to reach key policymakers directly and concisely. To this end he created the *National Intelligence Daily*, which presented the newest secrets in newspaper format, enabling consumers to scan headlines and read in depth only those stories of direct concern to them. "It became the journal with the smallest circulation (about 60), the largest reporting staff (the whole intelligence community), and the worst advertising in the world (none, because the content was highly classified)," Colby later quipped.[26] The old National Intelligence Estimates had focused almost exclusively on strategic and military issues; Colby wanted more breadth. He thus established two offices within the Directorate of Intelligence: the Office of Economic Research and the Office of Political Research. Those concerned with national security had long been aware that trade policies, strategic reserves of natural resources, and other economic factors, as well as long-term political trends, were of vital concern, but Colby believed that the new CIA had to give these topics more institutional visibility.

Colby would never abandon his faith in the value of human intelligence (HUMINT), but he was no Luddite either. He worked diligently to get up to speed on "the machine spies," as Richard Helms once dubbed them. By 1973, a lion's share of the intelligence community's budget was going into reconnaissance satellites and aircraft, ground stations, and ships at sea with highly sophisticated sight and sound monitoring devices. When Colby came on board as DCI, the Nixon administration was considering a new generation of spy satellite called KH-11. The United States already had equipment that could take detailed photographs, even at night, of the most discrete targets. The problem was how to transmit the images back to earth. Pre-KH-11 satellites transported their photographs physically by means of film capsules embedded in tiny reentry vehicles. The technique was fraught with problems. The planes sent to recover the capsules sometimes could not locate them; periodically, vehicles together with their film cargos burned up on reentry; and a satellite only could carry a finite number of capsules. There was the famous story of a satellite photo capsule accidentally landing in the steppes of Central Asia. When CIA agents tracked it down, they found that a reindeer herder had discovered it first, taken it apart, uncoiled the rolls of film, and used them to decorate his yurt. The KH-11 would solve the problem by means of a revolutionary process: pictures would be digitized on board the satellite and then read out to a ground station with the proper radio equipment. The development cost for KH-11 was enormous for that time, around $1.8 billion. Colby played a key role in securing congressional funding for what would become the mainstay of America's satellite surveillance system.[27]

The principal obstacle to Colby's plans for making the CIA the go-to intelligence agency for policymakers, and rendering it more accountable and thus acceptable to Congress and the American people, was Henry Kissinger. The former professor's reach sometimes exceeded his grasp. His success was largely due to his ability to exploit Nixon's insecurities, his skill at manipulating the bureaucracy, his ability to cultivate the press (he spent roughly half of every day talking to journalists), the personal relationships he had established while running his Harvard international seminar, and his penchant for claiming credit for the achievements of others. Détente with the Soviet Union, for example, had begun during the last months of the Kennedy administration and continued apace under Johnson. But without Nixon's iron-clad anticommunist credentials and the courage to risk them, the openings to Communist China and the Soviet Union could never have taken place. Like virtually all of his predecessors, Kissinger was an Atlanticist: "The Atlantic area is the key to our security," he declared in a meeting with the Joint Chiefs. "If we think that by competing in the Third World we can do anything but bring about the destruction of the Western World, we are wrong."[28]

Another key to Kissinger's success as a bureaucratic politician and a diplomat was a talent for making the straightforward complex and convincing those around him that only he could master the situation. His monologues during National Security Council meetings and his conversations with Nixon and, later, President Gerald Ford were dense, domineering, and generally nonsensical; the latter discussions focused far more on personalities than on policy—so-and-so is a bastard, this faction is out to get us (me), you don't understand the situation, he would tell Ford. During Strategic Arms Limitation Treaty negotiations in Moscow in the fall of 1974, Kissinger sent Ford a long memorandum including such observations as "Brezhnev enjoys power. . . . Like many Russians, Brezhnev is a mixture of crudeness and warmth. . . . He eschews Khrushchevian excursions into profanity. Brezhnev prides himself on being a sportsman." Unlike his predecessors McGeorge Bundy and Walt Rostow—men who, like Kissinger, came to the National Security Council with broad learning but little experience—Kissinger did not limit himself to ensuring that the president was kept thoroughly informed on key issues. He saw himself much as William Henry Seward did during his early days as secretary of state in the Lincoln administration: as president for foreign policy. From 1969 through 1972, Nixon taught him otherwise, but with the coming of Watergate, Nixon's eventual resignation, and Ford's accession, Kissinger's dream came true. His meetings with Ford were sometimes painful, with the national security adviser cum secretary of state lecturing his chief as if he were an ignorant schoolboy.[29]

Kissinger was especially warm personally with those he was about to manipulate to his own advantage. When Kissinger and Colby breakfasted together on June 18, 1973, Henry was gracious, complimentary, even reassuring. The two recalled their meetings in Vietnam. Demonstrating some insight into the new DCI's personality, Kissinger observed that US support for the coup against Diem had been a mistake. "We should never overthrow friendly governments," he said. Thinking that Colby was a Helms protégé, Kissinger expressed his regret over the latter's firing. Why hadn't he and Helms come to him when the White House was pressuring the Agency over Watergate? Because Kissinger was not involved, and Langley did not want to involve him, Colby replied. The dance continued. The national security adviser expressed the hope that Watergate "had not shaken CIA so that it might become subject to the same kinds of leaks that occur in other agencies." Kissinger did not know how much the CIA knew—about the fact that he had ordered wiretaps on members of his own staff and select journalists, for example—but his role in the war on Allende, among other things, could be clearly documented. Colby said he did not think Watergate had undermined security at the Agency, although the purge that had begun under Schlesinger (at Kissinger's and Nixon's behest) was causing some problems. Kissinger assured the new DCI that he looked forward to a long and productive relationship with him. Several things had to be made clear, however; Kissinger was to be the CIA's sole conduit to the White House. Moreover, he did not want policy recommendations made through the manipulation of information. ("That our analysis clearly bring out alternative interpretations and possible developments and that he not be subjected to any consensus language," as Colby put it.) Finally, Kissinger made it clear that Sino-Soviet relations were and would remain his top intelligence priority.[30]

Unfortunately, Colby's determination to be a good soldier caused him initially to let down his guard with Kissinger. (In this he was not alone. Kissinger thoroughly charmed J. William Fulbright, chair of the Senate Foreign Relations Committee, convincing him that he, Henry, was the light contending with Nixon's dark.) "He [Colby] came in saying we must have the confidence of the White House," Jenonne Walker recalled, "[that] the most important thing is to have the confidence of the White House. He had no idea of what it would take to gain the confidence of the Kissinger White House, which was to be a toady." He would quickly learn.[31]

Soon after becoming DCI, Colby was approached by top-level analysts complaining that Kissinger's team was cutting him, and consequently them, out of the information loop. Colby investigated and found that their charges were true. "Kissinger's direct links to the Soviet hierarchy, his negotiations with the North Vietnamese and, of course, his dazzling dances through the Middle East," Colby wrote, "all were reported in the most secret of channels with no copies coming to Langley." Colby went to Kissinger and complained. He recalled that Henry then allowed him to see his latest cables, but that access proved to be temporary. Colby caved. "I confess that I agreed with his action," he said in *Honorable Men*. "After Marchetti and Agee, I felt I could no longer say that it was inconceivable that anyone in CIA would be guilty of an information leak." He subsequently told the analysts to do the best they could with what they had and let Kissinger and the president use the reports as they wished.[32]

Jenonne Walker recalled that the daily briefings Colby provided to the president "became tips on how to make policy work rather than prodding policymakers to reexamine the premises of policy." Appeasement was not always the best course with the academic turned policymaker. After Nelson Rockefeller became Gerald Ford's vice president in 1974, the CIA did an assessment of world opinion that was overwhelmingly positive. One report quoted a foreign journalist who observed that because of their prior relationship, Rockefeller's ascendancy would surely enhance Kissinger's influence. For some reason, the national security adviser took umbrage at this. Kissinger called Colby on the phone and read him the riot act. "Bill's secretary took notes on calls—and this was absolutely foul and vile: 'If you allow criticism of me, I will ruin you.'"[33]

Colby was further marginalized as an adviser and policymaker when Kissinger, as secretary of state, named one of his protégés, William Hyland, to head State's intelligence division. Hyland had been an expert on the Soviet Union in the CIA's Office of National Estimates before he became a National Security Council staffer under Kissinger. As his assistant for intelligence, Hyland accompanied Kissinger to key meetings in Moscow and elsewhere. In addition, Hyland was present at a number of top decisionmaking meetings at the White House from which Colby was excluded. A State

Department official subsequently observed that "when Kissinger says 'Bill is doing a great job,' he is usually referring to Hyland and not to Colby."[34]

The irony was that to the extent there was a philosophy behind Kissinger's foreign policy, Colby was in tune with it. The DCI recalled in his memoir that as he became more confident in his knowledge of the intricacies of the Strategic Arms Limitation Treaty, "I found myself increasingly supporting Kissinger's efforts to keep the process of détente moving ahead with the comparatively cooperative Russian leadership then in power, and increasingly impatient with the Pentagon's insistence that all concessions be made by the Soviets."[35]

From 1969 onward, SALT had been pummeled by hawks on the right, led by Secretary of Defense Melvin Laird, as well as by a group on the left led by Senator Henry "Scoop" Jackson (D-WA), the "senator from Boeing." Shortly after his accession to the post of secretary of defense in 1973, Schlesinger became a prisoner of the Pentagon and a hardliner on SALT. Kissinger and Ford wanted to keep the ball rolling in hopes of signing a new, more comprehensive arms control agreement and in the process enhancing Ford's chances of winning the 1976 presidential election. To this end, Kissinger arranged for a Ford-Brezhnev summit meeting on arms control in Vladivostok for November 1974.[36]

Alarmed, the Pentagon began leaking stories to the press to the effect that the Soviets were cheating on the first SALT agreements concluded in 1972. Schlesinger proposed a two- to three-year moratorium on arms control negotiations. "Schlesinger is the big problem," Kissinger told Ford a month before the meeting with Brezhnev. "To go the Schlesinger route on SALT is I think impossible." Time after time, the CIA came down on the side of a new arms agreement and Colby more broadly on the side of détente. To the enragement of hardliners, a CIA report declared that "it is extremely unlikely that during the next ten years the Soviets will conclude that they could launch an attack which would prevent devastating U.S. retaliation." In various NSC meetings, Colby assured participants that if the Soviets cheated, American intelligence would catch them out. In one of his few departures from mere reporting, Colby urged decisionmakers in the Ford administration "to expand the subject under debate from narrow weapons counts to the politics of over-all Soviet policy."[37]

If Henry Kissinger was Colby's chief external problem, James Jesus Angleton was his principal internal headache. Colby came to the top floor at

Langley initially determined to do what Schlesinger had not had the courage to do—either move the CI chief into a totally innocuous position or fire him. The new DCI's experiences with his old adversary only strengthened his convictions. "I spent several long sessions doing my best to follow his tortuous theories about the long arm of a powerful and wily KGB at work, over decades, placing its agents in the heart of allied and neutral nations and sending its false defectors to influence and undermine American policy," Colby later recalled. The evidence did not support the theory. The DCI was not the only one who thought the CI chief somewhat removed from reality. "I watched Angleton as he shuffled down the hall," wrote David Phillips, "6 feet tall, his shoulders stooped as if supporting an enormous incubus of secrets . . . extremely thin, he was once described as 'A man who looks like his ectoplasm has run out.'"[38]

Not only was CI wasting its time, the new director believed, it continued to do positive harm to the clandestine services. Colby learned that on the unsubstantiated testimony of Angleton's favorite defector—Golitsin—an up-and-coming CIA officer had been transferred to a dead-end post. Shortly thereafter, while touring Agency stations abroad, Colby was taken aside and told by the head of the French intelligence service that counter-intelligence had told him that the American chief of station in his country, David Murphy, was a Soviet agent. Colby checked and found that Murphy, who had previously run afoul of CI when he had been head of the Soviet desk in the Directorate of Plans, had been tarred with the same Golitsin/Angleton brush. Colby ordered that his record be expunged of all damaging material. To his later regret, he did not immediately fire Angleton; Schlesinger had already shrunk his empire, and CI had experienced enough turmoil, Colby decided. He later confided to friends and family his fear that, given what he believed to be Angleton's unstable mental condition, dismissal might compel him to take his own life.[39]

If he could not fire Angleton, Colby reasoned, at least he could take the Israeli account away from him. The Middle East had developed into a major US policy concern following the 1967 Arab-Israeli war and the nation's growing dependence on Arab oil. Angleton had developed deeply personal relationships with the founders of the state of Israel, and particularly with Mossad, its intelligence service. The Israeli account, Colby noted with disapproval, was among the most compartmentalized in the CIA. Informed that he was to turn over the account to the Middle East

Division, Angleton dug in his heels. He threatened and pleaded: the Israeli connection was too valuable, too sensitive to be handled by the normal CIA bureaucracy. Again, Colby relented, again to his immediate regret.[40]

What Henry Kissinger was good at was personal diplomacy, but he thought he was also a master of crisis management. In Kissinger's first major test in this area, Bill Colby let him down badly.

Most of the Arab world had severed formal ties with the United States in the aftermath of the 1967 Six-Day War, in which the Israelis, utilizing American arms and supplies, had crushed Soviet-supplied Egyptian and Syrian forces. During the fighting, the Israelis had seized and occupied portions of Egypt, Syria, and Jordan, including the Sinai Desert, the Gaza Strip, and the Golan Heights. In 1970, Egyptian president Gamal Abdel Nasser, the founder of modern Egypt, had died, elevating his little-known vice president, Anwar Sadat, to the highest office in the land. Sadat seemed more pragmatic than his predecessor, tilting toward the West and evicting 15,000 Soviet advisers. By 1973, however, he had become totally frustrated with his inability to regain any of the ground lost in 1967. With the Syrian government of Hafez al-Assad—which assumed a position of implacable hostility toward Israel—threatening Cairo's leadership of the Arab world, Sadat appealed one last time to Washington to pressure Israel into concessions. Preoccupied with Great Power diplomacy and then Watergate, the Nixon administration did nothing. Aided by financial assistance from Saudi Arabia, Egypt and Syria launched a surprise attack on October 6, Yom Kippur, the highest of Jewish holy days. The Israelis were caught completely off guard, losing a thousand soldiers the first day and five hundred tanks the first week.[41]

Along with Israeli military intelligence, the CIA had completely missed the boat. Indeed, the Agency seemed amazingly uninformed, almost devoid of assets in the region. Colby recalled that earlier in the year a State Department analysis had warned that Sadat's patience was wearing thin; Arab nationalists in Egypt and Syria were demanding Israeli blood. There was also word of Egyptian troop movements into the Sinai and a high state of alert within the Egyptian and Syrian militaries. But, as Colby put it, "soothing words came from diplomatic circles."[42]

A few hours before the outbreak of hostilities, the Agency had assured the White House: "Exercises are more realistic than usual. But there will be no war." Colby accepted full responsibility. "We predicted the day before the war broke out that it was not going to break out," he subsequently told reporters. He did not say so, but the United States was deceived in part because, via Angleton, the CIA's intelligence was Tel Aviv's intelligence, and Cairo and Damascus had succeeded completely in deceiving Israel. "The mistake lay in the evaluation of the intelligence data and not in the absence of accurate and reliable information," Lieutenant Israeli General Haim Bar-Lev stated. Perhaps if the allegedly "pro-Arab" Middle East Division had been in the loop, the CIA might not have missed the mark so badly. Finally, according to William Quandt, then an NSC staffer responsible for handling Arab-Israeli matters, Kissinger had been warned privately by Brezhnev that the Arabs were serious and that war was coming, but he had chosen not to share that information with Langley. "I fully understand the need for secrecy in our government on these delicate subjects," Colby subsequently wrote Kissinger, "although it is clear that the back channel in many instances is becoming the main channel, causing lost and even counterproductive motion, aside from anguish, among many not in the circuit." Kissinger and Angleton—birds of a feather, Colby must have thought.[43]

The Yom Kippur War quickly escalated into a Great Power confrontation. The conflict came at an especially critical point in the Watergate scandal, and a beleaguered, depressed, and often inebriated Nixon was frequently sidelined. Kissinger took charge. At first, the National Security Council hesitated, but then in the second week of the war it ordered a massive resupply of Israel's armed forces. The infusion of tanks and other equipment enabled the Israelis to regain lost ground in the Sinai and attack the Golan Heights. In response, the Arabs, led by Saudi Arabia, clapped a crippling oil embargo on the United States and its allies. Facing defeat, Egypt and Syria appealed to the Soviets to intervene. Moscow and Washington brokered a cease-fire agreement, but when Kissinger allowed the Israelis to drag their feet, Brezhnev threatened to send troops to the area.

On October 24, while he and Barbara were at dinner at a friend's house in Virginia, Colby's pocket vibrator went off. He called Langley and was told that Kissinger, who had just added secretary of state to his national security adviser title, wanted him to come to the State Department at once to consult on a matter of great urgency. The DCI arranged a ride home for Barbara and set out for the capital. At the State Department, he learned that he was to go to the "situation room" in the basement of the White House. Together with Admiral Thomas Moorer, chairman of the Joint Chiefs of Staff, he drove over.

Kissinger had assembled the national security team. Nixon was indisposed; rumor had it that he was so intoxicated that he could not get out of bed. Kissinger outlined the situation. The Soviets were threatening to send troops into the Middle East to enforce a cease-fire agreement. Colby, representing the intelligence community, was asked to say whether Moscow had the capability to intervene (yes), whether it would (possibly, but not likely, except in token numbers, which, however, would still raise the specter of Israelis fighting Soviets), and finally, whether it was in the process of doing so (Soviet transport aircraft were on alert but had not yet moved to pick up their assigned troop cargoes). Before the night had ended, Kissinger had US military forces worldwide placed on DefCon 3, an alert status two steps short of war. Colby was not asked his opinion about how to proceed with the Soviets. Brezhnev kept his cool, however, and the cease-fire went into effect.[44]

In the months that followed, Kissinger engaged in his famous "shuttle diplomacy," flying back and forth between the Middle Eastern capitals. He helped negotiate permanent cease-fire lines between Israel and Egypt as well as between Israel and Syria. He subsequently persuaded Sadat to restore diplomatic relations with the United States, and in March 1974 he convinced the Arabs to lift their oil embargo. *Newsweek*'s cover the week following featured Kissinger as a cartoon character clad in a Superman-style costume with the caption, "It's Super K!"[45]

With Super K flying high and the image of the CIA taking a beating, the Agency and Bill Colby needed a victory in the worst possible way. A prospective triumph appeared in the spring of 1974 in the guise of Project Azorian, a CIA-led effort to recover the remains of a sunken Soviet submarine equipped with nuclear missiles. It is a story straight out of "Mission Impossible," but with a few more loose ends.

It all began on March 1, 1968, when a Soviet Golf-class submarine, the K-129, carrying three SS-N-4 nuclear-armed ballistic missiles, sailed from the Soviet naval base on the Kamchatka Peninsula to take up its patrol station northeast of Hawaii. If war broke out, the K-129 was under orders to launch its missiles, each carrying a 1-megaton nuclear warhead, at targets on the West Coast of the United States. In mid-March, the K-129 suffered a catastrophic accident and sank 1,560 miles northwest of Hawaii with the loss of all hands. US naval vessels, relying on their sonar surveillance system (SOSUS), detected the underwater explosion that led to the submarine's demise, but waited to move in while a flotilla of Soviet salvage ships milled helplessly in the area. By June, the US Navy was able to report that the K-129, with its hull apparently intact, lay on the ocean floor some 16,500 feet below the surface of the Pacific.

Throughout late 1968 and early 1969, a task force consisting of DCI Helms, his science and technology director, and high-ranking Defense Department officials met to discuss the possibility of raising the Soviet submarine. If the United States could recover the vessel's nuclear warheads, and with it the SS-N-4 missile system and its accompanying documents and codes, intelligence would have a much improved baseline for estimating the current and future Soviet threat. There might be other treasures on board as well, documents, for example, that would provide important insights into Soviet command and control systems and certain aspects of the Kremlin's strategic attack doctrine.[46]

On July 1, 1969, the CIA established a Special Projects Staff within the Directorate of Science and Technology to manage "Project Azorian." It was clear to all that security had to be airtight; leaks would surely lead to Soviet diplomatic and even physical interference. An elaborate security system, code-named Jennifer, encased the operation in absolute need-to-know secrecy. Helms informed both Nixon and Kissinger, and the president signed off on the project.

The first and most important task facing the CIA team was to come up with a feasible engineering scheme. The K-129 was huge—1,750 tons. The team considered and then discarded plans to refloat the vessel. Finally, in October 1970, CIA engineers and specially cleared private-sector contractors determined that the only feasible way to salvage the submarine was to lift it off the seafloor by slipping a custom-made sling composed of metal straps—called "pipe-strings"—around the vessel, then slowly raising it to the surface using heavy-duty winches mounted on a ship built specifically for this purpose.[47] As the CIA team developed its concept, it also worked on a cover story—deep-sea mining. It just so happened that one of the state-of-the-art deep-sea mining vessels of the time was an American vessel, the *Glomar Challenger*, owned and operated by the Summa Corporation. The

Glomar Challenger was of approximately the right size and shape for the job; moreover, the Summa Corporation was a subsidiary of Hughes Tool Company, which was owned by Howard Hughes, the reclusive billionaire, who had done work previously for the CIA. Indeed, Langley had for years viewed Hughes as one of its major assets. He may have been a paranoid schizophrenic and a crook, but he was a patriot, and that's what mattered.

On November 4, 1972, the *Hughes Glomar Explorer*, a specially modified version of the *Challenger*, was launched with the usual fanfare, including speeches by officials of the Ocean Mining Division of the Hughes Tool Corporation. (Hughes himself, in the last stages of decline, was holed up in his Las Vegas penthouse dosing himself with narcotics and laxatives and watching movies sixteen hours a day.) On August 11, the vessel departed for the 12,700-mile voyage around the southern tip of South America, destined for its next station at Long Beach, California.[48]

Once ensconced on the West Coast, however, the *Glomar* commenced its transformation from a purely "white" status, that is, commercial, to "black," a top-secret intelligence ship. The huge vessel measured 618 feet in length (almost twice the size of the sunken sub) and was equipped with a giant "moon pool" in the ship's hold, with doors that could open downward to accept bulky cargo from the ocean floor. Suspended beneath the ship was a clawlike apparatus that would be used to grapple the sub's hull, and beneath that a submersible barge where the wreckage could be stored. One shipyard worker later described the *Glomar*'s control room as "something out of James Bond, Jules Verne, '1984', and '2001: A Space Odyssey.'"[49]

As the vessel's crew tested the specialized equipment and readied everything for departure, pressure mounted. The ship would have to cast off by the second week in June to accommodate the only "good-weather window" available to salvagers working the North Pacific, a time frame that stretched from July through early September. Technicians estimated that raising the sub would require fourteen to twenty-one days. On June 7, 1974, Nixon gave final approval for Azorian, and the ship arrived at the recovery site 1,560 miles northwest of Hawaii on July 4.[50]

By this point, Project Azorian was Bill Colby's. His enthusiasm for the salvage operation knew no bounds. The top-secret attempt to raise the K-129, the largest salvage operation in history, had it all—danger, suspense, cutting-edge technology, high risk, and the promise of a huge payoff. Indeed, Azorian was potentially comparable to Ultra and Magic, the famous

World War II decoding operations that had allowed the Allies to intercept and read Axis communications. The salvage operation just might be the intelligence coup he and the Agency needed to recover from the Yom Kippur fiasco. Colby had huddled with the mission director and ship's captain just prior to the *Glomar*'s departure in June. Both men reported that morale among the crew was sky-high. Colby observed that he knew what it was like to conduct operations in the field with the enemy at hand and no help in sight. He would trust the men onsite to make whatever decisions needed to be made and take any action necessary. Whatever the outcome, he would back them up.[51]

When the *Glomar* arrived onsite, seas were running 7 to 8 feet high, and the captain postponed operations until the 14th, when the weather subsided. On the 17th, the *Glomar* learned that a Soviet naval vessel, the *Chazhma*, was approaching the recovery site. Throughout the next ten days, the *Chazhma* and another Soviet vessel hovered, but they failed to detect the real purpose of the *Glomar*'s mission.[52]

On July 26, the operation command center reported contact with the ocean floor. Several hours later, television cameras mounted on the recovery apparatus captured the image of a silt-covered hull and conning tower; the K-129 had been found. By August 1, the pipe-string cradle had been fitted underneath the submarine and the *Glomar*'s winches began hauling the huge payload to the surface. Then, when the sub was about two-thirds of the way up, it broke apart; the rear two-thirds of the ship, including the conning tower and the missiles, dropped back to the seafloor. The crew of the *Glomar* braced for a possible nuclear explosion, but there was none.[53]

Colby and his lieutenants followed every development with anxious interest. "Carl Duckett, who was the deputy director for science and technology," Jenonne Walker recalled, "would brief the group on how many inches or centimeters it had come up since the last meeting. There was enormous excitement about the possibility of capturing the gadgets that were on that sub. I remember the disappointment and desolation when it broke in two." The remaining one-third, which included the K-129's nuclear-tipped torpedoes and a cache of documents, was pulled up into the well of the *Glomar*. Back in Washington, the 40 Committee directed Colby to make a try at recovering the remains of the Soviet sub during the window of opportunity that would come in 1975. Unfortunately for US intelligence, there would be no second chance.[54]

In the fall of 1973, Seymour Hersh, the investigative reporter for the *New York Times* who had won a Pulitzer Prize for uncovering the My Lai massacre, pried the outlines of the secret effort to salvage the Soviet sub out of a high administration official. In search of additional information, the journalist called Assistant Attorney General Laurence Silberman. "He asked me about the *Glomar Explorer*," Silberman later recalled. "I knew nothing about it and called Colby. His response was, 'Oh shit!'" Colby told Silberman that any publicity about the Soviet submarine salvage operation would endanger one of the greatest intelligence coups in American history. Silberman got back to Hersh, who agreed to hold publication on condition that Colby meet and give him the full picture. At a White House meeting, the DCI asked permission to cooperate with the journalist. "Hersh has a story about the Soviet submarine," he told Kissinger, Secretary of Defense Schlesinger, and Admiral Thomas Moorer. "I would like to level with him and appeal to his patriotism." Kissinger's response was a terse no.[55]

Colby then met with Agency lawyers and his science advisers to plan a course of action. To hell with Henry, they decided; the DCI should take Hersh's deal. On February 1, 1974, Colby met with the journalist at the offices of the *New York Times* and briefed him on Azorian. "I went to see Seymour Hersh," Colby subsequently told White House aide Fred Buzhardt. "Henry thought I was crazy, but I had to." Hersh, who originally viewed the story as a study in CIA and Pentagon waste, was skeptical at first. He thought all the cloak-and-dagger stuff was just a cover. In the days that followed, Hersh and his superiors at the *Times* came around. But the journalist warned Colby that if he had gotten wind of Azorian, it would not be long before other enterprising reporters did, too.[56]

It then came to light that early on the morning of June 5, while the *Glomar Explorer* was making final preparations to depart Long Beach for a second try at salvaging the Soviet sub, a team of burglars had broken into the Los Angeles offices of Summa Corporation. According to the night watchman, who was bound and gagged, the intruders seemed to know what they were looking for. In the end, they departed carrying four footlockers of documents and an estimated $68,000 in cash. Summa executives subsequently informed Colby that among the things taken was a memo outlining negotiations between the Agency and the Hughes Corporation over construction of the *Glomar Explorer* and describing the scheme to raise the K-129.[57]

The Summa Corporation burglars might try to market the *Glomar Explorer* documents to one or more media outlets, but Colby comforted himself with the thought that it was going to be difficult to convince a reputable newspaper or magazine to publish a story based on them. But on Friday afternoon, February 7, 1975, the late edition of the *Los Angeles Times* carried banner headlines: "US Reported After Russian Submarine? Sunken Ship Deal by CIA, Hughes Told." The story reported that Hughes had contracted with the CIA to raise a sunken Soviet submarine "from the North Atlantic." It described the *Glomar Explorer* in a few sentences and then revealed that proof of the existence of "Project Jennifer" was included in the material stolen from Hughes's Romaine Street offices. With this, Colby leaped into action. The DCI had one of his West Coast operatives contact the publisher of the *Los Angeles Times*, who immediately expressed regret, had the story relegated to page eighteen in the second edition, and ordered his reporters not to write anything further. Colby managed to have a follow-up story published in the *New York Times* on the 8th buried on page thirty.[58]

But hadn't the damage already been done, hadn't the Kremlin been tipped off, and therefore hadn't plans to raise the remainder of the Soviet vessel, scheduled for the summer of 1975, been rendered moot? Perhaps not. Colby recalled that during World War II, the *Chicago Tribune* had reported in banner headlines that US Naval Intelligence had broken the Japanese diplomatic and military code. President Roosevelt had been beside himself with anger and anxiety, but the Japanese kept using the same code, and the Americans kept intercepting and deciphering their top-secret messages. It could have been that Tokyo simply did not get wind of the story; more probably, the Japanese High Command believed the article a ruse, assuming that no country would ever permit a secret of such magnitude to be published by a member of its national media.[59]

With the *Glomar Explorer*'s follow-up voyage just five months away, the director of the CIA waged an increasingly frantic war to keep the Soviet sub story out of print and off the airwaves. Finally, however, the dam broke. On the morning of March 18, 1975, Colby succeeded in persuading National Public Radio to hold its water. But that afternoon, he learned that syndicated columnist Jack Anderson was about to go public with news of Azorian. Colby called Anderson and, par for the course, appealed to his patriotism. Anderson was unmoved and proceeded to discuss the *Glomar*

Explorer on his radio program that evening, focusing on the Hughes connection. The next day the *New York Times* went with Hersh's full story. "C.I.A Salvage Ship Brought Up Part of Soviet Sub Lost in 1968, Failed to Raise Atom Missiles," the headline read.[60]

A flotilla of Soviet vessels rushed to the salvage site and parked itself there more or less permanently. Phase II of Project Azorian was canceled. The Ford administration debated how to react. Somewhat surprisingly, Colby argued for an absolute "no comment." He reminded Ford and Kissinger that during the U-2 crisis in 1960, it was Eisenhower's public admission that Gary Powers had been on a spy mission over the Soviet Union that had so angered Khrushchev and caused him to call off the Paris summit. "I think we should not put the Soviet Union under such pressure to respond," the DCI advised. And so, silence it was. Colby proved correct. Moscow was not forced to express outrage and wave the flag; détente continued uninterrupted.[61]

It was indicative of the widespread mistrust of the CIA that many journalists and public intellectuals were convinced that ulterior motives lay behind Colby's attempted cover-up. Hersh and Anderson continued to think that Jennifer/Azorian was not so much a case of espionage but a matter of government pork. Victor Marchetti told the *Village Voice* that the DCI had deliberately leaked the *Glomar* story in an effort to take some of the tarnish off of the Agency's image. "Project Jennifer was a put up job," he said. "I think the CIA leaked that story. They've been getting so much bad publicity. . . . Colby's a very clever man."[62]

A footnote to Project Azorian: The next year, Howard Hughes died. One of his chief mourners was Jim Angleton. "Howard Hughes!" he exclaimed to *Time* magazine. "Where his country's interests were concerned, no man knew his target better. We were fortunate to have him."[63]

17

REVELATIONS

B eing DCI changed Bill Colby; he had run large, complex operations before—the Saigon station, the Far East Division, CORDS, and Plans/Operations—but now he was a public figure who was expected to be on top of world events and a person of gravitas within and without the administration. He was a player on the Washington stage whether he liked it or not. Increasingly he did.

When Colby was not out of the country on an inspection tour or meeting with the head of a friendly foreign intelligence service, his day resembled that of a major cabinet officer. At 6:30 A.M. the alarm went off and he climbed out of bed. After retrieving and reading the *Washington Post*, it was calisthenics and a light breakfast. At 8:00 his driver and security officer picked him up in a dark blue, armor-plated Chevrolet. On the drive to the office he read the *New York Times* and the *Daily Intelligencer*. Colby wanted to know by the time he got to Langley what was going on in the world that would be of particular interest to the Agency and how American intelligence was being treated in that day's columns. At 8:25 A.M., his auto dropped him off; the director walked through the marble entrance hall and took his private elevator to the seventh floor. Huddling briefly with his secretary, Barbara Pindar, and his assistant, Jenonne Walker, he then walked into the conference room at 9:00 sharp to meet with his principal deputies. At 10:00, it was the turn of the US Intelligence Board, which he chaired. Frequently, before going to lunch in the general dining room, he would award a medal to some deserving operator just out of the bush in Southeast Asia or Africa. From 1:30 to 3:00, Colby might prepare for a National Security Council meeting in the White House basement; there, he would brief Kissinger and the other members of the national security team on the ongoing North Vietnamese buildup in South Vietnam or some other topic. Then it was back through rush-hour traffic to Langley, where he spent a couple of hours on crisis management. At 7:00 it was home to a quiet dinner and more document perusal, or to get dressed for one of Washington's ubiquitous dinners or receptions.[1]

By the fall of 1974, Colby's chief preoccupation had become defense of his beloved CIA from its growing number of critics. With President Richard Nixon's resignation in August over charges that he had obstructed justice in the Watergate affair, many Americans concluded that the government itself was not to be trusted. But what had gone wrong? There was a constitution, one of the most respected in the world; the United States, for better or worse, was a democracy. There must be an evil force working outside the grid, unseen and unaccountable to anyone. Perhaps what was wrong with American politics and foreign policy was that it was controlled by that "invisible government" that David Wise had talked about. The onslaught that had begun with the 1967 *Ramparts* article exposing CIA front organizations, then the Phoenix probe and Watergate, would continue with a massive congressional and media examination of America's role in the rise and fall of Salvador Allende.

In the spring of 1973, while Colby was still deputy director for plans, Senator Frank Church (D-ID), a key figure in the congressional anti–Vietnam War movement, had launched an investigation of multinational corporations. Chairing a special subcommittee of the Senate Foreign Relations Committee, Church and his team of investigators uncovered the fact that International Telephone and Telegraph had played a role in aiding opponents of Salvador Allende in Chile's 1970 presidential elections. The Senate Foreign Relations Committee, under J. William Fulbright, had long had its knife sharpened for what it considered illegal and immoral interference by the United States in the political affairs of other nations. Indeed, in 1970, as Richard Helms was leaving after testifying before the committee, Fulbright had pulled him aside and said, "Dick, if I catch you trying to upset the Chilean election, I will get up on the Senate floor and blow the operation."[2] DCI Schlesinger did not appear before the Church subcommittee, but he had testified to the CIA's oversight committees on the relationship between the Agency and ITT during the 1970 Chilean elections. He omitted any discussion of Track II, which, among other things, referred explicitly to US support for a coup. The previous month, Helms, during his confirmation hearings to be ambassador to Iran, had been asked by members of the Fulbright committee about the CIA's role in Chilean politics. Stuart Symington, who was a member of both the Senate Armed Services Committee, a CIA oversight body, and the Foreign Relations Committee, put the questions:

> "Did you try in the Central Intelligence Agency to overthrow the government of Chile?"
> "No, sir," Helms replied.
> "Did you have any money passed to opponents of Allende?"
> "No, sir."
> "So the stories you were in that war are wrong?"
> "Yes, sir."[3]

Later, Helms would recall that in authorizing Track II, Nixon had ordered him to keep it secret from anyone not directly involved, including the secretaries of state and defense. Perhaps so, but the CIA had clearly supplied funds to opposition parties under Track I, the plan to prevent Allende's election. Depending on one's interpretation of the law, Helms had perjured himself.

There matters rested until Allende's bloody overthrow on September 11, 1973. Allende's ouster, as luck would have it, occurred during Kissinger's confirmation hearings to be secretary of state. Fulbright and his colleagues asked him about Chile. "The C.I.A had nothing to do with the coup, to the best of my knowledge and belief," he said, "and I only put in that qualification in case some madman appears down there who without instructions talked to somebody. I have absolutely no reason to suppose it."[4]

At this point, Representative Michael J. Harrington (D-MA), long a critic of US foreign policy in Central and South America, decided to make the CIA and Chile his personal crusade. Convinced that the Agency, in alliance with multinational corporations and the Chilean military, had intervened to overthrow a democratically elected government, he persuaded the Subcommittee on Inter-American Affairs to hold hearings on Chile. Colby testified but would not discuss CIA activities in Chile. Frustrated, Harrington persuaded Lucien Nedzi, chair of the Intelligence Subcommittee of the House Armed Services Committee (a CIA oversight body), to hold full hearings on US activity in Chile. Nedzi, who knew of Track I, was not enthusiastic, but he felt he had no choice. On April 22, 1974, Colby appeared before the Nedzi subcommittee in secret session. Harrington was not present. The DCI began with Track I, revealing that the United States, acting through the CIA, had funneled $8 million to Allende's opponents and, following Allende's election, had worked to make conditions in Chile so uncomfortable that its citizenry would rebel against the new president. Colby made it clear that the CIA was not acting on its own but at the behest of President Nixon and the 40 Committee chaired by Henry Kissinger.

On his way to the hearing, Colby had debated what to do about Track II, which linked the United States to a coup attempt. Nixon had ordered Helms and the Agency to hold Track II in strictest confidence, but Colby had given assurances during his confirmation hearings that he would be absolutely frank with the oversight committees. "I considered it my responsibility to keep them informed," he wrote in *Honorable Men*, "even about CIA matters that they would have no way of even suspecting, and therefore would be unable to question me on."[5] Thus, after the formal hearings were over, Colby took Nedzi and the committee counsel aside and told them about Track II. The chairman, taken aback, paused and then demanded assurances that Track II had ended after Allende's election and that the Agency had had nothing to do with the coup that overthrew him in 1973. Colby gladly gave those assurances, and both men hoped that the matter had ended there.

Harrington had planned well. Taking advantage of the long-standing House rule that entitled any member to review the transcript of any committee of the House, he demanded to see Colby's secret testimony. Grudgingly, Nedzi agreed. On September 7, Harrington summarized Colby's testimony in a letter to Representative Thomas E. Morgan (D-PA), chair of the House Foreign Affairs Committee, and offered it as proof that the CIA had indeed worked to "destabilize" the Allende regime. Harrington subsequently had his letter published in the *Congressional Record*.[6]

Smelling new blood in the water, reporter Seymour Hersh launched himself. In September and October, claiming to have obtained the minutes of 40 Committee meetings, he wrote a series of articles in the *New York Times* on the CIA and Chile. This was the first the American public had ever heard of the 40 Committee's existence. With Kissinger once again threatened by the undertow of negative media coverage, his team at the

State Department pressured Colby to deny everything. Instead, the DCI gave an exclusive interview to *Time* magazine writer Strobe Talbott, admitting US interference in Chilean affairs but justifying it in the context of the Cold War.[7]

The previous summer, Colby had agreed to participate in a conference entitled "The Central Intelligence Agency and Covert Actions," sponsored by the Center for National Security Studies. The center was dedicated to uncovering the secrets of a presumably nefarious national security state; it was, among other things, an instrument of the New Left, and particularly the anti–Vietnam War movement. Colby was aware that he would be Daniel before the lions, but he had, "somewhat defiantly," as he put it, decided to make an appearance at the coliseum. Senator James Abourezk (D-SD) chaired the meeting, which was held in the cavernous congressional conference room on September 13. Other panelists included Daniel Ellsberg; Fred Branfman, a leading critic of the US air war in Indochina; David Wise; historian Richard Barnet; Congressman Harrington; and former CIA covert operative Paul Sakwa. Sakwa, whom journalist Neil Sheehan described as "nuts," had long believed that Desmond FitzGerald, Colby, and others were fathers of a scheme to deepen the crisis in Vietnam in order to provoke a showdown with Communist China. The audience ran the gamut of the antiwar movement, from hippies, Vietnam Veterans Against the War, and Quakers to Black Power advocates.[8]

The DCI led off with a short speech justifying the CIA and covert action from World War II through the Chilean election. He observed that thus far, the US clandestine services had succeeded in preventing World War III, implying that if there had been a CIA following the Great War, World War II might have been avoided. He then took questions. In response to a query from Harrington, Colby declared that the CIA had had nothing to do with the coup in Santiago. "We did look forward to a change in government," he said, an observation met with laughter and derisive hoots. "How many did you kill in Phoenix?" a young woman shouted from the audience. "I'd like to answer that," Colby said, "I didn't kill any." Another collective guffaw. He persisted: "The Phoenix program was designed and started in about 1968 in order to bring some degree of order and regularity to a very unpleasant, nasty war that had preceded it." Colby was asked if the CIA was above the law: Should Agency operatives be held to US statutes for actions taken outside the country? "There are a lot of illegal things done overseas by our standards," he retorted.[9]

Ellsberg was next. He questioned his old counterinsurgency colleague about the break-in to his psychiatrist's office. Why had the CIA destroyed taped conversations dealing with the incident? Standard procedure, the DCI replied. What about the "tiger cages" on Con Son Island? The Agency had moved expeditiously to get the South Vietnamese to end mistreatment at the facility, Colby replied. More laughter and catcalls. "What exactly was the morality of torture?" Branfman asked. "My morality is to try to help produce a better world," the former Jedburgh declared, "and not to insist on a perfect one, Mr. Branfman." At this point Branfman's wife, whom Sheehan described as "a skinny Vietnamese bitch," rose and began abusing Colby in "her strident, Vietnamese market-place voice." Another panelist: "The techniques of covert action include blackmail, burglary, subversion, and assassination. . . . Are these techniques justified in the name of national security?" Colby was unequivocal: "I think the use of an atomic bomb is justified in the interests of national security." Stunned silence. The gathering closed with another denunciation from an audience member: "You're not only a liar, you're not only a racist, you're a Nazi war criminal."[10]

That the director of the Central Intelligence Agency should be treated in such a manner in a public venue was stunning, almost as astounding as Colby's decision to volunteer for such punishment. Sheehan, who was as close to an unbiased observer as there was in the conference room, painted a picture of the DCI under fire and speculated on his motives: "Sharp features with a slightly receding hairline, piercing grey eyes, pursed lips and folded hands." Dressed in a light gray suit and a pink and red regimental tie, the DCI had remained the picture of composure, his hands trembling only slightly during one of the Phoenix queries. His facial expressions alternated between bemusement and sincerity. "He is really tough, extraordinarily tough," Sheehan wrote, "to stand up to that group and keep his cool. . . . There was an incredible venting of rage in that room, particularly from the young people, who really wanted Colby's blood." Sheehan and his wife, Susan, also a writer, speculated that Colby felt guilt over what he had been involved in, particularly the Phoenix program, and as a good Catholic was seeking redemptive punishment. Marcus Raskin, who, along with Barnet, had founded the Institute for Policy Studies, disagreed. "He's a cold-blooded killer," he told Sheehan. "Just look at those eyes."[11]

In the end, Sheehan returned to his thought of Colby as the American Felix Dzerzhinsky, the notorious founder and first head of the Soviet intelligence apparatus. Anything was permissible as long as it was authorized by the "duly constituted authority." Colby would not have disagreed with this last observation, but he would have pointed out that the duly constituted authorities he and Dzerzhinsky were serving were vastly different. And, in truth, Colby's actions in the ensuing days were designed to affirm the rule of law and the intelligence community's commitment to a liberal democratic system (in the United States, if not abroad), even above a White House determined to protect itself at all costs or a cold war against the Kremlin.

Chile continued to dominate headlines, columns, and editorials. The *Christian Science Monitor* in September 1974 accused the Agency of a double standard, acting against governments it did not like—usually left-leaning regimes such as Allende's—but abiding and even aiding governments it did like—generally rightwing regimes such as those in Greece and South Korea. The question is, columnist Tom Wicker declared in the *New York Times*, whether an administration had "the constitutional authority to order taxpayers' money spent for clandestine warfare against the legitimate government of a sovereign country." Daniel Schorr, a reporter who had covered Watergate for CBS, launched his own investigation, which led to a two-part television documentary on Chile, Allende, and the CIA. At a news conference on September 16, President Ford affirmed that CIA activities in Chile had been authorized by the White House; a few days later, he and Kissinger briefed top congressional leaders on Tracks I and II. Congress was not appeased. It subsequently enacted the Hughes-Ryan Amendment to the Foreign Assistance Act, stipulating that no funds could be expended on a covert operation unless the president declared it vital to the national security and the activity was vetted in advance before no fewer than eight congressional committees.[12]

The day after Ford's press conference, the staff of the Senate Foreign Relations Committee recommended that perjury charges be brought against Richard Helms for testimony given during his confirmation hearings. The principal piece of evidence in any trial would be Colby's testimony before the Nedzi Committee, subsequently made public by Harrington, as to the existence of Track II. The ball was in Colby's court. The issue, he recalled, "was about as welcome on my desk as a cobra, and as hard to handle. . . . Helms was a totally loyal servant of his President and his intelligence profession had manfully tried to keep the secret he had been directed to keep." But secrecy would not be possible. According to Colby, a "middle-grade officer" in the Agency, reacting to the Schlesinger-Colby directive that all "questionable" matters be reported, observed in a memo to the director that Helms might in fact have committed perjury and recommended an investigation. What Colby did not say in his memoirs was that the press would inevitably compare Colby's and Helms's testimonies and demand to know which one of them was lying. Colby's reputation and that of his Agency were on the line. Here was that question again: Was the CIA solely an instrument of the White House, or was it part of the executive branch and subject to constitutional checks and balances?[13]

Implicitly acknowledging that he was a party to the dispute, Colby had the Agency's inspector general put together a three-person panel to examine the record and submit a finding as to whether Helms had lied before a congressional committee. In the end, the panel could not decide, but advised the DCI that he was legally bound to turn the matter over to the Justice Department. Colby resisted; he recalled a 1954 "agreement" between the CIA and Justice to the effect that the Agency, and the Agency alone, would decide if and when any of its personnel—past or present—would be made available to the attorney general for prosecution. Both agencies had agreed that the overriding interest was national security, the need to cover trails from which intelligence sources and methods might be gleaned. If Colby stonewalled on this, the inspector general's panel advised, the matter would surely leak to the press, and the CIA would be accused of a cover-up. Reluctantly, Colby made an appointment to see Acting Attorney General Laurence Silberman.

The DCI began the meeting by bringing up the 1954 arrangement. "Come on, Bill," Silberman said. "You're a lawyer. You know better than that. I don't care what the past arrangements might have been. In this day and age, there's no way in the world the CIA is going to be given the extralegal privilege of deciding unilaterally which of its employees should be prosecuted and who shouldn't. . . . So come on now, let's get down to cases. Who or what are you talking about?" The next day, Colby had the files on Track II and Helms's testimony delivered to Justice. A year later, while he was ambassador to Iran, Helms pleaded "no contest" to a misdemeanor charge that he had misled Congress.[14]

Colby's decision to turn the Helms matter over to the attorney general split the CIA. Helms's followers—and they were still legion—viewed Colby's decision to go to Justice as nothing less than a betrayal of a mentor and colleague, and more important, a betrayal of the culture of secrecy. While the case against Helms was still under internal Agency review, one Directorate of Plans officer had written, "This mongoloid baby should have been strangled in its cradle," rather than being allowed to grow into "an irresponsible, uncontrolled and uncontrollable monster that threatens the integrity of the clandestine services." Another, referring to Colby's Catholicism, urged that the case be filed and forgotten, because it "has turned into a moralistic crusade to expiate our sins and exorcise the Satan from within the CIA corpus by sacrificing an as yet unknown number of officers." One thing was certain: from that point on, Richard Helms was Colby's sworn enemy, an enemy with influential friends.[15]

On the evening of February 1, 1975, journalist and former CIA officer Tom Braden hosted a dinner party. Among those present were Averell Harriman, Stuart Symington, Robert McNamara, Henry Kissinger, and celebrity journalist Barbara Walters. According to another guest, columnist William Greider, the group had assembled "to cheer up an old friend, a comrade wounded by recent events." The person in question was Richard Helms, whom Henry Kissinger pronounced an "honorable man." Kissinger added a few words of rebuke for Colby, who was not there. Greider compared the two DCIs in an article written shortly thereafter: "When old colleagues describe Helms, he emerges as a man of deeper intellect, more flexible, more cynical, quite skilled at crossing the sliding sands of Washington's bureaucratic struggles. Colby is more obvious, more straightforward and even moralistic, according to friends and non-friends. Helms is the urbanity of the Chevy Chase Club; Colby is the Boy Scouts in Springfield, Va, where he lives." (Greider was incorrect on that point at least.)[16]

Colby later wrote that he had not only had no choice but was proud of what he had done. "I was persuaded [by the inspector general's three-person panel] that I had no right to make a decision on this matter alone or to preempt a ruling by the proper authorities, whether the dangers to intelligence security would prevent prosecution or investigation in the case. And I am glad they did, requiring me to uphold my oath to the Constitution and really demonstrate that a new and American intelligence [community] had been born, not just talked about." As Colby was to learn, the labor pains had just begun.[17]

Meanwhile, the ongoing Colby-Angleton feud had come to a head. A few months after the Yom Kippur War, the DCI had paid a visit to the Middle East. At Kissinger's request, he had stayed away from East Jerusalem for fear of alienating the Arabs who disputed Israeli claims to the area. Privately, Angleton, who continued to view the Agency's Middle East Division as pro-Arab, rebuked Colby for giving in to Kissinger.

In late August 1974, a counterintelligence officer submitted a report to the CIA's security office in which an Agency informant fingered Angleton himself as a Soviet spy. According to the informant's story, Golitsin was a Soviet agent who had been dispatched to act as Angleton's case officer and to question the bona fides of subsequent Soviet defectors. Colby put together a panel under former deputy director Bronson Tweedy to investigate. Tweedy and his colleagues gave the counterintelligence chief a clean bill of health, but to Colby, the episode was just one more proof of the bizarre atmosphere that prevailed in the counterintelligence branch.[18]

On the morning of December 17, the DCI summoned Angleton to his office. He was relieving him of his duties both as Israeli liaison and chief of counterintelligence, he said. Colby offered Angleton "separate status" within the Agency, in which he could offer advice and act as a consultant, but without operational or policy control. Angleton protested—there was a "big fight," he later told a friend. Colby told him to take a couple of days to think about it and dismissed him.[19]

The day following his encounter with Angleton, Colby received a call from Seymour Hersh. "I've got a story bigger than My Lai," he told the DCI, adding that he needed to see him. Colby acceded and in the meeting that ensued, the reporter said he had uncovered a "massive effort" by the Agency to spy on the anti–Vietnam War movement, including wiretaps, break-ins, mail intercepts, and surveillances of American citizens. Colby later recalled that he was shocked but not surprised. Indeed, the call on December 18 was just the culmination of a drama that had begun two weeks earlier.

Hersh had telephoned Colby on December 9 to tell him he was working on a story on past illegal CIA operations within the United States. "I think if I crapped around long enough [on this] I could come up with a half-assed story," he said. "I understand there is nothing [earth-shaking]," Hersh

went on, that they were routine activities that were curtailed. Colby confided to Hersh that he had instructed his officers some months earlier to
report any instances of such illegalities or questionable activities: "We sent
out a memo to our people saying 'If you hear anything tell us.' We got a
few blips." Later that same day, Colby had informed House oversight committee chair Nedzi of the conversation, but Hersh, it seemed, had already
called the congressman.[20]

A week later, on December 16, former deputy director for operations
Tom Karamessines told Colby that he, too, had heard from Hersh, who
claimed that he could prove that both Helms and Angleton had engaged
in domestic operations in violation of the Fourth Amendment, which guaranteed citizens protection against "unreasonable searches and seizures."
The next day, Deputy Director for Operations William Nelson phoned to
tell his boss that Hersh had found out about the "family jewels" and was
about to hang Angleton. On the afternoon of the 18th, following the first
conversation of the day between Hersh and Colby, Hersh called again and
left a phone message for the DCI: "I figure I have about one-tenth of one
percent of the story which you and I talked about which is more than
enough. . . . I want to write it this weekend. I am willing to trade with you.
I will trade you Jim Angleton for fourteen files of my choice. I will be in
my office at the *Times* in 30 minutes."[21] The story linking counterintelligence to Operation MH/Chaos would not only further embarrass the CIA
but also lead to Angleton's ouster. Colby, Hersh reasoned, must have understood that a disgruntled officer, forced out of the CIA in disgrace, would
be more dangerous than one kept in-house under watch. This was particularly true of Angleton, who knew everything. From his point of view,
Hersh must have seen an advantage in Angleton's staying on; he could
blackmail him over MH/Chaos for more Agency secrets. Apparently, the
journalist was unaware that Colby hoped to get rid of Angleton.

In a conversation with Lucien Nedzi on December 19, Colby learned
that Angleton had confirmed the existence of the family jewels to Hersh.
"I talked with him [Hersh] a short time ago," Nedzi said. "Who is Jim
Angleton?"

> "He is the head of our counterintelligence," Colby replied. "He is kind
> of a legendary character. He has been around for 150 years or so. He
> is a very spooky guy. His reputation is one of total secrecy and no one

knows what he is doing. . . . He is a little bit out of date in terms of seeing Soviets under every bush."

"What is he doing talking to Hersh?" Nedzi asked.

"I didn't think he was."

"Sy showed me notes of what he said and claims he [Angleton] was drunk."

"You catch me twelve hours ahead of an unpleasant chore of talking to him about a substantial change of his [Angleton's] responsibilities."

"The problem that occurs to me right now is here is a guy who is trying to expose the Agency, and all of a sudden he gets sacked."

"Yes, I think what I'll do is talk to Hersh[,] . . . but brace myself for whatever he does write and be prepared to answer whatever comes out. Meanwhile, I have to proceed on the Angleton thing anyway. I wanted to do it about six to eight months ago and was dissuaded out of human compassion."[22]

The DCI later wrote that he had feelings of both trust and obligation toward Hersh. The journalist had gotten wind of the *Glomar Explorer* adventure early on, but after Colby implored him, he had sat on the story. Indeed, he was still sitting on the story. Jack Anderson's broadcast on the secret mission to raise the Soviet sub, and Hersh's follow-up article in the *Times*, would not appear until March 18 and 19, 1975. Colby must have decided that continued secrecy for the as-yet-to-be-revealed Project Azorian trumped confirming Hersh's impending story about the CIA and domestic spying. The best he could do was to try to get Hersh to put his story in context. "Look, Sy," Colby said during their December 20 meeting, "what you're onto here are two very separate and distinct matters that you've gotten mixed up and distorted." There was the effort at the behest of the White House to uncover foreign influence in the antiwar movement, but after none was discovered, the operation was terminated. Mail intercepts and surveillance of American citizens had to do with counterespionage against the Soviet Union. Overzealous agents may have overstepped the bounds of the Agency's charter, but there had been no further incidents since Schlesinger's orders of 1973, orders that had been reiterated by Colby after he became DCI.[23]

Later that same day, Colby called Angleton to his office and told him that Sy Hersh was going to go public with the Operation MH/Chaos story and that counterintelligence would be singled out. "This story is going to be tough to handle," the DCI said. "We've talked about you leaving before. You will now leave, period." Colby was not above a little turning of the knife: "I told him that no one in the world would believe his leaving his job was not the result of the article. But both Jim and I would know it was not, which was the important part to me." Peter Wright, MI-6 liaison with the counterintelligence branch, was waiting for Angleton in the latter's office. His face tinged with a gray-blue pallor when he returned, Angleton cried, "Peter, I've just been fired."[24]

When the story broke, the press rushed to Angleton's house in North Arlington. Daniel Schorr was first to ring the doorbell. "A groggy-looking man in pajamas opens the door," Schorr later wrote of the encounter. The journalist asked to come in, and Angleton admitted him. "It looks like the home of a somewhat disorderly professor," Schorr recalled, "books in many languages, memorabilia of Italy and Israel, a worn rug, pictures of wife and two sons. But no preparations for Christmas." For the next four hours, Angleton rambled on about the fiction of a divided communist camp. Holding up a picture of Yasser Arafat at Lenin's tomb, the former counterintelligence guru cited it as proof that the Palestinian leader was a KGB colonel. He then related the details of his firing.

Later that day, dressed in his black overcoat and fedora, Angleton emerged from his house to face the cameras and answer questions. He was so unsteady that he appeared drunk, Schorr wrote, but the journalist thought Angleton was shell-shocked rather than inebriated. Whatever the case, James Jesus Angleton would regain his balance. Bill Colby's longtime adversary had become a bitter and dangerous enemy.[25]

Meanwhile, Colby knew that Hersh was going to publish a major story on the family jewels, but he did not know how extensive it would be. The reporter's ability to acquire information was uncanny. On December 21, Larry Silberman called the DCI: the acting attorney general recalled that Hersh had told him that Colby was coming to see him, Silberman, about Helms's possible perjury even before the meeting took place. "I am absolutely staggered that he knew that I was going to see you," Colby said. "The SOB has sources that are absolutely beyond comparison." Jenonne Walker, Colby's assistant, later recalled that Hersh seemed to know more about the Agency's secrets than she and Colby did.[26]

The headline in the *New York Times* morning edition for Sunday, December 22, read: "Huge CIA Operation Reported in U.S. Against Anti-War

Forces, Other Dissidents in Nixon Years." The story described CIA activities undertaken in the course of MH/Chaos and cited various scholars on their legality or illegality. Hersh informed his readers that the contents of the story had been confirmed by a "high government official," and that MH/Chaos had been lodged in counterintelligence.

Paul Colby later recalled that his dad had decided to spend that Sunday at home with the family. It was snowing, and father and son walked to the corner to get the *Times* from a vending machine. Bill opened the paper, read the front page, folded the paper, and carried on the rest of the day as if nothing had happened. Paul told the story to demonstrate his father's calm under fire, but he may have had reason to be calm. The Hersh story had given him cover in his firing of Angleton, and it undercut to a degree Kissinger's ongoing effort to get Colby and the CIA to take the fall for various misdeeds of the Nixon administration.[27]

In his memoir, Colby recalled that he did not immediately foresee the huge flap that the Hersh article would cause. The Agency had been the subject of negative headlines before, and the ensuing outcry had quickly died down. Taken in context, the CIA's misdeeds were few and far between. If the Agency avoided the mistakes of the Watergate scandal—seeking to "distance" itself from the situation, thus arousing suspicion and eliciting charges of a cover-up—the crisis would pass. Colby decided to speak frankly and openly to Congress and the media (excluding sources and methods) and reiterate that nothing akin to MH/Chaos was going on at present—indeed such things had been explicitly prohibited by the Agency's leadership—and would not transpire in the future. And in fact, in the two or three days following publication of the Hersh article, the media hesitated. There were no substantive follow-up stories on Monday or Tuesday, and when Hersh published again it was largely to quote his own article: "A *New York Times* story reported . . ."[28]

Hersh had won a Pulitzer for his story on My Lai, but he had an unsavory reputation. "Hersh's technique is to wear down reluctant sources through tenacious pursuit by phone—often badgering, terrorizing, insulting," wrote a colleague. "I don't know of anyone other than Don Rickles who can be as disgustingly insulting, yet have the right touch for getting someone to respond." He did not feel constrained, as did some of his colleagues, by concerns about national security. "He was at a seminar at the Naval War College," CIA officer David Phillips recalled, "and one of the guys stood up and said, 'Mr. Hersh, if it were wartime and you found out about a troop ship sailing out of New York, would you break that information?' He said, 'You bet.' That's Hersh." Some suspected that the editorial board at the *New York Times*, having been repeatedly scooped by the *Washington Post* during the Watergate scandal, was making a mountain out of a molehill. There was certainly no question about the rivalry. Hersh, *Times* executive editor A. M. Rosenthal once said, "is like a puppy that isn't quite housebroken, but as long as he's pissing on [*Washington Post* editor] Ben Bradlee's carpet, let him go."[29]

For its part, the White House sensed the advent of a major scandal. In his memoir, Kissinger observed that the Hersh story had the effect of tossing "a burning match in a gasoline depot." When Colby called the White House that Sunday afternoon, he could feel the heat. What the hell was going on? Deputy National Security Adviser Brent Scowcroft asked. Was there more to come out? Another aide advised Colby to call the president, who was then on board Air Force One en route to a ski vacation at Vail, and fill him in. In due course, Colby had the White House operator put him through. As explicitly as he could over an unsecure circuit, the DCI attempted to bring Ford up to speed. "Mr. President," he said, "on the story in the *Times* this morning I want to assure you that nothing comparable to the article's allegations is going on in the Agency at this time." The material in the Hersh article was a distortion, and "all misdeeds of the past had been corrected in 1973." Ford thanked him and asked for a report. Upon landing at Vail, the president was besieged by reporters badgering him for comment on the Hersh article. He merely repeated what Colby had told him—that the Agency was not currently engaged in domestic spying or illegal activities of any other kind. He had asked Kissinger as his national security adviser to secure a report on the matter from the DCI.[30]

The White House was understandably stunned that this was the first it had heard of the "family jewels." When asked about the omission later, Colby said, "I never really thought about it. . . . I think I didn't think of it because Schlesinger was still in charge, and he didn't think of it. I asked him about it one time and he said something to the effect that, 'Oh, hell, with that bunch of characters down there.' So it was almost as though he had made a decision not to brief them."[31] Once he was in the saddle, Colby declared, he kept treating the issue as an internal matter. That the thought of briefing the president's men never crossed the DCI's mind is doubtful. He was dealing initially with the Nixon White House, which was in the process of trying to shift the blame for Watergate to the CIA, and during both the Nixon and Ford administrations with a national security adviser who was determined to marginalize the Agency. Why give the enemy bullets with which to fire at you?

By December 24 Colby had his report ready. It hit the high points of Operation MH/Chaos and then noted that the break-ins, surveillance of US citizens, and electronic bugs cited in Hersh's article had nothing to do with MH/Chaos. The report went on to describe those operations and attempted to justify them. "There are certain other matters in the history of the Agency which are subject to question," Colby warned.[32]

The cover letter and report had to go to Kissinger first. As soon as he received a copy, the national security adviser/secretary of state summoned the DCI. Colby had heard through the grapevine that Kissinger had been extremely critical of him—"making caustic comments about me," as Colby put it—for the previous two days. Kissinger was afraid of being linked to the Huston Plan for illegal spying on domestic "radicals" and to Allende's overthrow in Chile. As soon as the Hersh story broke, he had contacted Helms in Tehran using a backchannel. "This is an issue that's not going away," Kissinger declared, and ordered Helms home from Iran to help with damage control. Both men were convinced that Colby was Hersh's primary and only source.[33]

What else is there? Kissinger asked Colby. Colby handed him a document summarizing the family jewels. The CIA was linked to various assassination plots, especially the conspiracy to kill Castro, which also involved contacts with the Mafia. There were drug experiments on Americans, the Agency's involvement in the Huston Plan, and Angleton's imprisonment and torture of Yuri Nosenko. Kissinger thumbed through the report hurriedly, Colby recalled, but when he came to the section on assassinations, he stopped and read. Their meeting over, Kissinger hand-carried Colby's report to Ford in Colorado. "I have discussed these activities [the 'certain other matters' mentioned in Colby's cover letter] with him, and must tell you that some few of them clearly were illegal, while others— though not technically illegal—raise profound moral questions," he memoed Ford. "A number, while neither illegal nor morally unsound, demonstrated very poor judgment."[34]

Bill and Barbara had planned a family ski trip to Pennsylvania during the Christmas holidays, but in view of the emerging crisis over the Hersh article and the family jewels, Bill had opted to stay behind in Washington. He anticipated being summoned to Vail to be part of the team that was strategizing over damage control. What he hoped, he recalled in his memoir, was that the president would release his report verbatim—he had made sure that all of the material in it was declassified—and that it would stand as the administration's defense. But that was not to be; nor was Colby to be included in the decisionmaking process. The two things were related.

In Vail, Ford, Kissinger, Scowcroft, Chief of Staff Donald Rumsfeld, and Dick Cheney, his assistant, decided on a course of action. They considered doing as Colby wished, releasing the report and thus making it the White House's own. But that would saddle the Ford administration with the sins of past administrations. The president and his advisers decided to name an "independent Blue Ribbon Panel" composed of distinguished Americans and chaired by Vice President Nelson Rockefeller to investigate past CIA misdeeds and recommend reforms.[35]

Meanwhile, Colby grew increasingly uneasy. "The silence from there [Vail] was deafening," he later observed. The Ford administration was circling the wagons, and apparently he was to be left outside to deal with the hostiles by himself. "I felt very lonely," he recalled. "I decided that if I would have to fight the problem out alone, I at least would be free to use my strategy to save intelligence and not have to defer to every tactical move concocted in the White House."[36]

The die was cast.

18

DANCING WITH HENRY

Henry Kissinger's and Bill Colby's frames of reference and modi operandi could not have been more different. Kissinger, the academic turned diplomat, was secretive when he did not have to be, trusting only himself and a few subordinates. He was a master at deception, loved complexity for complexity's sake, and cared little about legal or constitutional niceties. Kissinger was skilled at acquiring and exploiting the influence he gained through personal relationships and cultivation of the media. Philosophically, he was a conservative internationalist with a Metternichian commitment to realpolitik. Like Metternich, the subject of his Ph.D. dissertation, he tended to confuse stability with the status quo. Colby was relatively simple by contrast—not simple-minded, but straightforward—often to a fault. He preferred friendship and trust in acquiring assets rather than threats and blackmail. He loved the clandestine world and covert operations because of the opportunity they provided for creativity. Colby was a liberal internationalist with all of the missionary baggage that went with the philosophy.

Colby's son John described his father's mindset well: "Up to 1973, [he] was less an intelligence professional than a special ops, covert action kind of guy. Here's a mission; go do it." First it was the Nazis, then the communists. In Italy he knew what to do, what was right. In Vietnam, the situation was murkier, but he pressed ahead. The problems he faced as DCI were more complicated. "In each case," John observed, "he looked at the situation, at his values and his perception of the national interest, and acted. If he believed in the value of intelligence and covert action—which he did all his life—then he was going to act to preserve it."[1]

Protecting the national security when confronted by totalitarian regimes bent on world domination meant frequently choosing the lesser of two evils—the Ngo brothers and Thieu over Ho Chi Minh in Vietnam, Sukarno over the PKI in Indonesia, Pinochet over Allende in Chile. In a perfect world, it was the responsibility of Americans and others who enjoyed the blessings of constitutional government, the rule of law, and respect for individual rights to take action to prevent gross abuses of human rights. He would throughout his life speak out against ethnic cleansing, whether it involved Nazi crimes against the Jews and Gypsies or Serbian campaigns against Balkan Muslims. He spoke of "an international conscience" and the duty of the international community to take action "even by overstepping longstanding prohibitions against intervening in the offending nation's 'internal affairs.'" The notion of an "international conscience" was, of course, absolutely foreign to Henry Kissinger.[2]

In *Honorable Men*, Colby claimed that during the Christmas holidays, while he was cooling his heels at Langley, Larry Silberman called him in. The deputy attorney general, who had acted as a go-between for Colby with Hersh during the *Glomar Explorer* episode, said that he had read the original *New York Times* article. "What else have you boys got tucked away up your sleeves?" he is said to have asked the DCI. Colby told him what he had told the president. "Tell me, did you turn over that list [the family jewels] to the Justice Department?" Silberman asked. After Colby said no, Silberman advised him that in withholding information concerning possible illegal action, the DCI himself was open to prosecution for obstruction of justice.[3]

The meeting may or may not have taken place. What is certain is that on December 31, Colby and CIA general counsel John Warner paid a visit to Silberman's office. According to Silberman, it was Colby who contacted him, not vice versa. Colby began by describing the management style of Richard Helms—based on "compartmentation"—comparing it to spokes on a wheel with Helms as the hub. Much had transpired in the Agency without the left hand knowing what the right was doing. Colby then summarized the "family jewels," including Operation MH/Chaos and other activities mandated by Ehrlichman, Huston, and their underlings; the Nosenko imprisonment; various wiretaps and break-ins; "personal surveillances" of Jack Anderson and other journalists; the mail-intercept program; the testing of experimental drugs on unwitting persons; and the fact that the CIA had "plotted" the assassination of foreign leaders, including Castro, Trujillo, and Lumumba.[4]

By January 3, 1975, Ford, Kissinger, and their staffs were back from Vail and ready to move on the family jewels matter. By this point, the White House had in its collective hands a report from Silberman on his meeting with Colby. He informed the president that the Justice Department had not yet decided "whether any of the items are prosecutable or appropriate for prosecution." The president should also be aware that as a result of another report from DCI Colby, former director Richard Helms might be indicted for perjury. Therefore, the White House should either avoid discussing possible CIA misdeeds with Helms or read him his rights if it did.[5]

At noon, President Ford, with Philip Buchen, counsel to the president, and Brent Scowcroft, Kissinger's deputy, met with former DCI and now secretary of defense James Schlesinger to discuss strategy. Schlesinger endorsed the decision to distance the White House from the Colby report and to appoint a blue-ribbon panel to investigate possible CIA wrongdoing. At 5:30 P.M. it was finally Colby's turn to meet with Ford, Scowcroft, and Buchen. "I think we have a 25-year-old institution which has done some things it shouldn't have," he began. He went over the charges in Hersh's article and then discussed some others, but not all the items on the "skeletons list," as he termed the family jewels. "We have run operations to assassinate foreign leaders," he declared. "We have never succeeded." Then, "A defector we suspected of being a double agent we kept confined for three years." The president pressed him to say who approved the various shady operations. Some occurred under the leadership of Dulles and Mc-Cone, but most were during Helms's watch and carried out by James Angleton and Richard Ober, the man in charge of Operation MH/Chaos, he said. Ford then instructed his DCI as to how the matter would be handled. First, the CIA would be told publicly to obey the law; second, the president would announce the formation of a panel of luminaries to investigate past misdeeds. And he would suggest that Congress establish a joint committee to carry out its own investigation. Meeting over.[6]

The following day found Kissinger in high dudgeon. "What is happening is worse than in the days of McCarthy," he exclaimed to Ford and Scowcroft. "He [Colby] has turned over to the FBI the whole of his operation. Helms said all these stories are just the tip of the iceberg. If they come out, blood will flow. . . . What Colby has done is a disgrace." It was his own blood that Kissinger was worried about. "The Chilean thing—that is not in any report," he noted, but that was because Colby was going to use it to "blackmail" him. Should he fire the DCI? Ford asked. Not until the investigation was over, Kissinger said, and then the president should move in someone of "towering integrity."[7]

Shortly afterward, Ford met with Helms, who had flown back from Tehran. The president assured him of his admiration. "I automatically assume what you did was right, unless it's proved otherwise," he told the man who kept the secrets. Helms declared that "a lot of dead cats will come out," and if they did, he would sling some of his own. Still later in the day, Ford met with Rockefeller to discuss the makeup of the blue-ribbon panel. Kissinger, who had once advised Rockefeller when he was governor of New York and had benefited enormously from his patronage, was present at this meeting. "Colby has gone to Silberman not only with his report but with numerous other allegations," Ford told Rockefeller. "At your request?" the latter asked. "Without my knowledge," the president responded. "Colby must be brought under control," Kissinger interjected.[8]

On January 6, the White House announced the formation of what became known as the Rockefeller Commission. The body included, in addition to the vice president, California governor Ronald Reagan; former secretary of commerce John T. Connor; retired army general Lyman Lemnitzer; Edgar F. Shannon Jr., a former president of the University of Virginia; former Treasury secretary Douglas Dillon; the AFL-CIO's Lane Kirkland; and former solicitor general Erwin A. Griswold. Ford, who had served on the Warren Commission to investigate the circumstances surrounding JFK's assassination, suggested David W. Belin, Warren's assistant counsel, as executive director of the commission's staff. It was a suggestion that he and Kissinger would live to regret.

The Rockefeller Commission's charge was carefully drawn, its charter limited to probing the CIA's alleged misdeeds in the domestic arena—Operation MH/Chaos, the mail-intercept program, and spying on journalists. Colby did not say so at the time, but he recognized that the Rockefeller Commission would not suffice. "The atmosphere in the nation had far too radically changed—in the aftermath of Vietnam and Watergate—for the Executive Branch to get away . . . with keeping the cloak-and-dagger world of intelligence strictly its own prerogative and affair," he subsequently wrote.[9]

That President Ford seemed to be inept rather than Machiavellian did not lessen the general anxiety. Putting Rockefeller in charge of a body to investigate the CIA was just one of President Ford's "latest blunders," columnist Nick Thimmesch wrote in the *Los Angeles Times*. The vice president was just "too, too close" to Henry Kissinger, who might very well be implicated in the scandal. Those reservations were reflected in a public opinion poll. Forty-nine percent of the people surveyed by Louis Harris believed that an executive commission would be too influenced by the White House, compared with 35 percent who supported Ford's action. Despite a reservoir of goodwill in Congress toward both Ford and Kissinger, the intelligence subcommittees of the Senate's Armed Services and Appropriations Committees announced that they, too, would hold hearings on Hersh's allegations against the Agency. Not to be outdone, the House announced it was launching its own probe. Over the course of the next year, Bill Colby would testify more than thirty-five times before various congressional bodies.[10]

As Colby recognized, the Ninety-fourth Congress, elected in 1974 in the wake of Richard Nixon's resignation, was not about to give way before claims of executive privilege. Barry Goldwater (R-AZ) termed the House and Senate that convened in January 1975 "probably the most dangerous Congress the country had ever known." Ten new senators were elected, and the House counted seventy-five freshmen, with the Democrats enjoying comfortable majorities in both chambers. In the House, the insurgents unseated four elderly committee chairmen, including longtime CIA friend and overseer Edward Hebert of Armed Services. The members of "the fighting Ninety-fourth," according to one observer, seemed "exultant in the muscle that they had used to bring a President down, willing and able to challenge the Executive as well as its own Congressional hierarchy, intense over morality in government [and] extremely sensitive to press and public pressures."[11]

More significant, by 1975 the Cold War consensus that had dominated US foreign policy for a quarter century was beginning to break apart. Within the anti–Vietnam War movement, doves had questioned the assumptions underlying the conflict in Southeast Asia—the monolithic communist threat, the Munich analogy, the domino theory—which were also the assumptions that underlay the broader Cold War. Hawks remained unshaken in their belief in the existence of an "evil empire," to anticipate a phrase made famous by a later president, but they began to recognize that there were limits on American power and to call for a more restrained foreign policy. Henry Kissinger seemed not to recognize the irony of his position. In urging détente, in engineering the openings to Beijing and Moscow, he, more than any other figure, had helped to undermine the Cold War consensus, thus making it politically possible to question the practicality and morality of institutions like the CIA.

In the wake of the publication of the Hersh article, Colby decided to attempt a preemptive strike that might head off a full-scale investigation. The senators before whom Colby had testified during his initial trip to Capitol Hill in January 1975 were comfortably familiar: Stennis, Symington, John McClellan of Arkansas, men who for years had listened to generalized reports delivered in executive session and then emerged not only to defend the CIA but to sing its praises. But these hoary-headed guardians of the nation's security were also aware of the nation's post-Watergate mood, and they asked Colby to give his testimony in open session. The DCI readily agreed. What he did was to lay before the committee and the public the report he had delivered to Ford on December 24. He saw it as a corrective to Hersh's sensationalized story, a refutation of the notion that the CIA had initiated a "massive" campaign of domestic spying. But the media chose to view his testimony, including information that the CIA had indeed sent out undercover agents to infiltrate dissident groups and had collected files on close to ten thousand American citizens, as confirmation of Hersh's story. The *New York Times* printed his statement verbatim beginning on the front page. The *Washington Post* and *Newsweek* noted that Colby had in fact confirmed much of what Hersh had reported. "On my way down from the Hill that afternoon," Colby wrote in *Honorable Men*, "I realized that I had not told the White House what was coming in the press the next day, so I stopped there to give Scowcroft a copy of the statement the Committee had released." Ford, Kissinger, and Helms continued to seethe.[12]

On January 27, 1975, the Senate voted 82–4 to establish the Select Committee to Study Governmental Operations with Respect to Intelligence Activities. Majority Leader Mike Mansfield had intended to appoint Philip Hart chair, but had to look elsewhere after the Pennsylvanian was diagnosed with cancer. He turned finally to a man who had actively campaigned for the post, Frank Church of Idaho. Not to be outdone, the House reconstituted its Select Committee on Intelligence with Lucien Nedzi as its chair, but the House body was much more divided than its Senate counterpart. Consequently, it was the Church Committee that would initially be the focus of the struggle between Congress and the executive branch over the family jewels.

The White House was deeply distrustful of Frank Church, viewing him as a man who intended to ride the investigation of CIA abuses—real and imagined—into the Oval Office. In Washington, the Idaho Democrat had a reputation as a straight arrow—and perhaps more. His penchant for moralizing speeches and his shunning of the Georgetown cocktail circuit earned him the sobriquets "Frank Sunday School" and "Frank Cathedral." Initially a strong supporter of the Cold War consensus, he—like Fulbright, McGovern, and others—had grown disillusioned during the Vietnam War. By 1966, he had emerged as one of the leading critics of the Indochinese conflict and a crusader on behalf of congressional prerogatives in foreign policy. Church, along with Fulbright, had led the way in demanding greater congressional oversight of the CIA.[13]

As soon as he learned of the Senate probe into the family jewels, Colby phoned Church and John Tower (R-TX), the ranking minority member, to offer his cooperation. He confided in his memoir that he had dreaded the process that would inevitably follow—the Agency's secrets would be gradually revealed to the Church Committee and inevitably leaked to the press. He shuddered to think, he wrote, of "the sensations created by everybody and his brother engaging in cheap TV theatrics at the expense of the CIA's secrets." And then there were the politics of the matter. The White House did not seem to understand that the center of power had shifted in Washington. Gone was the time when those who investigated the national security state would be labeled unpatriotic and turned out of office. Colby was determined to reverse the growing tendency to portray US intelligence as unconstitutional and improper. If those myths took root, he observed, "we can make our own mistaken Aztec sacrifice— American intelligence—in the belief that only thus can the democratic sun of our free society rise."[14]

On February 20, Schlesinger, Colby, and Silberman met with Kissinger to discuss how best to handle the looming inquiry. The national security adviser wanted to stonewall; it was especially dangerous to allow congressional investigators to delve into covert operations. "But we are doing so little in covert activities it is not too damaging," Colby declared. "Then disclosing them will show us to the world as a cream puff," Kissinger replied. Silberman backed Colby. Congress had the power of subpoena. The Justice Department had already announced that it was investigating possible illegal activity. Silberman, like David Belin of the Rockefeller Commission and Colby, thought that the White House was blowing the family jewels thing all out of proportion. For an intelligence agency of a major power that had functioned for twenty-five years at the height of the Cold War, the list of misdeeds was surprisingly mild, Colby again observed. Protect names and sources, ensure that America's sister services were not dragged into the affair. It wasn't going to be that simple, the stonewallers replied. Once the elephant got its nose under the tent . . . John Marsh, counselor to the president, subsequently told the CIA legislative liaison that the White House staff, "including the President," was afraid that the congressional probes would result in the disclosure of the links between the *Glomar Explorer* operation and the Hughes Corporation, and between covert US activities in Cuba and Robert Maheu of the Hughes Corporation, as well as Maheu's involvement in Watergate and the plots to kill Castro.[15]

Shortly thereafter, the White House attempted to co-opt the Justice Department. "Obviously, we need someone to corral this Silberman," Marsh told Ford.[16] "During the family jewels crisis," the deputy attorney general later recalled, "the President and Rumsfeld called me to the White House three days in a row and tried to persuade me to take the position of assistant to the President for intelligence. It would be my responsibility to deal with the exploding bombs." Each time he refused. On the third day, Ford said, "Would you at least talk to Henry?" The president was even weaker than he believed, Silberman thought at the time, but he went to see Kissinger. Kissinger pleaded with him:

> "Colby is going to give away the store."
>> "Would you take the job if you were me?" Silberman asked.
>> "I would if I trusted the President," Kissinger said.
>> "Exactly," said Silberman, and departed.[17]

In truth, Kissinger wanted to kill two birds with one stone. "Colby [is] . . . scared and out of control," he told Ford. "You should consider Silberman for Colby," he said. The president's other advisers scotched that idea. Firing Colby just as the congressional probe was getting underway would surely evoke memories of Watergate.[18]

The second week in March, Colby established a mechanism within the Agency to screen requests for classified and unclassified documents. Walter N. Elder, a twenty-four-year CIA veteran, headed the Church Committee team, and Donald Gregg, who had worked for Colby in Vietnam, was in charge of the Nedzi group. To his credit, Colby listened to all comers when it came to ground rules for releasing sensitive material. "Many long-time professionals in the Agency were anything but happy with my approach," he later observed. Angleton loyalists were for absolute secrecy. Helms's partisans continued to insist that intelligence was the prerogative of the executive and the executive alone. Both groups recalled the Doolittle Report and the directives of the early 1950s, when the CIA had been called upon to fight the Soviets on their own terms. They invoked Allen Dulles, who had once observed that it was absurd to argue that the CIA should be constrained by international law "or domestic law for that matter." Another group eschewed these extreme positions but argued that the Agency and the White House should contest each item requested by the congressional committees and that they be turned over only when there was no other option.[19]

Both George Carver and Deputy Director of Operations William Nelson, close colleagues of Colby, warned him that his commitment to openness was incompatible with the central mission of the Agency. "I believe it is almost impossible for the DCI to discuss operational matters including covert arrangements," Nelson wrote to him in a memo, "without inviting headlines and stories which seriously degrade the fabric of our security and no matter what the original intent, lead inevitably to a further exposure of intelligence sources and methods by persons inside and outside the Agency who take their cue from the man directly charged with this responsibility." Carver told his old friend from Vietnam days that he—Colby—was trying to educate people who did not understand the issues and who were not CIA's friends anyway.[20]

Colby directed the CIA's general counsel to employ a lawyer experienced in criminal and civil practice who could provide advice to any employee faced with questions of criminal liability. Some comfort! Langley's denizens thought; the very fact that such a step was necessary was demoralizing.

Most found the process of congressional investigation demeaning. Those in the Directorate of Operations "suffered the trauma of having total strangers from Congressional staffs ask for some of the Directorate's innermost secrets," Donald Gregg later recalled, "with the full expectation of receiving comprehensive replies. This experience ran counter to all that had been ingrained in Directorate personnel throughout their careers." Still others resented that everyone was being tarred with the same brush. "People on the clandestine side would come to me and say, 'How can I face my kids?'" Jenonne Walker remembered. "'For years I have told them that these stories were not true. As a senior official in the Agency, I would know.'"[21]

"I could not and would not agree [with those who wanted him to relent]," Colby wrote in *Honorable Men*. The guidelines he released on March 4 divided materials into four categories. Unclassified material, which dealt primarily with historical, organizational, and budget data, would be given to the committee staffs freely and could be retained in their files. More sensitive data would be "sanitized," that is, portions would be redacted, and rendered up. A third category would comprise material that could only be viewed by committee members and staff at Langley. Colby termed these "fondling" files. The last category, including 40 Committee documents and memoranda to the president, would not be revealed at all but used only to prepare briefs. At the same time, the DCI ordered Nelson to have his staff scour the records to ensure that there were no additional "surprises."[22]

To some, Colby's approach seemed reasonable under the circumstances, but not to the Agency diehards and the White House. David Atlee Phillips, a prominent operations officer who had played a large role in the Chilean affair, resigned in order to speak out publicly. On March 20, he and others formed the Association of Retired Intelligence Officers and launched a campaign to compel the CIA to keep its secrets. There were those who blamed Schlesinger. According to Ray Rocca, Angleton's deputy and no friend of Colby's, Schlesinger was guilty of "the most absurd act in completely losing his head in the 'tell me everything' matter of what became known as the 'family jewels.'" According to former CIA officer Ray Cline, Schlesinger had ordered the original search that unearthed the CIA's deepest secrets to "cover his ass. I've always seen this experience of Colby's as something of a Greek fate overcoming Bill, because, when he became DCI he couldn't get out from under, and because this caused him to run afoul of Dick Helms—who represented an entirely different world and a different time."[23]

Whatever the division of opinion within the Agency, Kissinger, Ford, and their staffs viewed Colby's guidelines as nothing less than a betrayal. "Bill Colby got off the reservation," Brent Scowcroft, Kissinger's factotum as deputy national security adviser, declared. "He wanted to open the files and I said no. These are executive files." Scowcroft told the DCI to respond only to specific requests for specific documents, an old catch-22 stratagem that had worked many times in the past. "What he did was to allow the committee staff to come down and look at the files and then go back and request specific documents they had seen and could identify. It defeated the whole purpose."[24]

While Colby and the Ford White House sparred over tactics for dealing with current and future congressional investigations, the issue of CIA involvement in the assassination of foreign leaders—long rumored—hit the front pages. On September 16, 1975, the president had granted an off-the-record interview to the editorial board of the *New York Times*. During lunch at the White House, the journalists observed that the composition of the blue-ribbon panel raised questions as to its credibility. The members had been carefully chosen, the president retorted, because if it was not careful, the Rockefeller panel would trip over matters—a "cesspool," Ford termed it—that might ruin America's image around the world. Like what? they asked. Like assassinations. Stunned, the *Times* people pleaded with the president to allow them to go on the record. Ford refused, but within days rumors began to circulate.[25] Daniel Schorr, who had termed the flap over the Hersh article "Son of Watergate," got wind of Ford's admission to the *Times* editors and arranged an interview with Colby. After a half-hour chit-chat about Watergate, E. Howard Hunt, and other matters, Schorr asked, "Has the CIA ever killed anybody?" Colby recalled that he was completely taken off guard. He did not know how specific the president had been.

"Not in this country," the DCI replied.

"Who?"

"I can't talk about it."[26]

Colby then volunteered the information that assassination plots had been banned since 1973 when they were uncovered by the inspector general and that the whole matter had been kept from President Ford.[27] When

Schorr subsequently published the meat of the interview, Kissinger and Helms cringed. Colby's response implied that the CIA had in fact conducted assassination operations against foreign citizens.

The evening following his interview with Colby at the director's Langley office, Daniel Schorr appeared in the middle of the *CBS Evening News* broadcast. He told viewers that President Ford had "reportedly warned associates that if current investigations go too far, they could uncover several assassinations of foreign officials in which the CIA was involved." He concluded with a delicious irony. "Colby is on the record saying, 'I think that family skeletons are best left where they are, in the closet.' He apparently had some literal skeletons in mind." "There was no stopping the press or Congress now," Colby later wrote in *Honorable Men*. "A hysteria seized Washington: sensation came to rule the day." "Abolish the CIA!" editorialized A. J. Langguth in *Newsweek*. Jim Garrison, that conspiracy theorist of yesteryear, emerged from the sidelines to pitch in. "John Kennedy, the murder of Robert Kennedy, the murder of Martin Luther King. . . . Each of them bears consistent earmarks of the involvement of government intelligence operations," he told the *Washington Star*.[28]

19

DEATH OF A DREAM

A s it happened, the siege of the CIA coincided with the siege of Saigon and the fall of South Vietnam to the communists. For Colby, who would become deeply involved in the final stages of that debacle, it was a tragedy almost beyond comprehension. Because of his long experience in Southeast Asia, Colby had remained a member of the Agency's Vietnam team even when he served as executive director and deputy director for operations. As DCI, he could only watch as Nixon and Kissinger proceeded with their plan to exit Vietnam posthaste. When the final collapse began in the spring of 1975, Colby was on the foreign policy team that worked frantically to secure a negotiated settlement that would allow the United States a dignified withdrawal and preserve the lives of those Vietnamese who had cooperated with America.

By 1972, it had become clear that time was running out for those waging the "other war" in Vietnam. The US presidential election was approaching, and both Nixon and Kissinger wanted to put the last nail in the Democrats' coffin by announcing a peace settlement. In the wake of the Soviet-American arms control summit that had unfolded without a hitch in Moscow in May, Kissinger for the first time indicated the administration's willingness to allow North Vietnamese troops to remain in South Vietnam following a cease-fire. CORDS personnel, those engaged in the day-to-day work of community-building, corruption-fighting, and counterinsurgency—Colby's people—began to receive signals to cease and desist, or at least indications that the US Mission Council in Saigon and Washington did not care whether they did anything or not. Said CIA analyst Frank Snepp, "I saw no indication from directives and so forth that Kissinger placed any importance on pacification, on security in the countryside." And he had no patience with efforts to reform the Thieu regime. "At that point something registered with me," Snepp later recalled. "They were really distant from the reality you could document with intelligence, and they were trying to remake reality to fit their own favorite vision."[1]

On October 31, 1972, just days before the general election, Kissinger announced that "peace was at hand." Having been secretly promised up to $7 billion in reparations payments by the United States, the North Vietnamese were ready to sign an accord that would leave Thieu in power. With North Vietnamese troops allowed to hold their positions in the south, however, Thieu would be irrelevant. According to the agreements, sixty days after the guns had stopped firing, all American troops were to be out of Vietnam, with US prisoners of war released sometime during this period. Ironically, the sticking point was Nixon. Seething with resentment at the attention Kissinger was getting as the architect of détente and the herald of peace, Nixon refused to abandon Thieu. He wanted "peace with honor," and that meant no sellout, he declared. And so peace turned out to be somewhere else than at hand.

The failure of the administration to conclude a cease-fire did nothing to damage Nixon politically, and he went on to defeat Democrat George McGovern in a landslide in the 1972 presidential contest. Following the election, Nixon ordered an additional $1 billion in aid to the South Vietnamese government, giving Thieu, among other things, the fourth-largest air force in the world. At the same time, he warned the South Vietnamese president that if he rejected the best peace agreement that could be obtained, the United States would "seek a settlement with the enemy that serves U.S. interests alone."[2] Then, during the 1972 Christmas holidays, Nixon ordered the most intensive and destructive bombing attacks of the war against North Vietnam. US aircraft dropped 36,000 tons of ordnance, more than the entire total for the period between 1969 and 1972. By December 30, the North Vietnamese had exhausted their stock of surface-to-air missiles. Peace negotiations resumed in Paris on January 8, 1973. Following six days of marathon sessions, the Americans and North Vietnamese signed an agreement that was essentially the same as the one Kissinger and Le Duc Tho, the North Vietnamese negotiator, had worked out the previous year, in October 1972.

By the end of March 1973, the 591 US prisoners of war held by North Vietnam were safely home, and the last American combat troops were gone. In reality, however, the "peace" agreements of 1973 merely established ground rules for the continuation of war in Indochina without direct US participation. The North Vietnamese Army retained control of a strip of territory in South Vietnam along the Laotian border, stretching from Kon Tum Province southward through Pleiku, Darlac, Quang Duc, and Phuoc Long. In this area, which American observers labeled the "Third Vietnam," the communists set up political shop and began recruiting settlers from areas controlled by the South Vietnamese government. At the same time, the North Vietnamese quietly infiltrated troops and equipment into the south, built a system of modern highways linking the Ho Chi Minh Trail to strategic staging areas, and began work on the 1,000-mile-long pipeline to ensure that its soldiers would have adequate supplies of fuel when it came time to attack.

In the autumn of 1974, Hanoi settled on a strategy that called for a series of offensives during 1975 to further weaken the ARVN, followed by a final assault and a call for popular uprising in South Vietnam the following year. The CIA reported as much to Washington and the US Mission in Saigon, that is, that there would be a rising level of violence in 1975 and a final push in 1976. In December 1974, main force units of the North Vietnamese Army and Viet Cong regional units attacked Phuoc Long, northeast of Saigon. Within three weeks, the communists had routed the ARVN defenders and captured large stockpiles of fuel and ammunition. Hanoi then held its collective breath, waiting to see if there would be a response, but no B-52 strikes or any hint of US ground activity materialized. Apparently, the Americans would not come to the rescue of South Vietnam. The CIA subsequently reported that it had evidence that "Hanoi regarded Phuoc Long as a test case for the Russian notion that we would not react to an offensive." The Russians, of course, had gotten that notion from none other than Henry Kissinger and passed it along to the North Vietnamese leadership.[3]

From January through February 1975, the communists continued to marshal their forces, and then on March 10, General Van Tien Dung attacked Ban Me Thuot in the Central Highlands. The city fell within two days. Encouraged, he ordered assaults on Pleiku and Kon Tum in hopes of securing control of the Highlands before the end of the dry season. At this point, Thieu made a fateful decision. Meeting secretly with his top military commanders at Cam Ranh Bay on March 14, he ordered them to withdraw from Kon Tum and Pleiku immediately. The ARVN was to prepare new defensive positions along South Vietnam's demographic frontier stretching along an arc northeastward from Saigon to Danang and Hue. Unfortunately, ARVN units in the Highlands had not prepared for a retreat, and the North Vietnamese Army had cut the main transportation routes. Strung out along country roads and paths, the South Vietnamese soldiers became sitting ducks for North Vietnamese artillery and tanks, which proceeded to indiscriminately shell them along with civilian refugees fleeing south. The withdrawal turned into a rout. Thieu's decision cost the government six provinces, at least two divisions, and "the confidence of his army and people," as historian George Herring put it. On March 18, Brent Scowcroft wrote to President Ford, "Unless the present trends are reversed, within the next few months the very existence of an independent non-Communist South Vietnam will be at stake. . . . The ultimate outcome is hardly in doubt."[4]

On March 26, Hue fell without a fight, and General Ngo Quang Truong, commander of Military Region IV, positioned his troops and artillery north of Danang for a last-ditch defense. The loss of Hue was particularly galling for South Vietnam's intelligentsia. "To think of South Vietnam without Hue," mourned a doctor in Saigon, "is to think of a body without a heart." Meanwhile, Danang, South Vietnam's second-largest city, became jammed with more than a million refugees who had fled in the wake of the North Vietnamese advance.[5]

On March 28, the US National Security Council commenced daily meetings on the situation in Southeast Asia. Each of these began with a briefing by Bill Colby. Three themes reappeared in the DCI's reports: the need for political and military decisions to be driven by current intelligence, his belief in the success of the pacification/counterinsurgency program, and his ongoing concern for the Vietnamese who were at risk for having worked for the US Mission, particularly for the CIA. At the March 28 meeting, he reported that Danang would not be able to hold out for more than a week or two. Colby observed with satisfaction that although "the refugees are placing a big burden on the government . . . it is interesting to note that they are all fleeing toward the government. That shows clearly how they really feel about the Communists." Incredibly, the DCI still believed that amid the chaos and bloodshed in South Vietnam, the average citizen was concerned with choosing sides. The refugees, the vast majority of whom had never cared about ideology, had nowhere else to flee but southward because of the battle lines. Colby remained a true believer to the end.[6]

The immediate question was what to do about Danang. "There have been terrible mob scenes, both at the airport where they stormed loading aircraft and at the port where they jammed aboard ships," Colby reported. "Some of the military have even shot their way on to the ships."[7] The US Mission chartered three Boeing 727s to ferry at-risk Vietnamese out of the beleaguered city. Meanwhile, Danang was running out of food, and sanitation facilities could not keep up with demand, causing a sickly, pervasive stench. Young women in soiled *ao dai* (long, sheathlike dresses, usually a pristine white) lined the streets begging for a place to sleep. Residents charged refugees $2 for a drink of water. One company of ARVN soldiers forced its way onto a plane, in the process trampling old men and women as well as children. The mobs finally became so dangerous that flights from the airport had to be suspended. Colby's focus for the moment was what to do about CIA people trapped in the city. Some of his colleagues, Kissinger in particular, warned against a "premature" evacuation of Americans lest it lead to a complete collapse of law and order. But Colby, after consulting with Chief of Station Tom Polgar, decided that Danang had reached the end of the line and ordered Agency personnel out. It was not an order that would be easy to follow.

On the 29th, the CIA personnel and consulate staff members still in Danang made their way to the port and boarded a tugboat, the Australian-owned *Osceola*. At one point, a sampan carrying South Vietnamese Marine deserters tried to board the tug by force but was repelled. The harbor was filled with barges, sailboats, sampans, and anything else that would float, carrying thousands of refugees who were without food or water. The captain of the *Osceola* radioed a freighter, the *Pioneer Commander*, and arranged a rendezvous so the Americans could be offloaded and taken to Saigon. The tugboat approached the vessel only to discover South Vietnamese Marine deserters, perhaps five hundred of them, already on board, busy robbing refugees alighting from a barge or knifing or shooting those who resisted. The Americans forced their way onto the ship and joined forces with the captain, whose armed sailors still controlled the bridge and engine room.

The CIA officers helped repel an attack on the bridge by renegade troops, but looting and raping continued throughout the night on the decks below. The next day, mercifully, the *Pioneer Commander* reached Saigon. On March 30, Danang fell to the North Vietnamese Army. The US rescue operation had extracted fifty thousand refugees from the city, but many Vietnamese who had worked for the US Consulate were left behind. All that remained of South Vietnam was Saigon and the delta to the south.[8]

Ford gave no serious thought to employing US air and naval power. He did ask Congress for $722 million in emergency aid for Thieu's beleaguered forces, arguing that this could stabilize the situation and lead to negotiations that would keep a remnant of South Vietnam alive. During the final, bitter debate that ensued, opponents of the bill pointed out that Thieu had already abandoned more equipment in Military Regions 1 and 2 than the $722 million could buy.

If Ford and Kissinger were playing to the galleries and making a record for history, Ambassador Graham Martin seemed to have actually believed that the South Vietnamese government and the ARVN were still viable and that South Vietnam could survive. He refused to accept the fall of Danang. When Polgar took an Agency officer just evacuated from the city in to report, the ambassador rejected his account and announced that he was going to go and see for himself. He was finally dissuaded by the fact that there would be nowhere to land, the airport being in North Vietnamese hands. Martin had convinced himself that the antiwar sentiment in the United States and Congress's accompanying unwillingness to appropriate more money for South Vietnam was the product of a media conspiracy. The ambassador was ranting about "a massive deception campaign" involving the *New York Times*, Polgar reported to Colby.[9]

Following the ARVN's withdrawal from the Highlands, Ford had created a Special Actions Group, including representatives from State, Defense, the CIA, and the Joint Chiefs, with Kissinger in the chair, to oversee the deepening crisis. By the first week in April, the Khmer Rouge (the Cambodian communists) had moved into Phnom Penh; meanwhile, the last American personnel were being airlifted out of the country in Operation Eagle Pull. On the morning of April 2, Kissinger met with his inner circle before convening the larger body. Why won't the ARVN stand and fight? he asked. Because they had been repeatedly ordered to withdraw, and the withdrawals had turned into routs, the military chiefs replied. Philip Habib, a career diplomat and former member of the US Mission in Saigon, pointed out that at a certain point South Vietnamese soldiers had become concerned primarily with protecting their families. Habib remarked that the CIA reports on the situation in South Vietnam had been quite good. Kissinger disagreed. "On whose side is Colby in this?" he asked. "I don't know what you mean by 'whose side.'" Habib replied. "I think Colby is one of those who is tremendously disappointed at what he sees happening. I don't think he anticipated that the ARVN would cave the way it did."[10]

The Special Actions Group convened that afternoon. "Okay, we just have to be prepared for the collapse of the South within the next three months," Kissinger declared. Three weeks would be more accurate, Colby interjected. The talk then turned to evacuation. "Tell Graham Martin to give us a list of those South Vietnamese we need to get out of the country," Kissinger instructed Habib. It could reach a million people, a participant observed, involving as it did not only relatives of Americans but the tens of thousands of people who had worked for the United States in some capacity. Colby said, "We're getting rumors and rumbles about some move to oust Thieu. Some of these rumbles indicate a military move, some of them indicate a move from other quarters like the Buddhists and politicians."

"Do you expect Thieu to survive?" Kissinger asked. Colby responded that it would "be very close." Kissinger said, "It really doesn't make any difference whether Thieu survives or not. . . . We can save nothing at this point."

"Nothing but lives," Colby interjected.

"How?" Kissinger asked.

Colby replied, "Talk to the North Vietnamese. Offer up Thieu for a negotiated release of people." Kissinger did not reply.[11]

Somewhat paradoxically, Colby made it clear that the CIA was not going to be involved in an internal coup against the South Vietnamese president. The same day that the Special Actions Group was meeting in Washington, Polgar and Shackley went to see Thieu. The president was not amenable to the creation of a new broad-based government that might be able to negotiate a cease-fire with the North Vietnamese, Chief of Station Polgar subsequently reported to Colby. It was all a plot by Ky to take control of the government, Thieu had said. It was obvious that the North Vietnamese were going to pursue victory through military means as long as Thieu stayed in office, Polgar observed, adding that a different government might be able to negotiate with the enemy while an evacuation proceeded. Colby immediately cabled back: "If there was any remote connection between US and such an event it would be an institutional and a national disaster. . . . Please make most clear to those you think it important to advise that they are to flatly reject even a hint that we would condone or participate in such action [a coup]."[12]

Colby was still haunted by the events surrounding the ouster and murder of the Ngo brothers. Moreover, with the family jewels issue front and center in the American press, and congressional investigations ongoing, CIA implication in the overthrow of a friendly government might sound the death knell for the Agency. But how to reconcile this with his willingness to sacrifice Thieu politically in order to save those Vietnamese who were tainted by contact with Americans? Colby thought that having Thieu resign to appease the communists was far different from ousting him through a coup. Following a resignation, while negotiations were ongoing with the North Vietnamese, Thieu could seek asylum in the United States. In a coup, there was a good chance that he would be killed, becoming in the process a monument to American hypocrisy in Vietnam.

If there were not enough angst in South Vietnam and the United States, on April 5 an American C-5 Galaxy aircraft crashed after taking off from Tan Son Nhut airport, killing 138 children and 35 Defense Attaché Office personnel who were on board. The children included war orphans as well as non-orphans whose parents just wanted their offspring out of a collapsing war zone. The flight was part of Operation Baby Lift, organized by a group of charitable organizations that included the Catholic Relief Fund. Eventually some 3,300 children would be evacuated, but the image that stuck in the world's collective mind was the horrific accident at Tan Son Nhut, to many the ultimate emblem of America's misguided idealism.

On April 8, a CIA agent in Tay Ninh reported that North Vietnam had decided to go for broke—even if Congress appropriated money for more aid to South Vietnam, even if the Thieu regime fell, there would be no negotiations or coalition government. "Communist forces will strike at Saigon at an appropriate time," he wrote. "The war is lost," Polgar declared. There were just four things to be done: accelerate the evacuation of US personnel, but not so precipitously as to generate a panic; persuade the Soviets or French to arrange a cease-fire; convince Thieu to step down, to be replaced by a government of national unity; and arrange the "orderly evacuation of those South Vietnamese who cannot reasonably be expected to survive under the new regime."[13]

By the second week in April, Colby's attention was increasingly focused on the evacuation of US personnel and their Vietnamese allies from South Vietnam. He had had to give up the idea of trading Thieu for safe passage. Colby wanted desperately to begin evacuation of at-risk Vietnamese; there would be grave difficulties even with the extraction of remaining American personnel. The Saigon station predicted that an ARVN collapse on any of the approaches to Saigon "could produce additional military disintegration as well as instability and social unrest in the capital that would make phased or orderly exfiltration impractical within two or three days." Any attempted large-scale evacuation of Vietnamese would produce a general panic, and, moreover, there were indications that "there are those in the Army who would hold the U.S. civilians hostage to their own safety and to insure their own evacuation." Indeed, Graham Martin reported to Kissinger via their backchannel line of communication that General Nguyen Ngoc Loan, the commander of South Vietnam's National Police, had told him that if the Americans tried to jump ship, the ARVN would turn its guns on them.[14]

By April 8, the nearest provincial capital east of Saigon, An Loc, was under siege. This time the embattled ARVN defenders put up fierce resistance, but the outcome was never in doubt. "The North Vietnamese now have 18 infantry divisions in South Vietnam supported by numerous armor, artillery, and air defense units," Colby informed the National Security Council. By contrast, the South Vietnamese could count at most seven divisions. South Vietnam's "long-term prospects are bleak, no matter how well Saigon's forces and commanders acquit themselves in the fighting that lies ahead," he said. Couldn't US forces execute a flanking movement and attack North Vietnam? Kissinger asked the chairman of the Joint Chiefs of Staff, General George Brown. The War Powers Act (Congress in 1973 had passed legislation restricting the executive branch's authority to commit troops to foreign conflicts) aside, Brown replied, there were no North Vietnamese soldiers left in North Vietnam.[15]

At a Special Actions Group meeting on April 17, Kissinger and Defense Secretary Schlesinger clashed over the rate of evacuation, with the former increasingly defending his ambassador. "I think he's getting the people out, don't you?" Kissinger said. No, Schlesinger replied. A little over a hundred a day were escaping, and there were still more than 5,000 US personnel in and around Saigon. Planes were flying in and out of Tan Son Nhut with only a handful of people on board. "Well, we have to leave some things to Graham's discretion," Kissinger said.

The discussion turned to the mechanics of evacuation. "It's our opinion that if this thing goes to a military operation—use of U.S. forces to get people out—the odds of success are very remote," General Brown remarked. Some members of the ARVN were going to resist the evacuation by force, and television footage of US Marines shooting down their erstwhile allies would be more than the nation could bear. He told the group that "certain South Vietnamese Airborne and Marine units" had offered to provide security for the extraction on the condition that the Americans took them with them. What about the at-risk South Vietnamese, Colby asked? Tan Son Nhut could come under North Vietnamese artillery fire anytime. Why not tell them to make the 60-mile trip to Vung Tau, where they could be evacuated by ship, someone suggested. There was but a single road for the estimated 93,000 South Vietnamese then in possession of identity cards entitling them to evacuation, Colby observed. There would be chaos, and anyway, the North Vietnamese Army was rapidly advancing on Vung Tau.[16]

In Saigon on April 18, Colonel Janos Toth, a Hungarian member of the International Control Commission Staff that had been put in place to monitor the 1973 cease-fire accords, came to see Polgar. The two had met at an embassy reception and were on friendly terms. Toth assured the station chief that Hanoi did not want to humiliate the United States. It preferred strangulation of Saigon rather than a full-scale assault. If Thieu could be gotten rid of, there was every possibility of a peaceful, negotiated settlement, which, among other things, would leave an American embassy—limited to normal diplomatic activities—to function in South Vietnam. The south had lost, he said, and the only question was whether the transfer of power would take place "under civilized circumstances," like those accompanying the abdication of Kaiser Wilhelm in 1918, or under conditions more like those associated with the fall of Berlin in 1945, when virtually the entire city was razed.[17]

As of April 21, there were still 2,000 Americans in Saigon. General Brown feared the imminent breakdown of law and order. He reminded members of the Special Actions Group that rebellious ARVN soldiers had shot three of their generals while they were trying to escape Nha Trang by helicopter: "There is every likelihood of armed mobs, and no leadership," he said. Colby continued to worry about the South Vietnamese. "If we don't make at least an attempt to get them out, you are going to have more bitterness than you can believe," he told the group.[18]

At last, on April 21, Thieu resigned. Accompanied by members of the Joint General Staff and their families, he boarded a plane for the United States. In his departure statement, Thieu blamed Henry Kissinger for having "led the South Vietnamese people to death."[19] He was replaced by his vice president, the feeble septuagenarian Tran Van Huong, whose lifelong anticommunism made him no more an acceptable negotiating partner for the North Vietnamese than Thieu. In Washington, all eyes turned to evacuation, all except those of Kissinger, who reported that he had asked the Soviets to intervene and restrain their North Vietnamese allies.

The third week in April, Congress appropriated $300 million for the evacuation of Americans from South Vietnam and endorsed President Ford's request to use troops to facilitate the air/sea lift. On the 22nd, Colby reported to the Special Actions Group that the fall of Saigon was imminent. "They [the North Vietnamese] are not interested in any interim deals," he said. "What they want is a full military victory and humiliation of the U.S. Tan Son Nhut is about to go." The next day, he told the national security team that CIA operatives had learned that the Khmer Rouge had instructed their cadres to "secretly eliminate all senior enemy commanders and those who owe us a blood debt." Would the North Vietnamese do no less? He also reported small arms firings on American planes but observed that it was unclear whether the fire was coming from the North or South Vietnamese. On the 24th, Colby informed the Saigon station that it was "safe to say that only Ambassador Martin, the COS, and to a lesser extent Dr. Kissinger" believed anything could come out of efforts at a negotiated settlement. He ordered Shackley to get with Polgar and see to the evacuation of all Vietnamese dependents of CIA officers. As far as other at-risk Vietnamese were concerned, the situation remained bleak. "We are amazed at the small number of Vietnamese being evacuated," the State Department complained to Martin, "considering the substantial amount of aircraft available.[20]

On April 27, Huong was succeeded by General Duong Van "Big" Minh, whom the Americans hoped would be acceptable to the communists. As of the 28th, Graham Martin was still holding out hope for a negotiated settlement, but the White House had had enough. The order was sent out that all Americans were to be out of Saigon by 3:45 A.M. on April 30. Miraculously, Tan Son Nhut remained open, and Kissinger reported to Ford on the 28th that 35,000 to 40,000 Vietnamese had been airlifted out.[21]

Early on the morning of the 28th, Tom Polgar was awakened by the thump of exploding artillery rounds. He phoned the embassy and learned that US Marines on the roof had reported seeing flames and explosions at Tan Son Nhut. The station chief arrived at the embassy to find that Martin was home, ill with bronchial pneumonia. He called the ambassador and insisted that he come in, which he did, arriving around 6:00 A.M. Polgar and Martin still wanted to talk about the Minh government and a negotiated settlement. At Langley, Colby would have none of it. Get your people ready to evacuate, he told the chief of station. The DCI was particularly insistent about destroying encryption equipment and CIA documents that would incriminate CIA informants. After the fall of South Vietnam, he expressed gratitude that "we have not been treated to the show trials that would have shamed us for the plight of our secret friends." By this point, however, a number of Agency officers who had served in Vietnam had arrived back in-country to help Vietnamese friends and coworkers escape through private means. Gage McAfee, who aided the owners of the Duc Hotel in getting out, would survive the ordeal. Others, such as covert ops officer Tucker Gougelmann, would not. Gougelmann was captured by the North Vietnamese Army, imprisoned, and subsequently beaten to death.[22]

Meanwhile, Martin refused to admit that the runways at Tan Son Nhut were unusable. After a hair-raising inspection by automobile, however, he accepted the inevitable and ordered the helicopter airlift to begin. At 1200 hours Polgar reported to headquarters that "all files and sensitive equipment [are] being destroyed. . . . We have started [to] lift surplus personnel from Embassy rooftop to warships off coast." By this time a large and anxious crowd had gathered outside the embassy gates; the crowd remained relatively calm, however, periodically parting to allow US personnel through. When he learned that Vietnamese were being mixed in with Americans during the by-now-continuous liftoff, Kissinger exploded: "Can someone explain to me what the hell is going on! The orders are that only Americans are to be evacuated. Now, what the hell is going on?" Colby explained that humanitarian considerations aside, the South Vietnamese might not allow the US Marine helicopters to land and take off if only Americans were being evacuated.[23]

At 4:40 P.M. Saigon time, Polgar radioed that "the die is cast. We are leaving. That means everybody, including Ambassador Martin." Some of the Marine C-46 helicopters were taking ground fire, apparently from disgruntled ARVN soldiers. The embassy, he said, was now a "beleaguered fortress" with an uncontrollable crowd of Vietnamese blocking all entrances. "There is no pretty ending to this," he said. While the last contingent of eight Americans, including Graham Martin, by then too sick to walk, waited to be ferried out, Polgar received a final message from DCI Colby: "The courage, integrity, dedication and high competence the Agency displayed in a variety of situations over these years has been fully matched and even surpassed by your performance during this difficult final phase. . . . Good luck and many thanks." Shortly after the last helicopter lifted off, North Vietnamese tanks and troops entered Saigon.[24]

In *Lost Victory*, Colby would write of the Vietnam conflict that "the ultimate irony was that the people's war launched in 1959 had been defeated, but the soldier's war, which the United States had insisted on fighting during the 1960s with massive military forces, was finally won by the enemy." It was, moreover, a clear-cut case of aggression, with a communist nation imposing its will by force of arms on a noncommunist one. "The political contest had been won," he wrote, "the Communists offered no attraction whatsoever. The Thieu Government had designed a program of economic and political improvement that meant a better life for the Vietnamese people."[25]

He was only partially right. The North Vietnamese Army had conquered South Vietnam by means of conventional warfare, but it had been able to do so because the South Vietnamese government and its supporters had failed to build a viable society, establish a separate identity, and capture the banner of Vietnamese nationalism. CORDS, working with select mid-level Vietnamese, had been able to bring a better life within reach of some rural Vietnamese, but their community-building efforts were no match for the relentless corruption and venality of the government in Saigon. The sickness that pervaded the regime in Saigon and the top levels of the ARVN was fully manifested during the final collapse. It was Thieu's "precipitous decisions and poor execution by his commanders," Tom Polgar

cabled Langley, "poor leadership, poor morale, indiscipline, and selfish-
ness[,] . . . that let the nation down and introduced a process of deteriora-
tion that led to results far in excess of what North Vietnamese military
pressure would have been capable of during this time frame."[26]

It was true that refugees fled mainly south rather than north to the communists, but there were areas in South Vietnam where Marxism-Leninism
remained deeply rooted. In Hau Nghia west of Saigon, in Quang Ngai on
the central coast, and in the Mekong Delta, communism had taken root in
the early 1930s in response to relentless exploitation of the peasantry by
absentee landlords and the Vietnamese lackeys who served their interests.
The Peoples' Revolutionary Government largely ceased its military activities after Tet, but the Viet Cong remained and became increasingly active
after the Easter Offensive of 1972. A Foreign Service Officer, James Nach,
recalled driving through My Tho that summer. He was headed for a nearby
district headquarters some 3 or 4 miles off of Highway 4. On maps in
Saigon, the area was rated "A"—most secure. "I came to this rather sad
looking town in the middle of the rice fields," he said. He then drove to
the American advisory compound and introduced himself to the senior
district adviser, a US Army major. For the next hour the officer harangued
Nach about everything that was wrong in his district. Government control
did not exist beyond the town boundaries. "He was basically sitting there
in his compound in a sea of red," Nach recalled.[27]

In May, after CIA personnel were safely back from what had been South
Vietnam, Colby presided over a welcome home and awards ceremony at
Langley. To the enragement of many there, he announced that counterinsurgency and pacification had been a complete success, and that if the
United States had not abandoned South Vietnam, victory could have been
won. A number of those present had been reporting for years on the pervasive corruption, the authoritarian nature of military rule, incompetence
within the ARVN, and the general hopelessness of the political and economic situation in South Vietnam. Several had had to leave friends and
lovers behind. Frank Snepp stood up and told the DCI that he was wrong.
But if the North Vietnamese Army had not invaded, . . . Colby began. That
was precisely the point, Snepp said. After $150 billion, more than 55,000
American lives and the best pacification/counterinsurgency program history had ever seen, South Vietnam, with the fourth-largest military in the
world, had not been able to defend itself.[28]

Colby the nation-builder could never admit that the dream of an independent, noncommunist South Vietnam was irreconcilable with the realities of Vietnamese culture, politics, and history. He had expected more of the South Vietnamese—and of the American people, for that matter—than they expected of themselves.

20

FIGHT FOR SURVIVAL

A fter the fall of South Vietnam, a return to the "family jewels" crisis was almost a relief for DCI Colby. There was another good fight to be fought. The reputation and perhaps the very existence of the Agency to which he had devoted his life were in peril. If he had not been able to save South Vietnam, he could save the Agency. At least, the DCI believed, there was a chance. To succeed, however, Colby was going to have to change the very culture of intelligence in the United States and overcome powerful opposition from within the intelligence community as well as the White House.

All of Henry Kissinger's worst fears were coming to pass in the late spring and early summer of 1975. There was not only the fall of Saigon and the accompanying humiliation, but the damned mess with the CIA to dog him. Both situations were undermining America's position in the world. A growing segment of the international community now saw the United States as the evil empire or a laughingstock—or both. And then there was always his personal reputation to worry about. Not only was there the Track II Chilean thing, but Kissinger had chaired the 40 Committee since he had come on board as national security adviser in 1969. Every covert operation initiated by the CIA since then had been undertaken with his personal approval. Perhaps his former patron, Nelson Rockefeller, could staunch the flow of damaging information. He tried in his own way to do just that. After one of Colby's appearances before the Rockefeller Commission, the vice president drew Colby aside. "Bill," he said, "do you really have to present all this material to us? We realize that there are secrets that you fellows need to keep." Not surprisingly, Rockefeller wanted nothing to do with the assassinations issue—but others with presidential ambitions, including President Ford and commission member Ronald Reagan, insisted on pursuing the matter. And so it was that the White House announced that the blue-ribbon panel's mandate was being extended two months so it could look into alleged plots to kill foreign leaders.[1]

David Belin, the Rockefeller Commission's executive director, took the commission's new charge seriously. He immediately requested all pertinent documents from the CIA, no matter how sensitive. Colby resisted. He could see no good whatsoever coming from this line of inquiry, he said. It would not matter that the CIA had never assassinated a foreign leader; it was clearly implicated in at least one plot—against Castro—and revelations concerning Mongoose would be enough to destroy the good name of not only the Agency but the United States. But he protested in vain. The commission, he was told, was part of the executive branch, and thus there was no reason to withhold anything from it, including information about sources and methods. Belin and his staff duly uncovered the Agency's involvement with Operation Mongoose, including attempts to enlist the Mafia, its connection to the deaths of Patrice Lumumba and Rafael Trujillo in 1961, and the abortive coup against President Sukarno of Indonesia in 1958. In April, Helms, called back once again from Tehran, testified before the commission in closed session for more than four hours. Exiting the committee room, he spotted Daniel Schorr, who had reported extensively on the assassination allegations, loitering with other reporters. "You son-of-a-bitch!" he yelled. "You killer! You cocksucker! Killer Schorr! That's what they should call you." On May 20, news of the plot against Castro and the Mafia connection hit the front pages.[2]

Belin and his staff had completed their work by the first week in June. Their draft report included an eighty-six-page section on CIA schemes to eliminate foreign leaders. "President Ford has firmly announced that assassination is not and should never be a tool of United States policy," read its conclusion. But that section would not see the light of day for some time.[3]

On June 5, the White House discussed what in the Rockefeller Commission report should be released and what should not. Belin and his staff pushed strongly for inclusion of the assassination material: "The omission of these findings will be viewed as a cover-up and will cast doubt upon the rest of the report." But Kissinger was adamant in his opposition to any mention in the report of plans to kill foreign leaders. A presidential commission admitting to assassination plots would be a disaster for US foreign policy, he declared. "Not since I have been here," he said, "has there been anything even thought of. There was the killing of the Chilean Chief of Staff, but we had dissociated from that group when we heard they were plotting to kidnap him." The assassinations were a "phenomenon of the Kennedys," he asserted, and advised Ford to "cover-up a little for Kennedy." Ford was persuaded. "I am not going to second guess my predecessors," he declared. "If Church wants to, let him. The Kennedys will get him."[4]

The report of the Rockefeller Commission was released on June 10. To the surprise of many observers, it was not a whitewash. The *Times* editorial board called the report "a trenchant, factual and plain-spoken document." "The Rockefeller Report is in," declared *Newsweek*, "and [it] found the agency guilty of nearly every serious allegation against it." There was nothing, however, on assassinations. "The Commission staff began the required inquiry," the document said, "but time did not permit a full investigation before this report was due." At a press conference the day before the release, President Ford announced that he was ordering all of the commission's assassination materials turned over to the Church Committee.[5]

Perhaps the most sensational family jewel exposed by the Rockefeller Commission was that concerning the drug experiments the CIA had conducted on individuals without their knowledge or permission in the 1950s. On July 17, a week after the commission issued its report, the surviving family of Dr. Frank Olson notified Colby that it was filing a wrongful-death suit against the Agency. Olson, a biochemist, had been a civilian employee of the US Army working on a cooperative effort with the CIA at Fort Detrick, Maryland. The task assigned to the team was to investigate the effects of mind-altering drugs on human behavior. On November 19, 1953, CIA personnel slipped a large dose of LSD into the drinks of Olson and other members of the group without their knowledge. By the time he was informed some twenty minutes later, Olson was hallucinating—experiencing "side-effects," as the CIA report on the matter termed them. He was rushed to New York for treatment by Dr. Harold Abramson, "a consultant to the agency on drug-related matters." Abramson prescribed hospitalization, but before Olson could be admitted, the terrified biochemist crashed through the closed window of his upper-floor hotel room and plunged to his death.

The CIA general counsel subsequently ruled that Olson had died from "circumstances arising out of an experiment undertaken in the course of his official duties for the U.S. Government." From 1953 through 1975, the family received survivor's benefits, but his family was never told the truth concerning his death. Colby recalled that he knew of a fatality connected to the drug research program, but he was "shocked and shamed" to learn of the circumstances. President Ford met with the family at the White House and issued a public apology. Colby followed suit and at the president's direction had the CIA's lawyers settle the family's claims. The press pounced on the story.[6]

In the early summer of 1975, in anticipation of his private confrontation with the White House over whether to cooperate with Congress, as well as his public one with the Church and Nedzi Committees over which CIA activities should be kept secret and which should not, Colby hired a personal lawyer. His choice was inspired—Mitchell Rogovin of the powerhouse Arnold and Porter law firm in Washington. The genius of the selection was that Rogovin had made his name as a civil liberties lawyer; for the previous twenty-five years, he had waged an almost constant war against the political establishment. A good friend of journalist Seymour Hersh, Rogovin had helped Common Cause successfully sue the Committee to Reelect the President, forcing the disclosure of Richard Nixon's campaign financing schemes. When John Warner, CIA's chief counsel, contacted Rogovin, he was representing the Institute for Policy Studies in its suit against former Nixon administration officials, including Kissinger, for wiretapping. Larry Silberman, whom Colby consulted, thoroughly approved: "Bill wanted a Democratic lawyer. He was a savvy operator." Rogovin was struck with Colby's sincerity; it seemed to him that the DCI was battling a corrupt political establishment, that Colby genuinely wanted an intelligence agency that conformed to the Constitution and obeyed the law. Throughout the summer and fall, the short, stocky forty-four-year-old attorney would be constantly at the DCI's side, advising him and mediating between him and committee staffs.[7]

On May 13, 1975, Kissinger and Secretary of Defense James Schlesinger met with Colby to set the ground rules for dealing with the Church Committee. Kissinger quoted Senator Henry "Scoop" Jackson: "The golden word of intelligence is silence. More can be lost by saying too much, too soon, than by saying too little, too slowly." In regard to past covert actions, the DCI should brief Church and Tower only in order to get them to appreciate the extreme sensitivity of much of the information. The purpose of this initial limited briefing "will be to induce the Chairman and Ranking Minority Member to impose limitations on the further investigation of the subjects covered." The national security adviser seemed oblivious to the fact that most of the cat was already out of the bag.[8]

Colby made his first appearance before the Church Committee on May 21. "All the questions were on assassination and it was like 'when did you stop beating your wife,'" he subsequently reported to the White House. He tried to put covert action in historical context, he said, and pointed out how little the Agency had been involved in would-be assassinations. He had pressed the committee to acknowledge "the delicacy of the problem," but had had no luck. One of the members had asked Colby if the Agency killed its own, referring to the Green Beret incident in Vietnam in which a double agent had been murdered in cold blood. No, the DCI had replied, noting that President Ford had given strict orders to the federal government to have nothing to do with assassinations. Church had wound up the proceedings by observing that what was needed was a law prohibiting the killing of foreign leaders in peacetime. Those in the Oval Office were stunned. "It is an act of insanity and national humiliation," Kissinger interjected during a meeting with Scowcroft and Schlesinger, "to have a law prohibiting the President from ordering assassinations."[9]

As the Church Committee hearings got underway, the CIA's reputation was approaching its nadir. A 1975 Gallup Poll registered an approval rating for the Agency of only 14 percent. Among college students, who constituted the Agency's prime recruiting pool, the figure stood at 7 percent.[10] But the US Senate was far from unanimous in its views on America's spies and their handlers. There were conservatives on both sides of the congressional aisle, such as Barry Goldwater and John Stennis, who continued to see the CIA as one of the nation's primary weapons in the ongoing struggle against international communism. Once they recognized that both Democratic and Republican presidents would be tarred with the assassination brush, mainstream politicians like Howard Baker (R-TN) and Church himself began to advocate restraint.

In addition, many of the most strident antiwar activists—those who had previously denounced the CIA as an instrument of the imperial presidency—were enthusiastic supporters of détente. Some, such as J. William Fulbright, had been captivated by Henry Kissinger and the openings to Moscow and Beijing. The two men developed what Fulbright thought was a personal as well as a professional relationship. Early on, Kissinger had cultivated the Foreign Relations Committee chair by showing deference to his views and appearing to confide in him. Thus it was that Fulbright, the author of *The Arrogance of Power*, published a 1975 article in the *Columbia Journalism Review* urging journalists to abandon what he called their "inquisition psychology." What the American people required, he wrote, was "restored stability and confidence." The accusations against the CIA might be true, "but I have come to feel of late that these are not the kind of truths we most need now," he added.[11]

In contrast to the Senate, the House was not interested in reform but rather sought a "thorough housecleaning" of agencies that had violated the law. The House Select Committee on Intelligence (different from the permanent subcommittee that Lucien Nedzi chaired) included five harsh critics of the CIA, including the ubiquitous Michael Harrington, three hardline defenders, and only one moderate. House Speaker Carl Albert named as chairman of the committee Otis Pike, a conservative Democrat and longtime representative of his Long Island district. Rather than being sanctimonious like Church, Pike was irreverent; he was also abrasive and confrontational. There was in him, however, a genuine concern that over the years Congress had gradually ceded its prerogatives to the executive branch, thus making abuses such as Watergate possible. Under his leadership, the House committee decided to focus on the answers to three questions: How much did the intelligence community cost the taxpayer? How effective was it? And what risks did its activities pose to the constitutional and political health of the country? Colby would view the Pike Committee with deep suspicion, sensing, as he later wrote, that the majority was determined to do a "hatchet job on the Agency."[12]

Harrington and Pike were not the only openly hostile House members that Colby had to deal with. Twice, on March 5 and then again on June 25, the DCI was called before the Subcommittee on Government Information and Individual Rights, chaired by the flamboyant and iconoclastic congresswoman from New York, Bella Abzug. Abzug had discovered that the CIA had included her name in its reports from Paris about visitors to the Vietnamese communist delegation, and she was furious. Colby had to endure a "day-long tongue-lashing," he later recalled, but kept his composure and held his ground. At one point he told Abzug "that if she visited such people abroad [North Vietnamese], such enemies of the United States, there was no way that I was going to keep her name out of our records." When Abzug declared at the second session that she had the right to call and compel testimony from anyone she chose, Colby quietly responded that she did not, and he would fight any effort to compromise the Agency's sources and methods.[13]

During the summer and fall of 1975, the DCI was forced to visit the Hill several times a week to testify. His colleagues marveled at his equanimity. "He looked like he had just been home for lunch and a nap," Deputy Director Vernon Walters remarked after one particularly contentious session. "Bill Colby could be doing a talk show on television with a mad dog chewing his leg off under the table and you would never know it," remarked longtime friend Stan Temko. In a 1976 interview with Colby, Italian journalist Oriana Fallaci asked, "What could shake your icy imperturbability? You never do show your emotions, do you?"

"I am not emotional," he replied. "I admit it. Just a few things bother me. For instance . . . when I was nominated and some people put posters around Washington. . . . They called me a murderer. And my children had to live with that. But it didn't really bother me. Oh, don't watch me like that. You're looking for something underneath which isn't there. It's all here on the surface, believe me."[14]

While the House tried to get itself in order, the Church Committee honed in on the assassination issue. It was the most sensational of the family jewels and the one most certain to garner headlines day after day. But the members of the committee immediately sensed a minefield. Both Democratic and Republican administrations were implicated. Idealists worried that the public's faith in the presidency and the federal government in general—already weakened by Vietnam and Watergate—would be further eroded. The simplest thing to do was to blame the Agency rather than the Kennedy, Johnson, and Nixon White Houses.

The concept of plausible deniability proved convenient to the task. This was a catch-22 that allowed the leaders of the intelligence community to shield political leaders from potentially embarrassing operations. Plausible deniability was one of the reasons why Eisenhower had set up the 5412 Group in 1955. That body, which morphed into the 303 Committee and then the 40 Committee in 1970, served the purpose of preserving the president's deniability while maintaining some White House control over Agency operations.[15] In this regard, there was a telling exchange between Republican senator Charles Mathias of Maryland and Richard Helms during the latter's testimony before the Church Committee:

> "Let me draw an example from history," Mathias offered. "When Thomas Becket was proving to be an annoyance, as Castro, the King said who will rid me of this man. He didn't say to somebody, go out and murder him."
>
> "That is a warming reference to the problem," Helms replied.
>
> "You feel that spans the generations and the centuries?"
>
> "I think it does, sir. . . . I think that any of us would have found it very difficult to discuss assassinations with a President of the U.S. . . . We all had the feeling that we're hired to keep those things out of the Oval Office."[16]

Kennedy after the Bay of Pigs, and Eisenhower after the downing of the U-2, had refused to hide behind plausible deniability—to the detriment of US foreign policy, some critics said. In his testimony before the Church Committee, Colby took the position that the CIA was and always had been an instrument of the president. He claimed that he had always been opposed to plausible denial and observed that it had become "outmoded and contentious in today's environment." Church and his colleagues took the easy way out, however. Following one meeting, Church told the press that the committee had not found any evidence "that would directly link the CIA involvement in this kind of activity with the President of the United States." The CIA, he subsequently observed, could be compared to a "rogue elephant on a rampage."[17]

On June 19, the night before he was to testify before the Church Committee, Sam Giancana, the Mafia figure who had been linked to the CIA plot to assassinate Castro, was murdered. The press went berserk. Senator John Tower (R-TX), who presided over hearings on the 20th, declared: "The committee, of course, notes with interest that Mr. Giancana was done away with." Colby, who testified later in the day on Phoenix, was cornered by reporters as he left the Capitol building and forced to deny that the CIA had anything to do with the former Mafia boss's murder.[18]

In contrast to its Senate counterpart, the Pike Committee was determined to trace CIA wrongdoings directly to the White House and to force a constitutional confrontation if the executive branch did not agree to give up all its secrets to Congress. Though a Democrat, Pike, a World War II bomber pilot and supporter of the Vietnam War, was not a liberal in the George McGovern–Michael Harrington vein. Like Senator Sam Ervin (D-NC), he was genuinely concerned with constitutional issues, such as separation of powers and checks and balances. He believed that Congress had failed in its duty to hold the White House accountable for its actions. As the House investigation began, Pike made no secret of the fact that he was convinced that the CIA had committed misdeeds and blunders that it was trying to cover up, and that the cover-up was being aided and abetted by the White House.

In his usual "come, let us reason together" mode, Colby called Pike and set up a meeting to work out ground rules for the upcoming investigation. The DCI quickly learned that, unlike Church and Rockefeller, Pike was not interested in compromise. The CIA had no right to withhold any document from the committee, he informed Colby. He refused to accept a classification system or to compel his staff to sign secrecy agreements. The chairman subsequently told a staff member: "Don't bring back anything the agencies want you to have; just get what they don't want you to have." A few days after their meeting, Pike wrote the DCI a sarcastic letter: "It's a delight to receive two letters from you not stamped 'Secret' on every page. . . . You are concerned with the concept of 'need to know' and I am concerned with the concept of 'right to know.'" Representative James Johnson (R-CO) set the tone for the relationship between the committee and the Agency when he told Seymour Bolten, chief of the CIA's Review Staff (the team Colby had assembled to decide which documents should be provided to Congress), "You, the CIA, are the enemy." Colby was appalled, particularly because he viewed the committee staff as a "ragtag" collection of "immature and publicity-seeking . . . children." Deputy Director for Intelligence Edward Proctor recalled that "a Pike committee staffer came to my office to interview me. She had on blue jeans that had been cut off at the calf and shredded, and she was barefoot." A more neutral observer, Church Committee counsel F.A.O. Schwarz Jr., observed that the Pike staff thought "they alone possessed virtue. They were all true believers." Colby feared that the Pike Committee would sensationalize at every opportunity and leak like a sieve. His fears were soon borne out.[19]

To help it prepare for hearings, Langley supplied Pike and his colleagues with a document listing the family jewels. The staff quickly began searching the document for gems that had not already been mined. A nugget, if not a jewel, soon appeared. One of the staffers discovered that over the years the Agency had detailed officers to various other bureaus and departments to act as liaisons. The sole object, Colby wrote in his memoir, was to enable the CIA to learn the ways of sister bureaucracies in order to better cooperate with them. Every agency head was aware of the officer's mission and identity, he claimed. Nevertheless, in 1973, Colby had issued an order terminating the liaison structure because, in a few "questionable" instances, the officers' activities "could be construed as involving the Agency in domestic activity [spying]." The wording of Colby's directive was unfortunate: the CIA "will not develop operations to penetrate another government agency, even with the approval of its leadership."[20]

On July 9, Searle Fields, staff director of the Pike Committee, sent a memo to committee members saying that the CIA had infiltrated other federal agencies, including the White House. The memo was immediately leaked to ABC News. Shortly thereafter, Colonel L. Fletcher Prouty, a CIA contract officer who had soured on the Agency, called reporter Daniel Schorr. The CIA had had a man in the Nixon White House, and he knew who he was: Alexander Butterfield. Schorr could hardly believe his ears—and his good luck. Butterfield was the man who had ratted out the Nixon White House on the existence of a secret taping system. His mind, Schorr later recalled, leaped back "to all the hints and rumors that the CIA pulled the plug on Nixon."[21]

On July 11, Bruce Morton and Schorr interviewed Prouty on the *CBS Morning News*. Prouty fingered Butterfield as the CIA's man in the White House and expressed the opinion that neither Nixon nor any of his aides knew his true mission, something that former White House aide Charles Colson subsequently affirmed. The program aired an interview with Colby, taped earlier, in which he declared: "I say that's outrageous and vicious nonsense. The CIA has never done anything with respect to the White House that's not known to the White House." Butterfield, who subsequently denied the allegation, might or might not have been the Agency's spy in the White House, but the CIA had penetrated the federal bureaucracy at a number of levels. Mole hunter Jim Angleton had spies everywhere. That fact was what lay behind Colby's 1973 decree terminating the liaison structure.[22]

The Pike Committee began its hearings by summoning budget director James Lynn in an attempt to uncover the CIA's money trail. Pike read Article 1, section 8, of the Constitution, which states, "No money shall be drawn from the Treasury but in consequence of appropriations made by law and a regular statement and account of the receipts and expenditures of all public money shall be published from time to time." Lynn stonewalled. Pike did not get any numbers, but the committee revealed that the General Accounting Office (GAO)—the independent arm of Congress that audits government agencies—had not been permitted to examine the CIA's books since 1962.[23]

When the misuse of taxpayer money issue did not strike a responsive chord with the media and the public, Pike and his colleagues moved on to more promising ground, namely, that the CIA was incompetent—that is, not only did the public not know how much it was spending on intelligence, but it wasn't getting much for its money. First up was the Yom Kippur War. There had already been reports that Langley's warriors had missed the boat badly, but Pike wanted to prove it. The committee subpoenaed a twenty-five-page internal postmortem prepared by the CIA. The retrospective was brutally frank—the Agency was not at all above learning from its mistakes—noting that intelligence on the crisis was "quite simply, obviously, and starkly wrong." To reveal the full extent of Agency incompetence, the committee wanted to make public the entire six-page summary of the report. The CIA, in turn, insisted that five paragraphs of the document be kept secret.[24]

The battle was joined at a committee meeting on the afternoon of September 11. Mitchell Rogovin represented the Agency. In an increasingly heated exchange, the staff insisted that Colby had ordered the five paragraphs struck not to protect sources and methods but to shield the Agency from further embarrassment. Repeatedly, Rogovin excused himself to phone Colby to ask for guidance. Time after time the DCI gave way, but he finally dug in his heels over four words—"and greater communications security." The words, referring to enhanced procedures to protect Egyptian military and diplomatic communications traffic, were part of the CIA station's report on the impending crisis in the Middle East; they implied that the Agency had the ability to monitor encrypted Egyptian traffic and, in fact, was doing so.[25]

Pike viewed the words not as a threat to sources and methods but as proof of how badly the Agency had blundered. America's spies were able to read Egypt's secret communications and still had not been able to predict the war. (President Anwar Sadat's regime knew of or suspected US surveillance and had sent misleading messages.) During a press conference at Langley shortly after the committee meeting, Colby explained why the seemingly innocuous words were potentially harmful to US interests. "Very expert analysts go over it," he said, referring to materials made public by congressional committees. "They examine their own machinery to see if there are chinks in the armor and whether there are gaps in their ability to keep secrets that they want to keep secret."[26]

As sources within the intelligence community would subsequently tell the *New York Times*, the Soviets and the Egyptians already knew about US spy capabilities. Indeed, Kissinger, in a very flattering biography written by Marvin and Bernard Kalb, had revealed that he had chosen to confide in the Soviets. Rogovin later reflected on Colby's reasoning: "Well, maybe those four words aren't that important, but if they disregard us on this, they'll disregard us on four other words." Disregard the administration is exactly what the Pike Committee did. Following a 6-to-3 vote, the chairman called a press conference to give a play-by-play account of the battle and then, over the formal protests of Rogovin and Assistant Attorney General Rex Lee, read the entire six-page report summary, including the four forbidden words, into the *Congressional Record*. "Obviously, we had reached a critical moment in the investigations," Colby wrote in *Honorable Men*.[27]

President Ford convened an emergency meeting at the White House to discuss the executive branch's response to the Pike Committee's challenge. He agreed that it wasn't so much the significance of the four words but the challenge inherent in the decision to release them. "For the committee to flatly ignore my protest and release what I regarded as legitimate secrets placed all our classified material and sensitive information at hazard," Colby later observed. Kissinger demanded a confrontation, insisting that no more classified material be turned over to the House committee and that everything of a sensitive nature that had been delivered be taken back. Schlesinger and Brent Scowcroft supported him. Ford's chief of staff, Donald Rumsfeld, and White House counsel John Marsh, both of whom had been congressmen, blanched at the prospect of a no-holds-barred show-down. How were documents already in the committee's hands to be recovered—through a contest of arms between the House sergeant at arms and a group of CIA operatives? "I was certainly with the 'doves,'" Colby later recalled, "holding that the committees should be given the material they requested with the exception of those that revealed the identities of our officers and agents, our relations with foreign intelligence services, and particularly sensitive technological data." The hardliners prevailed. "Bill, you know what you do when you go up to the Hill?" Kissinger cracked. "You go to confession."[28]

The morning following the gathering at the White House, Rex Lee arrived at the committee's public meeting to drop a bombshell. Until Chairman Pike promised that he would never again release classified information without permission, the executive branch would withhold classified documents. Moreover, the president would prohibit officials of the executive branch from testifying, and he had ordered that all sensitive materials be returned by the committee. Pike responded with righteous indignation. Sources and methods indeed! The issue was, "Shall Congress be a coequal branch of the Government?" It was secrecy versus democracy. Apparently, Pike declared, the CIA "would simply prefer that we operated in a dictatorship where only one branch of the Government has any power over secrecy." House members, disgusted with congressional pusillanimity during Vietnam and Watergate, temporarily rallied to the flag.[29]

Meanwhile, at the other end of Pennsylvania Avenue an appointed president was being urged to prevent any further erosion of executive power. "The House's action in releasing classified information over the protests of the executive," Kissinger wrote in a memo to Jack Marsh, "constitutes a challenge to the President's constitutional responsibility to conduct foreign affairs and protect the national security of the United States." Ford declared that he would ignore any subpoenas issued by the House for classified material. Pike retorted that, in that case, Congress would take the president to court. The *New York Times* declared the dispute "the most serious constitutional confrontation between the legislative and executive branches since the Watergate scandal."[30]

On Monday morning, September 29, the Pike Committee received a box of documents it had subpoenaed—the first such delivery since the committee had released the now-famous four words. To Pike's disgust, the Agency had heavily redacted the material and indicated that it would continue to censor such documents in the future. The committee then voted 10–3 to ask the House to cite Colby for contempt. "My sense of isolation, of being out on a limb all on my own, was rapidly growing," Colby wrote in *Honorable Men*. Morale at the Agency continued to deteriorate. Virtually all senior-level officials resented the congressional investigations, though for different reasons. Some were critical of the DCI for allegedly betraying Helms and breaking the Agency's code of secrets; others defended Colby, taking the position that he had had no choice in the matter and was being unfairly blamed for the sins of others. Regardless of their opinion of Colby, all of the Agency officials were offended not only by the Pike Committee but also by the irresponsible coverage by some media outlets. Colby was able to take some comfort from a blurb that Daniel Schorr read on the *CBS Evening News*: "Congress has its responsibilities, but Colby has his and he's prepared to take his chances. So, welcome Bill Colby to the club of potential jailbirds for principle!" But, surprisingly enough, it was aid and comfort—albeit indirectly—from another source—Henry Kissinger—that saved the DCI from a contempt citation.[31]

In line with its ongoing effort to prove CIA incompetence, the Pike Committee launched an investigation into the Greek-Turkish crisis that had temporarily gripped the world in the summer of 1974. In the course of the investigation, staff members learned of a memo written by Thomas Boyatt, the head of the State Department's Cyprus desk, critical of the intelligence he had received prior to the Turkish invasion of Cyprus. Subsequently fired from his post, Boyatt considered himself a whistle-blower and offered to help the committee. But on September 25, Lawrence Eagleburger, a Kissinger protégé and assistant secretary of state, appeared before Pike and his colleagues and informed them that the State Department would bar its personnel from testifying on policy matters and that no documents pertaining to Boyatt and the Cyprus crisis would be released to Congress. When Pike protested, Eagleburger compared the committee's demand for the Boyatt memo to the tactics employed by Senator Joe McCarthy during the Second Red Scare. Kissinger had ratcheted the confrontation between Congress and the executive branch up to a new level. Hitherto, Ford had not denied legislators the right to examine classified documents, only to release all or parts of them to the public.[32]

Having Colby and the CIA as an adversary was one thing; having Henry Kissinger was another. There was some mud from Watergate and the Allende coup still clinging to Kissinger's shoes, but in the fall of 1974, he was at the height of his power. No public official enjoyed a better press. The enormous amount of time he spent with journalists—rewarding allies, punishing enemies—was paying off in spades. *Time* called the secretary/adviser a "brilliant" policymaker with "diverse talents, energy and intellect." As the confrontation with the Pike Committee evolved, Kissinger rallied his troops in the press corps. Aaron Donner, chief counsel of the Pike Committee, recalled receiving a phone call from columnist James "Scotty" Reston in the midst of the brouhaha. "This is Scotty Reston of the [*New York*] *Times*," he growled into the phone. "What the hell are you guys doing down there? Are you reviving McCarthyism?" Both the *Times* and the *Washington Post* subsequently sided with Ford and Kissinger. Republicans on the committee began to get cold feet. Suddenly Pike's crusade was off the tracks. Though there was hardly a parallel, the ongoing comparison to McCarthyism proved devastating.[33]

It was time for a compromise, Bill Colby decided. While he, Rogovin, and Marsh worked on the White House, Pike Committee member Robert McClory, a moderate Illinois Republican hoping to avoid the humiliation of either his president or his committee, pushed Pike to be reasonable. Meanwhile, finally convinced that he had the upper hand, Kissinger agreed that "differences between the legislative and executive branches shouldn't be pushed to the point of law but decided on the basis of joint understanding and reconciliation." On September 30, Colby wrote Pike proposing an arrangement. In the future, there would be no disclosure of classified material by the committee without prior executive-branch review. In the event of a disagreement, the matter would be referred to the president. If he continued to object, the committee could still not release but would reserve the right to submit the matter to judicial review. That same day, Colby delivered a bundle of documents with only fifty words deleted. The committee subsequently agreed to the proposed compromise.[34]

Meanwhile, with the Pike Committee dominating the news, Church decided to hold public hearings, his committee's first. And the staff had a new jewel, one that was guaranteed to titillate. Sometime in the 1960s, zealous scientists in the technical branch of the Directorate of Operations—James Bond's "M" and his team—had collected 11 grams of shellfish toxin and

8 milligrams of cobra venom—enough, if dispersed widely, to kill thousands of people and, if applied discreetly, to assassinate a foreign leader. Indeed, one of the scenarios for doing away with Castro was to smear shellfish toxin on his scuba gear. In 1970, in the midst of negotiations over a multilateral treaty banning chemical and biological weapons, President Nixon had ordered all weapons-grade poisonous substances destroyed. The toxins and venom had been expensive and difficult to obtain, however, and a mid-level CIA officer took it upon himself to secret the poisons away in a secure storeroom. Shortly thereafter, the officer in question retired. His replacement assumed that the decision to retain the biological weapons had been approved by the DCI. Reacting to Colby's continual prodding to discover and divulge any and every CIA misdeed, Carl Duckett, deputy director for science and technology, came upon the cache of poisons and informed Colby. Aware that "we had something we should not have," Colby and Duckett reported the matter to the White House and subsequently to the Church Committee. "I unwittingly handed the committee a corker on a silver platter," Colby later recalled.[35]

On September 16, 1975, Colby and Rogovin appeared before the Church Committee in open session with the major networks televising the proceedings live. Colby calmly described the decision to retain the biological weapons and their subsequent discovery. The committee wanted the details of "Project Naomi," of which the toxins and venom were only a part. Were there other poisons? Yes, Colby replied—strychnine, cyanide, and a compound labeled "BZ" that attacked the nervous system. How were these agents to be delivered? Again Colby was prepared. He produced several dart guns and a .45-caliber-sized electric pistol capable of silently firing poison pellets. To the mirth of all present—except, of course, the CIA people—Colby referred to the pistol as "a nondiscernable microbioinoculator." Newspapers all across the country ran pictures of Church and Goldwater handling the dart guns. As Colby later wrote, "the overall impact was of the wildest hugger-mugger of the cloak-and-dagger world." Church subsequently used the CIA's "Show and Tell," as Newsweek dubbed it, to reinforce two points. The CIA was indeed in the business of assassination, and it was an Agency run amok, deliberately ignoring an order of the president. The New York Times agreed, terming the CIA handling of toxins and venom "the most reckless kind of insubordination." Times columnist Tom Wicker declared that the existence of the poisons was "only one more bit of evidence that this agency is a Frankenstein's monster that must be destroyed."[36]

According to Colby, the incident was "the last straw" as far as the White House was concerned. "From the outset," he later wrote, "I had been . . . aware that many in the administration did not approve of my cooperative approach to the investigations. I had been blamed for not categorically denying Hersh's story [concerning the CIA's role in spying on domestic radicals] at the very beginning; I had been criticized for turning material on Helms over to the Department of Justice; I had been chided for being too forthcoming to the Rockefeller Commission; I had been scolded for not stonewalling at every Congressional hearing." The White House had wanted to get rid of Colby ever since his January 1975 visit to Deputy Attorney General Laurence Silberman, when he—without Ford's knowledge—had delivered a list of possible criminal activities by Agency operatives. But in the wake of Hersh's revelations and those coming out of the congressional committees, firing the DCI then would have been seen as a cover-up. By summer, Washington was full of rumors that Colby's time had come. On June 20, CBS News had reported that Rockefeller and Kissinger were pressing for his dismissal. The vice president was quoted as saying that Colby was "a weak person who lacks strength of character." In the diary he wrote during the family jewels affair (later published in *Rolling Stone*), Dan Schorr speculated that "Kissinger is afraid that if Helms goes down, he'll be dragged down too."[37]

In fact, Kissinger had already misled the Church Committee. In testimony before that body, he had declared that Track II of the Chilean operation had ended on October 15, 1970, after he and Alexander Haig had met at the White House with Thomas Karamessines, the CIA's deputy director of plans. He was reminded that the DDP had recently testified that "as far as I was concerned, Track II was really never ended." Karamessines was misremembering, Kissinger replied. But the evidence said otherwise. Karamessines's cable to the CIA station in Chile, stating that "it is firm and continuing policy that Allende be overthrown by a coup," was dated October 16, 1970, the day after Track II had allegedly been terminated.[38]

Colby was not taking all this sitting down. On August 1, Mitch Rogovin told journalist Neil Sheehan that he and Colby had the goods on Kissinger. They had been able to obtain backchannel communications implicating him in the kidnapping and murder of Chilean general René Schneider.

"He's finished," Rogovin said. Later, in his notes on the conversation, Sheehan observed, "I wonder if Ford can afford to fire Kissinger. Perhaps it will be Mitch and Colby who will be fired."[39]

One Saturday morning in the early fall of 1975, Bill Colby, accompanied by two dark-suited security men, entered the back of a George Washington University auditorium. The distinguished classicist Bernard Knox, one of Colby's Jedburgh comrades-in-arms, was lecturing on Sophocles' *Antigone*. The title character was a young woman, the daughter of Oedipus and Jocasta, who defied the edict of her uncle, King Creon, by burying the body of her brother, who had led an enemy assault on his own city-state. In her eyes, she had done the honorable thing, but Creon condemned her to death. The gods sided with Antigone and reproached Creon. He, in turn, repented and went to free Antigone from prison, only to find that she had committed suicide. Creon's son, Haemon, who was in love with Antigone, then killed himself upon discovering her body. So, too, did his mother, appalled by the injustice of it all. The name Antigone was interpreted by many scholars to mean "unbending." You picked the appropriate lecture to attend, Knox remarked to his old friend after class. "Oh, I knew what you were going to talk about," Colby replied.[40]

On the evening of October 31, 1975, on *CBS Evening News*, Daniel Schorr revealed that the CIA, earlier in the year, with the Shah of Iran's approval, had been running a covert operation to help Kurdish tribesmen in their rebellion against the Iraqi government. "The operation had been described to the Pike committee only a few days before," Colby wrote in *Honorable Men*, "so there was very little doubt in any one's mind where the press had got hold of it."[41] The next morning, he went by the White House to discuss with Jack Marsh and others stratagems for keeping the Church Committee from issuing its report on assassinations and to commiserate over the irresponsibility of the Pike Committee. Shortly thereafter, Colby caught a plane for Jacksonville, Florida, where he was to discuss intelligence matters with Egyptian president Anwar Sadat. Sadat was so enthralled with journalist Barbara Walters, however, that Colby never got his audience.

When Colby returned to Washington that night, there was a message from Marsh waiting for him. He was to be at the White House at 8:00 sharp the next morning. When he arrived, the West Wing was deserted; there was no sign of the foreign policy team Colby had expected to see.

He was ushered into the Oval Office. As soon as Ford mentioned his intention to shake up his national security team, Colby realized that his tenure as DCI was over. He immediately offered his resignation. Ford accepted it and offered Colby the post of ambassador to the North Atlantic Treaty Organization. He said he would have to talk to Barbara. Ford confided that he was bringing George H. W. Bush back from China, where he was serving as ambassador, to run the Agency.

On his way out, Colby ran into James Schlesinger going in. He wasn't the only one being fired that day. Kissinger and Ford had had enough of the defense secretary's plotting against SALT II and his criticism of détente. The press later referred to the twin firings as the "Halloween Massacre." To undercut speculation that he was nothing more than Kissinger's lap dog, Ford announced that he was relieving Kissinger of his duties as national security adviser, though he would still be secretary of state. Kissinger's replacement would be Brent Scowcroft, his longtime deputy.

The first thing Bill did was call Barbara. The couple was scheduled to attend Mass at a Benedictine church where their sons had gone to school; instead, they received Communion at the parish church nearest their house and then began calling family and friends to break the news. Jenonne Walker later said that Colby knew from the outset of the family jewels crisis that he could not survive as DCI. Nevertheless, he was hurt and angry. "There goes twenty-five years just like that," he remarked to his wife when he arrived home. "He was pissed," Christine Colby, who was still in high school, later recalled.[42]

Bill and Barbara quickly decided that the NATO job was a dead end. He had the White House operator patch him through to Air Force One and so informed Ford, who was on his way to Miami for a dinner with Sadat. Dan Schorr called to check whether rumors he had heard of the twin firings were true. They were, Colby replied. "Colby, on the phone," Schorr subsequently wrote, "sounds as shaken as I've ever heard him." Late in the day, the Colbys paid a visit to the Schlesingers to commiserate. The newly ousted defense chief smiled at Bill and remarked, "It looks like Dick Helms outlasted both of us."[43]

Colby's firing precipitated a minor firestorm on Capitol Hill. Church called a press conference and, his voice quavering, declared that the decision to dismiss the DCI was just another part of a Watergate-style cover-up. "There seems to be a whole pattern developing of trying to thwart the committee's work and suppress its findings." At the time, the Church Committee was preparing its report on assassinations, and the White House was pulling every string to see that it was not made public. Church told reporters that there was no chance that the document would be suppressed. Other critics accused Ford of trying to politicize the CIA's top spot. Wasn't the president ignoring "the requirement that this be a non-partisan position?" a reporter subsequently asked White House press secretary Ronald Nessen, pointing out that George Bush was a former chair of the Republican National Committee.[44]

Kissinger and Ford had not thought matters out very well. It would be weeks, if not months, before Bush was ready to take over at Langley. Ford was scheduled to make a four-day visit to Beijing in December, and he wanted no changing of the guard at the American embassy there until after his trip. Even after Bush returned home, it would take time to have him confirmed. If Colby departed immediately, Vernon Walters would become acting DCI. The confrontations between the executive branch and the select committees were reaching a climax, and the White House did not want a man who had been tainted by the Watergate scandal to be chief spokesman for the intelligence community. According to Colby, it was Vernon Walters who pointed out the dilemma to the White House. This was probably not the case, but Walters did act as a go-between during the ensuing negotiations. Colby said he would agree to stay on, but he was scheduled to testify before various committees for at least the next six weeks, and he did not intend to be a mere pawn. Walters conveyed the message, and on Wednesday, November 5, Ford called Colby to the Oval Office once again.

Gracious as always, Colby took the initiative. "Mr. President, I don't want to make this in any way difficult. I am fully prepared to stay on until George Bush can get here, but the DCI serves at the pleasure of the President. In order to be effective he must have the President's full authority to act." Ford readily concurred and asked Colby if he wanted him to put it in writing. Colby said no. In his subsequent press release announcing that Colby would stay on, the president emphasized that during this period the DCI would act with "the full authority" of the President.[45]

The Halloween Massacre unfolded in the midst of the Ford administration's increasingly frantic effort to block publication of the Church Committee's report on assassinations, an effort in which Bill Colby played a leading role. On October 21, Colby had written to Ford arguing that release of the report would do irreparable damage to the foreign policy of the United States and threaten "the lives and livelihood of a number of officers of this Agency."

The Church Committee document examined in detail five alleged CIA plots to assassinate foreign leaders, in some cases naming names and in others re-creating scenarios that would enable foreign intelligence agencies to easily identify individuals. If the Church Committee were allowed to publish the results of the assassination investigation and its related probe into covert action, the CIA would in the future find it almost impossible to persuade citizens of foreign countries to cooperate with it, the DCI said. Some ten days later, Colby and Kissinger refused to testify at a public hearing that the Senate select committee had scheduled on Chile. Frustrated, Church reminded the White House that it was the president who had ordered the Rockefeller Commission's assassination materials to be turned over to the Senate committee. Yes, Ford replied, but not with the intention of having them made public. On November 2, just hours before Colby's firing, the Church Committee voted unanimously to approve the assassination report. But when members balked at making it public, Church threatened to resign. The committee then compromised by deciding to let the Senate as a whole decide.[46]

On November 19, Colby held only the second open press conference by a DCI in the CIA's history. He outlined the dire consequences to follow if the assassination report was released. Behind the scenes, the Agency pleaded for the deletion of eleven names. The committee agreed to only one—Dr. Sidney Gottlieb, who had been involved in the preparation of the poison designed to do away with Lumumba—but only because he had gone to court. Schorr learned the identity of some of the people whom Colby had hoped to shield from exposure, among them Robert Maheu and Johnny Roselli. "When you work with the Mafia and promise to try to protect them," Schorr observed in his diary, "I guess you have to go down the line with them." On the 20th in a closed-door session, the Senate refused to block the assassination report's release, but it would not approve its publication, either. That same day, on his own authority, Church released the results of the investigation, nine months after Dan Schorr had reported on the matter and six months after the Rockefeller Commission had suppressed its conclusions.[47]

The Church Committee's interim report on assassinations cleared the CIA of killing anyone, but it found that the Agency had tried and failed to assassinate Castro at least eight times, employing everything from toxic diving suits to syringes disguised as ballpoint pens. It also found that the CIA had acquired and dispatched an unnamed "lethal substance"—poisoned toothpaste—to the Congo to be used to eliminate Patrice Lumumba, but his enemies had killed him before US operatives could execute their plan. In three other cases, the CIA had encouraged the murders of foreign leaders—Rafael Trujillo, General René Schneider, and Salvador Allende—but was not complicit in their deaths. Washington had facilitated the overthrow of Ngo Dinh Diem, but did not advocate his assassination. But who was more to blame, the presidents or the CIA "rogue elephant"? The report equivocated.[48]

Shortly after releasing the report, Church filed papers with the Federal Election Commission to create an "exploratory" Church for President Committee. In February 1976, President Ford would issue an executive order—"Restrictions on Intelligence Activities"—declaring, "No employee of the United States shall engage in, or conspire to engage in, political assassination." In a 1978 *Playboy* interview, Bill Colby would observe that the Ugandan people would be morally justified in assassinating their brutal ruler, Idi Amin, and that if asked, the CIA would be justified in aiding such an effort.[49]

Meanwhile, the White House and the CIA had asked that they be allowed to review a draft of the Pike Committee report prior to its release. When it arrived the last week in October, President Ford and his advisers were appalled. The document was a litany of CIA failures substantiated by the Agency's postmortems, but without any mention of the spy agency's successes. More ominously, it contained specific information on covert operations in Iraq, Angola, and Italy. Shortly thereafter, portions of the report began leaking, and in the days that followed the trickle became a deluge. In a speech to the United States Navy League in October 1975, Colby asked rhetorically, "Is our intelligence to become mere theatre? Will it be exposed in successive re-runs for the amusement, or even amazement, of our people rather than being preserved and protected for the benefit of us all?"[50]

Even as leaks about the Pike Committee's report were occurring, it issued subpoenas for new material, including intelligence reports on the Soviet Union, Portugal, and the Cyprus crisis; decision memoranda of the 40 Committee; and documents on Russian compliance with nuclear arms control agreements. Both Colby and Kissinger dug in their heels, and on November 16, Ford claimed executive privilege. On that same day, the House select committee voted 10–2 to cite Kissinger for contempt of Congress. Ford's advisers told the president that they were not at all sure that the White House would win in the courts, and Kissinger, though likely to win, did not want to risk a contempt vote in the House. Ford proposed a compromise—a State Department official would read from the subpoenaed documents, but they would not be made available to committee members directly. Pike quickly accepted. His committee was deeply divided, and he sensed that the support he had in the House as a whole was crumbling. Then came the crowning blow.[51]

On December 23, 1975, Richard S. Welch, the CIA's chief of station in Athens, and his wife attended a Christmas party hosted by Ambassador Jack Kubisch. Both men were new to their jobs, two of the most difficult US posts in the world. In 1967, a group of neo-fascist colonels had staged a coup and seized power in Greece. They installed George Papadopoulos, who had been on the CIA payroll off and on since the 1950s, as president. Relations between Washington and Athens were cold during the Johnson administration but improved dramatically under Nixon. By 1973, the United States was the only nation in the developed world on friendly terms with the junta, which regularly jailed and tortured its political foes. By the time Welch and his family arrived, anti-American sentiment in Athens was reaching a fever pitch. Ever since the Agency had first established a presence in Athens, the chief of station had lived rather conspicuously in the same large house. "I had made arrangements for him to go into a different residence and to live in a different part of town, to try and help conceal who he was and to give him some cover," Kubisch later said. Welch refused. When the Christmas party at the ambassador's house broke up, the chief of station and his wife drove the few blocks to their CIA villa in the fashionable suburb of Palaio Psychiko. Parked in their driveway was a small car containing four people. Three got out, pulled Welch from his auto, and shot him three times in the chest with a .45. This was the first assassination of a station chief in the history of the Agency.[52]

Welsh's murder made the front page of newspapers across the United States. In still another press conference, Colby praised Welch and implied that he was a victim of the anti-CIA hysteria that was gripping the nation. More specifically, he pointed the finger at *Counterspy*, the magazine of an organization called The Fifth Estate. Among its members were disgruntled former CIA employees, including Philip Agee, as well as a number of anti–Vietnam War activists. In its winter 1974–1975 issue, *Counterspy* had listed Welch as the CIA chief of station at Lima, Peru. The magazine, whose chief financial angel was author Norman Mailer, was hardly repentant. "If anyone is to blame for Mr. Welch's death," the publication declared, "it is the CIA that sent him to Greece to spy and intervene in the affairs of the Greek people." Soon afterward, *Counterspy*'s winter 1975–1976 issue hit the stands. It quoted Agee as saying, "The most effective and important systematic efforts to combat the CIA that can be undertaken right now are . . . the identification, exposure, and neutralization of its people working abroad."[53]

Welch was buried with full military honors at Arlington National Cemetery on January 6, 1976. Ford, Kissinger, and Colby attended. "The funeral was a rare and glittering tableau of the American national security establishment," wrote Laurence Stern in the *Washington Post*, "with several generations of diplomats and spies gathered on the grassy slopes of Arlington to pay tribute to Welch and the institution he served." "Welch in death may have started the rollback that President Ford, Secretary Kissinger and the whole CIA seemed unable to accomplish," Daniel Schorr commented on *CBS Nightly News*. In 2002 a member of the radical Marxist organization 17 November (or 17N, for the date of an uprising in 1973) confessed to playing a role in Welch's murder and named his accomplices. But the statute of limitations had run out.[54]

On January 15, President Ford, riding the backlash that followed in the wake of Welch's murder, wrote Otis Pike, forbidding him to publish the details of various CIA covert operations. Colby called on the chairman to observe the terms of the "Colby compromise," but Pike insisted that it applied only to the release of specific documents, not to the committee's final report. With the committee's mandate set to expire on January 31, its staffers and a CIA team headed by Mitchell Rogovin negotiated frantically over specific deletions. Pike accepted some Agency redactions but rejected 150 others. The House select committee approved its report on January 23, but on the 29th the chamber as a whole voted 246–124 against releasing the document.[55]

By then, however, much of what was in the report had already leaked to the press. On February 13, the *Village Voice* published the results of the Pike investigation in their entirety. It listed the CIA's six most conspicuous "failures," released material on the 40 Committee that proved decidedly unspectacular, and dealt with some ongoing CIA covert operations. Ironically, the Pike report was an indictment of the presidency rather than the CIA. In his testimony before the committee, in an effort to deflect attention from himself, Kissinger had given the coup de grace to plausible deniability when he declared that every single covert operation carried out in recent years had been approved by the White House. "All evidence in hand," the committee report declared, "suggests that the CIA, far from being out of control, has been utterly responsive to the instructions of the President and the assistant to the president for National Security Affairs." It was soon revealed that the source for the *Village Voice* article was Daniel Schorr. CBS immediately fired him, and the House subsequently cited him for contempt.[56]

There were those within and without the media who took the position that the family jewels flap was a product of post-Watergate journalism. "Had Seymour Hersh not written his CIA domestic surveillance stories for *The New York Times* in December 1974 (indeed, had not *The Times* seen fit to splash the first story across five columns of page one headlined 'Massive Surveillance')," wrote Timothy Hardy, a Rockefeller Commission staffer, "there seems little doubt that there never would have been a Rockefeller Commission, a Pike 'Report,' a Church committee. . . . Hersh, and Hersh alone, caused the President, and then Congress . . . to make intelligence a major issue of 1975."[57]

Shortly after the original Hersh stories appeared, the respected *Washington Post* investigative reporter Walter Pincus wrote that "no series of news stories since Watergate has had so quick an impact on government, while generating so much discussion among journalists as the Hersh pieces." Like many other reporters of that time, Pincus had long used CIA personnel as sources of information for news stories; they were usually the best-informed Americans about any particular foreign situation. It was well known that the Agency sometimes solicited and received information from newspeople and used jobs in the industry as cover. Pincus, a friend of Hersh's, went on to show how Hersh and his editor, A. M. Rosenthal, had manipulated the scarce information they had—and had tricked Bill Colby into confirming information that they did not have—into a story that was at the least exaggerated and then helped prompt an investigation. Indeed, the first solon to demand a congressional probe was Senator William Proxmire (D-WI), whom Hersh had called seeking comments on his initial story. "Like it or not, he [Rosenthal] and his counterpart in *The Washington Post* are participants," Pincus declared. "The front page story selections set an agenda for government." In early 1976, shortly after the Pike report came out, Clare Boothe Luce observed to President Ford, "The press has arrogated to itself the right of secrecy . . . [and] no one else can have it."[58]

As George Bush prepared to return to the United States and face confirmation hearings, Colby did everything he could to ease the transition. "We have arranged a suitable office here and will organize secretarial, transportation, etc.," he cabled Bush, then en route from Beijing. Colby's own office staff and the Agency's senior officers would be at his service. "Also certainly would fully brief you on on-going ballgames with Senate and House Select Committees and, of course, the substantive business of intelligence." Bush replied that it would probably be best for him not to take up residence before his confirmation, but he gladly accepted the offer of consultations. After his arrival, the DCI-designate met almost daily with Colby and the deputy directors. "Bill Colby . . . has been extraordinarily thoughtful to me," Bush wrote President Ford.[59]

The Senate confirmed Bush as director on January 28, 1976; two days later, Colby received him and President Ford at Langley. The past and future DCIs were waiting at the entrance to the Agency's auditorium and greeted Ford as he pulled up in his limousine. The three then entered the great hall, where CIA employees had assembled. Colby began: "Mr. President and Mr. Bush, I have the great honor to present to you an organization of dedicated professionals. Despite the turmoil and tumult of the past year, they continue to produce the best intelligence in the world." He was treated to a standing ovation.

Following the swearing-in, the three emerged from the auditorium, but instead of accompanying Ford and Bush into the main office building, Colby inconspicuously walked away from them to the visitor's parking lot, where Barbara's rather dilapidated Buick Skylark was waiting. Ripples of applause followed him. An unassuming man making an unassuming exit. "It was an ending," wrote Laurence Stern in the *Washington Post*, "that would have done justice to George Smiley, the antihero of spy novelist John Le Carre: understated and not without its ironies."[60]

Shortly thereafter, journalist Neil Sheehan visited Langley and, viewing the portraits of past directors, was struck by the contrast between the ones of Bill Donovan and Bill Colby. "It was an interesting line . . . from Donovan, the somewhat flamboyant corporation lawyer/general to Colby, the self-effacing servant of the state, dressed in a business suit as Donovan was dressed in a warrior's garb."[61] In truth, there were far more similarities between Donovan and Colby than differences. Both were warriors and covert operations addicts. And, like Donovan, Colby would remain closely associated with the CIA long after he had officially departed its ranks.

EPILOGUE

I n the aftermath of his ouster as DCI, Bill Colby's most immediate concern was how to make a living. He had his pension from the Agency, but that would not suffice. He started a small law firm—Colby, Bailey, Werner & Associates—but also did work for the Washington firm of International Business-Government Counsellors, Inc. (IBC), doing risk analysis, that is, assessing the political stability of various nations on behalf of potential investors. He advised development projects in the Philippines, Thailand, and Malaysia, and did the same for Japanese businesses wanting to invest in the United States. He would write two books and numerous articles. Though it brought him little remuneration, Colby would continue to be involved with his beloved CIA for the remaining twenty years of his life. Indeed, he became a central figure in what one journalist termed "the wars of the CIA," with Colby at the head of one faction, and James Jesus Angleton and Richard Helms the standard-bearers for the other. The split was personal, but it was also political and ideological, pitting opponents of Soviet-American détente against its supporters, disciples of the counterintelligence culture versus its critics, and political conservatives against liberals.

The chickens of the early Cold War and the Colby-Angleton feud were coming home to roost. In various interviews and speeches, Angleton charged that Colby's decimation of CI, along with a new emphasis on détente, had opened the door to a horde of KGB agents in the West. Responding to charges by the gossip tabloid *National Enquirer* that there were no fewer than twenty-three Soviet agents working at the United Nations, Angleton told the *Washington Star* that "it's amazing . . . but that's a characteristic of this whole thing of détente. The Soviets have become very brazen about their spying and the FBI is having trouble keeping an eye on them. I don't think the FBI even has enough men to keep all KGB agents in this country under surveillance."[1]

Then followed two books from the Angleton-Helms camp, one— *Orchids for Mother*—fiction, and the other—*Legend: The Secret World of Lee Harvey Oswald*—nonfiction. The first, written by Aaron Latham and published in 1977, featured a CIA novice who was captivated by an Angleton character in all his orchid-growing, fly-fishing, poetry-reading glory. Eccentric though he might have been, the character based on Angleton, Francis Xavier Kimball, was dedicated and prescient, a man able to penetrate the schemes of the KGB. The character representing Colby, Ernest O'Hara, was a colorless bureaucrat, jealous of Kimball, and quite possibly a communist mole. In the climax, Kimball/Angleton set himself up to be assassinated by O'Hara/Colby and his henchmen, revealing the villain for what he was. The second book, *Legend*, by Edward J. Epstein in 1978, was a study of the Kennedy assassination and Lee Harvey Oswald's role in it. Epstein got the title from Angleton, who had written that "in the field of intelligence, a legend is an operational plan for a cover, or a cover itself, depending on the mission." The implication was that Oswald was living a legend at the time he shot Kennedy. He had not really returned from his sojourn in the Soviet Union disillusioned, but was acting as an agent of the KGB.[2]

According to Epstein's book, Soviet agents had managed to penetrate both British and American intelligence, including the CIA and the FBI, and flooded the West with pseudo-defectors, including Nosenko, to spread disinformation. The lie of lies was Nosenko's claim that the KGB had disassociated itself from Lee Harvey Oswald and had had nothing to do with the Kennedy assassination. Epstein alleged that at the time Nosenko was telling his story—a tale that Angleton and Golitsin never bought—a Soviet agent operating out of the United Nations (code-named "Fedora") had vouched for Nosenko with the FBI. Angleton's man, Golitsin, not Nosenko, was the real defector; it was his version of events, not Nosenko's, that was true. Epstein's book ended with the firing of Angleton and most of the counterintelligence staff, and readers were left with the impression that there was a major mole burrowing away within the CIA. In a subsequent interview, Epstein was asked if he thought there was a Soviet spy working within American intelligence. "He hasn't been caught yet, and it is entirely conceivable that one was planted," he replied. Did Angleton really know who the mole was? "Angleton refused to say, but one of his ex-staff members," Epstein said, "told me with a wry smile, 'You might find out who Colby was seeing in Rome in the early 1950s.'" One reviewer wrote, "Angleton's point of view fills the book [*Legend*] just as orchids now fill Epstein's New York apartment."[3]

In 1978, Simon and Schuster published *Honorable Men*, Colby's memoir, which he coauthored with Peter Forbath. In it Colby described his life and made the case against Angleton and the whole culture of counterintelligence. A reasonable vigilance for moles was necessary, the former DCI maintained, but in his paranoia Angleton had allowed counterintelligence to paralyze the CIA's efforts to gather intelligence on what was going on within the Soviet Union and the Eastern bloc. During the book tour that followed publication, Colby told an interviewer in Atlanta: "The KGB is something to be evaded, not to be mesmerized by. . . . For the CIA and the KGB to chase each other around like two scorpions is of no particular value to anyone." Angleton was not going to take this lying down. As a result of Colby's purge of CI, he declared, "there is tremendous [foreign espionage] going on and the bureau [FBI] and agency [CIA] simply do not have the assets in counterintelligence to contain them." Furthermore, he told a reporter, "the whole Colby ego trip is a hornswoggle on the American public."[4]

Thomas Powers, a journalist who was in the midst of writing a laudatory biography of Richard Helms, panned *Honorable Men* and raised the Colby-as-mole issue again. "Some CIA people" had looked him in the eye and told him, he said, that "Colby's decisions as Director of Central Intelligence were completely consistent with those one might expect of an enemy agent." Shortly afterward, Colby remarked ruefully to another interviewer, "Have you heard? . . . The latest story about me is that I'm the 'mole.' You know, on the side of the Russians."[5]

With Colby and Angleton at pen's point, the feud became entangled in the burgeoning debate over the SALT II agreement, with Colby siding with the "SALT sellers," as he put it, and Angleton with the "SALT shakers."

In January 1977, Jimmy Carter had succeeded to the presidency—having defeated Gerald Ford the previous November—and named Admiral Stansfield Turner to replace George Bush as DCI. Although Turner proceeded to cut Agency personnel by an additional 25 percent, and Langley censors brought suit against Colby for allowing a French edition of *Honorable Men* to be published without their approval (he agreed to pay a $10,000 fine), Colby got on well with Turner and the Carter administration in general. He was attracted by the White House's combination of toughness toward the Soviets on the issue of human rights and support for nuclear disarmament. He, like the president, seemed not to be bothered that the first policy impeded progress on the second.

Six days after his inauguration, Carter informed Soviet premier Leonid Brezhnev that he was deeply committed to détente. Carter had been an ardent supporter of the 1972 SALT I agreement, which had placed numerical limitations on different types of strategic missiles. The treaty was scheduled to expire in October 1977, and Carter desperately wanted to negotiate a new pact that would go beyond merely maintaining exit levels and mandated cuts. At the same time, the administration issued repeated calls for Moscow to stop persecuting dissidents such as Aleksandr Solzhenitsyn and Andrei Sakharov and to allow the free emigration of Jews from the Soviet Union to Israel. The Kremlin, of course, regarded the whole human rights campaign as an unwarranted attempt to meddle in Russia's internal affairs. Despite the ill will arising from Carter's castigation of Moscow over its treatment of dissidents and Jews, the two sides managed to sign an agreement on June 18, 1979. SALT II was the first nuclear arms treaty that assured real reductions in the strategic nuclear forces of both sides, imposing a maximum of 2,250 weapons. American and Soviet negotiators also agreed to severe restrictions on the development and deployment of American cruise missiles and the Russian Tu-22M "Backfire" bomber, which the Pentagon believed could be modified to attack the United States.

SALT II was anathema to conservatives and liberal hawks, such as Senator Henry "Scoop" Jackson of Washington. Angleton, now chair of the Security and Intelligence Fund—an organization dedicated to the resurrection of the clandestine services within the intelligence community—led a chorus of voices proclaiming that SALT II was unverifiable. Colby and Turner had gutted the Agency, rendering it incapable of keeping tabs on the treacherous Soviets, treaty opponents charged. In August 1978, a young CIA watch officer, William P. Kampiles, had been arrested and accused of selling an ultra-secret KH-11 spy satellite manual to the KGB. The FBI subsequently discovered that seventeen other KH-11 manuals were missing.

In the midst of the negotiations on SALT II, Richard Helms weighed in. "The Kampiles case raises the question of whether or not there has been infiltration of the US intelligence community or government at a significant level," he told the *Washington Post*. In that same month, May 1979, an article in *Penthouse* charged that more than 2,000 KGB agents were working out of New York using jobs at the United Nations as cover. "A large percentage of the KGB force operating from the United Nations," the magazine declared, "is known [to be] officers in Department V—the KGB elite specializing in murder, terrorism, and sabotage." SALT shakers cited other evidence to indicate that US intelligence had been so compromised that a new arms control agreement could not be safely negotiated with the Soviets. Topping things off was the death of CIA officer/consultant John Arthur Paisley.[6]

On the moonlit night of September 23, 1978, Arthur Paisley vanished into the waters of the Chesapeake Bay. His 31-foot sloop *Brillig*, named from Lewis Carroll's famous poem "Jabberwocky" in *Through the Looking Glass, and What Alice Found There*, was found run aground under full sail the next morning. Paisley had bought the vessel in 1974 following his retirement from the CIA, where he had worked as an expert on Soviet nuclear capabilities. A week later, on October 1, Paisley's bloated, decomposing body was discovered floating in the bay, a 9-millimeter gunshot wound in the back of his head and weighted divers' belts around his waist. The corpse was duly delivered to Maryland's chief medical examiner, but for seventeen days it went unidentified; the examiner looked high and low but could not come up with a set of fingerprints that would match. Finally, the hands were severed from the body and delivered to the FBI, which identified the corpse as Paisley's. The body was then cremated in a CIA-approved funeral home outside of Washington, DC. Langley strongly suggested that the death was a suicide, but the Maryland State Police later concluded that the cause of death was "undetermined."

Investigative reporters pounced on the Paisley story and discovered, among other things, that the deceased had originally been recruited by Angleton, had become a specialist on Soviet strategic research and deployment, had learned Russian in order to study Soviet technical journals, and had become one of the few men privy to the sources and methods of acquiring intelligence on Soviet nuclear developments. He was one of the agents Angleton had summoned to debrief Nosenko, and once Nosenko was cleared of charges that he was a Soviet double agent, in 1968, the two men had become friends. Paisley had also been deeply involved in the KH-11 spy satellite program, and when the *Brillig* washed ashore, journalist Tad Szulc noted ominously, it carried sophisticated communications equipment. It seems that the CIA had rehired Paisley as a consultant to work on nuclear arms verification matters some two years after his retirement. Speculation, of course, was rampant. Some said Paisley was the long-sought-after mole; others said he was a brilliant analyst who had been done in by the mole. All of the SALT naysayers agreed that the ability of the United States to monitor the Soviet nuclear arms industry, and hence verify SALT II, had been hopelessly compromised. On March 9, 1979, Scoop Jackson took to the floor of the Senate to announce that he might not vote for the disarmament agreement.[7]

In an article entitled "Verifying SALT," published in *Worldview*, Colby made the case for the SALT sellers. The CIA and the KGB both had agents busily at work gathering information on each other's arms programs, he wrote. That was probably a good thing. The notion that the Soviets could cheat in any meaningful way was absurd. US technology was equal to none. The Agency and other intelligence entities might miss something here and there, but any major violation of the treaty would be detected. "The question is this," he declared: "Are we pettyfoggers looking for absolute evidence for some little variation—a quarter of an inch on the side of an absolute scale—or are we interested in the protection of our country and the ability to make an agreement to move ahead to these kinds of new restraints that will help us as well as the Soviets?" He appealed to the naysayers to see the arms control debate in a larger context—the ongoing effort by the two major protagonists to ease tensions to the point where the Cold War could be ended. Stansfield Turner wrote to congratulate the former DCI on his *Worldview* article. "You make the case eloquently for expanding the scope of the debate," he said. "I hope I can induce others to see it your way." SALT II was never formally ratified by the Senate, although its terms were honored by both sides until 1986, when the Reagan administration disavowed the agreement, accusing the Soviets of massive violations.[8]

In the midst of the debate over nuclear disarmament, the anti-Angleton forces launched a new offensive. In 1979, DCI Turner hired Cleveland Cram, former station chief in Ottawa and one of the men upon whom CI had cast suspicion, to investigate the Angleton–Kim Philby connection. How could this supposed super-spy have been taken in so completely by the British traitor? In his report, Cram observed that Angleton had been "less than successful" in protecting the CIA from penetration by enemy agents. The following year, David Martin, a reporter for *Newsweek*, published *Wilderness of Mirrors*, which, à la Bill Colby, portrayed Angleton not as sleuth extraordinaire but as a tragic figure whose paranoia and mole-hunting destroyed his career. In his book, Martin revealed that in 1974, a member of Angleton's own staff had accused him of being a mole. Colby, who was DCI at the time, had dismissed the notion as just another manifestation of the overactive imaginations that pervaded CI.[9]

Then, hard on the heels of the December 1979 Soviet invasion of Afghanistan, came the election of Ronald Reagan; the Cold War was on again. The president-elect chose as his DCI William J. Casey, an OSS veteran and a hardline anticommunist. Casey came to Langley determined to further marginalize the analysts, who were continuing to argue that the Soviets did not possess superiority in nuclear weapons and had no intention of launching a first strike. He was equally determined to rebuild the clandestine services. Indeed, the Reagan transition team made Jim Angleton one of its principal consultants on intelligence matters. It was a logical move. Reaganites were convinced that the Soviets were cheating on SALT II and that first Colby and then Turner had so weakened counterintelligence that the country was being overrun by KGB operatives.[10]

Colby remained undaunted. In 1982, he came out publicly in favor of a nuclear arms freeze, identifying himself with the nuclear freeze movement generally and with a letter from the Catholic bishops calling for an end to the arms race specifically. A freeze agreement was eminently enforceable, he told a press conference. Indeed, any nuclear arms accord with Moscow would make it "easier rather than harder" to keep tabs on what the Soviets were doing by empowering the United States to demand an explanation of any suspicious Soviet arms behavior. In a subsequent article in the *Washington Post*, the former DCI accused the Reagan administration of appeasement—both of the Soviets, by making concessions that allowed the development of new weapons systems, and of the American "nuclear priesthood, which thinks only of building new and more complex weapons systems." In taking on the New Right and the military-industrial complex for which it spoke, Colby realized that he was running counter to form for a former DCI. "If I were taking the other side, nobody would bat an eyebrow about it," he said.[11]

On the matter of covert operations, however, Colby was more in agreement with William Casey and the Reagan White House than not. Noting that in 1983 only 3 to 4 percent of the Agency's budget was allocated to covert operations, both political and paramilitary, he told the *Los Angeles Times*: "I hope it will increase because I think there are areas of the world where a little covert action can forestall much more serious problems later." In an article in the *Washington Post*, he noted that the world was becoming an increasingly complex and dangerous place and called for the creation of an elite counterterrorist force. "Cuban, East German and other Soviet proxies proliferate in Africa, the Middle East and Central America, and ideologues such as Qaddafi, Khomeini, and Castro plot to isolate the United States by subverting its allies," he wrote. Carter's disastrous effort to rescue the American hostages in Iran revealed just how unprepared the United States was. What was needed was an antiterrorist unit composed of volunteers from the military services and appropriate civilian agencies, such as the Foreign Service and the CIA, that would train continuously and report directly to the Joint Chiefs of Staff.[12]

No high official ever really retires from the CIA, especially DCIs. Their experience and contacts are too valuable. Colby was called upon to facilitate dozens of schemes and operations, most of which are still shrouded in secrecy. But in 1980, his name popped up in connection with an Australian banking firm, Nugan Hand merchant bank, an enterprise that had laundered money for the Agency. It had also played a role in the 1975 fall of Australia's left-leaning prime minister Gough Whitlam. Australia was arguably America's most important ally in the Pacific. Oil tankers bound for Japan, Western Europe, and the United States regularly passed through an area north of Australia between Malaysia and Indonesia. The country was host to ten American military installations, including the ultra-secret satellite-monitoring facilities at Pine Gap.

In 1972, Whitlam had formed Australia's first Labor government in twenty-three years. He and his deputy prime minister, a self-described "fellow-traveler" named James Cairns, denounced the war in Vietnam and called for restrictions on CIA operations in Australia. The new government established diplomatic relations with Cuba, North Korea, and the German Democratic Republic and received leaders of the Palestine Liberation Organization. The Whitlam regime then began putting pressure on the Australian Security Intelligence Organisation (ASIO) to sever ties with its American counterpart. For once, Kissinger, Angleton, and Colby saw eye to eye. "We . . . entrusted the highest secrets of counter-intelligence to the Australian services and we saw the sanctity of that information being jeopardized by a bull in a china shop," Angleton later declared. For his part, Colby viewed the "left-leaning and . . . antagonistic government in Australia" as a problem equal in importance to the Cyprus crisis and the Yom Kippur War. "Whitlam's a bastard," James Schlesinger remarked at a 1973 White House meeting. "I agree," Kissinger added.[13]

When Whitlam indicated that he might not renew the contract for America's crucial Pine Gap listening post, the CIA and ASIO had had enough. Langley money began pouring into opposition parties. A CIA team headed by Edwin P. Wilson, later accused of selling arms to Libya, fabricated some cables implicating the Whitlam government in a financial scandal. In December 1975, the Australian House of Representatives passed a no-confidence vote, and the Commonwealth Governor-General asked Conservative Party leader Malcolm Fraser to form a new government. In 1980, it came to light that the paymaster for the CIA effort to unseat the Whitlam government had been Nugan Hand.[14]

The bank had been founded in 1973 by an Australian lawyer, Francis John "Frank" Nugan, who was reputedly associated with the Australian Mafia, and Michael Jon Hand, a former US Green Beret who had worked in Vietnam in the Phoenix program and in Laos training the Hmong army. In February 1980, Nugan was found dead, shot in the head with a .30 caliber rifle, in his Mercedes Benz some 90 miles north of his $1 million harborside residence in Sydney. The following July, Hand skipped the country with an estimated $5 million of what was left of the bank's assets. News articles would claim that Nugan Hand was an international dealer in heroin as well as a money launderer for the CIA. Bill Colby's business card—with his itinerary for a forthcoming Asian trip written on it—was found on Nugan's body. As it turned out, Colby had signed on as Nugan Hand's US attorney in 1976. Even more mysterious, Arthur Paisley had been investigating the financial ties between the Agency and Nugan Hand at the time of his death, apparently at the request of Langley, which was worried about the use of possible illicit funds in the financing of political action against the Whitlam government. When questioned by newsmen, Colby claimed that his connection with Nugan Hand was purely commercial, part of his international law practice.[15]

In 1982, at the age of sixty-two, Bill Colby fell in love. The object of his affection was a thirty-seven-year-old former US ambassador to Grenada, Sally Shelton. Smart, attractive, and self-assured, Shelton had been born in San Antonio in 1944, but had grown up in Monett, Missouri. She attended Southern Methodist University, earning a bachelor's degree in French. "I wanted to become an ambassador and change the world," she recalled. After garnering a master's degree in international relations from Johns Hopkins, she spent a year in Italy, and then enrolled in the Institut d'Etudes Politiques de Paris to complete her doctorate. She never finished, instead marrying a young Mexican from a politically prominent family. The union ended after a year, and Sally returned to Washington, where she went to work for the newly elected Democratic senator from Texas, Lloyd Bentson, as his foreign policy expert.

Politics would be her vehicle for advancement. "If I had gone into the Foreign Service," she later said, "I might still be waiting [for an ambassadorship]." Jimmy Carter named Shelton to be ambassador to Grenada and Barbados, where she served during the tumultuous period from 1979 to 1981. She remembered remarking to Secretary of State Cyrus Vance before her departure that she feared there would not be enough going on in the eastern Caribbean to occupy her time and energies. No sooner had the youthful ambassador arrived in Grenada, however, than the New Jewel Movement staged a military coup, replacing the existing pro–United States regime with a "People's Revolutionary Government" headed by Maurice Bishop. The new prime minister, who ruled by decree, immediately reached out to Cuba, which in turn dispatched economic and military aid. US forces would invade Grenada in 1983, but by then Shelton was gone, her tenure having ended with Reagan's election.

Shelton spent a year teaching and conducting research at the Kennedy School at Harvard University and then applied for a job with the International Business-Government Counsellors. Bill Colby was the person who interviewed her. "I remember the first time I laid eyes on him," she later recalled. "I had seen his picture in the newspapers many times. I thought he was so attractive, physically very attractive and just the nicest person." IBC offered Sally a job, and she and Bill quickly began an office romance.

"He was very troubled by the age difference," Sally recalled. "He was twenty-four and a half years older than I. I wasn't bothered by it at all. . . . It didn't take him very long to realize he wanted to marry me." Jenonne Walker, who had been friends with Sally before she met Colby, was surprised at the match. "I thought Bill Colby had all the charisma of a shoe clerk," she said. "Sally is a very outgoing woman, even flamboyant. She found him a sex object and with her he was."[16]

By the spring of 1983, Bill had decided to end his marriage to Barbara. His father, Elbridge, had died the previous December removing that Newmanite obstacle. Accounts differ as to where he broke the news. Barbara remembers him telling her in their living room at home; daughter Christine believes it was aboard *Eagle Wing II*. Apparently, Barbara was taken completely by surprise. "People like us don't get a divorce," she blurted out. A Catholic marriage conceived in the years immediately after World War II, replete with five children, should last. Paul remembered that his mother nearly died of humiliation: "In front of all of her friends, she is now repudiated. I say this only half in jest; she would rather have died than to have had inflicted on her that shame among all her friends."[17]

In June, Bill called the family together at the lodge at Thompson's Point, Vermont, on Lake Champlain. While Barbara was on a walk, he told the children that the marriage was over. The news did not go down well. John remembered standing at the foot of the stairs looking up at his father on the landing. "I'm disappointed in you," he said. He subsequently groused, "Why didn't you just do what the French do—have an affair?" Christine stayed mad. "He divorced my mother so that he could be free to be the person he wanted to be," she said. "He didn't have to obey the rules anymore." Her father had first sacrificed family to career and was now doing it to a midlife crisis. In the weeks after her husband moved out, Barbara became obsessed with the breakup. She would call Tom McCoy, Stan Temko, and their wives, old family friends, and talk for hours about her personal tragedy. Temko and his wife, Francine, remembered that Barbara was convinced that both she and Bill were going to hell.[18]

Bill and Sally were married in Venice on November 20, 1984. He insisted on having the ceremony abroad so the children would not have to choose whether or not to attend. "He organized the whole wedding, including my bouquet," Sally recalled. "He set up one of those special Venetian wedding gondolas draped in yellow and white silk, the wedding colors of Venice. And the gondola was full of flowers. He hired a musician to come along and play Venetian love songs." For her part, Sally believed that the love affair simply unleashed the romantic that had been hiding beneath the surface. Jenonne Walker agreed: "Sally had a great impact on Bill's personality."[19]

By this point, Sally had taken a job with Bankers Trust in New York. At the end of six months, she told her superiors that she wanted to live with her husband, and they agreed to let her work from home. The couple bought a brownstone in Georgetown and set up house. "We did not go to the movies very often," Sally said. "We never went to the theater. We liked to just talk about each other's days. We both had such public lives that at the end of the day we just wanted to be quiet and be private." The romance never seemed to lose its intensity. "You know he loved to dance," Sally recalled. "We frequently danced after dinner just right there in our dining room." There were the little touches. "He gave me a charm bracelet and the first little gold charm was a sailboat. . . . And everywhere we went together, he bought a little gold charm that reflected that place. . . . Once he gave me a diamond pin in the shape of the Big Dipper. And he said, that's so you'll always be able to find your way home."[20]

It did not hurt that the couple saw eye to eye on public issues. Both were Democrats, favored a nuclear freeze, supported measures to promote social and economic justice, and continued to speak out on foreign policy matters as liberal anticommunists. Colby kept driving his little red sports car, and the two got to New Orleans as often as possible to take in jazz performances at Preservation Hall. In the spring they would plant maroon and yellow tulips in their tiny garden in remembrance of South Vietnam. Sally never recalled Bill going to Mass after they were married.[21]

In May 1987, James Jesus Angleton died; the personal feud was over, but the larger issues that underlay it survived.

In 1989, Colby published *Lost Victory*, his revisionist account of the Vietnam War. The book argued that the United States had triumphed where it counted—in the countryside—and that if Congress and the American people had stood by South Vietnam, the 1975 North Vietnamese invasion could have been thwarted. *Lost Victory*, ironically, tended to identify Colby with Nixon, Reagan, and the New Right. The book elicited a long, anguished letter from Thomas Powers, who recited the orthodox litany: the Viet Minh, and subsequently the North Vietnamese, had captured the nationalist flag; the South Vietnamese government had been hopelessly un-democratic and corrupt; the strategic assumptions upon which the war was based were erroneous; and the whole damned mess had had little or no im-pact on the larger geopolitical situation and would not have had such an impact no matter who had won. Powers apologized for having earlier im-plied that Colby was a KGB mole and then closed by lamenting "the lack of feel in your books." In his reply, Colby passed over the "feel" comment and politely accused Powers of being a fatalist, of implying that man could not discern the difference between good and evil and was powerless to do anything about it if he could.[22]

In December 1989, the Berlin Wall came down and pundits pronounced the Cold War at an end. Shortly afterward, Colby attended a conference in Moscow. In between sessions, he took a stroll around Red Square. It was snowing, he remembered. He walked past St. Basil's Cathedral and then noticed something strange—nobody was following him; nobody cared. The Cold War really was over. "That was my victory parade," he later told his son John.[23]

It was Saturday, April 27, 1996. William Colby, a former director of the US Central Intelligence Agency, was alone at his weekend house on Chesa-peake Bay across from Cobb Island, Maryland. Colby, who was seventy-six years old, had worked all day on his sailboat at a nearby marina, putting it in shape for the coming summer . . .

ACKNOWLEDGMENTS

Several years ago, my son, Jeff Woods, who is also a professional historian, suggested that we write a book together. I readily agreed, and we chose as our subject William Egan Colby, one of the Cold War's great enigmas. For five years we researched and interviewed people, both in harness and separately. It soon became apparent that we were dealing with two potential books, one on Bill Colby and the other on the whole issue of counterinsurgency and pacification in the Vietnam War. In the end, we decided on a division of labor—I would do the Colby biography, and he would write on "the other Vietnam war." I recount all of this to make it clear that this book has been very much a joint effort between Jeff and me, although the original composition (as well as any errors) is mine.

All historians stand on the shoulders of others, but I owe a special debt to John Prados, whose *Lost Crusader: The Secret Wars of CIA Director William Colby* paved the way for this book. His superb research allowed me to start the project at a much more advanced stage than would otherwise have been possible.

I am also indebted to the entire Colby family—wives Barbara and Sally, sons Jonathan, Carl, and Paul, daughter Christine, daughter-in-law Susan, and grandson Elbridge—for their cooperation on this project. They have shared their memories and observations without once attempting to control the end product.

As usual, the staffs of National Archives II, the Library of Congress, and the Lyndon B. Johnson and Gerald Ford presidential libraries have behaved with the utmost professionalism. My research brought me for the first time to the Vietnam Archives at Texas Tech University and the George C. Marshall Library at the Virginia Military Institute. Both institutions exceeded my expectations. In addition, my thanks go out to the dozens of CIA veterans and personal friends of Bill Colby who agreed to be interviewed for this project. Of particular importance were the counterinsurgency/pacification personnel who worked for him in Vietnam and Laos, especially David Nuttle, Vinton Lawrence, Jean Sauvageot, and Frank Scotton.

Richard Immerman, Wesley Wark, Rhodri Jeffrey-Jones, Mark Lawrence, and my in-house editor, Rhoda Woods, have all read the book in manuscript and saved me from many errors in fact and style. Finally, I would like to pay tribute to the excellent team at Basic Books. Lara Heimert, publisher and editor-in-chief, has been an enthusiastic supporter and wise adviser from the start. Roger Labrie proved to be one of the most skilled textual editors with whom I have ever worked. Kudos, too, to Katy O'Donnell and Melissa Veronesi. Again, all errors in fact and judgment are mine and mine alone.

NOTES

CHAPTER 1

1. Tad Szulc, "The Missing CIA Man," *New York Times Magazine,* Jan. 7, 1989.

2. Zalin Grant, "Who Murdered the CIA Chief? William E. Colby: A Highly Suspicious Death," 2011, Zalin Grant's War Tales, www.pythiapress.com/wartales/colby.htm.

3. Some in the Agency, however, would view Colby as simply a man ahead of his time. See Douglas F. Garthoff, *Directors of Central Intelligence as Leaders of the U.S. Intelligence Community, 1946–2005,* rev. ed. (Washington, DC: 2007).

CHAPTER 2

1. "Obituaries," *Science* 45, no. 147 (1897): 628.

2. Author interviews with Paul Colby, Jan. 8 and June 10, 2007; author interview with Barbara Colby, Jan. 5, 2007; author interview with John Colby, Jan. 8, 2007.

3. The best biography of Baden-Powell is Tim Jael, *Baden-Powell: Founder of the Boy Scouts* (London: 1989).

4. "Minnesota Territorial and State Censuses, 1849–1905," Ancestry.com, http://search.ancestry.com/Places/US/Minnesota/Default.aspx; author interview with Christine Colby Giraudo, June 5, 2010; author interview with Barbara Colby, Jan. 5, 2007; "1900 United States Federal Census," Ancestry.com, http://search.ancestry.com/search/grouplist.aspx?group=usfedcen; Lieutenant James J. Egan, *Battle of Birch Cooley,* Oct. 2, 1889, Colby Family Papers; author interviews with John Colby, Jan. 12 and June 8, 2007.

5. Author interview with Paul Colby, Jan. 8, 2007; Lieutenant Colonel Ebenezer T. Colby to Charles A. Colby, April 10, 1863, Colby Family Papers; author interview with John Colby, Jan. 12, 2007.

6. John Prados, *Lost Crusader: The Secret Wars of CIA Director William Colby* (New York: 2003), 19.

7. Elbridge Colby and Margaret Egan, Marriage Certificate, Colby Family Papers.

8. William E. Colby, Birth Certificate, Colby Family Papers; William Colby and Peter Forbath, *Honorable Men: My Life in the CIA* (New York: 1978), 27; author interview with Paul Colby, Jan. 8, 2007.

9. Colby and Forbath, *Honorable Men,* 28; Prados, *Lost Crusader,* 20.

10. Alfred Emile Cornbise, *The United States 15th Infantry Regiment in China, 1912–1938* (Jefferson, NC: 2004), 1–2.

11. Ibid., 7–9.

12. Ibid., 13.

13. Ibid., 15.

14. Prados, *Lost Crusader*, 21; Cornbise, *15th Infantry*, 17.

15. Brian Power, *The Ford of Heaven* (New York: 1984), 10–11.

16. Ibid., 14–15.

17. Author interview with Sally Shelton Colby, June 12, 2007.

18. Ibid., 107.

19. W. E. Colby, Personnel File, CIA Records Search Tool (CREST hereafter), National Archives, Washington, DC; Prados, *Lost Crusader*, 22; William Colby, *Lost Victory: A Firsthand Account of America's Sixteen-Year Involvement in Vietnam* (Chicago: 1989), 19.

20. Author interview with John Colby, June 4, 2010; Prados, *Lost Crusader*, 22.

21. Prados, *Lost Crusader*, 23–24.

22. Author interview with Paul Colby, Jan.8, 2007; author interview with John Colby, June 8, 2007.

23. Author interview with John Colby, Jan. 12, 2007; author interview with Christine Colby Giraudo, June 5, 2010; author interview with Paul Colby, Jan. 8, 2007.

24. Author interview with John Colby, Jan. 12, 2007; author interview with Carl Colby, Jan. 9, 2007.

25. Author interview with Paul Colby, Jan. 8, 2007; Kenneth Roberts, *Northwest Passage* (Garden City, NY: 1937), 83, 98.

26. Roberts, *Northwest Passage*, 12.

27. Colby and Forbath, *Honorable Men*, 29; Prados, *Lost Crusader*, 24–25.

28. Author interview with Carl Colby, Jan. 9, 2007; Colby and Forbath, *Honorable Men*, 29; author interview with Christine Colby Giraudo, June 5, 2010.

29. Colby and Forbath, *Honorable Men*, 30.

30. Author interview with John Colby, Jan. 12, 2007; "What Attitude Toward Spain?" Jan. 21, 1938, Colby Family Papers.

31. Author interview with John Colby, Jan. 12, 2007.

32. Colby and Forbath, *Honorable Men*, 32; Zalin Grant, *Facing the Phoenix: The CIA and the Political Defeat of the United States in Vietnam* (New York: 1991), 282.

33. Prados, *Lost Crusader*, 27.

34. Colby and Forbath, *Honorable Men*, 31.

35. Author interview with Stan Temko, Jan. 6, 2007; author interview with Barbara Colby, Jan. 5, 2007; Colby and Forbath, *Honorable Men*, 32.

36. Colby and Forbath, *Honorable Men*, 32.

37. "Interview: William Colby, Former Director, Central Intelligence Agency," *Special Forces Magazine*, April 1994, 2; Colby and Forbath, *Honorable Men*, 32; Prados, *Lost Crusader*, 28.

38. Colby and Forbath, *Honorable Men*, 32; William E. Colby, Personnel File, CREST.

CHAPTER 3

1. William Colby and Peter Forbath, *Honorable Men: My Life in the CIA* (New York: 1978), 33.

2. For Donovan's background and his early relationship with Roosevelt, see Douglas Waller, *Wild Bill Donovan: The Spymaster Who Created the OSS and Modern American Espionage* (New York: 2011), 9–87.

3. Will Irwin, *The Jedburghs: The Secret History of the Allied Special Forces, France 1944* (New York: 2005), 32, 34; Richard Harris Smith, *OSS: The Secret History of America's First Central Intelligence Agency* (Berkeley, CA: 1972), 2; Anthony Cave Brown, *The Last Hero: Wild Bill Donovan* (New York: 1984); Waller, *Wild Bill Donovan*, 93.

4. Quoted in Smith, *OSS*, 1; Waller, *Wild Bill Donovan*, 6, 11, 16, 93.

5. Waller, *Wild Bill Donovan*, 29–31.

6. Arthur Lyton Funk, *Hidden Ally: The French Resistance, Special Operations, and the Landings in Southern France, 1944* (New York: 1992), 74.

7. John Prados, *Lost Crusader: The Secret Wars of CIA Director William Colby* (New York: 2003), 9; Irwin, *Jedburghs*, 38.

8. Anthony Cave Brown, *Bodyguard of Lies* (New York: 1975), 576.

9. Smith, *OSS*, 175; Irwin, *Jedburghs*, 40; Colby and Forbath, *Honorable Men*, 35.

10. Irwin, *Jedburghs*, 43–44.

11. Ibid., 44–45.

12. Quoted in ibid.; Colby and Forbath, *Honorable Men*, 35–36.

13. Irwin, *Jedburghs*, 46–53; Colby and Forbath, *Honorable Men*, 36.

14. Irwin, *Jedburghs*, 47–48, 62.

15. Ibid., 62–64, 77.

16. Irwin, *Jedburghs*, 65, 139; Colby and Forbath, *Honorable Men*, 38.

17. Colby and Forbath, *Honorable Men*, 37, 70–71.

18. T. E. Lawrence, *Seven Pillars of Wisdom: A Triumph* (Garden City, NY: 1938), 29.

19. Cave Brown, *Bodyguard*, 575; Funk, *Hidden Ally*, 74; Jeffrey Richelson, *A Century of Spies: Intelligence in the Twentieth Century* (New York: 1997), 154.

20. Prados, *Lost Crusader*, 11; Irwin, *Jedburghs*, 135.

21. Colby and Forbath, *Honorable Men*, 38–39.

22. Quoted in Cave Brown, *Bodyguard*, 575; quoted in Smith, *OSS*, 180.

23. Irwin, *Jedburghs*, 136–138.

24. Ibid., 138; Colby and Forbath, *Honorable Men*, 39.

25. Quoted in Colby and Forbath, *Honorable Men*, 26.

26. Irwin, *Jedburghs*, xiv.

27. Colby and Forbath, *Honorable Men*, 23; Operations, Team Bruce, OSS Microfilm, Roll 80, Frames 0925-0944, UK National Archives, Kew, London.

28. Operations, Team Bruce, OSS Microfilm, Roll 80, Frames 0925-0944, UK National Archives, Kew, London; Colby and Forbath, *Honorable Men*, 24.

29. Colby and Forbath, *Honorable Men*, 25, 39–40; Operations, Team Bruce, OSS Microfilm, Roll 80, Frames 0925-0945, UK National Archives, Kew, London.

30. Colby and Forbath, *Honorable Men*, 40.

31. Ibid., 41.

32. Irwin, *Jedburghs*, 142–143; Operations, Team Bruce, OSS Microfilm, Roll 80, Frames 0925-0944, UK National Archives, Kew, London.

33. Marcus Binney, *The Women Who Lived for Danger: The Agents of the Special Operations Executive* (New York: 2002), 247; Irwin, *Jedburghs*, 60–61.

34. Binney, *Women Who Lived*, 249–250, 255–266; Irwin, *Jedburghs*, 137–138.

35. Colby and Forbath, *Honorable Men*, 42; Operations, Team Bruce, OSS Microfilm, Roll 80, Frames 0925-0944, UK National Archives, Kew, London.

36. Operations, Team Bruce, OSS Microfilm, Roll 80, Frames 0925-0944, UK National Archives, Kew, London.

37. Quoted in Irwin, *Jedburghs*, 147, 149.

38. Author interview with John Colby, June 8, 2007; Irwin, *Jedburghs*, 147; Operations, Team Bruce, OSS Microfilm, Roll 80, Frames 0925-0944, UK National Archives, Kew, London.

39. Operations, Team Bruce, OSS Microfilm, Roll 80, Frames 0925-0944, UK National Archives, Kew, London; Colby and Forbath, *Honorable Men*, 43.

40. "Colby After Action Report," August 14/15, 1944, Files of the Special Operations Executive, File HS 7/17, UK National Archives, Kew, London; Binney, *Women Who Lived*, 262.

41. Colby and Forbath, *Honorable Men*, 43; Irwin, *Jedburghs*, 152.

42. Prados, *Lost Crusader*, 18; Operations, Team Bruce, OSS Microfilm, Roll 80, Frames 0925-0944, UK National Archives, Kew, London.

43. Colby and Forbath, *Honorable Men*, 44; Prados, *Lost Crusader*, 18.

44. Colby Military Personnel File, CREST.

CHAPTER 4

1. John Prados, *Lost Crusader: The Secret Wars of CIA Director William Colby* (New York: 2003), 28–29.

2. William Colby and Peter Forbath, *Honorable Men: My Life in the CIA* (New York: 1978), 44.

3. Prados, *Lost Crusader*, 29–30; Colby and Forbath, *Honorable Men*, 45.

4. Colby and Forbath, *Honorable Men*, 45.

5. Prados, *Lost Crusader*, 31; William E. Colby, "Skis and Daggers," CIA Historical Center, Washington, DC, 4.

6. "Recommendation for Silver Star, William E. Colby," June 29, 1945, CREST; Colby, "Skis and Daggers," 3; Colby and Forbath, *Honorable Men*, 46.

7. Colby, "Skis and Daggers," 6.

8. Ibid.

9. Ibid., 7–8.

10. Ibid.

11. Ibid.

12. Quoted in T. E. Lawrence, *Seven Pillars of Wisdom: A Triumph* (Garden City, NY: 1938), 30.

13. Colby, "Skis and Daggers," 9; Colby and Forbath, *Honorable Men*, 48. See also Patrick K. O'Donnell, *Operatives, Spies, and Saboteurs: The Unknown Story of the Men and Women of World War II's OSS* (New York: 2004), 275–276.

14. "Recommendation for Silver Star, William E. Colby," June 29, 1945, CREST; Colby, "Skis and Daggers," 9.

15. Colby, "Skis and Daggers," 10.

16. "Recommendation for Silver Star, William E. Colby," June 29, 1945, CREST; Colby, "Skis and Daggers," 11; Prados, *Lost Crusader*, 33.

17. Colby, "Skis and Daggers," 9–10.

18. Colby and Forbath, *Honorable Men*, 49; Prados, *Lost Crusader*, 33.

19. Colby and Forbath, *Honorable Men*, 50.

20. Ibid., 51.

21. "Recommendation for Silver Star, William E. Colby," June 29, 1945, CREST.

22. Cormac McCarthy, *Blood Meridian; or The Evening Redness in the West* (New York: 2001), 249.

23. Colby, "Skis and Daggers," 9–10.

24. McCarthy, *Blood Meridian*, 249.

25. Colby and Forbath, *Honorable Men*, 51.

26. Ibid., 52.

27. "OSS Personnel Evaluation, William E. Colby," Aug. 6, 1946, CREST; Colby and Forbath, *Honorable Men*, 52.

28. Prados, *Lost Crusader*, 37.

29. Quoted in ibid.

CHAPTER 5

1. Quoted in Anthony Cave Brown, *The Last Hero: Wild Bill Donovan* (New York: 1984).

2. Quoted in ibid.

3. Tom Braden, "The Birth of the CIA: When and How It Got the Green Light to Conduct 'Subversive Operations Abroad,'" *American Heritage* 28, no. 2 (1977); William Colby and Peter Forbath, *Honorable Men: My Life in the CIA* (New York: 1978), 60.

4. Braden, "Birth of the CIA"; Richard Helms, with William Hood, *A Look over My Shoulder: A Life in the Central Intelligence Agency* (New York: 2003), 66.

5. Quoted in Hugh Wilford, *The Mighty Wurlitzer: How the CIA Played America* (Cambridge, MA: 2009), 23; Braden, "Birth of the CIA"; Helms, *A Look over My Shoulder*, 73.

6. Quoted in Wilford, *The Mighty Wurlitzer*, 22.

7. Braden, "Birth of the CIA."

8. Quoted in Wilford, *The Mighty Wurlitzer*, 23–25.

9. Wilford, *The Mighty Wurlitzer*, 23–27; Colby and Forbath, *Honorable Men*, 71–72. For an excellent scholarly history of the CIA, see Rhodri Jeffreys-Jones, *The CIA and American Democracy*, 3rd ed. (New Haven, CT: 2003).

10. Colby and Forbath, *Honorable Men*, 62, 64.

11. Ibid., 64–65.

12. Quoted in Kati Marton, *The Polk Conspiracy: Murder and Cover-up in the Case of CBS News Correspondent George Polk* (New York: 1990), 14; see also 3–13.

13. Quoted in John Prados, *Lost Crusader: The Secret Wars of CIA Director William Colby* (New York: 2003), 41.

14. Ibid., 40–41.

15. Marton, *Polk Conspiracy*, 162, 289–290.

16. Ibid., 310.

17. Quoted in Prados, *Lost Crusader*, 41.

18. Colby and Forbath, *Honorable Men*, 76, 77; Prados, *Lost Crusader*, 43.

19. Author interview with Jenonne Walker, June 16, 2010.

CHAPTER 6

1. Author interview with Christine Colby and Jack Giraudo, June 5, 2010.

2. Author interview with Carl Colby, Jan. 9, 2007. Graham Greene, author of *The Third Man*, was engaging in a bit of literary license. The cuckoo clock was a German and not a Swiss invention.

3. William Colby and Peter Forbath, *Honorable Men: My Life in the CIA* (New York: 1978), 77.

4. Ibid., 65, 73; author interview with John Colby, Jan. 12, 2007; Cormac McCarthy, *Blood Meridian; or The Evening Redness in the West* (New York: 2001).

5. Colby and Forbath, *Honorable Men*, 77.

6. Author interview with Stan Temko, Jan. 6, 2007; Colby and Forbath, *Honorable Men*, 78.

7. Colby and Forbath, *Honorable Men*, 79, 87.

8. Ibid., 61, 104.

9. John Prados, *Lost Crusader: The Secret Wars of CIA Director William Colby* (New York: 2003), 44.

10. Richard Helms, with William Hood, *A Look over My Shoulder: A Life in the Central Intelligence Agency* (New York: 2003), 115; "Moscow Rules: Spy Tradecraft," Feb. 15, 2009, http://militaryhistorymatters.blogspot.com/2009/02/moscow-rules-spy-tradecraft.html.

11. Victor Marchetti, *The CIA and the Cult of Intelligence* (New York: 1974), 263.

12. Ibid., 260–264; Colby and Forbath, *Honorable Men*, 107; Norman Mailer, *Harlot's Ghost* (New York: 1991), 413.

13. Colby and Forbath, *Honorable Men*, 88–89.

14. See Helge Pharo, "Scandinavia," in David Reynolds, ed., *The Origins of the Cold War in Europe: International Perspectives* (New Haven, CT: 1994), 194–223; Colby and Forbath, *Honorable Men*, 83.

15. Colby and Forbath, *Honorable Men*, 91–92; Prados, *Lost Crusader*, 46.

16. Quoted in Hugh Wilford, *The Mighty Wurlitzer: How the CIA Played America* (Cambridge, MA: 2009), 45–46.

17. Colby and Forbath, *Honorable Men*, 98.

18. Ibid., 100; author interview with John Colby, June 4, 2010.

19. Prados, *Lost Crusader*, 48–49.

20. Colby and Forbath, *Honorable Men*, 90.

21. Author interview with Edward Ryan, Jan. 11, 2007.

22. Colby and Forbath, *Honorable Men*, 104.

23. Richard H. Shultz, *The Secret War Against Hanoi: Kennedy's and Johnson's Use of Spies, Saboteurs, and Covert Warriors* (New York: 1999), 11.

24. Colby and Forbath, *Honorable Men*, 8, 91.

25. Quoted in Prados, *Lost Crusader*, 51.

CHAPTER 7

1. James E. Miller, "Roughhouse Diplomacy: The United States Confronts Italian Communism, 1945–1958," *Storia Delle Relazioni Internazionali* 5 (1989–1992): 287–288; "Italian and French Struggle Against Communism: Summary for Secretary Marshall, May 26, 1947," National Archives and Records Administration (NARA hereafter), Secretary of State's Weekly Summary, 1947–1949, National Security Archive (NSA hereafter), Washington, DC.

2. "Summary for Secretary Marshall"; Miller, "Roughhouse Diplomacy," 290–291; Christopher Andrew and Vasili Mitrokhin, *The Sword and the Shield: The Mitrokhin Archive and the Secret History of the KGB* (New York: 1999), 276–277.

3. Miller, "Roughhouse Diplomacy," 300.

4. Mario Del Pero, "American Pressures and Their Containment in Italy During the Ambassadorship of Clare Boothe Luce, 1953–1956," *Diplomatic History* 18, no. 3 (2004): 412–413; Leopoldo Nuti, "The United States, Italy, and the Opening to the Left, 1953–1963," *Journal of Cold War Studies* 4, no. 3 (2002): 39–40.

5. Del Pero, "American Pressures," 417–418.

6. Author interview with Carl Colby, Jan. 9, 2007.

7. William Colby and Peter Forbath, *Honorable Men: My Life in the CIA* (New York: 1978), 109.

8. Ibid., 111.

9. John Prados, *Lost Crusader: The Secret Wars of CIA Director William Colby* (New York: 2003), 55.

10. Colby and Forbath, *Honorable Men*, 108; Martina A. Lee, "Colby of the CIA," *Mother Jones*, July 1983, 21–24.

11. Colby and Forbath, *Honorable Men*, 113.

12. Author interview with Tom McCoy, Jan. 11, 2007.

13. Author interview with John Colby, Jan. 12, 2007; Colby and Forbath, *Honorable Men*, 109.

14. Daniele Ganser, *NATO's Secret Armies: Operation GLADIO and Terrorism in Western Europe* (New York: 2005); Amos Elon, "A Shrine to Mussolini," *New York Review of Books*, Feb. 23, 2006. See also Prados, *Lost Crusader*, 56.

15. Colby and Forbath, *Honorable Men*, 115; quoted in Del Pero, "American Pressures," 417.

16. Quoted in David Corn, *Blond Ghost: Ted Shackley and the CIA's Crusades* (New York: 1994), 46. Sally Shelton-Colby, Bill's second wife, is convinced there was a physical relationship. Following their marriage, she recalled, she and Bill attended a reception where the incomparable Clare was also in attendance. She looked Sally up and down, clearly a sexual appraisal of a rival. Author interview with Sally Shelton-Colby, June 12, 2007.

17. Colby and Forbath, *Honorable Men*, 123; Burton Hersh, "Dragons Have to Be Killed," *Washingtonian*, September 1985, 4.

18. Del Pero, "American Pressures," 420–428; Colby and Forbath, *Honorable Men*, 123–124; William E. Colby, "Proposal to Establish US Contact with Pietro Nenni," memorandum, Oct. 24, 1956, CIA document obtained by author via Freedom of Information Act.

19. Tom Mangold, *Cold Warrior: James Jesus Angleton. The CIA's Master Spy Hunter* (New York: 1991), 32–34; "The Making of a Master Spy," *Time*, Feb. 24, 1975, 2.

20. Quoted in Mangold, *Cold Warrior*, 35; see also 36.

21. David Robarge, "Moles, Defectors, and Deceptions: James Angleton and CIA Counterintelligence," *Journal of Intelligence History* 3, no. 2 (2003): 28–29; Richard Helms, with William Hood, *A Look over My Shoulder: A Life in the Central Intelligence Agency* (New York: 2003), 146–147.

22. Hersh, "Dragons," 3; Mangold, *Cold Warrior*, 41, 49; Robarge, "Moles, Defectors," 27.

23. Mangold, *Cold Warrior*, 52.

24. Victor Marchetti, *The CIA and the Cult of Intelligence* (New York: 1974), 211.

25. Ibid., 211–213; quoted in Robarge, "Moles, Defectors," 30–31.

26. E. J. Epstein, "Disinformation: Or Why the CIA Cannot Verify an Arms Agreement," *Commentary*, July 1982, 4; Robarge, "Moles, Defectors," 34.

27. Helms, *A Look over My Shoulder*, 158; Ron Rosenbaum, "The Shadow of the Mole," *Harpers*, October 1983, 47–49; Robarge, "Moles, Defectors," 35; quoted in William F. Buckley Jr., "The Believable Need to Control Soviet Sympathizers," *New York Daily News*, Sept. 8, 1981.

28. Prados, *Lost Crusader*, 57; Colby and Forbath, *Honorable Men*, 125; Colby, "Proposal to Establish US Contact with Pietro Nenni."

29. Hersh, "Dragons," 4; Colby and Forbath, *Honorable Men*, 131.

30. Quoted in Prados, *Lost Crusader*, 57; Colby and Forbath, *Honorable Men*, 132.

31. Colby and Forbath, *Honorable Men*, 132–133.

32. Quoted in Randall Bennett Woods, *Fulbright: A Biography* (New York: 1995), 77; Del Pero, "American Pressures," 431–433; Colby, "Proposal to Establish US Contact with Pietro Nenni."

33. Henry S. Brasher, "U.S. Got 2 Copies of Speech by Khrushchev on Stalin's Sins," *Washington Star*, Dec. 7, 1976.

34. David Binder, "56 East European Plan of C.I.A. Is Described," *New York Times*, Nov. 30, 1976; Colby and Forbath, *Honorable Men*, 133–134; William E. Colby, "Proposed Approach to Pietro Nenni and the Italian Socialist Party," memorandum, June 6, 1956, CIA document obtained by author via Freedom of Information Act.

35. Colby and Forbath, *Honorable Men*, 134–135.

36. Quoted in Hugh Wilford, *The Mighty Wurlitzer: How the CIA Played America* (Cambridge, MA: 2009), 49; Prados, *Lost Crusader*, 61.

37. Colby and Forbath, *Honorable Men*, 134; Prados, *Lost Crusader*, 58.

38. Prados, *Lost Crusader*, 59; Colby and Forbath, *Honorable Men*, 127.

39. William E. Colby to DCI, April 1, 1958, CIA document obtained by author via Freedom of Information Act; Nuti, "Opening to the Left," 42–43, 45–47.

40. Colby and Forbath, *Honorable Men*, 139.

41. Wilford, *The Mighty Wurlitzer*, 74–75, 89.

CHAPTER 8

1. John Prados, *Lost Crusader: The Secret Wars of CIA Director William Colby* (New York: 2003), 61–62; William Colby and Peter Forbath, *Honorable Men: My Life in the CIA* (New York: 1978), 142.

2. Zalin Grant, *Facing the Phoenix: The CIA and the Political Defeat of the United States in Vietnam* (New York: 1991), 84–86, 91; Thomas L. Ahern Jr., *CIA and Rural Pacification in South Vietnam*, Center for the Study of Intelligence, August 2001, available at National Security Archive, www.gwu.edu/~nsarchiv/NSAEBB/NSAEBB284/index.htm, 4.

3. William Colby, *Lost Victory: A Firsthand Account of America's Sixteen-Year Involvement in Vietnam* (Chicago: 1989), 33.

4. Grant, *Facing the Phoenix*, 48; Records of the OSS, M1623, Roll 10, 61 ff., and M1623, Roll 8, National Archives II, Washington, DC; quoted in "National Archives Learning Curve," www.spartacus.schoolnet.co.uk/JFKconein.htm.

5. Ahern, *CIA and Rural Pacification*, 11–12.

6. Grant, *Facing the Phoenix*, 97–98; Ahern, *CIA and Rural Pacification*, 3.

7. Quoted in Ahern, *CIA and Rural Pacification*, 21.

8. Colby, *Lost Victory*, 19–20.

9. See "Saigon: A Booklet of Helpful Information for Americans in Vietnam," United States Operations Mission (Saigon: 1958), Douglas Pike Papers, Texas Tech University Virtual Archives.

10. Howard Simpson interview, Jan. 1, 1994, Foreign Affairs Oral History Collection, Library of Congress.

11. Author interview with Barbara Colby, Jan. 5, 2007; author interview with Paul Colby, Jan. 8, 2007; Colby, *Lost Victory*, 21.

12. Author interview with Carl Colby, Jan. 9, 2007; author interview with Barbara Colby, Jan. 5, 2007.

13. Colby, *Lost Victory*, 22.

14. Curtis C. Cutter interview, Feb. 3, 1992, Foreign Affairs Oral History Collection, Library of Congress; Colby and Forbath, *Honorable Men*, 149–150; Prados, *Lost Crusader*, 67.

15. Colby, *Lost Victory*, 28.

16. Colby and Forbath, *Honorable Men*, 147–148.

17. Ibid., 148–149.

18. Colby, *Lost Victory*, 29.

19. Colby and Forbath, *Honorable Men*, 154.

20. Colby, *Lost Victory*, 34.

21. Ibid., 39.

22. Kenton J. Clymer, *Troubled Relations: The United States and Cambodia Since 1870* (DeKalb, IL: 2007), 74–76; Milton Osborne, *Sihanouk: Prince of Light, Prince of Darkness* (Honolulu: 1994), 112.

23. Prados, *Lost Crusader*, 70.

24. Colby, *Lost Victory*, 43.

25. Author interview with John Colby, June 4, 2010.

26. Duong Van Mai Elliott, *The Sacred Willow: Four Generations in the Life of a Vietnamese Family* (New York: 1999), 232–235; William E. Colby Oral History, June 2, 1981, LBJ Library, Austin, Texas.

27. Colby, *Lost Victory*, 46.

28. Ibid., 54–57; Ahern, *CIA and Rural Pacification*, 32.

29. Colby, *Lost Victory*, 61.

30. Author interview with Paul Colby, Jan. 8, 2007.

31. Ibid.

32. Colby, *Lost Victory*, 63, 77; Prados, *Lost Crusader*, 72.

33. Quoted in Ahern, *CIA and Rural Pacification*, 36.

34. Quoted in Prados, *Lost Crusader*, 72; Colby, *Lost Victory*, 78.

35. Quoted in Colby, *Lost Victory*, 79.

36. Prados, *Lost Crusader*, 73.

CHAPTER 9

1. Quoted in Stanley Karnow, *Vietnam: A History* (New York: 1983), 247.

2. Thomas K. Adams, *US Special Operations Forces in Action: The Challenge of Unconventional Warfare* (London: 1998), 65; quoted in Richard H. Shultz Jr., *The Secret War Against Hanoi: Kennedy's and Johnson's Use of Spies, Saboteurs, and Covert Warriors in North Vietnam* (New York: 1999), 75. Counterinsurgency was one side of the coin. The other was pacification through modernization. The Kennedy White House turned to an emerging community of social scientists who saw nation-building in South Vietnam as part of a universal process of modernization. Advances in communications and transportation, new systems of trade and commerce, modern farming techniques, Western-style education, and modern medicine would shake "traditional" peoples out of their fatalism and complacency. Unfortunately, these prophets of modernity, typified by Walt Rostow, the MIT economist who would serve on both the Kennedy and Johnson foreign policy teams, tended to ignore the histories, political cultures, and entrenched interests of the countries with which they were working. See Michael E. Latham, "Redirecting the Revolution? The USA and the Failure of Nation-Building in South Vietnam," *Third World Quarterly* 27, no. 1 (2006): 27–41.

3. T. K. Adams, *US Special Operations Forces*, 19.

4. Ibid., 22, 54–55.

5. Ibid., 67.

6. Sedgwick Tourison, *Secret Army, Secret War: Washington's Tragic Spy Operation in North Vietnam* (Annapolis, MD: 1995), 8–9; John L. Plaster, *SOG: The Secret Wars of America's Commandos in Vietnam* (New York: 1997), 19.

7. John Prados, *Lost Crusader: The Secret Wars of CIA Director William Colby* (New York: 2003), 75.

8. Quoted in Tourison, *Secret Army, Secret War*, 19; quoted in Prados, *Lost Crusader*, 75.

9. Rene J. Defourneaux to William E. Colby, Nov. 21, 1989, Colby Collection, Box 6, F22, Vietnam Archives, Texas Tech University.

10. Plaster, *SOG*, 17–18; Prados, *Lost Crusader*, 76.

11. Quoted in Prados, *Lost Crusader*, 76; quoted in Plaster, *SOG*, 21.

12. Quoted in Prados, *Lost Crusader*, 77. Colby thought Air America a most inappropriate name for a secret air force. Tourison, *Secret Army, Secret War*, 19.

13. Tourison, *Secret Army, Secret War*, 20, 43. Kennedy had dismantled Eisenhower's 5412 committee, but then, seeing the need for such an oversight body, he had created his own.

14. Prados, *Lost Crusader*, 78; quoted in Tourison, *Secret Army, Secret War*, 37.

15. William Colby and Peter Forbath, *Honorable Men: My Life in the CIA* (New York: 1978), 173; Tourison, *Secret Army, Secret War*, 100; Plaster, *SOG*, 22; author interview with Robert Myers, June 11, 2007.

16. Tourison, *Secret Army, Secret War*, 8, 58; Prados, *Lost Crusader*, 80. See also Thomas A. Bass, *The Spy Who Loved Us: The Vietnam War and Pham Xuan An's Dangerous Game* (New York: 2009); Larry Berman, *The Perfect Spy: The Incredible Double Life of Pham Xuan An, Time Magazine Reporter and Vietnamese Communist Agent* (Washington, DC: 2007).

17. Harold Ford, *William E. Colby as Director of Central Intelligence, 1973–1976* (Washington, DC: 1993), 79, released under Freedom of Information Act, Aug. 11, 2011.

18. Quoted in Tourison, *Secret Army, Secret War*, 13.

19. William Colby, *Lost Victory: A Firsthand Account of America's Sixteen-Year Involvement in Vietnam* (Chicago: 1989), 84; Colby and Forbath, *Honorable Men*, 161.

20. Colby, *Lost Victory*, 88; Thomas L. Ahern Jr., *CIA and Rural Pacification in South Vietnam*, Center for the Study of Intelligence, August 2001, available at National Security Archive, www.gwu.edu/~nsarchiv/NSAEBB/NSAEBB284/index.htm, 39–40.

21. Colby, *Lost Victory*, 85.

22. Quoted in John A. Nagl, *Counterinsurgency Lessons from Malaya and Vietnam: Learning to Eat Soup with a Knife* (Westport, CT: 2002), 15, 22.

23. Quoted in ibid., 26.

24. Gregoire Potiron de Boisfleury, "The Origins of Marshal Lyautey's Pacification Doctrine in Morocco from 1912 to 1925," master's thesis, Fort Leavenworth, Kansas, 2010, 9–12, online at www.dtic.mil/cgi-bin/GetTRDoc?AD=ADA524341; Colby, *Lost Victory*, 91; Interview: William Colby, former director, Central Intelligence Agency, *Special Forces Magazine*, April 1994, 41.

25. Colby and Forbath, *Honorable Men*, 175–176; Zalin Grant, *Facing the Phoenix: The CIA and the Political Defeat of the United States in Vietnam* (New York: 1991), 166.

26. Author interview with Gilbert Layton Family, Oct. 13, 2006, Washington, DC.

27. Ken Conboy and James Morrison, "Early Covert Action on the Ho Chi Minh Trail," http://ngothelinh.150m.com/Early Covert Actions.html; Gilbert Layton to Frank Mallard, Nov. 1, 1961, Layton Family Papers.

28. Quoted in Tourison, *Secret Army, Secret War*, 24–25, 34; Ahern, *CIA and Rural Pacification*, 44.

29. Hugh Wilford, *The Mighty Wurlitzer: How the CIA Played America* (Cambridge, MA: 2009), 168–169; David A. Nuttle, "They Have Stone Ears, Don't They?" unpublished memoir, May 6, 1966; Nuttle to author, Sept. 21, 2006, 42–44.

30. Author interview with David Nuttle, Sept. 6, 2006.

31. Nuttle, "Stone Ears," 43.

32. Ibid., 5.

33. Quoted in Ahern, *CIA and Rural Pacification*, 45; Colby, *Lost Victory*, 89.

34. Colby and Forbath, *Honorable Men*, 165–166.

35. See Evan Thomas, *The Very Best Men: Four Who Dared. The Early Years of the CIA* (New York: 1995), 205–216, 237–272.

36. Quoted in Randall Bennett Woods, *Quest for Identity: America Since 1945* (New York: 2005), 213; quoted in Colby and Forbath, *Honorable Men*, 184; Tim Weiner, *Legacy of Ashes: The History of the CIA* (New York: 2007), 179; Richard Helms, with William Hood, *A Look over My Shoulder: A Life in the Central Intelligence Agency* (New York: 2003), 181.

37. Nuttle, "Stone Ears," 47. The conversation that follows is quoted from Nuttle's memoir.

38. Nuttle, "Stone Ears," 9.

39. Quoted in Prados, *Lost Crusader*, 73; Colby and Forbath, *Honorable Men*, 166.

40. Nuttle, "Stone Ears," 53.

41. Quoted in Ahern, *CIA and Rural Pacification*, 46–47.

42. Quoted in ibid., 46. Special Forces A-Teams consisted of twelve military personnel who had the collective mission of training local self-defense forces and conducting civil

affairs programs to improve hygiene, health care, education, and agriculture. Adams, *US Special Operations Forces*, 84–85.

43. Ahern, *CIA and Rural Pacification*, 52.

44. Dora Layton to Marsh and Family, December 1962, Layton Family Papers; Ahern, *CIA and Rural Pacification*, 54.

45. Ahern, *CIA and Rural Pacification*, 25.

46. Al Friendly to Gil Layton, Feb. 6, 1996, Layton Family Papers.

47. Ahern, *CIA and Rural Pacification*, 58; Nuttle, "Stone Ears," 57.

48. Quoted in Tourison, *Secret Army, Secret War*, 55.

49. Colby, *Lost Victory*, 91; author interview with Dora and Todd Layton, Oct. 23, 2006; Ahern, *CIA and Rural Pacification*, 76–77.

50. Tourison, *Secret Army, Secret War*, 24; author interview with Dora and Todd Layton, Oct. 23, 2006; Dora Layton to friend, Jan. 1963, Layton Family Papers.

51. Author interview with Carl Colby, Jan. 9, 2007.

52. Author interview with John Colby, Jan. 12, 2007.

53. "CIA Information Report," Nov. 28, 1961, *Foreign Relations of the United States* (FRUS hereafter), *1961–1963, Vietnam*, vol. 1, 689–691.

54. Quoted in Ahern, *CIA and Rural Pacification*, 78–79.

55. Colby, *Lost Victory*, 99.

56. Ahern, *CIA and Rural Pacification*, 80.

57. Ibid., 84; Colby, *Lost Victory*, 102.

58. Ahern, *CIA and Rural Pacification*, 80–82; Seth Jacobs, *Cold War Mandarin: Ngo Dinh Diem and the Origins of America's War in Vietnam, 1950–1963* (Lanham, MD: 2006), 127; A. J. Langguth, *Our Vietnam: The War, 1954–1975* (New York: 2000), 168–169.

59. Colby, *Lost Victory*, 93. This passage displays an amazingly cavalier attitude on the part of a CIA station chief whose job it was, in tandem with the chief of SEPES, the South Vietnamese security apparatus, to ferret out communist agents who had penetrated the South Vietnamese government and military.

CHAPTER 10

1. Stanley Karnow, *Vietnam: A History* (New York: 1983), 263.

2. William Colby, *Lost Victory: A Firsthand Account of America's Sixteen-Year Involvement in Vietnam* (Chicago: 1989), 117; author interview with Carl Colby, Jan. 9, 2007.

3. Quoted in Thomas L. Ahern Jr., *CIA and Rural Pacification in South Vietnam*, Center for the Study of Intelligence, August 2001, available at National Security Archive, www.gwu.edu/~nsarchiv/NSAEBB/NSAEBB284/index.htm, 60; David A. Nuttle, "They Have Stone Ears, Don't They?" unpublished memoir, May 6, 1966; David A. Nuttle to author, Sept. 21, 2006, 16.

4. Ahern, *CIA and Rural Pacification*, 61; Nuttle, "Stone Ears," 16–17; John Prados, *Lost Crusader: The Secret Wars of CIA Director William Colby* (New York: 2003), 87–88; two Montagnard representatives to Colonel Gilbert Layton, n.d., Layton Family Papers.

5. William Colby, *Lost Victory: A Firsthand Account of America's Sixteen-Year Involvement in Vietnam* (Chicago: 1989), 98; Richard H. Shultz Jr., *The Secret War Against Hanoi: Kennedy's and Johnson's Use of Spies, Saboteurs, and Covert Warriors in North Vietnam* (New York: 1999), 7; quoted in Ahern, *CIA and Rural Pacification*, 97.

6. Author interview with Barbara Colby, Jan. 5, 2007.

7. William Colby and Peter Forbath, *Honorable Men: My Life in the CIA* (New York: 1978), 178.

8. Ibid., 180, 183.

9. Lucien Vandenbroucke, *Perilous Options: Special Operations as an Instrument of US Foreign Policy* (New York: 1993), 30; Ted Shackley and Rickard A. Finney, *Spymaster: My Life in the CIA* (Dulles, VA: 1992), 57; quoted in Tim Weiner, *Legacy of Ashes: The History of the CIA* (New York: 2007), 185.

10. Weiner, *Legacy of Ashes*, 188.

11. Ibid., 182; Colby and Forbath, *Honorable Men*, 187.

12. Colby and Forbath, *Honorable Men*, 188.

13. Quoted in Ahern, *CIA and Rural Pacification*, 86.

14. Ibid., 86–87, 101, 114; unknown correspondent to Bonnie Layton, n.d., and Gil Layton to Colonel Barry Peterson, March 2, 1991, Layton Family Papers.

15. Ahern, *CIA and Rural Pacification*, 110; "Commentary on National Security Intelligence Estimate 53-2-64," Oct. 19, 1964, Box 2, F Colby-VN, Papers of James Srodes, Marshall Library, Virginia Military Institute; quoted in R. W. Komer, *Bureaucracy at War: U.S. Performance in the Vietnam Conflict* (Boulder, CO: 1986), 11; William E. Colby to Major Hardy Bogue, Jan. 31, 1992, Box 6, F20, Colby Papers, Vietnam Archives, Texas Tech University, Lubbock, Texas.

16. Shultz, *Secret War Against Hanoi*, 47–48.

17. Colby, *Lost Victory*, 122; quoted in Shultz, *Secret War Against Hanoi*, 39–40; author interview with Robert Myers, April 11, 2007.

18. See "Current Intelligence Memorandum, CIA," Jan. 11, 1963, *FRUS, 1961–1963, Vietnam*, vol. 3, 19–22.

19. "CIA Information Report," June 28, 1963, *FRUS, 1961–1963, Vietnam*, vol. 3, 423–425; quoted in Thomas L. Ahern Jr., *CIA and the House of Ngo: Covert Action in South Vietnam, 1954–1963*, Center for the Study of Intelligence, June 2000, available at National Security Archive, www.gwu.edu/~nsarchiv/NSAEBB/NSAEBB284/index.htm,167.

20. Ahern, *CIA and the House of Ngo*, 169–171; Ellen J. Hammer, *A Death in November: America in Vietnam, 1963* (New York: 1987), 167–168; David Halberstam and Daniel J. Singal, *The Making of a Quagmire: America and Vietnam During the Kennedy Era* (Lanham, MD: 2006), 143–145; Howard Jones, *Death of a Generation: How the Assassinations of Diem and JFK Prolonged the Vietnam War* (New York: 2003), 297–298.

21. Quoted in Ahern, *CIA and the House of Ngo*, 172, 173.

22. Quoted in ibid., 173; Colby, *Lost Victory*, 137.

23. Colby, *Lost Victory*, 133.

24. Quoted in Ahern, *CIA and the House of Ngo*, 174–175; Colby, *Lost Victory*, 119.

25. Quoted in Ahern, *CIA and the House of Ngo*, 183.

26. Quoted in Anne E. Blair, *Lodge in Vietnam: A Patriot Abroad* (New Haven, CT: 1995), 1.

27. Quoted in Zalin Grant, *Facing the Phoenix: The CIA and the Political Defeat of the United States in Vietnam* (New York: 1991), 196–197.

28. Blair, *Lodge in Vietnam*, 18; Grant, *Facing the Phoenix*, 186; William E. Colby Oral History, June 2, 1981, LBJ Library.

29. William E. Colby Oral History, June 2, 1981, 50–51; Ahern, *CIA and the House of Ngo*, 185.

30. William E. Colby to Director, "Possible Rapprochement Between North and South Vietnam," Sept. 19, 1963, Box 2, F Colby-VN, Srodes Papers, Marshall Library, Virginia Military Institute; Ahern, *CIA and the House of Ngo*, 187.

31. Ahern, *CIA and the House of Ngo*, 195 n. 3, 195.

32. Colby, *Lost Victory*, 137, 168. He would later compare the Buddhists to the followers of the Iranian Shiite leader Ayatollah Khomeini and their "fundamentalist obscurantism." Colby, *Lost Victory*, 145; William E. Colby Oral History, June 2, 1981. Of course, nothing could have been further from the truth. Buddhism is the most inclusive of religions.

33. Blair, *Lodge in Vietnam*, 28–29; see also Seth Jacobs, *Cold War Mandarin: Ngo Dinh Diem and the Origins of the American War in Vietnam, 1950–1963* (New York: 2006).

34. Colby, *Lost Victory*, 140.

35. Colby, *Lost Victory*, 144–145; Ahern, *CIA and the House of Ngo*, 191.

36. Author interview with Robert Myers, June 11, 2007, and Layton Family, Oct. 13, 2006; Ahern, *CIA and the House of Ngo*, 193.

37. Quoted in Ahern, *CIA and the House of Ngo*, 195, 200.

38. Ibid., 203; Jones, *Death of a Generation*, 393; Colby, *Lost Victory*, 149.

39. "Memorandum of a Conference with the President," White House, Oct. 29, 1963, *FRUS, 1961–1963, Vietnam*, vol. 4, 468–471; quoted in Ahern, *CIA and the House of Ngo*, 206; quoted in Colby, *Lost Victory*, 152.

40. Karnow, *Vietnam*, 307–322; Jones, *Death of a Generation*, 398–399; Patrick Lloyd Hatcher, *The Suicide of an Elite: American Internationalists and Vietnam* (Palo Alto, CA: 1990), 149.

41. "Telegram from the Embassy in Vietnam to the DOS," Nov. 1, 1963, *FRUS, 1961–1963, Vietnam*, vol. 4, 516–517; Ahern, *CIA and the House of Ngo*, 207.

42. Quoted in Ahern, *CIA and the House of Ngo*, 208; William E. Colby Oral History, June 2, 1981; quoted in Colby, *Lost Victory*, 153–154. Given Tung's widespread notoriety as the Diem regime's chief instrument of repression, Colby's observation here seems incredible.

43. Quoted in Jones, *Death of a Generation*, 429, 435.

44. Author interview with Barbara Colby, Jan. 5, 2007; quoted in Colby, *Lost Victory*, 156.

45. Colby, *Lost Victory*, 157.

46. Ibid., 158.

47. Ibid., 161.

48. Thomas L. Ahern Jr., *CIA and the Generals: Covert Support to Military Government in South Vietnam*, Center for the Study of Intelligence, October 1998, available at National Security Archive, www.gwu.edu/~nsarchiv/NSAEBB/NSAEBB284/index.htm, 10–11.

49. Colby, *Lost Victory*, 163.

50. Prados, *Lost Crusader*, 129.

51. Colby, *Lost Victory*, 169.

52. Ibid., 170.

53. Quoted in Randall Bennett Woods, *Quest for Identity: America Since 1945* (New York: 2005), 226.

54. Quoted in Prados, *Lost Crusader*, 133.

55. Ibid., 136.

56. Peer De Silva, *Sub Rosa: The CIA and the Uses of Intelligence* (New York: 1978), 211.

57. Ahern, *CIA and the Generals*, 13, 18 n. 11.

58. Quoted in ibid., 15.

59. Ibid., 18; quoted in Colby, *Lost Victory*, 171.

60. Quoted in Randall B. Woods, *LBJ: Architect of American Ambition* (New York: 2006), 509.

61. Author interview with Layton Family, Oct. 13, 2006.

62. Quoted in Prados, *Lost Crusader*, 140.

63. Ibid., 143.

64. Quoted in Ahern, *CIA and Rural Pacification*, 154.

65. Quoted in Woods, *LBJ*, 510; Ahern, *CIA and Rural Pacification*, 159–160; "NSC Meeting," May 16, 1964, John McCone Memoranda, Box 1, Papers of the National Security Council, LBJ Library; Richard Helms, with William Hood, *A Look over My Shoulder: A Life in the Central Intelligence Agency* (New York: 2003), 322.

66. Woods, *LBJ*, 510.

67. Colby, *Lost Victory*, 172–173.

68. Tran Van Don, *Our Endless War* (Novato, CA: 1978), 22–23, 122–123.

69. Ahern, *CIA and Rural Pacification*, 161.

70. Prados, *Lost Crusader*, 139; author interview with Frank Scotton, Oct. 10–12, 2007.

71. Ahern, *CIA and Rural Pacification*, 123.

72. Ahern, *CIA and Rural Pacification*, 140, 148, 154.

73. Quoted in ibid., 144.

74. Ibid., 161, 162–164.

75. Quoted in ibid., 166.

76. Ibid., 168–171.

77. Ibid., 175; author interview with Frank Scotton, Oct. 10–12, 2007.

78. Colby, *Lost Victory*, 179; quoted in ibid., 179.

79. Prados, *Lost Crusader*, 146; Weiner, *Legacy of Ashes*, 254.

CHAPTER 11

1. John Prados, *Lost Crusader: The Secret Wars of CIA Director William Colby* (New York: 2003), 158–159.

2. Theodore Friend, *Indonesian Destinies* (Cambridge, MA: 2003), 27; Roger M. Smith, ed., *Southeast Asia. Documents of Political Development and Change* (Ithaca, NY: 1974), 174–183.

3. Tim Weiner, *Legacy of Ashes: The History of the CIA* (New York: 2007), 142–143; see also Andrew Roadnight, *United States Policy Towards Indonesia in the Truman and Eisenhower Years* (New York: 2002).

4. Weiner, *Legacy of Ashes*, 259; Prados, *Lost Crusader*, 147.

5. *FRUS, 1964–1968, Indonesia*, vol. 26, 161, 163.

6. Author interview with Hugh Tovar, July 27, 2007; Weiner, *Legacy of Ashes*, 259; quoted in Kai Bird, *The Color of Truth: McGeorge Bundy and William Bundy: Brothers in Arms* (New York: 1998), 352.

7. M. C. Ricklefs, *A History of Modern Indonesia* (New York: 1982), 269.

8. *FRUS, 1964–1968, Indonesia*, vol. 26, 310–313; Adam Vickers, *A History of Modern Indonesia* (Cambridge, UK: 2005), 157–158.

9. Quoted in Bird, *Color of Truth*, 352, 353; Prados, *Lost Crusader*, 151; author interview with Hugh Tovar, July 27, 2007.

10. Quoted in Bird, *Color of Truth*, 353.

11. Roger Warner, *Backfire: The CIA's Secret War in Laos and Its Link to the War in Vietnam* (New York: 1995), 20–21.

12. Thomas L. Ahern Jr., *Undercover Armies: CIA and Surrogate Warfare in Laos, 1961–1973*, Center for the Study of Intelligence, 2006, available at National Security Archive, www.gwu.edu/~nsarchiv/NSAEBB/NSAEBB284/index.htm, 34.

13. Ibid., 8. The CIA never came up with a formal doctrine to guide operations in the Third World. The working assumptions that governed activity in Laos and Vietnam were shaped first by the OSS experience supporting partisan warfare in World War II and second by the Lansdale campaign against the Huk rebellion in the Philippines in the early 1950s. The thrust of Agency efforts was often a search for a charismatic leader who could mobilize his country's political and military resources for the struggle against the communists. Ibid., 5.

14. Ibid., 13, 22–23.

15. Ibid., 26–28.

16. Author interview with Vinton Lawrence, May 4, 2010; Zalin Grant, *Facing the Phoenix: The CIA and the Political Defeat of the United States in Vietnam* (New York: 1991), 142.

17. Warner, *Backfire*, 21; quoted in Ahern, *Undercover Armies*, 31.

18. Grant, *Facing the Phoenix*, 141.

19. Author interview with Vinton Lawrence, May 5, 2010.

20. Warner, *Backfire*, 40.

21. Ahern, *Undercover Armies*, 30–32.

22. Ibid., 34.

23. Ibid., 45, 49.

24. Ibid., 59. US intelligence reported that up to one-half of the soldiers in any given Pathet Lao unit were North Vietnamese. Ibid., 47.

25. Warner, *Backfire*, 59, 64.

26. Ahern, *Undercover Armies*, 73–77.

27. Ibid., 85–90.

28. Ibid., 109.

29. Prados, *Lost Crusader*, 98; Warner, *Backfire*, 83.

30. Ahern, *Undercover Armies*, 126.

31. William Colby, *Lost Victory: A Firsthand Account of America's Sixteen-Year Involvement in Vietnam* (Chicago: 1989), 194–196; William Colby and Peter Forbath, *Honorable Men: My Life in the CIA* (New York: 1978), 190–194.

32. Colby and Forbath, *Honorable Men*, 193.

33. Author interview with Vinton Lawrence, May 4, 2010.

34. Warner, *Backfire*, 76–79; Prados, *Lost Crusader*, 103–104; author interview with Vinton Lawrence, May 4, 2010.

35. Author interview with Vinton Lawrence, May 4, 2010; Warner, *Backfire*, 90.

36. Warner, *Backfire*, 89; author interview with Vinton Lawrence, May 5, 2010.

37. Colby, *Lost Victory*, 195–196; Ahern, *Undercover Armies*, 150–154; *FRUS, 1961–1963, Laos Crisis,* vol. 24, 972–973.

38. "Summary Record of the 512th NSC Meeting," April 20, 1960, *FRUS, 1961–1963, Laos Crisis,* vol. 24, 976–977; "NSCRA 2465," April 20, 1963, *FRUS, 1961–1963, Laos Crisis,* vol. 24, 989.

39. Ahern, *Undercover Armies*, 162; "Memorandum for the Record," June 19, 1963, *FRUS, 1961–1963, Laos Crisis,* vol. 24, 1030–1031.

40. Warner, *Backfire*, 74; Colby and Forbath, *Honorable Men*, 200; John F. Sullivan, *Gatekeeper: Memoirs of a CIA Polygraph Examiner* (Washington, DC: 2007), 19.

41. Ahern, *Undercover Armies*, 178–179.

42. Ibid., 181.

43. *FRUS, 1964–1968, Laos,* vol. 28, 129 n. 3.

44. "Colby Memorandum for the Record," June 4, 1964, and June 6, 1964, *FRUS, 1964–1968, Laos,* vol. 28, 130, 143–144.

45. Quoted in Warner, *Backfire*, 127.

46. Colby and Forbath, *Honorable Men*, 228, 229.

47. Prados, *Lost Crusader*, 161.

48. Warner, *Backfire*, 155.

49. Ahern, *Undercover Armies*, 195, 199, 206.

50. Author interview with Vinton Lawrence, May 4, 2010.

51. Colby and Forbath, *Honorable Men*, 199; see also Ahern, *Undercover Armies*, 63–64; Colby, *Lost Victory*, 198; Warner, *Backfire*, 178.

52. Colby, *Lost Victory*, 198.

53. Quoted in Ahern, *Undercover Armies*, 213, 215.

54. Richard H. Shultz Jr., *The Secret War Against Hanoi: Kennedy's and Johnson's Use of Spies, Saboteurs, and Covert Warriors in North Vietnam* (New York: 1999), 213–215; Ahern, *Undercover Armies*, 224–225.

55. Ahern, *Undercover Armies*, 67, 121–122, 213.

56. Interview with James R. Lilley, May 21, 1998, Foreign Affairs Oral History Collection, Library of Congress; author interview with Vinton Lawrence, May 4, 2010; Ahern, *Undercover Armies*, 261.

57. Ahern, *Undercover Armies*, 262; Warner, *Backfire*, 181–182.

58. Quoted in David Corn, *Blond Ghost* (New York: 1994), 135.

59. Interview with James R. Lilley, May 21, 1998, Foreign Affairs Oral History Collection, Library of Congress; Ahern, *Undercover Armies*, 265.

60. Warner, *Backfire*, 141.

61. John L. Plaster, *SOG: The Secret Wars of America's Commandos in Vietnam* (New York: 1998), 30.

62. Ibid., 37–39.

63. Ahern, *Undercover Armies*, 284; William E. Colby to Richard Helms, Aug. 16, 1966, *FRUS, 1964–1968, Laos,* vol. 28, 484–485.

64. William E. Colby to Lyndon B. Johnson, July 31, 1967, *FRUS, 1964–1968, Laos,* vol. 28, 608–609.

65. Ibid., 610.

66. Corn, *Blond Ghost*, 163; Colby, *Lost Victory*, 198.

CHAPTER 12

1. Richard Helms, with William Hood, *A Look over My Shoulder: A Life in the Central Intelligence Agency* (New York: 2003), 321; author interview with Frank Scotton, Oct.12–14, 2007.

2. Thomas L. Ahern Jr., *Undercover Armies: CIA and Surrogate Warfare in Laos, 1961–1973*, Center for the Study of Intelligence, 2006, available at National Security Archive, www.gwu.edu/~nsarchiv/NSAEBB/NSAEBB284/index.htm, 185, 187.

3. Ibid., 192.

4. Ibid., 196–197.

5. Zalin Grant, *Facing the Phoenix: The CIA and the Political Defeat of the United States in Vietnam* (New York: 1991), 282; Tran Ngoc Chau, "Hawks, Doves and the Dragon," unpublished memoir in the possession of author, 359.

6. Chau, "Hawks, Doves and the Dragon," 364.

7. Thomas L. Ahern Jr., *CIA and Rural Pacification in South Vietnam*, Center for the Study of Intelligence, August 2001, available at National Security Archive, www.gwu.edu/~nsarchiv/NSAEBB/NSAEBB284/index.htm, 206; William E. Colby Oral History, June 2, 1981, LBJ Library.

8. William E. Colby Oral History, June 2, 1981.

9. Quoted in Eric Bergerud, *The Dynamics of Defeat: The Vietnam War in Hau Nghia Province* (New York: 1993), 81–82; John Paul Vann to Keith Roberts, June 25, 1965, Box 41, F Hau Nghia Province, Papers of Neil Sheehan, Library of Congress.

10. Quoted in Ahern, *CIA and Rural Pacification*, 203.

11. Quoted in Randall B. Woods, *LBJ: Architect of American Ambition* (New York: 2006), 436.

12. Quoted in ibid., 608.

13. See Neil Sheehan, *Bright Shining Lie: John Paul Vann and America in Vietnam* (New York: 1988).

14. Author interview with Frank Scotton, Oct. 10–12, 2010; "Sheehan-Halberstam Conversation," May 23, 1975, Box 67, F4, Sheehan Papers, Library of Congress.

15. Douglas K. Ramsey, *Bees to the Honey, Flies to the Carrion, Moth to the Flame*, unpublished memoir in the possession of author, IIIA, 26, 55; author interview with Frank Scotton, Oct. 4, 2007.

16. "Vincent Demma Memo," Aug. 8, 1962, Box 62, F Vincent, D., Sheehan Papers, Library of Congress.

17. Quoted in Sheehan, *Bright Shining Lie*, 538.

18. Quoted in "Dunn-Sheehan Conversation," Dec. 31, 1979, Box 63, F Dunn, M., Sheehan Papers, Library of Congress.

19. Maxwell Taylor Oral History, Sept. 14, 1981, LBJ Library.

20. "Tactics," May 1968, Diary, Box 30, Papers of William Westmoreland, LBJ Library; Walter Rostow to Lyndon B. Johnson, April 5, 1966, *FRUS, 1964–1968, Vietnam*, vol. 6, 333.

21. "Sheehan-Halberstam Conversation," May 23, 1975, and July 16, 1972, F4, Sheehan Papers, Library of Congress.

22. Quoted in Woods, *LBJ*, 719.

23. William E. Colby to Michael Forrestal, Nov. 16, 1964, CREST, National Archives II.

24. Ibid.; "Commentary on Special National Intelligence Estimate 53-2-64," Oct. 19, 1964, Box 2, F Colby-Vietnam, Srodes Papers, Marshall Library, Virginia Military Institute.

25. "Notes of Meeting," Jan. 11, 1966, *FRUS, 1964–1968, Vietnam*, vol. 4, 43; "Memorandum of Conversation," Aug. 2, 1966, *FRUS, 1964–1968, Vietnam*, vol. 4, 542.

26. Quoted in R. W. Komer, *Bureaucracy at War: U.S. Performance in the Vietnam Conflict* (Boulder, CO: 1986), 81, 83.

27. William Colby, *Lost Victory: A Firsthand Account of America's Sixteen-Year Involvement in Vietnam* (Chicago: 1989), 205; quoted in Woods, *LBJ*, 683.

28. Robert Komer to Lyndon B. Johnson, May 9, 1966, NSF, Komer Files, Box 4, LBJ Library; Robert Komer to Lyndon B. Johnson, April 19, 1966, NSF, Komer Files, Box 2, LBJ Library; Robert Komer to Colonel Robert I. Channon, June 20, 1974, Box 22, Colby Papers, Texas Tech University.

29. Robert Komer to Lyndon B. Johnson, Aug. 2 and Aug. 30, 1966, NSF, Box 2, Komer Files, LBJ Library; John Paul Vann to Vince Davis, May 1, 1965, Box 26, F Davis, V., Sheehan Papers, Library of Congress. In 1966 alone, the ARVN experienced 135,000 desertions. "The South Vietnamese Army Today," CIA memorandum, Dec. 12, 1966, CREST, National Archives II.

30. George Carver to Richard Helms, July 7, 1966, *FRUS, 1964–1968, Vietnam*, vol. 4, 486–487; Richard Helms to Robert Komer, July 18, 1966, *FRUS, 1964–1968, Vietnam*, vol. 4, 505.

31. Robert Komer to William Porter, July 27, 1966, NSF, Komer Files, Box 4, LBJ Library.

32. "Memo from DOD to McNamara," Aug. 24, 1966, *FRUS, 1964–1968, Vietnam*, vol. 4, 591.

33. Woods, *LBJ*, 725–726; "Westmoreland Diaries," Sept. 18, 1966, Box 9, F History, Sept.-Oct. '66, Westmoreland Papers, LBJ Library; Lyndon B. Johnson to Henry Cabot Lodge, Nov. 16, 1966, NSF, Komer Files, Box 2, LBJ Library; George Carver to Richard Helms, Sept. 28, 1966, *FRUS, 1964–1968, Vietnam*, vol. 4, 669; Lyndon B. Johnson to Henry Cabot Lodge, Nov. 16, 1966, NSF, Komer Files, Box 2, LBJ Library.

34. Colby, *Lost Victory*, 206; Ahern, *CIA and Rural Pacification*, 205.

35. Chau, "Hawks, Doves, and Dragons," 368, 374.

36. Ahern, *CIA and Rural Pacification*, 216–217, 220, 230; "Pacification and Nation-Building in Vietnam: Present Status, Current Trends and Prospects," CIA, Feb. 17, 1967, CREST.

37. Thomas L. Ahern Jr., *CIA and the Generals: Covert Support to Military Government in South Vietnam*, Center for the Study of Intelligence, October 1998, available at National Security Archive, www.gwu.edu/~nsarchiv/NSAEBB/NSAEBB284/index.htm, 41, 48; "Memorandum for the Record," July 17, 1966, *FRUS, 1964–1968, Vietnam*, vol. 4, 497–498.

38. Quoted in Ahern, *CIA and Rural Pacification*, 244.

39. Thomas W. Scoville, *Reorganizing for Pacification Support* (Washington, DC: 1982), Chap. 4, p. 7; Lyndon B. Johnson to Secretary of State and Secretary of Defense, May 9, 1967, NSF Memos, Rostow, May 1967, vol. 27, LBJ Library; Ahern, *CIA and Rural Pacification*, 250.

40. John Roche to Lyndon B. Johnson, Nov. 4, 1966, Diary Backup, Box 49, LBJ Papers, LBJ Library.

41. Ellsworth Bunker Oral History, Dec. 9, 1980, LBJ Library.

42. Colby, *Lost Victory*, 121.

43. John Prados, *Lost Crusader: The Secret Wars of CIA Director William Colby* (New York: 2003), 182.

44. Ahern, *CIA and Generals*, 51–56.

45. See David E. Lilienthal, *The Journals of David E. Lilienthal, Creativity and Conflict* (New York: 1967), 379.

46. William E. Colby to Richard Helms, July 25, 1967, *FRUS, 1964–1968, Vietnam*, vol. 4, 633–637.

47. Author interview with Paul Colby, Jan. 8, 2007.

CHAPTER 13

1. Hugh Wilford, *The Mighty Wurlitzer: How the CIA Played America* (Cambridge, MA: 2009), 240–241.

2. Richard Helms, with William Hood, *A Look over My Shoulder: A Life in the Central Intelligence Agency* (New York: 2003), 380.

3. Quoted in William Colby and Peter Forbath, *Honorable Men: My Life in the CIA* (New York: 1978), 242; John Prados, *Lost Crusader: The Secret Wars of CIA Director William Colby* (New York: 2003), 192.

4. Colby and Forbath, *Honorable Men*, 242.

5. Quoted in Robert M. Hathaway and Russell Jack Smith, *Richard Helms as Director of the CIA* (Washington, DC: 2006), 101.

6. Tom Mangold, *Cold Warrior: James Jesus Angleton. The CIA's Master Spy Hunter* (New York: 1991), 154, 156–157.

7. Ibid., 56–57.

8. Hathaway and Smith, *Helms as Director*, 103; David Robarge, "Moles, Defectors and Deceptions: James Angleton and CIA Counterintelligence," *Journal of Intelligence History* 3, no. 2 (2003): 35.

9. Quoted in Hathaway and Smith, *Helms as Director*, 104.

10. "New Information on President Kennedy's Assassination," *Intelligence Digest*, April 1, 1975, 20; Robarge, "Moles, Defectors," 37–38; Hathaway and Smith, *Helms as Director*, 104–106.

11. Colby and Forbath, *Honorable Men*, 245. A subsequent investigation determined that both Golitsin and Nosenko had been authentic defectors. The investigation provided information on Soviet operations showing that both had been targeted for assassination by the KGB. Robarge, "Moles, Defectors," 39. David Blee, a later chief of central intelligence, believed that Angleton's unfounded suspicions cost some Soviet defectors their lives. Harold Ford, *William E. Colby as Director of Central Intelligence, 1973–1976* (Washington, DC: 1993), 87, released under Freedom of Information Act, Aug. 11, 2011.

12. Colby and Forbath, *Honorable Men*, 246.

13. Helms, *A Look over My Shoulder*, 335.

14. Author interview with Sally Shelton-Colby, Jan. 8, 2007.

15. Author interview with Paul Colby, June 10, 2007; author interview with Stan Temko, Jan. 6, 2007; author interview with Christine Colby Giraudo, June 5, 2010.

16. Author interview with Susan Colby, June 5, 2010.

17. Author interview with Barbara Colby, Jan. 5, 2007.

18. William Colby, *Lost Victory: A Firsthand Account of America's Sixteen-Year Involvement in Vietnam* (Chicago: 1989), 233.

19. Ibid.

20. Ibid., 227.

21. Quoted in Thomas L. Ahern Jr., *CIA and the Generals: Covert Support to Military Government in South Vietnam*, Center for the Study of Intelligence, October 1998, available at National Security Archive, www.gwu.edu/~nsarchiv/NSAEBB/NSAEBB284/index.htm, 74.

22. Lewis Sorley, *Vietnam Chronicles: The Abrams Tapes, 1968–1972* (Lubbock, TX: 2004), 13, 110.

23. Quoted in Randall Bennett Woods, *Quest for Identity: America Since 1945* (New York: 2005), 268.

24. Colby, *Lost Victory*, 233.

25. Thomas W. Scoville, *Reorganizing for Pacification Support* (Washington, DC: 1982), 67.

26. Author interview with Mike Hacker, Oct. 23, 2007; author interview with Louis Jankowski, Nov. 7, 2007; author interview with Bruce Kinsey, Sept. 20, 2007.

27. Thomas L. Ahern Jr., *CIA and Rural Pacification in South Vietnam*, Center for the Study of Intelligence, August 2001, available at National Security Archive, www.gwu.edu/~nsarchiv/NSAEBB/NSAEBB284/index.htm, 253, 257, 262; author interview with Frank Scotton, Oct. 12–14, 2007.

28. Ahern, *CIA and Rural Pacification*, 279.

29. Ibid., 284–285.

30. Ibid., 287; quoted in Thomas K. Adams, *US Special Operations Forces in Action: The Challenge of Unconventional Warfare* (London: 1998), 133.

31. Author interview with Tom Martin, Oct. 1, 2007; Ahern, *CIA and Rural Pacification*, 301, 303.

32. Quoted in Ahern, *CIA and Rural Pacification*, 297.

33. Colby, *Lost Victory*, 234.

34. Ahern, *CIA and Rural Pacification*, 313, 329; Colby, *Lost Victory*, 235.

35. Colby, *Lost Victory*, 238.

36. Sheehan interview with Colonel Carl Bernard, n.d., Box 120, F-Bernard, Sheehan Papers, Library of Congress.

37. Carl Bernard to Eric Bergerud, March 20, 1991, Box 22, Colby Papers, Texas Tech University; Sheehan interview with Colonel Carl Bernard, n.d., Box 120, F-Bernard, Sheehan Papers, Library of Congress.

38. Neil Sheehan, *Bright Shining Lie: John Paul Vann and America in Vietnam* (New York: 1988), 700–701.

39. Daniel Ellsberg, *Secrets: A Memoir of Vietnam and the Pentagon Papers* (New York: 2002), 117, 121–123.

40. Sheehan interview with Colonel Carl Bernard, n.d., Box 120, F-Bernard, Sheehan Papers, Library of Congress; author interview with Sally Shelton-Colby, Jan. 8, 2007.

41. Quoted in Randall B. Woods, *LBJ: Architect of American Ambition* (New York: 2006), 637.

42. Quoted in Woods, *Quest for Identity*, 271.

43. Quoted in Ahern, *CIA and the Generals*, 75.

44. Colby, *Lost Victory*, 239.

45. Ibid., 240.

46. Quoted in Ahern, *CIA and Rural Pacification*, 307.

47. Ibid., 307, 333.

48. Prados, *Lost Crusader*, 203; Colby, *Lost Victory*, 242–243.

49. Colby, *Lost Victory*, 254.

50. Quoted in Sorley, *Vietnam Chronicles*, 17, 26, 40, 44.

51. Colby, *Lost Victory*, 254; Sorley, *Vietnam Chronicles*, 50.

52. Colby, *Lost Victory*, 258–259; quoted in Ahern, *CIA and Rural Pacification*, 288 n. 28.

53. Quoted in ibid., 331.

54. Ellsworth Bunker to Walter Rostow, Oct. 9, 1968, NSF Memos to President, Rostow, Box 40, LBJ Library.

55. Colby, *Lost Victory*, 265; see also J. P. Vann, "Thoughts on GVN/VC Control," Nov. 1968, Box 64, F15, Sheehan Papers, Library of Congress.

56. Sorley, *Vietnam Chronicles*, 105; Ellsworth Bunker to Lyndon B. Johnson, Dec. 19, 1968, NSF Memos to President, Rostow, Box 39, LBJ Library; "Colby Memo on 1969 AAPC," June 28, 1969, RG 472, MACV-CORDS, Files of Harry Lee Braddock, Box 7, F Colby, National Archives II.

57. Author interview with Mike Hacker, Oct. 23, 2007.

58. Ibid.

59. Ibid.

60. Ibid.

61. Author interview with Bruce Kinsey, Sept. 20, 2007.

62. Ibid.

63. Sheehan interview with Lieutenant Colonel William Taylor, Nov. 11, 1975, Box 66, F4, Sheehan Papers, Library of Congress.

64. Author interview with Frank Scotton, Oct. 12–14, 2007; Sheehan interview with Colonel David Farham, Oct. 15, 1975, Box 22, F4, Sheehan Papers, Library of Congress; Julian Ewell Obituary, *Washington Post*, Aug. 5, 2009.

65. William E. Colby to Major Thomas K. Adams, Dec. 29, 1988, Box 6, F19, Colby Papers, Texas Tech University.

66. Author interview with Bruce Kinsey, Sept. 20, 2007.

CHAPTER 14

1. See Jeffrey Kimball, *Nixon's Vietnam War* (Lawrence, KS: 1998), 87–104; Henry Kissinger, *White House Years* (Boston: 1979), 272.

2. Quoted in Thomas L. Ahern Jr., *CIA and Rural Pacification in South Vietnam*, Center for the Study of Intelligence, August 2001, available at National Security Archive, www.gwu.edu/~nsarchiv/NSAEBB/NSAEBB284/index.htm, 336.

3. "Memo of Laird-Ky Conversation," April 4, 1969, Box C 31, Papers of Melvin Laird, Gerald Ford Library, Ann Arbor, Michigan; quoted in Randall Bennett Woods, *Quest for Identity: America Since 1945* (New York: 2005), 292.

4. Ahern, *CIA and Rural Pacification*, 337–338.

5. Lewis Sorley, *Vietnam Chronicles: The Abrams Tapes, 1968–1972* (Lubbock, TX: 2004), 55, 61, 64; author interview with Gage McAfee, Aug. 8, 2007.

6. John Prados, *Lost Crusader: The Secret Wars of CIA Director William Colby* (New York: 2003), 214–215; Victor Marchetti, *The CIA and the Cult of Intelligence* (New York: 1974), 246–247.

7. Thomas K. Adams, *US Special Operations Forces in Action: The Challenge of Unconventional Warfare* (London: 1998), 137, 139; William Colby, *Lost Victory: A Firsthand Account of America's Sixteen-Year Involvement in Vietnam* (Chicago: 1989), 281.

8. Author interview with Gage McAfee, Aug. 8, 2007; author interview with Frank Snepp, May 21, 2008.

9. Quoted in Prados, *Lost Crusader*, 219.

10. Ibid., 216.

11. Ibid., 218.

12. Author interview with Gage McAfee, Aug. 8, 2007; author interview with Frank Snepp, May 21, 2008.

13. Prados, *Lost Crusader*, 216, 225.

14. Sorley, *Vietnam Chronicles*, 220; author interview with Gage McAfee, Aug. 8, 2007; USMACV to Phoenix Directorate, n.d., Box 22, Colby Papers, Texas Tech University.

15. Prados, *Lost Crusader*, 220; Zalin Grant, *Facing the Phoenix: The CIA and the Political Defeat of the United States in Vietnam* (New York: 1991), 32–33.

16. Quoted in Prados, *Lost Crusader*, 221.

17. Quoted in ibid., 225.

18. Sorley, *Vietnam Chronicles*, 389.

19. "President Thieu's Concern," CIA Information Cable, March 18, 1968, NSF Memos to President, Rostow, Box 31, LBJ Library; see Ellsworth Bunker to Lyndon B. Johnson, Dec. 19, 1968, NSF Memos to President, Box 43, Rostow, LBJ Library.

20. Ed Lansdale to Ellsworth Bunker, June 7, 1968, NSF Memos to President, Rostow, Box 35, LBJ Library; author interview with James Nach, Sept. 2, 2008. See also Douglas Blaufarb to William E. Colby, Dec. 1, 1989, Box 6, F20, Colby Papers, Texas Tech University. Blaufarb lamented "the failure of the Thieu government to develop a popular political base, choosing instead to rely on the officer corps as its base. That led to the massive corruption within the military and the assignment and promotion of unqualified leaders. . . . It also led to an immense gap between the provincial and district governments and the peasant population."

21. William E. Colby to Nguyen Van Thieu, Feb. 2, 1969, Box 2, F Colby/VN Traffic, Srodes Papers, Marshall Library, Virginia Military Institute.

22. "Memorandum by Chief of Far East Division, CIA," July 25, 1967, *FRUS, 1964–1968, Vietnam*, vol. 6, 636; William E. Colby to Robert Komer, April 3, 1973, Box 6, Colby Papers, Texas Tech University; author interview with Frank Scotton, April 10–14, 2008.

23. Tran Ngoc Chau, "Hawks, Doves and the Dragon," unpublished memoir in possession of author, 446–447, 515–520, 460.

24. Thomas L. Ahern Jr., *CIA and the Generals: Covert Support to Military Government in South Vietnam*, Center for the Study of Intelligence, October 1998, available at National Security Archive, www.gwu.edu/~nsarchiv/NSAEBB/NSAEBB284/index.htm, 94; Chau, "Hawks, Doves and the Dragon," 492.

25. Chau, "Hawks, Doves and the Dragon," 496, 499–501.

26. Jeff Woods interview with Jean Sauvageot, Saigon, July 16, 2010.

27. Author interview with Frank Scotton, April 10–14, 2008; author interview with Frank Snepp, May 21, 2008; Ahern, *CIA and the Generals*, 93. See also Sheehan Interview with Carl Bernard, n.d., Box 120, F Carl Bernard, Sheehan Papers, Library of Congress.

28. Author interview with Frank Scotton, April 10–14, 2008.

29. Quoted in Prados, *Lost Crusader*, 223; William E. Colby Oral History, March 1, 1982, Interview II, LBJ Library.

30. Author interview with Tony Cistaro, Jan. 15, 2008; John F. Sullivan, *Gatekeeper: Memoirs of a CIA Polygraph Examiner* (Washington, DC: 2007), 34–35; author interview with Gage McAfee, Aug. 8, 2007.

31. Author interview with Steve Young, July 7, 2010.

32. Steve Young to William E. Colby, July 15, 1971, Box 6, Colby Papers, Texas Tech University; author interview with Paul Colby, June 1, 2007.

33. Sorley, *Vietnam Chronicles*, 420.

34. Colby, *Lost Victory*, 288, 310; Prados, *Lost Crusader*, 211.

35. James Nach to author, July 25, 2010, e-mail.

36. Prados, *Lost Crusader*, 231–233.

37. Colby, *Lost Victory*, 309–310.

38. Sorley, *Vietnam Chronicles*, 456.

39. Ahern, *CIA and the Generals*, 94–95, 97; Prados, *Lost Crusader*, 230.

40. Quoted in Ahern, *CIA and the Generals*, 102.

41. Author interview with Frank Snepp, May 21, 2008. They were correct; Colby had not severed his ties with the Agency. In 1971, when Jean Sauvageot, liaison to the prime minister, was being considered for a job with the CIA, Colby advised him against taking it. "Why?" Sauvageot asked. "If you took the job and I asked you to sneak a look at documents on Khiem's desk or plant listening devices in the Palace, would you?" No, Sauvageot said, that would be a betrayal of trust. "Then don't take the job," Colby said. Jeff Woods interview with Jean Sauvageot, Saigon, July 18, 2010.

42. T. E. Lawrence, *Arab Bulletin*, 1917, for Foreign Service Agents, in Carl Colby film script, *The Man Nobody Knew*, in possession of author.

43. Author interview with Jenonne Walker, June 6, 2010; author interview with Paul Colby, Jan. 8, 2007.

CHAPTER 15

1. Joseph B. Treaster, "Phoenix Murders," *Penthouse*, December 1975.

2. Quoted in John Prados, *Lost Crusader: The Secret Wars of CIA Director William Colby* (New York: 2003), 235.

3. Ibid., 232–233; William Colby, *Lost Victory: A Firsthand Account of America's Sixteen-Year Involvement in Vietnam* (Chicago: 1989), 333.

4. Prados, *Lost Crusader*, 237; author interview with Gage McAfee, Aug. 8, 2007.

5. William Colby and Peter Forbath, *Honorable Men: My Life in the CIA* (New York: 1978), 291–293.

6. Quoted in Robert M. Hathaway and Russell Jack Smith, *Helms as Director of the CIA* (Washington, DC: 2006), 9.

7. Quoted in Richard Helms, with William Hood, *A Look over My Shoulder: A Life in the Central Intelligence Agency* (New York: 2003), 38; Harold Ford, *William E. Colby as Director of Central Intelligence, 1973–1976* (Washington, DC: 1993), 17, released under

Freedom of Information Act, Aug. 11, 2011, quoted in Hathaway and Smith, *Helms as Director*, 10.

8. Hathaway and Smith, *Helms as Director*, 85.

9. Ibid., 81–86.

10. Colby and Forbath, *Honorable Men*, 303; quoted in Hathaway and Smith, *Helms as Director*, 88.

11. "DCI Briefing for Nov. 6 Meeting," Nov. 5, 1970, Box 32, President's Handwriting File, Ford Papers, Ford Library; Tim Weiner, "All the President Had to Do Was Ask: The CIA Took Aim at Allende," *New York Times*, Sept. 13, 1998.

12. Hathaway and Smith, *Helms as Director*, 92–94.

13. Colby and Forbath, *Honorable Men*, 304.

14. Ibid., 305.

15. Ibid., 312.

16. Prados, *Lost Crusader*, 247.

17. Colby and Forbath, *Honorable Men*, 314.

18. Ibid., 313.

19. See William E. Colby, "Memo for the Record," Feb. 15, 1973, F–Mail Intercepts, Box 1, Srodes Papers, Marshall Library, Virginia Military Institute.

20. Quoted in Tim Weiner, *Legacy of Ashes: The History of the CIA* (New York: 2007), 287; quoted in Helms, *A Look over My Shoulder*, 280.

21. Quoted in Hathaway and Smith, *Helms as Director*, 16; quoted in Hugh Wilford, *The Mighty Wurlitzer: How the CIA Played America* (Cambridge, MA: 2009), 23.

22. Thomas Karamessines to James Angleton, Aug. 15, 1967, Box 6, Richard Cheney Files, Ford Library; Helms, *A Look over My Shoulder*, 280; Colby and Forbath, *Honorable Men*, 314.

23. Victor Marchetti, *The CIA and the Cult of Intelligence* (New York: 1974), 228; Hathaway and Smith, *Helms as Director*, 16–17; "Memo for Record, Colby, Scowcroft, Kissinger Breakfast," June 18, 1973, CREST, National Archives II.

24. William E. Colby to Gerald Ford, Dec. 24, 1974, Box 1, Cheney Papers, Ford Library.

25. Ibid.

26. William E. Colby to Nelson Rockefeller, June 26, 1975, CREST, National Archives II; Intelligence Evaluation Committee and Staff, May 14, 1973, Box 2, F–Family Jewels, Srodes Papers, Marshall Library, Virginia Military Institute.

27. Colby and Forbath, *Honorable Men*, 310.

28. Thomas Powers, *The Man Who Kept the Secrets: Richard Helms and the CIA* (New York: 1979).

29. Prados, *Lost Crusader*, 241–243; Colby and Forbath, *Honorable Men*, 318.

30. Neil Sheehan, *Bright Shining Lie: John Paul Vann and America in Vietnam* (New York: 1988), 786; author interview with Paul Colby, Jan. 8, 2007.

31. Quoted in Sheehan, *Bright Shining Lie*, 21.

32. See Weiner, *Legacy of Ashes*, 318–319.

33. Hathaway and Smith, *Helms as Director*, 189.

34. Helms, *A Look over My Shoulder*, 4–5.

35. Marchetti, *The CIA and the Cult of Intelligence*, 226; Helms, *A Look over My Shoulder*, 5–6.

36. Colby and Forbath, *Honorable Men*, 323.

37. Curt Gentry, *J. Edgar Hoover: The Man and His Secrets* (New York: 1991), 327, 380, 391–392, 645; Andrew St. George, "The Cold War Comes Home," *Harper's Magazine*, November 1973, 76; Helms, *A Look over My Shoulder*, 269–270.

38. Quoted in Stephen Ambrose, *Nixon*, vol. 2, *The Triumph of a Politician, 1962–1972* (New York: 1991), 567.

39. Hathaway and Smith, *Helms as Director*, 189.

40. Helms, *A Look over My Shoulder*, 9–10.

41. "Testimony of General Vernon Walters, Senate Watergate Hearings," Aug. 3, 1973, CREST, Archives II ("Walters Testimony" hereafter); Colby and Forbath, *Honorable Men*, 324.

42. "Walters Testimony."

43. Helms, *A Look over My Shoulder*, 12–13.

44. "Walters Testimony"; Hathaway and Smith, *Helms as Director*, 191–192.

45. Weiner, *Legacy of Ashes*, 322; Richard Helms to Deputy Director, June 28, 1972, CREST, National Archives II.

46. Helms, *A Look over My Shoulder*, 410.

47. Colby and Forbath, *Honorable Men*, 328; Hathaway and Smith, *Helms as Director*, 208–209; quoted in Helms, *A Look over My Shoulder*, 410.

48. Quoted in Hathaway and Smith, *Helms as Director*, 210.

49. Colby and Forbath, *Honorable Men*, 329.

50. Prados, *Lost Crusader*, 252; Colby and Forbath, *Honorable Men*, 331–333.

51. Colby and Forbath, *Honorable Men*, 296–298.

52. Quoted in ibid., 332.

53. Author interview with Jenonne Walker, June 16, 2010.

54. Colby and Forbath, *Honorable Men*, 333; Prados, *Lost Crusader*, 256.

55. Colby and Forbath, *Honorable Men*, 335.

56. Author interview with Susan Colby, June 5, 2010; author interview with Christine Colby Giraudo, June 5, 2010; Carl Colby film script, *The Man Nobody Knew*, in possession of author; author interview with John Colby, June 4, 2010.

57. DCI to All CIA Employees, May 9, 1973, Colby Papers, Box 7, F1, Texas Tech University.

58. Colby and Forbath, *Honorable Men*, 339.

59. See William Broe to William E. Colby, May 21, 1973, Colby Papers, Box 7, F1, Texas Tech University. The full text of the "Family Jewels" document was only released in 2007. See "The CIA's Family Jewels," June 26, 2007, National Security Archive, www.gwu.edu/~nsarchiv/NSAEBB/NSAEBB222/index.htm.

CHAPTER 16

1. Quoted in William Colby and Peter Forbath, *Honorable Men: My Life in the CIA* (New York: 1978), 343.

2. Ibid.

3. Richard M. Nixon to William E. Colby, Feb. 20, 1973, Box 7, Colby Papers, Texas Tech University; author interview with Brent Scowcroft, June 3, 2010; author interview with Robert Myers, April 11, 2007.

4. Colby and Forbath, *Honorable Men*, 344; author interview with Barbara Colby, Jan. 5, 2007.

5. Colby and Forbath, *Honorable Men*, 346.

6. Ibid., 347.

7. Ibid., 348.

8. "Exchange of Remarks Between President Nixon and WEC," Sept. 4, 1973, Box 1, F–Mail Intercepts, Srodes Papers, Marshall Library, Virginia Military Institute.

9. David Wise, "Colby of the CIA," July 1, 1973, CREST, National Archives II; "Sheehan Notes of Interview with WEC," March 15, 1975, Box 62, F Colby, W. E., Sheehan Papers, Library of Congress.

10. Quoted in Harold Ford, *William E. Colby as Director of Central Intelligence, 1973–1976* (Washington, DC: 1993), 204, released under Freedom of Information Act, Aug. 11, 2011.

11. Ibid., 7, 205.

12. William E. Colby to Henry A. Kissinger, Sept. 13, 1973, Box 1, and "William E. Colby Memo," n.d., Srodes Papers, Marshall Library, Virginia Military Institute.

13. Hinchey Report, "CIA Activities in Chile," US Department of State, Sept. 18, 2000.

14. James Pringle, "The Year of the Generals," *Newsweek*, Sept. 16, 1974, and "Gentlemen of Torture," *Newsweek*, March 31, 1975.

15. Quoted in Ford, *Colby as Director*, 71, 204.

16. William E. Colby Oral History Project, July 27, 1976, CREST, Archives II.

17. William E. Colby, "American Intelligence Today and Tomorrow," Sept. 6, 1973, CREST, Archives II.

18. Ronald Radosh, "The CIA in the Job Market," *Nation*, Feb. 8, 1975; "Nixon, Brezhnev, Colby Conversation," June 22, 1973, CREST, Archives II.

19. Daniel Gilmore, "WEC Interview," n.d., CREST, Archives II; John Blake to William E. Colby, Dec. 5, 1974, CREST, Archives II.

20. Harold L. Brownman to William E. Colby, May 9, 1974, CREST, Archives II.

21. William E. Colby, "American Intelligence Today and Tomorrow," Sept. 6, 1973, CREST, Archives II; William E. Colby Oral History, July 27, 1976, CREST, Archives II.

22. William E. Colby Oral History, July 27, 1976, CREST, Archives II; author interview with Jenonne Walker, June 16, 2010.

23. Colby and Forbath, *Honorable Men*, 353; Ford, *Colby as Director*, 45.

24. John Prados, *Lost Crusader: The Secret Wars of CIA Director William Colby* (New York: 2003), 353.

25. Author interview with Jenonne Walker, June 16, 2010; "Advanced Management Students Discussion with DCI," Sept. 26, 1973, CREST, Archives II.

26. Colby and Forbath, *Honorable Men*, 354.

27. Prados, *Lost Crusader*, 265.

28. "Memo of Conversation Between HAK, Schlesinger and Joint Chiefs," March 11, 1974, National Security Adviser Memcons, Box 3, Ford Library.

29. Henry A. Kissinger to President Gerald Ford, Oct. 24, 1975, National Security Adviser, Outside the System, Box 1, Ford Library. See also Robert M. Hathaway and

Jack Russell Smith, *Helms as Director of the CIA* (Washington, DC: 2006), 11. In September 1975, Kissinger observed to reporters that Ford was not "tough enough" on foreign policy. "Memo of Conversation Between President Ford and HAK," Sept. 26, 1975, National Security Adviser, Memos of Conversations, Box 23, Ford Library.

30. William E. Colby, "Memo for the Record," June 15, 1973, CREST, Archives II.

31. Author interview with Jenonne Walker, June 16, 2010.

32. Colby and Forbath, *Honorable Men*, 356.

33. Author interview with Jenonne Walker, June 16, 2010.

34. Quoted in Ford, *Colby as Director*, 22.

35. Colby and Forbath, *Honorable Men*, 375.

36. See Douglas Brinkley, *Gerald R. Ford* (New York: 2007), 82–84.

37. "Memo of Conversations Between Ford and Kissinger," Oct. 21, 1974, and Nov. 10, 1974, National Security Adviser, Memos of Conversations, Box 7, Ford Library; Lodl /Richard Ober to Henry A. Kissinger, Sept. 5, 1975, Box 1, F-CIA, Srodes Papers, Marshall Library, Virginia Military Institute; Colby and Forbath, *Honorable Men*, 375.

38. Quoted in Ford, *Colby as Director*, 79.

39. See Burton Hersh, "Dragons Have to Be Killed," *Washingtonian*, September 1985; author interview with Paul Colby, Jan. 6, 2007.

40. Colby and Forbath, *Honorable Men*, 365.

41. George C. Herring, *From Colony to Superpower: U.S. Foreign Relations Since 1776* (New York: 2008), 804–805.

42. Colby and Forbath, *Honorable Men*, 366.

43. Quoted in Tim Weiner, *Legacy of Ashes: The History of the CIA* (New York: 2007), 329; Deputy Director for Administration to William E. Colby, Sept. 24, 1975, CREST, Archives II; Ford, *Colby as Director*, 26, 30, 34.

44. Colby and Forbath, *Honorable Men*, 366.

45. Herring, *From Colony to Superpower*, 805–806.

46. "Project Azorian: The Story of the Hughes Glomar Explorer," *Studies in Intelligence*, Fall 1985, 36.

47. Ibid., 9.

48. Ibid., 23–24.

49. Quoted in "The CIA's Mission Impossible, *Newsweek*, March 31, 1975.

50. Author interview with Brent Scowcroft, June 3, 2010.

51. "Project Azorian," 48.

52. Quoted in ibid., 39.

53. Prados, *Lost Crusader*, 266.

54. Author interview with Jenonne Walker, June 16, 2010; "Project Azorian," 44–46.

55. Author interview with Laurence Silberman, June 3, 2010; "Memo of Conversation Between Kissinger, Colby, Schlesinger, and Moorer," Jan. 22, 1974, National Security Adviser, Memos of Conversations, Box 3, Ford Papers.

56. "DCI Colby Meeting Regarding News Media Knowledge of the Glomar Story," Jan. 9, 1974, CREST, National Archives II; "Memo of Conversation Between DCI Colby and Fred Buzhardt," Feb. 2, 1974, CREST, National Archives II; "Memo of Conversation Between Colby and Sulzberger," Jan. 30, 1974, CREST, National Archives II.

57. Quoted in Donald L. Bartlett and James B. Steele, *Howard Hughes: His Life and Madness* (New York: 1979), 531–532.

58. Colby and Forbath, *Honorable Men*, 414, 415.

59. Ibid., 415.

60. Bartlett and Steele, *Howard Hughes*, 536, 541; "Memo of Conversation Between WEC and Brent Scowcroft," March 18, 1975, CREST, National Archives II; Seymour Hersh, "Hughes Built Ship," *New York Times*, March 19, 1975.

61. "Memo of Conversation Between Ford, Schlesinger, Colby et. al.," March 19, 1975, National Security Adviser Memos, Box 5, Ford Library.

62. "CIA as White-Collar Mafia," *Village Voice*, June 16, 1975.

63. "The CIA Partner," *Time*, April 19, 1976.

CHAPTER 17

1. See William Colby and Peter Forbath, *Honorable Men: My Life in the CIA* (New York: 1978), 371–373.

2. Quoted in Richard Helms, with William Hood, *A Look over My Shoulder: A Life in the Central Intelligence Agency* (New York: 2003), 399.

3. Ibid.

4. Quoted in "CIA Chief Tells House of $8 Million Campaign Against Allende in '70–73," *New York Times*, Sept. 8, 1974.

5. Colby and Forbath, *Honorable Men*, 380.

6. "CIA Chief Tells House."

7. Lawrence Eagleburger and Pete McClosky to Henry A. Kissinger, Sept. 24, 1974, Srodes Papers, Box 2, Marshall Library, Virginia Military Institute; "Director Colby on the Record," *Time*, Sept. 30, 1974.

8. John Prados, *Lost Crusader: The Secret Wars of CIA Director William Colby* (New York: 2003), 73.

9. "CIA and Covert Operations Conference," Sept. 13, 1974, CREST, National Archives; "Colby and CIA Conference," Sept. 13, 1974, Box 62, F Colby, Sheehan Papers, Library of Congress.

10. "CIA and Covert Operations Conference," Sept. 13, 1974, CREST, National Archives; "Colby and CIA Conference," Sept. 13, 1974, Box 62, F Colby, Sheehan Papers, Library of Congress.

11. "Colby and CIA Conference," Sept. 13, 1974, Box 62, F Colby, Sheehan Papers, Library of Congress.

12. "CIA and Chile," *Christian Science Monitor*, Sept. 11, 1974; Tom Wicker, "Secret War on Chile," *New York Times*, Sept. 13, 1974; Daniel Schorr, "My 17 Months on the CIA Watch," *Rolling Stone*, April 8, 1976; Prados, *Lost Crusader*, 291–292.

13. Laurence Stern, "Perjury Inquiry Urged on Chile Data," *Washington Post*, Sept. 17, 1974; Colby and Forbath, *Honorable Men*, 383.

14. Quoted in Colby and Forbath, *Honorable Men*, 385.

15. Quoted in Harold Ford, *William E. Colby as Director of Central Intelligence, 1973–1976* (Washington, DC: 1993), 116, released under Freedom of Information Act, Aug. 11, 2011.

16. Quoted in ibid., 142.

17. Colby and Forbath, *Honorable Men*, 386.

18. Ford, *Colby as Director*, 88–89.

19. Burton Hersh, "Dragons Have to Be Killed," *Washingtonian*, September 1985.

20. Ford, *Colby as Director*, 100.

21. Quoted in ibid., 101.

22. Quoted in ibid., 101–102.

23. Colby and Forbath, *Honorable Men*, 390–391.

24. Quoted in Prados, *Lost Crusader*, 298; Colby and Forbath, *Honorable Men*, 396.

25. Schorr, "My 17 Months."

26. Quoted in Ford, *Colby as Director*, 119; author interview with Jenonne Walker, June 6, 2010.

27. Author interview with Paul Colby, Jan. 8, 2007.

28. Colby and Forbath, *Honorable Men*, 392; see also Walter Pincus, "Covering Intelligence," *The New Republic*, Feb. 1, 1975.

29. "Seducing the Source," *Washington Monthly*, April 1975; Ford, *Colby as Director*, 97; quoted in Kathryn S. Olmsted, *Challenging the Secret Government: The Post-Watergate Investigations of the CIA and FBI* (Chapel Hill, NC: 1996), 33.

30. Henry Kissinger, *Years of Renewal* (New York: 1999), 320; quoted in Colby and Forbath, *Honorable Men*, 393.

31. Ford, *Colby as Director*, 104.

32. William E. Colby to Gerald Ford, Dec. 24, 1974, Box 6, Files of Richard Cheney, Ford Library.

33. Colby and Forbath, *Honorable Men*, 395; "Oral History: Reflections of DCI Colby and Helms on the CIA's 'Time of Troubles,'" Feb. 2, 1988, Center for the Study of Intelligence, Box 2, F-Colby, Srodes Papers, Marshall Library, Virginia Military Institute.

34. Henry A. Kissinger to Gerald Ford, Dec. 25, 1974, Box 6, Files of Richard Cheney, Ford Library.

35. "CIA: The Colby Report," Dec. 27, 1974, Box 6, Files of Richard Cheney, Ford Library.

36. Colby and Forbath, *Honorable Men*, 398; see also "Oral History: Reflections of DCI Colby and Helms on the CIA's 'Time of Troubles,'" March 15, 1988, Center for the Study of Intelligence, Box 2, F-Colby, Srodes Papers, Marshall Library, Virginia Military Institute.

CHAPTER 18

1. Author interview with John Colby, June 4, 2010.

2. William E. Colby to Alain Chevalerias, Aug. 21, 1992, Box 6, F21, Colby Papers, Texas Tech University.

3. William Colby and Peter Forbath, *Honorable Men: My Life in the CIA* (New York: 1978), 395–396.

4. Author interview with Laurence Silberman, June 3, 2010; James Wilderotter, "Memo for the File," Jan. 3, 1975, Box 7, Files of Richard Cheney, Ford Library.

5. Laurence Silberman to Gerald Ford, Jan. 3, 1975, Box 7, Files of Richard Cheney, Ford Library.

6. "Memo of Conversation Between Ford, Buchen, Scowcroft, and Schlesinger," Jan. 3, 1975, Box 7, Memos of Conversations, 1973–1977, National Security Adviser, Ford Papers; "Conversation Between Ford, Colby, Buchen, and Scowcroft," Jan. 3, 1975, Box 8, Memos of Conversations, 1973–1977, National Security Adviser, Ford Library.

7. "Conversation Between Ford, Kissinger, and Scowcroft," Jan. 4, 1975, Box 8, Memos of Conversations, National Security Adviser, Ford Library.

8. "Conversation Between Ford, Helms, Buchen, and Scowcroft," Jan. 4, 1975, Box 8, Memos of Conversations, National Security Adviser, Ford Library; "Conversation Between Ford, Rockefeller, Kissinger, Rumsfeld, Buchen, and Scowcroft," Jan. 4, 1975, Box 8, Memos of Conversations, National Security Adviser, Ford Library.

9. Colby and Forbath, *Honorable Men*, 399, 401.

10. Nick Thimmesch, "Rockefeller Wrong Man to Investigate CIA," *Los Angeles Times*, Jan. 11/12, 1975; Kathryn S. Olmsted, *Challenging the Secret Government: The Post-Watergate Investigations of the CIA and FBI* (Chapel Hill, NC: 1996), 50; Colby and Forbath, *Honorable Men*, 309.

11. Quoted in Olmsted, *Challenging the Secret Government*, 48.

12. Olmsted, *Challenging the Secret Government*, 35; Colby and Forbath, *Honorable Men*, 402.

13. Colby and Forbath, *Honorable Men*, 52–57.

14. Ibid., 404; quoted in Harold Ford, *Colby as Director of Central Intelligence, 1973–1976* (Washington, DC: 1993), 10, released under Freedom of Information Act, Aug. 11, 2011.

15. "Memo of Conversation Between Kissinger, Schlesinger, Colby, Silberman, and Scowcroft," Feb. 20, 1975, Box 9, Memos of Conversations, National Security Adviser, Ford Library; Ford, *Colby as Director*, 147.

16. "Conversation Between Ford, Rumsfeld, Marsh, and Kissinger," Feb. 21, 1975, Box 9, Memos of Conversations, National Security Adviser, Ford Library.

17. Author interview with Laurence Silberman, June 3, 2010.

18. "Conversation Between Ford, Kissinger, and Scowcroft," Feb. 28, 1975, Box 9, Memos of Conversations, National Security Adviser, Ford Library.

19. Brent Scowcroft to Jack Marsh, July 24, 1975, CREST, National Archives II.

20. Quoted in Ford, *Colby as Director*, 11.

21. Ford, *Colby as Director*, 129; author interview with Jenonne Walker, June 16, 2010.

22. Colby and Forbath, *Honorable Men*, 407; John Prados, *Lost Crusader: The Secret Wars of CIA Director William Colby* (New York: 2003), 311; "Conversation Between Kissinger, Schlesinger, Colby, Silberman, and Scowcroft," Feb. 20, 1975, Box 9, Memos of Conversations, National Security Adviser, Ford Library; William Nelson to William E. Colby, April 16, 1975, CREST, Archives II.

23. Prados, *Lost Crusader*, 310–311; quoted in Ford, *Colby as Director*, 99.

24. Author interview with Brent Scowcroft, June 3, 2010.

25. Prados, *Lost Crusader*, 300–301; Daniel Schorr, "My 17 Months on the CIA Watch," *Rolling Stone*, April 8, 1976.

26. Colby and Forbath, *Honorable Men*, 419–420.

27. Schorr, "My 17 Months."

28. Quoted in Olmsted, *Challenging the Secret Government*, 59–60; Colby and Forbath, *Honorable Men*, 410; A. J. Langguth, "Abolish the CIA!" *Newsweek*, April 7, 1975; "Jim Garrison and His War with the CIA," *Washington Star*, April 18, 1975.

CHAPTER 19

1. Jeffrey Kimball, *Nixon's Vietnam War* (Lawrence, KS: 1998), 240; author interview with James Nach, Sept. 9, 2008; author interview with Frank Snepp, May 21, 2008.

2. Quoted in George C. Herring, *America's Longest War* (New York: 1979), 315.

3. Ibid., 149–150; quoted in Herring, *Longest War*, 332; William Smyser to Henry A. Kissinger, March 31, 1975, *FRUS, 1969–1976, Vietnam*, vol. 10, 720.

4. See Thomas L. Ahern Jr., *CIA and the Generals: Covert Support to Military Government in South Vietnam*, Center for the Study of Intelligence, October 1998, available at National Security Archive, www.gwu.edu/~nsarchiv/NSAEBB/NSAEBB284/index.htm, 157–159; Herring, *Longest War*, 333; Brent Scowcroft to Gerald Ford, March 18, 1975, *FRUS, 1969–1976, Vietnam*, vol. 10, 682.

5. Quoted in "A New Dunkirk in Indochina," *Newsweek*, April 7, 1975; "Special National Intelligence Estimate," March 27, 1975, *FRUS, 1969–1976, Vietnam*, vol. 10, 702–704.

6. "Minutes of National Security Council Meeting," March 28, 1975, *FRUS, 1969–1976, Vietnam*, vol. 10, 707–708.

7. Ibid.

8. Ahern, *CIA and the Generals*, 168–169.

9. Quoted in ibid., 144.

10. "Minutes of the Secretary of State's Regional Staff Meeting," April 2, 1975, *FRUS, 1969–1976, Vietnam*, vol. 10, 725–726.

11. "Minutes of Washington Special Actions Group Meeting," April 2, 1975, *FRUS, 1969–1976, Vietnam*, vol. 10, 732–737.

12. Quoted in John Prados, *Lost Crusader: The Secret Wars of CIA Director William Colby* (New York: 2003), 287.

13. Quoted in Ahern, *CIA and the Generals*, 175, 177.

14. Quoted in ibid., 178; Graham Martin to Henry A. Kissinger, April 15, 1975, Box 8, National Security Adviser, Papers of Graham Martin, Ford Library.

15. "Minutes of National Security Council Meeting," April 9, 1975, *FRUS, 1969–1976, Vietnam*, vol. 10, 764; "Minutes of Washington Special Actions Group Meeting," April 19, 1975, *FRUS, 1969–1976, Vietnam*, vol. 10, 850.

16. "Minutes of Washington Special Actions Group Meeting," April 17, 1975, *FRUS, 1969–1976, Vietnam*, vol. 10, 833–838.

17. Ahern, *CIA and the Generals*, 185.

18. "Minutes of WSAG Meeting," April 21, 1975, *FRUS, 1969–1976, Vietnam*, vol. 10, 872; "Minutes of Washington Special Actions Group Meeting," April 19, 1975, *FRUS, 1969–1976, Vietnam*, vol. 10, 855.

19. Ahern, *CIA and the Generals*, 191.

20. "Minutes of WSAG," April 22, 1975, *FRUS, 1969–1976, Vietnam*, vol. 10, 884; "Minutes of WSAG," April 23, 1975, *FRUS, 1969–1976, Vietnam*, vol. 10, 891; Ahern, *CIA and the Generals*, 196; Henry A. Kissinger to Graham Martin, April 23, 1975, Box 8, National Security Adviser, Papers of Graham Martin, Ford Library.

21. "Minutes of WSAG Meeting," April 28, 1975, *FRUS, 1969–1976, Vietnam*, vol. 10, 915–917; William Colby, *Lost Victory: A Firsthand Account of America's Sixteen-Year Involvement in Vietnam* (Chicago: 1989), 353; "Memorandum of Conversation," April 28, 1975, *FRUS, 1969–1976, Vietnam*, vol. 10, 921.

22. Colby, *Lost Victory*, 353.

23. Ahern, *CIA and the Generals*, 212; "Minutes of WSAG Meeting," April 29, 1975, *FRUS, 1969–1976, Vietnam*, vol. 10, 934.

24. Ahern, *CIA and the Generals*, 216; William Colby to Saigon Station, April 29, 1975, CREST, National Archives II.

25. Colby, *Lost Victory*, 343–344, 355.

26. Quoted in Ahern, *CIA and the Generals*, 161.

27. Author interview with James Nach, Sept. 2, 2008.

28. Jeff Woods interview with Merle Pribenow, Jan. 10, 2007.

CHAPTER 20

1. Quoted in William Colby and Peter Forbath, *Honorable Men: My Life in the CIA* (New York: 1978), 400; John Prados, *Lost Crusader: The Secret Wars of CIA Director William Colby* (New York: 2003), 301–302.

2. Prados, *Lost Crusader*, 301–302; quoted in Daniel Schorr, "My 17 Months on the CIA Watch," *Rolling Stone*, April 8, 1976; Nicholas Horrock, "Files Said to Link Mafia to C.I.A. in Plot on Castro," *New York Times*, May 20, 1975.

3. Quoted in Prados, *Lost Crusader*, 302.

4. Pete Clapper to David Belin, May 29, 1975, Box 5, Files of Richard Cheney, Ford Library; "Conversation Between Ford, Kissinger, and Scowcroft," June 5, 1975, Box 10, Memos of Conversations, National Security Adviser, Ford Library.

5. Kathryn S. Olmsted, *Challenging the Secret Government: The Post-Watergate Investigations of the CIA and FBI* (Chapel Hill, NC: 1996), 58; "The Cloak Comes Off," *Newsweek*, June 23, 1975; quoted in Prados, *Lost Crusader*, 303.

6. Alice W. Olson et. al. to William E. Colby, July 17, 1975, CREST, National Archives II; "The Rockefeller Report," n.d., Box 9, Presidential Handwriting File, Ford Library; William E. Colby to Alice Olson, July 24, 1975, CREST, National Archives II.

7. Author interview with Laurence Silberman, June 3, 2010; Colby and Forbath, *Honorable Men*, 427.

8. "Buchen Notes on Meeting Between Kissinger, Schlesinger, and Colby," May 13, 1975, Presidential Handwriting File, Box 30, Ford Library.

9. Quoted in Prados, *Lost Crusader*, 314.

10. Olmsted, *Challenging the Secret Government*, 17.

11. Quoted in ibid., 39.

12. Ibid., 56–57; Colby and Forbath, *Honorable Men*, 408.

13. Quoted in Harold Ford, *William E. Colby as Director of Central Intelligence, 1973–1976* (Washington, DC: 1993), 177, released under Freedom of Information Act, Aug. 11, 2011.

14. Quoted in ibid., 3.

15. Olmsted, *Challenging the Secret Government*, 86.

16. Quoted in Ford, *Colby as Director*, 156–157.

17. "DCI Appearance Before Murphy Commission," Nov. 18, 1974, CREST, National Archives II; quoted in Olmsted, *Challenging the Secret Government*, 87.

18. Schorr, "My 17 Months."

19. Colby and Forbath, *Honorable Men*, 431–432; quoted in Olmsted, *Challenging the Secret Government*, 120–121; quoted in Prados, *Lost Crusader*, 319; quoted in Gerald K. Haines, "The Pike Committee Investigation and the CIA," Sept. 21, 1977, Center for Study of Intelligence, 4; quoted in Ford, *Colby as Director*, 166.

20. Colby and Forbath, *Honorable Men*, 432.

21. "The CIA and the White House," World News Wrap-up, July 9, 1975, CREST, National Archives II; Schorr, "My 17 Months."

22. "An Interview with Fletcher Prouty," July 11, 1975, *CBS Morning News*, CREST, National Archives II.

23. Quoted in Olmsted, *Challenging the Secret Government*, 119.

24. Quoted in Haines, "The Pike Committee Investigation," 7; quoted in Olmsted, *Challenging the Secret Government*, 121.

25. See "WEC Press Conference," Sept. 24, 1975, CREST, National Archives II.

26. Ibid.

27. Olmsted, *Challenging the Secret Government*, 122; Colby and Forbath, *Honorable Men*, 435.

28. Colby and Forbath, *Honorable Men*, 435, 437; quoted in Olmsted, *Challenging the Secret Government*, 92.

29. Quoted in Olmsted, *Challenging the Secret Government*, 123–124.

30. Henry A. Kissinger to John Marsh, Sept. 23, Box 13, Congressional Relations Office, Leon Leppert Files, Ford Library; Olmsted, *Challenging the Secret Government*, 124.

31. Colby and Forbath, *Honorable Men*, 432; Michael J. Malenick to Deputy Director for Administration, Sept. 24, 1975, CREST, Archives II; "Dan Schorr Gave This to Me[,] . . ." Sept. 30, 1975, CREST, Archives II.

32. Olmsted, *Challenging the Secret Government*, 126.

33. Quoted in ibid., 127.

34. "Conversation Between Ford, Kissinger, and Scowcroft," Oct. 31, 1975, Box 16, Memos of Conversations, National Security Adviser, Ford Library; William E. Colby to Otis Pike, Sept. 30, 1975, CREST, National Archives II.

35. Colby and Forbath, *Honorable Men*, 440.

36. "CIA Tells of Exotic Weapons," *Washington Post*, Sept. 17, 1975; Colby and Forbath, *Honorable Men*, 442; quoted in Olmsted, *Challenging the Secret Government*, 93.

37. Colby and Forbath, *Honorable Men*, 444–445; quoted in "Rockefeller and Kissinger Said to Seek Colby's Ouster," *New York Times*, June 21, 1975; Schorr, "My 17 Months."

38. Ford, *Colby as Director*, 109, 111.

39. Sheehan interview with Mitchell Rogovin Aug. 1, 1975, Box 70, F-Kissinger, Sheehan Papers, Library of Congress.

40. Bernard Knox, Eulogy for William Colby, Courtesy of Paul Colby.

41. Colby and Forbath, *Honorable Men*, 445.

42. Author interview with Barbara Colby, Jan. 5, 2007; author interview with Christine Colby Giraudo, June 5, 2010.

43. Schorr, "My 17 Months"; quoted in Colby and Forbath, *Honorable Men*, 445.

44. Norman Kempster, "Senators Flay Colby Firing as Part of 'New Cover-up,'" *Washington Post*, Nov. 3, 1975; "White House News Conference No. 370," Nov. 12, 1975, CREST, National Archives II.

45. Colby and Forbath, *Honorable Men*, 446–447; "White House News Conference No. 370," Nov. 12, 1975, CREST, National Archives II.

46. William E. Colby to Gerald Ford, Oct. 20, 1975, Box 1, Papers of Richard Cheney, Ford Library; Prados, *Lost Crusader*, 327.

47. Schorr, "My 17 Months"; Olmsted, *Challenging the Secret Government*, 106.

48. "Alleged Assassination Plots Involving Foreign Leaders: An Interim Report," Nov. 20, 1975, CREST, National Archives II.

49. Richard Helms, with William Hood, *A Look over My Shoulder: A Life in the Central Intelligence Agency* (New York: 2003), 171; CIA Operations Center–News Service, May 24, 1974, CREST, National Archives II.

50. Quoted in Richard Beeston, "CIA Lose [*sic*] Allies 'Because of Congress Inquiries,'" *London Daily Telegraph*, Oct. 22, 1975.

51. Prados, *Lost Crusader*, 328; Olmsted, *Challenging the Secret Government*, 141.

52. Quoted in Tim Weiner, *Legacy of Ashes: The History of the CIA* (New York: 2007), 334.

53. Laurence Stern, "CIA Agent's Murder Spurs Accusations," *Washington Post*, Dec. 25, 1975; "On the Assassination of a CIA Station Chief in Athens," Jan. 7, 1976, CREST, National Archives II.

54. Stern, "CIA Agent's Murder Spurs Accusations"; *CBS Nightly News*, Dec. 26, 1975, CREST, National Archives II.

55. Gerald Ford to Otis Pike, Jan. 15, 1976, Box 1, F–Pike Com., Srodes Papers, Marshall Library, Virginia Military Institute; Colby and Forbath, *Honorable Men*, 439.

56. Quoted in Olmsted, *Challenging the Secret Government*, 142.

57. Quoted in Ford, *Colby as Director*, 125.

58. Walter Pincus, "Covering Intelligence," *The New Republic*, Feb. 1, 1975; "Ford-Luce Conversation," Feb. 25, 1976, Memoranda of Conversations, Box 18, National Security Adviser, Ford Library.

59. William E. Colby to George Bush, n.d., CREST, National Archives II; George Bush to William E. Colby, n.d., CREST, National Archives II; George Bush to Gerald Ford, Jan. 3, 1976, CREST, National Archives II.

60. Quoted in Ford, *Colby as Director*, 193.

61. "Sheehan Notes on Luncheon Conversation with Dave Farnham," May 7, 1976, Box 62, F Colby, Sheehan Papers, Library of Congress.

CHAPTER 21

1. "23 Soviets Tabbed as Spies," *Washington Star*, March 15, 1976.

2. Aaron Latham, *Orchids for Mother* (New York: 1977); Edward J. Epstein, *Legend: The Secret World of Lee Harvey Oswald* (New York: 1978); Aaron Latham, "Under Several Hats," *Nation*, April 29, 1978.

3. "J. Edgar Hoover Was Feeding . . ." n.d., CREST, National Archives II; Latham, "Under Several Hats."

4. Latham, "Under Several Hats."

5. Thomas Powers, "Looking for Moles," *Commonweal* 106, no. 4 (1979); Thomas Powers, *Intelligence Wars: American Secret History from Hitler to Al-Qaeda*, rev. ed. (New York: 2004), 280; see also Charles Osolin, "Spying on the Spies," *Atlanta Constitution*, May 28, 1978.

6. Jeff Stein, "Poisoning SALT," *Inquiry*, May 1, 1979; Joe Trento and Dave Roman, "KGB in New York," *Penthouse*, August 1978.

7. See Tad Szulc, "The Missing C.I.A. Man," *New York Times Magazine*, Jan. 7, 1979; see also Powers, "Looking for Moles"; William Safire, "Slithy Toves of C.I.A.," *New York Times*, Jan. 22, 1979.

8. Quoted in "Ex-Director of CIA Says Senate Must Ratify the SALT II Treaty," *Indianapolis Star*, June 29, 1979; William E. Colby, "Verifying SALT," *Worldview*, April 1979; Stansfield Turner to William E. Colby, May 2, 1979, CREST, National Archives II.

9. Quoted in Joe Trento, "CIA Mole Probe Focuses on Ex-Counterspy Chief," *Wilmington News Journal*, May 5, 1979; David Ignatius, "James Angleton: Superspook or Tragic Hero?" *Wall Street Journal*, April 23, 1980.

10. See Robert Moss, "The Intelligence War: Putting the Muscle in the CIA," *London Daily Telegraph*, Dec. 20, 1980.

11. "Ex-CIA Chief Favors Nuclear Arms Freeze," *Baltimore Sun*, June 27, 1982; quoted in United Press International, Aug. 10, 1983, CREST, National Archives II; Paul Gailey, "Ex-C.I.A. Head Now Works for a Nuclear Freeze," *New York Times*, June 14, 1983.

12. David Wise, "The Once and Future CIA," *Los Angeles Times*, Feb. 15, 1983; William E. Colby, "An Elite Fighting Force—At the Ready," *Washington Post*, Feb. 10, 1981.

13. "Memo of Conversation Between Kissinger, Schlesinger, Scowcroft, and Wickham," Sept. 5, 1973, Memoranda of Conversations, National Security Adviser, Box 2, Ford Library.

14. James A. Nathan, "Dateline Australia: America's Foreign Watergate?" *Foreign Policy*, Winter 1982–1983, 168–175.

15. See Nathan, "Dateline Australia: America's Foreign Watergate?" 171; Alan Berger, "Heroin, Banking, and the CIA," *Boston Globe*, Sept. 7, 1980; James Dooley, "Australian Banker's Death Sparks Saga . . ." *Honolulu Advertiser*, Nov. 2, 1980; A. McCoy, *The Politics of Heroin: CIA Complicity in the Global Drug Trade* (New York: 1991).

16. Author interview with Sally Shelton-Colby, Jan. 8, 2007; author interview with Jenonne Walker, June 16, 2010.

17. Author interview with Paul Colby, Jan. 8, 2007.

18. Author interview with Christine Colby Giraudo, June 5, 2010; author interview with Susan Colby, June 5, 2010.

19. Author interview with Sally Shelton-Colby, Jan. 8, 2007; author interview with Jenonne Walker, June 16, 2010.

20. Author interview with Sally Shelton-Colby, Jan. 8, 2007.

21. Ibid.

22. Thomas Powers to William E. Colby, Dec. 8, 1989, and William E. Colby to Thomas Powers, Dec. 26, 1989, Box 6, F34, Colby Papers, Vietnam Archive, Texas Tech University.

23. Author interview with John Colby, Jan. 2, 2007.

INDEX